LET'S GO:
NEW YORK CITY

is the best book for anyone traveling on a budget. Here's why:

No other guidebook has as many budget listings.

We list over 17 places in or near New York City where you can spend the night for under $36. We tell you how to get there the cheapest way, whether by bus, plane, or thumb, and where to get an inexpensive and satisfying meal once you've arrived. There are hundreds of money-saving tips for everyone plus lots of information on student discounts.

LET'S GO researchers have to make it on their own.

Our Harvard-Radcliffe researchers travel on budgets as tight as your own—no expense accounts, no free hotel rooms.

LET'S GO is completely revised every year.

We don't just update the prices, we go back to the places. If a charming café has become an overpriced tourist trap, we'll replace the listing with a new and better one.

No other budget guidebook includes all this:

Coverage of both the city and daytrips out of the city; directions, addresses, phone numbers, and hours to get you in and around; in-depth information on culture, history, and inhabitants; tips on work, study, sights, nightlife, and special splurges; detailed city maps; and much, much more.

LET'S GO is for anyone who wants to see New York City on a budget.

Books by Let's Go, Inc.

Let's Go: Europe
Let's Go: Britain & Ireland
Let's Go: France
Let's Go: Germany, Austria & Switzerland
Let's Go: Greece & Turkey
Let's Go: Israel & Egypt
Let's Go: Italy
Let's Go: London
Let's Go: Paris
Let's Go: Rome
Let's Go: Spain & Portugal

Let's Go: USA
Let's Go: California & Hawaii
Let's Go: Mexico
Let's Go: New York City
Let's Go: The Pacific Northwest, Western Canada & Alaska
Let's Go: Washington, D.C.

LET'S GO:

The Budget Guide to

NEW YORK CITY

1993

Michael C. Vazquez
Editor

Alexander E. Marashian
Assistant Editor

Written by
Let's Go, Inc.
a wholly owned subsidiary of
Harvard Student Agencies, Inc.

ST. MARTIN'S PRESS
NEW YORK

Helping Let's Go

If you have suggestions or corrections, or just want to share your discoveries, drop us a line. We read every piece of correspondence, whether a 10-page letter, a tacky Elvis postcard, or, as in one case, a collage. All suggestions are passed along to our researcher/writers. Please note that mail received after May 5, 1993 will probably be too late for the 1994 book, but will be retained for the following edition. Address mail to:

> *Let's Go: New York City*
> **Let's Go, Inc.**
> **1 Story Street**
> **Cambridge, MA 02138**

In addition to the invaluable travel advice our readers share with us, many are kind enough to offer their services as researchers or editors. Unfortunately, the charter of Let's Go, Inc. and Harvard Student Agencies, Inc. enables us to employ only currently enrolled Harvard students.

Maps by David Lindroth, copyright © 1993, 1992, 1991 by St. Martin's Press, Inc.

Distributed outside the U.S. and Canada by Pan Books Ltd.

ISBN: 0-312-08245-2

First edition
10 9 8 7 6 5 4 3 2 1

Let's Go: New York City is written by the Publishing Division of
Let's Go, Inc., 1 Story Street, Cambridge, Mass. 02138.

Let's Go® is a registered trademark of Let's Go, Inc.
Printed in the U.S.A. on recycled paper with biodegradable soy ink.

Editor	Michael Colin Vazquez
Assistant Editor	Alexander Edward Marashian
Managing Editor	July Paisley Belber
Publishing Director	Paul C. Deemer
Production Manager	Mark N. Templeton
Office Coordinator	Bart St. Clair
Office Manager	Anne E. Chisholm

Researcher-Writers

Manhattan	Steven Burt
Long Island	Jennifer Cox
Manhattan, Brooklyn, Queens	Jim Ebenhoh
Manhattan; Staten Island; New Haven, CT	
Atlantic City and Princeton, NJ	Dara Mayers
Manhattan, The Bronx	Woden Sorrow Teachout

Sales Group Manager	Tiffany A. Breau
Sales Group Representatives	Frances Marguerite Maximé
	Breean T. Stickgold
	Harry J. Wilson
Sales Group Coordinator	Aida Bekele
President	Brian A. Goler
C.E.O.	Michele Ponti

Acknowledgments

To Alex "Hively" Marashian goes my most heartfelt and honest thanks and comradely greetings. I never imagined that two minds could meet at such an explosive loggerhead; the scattered remains of our combination are the meat and substance of this book.

Andrew Kent returned from the European midlands to help clean up our mess, proofing, calling, and chumbling with dead-on wit and straight-arrow eyes. In this he redoubled his performance on the *Slit* and once-again revealed to me one of the essential wellsprings of friendship: being around for the stupid shit.

Another community, our trusty office group, kept us in shape, making the days pass with ease and curtailling our excesses. Moondog, Elijah "Döh" Siegler, David, Kayla, Jane, Nell, and July kept us honest, or at least credible. July put up with our aggressive disorganization without freaking; she also accepted most of our glib linguistic trinkets, shared a grin and a cackle, and allowed us to swing lightly through our forested prose. We would have produced a sadder book without her.

Our ragtag team of researchers performed admirably under weird conditions.

Trusty stalwart Dara Mayers spent the whole summer writing and thinking about art; her keen eye and sardonic prose ravaged the city and its fashionable inhabitants. She dug deep into the Village, daytripped, and explored vasty Harlem. Her hospitality and guidance made my working vacation in Manhattan a pleasure.

Groundhog Jim Ebenhoh took on the long-neglected boroughs, wrote precise and painstakingly detailed copy, and literally ate the sheep's head in Queens. His task completed before anyone else's had begun, he spent countless summer hours working on maps, fielding stupid questions, and priming us with oven-baked pizza.

Steve "Blueboy" Burt kicked ass, as predicted. The Upper West Side, Central Park, and MoMA flowered as a result of his patient, inspired care. His generosity and unflagging committment amazed me this summer, as in the spring, when he provided similarly sterling support during Rough Trade.

Wodensorrow Teachout went off kicking and screaming, blitzkrieged through Midtown and the Upper East Side, then packed up for the puritan wilds of Vermont to shuck peas and coddle. Her easy laugh, eye-sparkling smile, and euphonic siblings made the long, hard spring a little more human; her box-cot cubbyhole and sheepskin rugs served me in good if fitful stead in the early summer. I miss you, Wod.

Jen Cox stayed home and sent back funny, informative copy while summering on Long Island. Mike Sonnenshein took a little time out of his vacation to check some facts. Graham "Beautiful Loser" Cassano told us a thing or two about the Bronx, and clued us in to a few bookstores that would otherwise have escaped our attention.

Others performed integral tasks: Deedee Richardson, Jill Kamin, and Charles "Honey" Honig typed and proofed for us, Andrew and Nora plied us with food, rubbings, and voicemail, Bart did just what we told him to, even when it was lame, Jane made us happy, Mark "Candyman" Templeton kept us up and running, and David kept our cynicism from getting the better of us.

Thanks, finally to a host of others: Marlies and Minna, longtime friends who directly or indirectly lent inrigue to my summer; Nell of the smiling curls and zebra skull, whose plotting grin and gypsy spirit were my most treasured find; Jason Sure, my grandmother; Milena, whose grizzled sweetness kept me company at odd times; Ethan, who took me and Al through a North End carnival and into the urban blightscape; and Orah, whose warm company rounded out my summer in Cambridge.

Like most of the things I do, this book is offered to my parents, Lois and John. With love, thanks, and longing.

—MCV

How to thank Mike Vazquez, who urged our overkill and oversaw our urges to slamhandle language, jumpstart the summer, and junket the days away? Wishbone headphones linked us to *Lost and Found* (88.1) and to a molten substratum of language where mutual upchuckle is community agreement and a neighborly guffaw the signal for further excavations. I really wouldn't have done this for anyone else. Next is Mark Nevins PhD, medievalist, neologist. Thanks for putting me up and keeping me up and for reminding me, every time we meet, what and how it is to be a friend. Time and space constraints will constipate the brain; I love all of you who didn't slip through—here are those who did: my brother Ed who shEd his fresno for a gotham on it's last gasps; thanks for, mongotherthings, clearing off your floor for Purcell and me/ my sister Julianne for bringing joy to Cambridge/ my other sister Kayla Alpert/ John and Barbara Knight for friendship and square meals/ Nick Pirok (never lose your fresno)/ Cookieboy Dave Thorpe/ July Belber/ Muneer the hustler/ Elijah (though he shaved it)/ Geoff Rodkey/ Becca Knowles/ Thomas Lauderdale for reminding me of the possibilities/ Rump Inglenook/ Andrew Kent for officeball/ Will and Sne for the trip through the fens/ Gin Soon T'ai Chi Club/ Steve McCauley, for the pinpoint of light at the end of the summer/ Robert Kiely and Vicky Macy/ John/ Gelcap, Gameboy, and the Kid/ Paul/ the Gold Star 5 (jizzes of thank go out to Troy and Tanya for towing me two years back over a plate of enchiladas)/ George/ Tuli Kupferberg, Noah, and fam for my hosting my first visit to the City/ Ringo/ Josh Pashman and Dmitri Tymoczko, my fellow curmudgeons/ Turf Butswang/ Radio AM 1430 / the pit at Shays, where we hatched our nuts and mahfoozed away the days/ John Kelly and Rick Hawkins for the occasional pint/ Craig Mullen and Liz/ last, my girlfriend, Melba Petal, who indulged my poolside manqué. And other fancies.
For my part this book is dedicated to my parents, Edward and Janet, who are beyond thanks.

—AEM

Contents

x   Contents

List of Maps

About Let's Go

A generation ago, Harvard Student Agencies, a three-year-old nonprofit corporation dedicated to providing employment to students, was doing a booming business booking charter flights to Europe. One of the extras offered to passengers on these flights was a 20-page mimeographed pamphlet entitled *1960 European Guide,* a collection of tips on continental travel compiled by the HSA staff. The following year, students traveling to Europe researched the first full-fledged edition of *Let's Go: Europe,* a pocket-sized book with tips on budget accommodations, irreverent write-ups of sights, and a decidedly youthful slant.

Throughout the 60s, the series reflected its era: a section of the 1968 *Let's Go: Europe* was entitled "Street Singing in Europe on No Dollars a Day." During the 70s *Let's Go* gradually became a large-scale operation, adding regional European guides and expanding coverage into North Africa and Asia. Now in its 33nd year, *Let's Go* publishes 17 titles covering more than 40 countries. This year *Let's Go* proudly introduces two new guides: *Let's Go: Paris* and *Let's Go: Rome.*

Each spring 80 Harvard-Radcliffe students are hired as researcher-writers for the summer months. They train intensively during April and May for their summer tour of duty. Each researcher-writer then hits the road on a shoestring budget for seven weeks, researching six days per week, and overcoming countless obstacles in a glorious quest for better bargains.

Back in a basement deep below Harvard Yard, an editorial staff of 32, a management team of six, and countless typists and proofreaders—all students—spend four months poring over more than 75,000 pages of manuscript as they push the copy through a rigorous editing process. High tech has recently landed in the dungeon: some of the guides are now typeset in-house using sleek black desktop workstations.

And even before the books hit the stands, next year's editions are well underway.

A NOTE TO OUR READERS

The information for this book is gathered by Let's Go's researchers during the late spring and summer months. Each listing is derived from the assigned researcher's opinion based upon his or her visit at a particular time. The opinions are expressed in a candid and forthright manner. Other travelers might disagree. Those traveling at a different time may have different experiences since prices, dates, hours, and conditions are always subject to change. You are urged to check beforehand to avoid inconvenience and surprises. Travel always involves a certain degree of risk, especially in low-cost areas. When traveling, especially on a budget, you should always take particular care to ensure your safety.

LET'S GO: NEW YORK CITY

This rural America thing. It's a joke.
—Edward I. Koch, former mayor of New York City

Life and Times

History

Since New York's early days, outsiders have regarded it with wonder and alarm. The city has a history of dramatic and often ungainly growth; services and infrastructures have rarely kept up with the rapid pace of expansion. In the 1600s, root pigs ran wild in the streets. In the 1700s, the city's water supply was so fouled that even the horses refused to drink. And in the 19th and 20th centuries, New York's mean streets and corrupt bosses became emblems of troubled urbanity, of the malignant, treacherous torpor of life in the big city. But for the city's long-term residents, and for the constantly replenished stock of new arrivals, the magic produced by that stunning growth compensates for the drawbacks. New York scoffs at the timid compromises of other cities. It boasts the most immigrants, the tallest skyscrapers, the trickiest con artists. Even the vast grey blocks of concrete have an indomitable charm. "There is more poetry in a block of New York than in 20 daisied lanes," said O. Henry, returning from a prosaic and dull vacation in rural Westchester. In the country, he said, "There was too much fresh scenery and fresh air. What I need is a steam heated flat and no vacation or exercise."

New York's vaunted self-sufficiency began early. The colony was founded in 1624 by the Dutch West Indies Company as a trading post, but England soon asserted rival claims to the land. While the home countries squabbled, the colonists went about their business: trading beaver skins, colorful wampum, and silver with the neighboring Indians. In 1626, in a particularly infamous swap, they traded Manhattan as well: Peter Minuit bought the island for 60 guilders, or just under $24.

The land was rich and abundant, and European guidance was hardly necessary. "Wild pigeons are as thick as the sparrows in Holland...Children and pigs multiply here rapidly," gloated one colonist. When the Dutch West Indies Company did try to interfere, the settlers resented it. Calvinist Peter Stuyvesant, the governor appointed by Holland in the middle of the 17th century, instituted rigid reforms on the happy-go-lucky settlement. He shot hogs, closed taverns, and whipped Quakers, while the citizens protested and complained. Inexplicably, the physically challenged Stuyvesant has since become a local folk hero. Schools and businesses in New York are named for him and people refer to him fondly as "Peg-Leg" Peter.

By and large, though, the early colonists were less than enthralled with Dutch rule; they put up only token resistance when the British finally invaded the settlement in 1664. The new British governors were less noxious if only because they were less effective; an astounding number never even made it to the colony: some got lost en route from England, a handful went down at sea, some died outright, and others decided that New England was a more attractive spot, and went there. Between 1664 and 1776, there were 22 hiatuses in governance.

Left to its own devices, the city continued to grow. It founded King's College (later Columbia) in 1754. By the late 1770s the city had become a major port with a population of 20,000. New York's primary concern was maintaining that prosperity, and it reacted apathetically to the first whiffs of revolution. British rule was good for business, so.... The new American army, understandably, made no great efforts to protect the ungrateful city, and New York was held by the British throughout the war.

The American Revolution was a rough time for poor New York. It had "a most melancholy appearance, being deserted and pillaged," wrote one observer. Fire destroyed a quarter of the city in 1776, ships spontaneously exploded, and the general atmosphere was one of chaos interspersed with games of cricket. When the defeated British army finally left in 1783, most people were relieved—except for 6000 Tory loyalists, who followed the British out of New York and went on to Nova Scotia.

With its buildings in heaps of rubble and a third of its population off roaming Canada, New York made a valiant effort to rebuild. It succeeded, somewhat unexpectedly. "The progress of the city is, as usual, beyond all calculations," wrote one rapturous citizen. New York served a brief stint as the nation's capital; about the same time it acquired a bank and the first stock exchange, which met under a buttonwood tree on Wall Street. The Randel Plan simplified the organization of the city streets in 1811, establishing Manhattan's grid scheme. Merchants built mansions on the new streets, along with tenements for the increasing numbers of Eastern and Northen European immigrants.

Administration and services continued to lag behind growth. New York became the largest U.S. city early in the 19th century, but pigs, dogs, and chickens continued to run freely. Fires and riots lent zest to the streetlife, while the foul water supply precipitated a cholera epidemic. The world-famous corruption of Tammany Hall, a political machine set in motion in the 1850s and operative for nearly a century, complicated the already desperate situation. "The New Yorker belongs to a community worse governed by lower and baser scum than any city in Western Christendom," complained George Strong.

Still, New Yorkers remained loyal to the city, often neglecting national concerns in favor of local interests. New York initially opposed the Civil War, its desire to protect trade with the South outweighing abolitionist principles. Lincoln, the *New York Times* wrote dismissively in 1860, was "a lawyer who has some local reputation in Illinois." The attack on Fort Sumter made New York rally to the Northern side, but a conscription act in 1863 led to the infamous Draft Riots, which cost a thousand lives.

After the war, New York entered a half-century of peace and prosperity; during this time the elements of urban modernity began to coalesce. The Metropolitan Museum of Art was founded in 1870, Bloomingdale's in 1872. Frederick Law Olmsted created Central Park on 82 rolling acres in the last part of the century; the Flatiron building, the first (intriguing triangular) skyscraper, was erected in 1902. The city spread out, both horizontally and vertically. "It'll be a great place if they ever finish it," O Henry quipped.

Booming construction and burgeoning culture industries helped generate a sort of urban bliss. Mayor Fiorello LaGuardia brought the city safely out of the Great Depression, and post-World War II prosperity brought still more immigrants and businesses to the city. But even as the country—and the rest of the world—celebrated New York as the capital of the 20th century, the cracks in the city's foundations became apparent. By the 1960s, crises in public transportation, education, and housing exacerbated ethnic tensions and fostered the consolidation of a criminal underclass.

City officials raised taxes to provide more services, but higher taxes drove middle class residents and corporations out of the city. As a series of recessions and budget crises swamped the government, critics charged that Mayor Robert Wagner's only response was "dedicated inactivity." By 1975, the City was pleading with the Federal Government to rescue it from impending bankruptcy—and was rebuffed. The *Daily News* headline the next day read "Ford to New York: Drop Dead."

New York rebounded. Budget wizard Felix Rohatyn trimmed the city's budget. The city's massive (if goofy) "I Love New York" campaign spread cheery hearts on bumper stickers. Large manufacuring interests were superseded by fresh money from high finance and infotech, big Reaganaut growth industries. In the 80s Wall Street was hip again, or at least grotesquely profitable; the city seemed to recover some of its lost vitality.

As the rosy blush of the 80s fades to grey 90s recession, the city's problems have re-appeared. Bizarre outbreaks of violence, particularly violence against women, have gotten national attention; racial bigotry, and threats of violent direct action, litter the newspapers and street-corners; and budget problems have necessitated cuts in education and the police force. Still, there are signs of life and renewed committment in the urban blightscape: a recent resurgence of community activism and do-it-yourself politics is a glimmer of hope. New York's history of heroic comebacks is not yet over, at least in the hearts of its citizens. Former Mayor Ed Koch's inaugural speech echoes the sentiments of generations. "New York is not a problem," said Koch. "New York is a stroke of genius."

Ethnic New York

> To Europe she was America, to America she was the
> gateway of the earth. But to tell the story of New
> York would be to write a social history of the world.
> —H.G. Wells

In 1643, Jesuit missionary Isaac Jogues wrote a description of a lively New Amsterdam fort. Among the 500 people living in this 17th-century melting-pot community were artisans, soldiers, trappers, sailors, and slaves—and they spoke 18 languages among them.

New Yorkers have always claimed a wide range of national origins. The first Black settlement began in today's SoHo in 1644; by the time of the American Revolution the city had a Black population of 20,000. Germans and Irish came over between 1840 and 1860; in 1855 European-born persons constituted nearly half of New York's population.

After the Civil War, a massive wave of immigration began, cresting around the turn of the century. Europeans left famine, religious persecution, and political unrest in their native lands for the perils of seasickness and the promise of America. Germans and Irish immigrants were joined, beginning in 1890, by Italians, Russians, Poles, and Greeks.

Immigrants worked long hours in disgusting and unsafe conditions for meager wages; only the Triangle Shirtwaist Fire of 1911, which killed 146 female factory workers, brought about enough public protest to force stricter regulations on working conditions. Meanwhile, Tammany Hall-based "ward bosses" stepped in to take care of the confused new arrivals, helping them find jobs and housing and even providing them with emergency funds in cases of illness or accident. All the immigrants needed to produce in return were their votes for the incumbent city government. But the U.S. Congress restricted immigration from Europe in the 1920s, and the Great Depression of the 30s brought it to a virtual halt.

Today New York has more Italians than Rome, more Irish than Dublin, and more Jews than Jerusalem. Immigrants from Asia and the Caribbean still come to the city. Today, the melting pot simmers with nine million people speaking 80 languages. New York continues to easily absorb those who navigate to its shores; while it takes years or lifetimes to blend into other cities, newcomers become New Yorkers almost instantly.

Politics

New York's political history is a murky one. Corruption, typified by "Boss" William Tweed and Tammany Hall, was long its hallmark, and honest politicians have had difficulty being effective.

In the 1850s, Tweed took charge of Tammany and began promising money and jobs to people—often new immigrants—who agreed to vote for his candidates. With Tweed's men ruling city government, embezzling and obtaining kickbacks were a simple matter. Tweed managed to rob the city of somewhere between 20 and 300 million dollars. When citizens complained in 1871, Tweed said defiantly, "Well, what are you going to do about it?" Although a *New York Times* exposé led to Tweed's downfall in 1875, Tammany continued to try to influence elections without him.

Occasional reform movements bucked Tammany's power. In 1894, for example, Teddy Roosevelt was appointed to the police department. Dressed in a cape, he sallied forth at night like a judicial Masked Avenger, searching for policemen who were sleeping on the job or consorting with prostitutes. A truly successful reformer was Fiorello LaGuardia, New York's immensely popular mayor from 1933-1945. "Nobody wants me but the people," he said as he reorganized the government and revitalized the city.

Since the 1960s, politicians have grappled with social and economic problems. Lindsay ran in 1965 with the slogan "He is fresh and everyone else is tired," but even his freshness wilted under the barrage of crime, drought, race problems, and labor unrest. After its bankruptcy crisis, the city slowly began to rebound. Ed Koch became America's most visible mayor, appearing on *Saturday Night Live* and providing an endless stream of quotables. And the economic boom of the late 80s made Wall Street—and, by extension, New York—seem glamorous and fashionable. In 1988, David Dinkins was elected on a platform of harmonious growth and continued prosperity.

New York reflects, in heightened form, the mood of the country. When America flourishes, New York does too. And as America entered recession in the early 1990s, New York was especially hard hit. Once again, residents are fleeing for the suburbs and New Jersey. Budgetary problems may force the city to cut education and services. And recent acts of random violence—against Yusef Hawkins, the Central Park Jogger, and many others—have drawn new attention to social unrest.

One optimistic note is the reform of the city government. In 1989, the Supreme Court abolished the Board of Estimate system, under which each borough president had one vote. The system was blatantly unfair, since borough populations range from Brooklyn's 2.8 million to Staten Island's 350,000. Now, a 35-member City Council runs New York and each borough can initiate zoning, propose legislation and deal with contractors on its own. A more streamlined government may allow the city to respond more quickly to the crises that imperil it.

Architecture

> *A hundred times have I thought New York is a catastrophe and fifty times: It is a beautiful catastrophe.*
> —Le Corbusier

The Early Years and the European Influence

New York has always warmed to the latest trends in architecture, hastily demolishing old buildings to make way for their stylistic successors. In the 19th century the surging rhythm of endless destruction and renewal seemed to attest to the city's vigor and enthusiasm. Walt Whitman praised New York's "pull-down-and-build-over-again spirit," and *The Daily Mirror* was an isolated voice when, in 1831, it criticized the city's "irreverence for antiquity."

By the 20th century, many found that irreverence troubling. New York's history was quickly disappearing under the steamroller of modernization. Mounting public concern climaxed when developers destroyed gracious Penn Station in 1965; the Landmarks Preservation Commission was created in response. Since then, the LPC has been vigorously designating buildings to protect. Developers, meanwhile, seek loopholes and air-rights to explode city buildings into the sky.

Despite the rear-guard efforts of the LPC, traces of pre-Revolutionary New York are hard to find. The original Dutch settlement consisted mostly of traditional homes with gables and stoops. One example from 1699, the restored Vechte-Cortelyou House, stands near Fifth Ave. and 3rd St. in Brooklyn. The British, however, built over most of these with Federal-style buildings like St. Paul's Church on Madison Ave.

Even after the British had been forced out, their architectural tastes lingered, influencing the townhouses built by their prosperous colonists. Through the early 19th century, American architects continued to incorporate such Federal details as dormer windows, stoops, and doors with columns and fan lights. Federal houses still line Charlton St. and Northern Vandam St., while the old City Hall, built by goodtiming DC mastermind Pierre L'Enfant (see *Let's Go: Washington, DC*) in 1802, applies Federal detailing to a public building.

The Greek Revival of the 1820s and 30s added porticoes and iron laurel wreaths to New York's streets. If you see a house with uneven bricks, it probably predates the 1830s, when machines started making bricks. Greek Revival prevails at Washington Square North. It also pops up on Lafayette St. and on W. 20th St. Grey granite St. Peter's, built in 1838, was the first Greek Revival Catholic Church in New York.

While cadging from the old country and the classical tradition, Americans did manage to introduce some architectural innovations. Beginning in the 1850s, thousands of brownstones (made from cheap stone quarried in New Jersey) sprang up all over New York. Next to skyscrapers, the brownstone townhouse may be New York's most characteristic structure. Although beyond most people's means today, the houses were middle class residences back then—the rich lived in block-long mansions on Fifth Avenue, and apartments were for the poor.

The tidy social hierarchy of buildings was scandalized in 1883, when the luxurious Dakota apartment house (later John Lennon's home) went up. The building's name derives from its location on the far side of Central Park; it was so far removed from the social center of town, local wits joked, that it might as well be in Dakota Territory. But the relatively cheap, sumptuously appointed apartments offered an attractive alternative to the soaring real estate prices of Central Midtown. Soon, similar apartment buildings, like the Ansonia, were built in Harlem and on the Upper West Side.

In the 1890s American architects studying abroad brought the Beaux-Arts style back from France and captivated the nation. Beaux Arts, which blended classic details with lavish decoration, stamped itself on structures built through the 1930s. Especially fine examples are the New York Customs House, built by Cass Gilbert, and the New York Public Library, originally built to house James Lenox's overflowing book collection. Lenox, a wealthy recluse, accumulated so many books that keeping track of them in his apartment was nearly impossible; when he wanted to read one he already possessed, he often had to go out and buy another copy. He donated his collection to the city in 1895.

Architects lavished gracious Beaux Arts detailing on the first specimens of New York's quintessential structure, the skyscraper. Made possible by the invention of the elevator in 1857, skyscrapers soon became the city's architectural trademark.

The Skyscraper: An American Tallboy

Permissive new building codes at the turn of the 20th century allowed the first skyscrapers to sprout. Initial response was mixed. The Flatiron building, erected in 1902, was triangular in shape and only six feet wide at its point; its wind currents blew women's skirts up, and people feared it would topple. But tall buildings proved a useful invention in a city forever short on space, and others soon joined the Flatiron.

In 1913, Cass Gilbert gilded the 55-story Woolworth Building with Gothic flourishes, piling terracotta salamanders onto antique "W"s. The Empire State Building and the Chrysler Building, fashioned from stone and steel and built like rockets, stand testimony to America's romance with science and space. Over the years, more dizzying buildings have joined the throng.

But not all New York monoliths look the same, and the urban landscape does have quirks and personality. Learn to read between the skylines and you'll be able to distinguish and date just about every tower. New York's succession of zoning laws can be a better architectural guide than I.M. Pei.

Does the building have a ziggurat on top? Look like a wedding cake? Zoning restrictions of the late 1940s stipulated that tall buildings had to be set back at the summit. New York's first curtain of pure glass was the 1950 United Nations Secretariat Building, an air-conditioning nightmare. The building quickly inspired Lever House, a 24-story glass box. Then, in 1958, Mies Van der Rohe and Philip Johnson created the Seagram Building, a glass tower set behind a plaza on Park Avenue. Crowds soon gathered to mingle, sunbathe, and picnic, much to the surprise of planners and builders. A delighted planning commission began offering financial incentives to every builder who offset a highrise with public open space. Over the next decade, many architects stuck empty plazas next to their towering office complexes. Some of them looked a little too empty to the picky planning commission, which changed the rules in 1975 to stipulate that every plaza should provide public seating. By the late 70s, plazas were moved indoors: high-tech atriums with gurgling fountains, bevis fronds, and pricey cafés began to flourish.

The leanest skyscrapers you will see date from the early 80s, when shrewd developers realized they could get office space, bypass zoning regulations, *and* receive a bonus from the commission, if they hoisted up "sliver" buildings. Composed largely of elevators and stairs, the disturbingly anorexic newcomers were generally disliked. Those tired of living in the shadow of shafts altered zoning policy in 1983 so that structural planning would encourage more room for air and sun.

Builders have finally recognized the overcrowding problem in East Midtown and expanded their horizons somewhat. New residential complexes have risen on the Upper East Side above 95th St.; in the near future you can expect high-flying office complexes to stomp out the West mid-town culture of the 40s and 50s. Some developers have even ventured into the sagebrush splendor of Queens. And with the restructuring of the city government in 1989, citizens now have a greater say in development projects in their community.

The planning commission that oversees the beautiful catastrophe now takes overcrowding and environmental issues into account when it makes its decisions. As an added safeguard, the Landmarks Preservation Commission lurks ever-vigilant, ensuring that New York does not destroy its past as it steamrolls into the future.

Music

Music in New York City rocks, hard, in every genre and style. Classical music-related performances flourish uptown, especially at the series of halls comprising Lincoln Center (Avery Fisher Hall is home to the **New York Philharmonic**). The 92nd St. Y is another showcase for serious music. Each summer the **Next Wave Festival** takes over the Brooklyn Academy of Music, offering spectacular, offbeat happenings, crackpot fusions of classical music, theater, and performance art.

In 1976 ambitious avant-garde poets and sometime musicians took over the campy glamrock scene in downtown bar-room clubs like **CBGB's** and **Maxwell's Kansas City**: bands and performers like the Ramones, Patti Smith, Richard Hell, Television, and Blondie combined venom, wit, and a calculated stupidity to invent **punk**. Ever since, New York has convulsed with musical shocks: the New Wave became the **No Wave** when speed-freaking bizarro intellectuals (in bands like DNA, the Contortions, Teenage Jesus and the Jerks, and Red Transistor) pared rock down to a minimum and added honking saxophone squalor. In the 80s angry kids imported **hardcore** from Washington, DC: a bevy of fast-rocking, non-drinking, non-smoking bands like Youth of Today, Sick of It All, and Gorilla Biscuits packed Sunday all-ages shows at CBGB's. In the 80s and early 90s the **"post-punk"** scene crystallized around bands like Sonic Youth, Yo La Tengo, Pussy Galore, and Helmet; today smaller outfits like girlnoise God Is My Co-Pilot, the Airlines, and the Mad Scene produce short, finely-crafted bursts of musical energy. You can find obscure or out-of-print vinyl in one of the city's many used record stores: prices are absurd, but the selection far surpasses that of any other North American city. (See Shopping: Record Stores.)

Rap and **hip-hop** began here, on the streets of New York's neighborhoods, and the list of New York artists reads like the text of *Who's Who in Urban Music:* KRS-1, Chuck D, MC Lyte, LL Cool J, Run-DMC, EPMD, and—the one true queen—Queen Latifah, from across the river in Jersey. Grandmaster Caz and Bronx DJ Afrika Bambaataa laid the foundations in the late 70s and early 80s with records rooted deeply in electronic processing, scratching, and sampling. In 1979, the Sugarhill Gang (see Harlem: Sights for more on Sugar Hill) released *Rapper's Delight*, widely considered the first true rap song. For a clearer glimpse of the hip-hop scene in New York (and across the country) pick up a copy of New York-based *The Source*, the genre's premier fanzine (new, thicker, glossier than before).

Jazz has been associated with the sound of the big city since the music's inception. Duke Ellington played here in the 20s and 30s. **Minton's Playhouse** in Harlem was home to Thelonious Monk and one of the birthplaces of **be-bop**, a highly-sophisticated jazz variant with a hard-edged sensibility. Miles Davis, Charlie Parker, Dizzy Gillespie, Max Roach, Tommy Potter, Bud Powell, and many others contributed to the New York sound of the late 40s and 50s, when beatniks, hepcats, and poor old souls filled 52nd St. clubs, especially the Village Vanguard. **Free-jazz** pioneer Cecil Taylor and spaceman Sun Ra set up shop here during the 60s and 70s. Today, wonko experimentalists like John Zorn and James Blood Ulmer plot to destroy music at clubs like the **Knitting Factory**; meanwhile, in Brooklyn, a loose grouping of like-minded musicians called M-Base mixes hot funk with cool jazz, to good effect.

This is the place to catch new music: nearly every performer who comes to the States plays here, and thousands of local bands compete to make a statement and (rarely) win an audience. Venues range from stadiums to concert halls to back-alley sound-systems. Whatever your inclination, New York's expansive musical scenes should be able to satisfy your desire for stimulation. (See Entertainment: Music.)

Literary New York

New York's reputation as literary capital of the Americas has deep historical roots. English-born **William Bradford,** perhaps the city's first literary man of note, was appointed public printer—America's first—here in 1698. He went on to found the country's first newspaper, the *New York Gazette,* in 1725. See the spot—down on the corner of Hanover, Stone, and William Streets in Lower Manhattan—where New York's tabloid tradition took hold.

Even before it had become the publishing center of the country (supplanting Boston some time in the mid-19th century) New York was home to many of the pioneers of the national literature. Some of these writers—**Herman Melville** for example—knew neither of their own nor of New York's impending literary fame. Melville, born in 1819 at 6 Pearl St. (also in Lower Manhattan), was so disheartened by the critics' response to *Moby Dick* that he took a job at a New York customs house for four dollars a day and died unrecognized and unappreciated. To top it off, the *Times* called him Henry in his obituary. **Washington Irving** knew better how to work a room. Born at 131 William St., the author of *Knickerbocker's History of New York* made a name for himself penning satirical essays on New York society "from the beginning of the world to the end of the Dutch dynasty." In a moment of classic coinage Irving gave New York its enduring pen-name, Gotham City. Other Lower Manhattan writers of the times included **William Cullen Bryant, James Fenimore Cooper,** and **Walt Whitman,** who hung around for a while to work on the magazine *Aurora* and to rhapsodize freeversely on the Brooklyn Bridge and "Manahatta."

American writers have traditionally lived on the fringes of the culture. Appropriately, most New York writers have lived on the *geographic* fringes of their city–either well above (in Harlem) or below (in the Village and on the Lower East Side) New York's social and commercial centers. Maybe these writers have sought the critical perspective that comes with living at a distance. Maybe, as in **Edgar Allen Poe's** pitiful case, they were so brutally poor they had no choice in the matter. Poe, who rented a house all the way out in the rural Bronx, earned so little he used to send his aging mother-in-law to scour nearby fields for edible roots to feed the family.

Literary deadbeats, hacks, and bohunks followed the wave of mostly Italian immigrants and Bohemians streaming into Greenwich Village and its surroundings in the early 20th century. Among the young-and-poor crowd were **Willa Cather, John Reed,** and **Theodore Drieser,** pioneers of the mature American novel. For over fifty years the Village would be one of America's most important neighborhoods, hosting a full spectrum of poets, essayists, and novelists: **Marianne Moore, Hart Crane, e.e. cummings, Edna St. Vincent Millay, John Dos Passos, Thomas** *(Look Homeward, Angel)* **Wolfe.**

Although too expensive for most Village writers, spiffy Washington Square—immortalized by **Henry James's** *Washington Square* (duh) and **Edith Wharton's** *Age of Innocence*—was neverthless the center of the literary scene. Radiating off the Square to the north were the legendary **Salamagundi Club** (47 Fifth Ave. at 11 St.); the Cedar Tavern, one time gathering place for degenerate **Allen Ginsburg** and **Jack Kerouac;** and the cobblestoned Washington Mews, home over the years to **Sherwood Anderson** (No. 54), **"Jaundice" John Dos Passos** (in the studio between No. 14 and 15), and innumerable others. To the south of the Square once stood the boarding houses where **O. Henry** and **Eugene O'Neill** kicked it, and at 133 MacDougal, the spot where O'Neill revved up his **Provincetown Players.** Down Bleecker and MacD you'll find some of the coffee houses the Beats made famous, along with former residences of James Fenimore Cooper (145 Bleecker), Theodore Drieser, and **James Agee** (172 Bleecker). West of the Square are the former pads of **Richard Wright, Edward Albee** (238 W. 4th St.), **Sinclair Lewis** (69 Charles St.), **Hart Crane** (79 Charles St.) and **Thomas** *(Look Homeward, Angel)* **Wolfe** (263 West 11 St.). **Dylan Thomas** was one many writers who gassed up at the White Horse Tavern (567 Hudson St.). Few, however, were so unfortunate as Thomas, who, after pumping a purported 18 shots of scotch through his shredded gut, stepped outside, stumbled a few feet, then dropped dead. To this day **Troy Selvaratnam** stops by the White Horse for a quickie.

The West Village, of course, did not have exclusive rights on New York's writerly set. On the other side of Broadway, the now-thriving, once-affordable East Village was headquarters to Kerouac and Ginsberg, **Amiri Baraka (Le Roi Jones),** and **W.H. Auden** (who spent a couple of decades at 77 St. Mark's Place, basement entrance.). Many a writer has whiled away his dying days in relative obscurity at the **Chelsea Hotel** (on 23rd St. between 7th and 8th St.). It's up in Chelsea. Among the luckier of tenants have been **Arthur Miller** and **Vladimir Nabokov.** In midtown lurks the legendary **Algonquin Hotel** (59 W. 44th St.). In 1919 the wits of the Round Table— writers like **Robert Benchley, Dorothy Parker, Alexander Woollcott,** and **Franklin P. Adams**—made this hotel the site of their famous weekly lunch meetings. The Algonquin is birthplace of the *New Yorker* magazine.

The **Gotham Book Mart** (41 W. 47th St.), established in 1920, has long been one of New York's most important literary hangouts. The store is famous for its second-story readings, which hosted some of the biggest writers of the century and attracted all of literary New York. During the years when *Ulysses* was banned in the U.S., those in the know came to the Gotham to buy imported copies under the counter. Check out the memorabilia and old photographs that document the bookstore's history. **Columbia University** has been the intellectual magnet of the Upper West Side. The roving Beat crowd contaminated the area in the late Forties while Ginsberg was studying at the college. His friends were known to join him at the West End Cafe (2911 Broadway). Unlike the White Horse, this delicatessen/bar doesn't play up its high-falutin' past. Ask Ed or Dan or any of the West End regulars to hear some stories of the glory days.

The Renaissance that exploded in the Harlem of the Twenties is one of the most important moments in American literary history. Novels like **George Schuyler's** *Black No More* and **Claude McKay's** *Home to Harlem* are energized accounts of the throbbing, grizzled underworld of speakeasies and nightclubs. **Zora Neale Hurston,** an anthropology student at Columbia, helped plug the college intellectual scene into the hypercreative buzz up in Harlem, while **Langston Hughes** and his circle were busy founding radical journals. A downtown crowd of lefties, artists, and alternative lifestylists bypassed Midtown altogether in their relentless (often ignorantly condescending) explorations into Black culture. For the next generation's impressions of this amazing neighborhood, look to the writings of **James Baldwin, Anne Petry,** and **Ralph Ellison**, whose *Invisible Man* captures a tense and disappointed post-Renaissance Harlem. Also see **Nathan Huggins's** *Harlem Renaissance*.

Journalism and Publications

New York, the premiere society of information abundance, is a sounding board for the rest of the global village. ABC, CBS, NBC, two wire services, umpteen leading magazines, and more newspapers than anywhere else in the world have taken up residence here. Publicists, preachers, advertisers, sociologists, and community activists jockey for position, hoping to make enough noise to be heard above the information din. The stakes are immense, the opportunities unparalleled: the high concentration of media here amplifies every sound. Broadsheets, graffiti, posters, and billboards provide additional media outlets, public spaces for high-profile intervention. Meanwhile, a strange underground world opens up on public access television, if you can find a friend with cable.

New York's romance with the media began almost three centuries ago. The city's first newspaper, the *Gazette,* appeared in 1725. Ten years later, John Peter Zenger, editor of the *New-York Weekly Journal,* was charged with libel for satirizing public officials. His description of the city recorder as "a large spaniel...that has lately strayed from his kennel with his mouth full of fulsome panegyrics" was seen as especially offensive. The governor threw Zenger into jail and burned copies of his paper in public. When the court acquitted him, it set a precedent for what would become a great U.S. tradition, the freedom of the press.

The city soon became the center of the nation's rapidly developing print network. Horace Greeley's *Tribune,* based in New York, became America's first nationally distributed paper; Greeley told young men all around the country to Go West. In the mid-19th century, Nassau Street was dubbed "Newspaper Row."

Today New York supports well over 100 different newspapers, reflecting the diversity of its urban landscape. Weekly ethnic papers cater to the Black, Hispanic, Irish, Japanese, Chinese, Indian, Korean, and Greek communities, among others. Candidates for local office frequently court voters in these communities by seeking endorsements from their papers. Other papers cater to the patrician, the pensive, and the prurient.

The *New York Post* and the *Daily News,* the city's two major tabloid dailies, are famous for their less-than-demure sensibilities. The *News,* recently "rescued" by now-dead Robert Maxwell, has slightly better taste—it doesn't use red ink, and it reports fewer gruesome murders. *Post* headlines, often printed in unwieldy lettering three inches high, can have a nasty, toothsome ring. One of the *Post's* more brilliant offerings read "Headless Body Found in Topless Bar." Both papers have editorial policies more conservative than their headlines, as well as comics, advice pages, gossip columns, and horoscopes. The *Post* has a great sports section and both have good metropolitan coverage. *New York Newsday* also offers thorough local coverage. After more than 40 years as a successful Long Island paper—with a youngish staff, some entertaining columnists and a special Sunday section just for the kids—*Newsday* recently decided to make the jump to city tabloid and is trying hard to compete with the worst of its peers.

If you do want to read about headless bodies, the *New York Times* will not satisfy you. The distinguished elder statesman of the city papers, the *Times* deals soberly and thoroughly with the news. Its editorial page provides a nationally respected forum for policy debates and its political endorsements are prized by candidates across the country. Praise from its Book Review section can revitalize living authors and immortalize dead ones, and its Sunday crossword puzzles enliven brunches from Fresno to Tallahassee. Recently, the *Times* increased its regional coverage with "National Editions" geared toward audiences outside the city. But it remains centered on New York. Theater directors, nervous politicians, and other fervent readers even make late-night newsstand runs to buy the hefty Sunday *Times* around midnight on Saturday.

The largest weekly leftist newspaper in the country, the *Village Voice* captures a lot of the spirit of the city you won't find in the dailies. Printed on the same kind of paper as the conservative *Post* and *Daily News,* it has nothing else in common with them. Don't search here for syndicated advice columnists, baseball statistics, or the bikini-clad woman du jour. The *Voice* prefers to stage lively political debates and print quirky reflections on New York life. It also sponsors some good investigative city reporting— and the city's most intriguing set of personal ads. Twice-yearly special editions examine new music and literary trends. Aging rock-modernist Robert Christgau's music columns grace the *Voice* every week, while the movie reviews are some of the most substantial (and sometimes, considered) in the nation.

The *Wall Street Journal* and the Upper East Side's *New York Observer* fill out the news spectrum. The *Observer* prints articles and commentary on city politics on its dapper pink pages. The *Journal* gives a quick world news summary on page one for breakfasting brokers more interested in the market pages. With its pen-and-ink drawings, market strategies, and continual obsession with the price of gold, the *Journal* offers an alternate view of the world.

Magazines rise and fall constantly in New York, but a few have managed to endure. The rarefied *New Yorker* publishes fiction and poetry by well-known authors and the occasional fledgling discovery. Even its ads contain measured prose. Its world-famous cover by Saul Steinberg, showing the rest of the world dwarfed by New York, reflects the perspective of typical New Yorker and of the city's literary scene. *The New Yorker* also carries the most thorough listings and reviews of films and events—and the finest cartoons—in the tri-state area. *New York* magazine also prints extensive listings but focuses on the city's (wealthy) lifestyle. Its final pages can prove very entertaining: they hold impossible British crossword puzzles, monthly word game contests, and a slew of desperate personal ads.

Spy magazine, famous for calling Donald Trump a "garden gnome" and for popularizing the Bush adultery story, has gotten a lot of mileage out of its implicit belief that readers will peruse even the tiniest of type as long as it is trenchant. *Spy's* writing is tiny, but it takes witty jabs at city figures and styles. Its "Separated at Birth" series (pairing, say, Leona Helmsley with the Joker) has proved especially successful. *Spy* also occasionally mocks other journals, amusing those in the know and invariably baffling laypeople.

Etiquette

New Yorkers have a widespread reputation for rudeness. For most of them, lack of politeness is not a matter of principle; it's a strategy for survival. Nowhere is the anonymous rhythm of urban life more pronounced than in New York City. Cramped into tiny spaces, millions of people find themselves confronting one another every day, rudderless in a vast sea of humanity. If the comfort of strangers seems particularly meager here, keep in mind that it's partly a question of scale. The city is just too goddamn big, too heterogeneous, too jumbled. People tend to keep to themselves, especially in public.

If you feel that the city is unfriendly, try to note the small humanitarian gestures that transpire in unlooked-for places. On the subway, for example. Watch as those reclining give up their seats for the elderly, the handicapped, and the compulsive shoppers. And watch the Great Door Wrestle, staged daily in subway stops near you. "Hold the door!" yells a laggardly person, running down the stairs towards the train. Another passenger leaps from his seat and places his sturdy frame between the doors. "Close the door!" yells the conductor, eager to leave. "Hold the door!" yell other passengers, rallying to the cause. And as the pedestrian, gasping, hurtles into the subway car, the other passengers smile for a moment, happy at the drama's resolution.

New Yorkers don't greet everyone they see with a friendly smile, but some do save up a little warmth for the familiar faces in their building or neighborhood; many know their local grocer, or stationer, or dry cleaner. You won't make friends with the person sitting next to you on the bus, but many a cabdriver can chat engagingly through eons of gridlock. Most preciously, New Yorkers have great respect for privacy and intimacy. You can get away with almost anything on the streets of the city, and that's not simply rude evasiveness; the universal experience of being a stranger makes everyone live according to an uneasy ethos of toleration.

Clothing shouldn't be of great concern, unless you're hoping to impress someone. City dwellers dress in every sort of garb; you're sure to fit in (somewhere) no matter what you wear; women should avoid wearing extremely short skirts or shorts in seedier parts of town. When departing for a night out, remember that most moviehouses and theaters air condition their little velvet hearts out. Dance clubs can get very hot; you may want to wear a jacket or sweater, something you can take off later. Even theater dress is casual. Unless it's opening night, Broadway shows are casual affairs. If you want to know what's in style at the top, just check out a French fashion magazine from about a year ago.

Remember that service is never included on a New York tab. Sales tax is 8.25%; your tip should be about twice the tax. Tip hairdressers 10%, and bellhops around $1 a bag. Cab drivers and waiters expect 15%.

Planning Your Trip

Millions of penniless immigrants disembarked at Ellis Island with visions of streets paved with gold, but they quickly learned to survive in New York. You can too.

Use your address book as a supplementary travel guide; staying with friends, enemies, and remote acquaintances reduces the cost of living. The off-season helps too: in May and September, the weather improves, the crowds of tourists thin, and prices plummet. Facilities and sights don't close in the off-season—the city is a year-round attraction.

Travel offices, tourist information centers, chambers of commerce, and special interest organizations conspire to barrage you with an overwhelming amount of free information; it's best to write with specific requests. (See Practical Information for addresses.) Travel agents can advise you on the cheapest transportation options, but don't rely exclusively on their information. Do some calling on your own, scan newspaper travel sections, or consult your local bulletin boards.

Documents

Carry at least two forms of identification, one of which should be a photo ID. Banks, in particular, will want to see more than one form of identification whenever you cash a traveler's check. Before you leave, photocopy both sides of your important documents, such as ID and credit cards, and leave them with someone you can contact easily. Students should bring proof of their status. (Don't, however, expect the extensive student discounts on museum admission, entertainment, transportation, and accommodations available in Europe.) A current university ID card will generally suffice for U.S. students. Foreign students may want to purchase an **International Student Identification Card (ISIC),** available through several sources (see International Visitors below), although the cards tend not to carry much weight, especially with bouncers; they're notoriously easy to counterfeit.

Money

No matter how tight your budget or how short your trip, you won't be able to carry all your cash with you. Even if you think you can—don't. Non-cash reserves are necessary. Personal checks will not be readily accepted out of state, no matter how many forms of identification you have.

If you're visiting New York for more than a month, your best bet is to open a savings account in one of the local banks and get an **Automatic Teller Card (ATM)** which you can use 24 hrs. all over the City (see the list of NYC banks below). Your money will earn interest in the safety of the bank and be at your fingertips when you need it (albeit only about $250 per day). Shop around for banks without service and start-up charges. Most banks also belong to ATM networks, so you will be able to use the card in other cities if you travel on the weekends. Before you leave, you might also want to find out if your home bank is networked with any NYC banks; **Cirrus** (800-424-7787) and **Plus** (800-843-7587) are both popular. Be careful not to rely too heavily on your hometown card, though: heavy surcharges attach to such luxuries as using your Sporkie, Wyoming bank card in a New York bank.

If you're only passing through the city or if you're on the road a lot, **traveler's checks** will be most useful. Most tourist establishments accept them (though some cynical New York types might require the same kinds of ID—driver's license, major credit card—needed to cash personal checks), and almost all banks will cash them. Get your checks in your hometown bank, usually with a 1-2% surcharge; the surcharge may be waived if you have a large enough balance or a certain type of account. Certain travel organizations, such as the **American Automobile Association (AAA)**, offer commission-free traveler's checks to their members, but you must go to one of their offices to purchase them. While checks are available in denominations from $10 to $1000, try to get them in small denominations ($20 is best, never larger than $50)—otherwise, if you make a small-to-medium purchase you'll again find yourself carrying a large amount of cash. Remember that most exchangers will expect you to convert at least US$100 into traveler's checks.

Always hold onto the receipt from the purchase of your traveler's checks, a list of their serial numbers, and a record of which ones you've cashed. Keep these in a separate pocket or pouch from the checks themselves, since they contain the information you will need to replace the checks if they are stolen. It's also a good idea to leave the serial numbers with someone at home as a back-up in case of luggage loss.

American Express traveler's checks are perhaps the most widely recognized in the world, and the easiest to replace if lost or stolen—just contact the nearest AmEx Travel office or call the (800) number below. Other well-known banks market their own brands. Major traveler's check or credit card companies offer a variety of free services when you buy their checks or apply for their cards, including emergency cash advances; travel information hotlines; medical, legal, and interpreter referrals; emergency message relays; guaranteed hospital entry payments; lost document and credit card cancellation assistance; travel insurance; and help with travel arrangements.

The following are reliable and well-known traveler's check companies:

American Express, 800-221-7282 in U.S. and Canada; from elsewhere, call collect at 800-964-6665, or contact the U.K. office at (0800) 52 12 12 and ask for the *Traveler's Companion*, which lists the addresses of all their travel offices. The *Check for Two* option allows for double signing with a travel partner.

Bank of America, 800-227-3460; outside the U.S. call collect 415-624-5400. Connected with Visa/Barclay's under Interpayment. 1% commission for non-Bank of America customers. Checkholders may use the Travel Assistance hotline (800-368-7878 from U.S., 202-347-7113 collect from Canada), which provides free legal assistance, urgent message relay, lost document services, and, if you provide them with a credit card number, up to $1000 advance for prompt medical treatment.

Barclay's, 800-221-2426 in U.S. and Canada; in the U.K., (202) 67 12 12; from elsewhere call collect (212) 858-8500. Connected with Bank of America and Visa under Interpayment. Checks issued in US$ in Canada and U.S., CDN$ as well in Canada. 1% commission. Any branch will cash Barclay's checks free Mon.-Fri.; surcharge on Sat.

Citicorp, 800-645-6556; outside the U.S. call collect 813-623-4100. Commission 1%. Checks available in four currencies including both U.S. and CDN$. Commission of 1-2%. Checkholders enrolled automatically in Travel Assist Hotline (800-523-1199) for 45 days after purchase.

MasterCard International, 800-223-9920; outside the U.S. call collect 609-987-7300. Free from MasterCard, though bank commissions may run 1-2%.

Don't forget to write.

Now that you've said, "Let's go," it's time to say, "Let's get American Express® Travelers Cheques." Because when you want your travel money to go a long way, it's a good idea to protect it. So before you leave, be sure and write.

Thomas Cook, 800-223-7373; outside the U.S. call collect 212-974-5696. Available at any bank displaying a MasterCard sign.

Visa, 800-227-6811 in U.S. and Canada; from abroad, call collect 212-858-8500 (New York) or 71 937 80 91 (London). No commission if purchased at Barclay's.

Even the best-budgeted trip will present unexpected expenses and emergencies, and **credit cards** are the best way to make sure you're not sent home because of them. Many of the places *Let's Go* lists won't accept plastic, but virtually all transportation companies do. The cards are especially handy for renting cars, making reservations, and obtaining cash advances at most banks. Or use them for large purchases to avoid depleting your money at hand. American Express tends to be accepted by more up-scale establishments, while almost any place that accepts credit cards will take Visa or MasterCard.

American Express cardholders pay a hefty annual fee ($55), but membership has its privileges: local AmEx offices will cash one personal check, domestic or foreign, per person per 7-day period. They can also cancel stolen credit cards, arrange for temporary identification, help change airline, hotel, and car rental reservations, send mailgrams and international cables, and hold your mail if you contact them well in advance. American Express operates machines at some major airports through which you can purchase traveler's checks with your card. For more information, call the American Express Card Division, 770 Broadway, New York, NY 10003 (800-528-4800) or AmEx Global Assist (800-333-2639), a 24-hr. helpline that provides legal and medical assistance.

Visa (800-227-6811) and **MasterCard** (800-223-9920) are accepted in more establishments than other credit cards, and they are also the most useful for getting an instant cash advance. Visa holders can generally obtain an advance up to the amount of the credit line remaining on the card, while MasterCard imposes a daily limit. Be sure to consult the bank that issues your card, however, since it may impose its own rules and restrictions. At a bank, you should be able to obtain cash from a teller, who will essentially "charge" you as if you had made a purchase. Not all ATMs will honor your credit card; those that do require you to enter your personal code number. You will have the option to set up a personal code when you receive a new card; if you do not have a code number for an old account, contact the credit card company to establish one. Expect a service charge for electronic cash advances.

Students or those with low income levels may run into problems trying to acquire a major credit card. Some of the larger, national banks have credit card offers geared especially toward students, even those who bank elsewhere. Otherwise, you may have to find someone older and more established (a parent or guardian, for example) to co-sign your application or request an extra card in your name.

Should you run out of money on the road and not have a credit card, you are at the mercy of the cash transfer and cabling systems, both reliable and costly choices. The most inexpensive option, and the one that makes the most sense within North America, is to have a **certified check** or **postal money order** mailed to you. It should arrive in about two days. All banks will cash certified checks, and post offices will redeem money orders upon presentation of two forms of identification (one with photo). Be sure the sender keeps the receipt for the money order, as they are refundable if lost.

Cabling money is a more costly alternative. **Bank of America** (800-346-7693) will do the job. Have someone bring cash, a credit card, or a cashier's check to the sending bank—you don't have to have an account. You can pick up the money three to five working days later with ID, and it will be paid out to you in traveler's checks. If you do not have a Bank of America account, there is a $40 fee for domestic cabling, $45 for international. Other fees apply, depending on the bank at which you receive the money. **American Express' Moneygram** service (800-543-4080) will cable money domestically for $49 per $750-1000 and internationally for $70 per $750-1000. The first $200 may be received in cash, the rest in traveler's checks or as a money transfer check. Non-cardholders may use this service for no extra charge, but money can only be sent from England, Germany, and some locations in France; other European and

Australian AmEx offices can only *receive* Moneygrams. **Barclay's** will wire money for their customers for the slight fee of $15 for sums under $3000 within the U.S.; for larger sums you may pay as much as $35-40. To take advantage of a classic, reliable, and expensive service, use **Western Union** (800-325-6000). You or someone else can phone in a credit card number, or else someone can bring cash to a Western Union office. As always, you need ID to pick up your money. Their charge is $40 for $500, $50 for $1000. There is an additional surcharge on money sent from Europe to the U.S., but it will usually be available within two days.

If time is of the essence, you can have money wired directly, bank to bank. A **cable transfer** is the fastest method of transport, requiring 24 or 48 hours to get to a major city or a bit longer to a more remote location. Cabling costs average $30 for amounts less than $1000, plus the commission charged by your home bank. Cheaper but slower is a **bank draft** or **international money order.** You pay a commission ($15-20) on the draft, plus the cost of sending it airmail (preferably registered). If nothing else works, your consulate will wire home for you and deduct a charge from the money you receive. Don't expect them to be happy about it.

New York banks are usually open Mon.-Fri. 9am to 5pm. Some may also be open Saturdays 9am to noon or 1pm. All banks, government agencies, and post offices are closed on legal holidays (see Holidays below).

The prices quoted throughout *Let's Go: New York City* are the amounts before **sales tax** has been added. Sales tax in New York state is 8.25%, depending on the item. Hotels have begun to charge a special tax of 5% on rooms costing over $100 per night, on top of sales tax.

Packing

Pack light if New York is just a stop on a longer trip for you, or if you'll be moving around the area a lot. But if you're planning to stay in the city for a long time, you might want to bring more clothes along, and you might also prefer a suitcase or duffel bag to a backpack.

Bring good footwear and rainwear. You may need an outfit for going out in the evening—some restaurants, theaters, and events require (or at least seem to require) an upscale outfit. Clothing should be comfortable and should require minimal care. Laundromats can be found throughout the city, but if you don't want to spend your valuable vacation time planted in front of a Maytag, consider doing laundry by hand. Pack a plastic clothesline that can be hung up in your room; your clothes can dry while you enjoy the sights.

Travelers are sometimes separated from their luggage, temporarily or permanently. Always keep valuable items (traveler's checks, tickets, credit cards) and identification on your person. Stow a change of clothes, medication, and any other irreplaceable items in a carry-on bag.

Bring appropriate camera equipment; you'll probably want to leave the tripod at home. If you only want snapshots, bring a pocket camera or a small automatic 35mm camera. Buy film at supermarkets or drugstores, since tourist shops often charge ridiculous prices. Steer clear of film (even of well-known name brands) manufactured in underdeveloped nations, since it can be of dubious quality. Have your film handchecked at airport X-ray machines. Prices for camera equipment in New York City are the lowest in the country. (See Shopping.)

Health

New York's sights are plentiful enough to make racing through them doubly a blunder: not only will you exhaust yourself, but you'll have missed most of what you tried to see. Drink fluids in July and August, when heat exhaustion can become a real danger. Be especially good to your feet—some good walking shoes, clean socks, and a bit of talcum powder will go a long way. If you wear glasses or contact lenses, bring a prescription and/or an extra pair. Lens wearers can avoid dried-out contacts by drinking sufficient fluids and switching to glasses where the air is dry or smoky. Be sure all immunizations, such as tetanus shots, are up to date. All travelers should be concerned about Acquired Immune Deficiency Syndrome (AIDS), transmitted through the exchange of body fluids with an infected individual. Avoid unprotected sex and the sharing of intravenous needles. For more information you can call the AIDS Hotline at the **Center for Disease Control** (800-342-2437).

Before you leave, check whether your insurance policy (if you have one) covers medical costs incurred while traveling (see Insurance). Always have proof of insurance and policy numbers with you. If you're a student, you may be covered by your family's policy. If you have insurance through your school, find out if the policy includes summer travel. If you choose to risk traveling without insurance, you still have avenues for health care that bypass hospitals and private practice. Call the local hotline or crisis center listed in this book under Practical Information. Operators at these organizations have numbers for public health organizations and clinics that treat patients without demanding proof of solvency. University teaching hospitals usually run inexpensive clinics as well. If you require **emergency treatment,** call 911 or go to the emergency room of the nearest hospital.

If you have a chronic medical condition that requires medication on a regular basis, consult your physician before you leave. Carry copies of your prescriptions and always distribute medication and/or syringes among all your carry-on and checked baggage in case any of your bags is lost. If you are traveling with a medical condition that cannot be easily recognized—such as diabetes, an allergy to antibiotics or other drugs, epilepsy, or a heart condition—you should obtain a **Medic Alert identification tag** (about $30) to alert both passersby and medical personnel of your condition in case of emergency. Such a tag is engraved with the wearer's primary medical condition, an identification number, and a 24-hr. hotline number that can provide critical medical information in an emergency. Contact Medic Alert Foundation International, Turlock, CA 95381-1009 (800-ID-Alert or 800-432-5378).

The **American Diabetes Association** (Attention: Patient Services, 1660 Duke St., Alexandria, VA 22314, (800-232-3472)) provides copies of the article "Travel and Diabetes" and diabetic ID cards. Contact your local ADA office for information. For more health-related advice, consult The *Pocket Medical Encyclopedia and First-Aid Guide* (Simon and Schuster, $5; write to Mail Order Dept., 200 Old Tappan Rd., Old Tappan, NJ 07675, or call 800-223-2348). In addition, the International Association for Medical Assistance to Travellers (IAMAT) provides members with free pamphlets and a directory of fixed-rate English-speaking physicians throughout the world. Membership is free, although donations are appreciated. Contact IAMAT at 415 Center St., Lewiston, NY 14092 (716-754-4883), or in Canada at 40 Regal St., Guelph, Ont. N1K 1B5 (519-836-0102). If you would like more information concerning health problems you may encounter in your travels, you can send away for the First-Aid and Safety Handbook ($14.95) from the American Red Cross. Write to 99 Brookline Ave., Boston, MA 02215, or to any local office in the U.S. to purchase the book. If you are interested in taking one of the many first-aid and CPR courses that the American Red Cross offers, contact one of their local offices. Courses are relatively inexpensive, and are usually very well taught.

If you are in the New York area and need an abortion, you may want to contact the **National Abortion Federation**. NAF is a professional association of abortion providers. Call their toll-free hotline (800-772-9100, Mon.-Fri. 9:30am-5:30pm) for information, counseling, and the names of qualified medical professionals in the area. NAF has developed informational publications for individuals and health care clinics alike. Clinics they'll refer you to must maintain certain safety and operational standards. In New York NAF will refer you to the Planned Parenthood clinics. The number of the Manhattan clinic is 212-677-6474; the Brooklyn number is 718-858-1819; in the Bronx it's 212-292-8000.

Insurance

Before leaving home, check to see if your homeowner's insurance (or your family's coverage) will cover theft and accident while you're on the road; coverage usually includes loss of travel documents such as passports, plane tickets, and rail passes up to $500. For U.S. residents, **Medicare** covers travel in the U.S., Canada, and Mexico. **American Express** cardmembers automatically receive car-rental and flight insurance on purchases made with the card. If you need additional insurance, the **Council on International Educational Exchange (CIEE)** (212-661-1414) offers a **Trip-Safe Plan** that covers the entire U.S. for **ISIC** cardholders (see For International Visitors, below) and non-holders alike. The Trip-Safe plan includes US$3000 of accident-related coverage and US$100 per day of in-patient health coverage for up to 60 days, US$1000 for 24-hr. all-risk death and dismemberment, as well as $25,000 for accidental death and dismemberment as an airline passenger. The plan also provides insurance for baggage loss, trip cancellation, and many other infelicities.

Most of the following insurance companies offer coverage for trip cancellation/interruption, baggage loss, accidents, and sickness, but ask individual firms for specifics. Some also provide on-the-spot hospital expenses, emergency cash advances, and guaranteed transferals, and most have 24-hr. hotlines. Senior citizens should be aware that many policies have an upper age limit of 70.

You can buy a policy directly from these firms or through a travel agent operating on their behalf:

Access America, Inc., P.O. Box 90310, Richmond, VA 23230-9310 (800-284-8300). A subsidiary of Blue Cross/Blue Shield. Covers trip cancellation/interruption, on-the-spot hospital admittance costs, emergency medical evacuation, and a 24-hr. hotline.

Carefree Travel Insurance, 120 Mineola Blvd., Mineola, NY 11501 (800-645-2424). Package includes coverage for baggage loss, accidents, medical treatment, and trip cancellation or interruption; the last can also be purchased separately. 24-hr. hotline.

Edmund A. Cocco Agency, 220 Broadway, #201, Lynnfield, MA 01940 (800-821-2488, in MA 617-595-0262). Coverage against accident, sickness, baggage loss, and trip cancellation or interruption. Emergency medical evacuation covered as well. Payment of medical expenses on-the-spot anywhere in the world. Protection against bankruptcy or default of airlines, cruise lines, or charter companies. Trip cancellation/interruption coverage $5.50 per $100 of coverage. Group rates available. 24-hr. hotline.

The Traveler's Insurance Co., 1 Tower Sq., Hartford, CT 06183-5040 (800-243-3174, in CT, HI, or AK 203-277-2318). Insurance against accident, baggage loss, sickness, trip cancellation or interruption, and company default. Covers emergency medical evacuation as well. Available through most travel agencies.

Travel Guard International, 1145 Clark St., Stevens Point, WI 54481 (715-345-0505 or 800-782-5151). Basic ($19), deluxe ($39), and comprehensive "Travel Guard Gold" (8% of total trip cost) packages cover baggage delay, car rental, accidental death, and trip cancellation or interruption. 24-hr. hotline for policy-holders.

Average Monthly Temperatures

> *"Oh dear, I'm so hot and thirsty—and what a hideous place New York is!" She looked despairingly up and down the dreary thoroughfare. "Other cities put on their best clothes in summer, but New York seems to sit in its shirt-sleeves."*
> —Edith Wharton, The House of Mirth

City summers have been getting hotter, but in general New York weather stays mild. In cold weather, gusts of wind swirl near the rivers and Central Park, but pretty much come to a halt at the unperturbed edifices of Midtown. Umbrellas are nice to have, though strategic walkers can often find enough construction and canopies to keep dry all the way home.

month	high	low
January	38°	26°
February	40°	27°
March	49°	34°
April	61°	44°
May	72°	53°
June	80°	63°
July	85°	68°
August	84°	67°
September	76°	60°
October	66°	50°
November	54°	41°
December	42°	30°

Travelers with Specific Concerns

Student Travelers

Students are often entitled to special discounts on admission prices, hotel rates, and airfares. Most places accept a current university ID or an **International Student Identity Card (ISIC)** as sufficient proof of student status. An ISIC for 1993 will cost around $14 and can be obtained at your university's student travel office (if it has one) or else from one of the organizations listed below. When you apply for an ISIC, be sure to have up-to-date proof of full-time student status (usually a student ID, but sometimes official university documents), a vending-machine photograph (1 1/2 x 2-inch) with your name printed and signed in pencil on the back, and proof of your birthdate and nationality. The ISIC card is valid for up to 16 months, always expiring in December. Students must be at least 12 years old to be eligible. Non-students under 26 years of age should look into the **International Youth Card** from the **Federation of International Youth Travel Organizations (FIYTO),** which may help you take advantage of age-based discounts. Applicants must submit proof of birthdate, a photo, and a fee of $10. For further information, write to the FIYTO at Islands Brygge 81, DK-23X Copenhagen S, Denmark (tel. 31 54 60 80).

The following agencies specialize in travel for high school and university students. They sell ISIC cards and have tips on transportation discounts. For listings of similar organizations that serve foreign travelers, see For International Visitors.

Council on International Educational Exchange (CIEE) Travel Services. Advice on questions ranging from package tours and low-cost travel to work opportunities and long-distance hiking. Special academic and employment exchange programs. ISIC and International Youth cards. Write for *Student Travels* (free), CIEE's new biannual travel magazine for college students. **Council Travel,** a budget travel subdivision of CIEE, operates 30 offices throughout the U.S., including the following: **Boston,** 729 Boylston St. #201, MA 02116 (617-266-1926); **Chicago,** 1153 N. Dearborn St., IL 60601 (312-951-0585); **New York,** 205 E. 42nd St., NY, NY 10017 (800-223-7402 or 212-661-1450; one of three offices in the City (another is located in the HI/AYH hostel)—write or call the NY office for general information and for the address and phone of an office closer to you); **Los Angeles,** 1093 Broxton Ave. #220, CA. 90024 (213-208-3551); **San Francisco,** 919 Irving St. #102, CA 94122 (415-566-6222).

Let's Go Travel Services, Harvard Student Agencies, Inc., Thayer Hall-B, Harvard University, Cambridge, MA 02138 (617-495-9649). Sells railpasses, American Youth Hostel memberships (valid at all IYHF/HI youth hostels), International Student and Teacher ID cards, International Youth Cards for non-students, travel guides (including the *Let's Go* series), swell maps, discount airfares and a complete line of budget travel gear. All items are available by mail.

STA Travel, 17 E. 45th St., New York, NY 10017 (800-777-0112 or 212-986-9470) operates 10 offices in the U.S. and over 100 around the world. Offers discount airfares for travelers under 26 and full-time students under 32.

Travel CUTS (Canadian Universities Travel Service, Ltd.): 187 College St., Toronto, Ont. M5T 1P7 (416-979-2406). Canadian distributor of the ISIC, IYHF/HI, and International Youth Cards. Offers discount travel services and publishes a quarterly newsletter, *Canadian Student Traveler.* Write for address and phone number of branches in Burnaby, Calgary, Edmonton, Halifax, Montreal, Ottawa, Quebec, Saskatoon, Sudbury, Victoria, Waterloo, Winnipeg, and London.

Senior Travelers

Discounts abound for the mature traveler. Don't lie about your age; take advantage of reduced rates on public transportation, museum, movie, theater and concert admissions, accommodations, and even dining. All you need is identification proving your age (a driver's license, a Medicare card, or a membership card from a recognized society of retired people).

Eight dollars will enroll you and your spouse in the **American Association of Retired Persons (AARP)**, open to U.S. residents aged 50 and over. As members you can take advantage of **AARP's Purchase Privilege Program** with discounts at major hotel/motel chains, from car-rental and sight-seeing companies. For more information, write 601 E St. NW, Washington, DC 20049 (202-434-2277). For a fee, membership in the **September Days Club**, 2571 Buford Highway, Atlanta, GA 30324 (800-241-5050) entitles you to a 15-40% discount at Days Inns across the U.S. They also have a travel service for senior citizens.

Through the **National Council of Senior Citizens,** 1331 F St. NW, Washington, DC 20004 (202-347-8800), anyone of any age can get hotel and auto rental discounts, a senior citizen newspaper, use of a discount travel agency, and members over 65 years of age receive supplemental Medicare insurance. Fees are $12 per year or $150 for lifetime membership.

The **Hostelling International/International Youth Hostel Federation** sells membership cards ($15) at a discount to those over 54. Write the AYH National Headquarters, P.O. Box 37613, Washington, DC 20013-7613 (202-783-6161). The IYHF is currently in the process of adopting a new seal of approval. Members of the network will soon be using the trademark blue triangle and the name "Hostelling International" ("HI"). Look for these symbols to insure that you are staying at IYHF/AYH-affiliated hostels. (See Accommodations for information on hostels.) To explore the outdoors, U.S. citizens and permanent residents 62 and over can buy a **Golden Age Passport** ($20 at park entrances), that gives you free entry into all national parks and a 50% discount on recreational activities. Write or stop by the U.S. Department of the Interior, National Park Service, P.O. Box 37127, Washington, DC 20013-7127 or call 202-208-4747.

Elderhostel uses the facilities of colleges and universities in New York (and worldwide). Participants in domestic programs spend a week studying subjects ranging from music appreciation to beekeeping at a cost of around $300. International programs last two to four weeks at costs ranging from $900-5000 including airfare. The fee covers room, board, tuition, use of campus facilities, and extracurricular activities. Hostelships are available to those requiring financial assistance (domestic programs only). You must be at least 60 to enroll and may bring a companion who is over 50; spouses may be any age. For a free catalog listing course descriptions for the current season, contact Elderhostel, 75 Federal St., Boston, MA 02110 (617-426-7788). Unaffiliated with the Elderhostel program is the publication *Elderhostels: The Students' Choice,* by Mildred Hyman ($15.95 plus $2.75 postage), a guide to 100 popular hostels, from John Muir Publications, P.O. Box 613, Santa Fe, NM 87504 (800-888-7504).

Helpful publications regarding travel for senior citizens are legion. *Travel Tips for Older Americans,* a pamphlet put out by the U.S. Government, may be useful. For a copy, send $1 to the **Bureau of Consular Affairs,** Superintendent of Documents, U.S. Government Printing Office, Washington, DC 20402 (202-783-3238). The *International Directory of Access Guides* ($5) has listings specifically for the elderly; order from **Rehabilitation International USA,** 112 Broadway #704, New York, NY 10010.

Pilot Books puts out two travel books for senior citizens: *Senior Citizen's Guide to Budget Travel in the United States and Canada* ($6 ppd.) and *The International Health Guide for Senior Citizen Travelers* ($5). Order from Pilot Books, 103 Cooper St., Babylon, NY 11702 (516-422-2225) and add $1 for postage. *Get Up & Go: A Guide for the Mature Traveler* ($10.95 plus $1.50 postage), by Gene and Adele Malott, is available from **Gateway Books,** 13 Bedford Cove, San Rafael, CA 94901 (415-454-5215). **Penguin USA,** 120 Woodbine St., Bergenfield, NJ 07621 (800-331-4624) distributes the *Discount Guide for Travelers over 55,* by Caroline and Walter Weintz (Dutton, $8 plus $1.50 postage).

Women Travelers

Women exploring any area on their own inevitably face additional safety concerns. Forgo cheap accommodations in city outskirts—the risks outweigh any savings—and stick to youth hostels, university accommodations, bed-and-breakfasts, and organizations offering rooms for women only. A woman should *never* hitchhike alone; it's dangerous even for two women together.

If you find yourself the object of catcalls or unwelcome propositions, your best answer is no answer. Always look as if you know where you're going (even when you don't), and maintain an assertive, confident posture wherever you go. If you feel uncomfortable asking strangers for information or directions, it may be easier to approach other women or couples. Always carry enough change for a bus, taxi, or phone call. And in emergencies, don't hesitate to yell for help.

Know the emergency numbers for the area you're visiting; *Let's Go* lists them in the Practical Information section of each area. More information and safety tips can be found in the *Handbook for Women Travelers,* available from **Judy Piatkus** (Publishers) Ltd., 5 Windmill St., London W1P 1HF, England (07 16 31 07 10). The folks who produced *Gaia's Guide* (no longer available) are now publishing *Women Going Places,* a new women's travel/resource guide, emphasizing women-owned and operated enterprises. The guide is aimed at lesbians, but useful to all women. Available from **INLAND Book Company,** P.O. Box 120261, East Haven, CT 06512 (203-467-4267).

Gay and Lesbian Travelers

New York City has a large, active, out, and supportive gay and lesbian population. Gay and lesbian visitors will have no trouble finding bars and clubs, bookstores, and special events in the City. (The NYC Gay Pride Parade, late June each year, is one of the biggest in the world; 1992's was the largest queer happening in U.S. history.) Wherever possible, *Let's Go* lists information lines, community centers, entertainment, and special services for gays and lesbians. You'll definitely want to consult New York's many gay papers, most of them available at corner newsstands (especially in the Village), for the most current information. *NY Native* and *Queer Weekly* are two of the most useful. *Homo-Xtra,* which bills itself as the "politically incorrect" weekly, directs its readers to all kinds of sexy services. The nationally-distributed *Advocate* magazine has a New York section, and you might also check the *Village Voice,* which lists events, services, and occasional feature articles of interest to gays and lesbians. *Metrosource,* issued every six months, covers bars, bookstores, and various gay resources. It is available at most gay bookstores.

For a continental directory of gay and lesbian establishments and services, consult the *Gayellow Pages* ($12). Order a copy from **Renaissance House,** P.O. Box 292, Village Station, New York, NY 10014-0292 (212-674-0120). Ask them about the spin-off *NY Gayellow,* which focuses exclusively on New York City. Two excellent sources of books for gay and lesbian travelers are **Giovanni's Room,** 345 S. 12th St., Philadelphia, PA 19107 (215-923-2960), which charges $3.50 postage per book in the U.S., and **Bob Damron Company, Inc.** P.O. Box 11270, San Francisco, CA 94101 (800-462-6654 or 415-777-0113). All of the following books are available through Giovanni's Room or the address listed under each book.

Spartacus International Gay Guide. $28; c/o Bruno Gmünder, Worldwide Advertising Sales, Lutzowstrasse 106, P.O. Box 30 13 45, D-1000, Berlin 30, West Germany. U.S. address: 100 East Biddle St., Baltimore, MD 21202 (301-727-5677). International guide for gay men, listing bars, restaurants, hotels, bookstores, and hotlines throughout the world.

Bob Damron's Address Book. $13; P.O. Box 11270, San Francisco, CA 94101 (415-777-0113). Over 6000 listings of bars, restaurants, guest houses, and services catering to the gay community.

Inn Places: USA and Worldwide Gay Accommodations. $14.95; available from Giovanni's.

The Women's Traveler. $10 plus $4.50 shipping; available from Giovanni's. A travel guide for lesbians. Maps of 50 major U.S. cities; listings of bars, restaurants, accommodations, bookstores, and services.

Places of Interest. A series of three books for men ($11), women ($10), and general ($12.50), including maps. Ferrari Publications, P.O. Box 35575, Phoenix, AZ 85069 (602-863-2408).

The number for the Gay and Lesbian Switchboard in New York is 777-1800; the number for the Lesbian Switchboard is 741-2610. When you first arrive in the City, you may want to stop by the Gay and Lesbian Community Center (620-7310), located at 208 W. 13th St. Over 150 meeting groups hold their gatherings in this three-story converted school house. The Center oversees an anti-violence project, houses a medical walk-in clinic (four nights a week), holds dances almost every other Saturday, and will refer you to various support groups.

Disabled Travelers

Most modern-day cities have been built by the physically-abled, for the physically-abled. Times are gradually changing, though, and with a little research and planning ahead, the disabled traveler can gain access to all but the most awkwardly built establishments. Your primary resource should be brand-new *Access for All* guide to New York cultural institutions, aimed at people with mobility, visual, or hearing impediments. It describes, in detail, over 180 locations throughout the city. For a free copy, write to **Hospital Audiences, Inc.**, Access Department, 220 W. 42nd St, New York, NY 10036. If it's not listed call restaurants, hotels, parks, and other facilities to find out about ramps, the presence of easy trails, the width of doors, the dimensions of elevators, etc. Also inquire about restrictions on motorized wheelchairs. *Let's Go* indicates disabled access whenever possible.

You can root around in a number of books helpful to disabled travelers. One good resource is *Access to the World,* by Louise Weiss ($17). For a copy, contact **Facts on File, Inc.,** 460 Park Ave., New York, NY 10016 (800-322-8755). **Twin Peaks Press** publishes three books: *Directory for Travel Agencies for the Disabled* ($20), *Travel for the Disabled* ($20), and *Wheelchair Vagabond* ($10), which discusses camping and travel in cars, vans, and RVs. Order from Twin Peaks Press, P.O. Box 129, Vancouver, WA 98666 (800-637-2256 or 206-694-2462). Add $2 shipping per book for the first three ordered, $1 for each book after that. Twin Peaks also operates a worldwide traveling nurse network.

If you are planning to visit a national park or attraction run by the National Park Service, you should obtain a **Golden Access Passport** ($20) available at all park entrances and from Federal offices whose functions relate to land, forests, or wildlife. The Golden Access Passport entitles disabled travelers and their families to enter the park for free and provides a 50% reduction on all campsite fees.

Arrange transportation well in advance to ensure a smooth trip. If you give sufficient notice, some major car rental agencies have hand-controlled vehicles at select locations. Call **Avis** (800-331-1212, at least 24 hrs. notice), **Hertz** (800-654-3131, 2-3 days notice), or **National** (800-328-4567, at least 24 hrs. notice). Both **Amtrak** and the airlines will accommodate disabled passengers if notified in advance—when booking your flight or train, tell the ticket agent which services you require. Hearing-impaired travelers may contact Amtrak (800-872-7245, in PA 800-322-9537) using teletype printers. **Greyhound** buses will also provide free travel for a companion; if you are without a fellow-traveler, call Greyhound (800-752-4841) at least 48 hrs. before you plan to leave and they will make arrangements to assist you. Seeing-eye and hearing-ear dogs also ride Greyhound without charge. For information on transportation availability in NYC (or any other U.S. city), contact the **American Public Transit Association,** 1201 N.Y. Ave. NW, Suite 400, Washington, DC 20005 (202-898-4000).

The **Travel Information Service** at the **Moss Rehabilitation Hospital,** 1200 W. Tabor Rd., Philadelphia, PA 19141 (215-329-5715), is an excellent source of information on tourist sights, accommodations, and transportation for the disabled; it charges only a nominal postage fee if you request the packet of information on travel accessibility. The **Society for the Advancement of Travel for the Handicapped,** 345 Fifth Ave., Suite #610, New York, NY 10016 (212-447-7284; fax 212-620-2159), provides several useful booklets as well as advice and assistance on trip planning. Membership is $45 per year, $25 for senior citizens and students; non-members may obtain publications by sending a self-addressed stamped envelope and $2 to cover expenses. The **American Foundation for the Blind** recommends travel books and issues identification discount cards ($10) for the legally blind. For an ID application or for other information, contact the American Foundation for the Blind, 15 W. 16th St., New York, NY 10011 (800-232-5463 or 212-620-2159).

Other organizations specialize in arranging tours. **Evergreen Travel Service,** 4114 198th St., SW #13, Lynnwood, WA 98036 (800-435-2288), offers tour programs for travelers in wheelchairs, blind travelers, deaf travelers, and "slow walkers." **Directions Unlimited,** 720 N. Bedford Rd., Bedford Hills, NY 10507 (800-533-5343; in NY, 914-241-1700), also conducts tours for the physically disabled. To inquire about other organizations that plan tours for disabled travelers, write to the **Handicapped Travel Division, National Tour Association,** P.O. Box 3071, Lexington, KY 40596 (606-253-1036). The **Federation of the Handicapped,** 211 W. 14th St., New York, NY 10011 (212-727-4268), leads tours for physically-disabled members, including daytrips, weekend outings, and longer excursions. **Flying Wheels Travel,** 143 W. Bridge St., P.O. Box 382, Owatonna, MN 55060 (800-535-6790, in MN 800-722-9351), provides general information and arranges domestic or international tours for groups and individuals. **Whole Persons Tours,** P.O. Box 1084, Bayonne, NJ 07002-1084 (201-858-3400), conducts tours and publishes the *Itinerary,* a bimonthly magazine for disabled travelers. (Subscriptions: $10 for 1 year, $18 for 2 years.)

Travelers with Special Diets

Vegetarians won't have any problem eating well and cheaply in New York. (Vegetarian meals are almost always cheaper anyway—the ecosystem and your wallet are on the same side.) *Let's Go* lists a number of great, cheap vegetarian restaurants, but discriminating travelers will want more. You can order key books like the *International Vegetarian Travel Guide* and/or the *Vegetarian Times Guide to Natural Foods Restaurants in the U.S. and Canada* (each costs $15.95 plus $3 postage) from the **North American Vegetarian Society,** P.O. Box 72, Dolgeville, NY 13329 (518-568-7970).

Kosher travelers should contact NYC synagogues for information about kosher restaurants and advice on how to eat kosher in non-kosher restaurants; your own synagogue or college Hillel should have access to lists of Jewish institutions across the continent. *The Jewish Travel Guide* ($11.50 with a $1.50 shipping charge) is available in the U.S. from **Sepher-Hermon Press,** 1265 46th St., Brooklyn, NY 11219 (718-972-9010). It lists Jewish institutions, synagogues, and kosher restaurants in over 80 countries. Muslim travelers seeking **halal** foods should visit Islamic neighborhoods and stores or check the local Yellow Pages listings under "halal."

For International Visitors

United States Tourist Offices, found in many countries, can provide you with armloads of free literature. If you can't find a U.S. Tourist Office in your area, write the

U.S. Travel and Tourism Administration, Department of Commerce, 14th St. and Constitution Ave. NW, Washington, DC 20230 (202-377-4003 or 202-377-3811). USTTA has branches in Australia, Belgium, Canada, France, Germany, Japan, Mexico, and the United Kingdom; contact the Washington office for information about the branch in your country. For general tourist information, you may also want to direct inquiries to the state and city tourist offices listed throughout the book and under *Tourism Bureaus* above. In Canada, contact **Travel CUTS,** 44 George St., Toronto, Ont. M5T 1P7 (416-979-2406).

If you wish to stay in a U.S. home during your vacation, many organizations can help you. The **Experiment in International Living** coordinates homestay programs for international visitors wishing to join a U.S. family for 3-4 weeks. Visitors over 14 live with host families. Homestays are arranged for all times of the year. For the appropriate address in your country, write to the U.S Headquarters, P.O. Box 676, Kipling Rd., Brattleboro, VT 05302-0676 (800-327-4678 or 802-257-7751). The **Institute of International Education (IIE)** publishes their "Homestay Information Sheet" listing many homestay programs for foreign visitors. Write to them at 809 United Nations Plaza, New York, NY 10017-3580 (212-883-8200). See Accommodations above for information on **Servas,** a similar inter-nation travel organization, which coordinates short (2-3 day) homestays.

Student Travelers

The **Council on International Educational Exchange (CIEE)** has affiliates abroad that charter airline tickets, arrange homestays, sell international student ID cards, travel literature, travel insurance, and hostel cards. CIEE also helps students secure work visas and find employment through its work-exchange programs. In **Australia,** contact SSA/STA Swap Program, P.O. Box 399 (1st Floor), 220 Faraday St., Carlton South, Melbourne, Victoria 3053 (03 347 69 11). In the **United Kingdom,** contact London Student Travel, 52 Grosvenor Gardens, London WC1 (tel. (071) 730 34 02). In **Canada** write to Travel CUTS (Canadian University Travel Services Ltd.), 187 College St., Toronto, Ont. M5T 1P7 (416-979-2406). If you can't locate an affiliated office in your country, contact CIEE's main office: 205 E. 42nd St., New York, NY 10017 (212-661-1450; 800-223-7402 for charter flight tickets only) or the **International Student Travel Confederation,** Gothersgade 30, 1123 Copenhagen K, Denmark (tel. 45 33 99 93).

The **Federation of International Youth Travel Organization (FIYTO)** issues the **International Youth Card (IYC)** to anyone under 26, as well as a free catalog that lists special services and discounts for IYC cardholders. Write or call Council Travel.

STA Travel, based in the U.K., has over 100 offices worldwide to help you arrange discounted overseas flights. In the U.S. call 800-777-0112; if the number does not work, call local information for an office near you, or write to 74 and 86 Old Brompton Rd., London SW7 3LQ, England, or call (071) 937 99 71 for flights to North America.

Documents and Formalities

Foreign visitors who wish to travel to the United States should plan early so they can complete all the necessary paperwork in time.

Visas

Foreign visitors to the United States are required to have a **passport, visitor's visa,** and **proof of intent to leave.** That said, there are a number of exceptions. Visitors from the following nations do not need a visa to enter the U.S.: Japan, Italy, Germany, France, the U.K., the Netherlands, Sweden, and Switzerland. Without a visa, however, these travelers must fly into the country on one of a specified list of carriers, have with them a ticket to leave the U.S., and stay not more than 90 days. For more information, contact the nearest U.S. consulate.

Canadian citizens who enter the U.S. from Canada or Mexico do not need a visa or passport, nor do Mexican citizens with a form I-186. Mexican border crossing cards (non-immigrant visas) limit you to 72 hours or less in the U.S. within 25 mi. of the border. Always carry proof of citizenship (a driver's license or birth certificate).

Most visitors obtain a B-2 or "pleasure tourist" visa, valid for six months. If you lose your I-94 form (arrival/departure certificate attached to your visa upon arrival), replace it at the nearest **U.S. Immigration and Naturalization Service** office. (If you lose your passport in the U.S., you must replace it through your country's embassy.) Extensions for visas (maximum 6 months) require form I-539 as well as a $35 fee and are also granted by the INS. For a list of offices, write the Immigration and Naturalization Service, Central Office Information Operations Unit, 425 I St. NW #5044, Washington, DC 20536 (202-633-4316).

In most cases, no special vaccinations are required to enter the U.S. For exceptions contact a U.S. embassy or consulate.

Non-Tourist Visas for Work and Study

Working in the U.S. with only a B-2 visa is grounds for deportation. You must obtain a work visa. Apply at the U.S. consulate in your country with a letter from an American employer stating that you have been offered a job and listing its responsibilities, salary, and employment period. An American employer can also obtain an H visa (usually an H-2) for you.

To **study** in the U.S., foreigners must apply for a F-1 or J-1 visa, depending on whether they are exchange students or full-time students enrolled in degree-granting programs. F-1 and J-1 students may apply to the INS through their school for full-time **practical training,** employment at the school closely related to a student's field of study, beneficial to a student's professional development, and unavailable in the home country. Many foreign schools—and most U.S. colleges—have offices that give specific advice on study and employment in the U.S. Almost all institutions accept applications from international students directly. If English is not your native tongue, you will generally be required to take the **Test of English as a Foreign Language and Test of Spoken English (TOEFL/TSE),** administered in many countries. Actual requirements are determined by each U.S. college or university. For more information, contact the TOEFL/TSE Application Office, P.O. Box 6155, Princeton, NJ 08541 (609-951-1100).

Before leaving the United States, foreigners holding some work or student visas must obtain a "Sailing Permit" from the **Internal Revenue Service** within 30 days prior to departure. (This is to ensure that you do not owe taxes to the U.S. government.) If you have any questions, write to the Director of International Operations, Internal Revenue Service, Washington, DC 20225.

International Driver's License

If you plan to drive during your visit, be sure to obtain an International Driver's License from your national automobile association before leaving (you can't get one here) and make sure you have proper insurance (required by law). To obtain a domestic driver's license, you must apply and be tested, a process that often takes weeks or months. Some foreign driver's licenses will be valid here for up to one year (check before you leave). And be careful: authorities may not realize that your license is valid.

Members of national automobile associations affiliated with the **American Automobile Association** (800-222-4357) can receive services from the AAA while they are in the U.S. Automobile associations in 19 countries have full reciprocity agreements with the AAA. Check your country's association for details.

In addition to a **passport,** almost all visitors to the U.S. must have a visitor's **visa** and proof of plans to leave the U.S. For stays of only a few days, Canadian citizens bearing proof of citizenship do not need a visa. Other travelers have to apply for visas at a U.S. consulate. International visitors usually obtain a B-1 or B-2 (non-immigrant traveling for pleasure) visa valid for a maximum of six months. The citizens of eight countries—the U.K., Japan, Italy, Germany, France, the Netherlands, Sweden, and

Switzerland—do not need visas to enter the U.S.; however, they must meet certain criteria, such as being in possession of a ticket to leave the U.S. within 90 days and flying on one of a specified group of air carriers. For more information, contact a U.S. consulate near you.

If you lose your passport once in the U.S., replace it through the embassy of your country. If you lose your visa or your I-94 form (the arrival/departure certificate attached to your visa upon arrival), replace it at the nearest **U.S. Immigration and Naturalization Service** office. You can procure a list of offices from the INS, Central Office Information Operations Unit, #5044, 425 I St. NW, Washington, DC 20536 (202-514-4316). This information does not necessarily apply for work or study in the U.S. (see Work and Study above). To extend your length of stay in the U.S., you must acquire separate INS forms. An application for an extension must be filed well before your original departure date; plan ahead.

Foreign students should obtain an **International Student Identification Card (ISIC)** as proof of student status. Obtain the ISIC at local travel agencies, from the International Student Travel Confederation, from CIEE, or from **Let's Go Travel Services.** Let's Go Travel also sells Hostelling International/American Youth Hostel memberships. The HI/ISIC and the HI/AYH card are available by mail.

If your home country signed the Geneva Road Traffic Convention back in 1949, you can legally drive in the U.S. for one year from the date of your arrival (unless you take a job or study). You can drive either a personal or rental car. However, unless you are from Canada or Mexico, your personal cars must exhibit the International Distinguishing Sign, which must be obtained in your home country. If your home country is not a signatory of the Convention, it is illegal for you to drive in the U.S. without obtaining a U.S. license and license plates/registration for your car, even if you have an international license. Consult the resident sages at your national automobile association before you leave. Remember that the usual minimum age for car rental and auto transport services is 21; recently a number of New York rental agencies were charged with violating state business codes by setting minimums as high as 25.

Customs

You may bring the following into the U.S. duty free: 200 cigarettes, $100 in gifts, and personal belongings such as clothes and jewelry. Travelers aged 21 and over may also bring up to one liter of alcohol, although state laws may further restrict the amount of alcohol you may carry.

You can bring any amount of currency, but if you carry over $10,000, you'll need to report it. In general, customs officers ask how much money you're carrying and your planned departure date in order to ensure that you'll be able to support yourself while here. In some cases they may ask about traveling companions and political affiliation. Travelers should carry any prescription drugs in clearly labeled containers and have a written prescription or doctor's statement ready to present to the customs officer. For more information, including the helpful pamphlet *Know Before You Go*, contact the nearest U.S. embassy or write the U.S. Customs Service, 1301 Constitution Ave. NW, Washington, DC 20229 (202-566-8195).

Currency and Exchange

> In Boston they ask, How much does he know? In
> New York, How much is he worth?
> —Mark Twain

U.S. currency uses a decimal system based on the **dollar ($).** Paper money ("bills") comes in six denominations, all the same size, shape, and dull green color. The bills now issued are $1, $5, $10, $20, $50, and $100. You may occasionally see funny denominations of $2 and $500 which are no longer printed, but are still acceptable as

FOR $20 YOU CAN STAY HERE OR GET YOUR SHOES SHINED AT THE HOTEL DOWN THE STREET.

currency. Some restaurants and stores may be squeamish about accepting bills larger than $50. The dollar is divided into 100 cents (¢). Pick your favorite notation for values of less than a dollar: 35 cents can be represented as 35¢ or $0.35. U.S. currency uses six coins. The penny (1¢), nickel (5¢), dime (10¢), and quarter (25¢) are the most common. Half-dollar (50¢) and one-dollar coins are rarely seen and make excellent souvenirs.

Convert your currency infrequently and in large amounts to minimize exorbitant exchange fees. Try to buy traveler's checks in U.S. dollars so that you won't have to exchange them. Personal checks can be difficult to cash in the U.S. Most banks require that you have an account with them before they will cash a personal check, and opening an account can be a time-consuming affair.

Holidays

Some listings in *Let's Go: New York City* refer to holidays that may be unfamiliar to foreign travelers. **Martin Luther King Jr.'s Birthday** is celebrated on the third Monday in January, **Presidents' Day** on the third Monday in February. **Memorial Day,** falling on the last Monday of May, honors all U.S. citizens who have died in wars and signals the unofficial start of summer. Halfway through summer, **Independence Day** explodes on July 4. Americans celebrate their independence from England with barbecues and fireworks. Summer ends with another long weekend, **Labor Day,** on the first Monday of September, occasioning a flurry of back-to-school sales. **Columbus Day** comes on the second Monday in October. **Thanksgiving,** the fourth Thursday of November, celebrates the arrival of the Pilgrims in New England in 1620. Thanksgiving unofficially marks the start of the holiday season that peaks at **Christmas** (Dec. 25) and runs through **New Year's Day** (Jan. 1). All public agencies and offices and many businesses close on these holidays, as well as on several others scattered throughout the calendar.

Measurements

The British system of weights and measures is still in use in the U.S., despite half-hearted efforts to convert to the metric system. The following is a list of American units and their metric equivalents:

1 inch = 25 millimeters
1 foot = 0.30 meter
1 yard = 0.91 meter
1 mile = 1.61 kilometers
1 ounce = 25 grams
1 pound = 0.45 kilogram
1 quart (liquid) = 0.94 liter

12 inches equal 1 foot; 3 feet equal 1 yard; 5280 feet equal 1 mile. 16 ounces (weight) equal 1 pound (abbreviated as 1 lb.). 8 ounces (volume) equal 1 cup; 2 cups equal 1 pint; 2 pints equal 1 quart; and 4 quarts equal 1 gallon. Confusing? Yes.

Electric outlets throughout the U.S. provide current at 117 volts, 60 cycles (Hertz). European voltage is usually 220; you might need a transformer in order to operate your non-U.S. appliances. This is an extremely important purchase for those with small appliances such as electric systems for disinfecting contact lenses. Transformers are sold to convert specific wattages (e.g. 0-50 watt transformers for razors and radios; larger watt transformers for hair dryers and other appliances). You might also need an adapter to change the shape of the plug; U.S. plugs usually have two rectangular prongs, but plugs for larger appliances often have a third, circular prong.

The U.S. uses the Fahrenheit temperature scale rather than the Centigrade (Celsius) scale. To convert Fahrenheit to approximate Centigrade temperatures, subtract 32, then divide by 2. To convert them properly, subtract 32 then multiply by 9 and divide by 5. Or just remember that 32° is the freezing point of water, 212° its boiling point, normal human body temperature 98.6°, and room temperature around 70°.

Time

Americans tell time on the 12-hour, not 24-hour, clock. Hours after noon are post meridiem or pm (e.g. 2pm); hours before noon are ante meridiem or am (e.g. 2am). Noon is 12pm and midnight is 12am. (To avoid confusion, *Let's Go: New York City* uses only "noon" and "midnight.") The Continental U.S. divides into four time zones: Eastern, Central, Mountain, and Pacific. When it's noon Eastern time, it's 11am Central, 10am Mountain, 9am Pacific, and 7am central Alaskan and Hawaiian.New York follows Eastern Time. NB: Most areas of the country switch to Daylight Saving Time (1 hr. ahead of standard) from mid-April to October.

Alcohol and Drugs

You must be 21 years old to purchase alcoholic beverages legally. Many places will want to see a photo ID (preferably a driver's license or other valid government-issued document) when ordering or buying alcohol. Possession of marijuana, cocaine, and most opiate derivatives (among many other chemicals) is punishable by stiff fines and/or imprisonment. Check with the U.S. Customs Service before your trip (see Customs above) about any questionable drugs.

Getting to the U.S.

Transportation to and from New York City, especially from outside the U.S., will probably be your major expense. The alternative to research and early planning is exorbitant rates; talk to a travel agent you trust. In addition, check the travel section of any major newspaper for bargain fares, and consult CIEE or your national student travel organization—they sometimes have special deals that regular travel agents can't offer.

From Canada and Mexico

Canadians and Americans are very welcome in each other's countries—border officials will accept a valid driver's license or passport as proof of citizenship (just don't carry any mace), and they sometimes won't even ask to see it. (Don't try to joke around with the border official, though; it can only get you in trouble.) Crossing the Mexican-American border can be more difficult. Mexican citizens may need a tourist visa for travel in the U.S.; contact the U.S. Embassy in Mexico City with questions.

Finding bargains on travel in the States may not be easy for residents of its neighboring countries. Residents of North America are rarely eligible for the discounts that U.S. airlines, bus, and train companies offer visitors from overseas (see Getting Around below). Canadian and Mexican carriers often fly to and from the U.S. and their respective country, as do U.S. airlines. Mexican residents who live more than 100 miles from the border may be eligible for "Visit USA" discount flight passes on some carriers. Otherwise, because flying in the U.S. is expensive, it may be cheaper to fly on a Mexican airline to one of the border towns, then travel by train or bus from there.

Most buses and trains from Mexico travel no farther than the U.S. border, but it's possible to arrange connections at San Diego, CA; Nogales, AZ; and El Paso, Eagle Pass, Laredo, or Brownsville, TX. **Amtrak, Greyhound,** and their subsidiaries serve the towns along the U.S.-Mexico border.

From Europe

Travelers from Europe can get terrific deals on seats during the off-season. Peak season rates are generally set on either May 15 or June 1 and run until about September 15. You can take advantage of cheap off-season flights within Europe to reach an advantageous port of departure for North America. (London is an important connecting point for budget flights to the U.S.)

Charter flights can save you a lot of money. You can book charters up to the last minute—some will not even sell tickets more than 30 days in advance. Many flights fill up well before their departure date, however. You must choose your departure and return dates when you book, and you will lose all or most of your money if you cancel your ticket. (Travel agents will cover your losses only in case of sudden illness, death of a close family member, or natural disaster.) Charter companies themselves reserve the right to change the dates of your flight or even cancel the flight a mere 48 hours in advance. Delays are not uncommon. To be safe, get your ticket as early as possible and arrive at the airport several hours before departure time. When making plans, try to investigate each charter company's reputation.

If you decide to fly with a scheduled airline, you'll be purchasing greater reliability, security, and flexibility. Major airlines do offer reduced-fare options. **APEX (Advanced Purchase Excursion Fare)** is one of the more sensible ways to go. It provides you with confirmed reservations, and you can make connections through different cities and travel on different airlines. Drawbacks include restrictions on the length of your stay (from 7-14 days minimum to 60-90 days maximum) and the requirement that you make reservations two weeks in advance (hence the name). APEX fares are generally not refundable, nor may you change your flight. You might also investigate unusual airlines that undercut the major carriers on regularly scheduled flights to an extremely limited number of cities. **Virgin Atlantic Airways** (800-862-8621) and **Icelandair** (800-223-5500) have particularly low fares. Competition for seats on these small carriers is usually fierce, so book early.

Student discounts will appear with magical ease if you look around for them. Many major carriers will sell off un-purchased APEX seats at a further discount to persons under age 24, beginning 72 hours before the flight. These fares allow an open return date, but restrict your stay to a maximum of two weeks—the last part of which you will have to spend trying to secure your ticket back. Such deals are never really a predictable way to travel, and are especially risky in high season. They can, however, save you a considerable amount of money if your schedule is flexible enough for you to take advantage of them.

From Asia, Australia, and New Zealand

Whereas European travelers may choose from a variety of regular reduced fares, their counterparts in Asia and Australia must rely on APEX flights. From Japan, U.S. airlines such as **Northwest** and **United Airlines** offer cheaper flights than Japan Airlines. **Qantas, Air New Zealand, United, Continental,** and **UTA French Airlines** fly between Australia or New Zealand and the United States. Prices are roughly equivalent among the five (American carriers tend to be a bit less) although they vary seasonally, and the cities served by each carrier differ slightly. Super Saver fares from Australia have extremely tough restrictions. If you are uncertain about your plans, pay extra for a Super Saver that has only a 50% penalty for cancellation.

Once There

> *The Americans are justly very proud of it, and its residents passionately attached to it...a young New Yorker, who had been in Europe for more than a year, was in the same sleigh with me. "There goes the old city!" said he in his enthusiasm, as we entered Broadway; "I could almost jump out and hug a lamp-post!"*
> —Alexander Mackay, The Western World, 1849

Safety

New York City is widely perceived to be the most dangerous city in the U.S. While it is clear that danger exists—street robbery and mugging statistics are the worst in the country—many tourists and would-be adventurers are unduly terrified by the streets of the city. With some precautions, you can emerge from your vacation in the city enriched, unscathed, and maybe even more confident.

Safety on Foot

Acting like a native (read: rude) may be your best protection. Petty criminals often attack tourists because they seem naive and hapless. In a recent interview, a city cop told reporters, "They go for the gawkers"—which means that small-time crooks scam the unwary, the wide-eyed, and the slow-moving. The New Yorker walks briskly; the tourist wanders absently. Maintain at all times the fiction that you know where you are going. Keep a blank stare or a silent, knowing grin on your face. Be discreet with street maps and cameras and address questions about directions to policemen or store-owners. Consider covering your trusty *Let's Go: New York City* with plain brown paper. And like a true New Yorker, stay out of public bathrooms; they tend to be filthy and unsafe. Instead, try department stores, hotels, or any restaurant without a sign on the door saying "restrooms for patrons only." (See Bathrooms under Practical Information).

If, despite your confident swagger, you suspect you're being followed, duck into a store or restaurant. Some East Side shops near school districts have yellow and black signs that say "safe haven" in their windows. The signs mean that shop managers have agreed to let people—especially students—who feel unsafe remain in their stores for long periods of time or call the police.

Rip-off artists seek the rich as well as the unwary, so hide your wealth. Conceal watches, necklaces, and bracelets under your clothing if you're in a dangerous neighborhood. Turn that huge diamond ring around on your finger so jewelry-swipers can only see the band. Grip your handbag tightly and wear the strap diagonally. If you keep the bag and the strap on one side, it can easily be pulled off—or a clever thief with scissors may cut the strap so adeptly that you don't even notice.

Tourists are especially juicy prey because they tend to carry large quantities of cash. Transfer your money into traveler's checks and be careful with it. Don't count your money in public or use large bills. Tuck your wallet into a discreet pocket and keep an extra 10 bucks or so in a more obvious one. Many New Yorkers invest in a cheap extra wallet designated for "mugging money." Keep an extra bill for emergencies in an unlikely place, such as your shoe, sock, or inner ear.

New York's streets are rife with con artists. Their tricks are many. Beware of hustlers working in groups. No one ever wins at three-card monte. If someone spills ketchup on you, someone else may be picking your pocket. Ignore people who claim to have found a huge pile of unmarked $20 bills. Be mistrustful of sob stories that require a donation from you.

Pay attention to the neighborhood that surrounds you. A district can change character drastically in the course of a single block. The haughty Upper East Side, for example, segues into a nasty bit of Harlem up in the triple digits. Note, however, how attention to the neighborhood, to the flow of people on the street, can tell you about the relative safety of the area. Many notoriously dangerous districts have safe sections; look for children playing, women walking in the open, signs of an active community. If you feel uncomfortable, leave as quickly and directly as you can, but don't allow your fear of the new to close off whole worlds to you. Careful, persistent exploration will build confidence, undergird your emerging NYC attitude, and make your stay in the city that much more rewarding.

At night, of course, it's even more important to keep track of your environment. Avoid poor or drug-ridden areas like the South Bronx, Washington Heights, Harlem, Fort Greene, Bedford-Stuyvesant and Alphabet City, the segment of lower east Manhattan where numbered avenues become ominously lettered. West Midtown and the lower-middle East Side, both well populated commercial centers during the day, can be foreboding at night. Follow the main thoroughfares; try to walk on avenues rather than streets. Residential areas with doormen are relatively safe even in the twilight. Fifth and Park are the least dangerous avenues in the evening on the East Side, Central Park West and Broadway the safest on the West.

Central Park, land of frisbees and Good Humor trucks by day, becomes dangerous and forbidding after sunset. If you find yourself penniless, tokenless, and on the wrong side of the park, walk around it by Central Park South rather than north of it or through it. If you're uptown, walk through the 85th St. transverse by the police station. Avoid the woodsy deserted areas far from the main path. If you are visiting the gay bars near the West Side docks along the Hudson River, stay away from the abandoned waterfront area. Although the bars are trendy, the surrounding areas are purported to be unsafe. Bars and clubs in the Village may be a better bet. Further inland, the areas around Times Square and Penn Station are also dangerous.

Safety in Vehicles

If you take a car into the city, try not to leave valuable possessions—such as radios or luggage—in it while you're off rambling. Radios are especially tempting; in fact, most thieves in New York actually make their living stealing only radios. (Thus the many "No Radio" or "Radio Already Stolen" signs adorning car windows.) If your tape deck or radio is removable, hide it in the trunk or take it with you. If it isn't detachable, at least conceal it under junk. Similarly, hide baggage in the trunk—although some savvy thieves can tell if a car is heavily loaded by the way it is settled on its tires. Park your vehicle in a garage or well-traveled area. Sleeping in a car or van parked in the city is extremely dangerous—even the most dedicated budget traveler shouldn't consider it an option.

Late at night, take the bus rather than the subway; buses are safer because the driver is in plain view. On weekends, taking the subway in the evening is less dangerous since most major lines are quite crowded then. If a station seems empty, stand near the token counter or look for a Guardian Angel, one of the self-appointed crime-fighters clad in red berets. Or treat yourself to a taxi; although more expensive, they are probably the safest mode of travel at night.

In taxis, the dangers are financial rather than physical. Don't let the driver take advantage of you. Cab fares can only be paid at the end of the ride. New York taxis must drop off individuals and charge a bulk fare at the end; any driver who tries to charge you per person by location has no business doing so. Take a yellow cab with a meter and a medallion on the hood rather than an illegal "gypsy" cab, which isn't yellow and doesn't have a meter. The driver's name should be posted over the glove compartment, and when you get out you can request a receipt with a phone number to call about complaints or lost articles. State your destination with authority, and suggest the quickest route if you know it. If you hesitate or sound unsure, the driver will know that you can be taken out of your way without noticing.

When disembarking from a plane or train, be wary of unlicensed taxi dispatchers. At Grand Central or Penn Station, a person may claim to be a porter, carry your bags, hail you a cab, and then ask for a commission or share of the fare. Don't fall for this baggage-carrying scam—give directions to the driver as fast as you can and drive off in style. Official dispatchers do not need to be paid.

Accommodations

Hotels, Motels, and Bed & Breakfasts

Put those images of a beneficent Leona Helmsley out of your head. No chocolate dainties for you, o budget traveler. Instead, count yourself lucky to have found a reasonably-priced room in this sybaritic city.

Let's Go: New York City determines the best budget hotels and ranks them in order of value, based on price, safety, and location. Ask the hotel owner if you can see a room before you pay for it.

A single in a cheap hotel should cost about $30. You will be told in advance if the bathroom is communal. Most hotels require a key deposit when you register. Check-in usually takes place between 11am and 6pm, check-out before 11am. You may be able to store your gear for the day even after vacating your room and returning the key, but

most proprietors will not take responsibility for the safety of your belongings. Most hotel rooms can be reserved in advance.

If you have a particular fondness for Hiltons and Marriotts beyond your means, consider joining **Discount Travel International,** Ives Bldg., #205, 114 Forrest Ave., Narberth, PA 19072 (215-668-7184). For an annual membership fee of $45, you and your household will have access to a clearing house of unsold hotel rooms (as well as airline tickets, cruises, and the like), which can save you as much as 50%.

Bed and Breakfasts (private homes which rent out one or more spare rooms to travelers) are a great alternative to impersonal hotel and motel rooms. B&Bs may provide an excellent way to explore with the help of a host who knows the region well, and some go out of their way to be accommodating—accepting travelers with pets or giving personalized tours. The best part of your stay will often be a home-cooked breakfast (and occasionally dinner). Many B&Bs do not provide phones, TVs, or showers with their rooms. Some homes give special discounts to families or senior citizens. Reservations are almost always necessary, although in the off-season you can frequently find a room on short notice. Many bed and breakfasts close down during the winter, though.

As an alternative to standard B&Bs, contact the **U.S. Servas Committee,** 11 John St. #407, New York, NY 10038 (212-267-0252), an international cooperative system of hosts and travelers. This non-profit organization provides travelers with hosts for two nights. Letters of reference and an interview are required. Participation in the program costs $45 per year per traveler, with a $15 deposit on host lists, but travelers and hosts do not exchange money.

Hostels

Hostels offer unbeatable deals on indoor lodging, and are great places to meet budget travelers from all over the world. Hostels as a rule are dorm-style accommodations where the sexes sleep apart, often in large rooms with bunk beds. Expenses and frills are kept to a minimum. You must rent or bring your own sheets or sleep sacks (two

sheets sewn together); sleeping bags are often not allowed. Hostels often have kitchens and utensils for your use, and some have storage areas and laundry facilities.

Hostelling International/American Youth Hostels (HI/AYH) is the leading organization of U.S. hostels. They have an excellent hostel in New York, with much space and many amenities. (AYH is affiliated with IYHF and treats IYHF cards just like AYH's. Note that IYHF is currently in the process of adopting a new seal of approval for the hostels that belong to its network. Soon AYH and IYHF cards will be phased out and replaced by the new "Hostelling International" ("HI") cards. Look for the trademark blue triangle to identify IYHF-affiliated hostels.) Most HI/AYH hostels have strict check-in and check-out times, a maximum stay of less than a week, and rules against pets and alcohol. All ages are welcome. Prices usually run $7-12 a night. HI/AYH membership is annual: $25 for adults, $15 for those over 54, $10 for those under 18, $35 for families. Nonmembers who wish to stay at an HI/AYH hostel usually pay $3 extra, which can be applied toward membership. For more information, contact HI/AYH, 425 Divisadero St. #310, San Francisco, CA 94117 (415-863-9939).

YMCAs and YWCAs

Don't overlook the **Young Men's Christian Association (YMCA).** Their rates are often better those of city hotels. Singles average $25-35 per night, around $110 per week; rooms include use of a library, pool, and other facilities. You may have to share a room with another sleeper and use a communal bath or shower, however. The five YMCAs in New York accept women and families as well as men.

Make reservations at least two months in advance, and expect to pay a refundable key deposit of about $5. Economy packages (4-8 days, $160-290) that include lodging, breakfast, dinners, and excursions are available. The YMCA of Greater New York offers an **International Program,** accommodation centers for students and young adults. For information and reservations, write or call **The Y's Way,** 224 E. 47th St., New York, NY 10017 (212-308-2899).

Dormitories

Miss that boxlike dorm ambience? Now you can experience it on vacation, too. Some colleges and universities open their residence halls to conferences and travelers, especially during the summer. You may have to share a bath, but rates are often low and facilities are usually clean and well-maintained. If you hope to stay at a school, contact its housing office before your vacation.

Staying in Touch

Mail

Individual offices of the U.S. Post Office are usually open Monday to Friday from 8am to 5pm and sometimes on Saturdays until about noon. All are closed on national holidays. **Postcards** mailed within the U.S. or to Canada or Mexico cost 19¢, **letters** up to one ounce 29¢. Postcards mailed overseas cost 40¢, letters 50¢ (up to 1/2 oz.). **Aerograms** are available at the post office for 45¢. Mail from one coast to the other usually takes three days; to northern Europe, a week to 10 days; to southern Europe, North Africa, and the Middle East, two weeks; to South America or Asia, a week to 10 days. Of course, all of the above travel times for mail are dependent on the particular foreign country's mail service as well. Be sure to write "Air Mail" clearly on the front of the envelope for the speediest delivery. Large city post offices offer an **International Express Mail** service (delivery to a major city overseas in 48-72 hrs.).

The U.S. is divided into postal zones, each with a five-digit **ZIP code** particular to a region, city, or part of a city. Some addresses have nine-digit ZIP codes, used primarily for business mailings to speed up delivery. Writing this code on letters is essential for delivery. The normal form of address is as follows:

Turf Butswang (name)
White Horse Health Club (name of organization, optional)
2608 Coaster Ave, Suite 301 (address, apartment number)
Nywas Falls, CA 93711 (city, state abbreviation, ZIP)
USA (country, if mailing internationally)

When ordering books and materials from the U.S., always include an **International Reply Coupon** with your request. IRCs should be available from your home post office. Be sure that your coupon has adequate postage to cover the cost of delivery.

Depending on how neurotic your family is, consider making arrangements for them to get in touch with you. The General Post Office at 390 9th Ave. is the only address to which general delivery mail can be sent (subway: A, C, or E to 34th St./Penn Station); it wields the easy-to-remember zip code 10001. Plan your mailstops for mid-week. Once a letter arrives it will be held for about a week, but may be held longer if it has an arrival date marked clearly on the front of the envelope. Family and friends can send letters to you in labeled like this:

Mr. Ivor <u>Cutler</u> (underline last name for accurate filing)
c/o General Delivery
Main Post Office
James A. Farley Building
390 9th Ave.
New York City, NY 10001

If you've reserved accommodations in advance, you can have mail sent to their addresses, with your arrival date marked on the envelope.
Station Address Zip Code

Station	Address	Zip Code
James A. Farley Bldg.	421 Eighth Ave.	10001
Knickerbocker	130 E. Broadway	10002
Cooper	93 Fourth Ave.	10003
Bowling Green	25 Broadway	10004
Wall Street	73 Pine St	10005
Church	90 Church St.	10007
Peter Stuyvesant	432 E. 14th St.	10009
Madison Square	149 E. 23rd St.	10010
Old Chelsea	217 W. 18th St.	10011
Prince103	Prince St.	10012
Canal St.	350 Canal St.	10013
Village	201 Varick St.	10014
Murray Hill	115 E. 34th St.	10016
Grand Central	450 Lexington Ave.	10017
Midtown	221 W. 38th St.	10018
Radio City	322 W.52nd St.	10019
Rockefeller Center	610 Fifth Ave.	10020
Lenox Hill	217 E. 70th St.	10021
Franklin Delano Roosevelt	909 Third Ave.	10022
Ansonia	1980 Broadway	10023
Planetarium	127 W. 83rd St.	10024
Cathedral	215 W. 104th St.	10025
Morningside	232 W. 116th St.	10026
Manhattanville	365 W. 125th St.	10027
Gracie	229 E. 85th St.	10028
Hell Gate	153 E. 110th St.	10029
College	217 W. 140th St.	10030
Hamilton Grange	521 W. 146th St.	10031
Audubo	515 W. 165th St.	10032
Washington Bridge	555 W. 180th St	10033
Inwood	90 Vermilyea Ave.	10034
Triborough	167 E. 124th St.	10035
Times Square	340 W. 42nd St.	10036
Lincolnton	2266 Fifth Ave.	10037
Peck Slip	1 Peck Slip	10038
Colonial Park	99 Macombs Pl.	10039

Fort George	4558 Broadway	10040
Island	694 Main St., Roosevelt Island	10044
Yorkville	1591 Third Ave.	10128

American Express does not automatically offer a Poste Restante service as it does in Europe, but the offices in New York City will act as a mail service for cardholders if you contact them in writing in advance. Under this "Client Letter Service," they will hold mail for one month, forward upon request, and accept telegrams. For a complete list of offices and instructions on how to use the service, call 800-528-4800. Sometimes cabling may be the only way to contact someone overseas quickly (usually by the next day). **Western Union** (800-325-6000) charges a base fee of $8, in addition to 51-66¢ per word, including name and address (the rate varying according to destination). If you're contacting England, Argentina, the Netherlands or the Philippines, you can send a **Telemessage** ($8.50 for the first 50 words or less, including name and address, $3.25 for each additional 50 words or less). Call to check rates to specific countries.

Telephones

Americans pride themselves on their many telephones, and communication within the country is speedy and simple. **AT&T** is the leading company but competes with other long-distance phone companies such as **MCI** and **Sprint.** Telephone numbers in the U.S. consist of a three-digit area code and a seven-digit number, usually written as (212) 853-5806. Normally only the last seven digits are used in a **local call. Non-local calls** within the area code from which you are dialing require a "1" dialed before the last seven digits. **Long-distance calls** require a "1," the area code, and then the seven-digit number. Canada and the greater part of Mexico share the same area code system. The area code "800" indicates a toll-free number, usually for a business. A "1" must be dialed before the "800." For information on specific toll-free numbers, call 1-800-555-1212. Be careful—the age of information technology has recently given birth to the "900" number. Its area code is deceptively similar to the toll-free code, but "900" calls are staggeringly expensive. Average charges range from $2-5 for the first minute, with a smaller charge for each additional minute. You can have phone sex, make donations to political candidates, or hear about Teenage Mutant Ninja Turtles, but it'll cost you.

If you plan to rely on the phone, a **calling card** offered by AT&T or one of its various competitors, or a Visa, Mastercard, or American Express card, can save money over calling collect.

The New York telephone directory contains most of the information you will need about telephone usage, including area codes for the U.S., many foreign country codes, and rates. To obtain local phone numbers or area codes of other cities, call directory assistance (411 within your area code; otherwise, 1-(area code)-555-1212). From any phone you can reach the **operator** by dialing "0." The operator will help you with rates and other information and give assistance in an emergency. Both directory assistance and the operator can be reached from any pay phone without payment.

Pay phones hang out on street corners (usually every two blocks on avenues) and in public areas. Be wary of private, more expensive pay phones—the rate they charge per call will be printed on the phone. Put your coins (25¢ for a local call) into the slot and listen for a dial tone (a buzzing hum) before dialing; if there is no answer or if you get a busy signal (a rapid beep), you will get your money back after hanging up. To make a long-distance direct call, deposit the coins and dial; an operator will tell you the cost of the first three minutes. The operator will cut in after your time is up and tell you to deposit more money. Long-distance rates usually take a nose-dive after 5pm on weekdays and plummet even further between 11pm and 8am on weekends.

If you don't carry around barrels of change or have a calling card, you may want to make a **collect call** (i.e. charge the call to the recipient). First dial "0" and then the area code and number you wish to reach. An operator will cut in and ask to help you. Tell her or him that you wish to place a collect call from Blackie Onassis, or whatever your name happens to be. You might opt for a **person-to-person** call, which costs more than collect but cuts right to the heart of things. To call person-to-person, you must also give the recipient's name to the operator, but you will only be charged if the person you want to speak with happens to be there. (Another party may accept collect charges.) In some areas, particularly rural ones, you may have to tell the operator what number you wish to reach, and he or she will put the call through for you.

You can place **international calls** from any telephone. To call direct, dial the international access code (011), the country code, the city code, and the local number. Country codes may be listed with a zero in front (e.g. 044), but when using 011, drop the zero (e.g. 011-44). In some areas you will have to give the operator the number and she or he will place the call. To find out the cheapest time to call various countries in Europe or the Middle East, call the operator (dial "0"). The cheapest time to call Australia and Japan is between 3am and 2pm, New Zealand 11pm and 10am.

Getting Around the U.S.

In the 50s, President Dwight D. Eisenhower envisioned an **interstate system,** a national network of highways that would aid the military in defending U.S. soil against foreign invasion. Eisenhower's asphalt dream has gradually been realized, although Toyotas far outnumber tanks on the federally funded roads. Even-numbered roads run east-west and odd run north-south. If the interstate has a three digit number, it is a branch of another interstate (i.e., I-285 is a branch of I-85). An even digit in the hundreds place means the branch will eventually return to the main interstate; an odd digit means it won't. North-south routes begin on the West Coast with I-5 and end with I-95 on the East Coast. I-10 stretches across the entire southern border, from Los Angeles along the coast of the Gulf of Mexico to Jacksonville, FL. The northernmost east-west route is I-94. The national speed limit of 55 miles per hour (88km per hour) has been raised to 65 mph in some areas. The main routes through most towns are **U.S. highways,** often locally referred to by non-numerical names. **State highways** are usually less heavily traveled and may lead travelers to down-home farming communities. Of course U.S. and state highway numbers don't follow any particular numbering pattern.

By Plane

Flight listings and airfares can leave you in a gnarly swamp of numbers, all but impossible to wade through. Again, your best bet is to ask a knowledgeable travel agent to help you; then check the weekend travel sections of major newspapers for bargain fares.

Super Saver fares can save you hundreds of dollars over the regular coach price. On the average, you save more than half on a 14-day advance-purchase fare, and a still-considerable amount on the 7-day advance-purchase fare. To obtain the cheapest fare, buy a round-trip ticket (not necessarily returning on the same route, if you want a stopover) and stay over at least one Saturday. You will need to pay for the ticket within 24 hours of booking the flight, and you will not be able to change your flight reservation; the fare is also entirely non-refundable. By paying a bit extra, you can buy the ability to alter your plans, though there will still be some penalties for doing so. Also check with your travel agent for system-wide air passes and excursion fares.

There are a few principles to keep in mind when booking a flight. Traveling at night and during the wee hours of the morning is generally cheaper than during the day, and traveling on a weekday (between Monday and Thursday at noon) is cheaper than traveling on the weekend. Since airline travel peaks between June and August and around holidays, reserve a seat several months in advance for these times. Given the occasional appearance of sudden bargains and the availability of standby fares, advance purchase may not guarantee the lowest fare, but you will save some money and be assured a seat. The best deals usually appear between January and mid-May.

Many airlines offer special rates (usually 50% off regular fares) to children accompanied by an adult. These may still be higher than Super Savers, though. Very few airlines offer discounts for seniors. Chances of receiving discount fares increase on competitive routes.

Many major airlines offer special "**Visit USA**" passes and fares to foreign travelers. Purchase these tickets at home; one price pays for a certain number of "flight coupons," each good for one flight segment on a particular airline's domestic system within a certain time period. Often, the passes must be purchased when you buy a ticket to or from the States. Many different airlines offer these passes, but they come with innumerable restrictions and guidelines. Prices therefore vary a great deal. Consult a travel agent before you purchase any of these coupons to see whether you're really getting the best deal. Depending on the airline, the passes may be valid from 30 to 90 days. United Airlines offers special fares for travelers departing from many different regions of the world, including Asia, Europe, and Australia. When you purchase a pass, keep in mind the size of the airline. Eastern, United, American, and Northwest fly over the entire continent, while other airlines offer more limited or regional service.

Another discount option is to travel as a **courier.** In return for carrying packages with you, you receive dramatically reduced airfares. There are two catches, though. Only carry-on luggage is permitted (the company needs your luggage space), and flights mostly originate from New York City. Still, for the adventurous and the resourceful, courier services present opportunities for inexpensive travel. For more information, contact **Now Voyager,** 74 Varick St. #307, New York, NY 10013 (212-432-1616), or **Halbert Express,** 147-05 176th St., Jamaica, NY 11434 (718-656-8189).

Ticket consolidators sell unbooked commercial and charter airline tickets. The membership fee is $30-50, but fares can be extremely cheap. Inquire about cancellation fees and advance purchase requirements, and be prepared to be flexible about your dates of arrival and departure. For more information, contact **Air Hitch,** 2790 Broadway #100, New York, NY 10025 (212-864-2000). Or try **Unitravel Corporation**. Unitravel has departures from over 70 U.S. cities to more than 50 cities in Europe. The company holds all payments in a bank escrow until completion of the trip. Call 1-800-325-2222 and they will send a memo listing all of the flights departing from your city.

By Bus

If you are coming from rural America or have a seriously tight budget, buses may be your best bet. In the U.S., **Greyhound** (800-752-4841) operates the largest number of lines. Seniors receive a 5-10% discount off standard-fare tickets; children ages 5-11 travel for half-fare on standard-fare tickets; children ages 2-4 travel for 10% of the standard fare, and children under 2 travel free on laps. Restrictions do apply. If you plan to tour a great deal by bus within the U.S., you may save money with the **Ameripass.** Passes can be purchased for seven days ($299), 15 days ($319), or 30 days ($429), and each can be extended for $15 per day.

Always check bus schedules and routes personally, and don't rely on old printed schedules since listings change seasonally. Don't count on flagging down buses between stops—the driver might not stop. By all means avoid spending the night in a bus station. Though generally guarded, bus stations can be hangouts for deadbeats and down-and-outs. Try to arrange your arrivals for reasonable day or evening times. This will also make it easier for you to find transportation out of the station and another place to stay.

By Train

The train is one of the cheapest and most comfortable ways to travel in the U.S. Within the lower 48 states, **Amtrak** offers the "**All Aboard America**" fares for long-distance travel. Dividing the U.S. into three regions, Amtrak charges the same rate for both one-way and round-trip travel: $199 within one region, $279 between two regions, $339 between three (from Sept. 1-Dec. 17 and Jan. 4-May 27, rates are $179, $229, and $259). Amtrak discounts allow children ages 2-15 to travel for half-fare when accompanied by an adult. Senior citizens and disabled travelers may save up to 25% on regular one-way fares. Watch for special holiday packages as well. For information and reservations, call 800-872-7245 or look up Amtrak's local number in your area. Travelers with hearing impairments may use a **teletypewriter** (800-523-6590;

800-562-6960 in PA). Keep in mind that discounted air travel, particularly for longer distances, may be cheaper than train travel.

Airline, bus, and train companies offer discounts to foreign visitors within the U.S. **Greyhound** offers an **International Ameripass** for foreign students and faculty members. They primarily peddle in foreign countries, but you can purchase 'em for a slightly higher price in New York, Los Angeles, San Francisco, or Miami. You part with $69 for a 4-day pass ($80 in the U.S.), $125 for a 7-day pass ($140 in the U.S.), $199 for a 15-day pass ($215 in the U.S.), and $250 for a 30-day pass. You need a valid passport and proof of eligibility; the pass cannot be extended. Those without school affiliation must pay $199 for seven days, $269 for 15 days, and $369 for 30 days, with optional extensions of $10 per day. Call Greyhound at 800-237-8211 for information or to request their *Visit USA Vacation Guide,* which details services for foreigners.

Amtrak's **USA Rail Pass,** similar to the Eurailpass, entitles foreigners to unlimited travel anywhere in the U.S. A 45-day pass costs $299. Purchase a Regional Rail Pass instead to travel around a particular area. Each pass serves a single region, including Western ($229) and Eastern, Far Western, and Florida ($179 each). USA Rail Passes for children (ages 2-11) are half-fare. With a valid passport, purchase the USA Rail Pass outside the country or in New York, Boston, Miami, Los Angeles, or San Francisco. Check with travel agents or Amtrak representatives in Europe. Or call Amtrak in the U.S. of A. at 800-872-7245. Be sensible when buying passes; they're a rip-off unless you make a multitude of stops. Remember that many U.S. cities are not accessible by train.

Many major U.S. airlines offer special **Visit USA** air passes and fares to foreign travelers. Purchase passes outside the U.S., paying one price for a certain number of "flight coupons" good for one flight segment on an airline's domestic system within a given time period; cross-country trips may require two segments. Most airline passes can be purchased only by those living outside the Western Hemisphere, though a few crop up for Canadians, Mexicans, and residents of Latin America if they purchase a pass from a travel agent located at least 100 miles from the U.S. border. Those who do buy "Visit USA" fares instantly enter a maze of restrictions; consult a travel agent for guidance out of the shrubbery.

Practical Information

Visitor Information: New York Convention and Visitors Bureau, 2 Columbus Circle (397-8222 or 484-1200), 59th St. and Broadway. Subway: #1, 9 or A, B, C, D to Columbus Circle/59th St. Multilingual staff will help you with directions, hotel listings, entertainment ideas, safety tips, and "insiders'" descriptions of New York's neighborhoods. Request two invaluable maps: the *MTA Manhattan Bus Map,* and the *MTA New York City Subway Map.* Try to show up in person; the phone lines tend to be busy, the maps and brochures worthwhile. Open Mon.-Fri. 9am-6pm, Sat.-Sun. and holidays 10am-6pm.

New York State Department of Economic Development, 1515 Broadway near Times Sq. Subway: #1, 2, 3, 7, 9 or N, R, S to 42nd St./Times Sq. Tourist Division (827-6250) open Mon.-Fri. 9am-5pm. Or call their toll-free *I Love New York* number (800-342-3810) for statewide information about sights and events.

Travelers' Aid Society: at 158-160 W. 42nd St. (944-0013) between Broadway and Seventh Ave.; and at JFK International Airport (718-656-4870), in the International Arrivals Building. JFK office provides general counseling and referral to travelers, as well as emergency assistance (open Mon.-Thurs. 10am-7pm, Fri. 10am-6pm, Sat. 11am-6pm, Sun. noon-5pm). 42nd St. branch specializes in crisis intervention services for stranded travelers or crime victims (open Mon.-Fri. 9am-5pm; Wed. closes at noon. Subway: #1, 2, 3, 7, 9 or N, R, S to 42nd St.).

Entertainment Information: Free Daily Events in the City, 360-1333, 24 hrs. **NYC Onstage,** 768-1818; updates on theater, dance, music, children's entertainment, and other events; 24 hrs. **TKTS** 354-5800; at Broadway and 42nd St. (open Mon.-Sat. 3-8pm, Wed. and Sat. matinees 10am-2pm, Sun. from noon); and at 2 World Trade Center (open Mon.-Fri. 11am-5:30pm, Sat. 11am-1pm). Half-price tickets for Broadway and Off-Broadway shows sold the day of the performance only. Tickets for Wed., Sat., and Sun. matinees sold 11am-closing on the day before the performance.

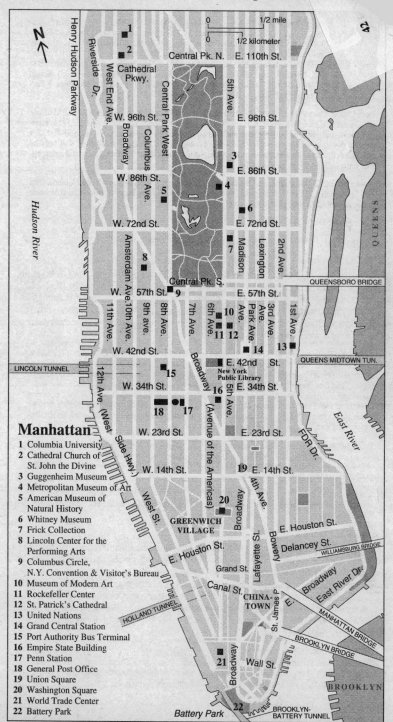

N

Henry Hudson Parkway

Riverside Dr.

Hudson River

1
2

Cathedral Pkwy.

Central Pk. N.   E. 110th St.

West End Ave.

W. 96th St.

Broadway

Columbus Ave.

Central Park West

5th Ave.

E. 96th St.

W. 86th St.

3

E. 86th St.

4

5

W. 72nd St.

6

E. 72nd St.

Madison

Lexington

2nd Ave.

7

Amsterdam Ave.

10th Ave.

8

9th ave.

Central Pk. S.

W. 57th St.

9

QUEENSBORO BRIDGE

QUEENS

8th Ave.

7th Ave.

6th Ave.

10

5th Ave.

Park Ave.

3rd Ave.

1st Ave.

11   12

14

13

Broadway

W. 42nd St.

E. 42nd St.

QUEENS MIDTOWN TUN.

11th Ave.

12th Ave. (West Side Hwy.)

LINCOLN TUNNEL

15

New York
Public Library

W. 34th St.

16

E. 34th St.

18   17

West St.

W. 23rd St.

E. 23rd St.

East River

W. 14th St.

19   E. 14th St.

20

GREENWICH
VILLAGE

Broadway

4th Ave.

(Avenue of the Americas)

5th Ave.

E. Houston St.

Bowery

Delancey St.

WILLIAMSBURG BRIDGE

E. Houston St.

Lafayette St.

Grand St.

Broadway

East River Dr.

Canal St.

HOLLAND TUNNEL

CHINA-
TOWN

St. James

MANHATTAN BRIDGE

BROOKLYN BRIDGE

21   Wall St.

Broadway

22

Battery Park

BROOKLYN-
BATTERY TUNNEL

BROOKLYN

42

Manhattan

1 Columbia University
2 Cathedral Church of
  St. John the Divine
3 Guggenheim Museum
4 Metropolitan Museum of Art
5 American Museum of
  Natural History
6 Whitney Museum
7 Frick Collection
8 Lincoln Center for the
  Performing Arts
9 Columbus Circle,
  N.Y. Convention & Visitor's Bureau
10 Museum of Modern Art
11 Rockefeller Center
12 St. Patrick's Cathedral
13 United Nations
14 Grand Central Station
15 Port Authority Bus Terminal
16 Empire State Building
17 Penn Station
18 General Post Office
19 Union Square
20 Washington Square
21 World Trade Center
22 Battery Park

0   1/2 mile
0   1/2 kilometer

Practical Information

Consulates: Australian, 636 Fifth Ave. (245-4000). **British,** 845 Third Ave. (745-0202). **Canadian,** 1251 Sixth Ave. (768-2400). **Danish,** 825 Third Ave. (223-4545). **Dutch,** 1 Rockefeller Plaza (246-1429). **Egyptian,** 1110 Second Ave. (759-7120). **Finnish,** 380 Madison Ave. (573-6007). **French,** 934 Fifth Ave. (606-3600). **German,** 460 Park Ave. (308-8700). **Indian,** 3 E. 64th St. (879-7800). **Israeli,** 800 Second Ave. (351-5200). **Italian,** 690 Park Ave. (737-9100). **Japanese,** 299 Park Ave. (371-8222). **Norwegian,** 825 Third Ave. (421-7333). **South African,** 326 E. 48th St. (213-4880). **Spanish,** 150 E. 58th St. (355-4090). **Swedish,** 1 Dag Hammerskjold Plaza (751-5900). **Swiss,** 665 Fifth Ave. (758-2560).

Post Office: Central branch 380 W. 33rd St. (967-8585), at Eighth Ave. across from Madison Sq. Garden. To pick up general delivery mail, use the entrance at 390 Ninth Ave. C.O.D.s, money orders, and passport applications are also processed at some branches. Call 330-4000 for general postal inquiries; questions concerning other branch locations and hours. will only be handled at the main information number. Open Mon.-Fri. 8:30am-7:45pm. For postal emergencies only, call the 24-hr. postal hotline (330-2671).

Area Code: 212 (Manhattan and the Bronx); 718 (Queens, Brooklyn, and Staten Island). Dial "1" first when making calls between these area codes. **All telephone numbers in this book are area code 212 unless otherwise noted.**

Emergency: Dial 911.

Police: 212-374-5000. Use this for inquiries that are not urgent. 24 hrs.

Financial Services

Travelers visiting New York have easy access to exchange of foreign currencies and traveler's checks. Large banks—Citibank (627-3999), Chase Manhattan (552-2222), Chemical (270-6000), for example—blanket the city with subsidiary branches and ATM machines, and fall over each other claiming to be the largest, biggest, nicest...-bank in town. Other companies specialize in providing foreign exchange services up to seven days a week, often quoting rates by phone.

American Express: Multi-task agency providing tourists with traveler's checks, gift checks, cashing services, and other financial assistance. Branches scattered throughout Manhattan include: **American Express Tower,** 200 Vesey St. (640-2000), near the World Financial Center (open Mon.-Fri. 9am-5pm); **Macy's Herald Square,** 151 W. 34th St. (695-8075), between Sixth and Seventh Ave. (open Mon.-Fri. 10am-6pm); **150 E. 42nd St.** (687-3700), between Lexington and Third Ave. (open Mon.-Fri 8:30am-5:30pm); in **Bloomingdale's,** 59th St. and Lexington Ave. (705-3171; open Mon.-Fri. 10am-6pm); **822 Lexington Ave.** (758-6510), between 63rd and 64th St. (open Mon.-Fri. 9am-5pm).

Bank Leumi, 579 Fifth Ave. (382-4407), on 47th St. One need not have an account to buy or sell foreign currencies and traveler's checks, issue foreign drafts, or make payments by wire, although Bank Leumi does charge for its services. Latest exchange rates are available by phone (912-6262). Open Mon.-Fri. 9am-3:30pm.

Chequepoint USA, 551 Madison Ave. (980-6443), between 55th and 56th St. Wire funds to foreign countries at rates cheaper than American Express's. Open Mon.-Fri. 8am-6pm, Sat.-Sun. 10am-6pm.

Car Rental

All agencies maintain varying minimum age requirements and require proper ID as well as a security deposit. Call to check on fluctuating prices and to reserve in advance, especially on weekends or holidays when cars can be scarce. If possible, look into some of the local Queens agencies. While less liberal with their free mileage policies, they usually have fewer age restrictions and offer considerably lower rates. Also, get complete information on collision-damage insurance. Some credit cards like Chase Visa take care of your rental insurance costs if you've charged the vehicle to their card, thereby saving you $9-12 a day.

Thrifty, 330 W. 58th St. (867-1234), between Eighth and Ninth Ave; 213 E. 43rd St. (867-1234), between Second and Third Ave. Large, reputable nationwide rental chain. Midsized domestic sedan: $42 per day, $255 per week, with unlimited mileage. Open Mon.-Fri. 7am-7pm, Sat. 7am-5pm, Sun. 8am-4pm. Must be 23 with a major credit card. No returns.

Payless, 189-08 Northern Blvd. (718-886-0058), near Utopia Pkwy. in Flushing, Queens. Take the #7 subway to Main St., Flushing, then the Q13 Bus. Mon.-Thurs. $36 per day, Fri.-Sun. $49 per day, 100 free mi., 17¢ each additional mi. Weekly $235, 1000 free mi., 17¢ each additional mi. Open Mon.-Fri. 7am-7pm, Sat. 7am-5pm, Sun. 8am-4pm. Must be 23 with a major credit card.

ABC Car Rental, 12 E. 13th St. (989-7260), between Fifth Ave. and University Pl. Current midsized Plymouth sedans available: $60 per day, Mon.-Thurs.; $70 per day, Fri.-Sun., $273 per week. Open daily 8am-6:30pm. Must be 23 with a major credit card.

Discount Car Rentals, 315 W. 96th St. (222-8500), between West End Ave. and Riverside Dr. Japanese midsized sedans: $49 per day, 200 free mi., 25¢ each additional mi.; $289 per week with unlimited mileage. No one-day rentals Sat.-Sun. Open Mon.-Fri. 8am-7:30pm, Sat.-Sun. 9am-5pm. Must be 25 with a major credit card.

All-Star Rent-A-Car Inc., 325 W. 34th St. (714-0556), between Eighth and Ninth Ave. Mid-sized Dodge sedan $50 per day with 100 free miles; $169 per weekend with 600 free miles; $229 per week with 800 free miles. Open Mon.-Fri. 7:30am-6:30pm. Must be 25 with a major credit card.

Goldie's Leasing Corp., 46-44 11th St., Long Island City, Queens (718-392-5435 or 718-392-5339), across the Queensborough Bridge, south of Astoria. Subway: E or F to 23rd St./Ely Ave. Mon.-Thurs. $37 per day, 100 free mi., 20¢ each additional mi. Fri.-Sun. $45 per day, 100 free mi., 20¢ each additional mi.; Weekly $226, 700 free mi., 20¢ per additional mi. Open Mon.-Sat. 8am-5pm, Sunday drop-off possible. Must be 21 with a major credit card.

Yonkers Datsun Leasing Inc., 84 Ashburton Ave., Yonkers, NY (914-423-0200). Take the Bronx Liberty Line Express Bus (see Getting There below), which stops right in front. Remotely located on a steep hill, this Nissan dealership doubles as a car rental agency, with an adjacent parking lot filled with late-model Nissans and Datsuns. Rental rates on a daily basis only. $15 per day for '84-'86 Nissan Sentra; $20 per day for '87-'88 Nissan Sentra; $25 per day for '89 Nissan Sentra or newer, 50 free mi., 25¢ each additional mi. Open Mon.-Sat. 9am-7pm, Sun. 9am-5pm. Must be 18 with major credit card or proof of residence somewhere and $500 deposit.

Auto Transport Companies

New York serves as one of the major departure points for auto transport companies. The length of time for application processing varies considerably from place to place. Nearly all agencies require references and a cash deposit, refundable upon safe delivery.

All American Auto Transport (800-227-7447 or 800-942-0001). Must be 18 or older with a valid license and at least 3 references. Application verification in 2-3 days; $150 deposit required for drive-away. Open Mon.-Fri. 9am-8pm, Sat. 11am-5pm.

Dependable Car Services, 801 E. Edgar Rd., Linden, NJ (840-6262 or 908-474-8080). Recently moved after 37 years in New York, but will still process your application immediately. Must be 21, have 3 personal references, and a valid license without major violations. $150-200 deposit. Open Mon.-Fri. 8:30am-4:30pm, Sat. 9am-1pm.

Auto Driveaway, 264 W. 35th St., Suite 500 (967-2344); 33-70 Prince St., Flushing, Queens (718-762-3800). Must be 21 years old, with 2 local references and a valid driver's license. Application processed immediately. $250 deposit, $10 application fee. Open Mon.-Fri. 9am-5pm.

Bicycle Rentals

City streets are busy at virtually any time of the day. But on weekends from May-Oct. and on weekdays from 10am-3pm and 7-10pm, parts of Central Park close to cars, allowing bicycles to rule the roads.

Pedal Pushers, 1306 Second Ave. (288-5594), between 68th and 69th St., rents 3-speeds for $4 per hr., $10 per day; 10-speeds for $5 per hr., $14 per day; mountain bikes for $6 per hr., $17 per day. 3-speeds overnight rental $39. Open daily 10am-6pm. No cash deposit required; leave passport, driver's license, or a major credit card.

Gene's, 242 E. 79th St. (288-0739), near Second Ave. This one-stop discount bike shop also rents 3-speeds for $3 per hr., $10.50 per day; mountain bikes for $6 per hr., $21 per day. Open Mon.-Fri. 9:30am-8pm, Sat.-Sun. 9am-7pm. $20 deposit required for 3-speeds, $40 deposit required for mountain bikes, as well as a driver's license or major credit card. $250 cash deposit required for overnight rentals.

Metro Bicycle, 332 E. 14th St. (228-4344), between First and Second Ave. Rents 3-speeds for $4 per hr. Credit card or $50 deposit with driver's license required. Other locations throughout the city.

Libraries

Whether grappling with a difficult paper, looking for a date, admiring one of the many free and constantly changing exhibits, or just sinking into the latest best-sellers, millions of people, young and old, utilize the city's vast public library networks each year. The New York Public Library System, with 82 locations scattered throughout Midtown, The Bronx, and Staten Island, is the oldest and largest. Queens and Brooklyn maintain separate systems. Call the respective central branches for locations and opening hours, which vary greatly from branch to branch and from year to year (along with the annual library budget).

New York Public Library, 11 W. 40th St. (930-0830), entrance at Fifth Ave. on 42nd St. Nonlending central research library. Wide variety of exhibits on display. Open Tues.-Wed. 11am-7:30pm, Thurs.-Sat. 10am-6pm.

Midtown Manhattan, 455 Fifth Ave. at 40th St. (340-0934). Largest circulation library branch; specialized sections include Folklore and Women's Studies. Numerous events and exhibits; pick up a free events calendar at any NYPL location. Open Mon. and Wed. 9am-9pm, Tues. and Thurs. 11am-7pm, Fri.-Sat. 10am-6pm.

Donnell Library Center, 20 W. 53rd St. (621-0618), between Fifth and Sixth Ave. Central Children's Room for "Curious George" fans. Largest circulation of foreign language books. Open Mon. and Wed. noon-6pm, Tues. and Thurs. 9:30am-8pm, Sat. 10am-5:30pm.

Performing Arts Research Center, at Lincoln Center, 111 Amsterdam Ave. (870-1630), entrance at 65th St. Specializes in theater, music, dance, film, and TV. Circulation section includes CDs, CD-ROMs, tapes, and records. Tour (870-1670) Wed. at 2pm. Open Mon. and Thurs. noon-8pm, Wed. and Fri.-Sat. noon-6pm.

Library for the Blind and Physically Handicapped, 166 Sixth Ave. (206-5499), between Prince and Spring St. Braille and large-type books. Call first for hours.

Schomburg Center for Research in Black Culture, 515 Malcolm X Blvd. (491-2200), on the corner of 135th St. Largest collection of books by and about African-Americans anywhere in the world. Open Mon.-Tues. noon-8pm, Wed.and Fri. noon-6pm, Sat. 10am-6pm.

The other boroughs' head branches are: the **Bronx Reference Center,** 2556 Bainbridge Ave. (220-6565); the **St. George Library Center,** 5 Central Ave., Staten Island (718-442-8560); the **Queensborough Public Library,** 89-11 Merrick Blvd., Jamaica, Queens (718-990-0700); and the **Brooklyn Public Library,** Grand Army Plaza, Brooklyn (718-780-7722).

Help Lines

Crime Victim's Hotline, 577-7777. 24-hr. counseling and referrals.

Sex Crimes Report Line, New York Police Department, 267-7273. 24-hr. help, counseling, and referrals.

Samaritans, 673-3000. 24-hr. suicide prevention, confidential counseling.

Helpline Telephone Services, 532-2400. 24-hr. crisis intervention, counseling.

New York Gay and Lesbian Anti-Violence Project, 807-0197. 24-hr. crisis intervention hotline, counseling, referrals to support groups, and legal services.

Crisis Counseling, Intervention, and Referral Service, 516-679-1111. Includes the Gay Peer Counseling Network. 24 hrs.

Gay and Lesbian Switchboard, 777-1800. Daily 10:30am-midnight.

Lesbian Switchboard, 741-2610. Mon.-Fri. 6-10pm.

Drug Abuse Information Line, 800-522-5353. 24-hr. information and referrals on all drug-related problems.

Alcoholics Anonymous, 683-3900. Counseling and referrals, daily 9am-10pm. **Drugs Anonymous,** 874-0700; 24 hrs. **Gamblers Anonymous,** 265-8600.

New York City Department for the Aging, 577-0800. Information and referrals, Mon.-Fri. 9am-5pm.

Legal Aid Society, 577-3300. Referrals, Mon.-Fri. 9am-5pm.

Department of Consumer Affairs, 487-4398. For complaints, not advice, Mon.-Fri. 9am-4:30pm.

Consumer's Union, 914-378-2000. Consumer advice, reports.

MLM Talking Yellowbook, (718-921-1400). Unlike notorious (900) lines, this continually up-dated service provides quick information on a variety of topics for the cost of a local phone call. Simply punch in the 4-digit code after the intial greeting to access the rich store of available data, such as: Today's Top Stories (2277), New York Local Weather Forecast (2777), Sports Report (1278).

Medical Care

Beth Israel Medical Center, First Ave. and 16th St. Emergency Room 420-2840. **Mount Sinai Medical Center,** 100th St. and First Ave. Emergency Room 241-7171. **New York Infirmary Beekman Downtown Hospital,** 170 William St. Emergency Room 312-5070.

Walk-in Clinic, 57 E. 34th St. (683-1010), between Park and Madison Ave. Open Mon.-Fri. 8am-6pm, Sat. 10am-2pm. Affiliated with Beth Israel Hospital.

24-hour Emergency Doctor, 718-745-5900; will send doctor to home or hotel in all boroughs.

Kaufman's Pharmacy, 557 Lexington Ave. (755-2266), at 50th St. Open 24 hrs.

Eastern Women's Center, 40 E. 30th St. (686-6066), between Park and Madison Ave. Gynecological exams and surgical procedures for women, by appointment only. **Women's Health Line,** 230-1111; New York City Department of Health. Information and referrals concerning reproductive health. Open Mon.-Fri. 8am-6pm.

AIDS Information, 807-6655. **VD Information,** 427-5120. **Aids Info Hotline,** New York City Department of Health, 447-8200.

Bathrooms

By law, public buildings in New York City must have public facilities. Some of the cleanest and safest restrooms are located at **Trump Plaza,** 56th St. and Fifth Ave.; **Citicorp Center,** 153 Lexington Ave. at 53rd St., lower level; **Forbes Building,** Fifth Ave. at 12th St.; **Royalton Hotel,** 44 W. 44th St., between Fifth and Sixth Ave. Large department stores like **Macy's** or **Bloomingdale's** are also good bets. There has also been some progress lately in planting snazzy new designer pay-toilets (some with disabled access) on Manhattan's sidewalks: tinkle on 34th St. in front of Macy's, for example, or on 125th St. by the Municipal Building.

Getting Here

By Plane

Not only will you have to choose a carrier, but an airport as well. Three airports service the New York Metropolitan Region. The largest, John F. Kennedy Airport, or JFK (718-656-4520), 12 miles from Midtown in southern Queens, handles most international flights. LaGuardia Airport (718-476-5072), six miles from midtown in northwestern Queens, is the smallest, offering domestic flights and air shuttles. Newark International Airport (201-961-2000), 12 miles from Midtown in Newark, NJ, offers both domestic and international flights at budget fares often not available at the other airports.

There are plenty of inexpensive flights to and from New York but finding them takes time. Time of year, traveler's age, the economy, and international affairs all affect pric-

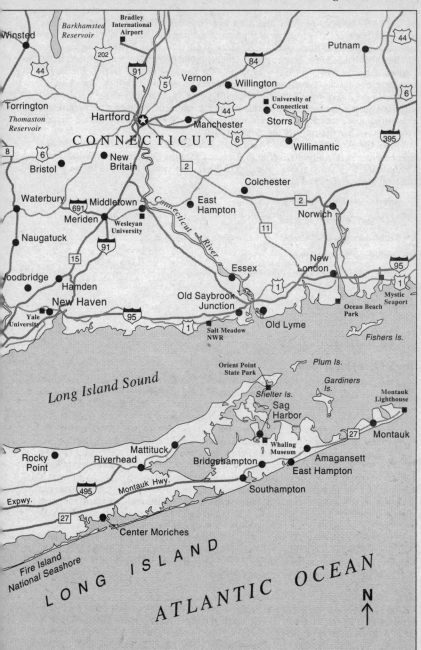

New York Metropolitan Area

es. Try to fly between Monday afternoon and Thursday afternoon, and stay over one weekend. Book your flight early, even if you don't pay until a few days before departure. Booking two to three weeks in advance usually qualifies for the cheapest seats. On the other hand, some airlines give discounts if you book less than 48 hr. before departure. Scan the *New York Times,* especially the Sunday "Travel" section, for the latest deals, or consult a travel agent with computer access to all airlines. Travel agents won't always direct you to the dirt-cheap flights because commissions are low; call airlines yourself. Be sure to tell agents if you are a student, a senior citizen, or if you are willing to travel standby. Keep in mind travel costs to and from different airports (see below) when figuring out the cheapest flight.

Three *Airport Guides,* put out by the Port Authority, have comprehensive information on New York's airports. Write to Airport Customer Services, One World Trade Center 65N, New York 10048, or call 435-7000. The guides cost $1.95 through the mail but are free if picked up in person.

American Airlines: 800-433-7300

Air France: 247-0100

British Airways: 800-247-9297

Continental Airlines: 319-9494

Delta Airlines/Delta Shuttle: 239-0700

Northwest: 736-1220

TWA: 290-2121

United: 800-241-6522

USAir/USAir Shuttle: 800-428-4322.

To and From the Airports

Travel between each of the airports and New York City without a car of your own becomes simpler as cost increases; you pay in time or money. The cheapest way in dollars is public transportation. This option usually involves changing mid-route from a bus to a subway or train, but service is frequent. Moving up the price scale, private bus companies will charge slightly more, but will take you directly from the airport to one of three destinations: Grand Central Station (42nd St. and Park Ave.), the Port Authority Bus Terminal (41st St. and Eighth Ave.) or the World Trade Center (1 West St.). Private companies run frequently and according to a set schedule (see below). Some services peter out or vanish entirely between midnight and 6am. If you want to set your own destination and schedule, however, and if you're willing to pay, you can take one of New York's infamous yellow cabs. Heavy traffic makes the trip more expensive: traveling during rush hour (7:30-9:30am and 4:30-7pm) can devastate a wallet. You are responsible for paying bridge and tunnel tolls. For the most up-to-date information on reaching the airports, call AirRide, the Port Authority's airport travel hotline, at 800-247-7433. Finally, if you make lodging reservations ahead of time, be sure to ask about limousine services—some Ys and hostels offer door-to-door transportation from the airports for reasonable fares.

JFK

The vanilla route into the city is on the subway. Catch a brown and white JFK long-term parking lot bus from any airport terminal (every 15 min.) to the **Howard Beach-JFK Airport subway station** (718-330-1234). You can take the A train from there to the city (1hr.). The A stops at Washington Sq., 34th St./Penn Station, 42nd St./Port Authority, and 59th St./Columbus Circle ($1.25). Heading from Manhattan to JFK, take the Far Rockaway A train. Or you can take one of the local buses (Q10 or Q3; fare $1.25, exact change required) from the airport into Queens. The Q10 bus heads to Lefferts Blvd. where it connects with the A train, and to Kew Gardens where it connects with the E, F, and R trains. You can then take the subway into Manhattan ($1.25). The

Q3 connects JFK with the F and R trains at 179 St./Jamaica. Ask the driver where to get off, and be sure you know which subway line you want. Some of the areas serviced by these buses are unsafe.

Those willing to pay more can take the **Carey Airport Express** (718-632-0500 or -0509), a private line that runs between JFK (also LaGuardia, see below) and Grand Central Station and the Port Authority Terminal. Buses leave every 30 minutes from Kennedy to Manhattan from 6am to midnight daily (1 1/4hr., $11) If you want to save a few dollars, Carey will take you to Jamaica station in Queens ($5), from where you can catch the Long Island Railroad to Penn Station (fare $3.50). If you are heading to Kennedy from Manhattan get on the Carey bus at 125 Park Ave. at Grand Central Station (every 30min., 5am to 1am; 1 1/4hr.) or at the Port Authority Terminal (1 1/2hr.). The **Gray Line Air Shuttle,** (757-6840), will drop you off (not pick you up) anywhere in Manhattan between 23rd and 63rd St. ($14). Inquire at a Ground Transportation Center in JFK to facilitate pick-up. A taxi from JFK to mid-Manhattan costs about $35; to LaGuardia about $18; and to Newark a whopping $60-65...plus tip and tolls.

LaGuardia

The journey to LaGuardia takes about two-thirds as long as the trek out to JFK. If you have extra time and light luggage, take the MTA Q33 bus ($1.25) to the 74th St./Broadway/Roosevelt Ave./Jackson Hts. subway stop in Queens. From there, take the #7, E, F, G, or R train into Manhattan ($1.25). You can catch the Q 33 from the lower level of the terminal. Allow at least 90 minutes travel time. The same word of caution applies here as with the Q buses above. The **Carey** bus also runs to and from LaGuardia every 30 minutes, stopping in Manhattan at Grand Central Station and the Port Authority. (55min., fare $8.50.) If you can't afford a cab but you still crave door to door service, the **Gray Line Air Shuttle** (757-6840) will take you anywhere between 23rd and 63rd for $11 (6am-midnight). A taxi to Manhattan costs around $18 dollars.

Newark

The commute from Newark Airport, in New Jersey, takes about as long as from JFK. **New Jersey Transit Authority (NJTA)** (201-460-8444) runs a fast, efficient bus (NJTA #300) between the airport and Port Authority every 15 minutes during the day, less frequently at night (24 hrs., $7). For the same fare, the **Olympia Trails Coach** (212-964-6233) travels between either Grand Central or the World Trade Center and the airport. (Mon.-Fri. 6am-1am, Sat.-Sun. 7am-8pm, every 20min., 45 min.-1 hr. depending on traffic, $7.) **NJTA Bus #107** will take you to Midtown for $2.60 (exact change required), but don't try it unless you have little luggage and lots of time. The NJTA also runs an **Air Link bus** ($4) between the airport and Newark's Penn Station (*not* Manhattan's), and from there **PATH** trains ($1) run into Manhattan, stopping at the World Trade Center, Christopher St., Sixth Ave., 9th St., 14th St., 23rd St. and 33rd St. For PATH information call 1-800-234-7284. Don't even bother trying to take a taxi—if you've got the $70 for the cab ride, why'd you fly into Newark in the first place?

By Bus or Train

Getting in and out of New York can be done less expensively and more scenically by bus or train than by plane. The **Port Authority Terminal,** 41st St. and Eighth Ave. (435-7000; Subway: A, C, or E to 42nd St./Port Authority), is a tremendous modern facility with labyrinthine bus terminals. Port Authority has good information and security services, but is located in an unsafe neighborhood. Be wary of pickpockets, and call a cab at night. Forsake its bathrooms at all times. The station is the hub of the Northeast bus network, and **Greyhound** (971-6363 or 730-7460) is the titan here. There are frequent buses to most other Eastern cities. Special offers do exist; ask about student specials. Greyhound races to Boston (5hr., $19 one-way, $30 round-trip), Philadelphia (2hr., $16 one-way, $32 round-trip), Washington, DC (5 1/2 hr., $34 one-way, round-trip $67.50), and Montreal (10hr., $67 one-way, $124 round-trip).

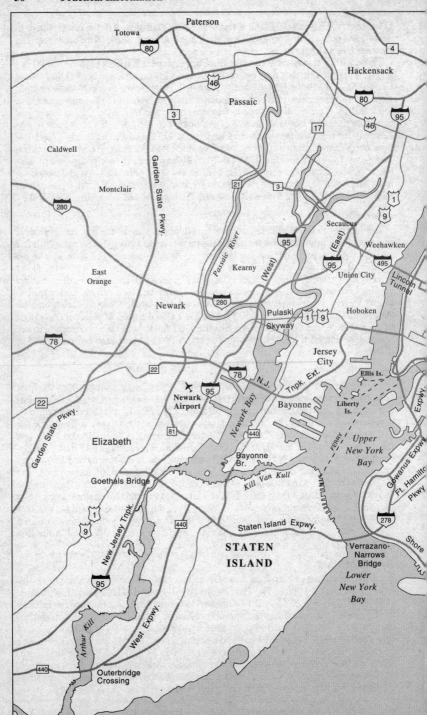

N

| 0 | 2 miles |
| 0 | 2 kilometers |

Grand Central Station, 42nd St. and Park Ave. (Subway: #4, 5, 6, 7 or S to 42nd St./Grand Central), the transportation colossus of the metropolis, has more than 550 trains running daily on its two levels of tracks. It handles the four **Metro-North** (800-638-7646 or 532-4900) commuter lines to Connecticut and New York suburbs (the Hudson, Harlem, New Haven and Port Jervis Lines). Longer train routes run out of the smaller **Penn Station,** 33rd St. and Eighth Ave. (Subway: #1, 2, 3, 9, or A, C, E to 34th St./Penn Station); the major line is **Amtrak** (800-872-7245 or 582-6875), serving upstate New York and most major cities in the U.S. and Canada, especially those in the Northeast (to Washington, DC 4hr., $64; Boston 5hr., $55). Penn Station also handles the **Long Island Railroad (LIRR)** (718-217-5477, see Long Island) and **PATH** service to New Jersey (732-8920 for recorded info.; 466-7649 for travel assistance, Mon-Fri 9am-5pm.).

By Car

Driving in New York City is not something to anticipate with glee. Most New Yorkers only learn to drive in order to escape from the city, and many forgo driving altogether as a means of transportation. When behind the wheel in New York, you are locked in combat with thousands of aggressive taxis, millions of careless pedestrians, and dozens of balls-out bicycle messengers. Stopped in traffic, you may have to fight off over-eager windshield washers who expect to be paid either to wash the windshield or not to wash the windshield.

Driving into New York there are several major approaches. From New Jersey there are three choices. The Holland Tunnel connects to lower Manhattan, exiting into the SoHo and TriBeCa area. From the New Jersey turnpike you'll probably end up at the Lincoln Tunnel which exits in midtown in the West 40s. The third option is the George Washington Bridge, which crosses the Hudson River at northern Manhattan, giving fairly easy access to either the Harlem River Drive or the West Side Highway. Coming from New England or Connecticut on I-95, follow signs for the Triboro Bridge. From there get onto the FDR Drive, which runs along the east side of Manhattan and exits onto the city streets every 10 blocks or so. No matter how you enter Manhattan, expect to pay a toll ($1-5).

Once in Manhattan, traffic continues to be a problem, especially between 57th and 34th St. The even greater hassle of parking joins in to plague the weary. Would-be parallel parkers can rise to this challenge in one of three ways. **Parking lots** are the easiest but the most expensive. In midtown, where lots are the only option, expect to pay at least $25 per day and up to $15 for two hours. The cheapest parking lots are downtown—try the far west end of Houston St.—but make sure you feel comfortable with the area and the lot. Is it populated? Is the lot guarded? Is it lit?

The second alternative is short-term parking. On the streets, **parking meters** cost 25¢ per 15 minutes, with a limit of one or two hours. Competition is ferocious for the third option, **free parking** at spots on the crosstown streets in residential areas. Read the signs carefully; a space is usually legal only certain days of the week. The city has never been squeamish about towing, and recovering your car once it's towed will cost $100 or more. Break-ins and car theft are definite possibilities, particularly if you have a flashy radio. The wailing of a car alarm, a noise as familiar and ritualistic to city residents as the crowing of a rooster is to rural Americans, attracts little if any attention.

Hitchhiking is illegal in New York State and the laws tend to be strictly enforced within New York City. Offenders will usually be asked to move on. It's best to take the train or bus out of the metropolitan area; hitching in and around New York City is dangerous. If someone you don't know offers you a free ride, don't accept it.

Orientation

New York City is composed of five boroughs: Brooklyn, the Bronx, Queens, Staten Island, and Manhattan. But plenty of tourists and Manhattanites have been known to confuse Manhattan with New York. This Manhattancentric perspective has historical roots. The island's original inhabitants, the Algonquin, called it "Man-a-hat-ta" or "Heavenly Land." The British were the first to call the island "New York," after James,

Duke of York, the brother of Charles II. It was only in 1898 that the other four boroughs joined the city's government. No matter how often you hear Manhattan referred to as "The City," each of the other boroughs has a right to share in the name. Flanked on the east by the East River (actually a strait) and on the west by the Hudson River, Manhattan is a sliver of an island. It measures only 13 miles long and 2 1/2 miles wide. Fatter Queens and Brooklyn look onto their svelte neighbor from the other side of the East River, and pudgy, self-reliant Staten Island averts its eyes in the south. **Queens,** the city's largest and most ethnically diverse borough, is dotted with light industry, airports, and stadiums. **Brooklyn,** the city's most populous borough (with 2.24 million residents), is even older than Manhattan. Founded by the Dutch in 1600, the borough today cradles several charming residential neighborhoods along with pockets of dangerous slums. **Staten Island** has remained a staunchly residential borough, similar to the suburban bedroom communities of outer Long Island. North of Manhattan nests the **Bronx,** the only borough connected by land to the rest of the U.S. Originally a Dutch estate owned by Jonas Bronck, an excursion to his family's farm was referred to as a visit to "the Broncks'." Today's Bronx encompasses both the genteel suburb of Riverdale and New York's most devastated area, the South Bronx.

Districts of Manhattan

New York is a sucked orange.
—Ralph Waldo Emerson

Glimpsed from the window of an approaching plane, New York City can seem a monolithic jungle of urbania. But up close, New York breaks down into manageable neighborhoods, each with a history and personality of its own. As a result of city zoning ordinances, quirks of history, and random forces of urban evolution, boundaries between these neighborhoods can often be abrupt.

The city began at the southern tip of Manhattan, in the area around **Battery Park** where the first Dutch settlers made their homes. The nearby harbor, now jazzed up with the **South Street Seaport** tourist magnet, provided the growing city with the commercial opportunities that helped it succeed. Historic Manhattan, however, lies in the shadows of the imposing financial buildings around **Wall Street** and the civic offices around **City Hall.** A little farther north, neighborhoods rich in the ethnic culture brought by late 19th-century immigrants rub elbows below Houston Street—**Little Italy, Chinatown,** and the southern blocks of the **Lower East Side.** Formerly the home of Russian Jews, Delancey and Elizabeth Streets now offer pasta and silks. To the west lies the newly fashionable **TriBeCa** (Triangle Below Canal St.). **SoHo** (for "South of Houston"), a former warehouse district west of Little Italy, has transformed into a pocket of gleaming art studios and galleries. Above SoHo huddles **Greenwich Village,** an actual village of lower buildings, jumbled streets, and neon glitz that has for decades been home to intense political and artistic activity.

A few blocks north of Greenwich Village, stretching across the West teens and twenties, lies **Chelsea,** the late artist Andy Warhol's favorite hangout and former home of Dylan Thomas and Arthur Miller. East of Chelsea, presiding over the East River, is **Gramercy Park,** a pastoral collection of elegant brownstones immortalized in Edith Wharton's *Age of Innocence.* **Midtown Manhattan** towers from 34th to 59th St., where traditional and controversial new skyscrapers stand side by side, supporting over a million elevated offices. Here department stores outfit New York while the nearby **Theater District** attempts to entertain the world, or at least people who like musicals.

North of Midtown, **Central Park** slices Manhattan into East and West. On the **Upper West Side,** the gracious museums and residences of Central Park West neighbor the chic boutiques and sidewalk cafés of Columbus Ave. On the **Upper East Side,** the galleries and museums scattered among the elegant apartments of Fifth and Park Ave. create an even more rarefied atmosphere.

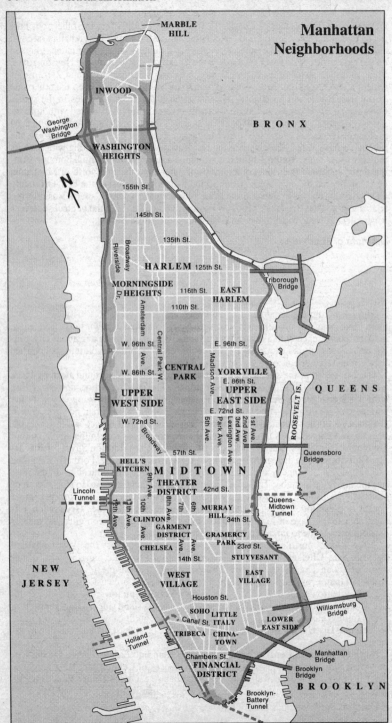

Manhattan Neighborhoods

Above 97th St., the Upper East Sides opulence ends with a whimper where commuter trains emerge from the tunnel and the *barrio* begins. Above 110th St. on the Upper West Side sits majestic **Columbia University** (founded as King's College in 1754), an urban member of the Ivy League. The communities of **Harlem, East Harlem,** and **Morningside Heights** produced the Harlem Renaissance of black artists and writers in the 1920s and the revolutionary Black Power movement of the 1960s. Although torn by crime, **Washington Heights,** just north of St. Nicholas Park, is nevertheless somewhat safer and more attractive than much of Harlem, and is home to Fort Tryon Park, the Met's Medieval Cloisters, and a quiet community of Old World immigrants. Still farther north, the island ends in a rural patch of wooded land with caves inhabited at various times by the Algonquin and homeless New Yorkers.

Manhattan's Street Plan

> *The city of right angles and tough, damaged people.*
> —Pete Hamill

Most of Manhattan's street plan was the result of an organized expansion scheme adopted in 1811, and the major part of the city grew in straight lines and at right angles. Above 14th St., the streets form a grid that a novice can quickly master. In the older areas of Lower Manhattan, though, the streets are named rather than numbered. Here, the orderly grid of the northern section dissolves into a charming but confusing tangle of old, narrow streets. Bring a map: even long-time neighborhood residents may have trouble directing you to an address.

Above Washington Square, avenues run north-south and streets run east-west. Avenue numbers increase from east to west, and street numbers increase from south to north. Traffic flows east on most even-numbered streets and west on most odd-numbered ones. Two-way traffic flows on the wider streets—Canal, Houston, 14th, 23rd, 34th, 42nd, 57th, 72nd, 79th, 86th, 96th, 110th, 116th, 125th, 145th, and 155th. Four transverses cross Central Park: 65/66th St., 79/81th St., 85/86th and 96/97th St. Most avenues are one-way. Tenth, Amsterdam, Hudson, Eighth, Avenue of the Americas (Sixth), Madison, Fourth, Third, and First Avenues are northbound. Ninth, Columbus, Broadway below 59th Street, Seventh, Fifth, Lexington, and Second Avenues are southbound. Some avenues allow two-way traffic: York, Park, Central Park West, Broadway above 59th Street, Third below 24th Street, West End, and Riverside Drive.

New York's east/west division refers to an address's location in relation to the two borders of Central Park—**Fifth Avenue** along the east side and **Central Park West** along the west. Below 59th St. where the park ends, the West Side begins at Fifth Ave. Looking for adjectives to describe where you are relative to something else? Uptown is anywhere north of you, downtown is south, and crosstown means to the east or the west. Want to use nouns? Uptown (above 59th St.) is the area north of Midtown. Downtown (below 34th St.) is the area south of Midtown.

Now for the discrepancies in the system. You may still hear the **Avenue of the Americas** referred to by its original name, **Sixth Avenue.** Lexington, Park, and Madison Ave. lie *between* Third and Fifth Ave–and (get this) there is no Fourth Ave. On the Lower East Side, there are several avenues east of First Avenue that are lettered rather than numbered: Avenues A, B, C, and D. Finally, above 59th St. on the West Side, Eighth Avenue becomes Central Park West, Ninth Avenue becomes Columbus Avenue, Tenth Avenue becomes Amsterdam Avenue, and Eleventh Avenue becomes West End Avenue. **Broadway,** which follows an old Algonquin trail, cavalierly defies the rectangular pattern and cuts diagonally across the island, veering west of Fifth Ave. above 23rd St. and east of Fifth Ave. below 23rd St.

Tracking down an address in Manhattan is easy. When given the street number of an address (e.g. #250 E. 52nd St.), find the avenue closest to the address by thinking of Fifth Ave. as point zero on the given street. Address numbers increase as you move east or west of Fifth Ave., in stages of 100. On the East Side, address numbers are 1 at

Fifth Ave., 100 at Park Ave., 200 at Third Ave., 300 at Second Ave., 400 at First Ave., 500 at York Ave. (uptown) or Avenue A (in the Village). On the West Side, address numbers are 1 at Fifth Ave., 100 at the Avenue of the Americas (Sixth Ave.), 200 at Seventh Ave., 300 at Eighth Ave., 400 at Ninth Ave., 500 at Tenth Ave., and 600 at Eleventh Ave. In general, numbers increase from south to north along the avenues, but you should always ask for a cross street when you are getting an avenue address. Or you can figure it out for yourself using the following simple formula: take the address number, cancel its last digit, divide by two, and add or subtract the number from the following list:

First Avenue: Add 3.

Second Avenue: Add 3.

Third Avenue: Add 10.

Fourth Avenue: Add 8.

Fifth Avenue: Up to 108, add 11; 108-200, add 13; 200-400, add 16; 400-600, add 18; 600-775, add 20; 775-1286, eliminate the last digit, do not divide by two, subtract 18; 1286-1500, add 45; above 2000, add 24.

Sixth Avenue: Subtract 12.

Seventh Avenue: Up to 1800, add 12; above 1800, add 20.

Eighth Avenue: Add 9.

Ninth Avenue: Add 13.

Tenth Avenue: Add 14.

Amsterdam Avenue: Add 59.

Broadway: Subtract 30.

Central Park West: Divide number by 10 and add 60.

Columbus Avenue: Add 60.

Lexington Avenue: Add 22.

Madison Avenue: Add 26.

Park Avenue: Add 35.

West End Avenue: Add 60.

Riverside Drive: Divide number by 10 and add 72.

Getting Around

> *I have two faults to find with New York. In the first place, there is nothing to see; and in the second place, there is no mode of getting about to see anything.*
> —Anthony Trollope, *North America, 1862.*

To be equipped for the New York City navigation experience, you will need more than an understanding of the logic underlying its streets. You will need to know how to use the public transportation system. Get a free subway or bus map from station token booths or the visitors bureau, which also has a free street map (see Practical Information above). Ask at the visitors bureau first, since token booth operators are usually less cooperative. For a more detailed program of interborough travel, find a Manhattan Yellow Pages, which contains detailed subway, PATH, and bus maps. Since bus routes vary for each of the boroughs, you may want to get other bus maps; send a self-addressed, stamped envelope to **NYC Transit Authority,** 370 Jay St. Brooklyn, NY 11201. Their reply takes about a month. In the city, round-the-clock staff at the **Transit Authority Information Bureau** (718-330-1234) dispenses subway and bus information.

Subways

The 230-mile New York subway system operates 24 hrs. a day, 365 days a year. It handles over 3.5 million commuters daily, and has 468 stations with 25 free transfer points.

The fare for Metropolitan Transit Authority (MTA) subways is a hefty $1.25, so groups of four or more may find a cab ride to be cheaper and more expedient for shorter distances. However, once inside, a passenger may transfer onto any of the other trains without restrictions.

Although by far the quickest means of transportation in Manhattan, the subways are far more useful for traveling north-south than east-west, as there are only two crosstown shuttle trains (42nd and 14th St.). In upper Manhattan and in Queens, Brooklyn, and the Bronx, some lines become "El" trains (for "elevated") and ride above street level to the city's nether regions.

Token clerks can tell you how to get anywhere, but can be impatient and uncooperative during rush hour. Don't lose your cool, but if you're not gaining any ground turn to a transit police officer for advice. "Express" trains stop only at certain major stations; "locals" stop everywhere. Be sure to check the letter or number and the destination of each train, since trains with different destinations often use the same track. When in doubt, ask a friendly passenger or the conductor, who usually sits near the middle of the train. Even once you're on the train, pay attention to the often garbled announcements—trains occasionally change mid-route from local to express.

Oft-maligned in the past for their squalor, the stations are slowly being rehabilitated, but some are still dirty and filled with the stench of stale urine and vintage filth. A major subway clean-up campaign, including new spray paint-resistant shiny cars, has erased much of the graffiti and made the atmosphere more aesthetically pleasing. However, the modernization also wiped out truly creative underground art, remnants of which can still be viewed on the few old cars that remain in service.

But it will take more than paint-resistant cars to erase subway crime. In crowded stations (most notably those around 42nd St.), pickpockets find plenty of work; violent crimes, although infrequent, tend to occur in stations that are deserted. Always watch yourself and your belongings, and try to stay in lit areas near a transit cop or token clerk. Some stations have clearly marked "off-hours" waiting areas that are under observation and significantly safer. At any time and at any place, don't stand too close to the platform edge (some people have been pushed, though others, clumsy, have fallen in of their own accord) and keep to well-lit areas when waiting for a train. When boarding the train, make sure to pick a car with a number of other passengers in it.

For safety reasons, try to avoid riding the subways between 11pm and 7am, especially above E. 96th St. and W. 120th St. Try also to avoid rush-hour crowds, where you'll be fortunate to find air, let alone seating—on an average morning, more commuters take the E and the F than use the entire rapid transit system of Chicago (which has the nation's second largest system). If you must travel at rush hour (7:30-9:30am and 5-6:30pm on every train in every direction.), the local train is usually less crowded than the express. Buy a bunch of tokens at once: you'll not only avoid a long line, but you'll be able to use all the entrances to a station (some lack token clerks).

The subway network integrates once-separate systems known as the **IRT, IND,** and **BMT** lines, now all operated by the NYC Transit Authority. The names of these lines are still in use, although they are no longer of any functional significance. The IRT (#1-#7) and the IND (A, C, D, E, F, Z) are two lines that run through Manhattan; the BMT (B, J, L, M, N, Q, R) runs mostly from lower Manhattan to adjoining Queens and Brooklyn. Certain routes also have common, unofficial names based on where they travel, such as the "7th Ave. Line" or the "Broadway Line" for the #1, 2, 3, or 9;

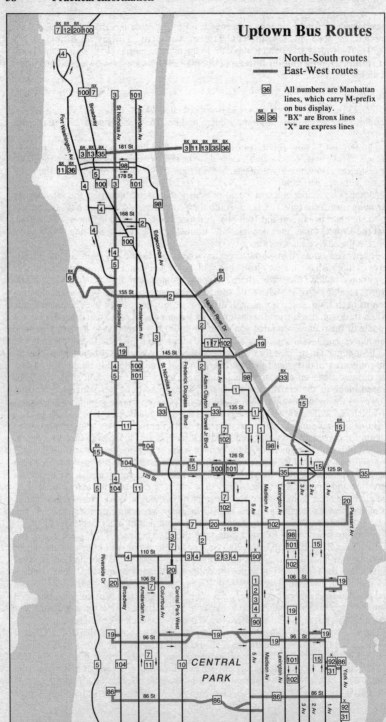

Uptown Bus Routes

— North-South routes

— East-West routes

All numbers are Manhattan lines, which carry M-prefix on bus display.
"BX" are Bronx lines
"X" are express lines

CENTRAL PARK

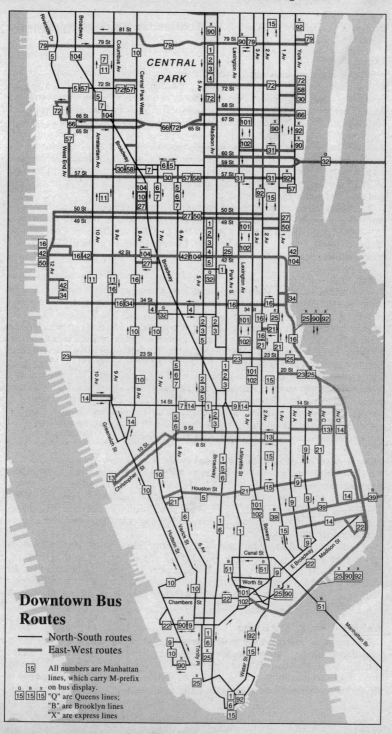

Downtown Bus Routes

—— North-South routes

≈≈≈ East-West routes

15 All numbers are Manhattan lines, which carry M-prefix on bus display.

15 15 15 "Q" are Queens lines; "B" are Brooklyn lines "X" are express lines

the "8th Ave. Line" for the A and C; the "Lexington Line" for the #4, 5, or 6; and the "Flushing Line" for the #7.

Buses

Because buses are often mired in traffic, they can take twice as long as subways, but they are almost always safer, cleaner, and quieter. They'll also get you closer to your destination, since they stop every two blocks or so and run crosstown (east-west), as well as uptown and downtown (north-south). The MTA transfer system provides north-south travelers with a slip good for a free ride east-west, or vice-versa. Just ask the driver for a transfer when you pay. Make sure you ring when you want to get off. Bus stops are indicated by a yellow-painted curb, but you're better off looking for the blue sign post announcing the bus number or for a glass-walled shelter displaying a map of the bus's route and a schedule (usually unreliable) of arrival times. A flat fare of $1.25 is charged when you board; either exact change or a subway token is required; dollar bills are not accepted.

Queens is served in addition by five private bus lines: **Metropolitan Suburban Bus Authority** (516-776-6722), **Green Bus Lines** (718-995-4700), **Jamaica Buses, Inc.** (718-526-0800), **Queens Surface Corp.** (718-445-3100), and **Triboro Coach Corp.** (718-335-1000), while the Bronx has two: **Liberty Lines Express** (652-8400) and **New York Bus Service** (994-5500).

Taxis

With drivers cruising at warp speed along near-deserted avenues or dodging through bumper-to-bumper traffic, cab rides can give you ulcers. And even if your stomach survives the ride, your budget may not. Still, it's likely that you'll have to take a taxi once in a while, in the interest of convenience or safety. Rides are expensive: The meter starts at $1.50 and clicks 25¢ for each additional fifth of a mile; 25¢ is tacked on for every 75 seconds spent in slow or stopped traffic; a 50¢ surcharge is levied from 8pm to 6am; and passengers pay for all tolls. Don't forget to tip 15%; cabbies need and *expect* the dough. Before you leave the cab, ask for a receipt, which will have the taxi's identification number. This number is necessary to trace lost articles or to make a complaint to the **Taxi Commission** (221 W. 41st St. (221-TAXI), between Times Sq. and the Port Authority Bus Terminal). Since some drivers may illegally try to show the naïve visitor the "scenic route," quickly glance at a street map before embarking, so you'll have some clue if you're being taken to your destination, or just being taken for a ride.

Use only yellow cabs—they're licensed by the state of New York and are safe to ride. If you can't find anything on the street, or if you like to plan ahead, commandeer a radio-dispatched cab (such as UTOC, 718-361-7270, or see Yellow Pages under "Taxicabs"). Use common sense to make rides cheaper—catch a cab going your direction and get off at a nearby street corner. When shared with friends a cab can be cheaper, safer, and more convenient than the subway. But don't expect to be allowed to cram more than four people into the cab.

To hail a cab, stand on the curb and raise your arm. Yelling worked for Dustin Hoffman in *Tootsie*, but will attract more critical glances from New Yorkers than if you too were in drag. An available cab has only the center of its rooflight lit up. When the rooflight is completely off, the cab is already occupied. A cab that has its entire rooflight lit up is off-duty. Got it? Taxis seem to be an endangered species during rush hours, holidays, and inclement weather.

Walking, Running, and Biking

Walking is the cheapest, the most entertaining, and often the fastest way to get around town. During rush hours the sidewalks are packed with suited and sneakered commuters. In between rush hours, the sidewalks are still full of street life. Twenty street blocks (north-south) make up a mile; the distance east-west from one avenue to the next is about triple the distance of a north-south, street-to-street block. For scenic strolls and educational excursions, try a walking tour of Manhattan (see Guided Tours below).

If you plan on running along the street, be prepared to dodge pedestrians and to break your stride at intersections. Women may prompt cat calls. A better alternative to the sidewalk are paths along the rivers or in Central Park—most are pavement, but there is a 1.57 mile cinder loop that circles the Reservoir (between 84th and 96th St.). Joggers pack this path from 6-9am and 5-7pm on weekdays and all day on weekends. For information on running clubs, call **Hostelling International/American Youth Hostels** (932-2300) or the **New York Roadrunner's Club** (860-4455). The Roadrunner's Club hosts races in Central Park every weekend and the Marathon every fall.

Weekday biking in commuter traffic poses a mortal challenge even for veterans. But on weekends, when the traffic thins, cyclists who use helmets and caution can tour the Big Apple on two wheels. From May-Oct., the park (except the lower loop) is closed to traffic on weekdays from 10am-3pm and 7-10pm, and from Fri. 7pm-Mon. 6am. Otherwise, Sunday mornings are best. For a challenging and aesthetic traffic-free course, try circumnavigating the 3.5-mile path within Central Park. If you must leave your bike unattended anywhere in Manhattan, use a strong "U" lock (Tiogas are good). Thieves laugh at weaker chain locks. Don't leave quick-release items unattended; you will find them very quickly released.

Those who can't bring their bikes can rent them by the hour or the day (see Practical Information above). For the more coordinated, roller blades are available at **Peck and Goodie Skates**, 917 Eighth Ave. (246-6123), between 54th and 55th St. They'll hold your shoes while you whiz past your favorite New York sights for $12 per 2hr., $15 per weekday (24-hr.), $17 per 4hr. on weekends, and $25 per day on weekends (24-hr.). Rates include all protective gear. $100 deposit or credit card required. Lessons for all levels of skill offered Sat.-Sun. at 11am in Central Park, $6 per hr. (Open Mon.-Tues., Thurs., Sat.-Sun. 10am-6pm, Wed. and Fri. 10am-8pm.)

Accommodations

If you know someone who knows someone who once heard of someone who lives in New York—get that person's phone number. The cost of living in New York can rip the seams off your wallet. Don't expect to fall into a hotel; if you do, odds are it will be a pit. At true full-service establishments, a night will cost you around $125, plus the hefty 14.25% hotel tax. However, many reasonable choices are available for under $60 a night; it depends upon your priorities. People traveling alone may want to spend more to stay in a safer neighborhood. The young and the outgoing may prefer a budget-style place crowded with students. Honeymooning couples will not.

Cheap YMCAs and hostels offer fewer amenities than more commercial establishments, yet manage to preserve a greater feeling of homeyness and camaraderie. These places advise you to reserve in advance—even once you get to New York, you should call to make sure there are rooms available before trekking any place with large bags. Cheap hotels lasso in hapless innocents and ingenues around the Penn Station and Times Square areas of midtown. Avoid these sleazy, honky-tonk spots. The neighborhoods possess no redeeming qualities, and the hotel rooms often rent by the hour. Another high concentration of budget hotels can be found in lower midtown, on the East Side, the area just below the Empire State Building. These spots, around Park Avenue South in the 20s, vary widely in quality, as the neighborhood changes drastically from block to block. You may encounter some unpleasantness or a good deal.

Crime-free neighborhoods in the city exist only in dreams; never leave anything of value in your room. Most places have safes or lockers available, some for an extra fee. And never, ever sleep outdoors, anywhere in Manhattan. The city has a hard enough time protecting its vast homeless population—tourists would simply not stand a chance.

Student Accommodations

Student accommodations can run as cheap as $15 per night, but don't expect luxury or intimacy. You can pay a little more for a room with fewer occupants and more conveniences. University housing, although usually reserved for affiliated students, becomes a viable option in the summer. Whenever possible, call or write ahead of time.

New York International HI/AYH Hostel-CIEE New York Student Center, 891 Amsterdam Ave. (932-2300) at 103rd St. Subway: #1, 9, B, or C to 102nd St. Located in a block-long, landmark building designed by Richard Morris Hunt, the HI/AYH Hostel shares its site with the CIEE Student Center, an information depot for travelers abroad and U.S. citizens looking to get away (call 666-3619 for information), as well as a Council Travel office. The largest hostel in the U.S., with 90 dorm-style rooms and 480 beds. Spiffy new soft carpets, blondewood bunks, spotless bathrooms. Members' kitchens and dining rooms, coin-operated laundry machines, communal lounges, and a large outdoor garden. Separate and secure indoor storage for belongings and bicycles. Open 24hr. Check in any time, check out 11am. No curfew. Max. stay 29 days. $20 per night, nonmembers $23. Family room $60. Groups of 4-12 may get rooms to themselves, esp. if they call ahead. Linen rental $3. Towel $2. Late check-out fee (after 11am) $5. Excellent disabled access.

International Student Hospice, 154 E. 33rd St. (228-7470), between Lexington and Third. Subway: #6 to 33rd St. An inconspicuous converted brownstone with a brass plaque saying "I.S.H." by the door. Good location in Murray Hill. An institution with character. Twenty very small rooms with bunk beds bursting with crusty bric-a-brac, cracked porcelain tea cups, and clunky oak night tables. The ceilings are crumbling and the stairs are listing precariously, but the house is slowly being restored by willing inmates. Loquacious and friendly proprietor Art Stabile watches over his visitors like a mother hen, prepping them on how to be street smart. Not for the fastidious. Preference for internationals and students. Two to four person rooms. Hall bathroom. Large common room, lounge, and enough dusty books to last a summer. Strict midnight curfew. $30 per night, some weekly discounts.

YMCA—Vanderbilt, 224 E. 47th St. (755-2410), between Second and Third Ave. Subway: #6 to 51st St. or E, F to Lexington/Third Ave. Internationals jabber in the clean, brightly lit lobby. The 750 cramped rooms are a strange hybrid of hotel and hostel: TV, A/C, and sheets on beds imply hotel, but the linoleum floor, grungy walls, and severely limited bathroom facilities detract. Nonetheless, a good deal. Lockers, Nautilus equipment, pool, luggage storage for early arrivals, and safe deposit boxes. The front desk and 24-hr. security guard keep close tabs on who is doing what. It's popular: make reservations and guarantee them with a deposit. VISA, MasterCard, and money orders accepted; personal checks taken only for reservations. Check in 1-6pm. 25-day max. stay. $10 key deposit. Singles $39. Doubles $49. Triples $63-67. Quads $84. Rates lower off season.

International Student Center, 38 W. 88th St. (787-7706). Subway: B or C to 86th St. Between Central Park West and Columbus Ave. Open only to foreigners, preferably students; you must show a foreign passport to be admitted. A once-gracious, welcoming brownstone on a cheerful, tree-lined street noted for frequent celebrity sightings. Single-sex no-frills bunk rooms. Large basement TV lounge with affable, satisfied guests. No curfew; open daily 8am-11pm (guests have keys). Seven-day max. stay, when full. No reservations; call by 10pm for a bed. A bargain: $10 a night (may have risen to $12 by summer '93.)

International House, 500 Riverside Dr. (316-8436) at 123rd St. Subway: #1 or 9 to 116th St. or 125th St. Very large hostel fairly close to Columbia University; single women should still take extra precaution. Great facilities: gymnasium, TV lounge, cafeteria, coin-op laundry. 24-hr. security. Singles $25 per night, $18 per night for a stay of 2 weeks or longer. Communal bath. Make reservations 8am-10pm. Often vacancies, but try to call in advance. Open Mon.-Fri. 9am-5pm in the winter, Mon.-Fri. 8am-6:45pm in the summer.

Hotel Gershwin, 3 E. 27th St. (545-8000), between Fifth and Park Ave. Attractive hotel with a popish Art Deco design scheme. Although open continuously, the hotel is currently undergoing ambitious renovations which will result in a rooftop garden and an expanded lobby. Friendly management. Passport required for dorm beds; all dorm rooms have lockers. Free tea and coffee. 24-hr. reception and no curfew. Private room $45; 4-bed rooms $17 per bed. 20-day max. stay.

Sugar Hill International House, 722 Saint Nicholas Ave. (246-6644) at 146th St. in Harlem. Subway A, B, C, or D to 145th St. Located on Sugar Hill near the Harlem Dance Theatre, the Schomburg Center, and Yankee Stadium, the neighborhood is a lively mix and busy at all hours. 30-person occupancy with 2-10 people per room in standard bunkbeds. A hostel with few rules, no curfew, no chores, and no lockout. Staff is incredibly friendly and helpful, with a vast knowledge of NYC which they are more than willing to share. Facilities include kitchens, TV, stereo, and paperback library. Beautiful garden in back. All female room available. Europeans preferred, but well-traveled Americans accepted as well. Check in 9-11am, or call. $12 per person per night. Call in advance.

Big Apple Hostel, 109th W. 45th St. (302-2603) between 6th and 7th Ave. Centrally located (in same building as St. James Hotel). Small, clean rooms. 24-hr. reception. Free coffee. Lockers in rooms. Private room $45, $17 per bed.

Mid-City Hostel, 608 Eighth Ave. (704-0562) between 39th and 40th St., on the 3rd and 4th floors. No sign: look for the small red building in the middle of the block. People walking up the creaky, uneven steps in this even shakier neighborhood will be pleasantly surprised by the comfortable, homey hostel: the skylights, brick walls, and old wooden beams make it feel like a friend's apartment. Charismatic owner Donna aims to attract international backpackers; backpack and passport ID required. Call in advance. Lockout noon-6pm. Curfew Sun.-Thurs. midnight, Fri.-Sat. 1am. Only 25 beds. Dorm-style beds $15, $18 during peak season, including a light breakfast of fruit salad.

YMCA—West Side, 5 W. 63rd St. (787-4400). Subway: #1, 9, A, B, C, or D to 59th St./Columbus Circle. Small, well-maintained rooms but dilapidated halls in a big, popular Y whose impressive, Islamic-inspired façade belies its functional innards. Free access to 2 pools, indoor track, racquet courts, and Nautilus equipment. Shower on every floor. A touch grim. Check out noon; lockout at 11pm. Singles $39, doubles $49, $3 extra for A/C.

YMCA—McBurney, 206 W. 24th St. (741-9226), at Seventh Ave. Subway: #1, 9, C, or E to 23rd St. A working YMCA with a lot of activity on the ground floor, but the no-frills rooms upstairs are clean and liveable. Good security and friendly staff. Singles $28-35. Doubles $47. Usually has rooms available.

YMCA, 138-46 Northern Blvd. (718-961-6880), in Flushing, Queens. Subway: #7 to Main St. About 1/2 hr. from Manhattan. Walk down Main St. and turn right onto Northern Blvd. Men only. Convenient to the Flushing central shopping district, but the neighborhood quickly deteriorates past Northern Blvd. Gym, Nautilus, squash, and swimming facilities. $25 per person, $110 per week. Key deposit $20. Passport or driver's license required.

YMCA—Central Queens, 89-25 Parsons Blvd. (718-739-6600), in Jamaica, Queens. Subway: F or R to Parson Blvd., or E or J to Jamaica Center. Men only. In the bustling, noisy downtown of Jamaica. Gym, Nautilus, racquetball, and swimming facilities. $28 per person per day, $110 per week. Key deposit $10. Passport or driver's license required.

YWCA—Brooklyn, 30 Third Ave. (718-875-1190), near Atlantic Ave. in Brooklyn. Subway: #2, 3, 4, 5 B, D, M, N, or R to Atlantic Ave./Pacific St. Women only. An octogenarian building still in good shape. Plain rooms with access to kitchen facilities. Rough neighborhood draws residents of varying respectability. Singles $68-90 per week plus mandatory annual YWCA membership ($38, students $23). Application necessary—guests must be 18-55 and employed—but can be filed on the day of arrival.

Chelsea Center Hostel, 313 W. 29th St. (643-0214) between 8th and 9th Ave. Subway: #1, 2, 3, 9, A, C, E. Gregarious, knowledgeable staff will help you out with New York tips in multiple languages. 25 bunks in low-ceilinged room makes for a slightly cramped setup; the decor and lighting are being improved and may be inviting by summer 1993. Their pride and joy is the tiny backdoor garden, replete with ivy and picnic table. Lockout 11am-4pm, but check in anytime. Definitely call ahead. $20 in summer, $18 in winter, light breakfast included.

Fashion Institute of Technology, 210 W. 27th St. (760-7885). Subway: #1 or 9 to 28th St. Decent neighborhood, but adjacent to a bad one; exercise caution at night. Spartan dorm-style doubles with communal baths in a fairly modern building. Application required: call or pick one up, but expect to wait a couple days for processing. Office open Mon.-Fri. 8am-7pm. $122 per person per week, 1-week min. stay. Double occupancy suites with kitchen and a bath, $640 per person per month, 1-month min. stay. Housing offered from the second week of June until July 31. Reservations necessary for suites; full payment in advance.

Allerton House, 130 E. 57th St. (753-8841), between Park and Lexington Ave. Subway: #6 to 59th St. or N, R to Lexington Ave. Women only. A safety-conscious operation in a swanky district. Small flowery private rooms, about the size of a walk-in closet. Slightly musty in the hallways, but still an incredible deal. Check in 11am; check out 1pm. Singles $35, with connecting bath $40, with private bath $50. Doubles $65.

Whittier Hall, 1230 Amsterdam Ave. (678-3235) at 120th St. Subway: #1 or 9 to 116th St. Columbia dorm sets aside some rooms for visitors. Rooms are small but clean. Tight security. Bad neighborhood, but well populated until fairly late. Predominantly student clientele. Singles $30. Doubles with A/C, bath, and kitchen $50. Reserve in advance.

Hotels

Carlton Arms Hotel, 160 E. 25th St. (679-0680), at Third Ave. Subway: #6 to 23rd St. The funkiest hotel in Manhattan, and possibly the world. Stay inside a submarine and peer through windows at the lost city of Atlantis, travel to Renaissance Venice, or stow your clothes in a dresser suspended on an astroturf wall. Each room has been designed by a different avant-garde artist, not one of whom has left many motel pastels around. "I sought to create a resounding rhythm that echoed wall-to-wall, layer upon layer, to fuse our separate impressions into one existence," writes the artist of Room 5B. Hmm. Aggressive adornment doesn't completely obscure the age of these budget rooms, or their lack of air, but it goes a long way toward providing distractions. Strong sense of solidarity among the guests. The artist staff might be wearing pins saying "I'd Rather Be Sculpting," but they get the job done. Not the best of neighborhoods, especially at night, but 3rd Ave. is well-traveled. Discounts for students and foreign tourists. Confirm reservations at least 10 days in advance. Singles $40 (with student/foreign discount $37). Doubles $54 ($48), with private bath $62 ($56). Triples $65 ($58), with private bath $74 ($64). Pay for 6 nights at once and get the 7th free. Visa and Mastercard accepted for stays of 2 nights or more. Most major traveler's checks accepted.

Martha Washington, 30 E. 30th St. (689-1900), near Madison. Subway: #6 to 28th St. Women-only dormitory with over 400 reasonably sized rooms identically decked out in floral bedspread and wallpaper. "Gentlemen callers" not allowed beyond the lobby, and all men are banished from the building when the clock strikes twelve. Pleasant if vaguely impersonal. Laundry room. Rental TV and books available in lobby. Doors locked midnight-7am, but residents get keys. Singles $35, with private lavatory $39, with private bath $54. Doubles $50, with private bath $69. Weekly: singles $140, with private lavatory $154, with private bath $175; doubles $112, with private bath $122.50, with bath and kitchenette $136.50. Astonishing discounts for longer stays.

Hotel Esplanade, 305 West End Ave. (874-5000), at 74th St. Less pricey than it looks or feels, perhaps due to the quiet block (and street) it occupies. Kitchenettes, TVs, and bouncy beds; boring, but in a reassuring way. Roomy-enough singles and doubles with bath $55-80 depending on day, month, and how full they are (cheaper on weekdays); "suites" from $75.

Roger Williams Hotel, 28 E. 31st St. (684-7500), at Madison in pleasant Murray Hill area. Subway: #6 to 33rd St. The wavering paint job and the scent of disinfectant may deter some guests, but these rooms have all the amenities: kitchenettes, 2-burner gas stoves, sink, refrigerator, full bath, and color cable TV. 24-hr. security. Singles $55-65. Doubles $60-70. Triples $75-80. Quads $80-90.

Rutledge Hotel, 161 Lexington Ave. (532-2255), at 30th St. Subway: #6 to 28th St. Linoleum-tiled corridors, tiny hallway toilets, and drably decorated bare-bones rooms contribute to the feel of a rooming house. Many of the guests stay for extended periods. Singles $40, doubles $50; singles $150 per week, doubles $180.

Hotel Grand Union, 34 E. 32nd St. (683-5890), between Madison and Park. Subway: #6 to 33rd St. A real hotel, centrally located but reasonably priced. All rooms and bathrooms have recently been renovated and redecorated, and come equipped with TV, electronic phones, A/C. Major credit cards accepted. Singles $57-68. Doubles $80. Quad $95. YIEE discount 15%. ISIC discount 10%.

Pickwick Arms Hotel, 230 E. 51st St. (355-0300 or 800-742-5945), between Second and Third Ave. Subway: #6 to 51st St. or E, F to Lexington/Third Ave. Chandeliered, marbled lobby filled with the silken strains of "Unforgettable You" contrasts with disenchantingly dark and minuscule rooms and equally microscopic bathrooms. Nonetheless, a clean hotel with unbeatable rates in a great neighborhood. Roof garden, parking, and airport service available. Even with nearly 400 rooms to fill, the Pickwick Arms gets very busy, so make reservations. Check in 2pm; check out 1pm. Singles $40, with shared bathrooms $50. Doubles $80. Studios $99.50. $12 each additional person.

Portland Square Hotel, 132 W. 47th St. (382-0600), between Sixth and Seventh Ave. Pleasant lobby painted dusty rose lures guests up to carpeted rooms with firm beds, TVs, and bathrooms big enough to turn around in. Framed scenes of Times Square in days of yore scattered about. Keycard entry. Singles $40, with bath $60. Doubles $85. Triples $90. Quads $95.

Herald Square Hotel, 19 W. 31st St. (279-4017 or 800-727-1888), just west of Fifth Ave. Quartered in the original Beaux-Arts home of *Life* magazine, built in 1893; today, the reception desk is shielded in glass while sirens blare outside. Above the entrance note the reading cherub entitled the "Winged Life," carved by Philip Martiny. The sculpture was a frequent presence on the pages of early *Life* magazines. The work of some of America's most noted illustrators adorns the walls of the lobby, halls, and rooms. Immaculate, newly renovated rooms with color TV and A/C. Singles (1 person only) $40, single/double (1 bed, 1 bathroom) $50. Larger singles with bath $65. Larger doubles (1 bed) with bath $85.

Hotel Iroquois, 49 W. 44th St. (840-3080 or 800-332-7220), off Fifth Ave. Pink and blue, slightly worn but spacious rooms host Greenpeace activists when they come to town. Lucky first-comers get kitchen in their suite at no extra charge. Special student rates: singles $65, doubles $80, suite for 2 $99, for 5 $125. $10 extra per person.

Hotel Remington, 129 W. 46th St. (221-2600), between Broadway and Sixth. Plush carpeting, bedspread and curtains in matching orange hang in reasonably large rooms. Spotless bathrooms. Out of the window you get a beautiful view of the individual bricks which compose the adjacent building; they are so close, you can reach out and touch for extra pleasure. All rooms with color TV and A/C; no bath. Singles or doubles $60. Triples $65. With bath: singles $75, doubles $80, triples $85.

Washington Square Hotel, 103 Waverly Pl. (777-9515), at MacDougal St. Subway: A, B, C, D, E, F, or Q to W. 4th St. Fantastic location. Glitzy marble and brass lobby; dingy halls. TV, A/C, and key card. Clean, comfortable rooms. Friendly and multilingual staff. Singles and Doubles $85. Quads (2 double beds) $105. Reservation and deposit required 2-3 weeks in advance.

Mansfield Hotel, 12 W. 44th St., (944-6050 or 800-255-5167), off Fifth Ave. A dignified establishment housed in a turn-of-the-century building with comfortable leather couches in the lobby and beautiful oak doors in the hallways. Rooms in process of renovation: new lighting, new paint, and sauna whirlpool. Make sure you get one of the fixed-up ones. Checkout at noon. Reservations and 1 night's deposit required. Singles $65. Doubles $80. Triples $95. Quads $100. Large suites $120 for 5, $140 for 6. Call for special student rates.

Riverview Hotel, 113 Jane St. (929-0060), near West St. in the West Village, on the Hudson. Subway: #1 or 9 to Christopher St. Moderately safe area, particularly for 2 or more. No frills. Rooms vary in quality and price. Shared bathrooms on the hall. Clean and friendly. Singles $19.50. Doubles $32.80.

Senton Hotel, 39-41 W. 27th St. (684-5800), at Broadway. Subway: R to 28th St. Comfortable beds in spacious quarters, amidst a bevy of large-print floral wallpapers. TV, including HBO, cable, and dirty movies. Basic accommodations, spartan but newly renovated. No guests. Singles with communal hall bath $40. Doubles $50. Suites (2 double beds) $65.

Malibu Studios Hotel, 2688 Broadway (222-2954), at 103rd St. Subway: #1 or 9 to 103rd St. Tropical motif. Second and higher floors on a funky block. Unremarkable, brightly-lit blue rooms with refrigerator and hot plate. Variable rates hover around $35 for a single with shared bath, $70 for private bath; doubles $70. Ask about student or off-season discounts.

Broadway-American Hotel, 222 W. 77th St. (362-1100; 800-446-4556), at (surprise) Broadway. Subway: #1 or 9 to 79th St. Cool, clean, ultra-modern quarters with few right angles and lots of charcoal-grey; if it were roomier, it might be a corporate law office. Singles $45, with private bath $80. Doubles $65, with bath $90.

Arlington Hotel, 18-20 W. 25th St. (645-3990), between Fifth and Sixth Ave. Subway: F or R to 23rd St. Prides itself on hospitality and courteous service. Clean-smelling refurbished rooms, all with TV and A/C. Free transportation to Jacob Javits Convention Center during trade shows. Singles or doubles $65. Twin or Triple $77. Quads $105. ISIC 10% discount.

The Aberdeen, 17 W. 32nd St. (736-1600 or 800-826-4667), between Fifth Ave. and Broadway. Subway: R to 28th St., or B, D, F, N, Q, R to 34th St. A small Korean community around the hotel offers good food. Dignified Beaux-Arts façade of limestone and brick leads into a clean and simple lobby with tight security; a guard at the door questions all newcomers. Rooms are adequately sized and pleasant, if unexceptional. Check out at noon, check in at 3pm. Singles $65. Doubles $75. Triples $85. Quads $95. Discounts on groups of 10 or more. Make reservations early.

Hotel Stanford, 43 W. 32nd St. (563-1480), between Fifth Ave. and Broadway. Slightly ritzier than The Aberdeen up the street, but quite a bit more expensive. The lobby glitters with sparkling ceiling lights and a well-polished marble floor. Korean restaurant and teahouse connected to the hotel. Rooms small and L-shaped, but clean and comfortable, with firm mattresses and plush carpeting. TV, A/C, refrigerator. Check out at noon. Singles $80. Doubles $90. Twins $100. 10% off for students with ID.

Milford Plaza, 270 W. 45th St. (869-3600 or 800-221-2690), between 44th and 45th. Smack in the heart of the theater district, this hulking 1300-room hotel's greatest asset is its prime location. Rooms are average in every respect, with A/C and TV. Check in 3pm, check out noon. Singles $95-135. Doubles $110-150. Take advantage of the seen-on-TV **Lulla "buy" Package,** which includes doubles accommodations, breakfast, and dinner meal tickets for $99 per night ($85 for students). Advance reservations and prepayment are required.

Hotel Belleclaire, 250 W. 77th St. at Broadway (362-7700). Shabby yellow-orange rooms with high ceilings in an old 12-story building, Singles $55 with bath, $150 weekly.

Bed and Breakfasts

Referral services can help you find private individuals who will rent out part or all of their apartment to you and provide a breakfast as well. Although not your stereotypical bed and breakfasts—no sleepy New England village squares or big front porches—Manhattan has its share of B&Bs. Reservations should be made a few weeks in advance, usually with a deposit. A cancellation fee may be levied. Most of the apartments listed have two-night minimums. Listings are divided into "hosted," meaning traditional B&B arrangements, and "unhosted," meaning that the people renting you the apartment will not be there. Most agencies offer a wide range of prices, depending upon the accommodation's size and quality and the neighborhood's safety. Apartments in the West Village and the Upper East Side cost the most. Most agencies also list accommodations in boroughs other than Manhattan; these can often be an excellent budget alternative.

New World Bed and Breakfast (675-5600 or toll-free: from U.S. and Canada, 800-443-3800; from Australia, 0014-800-125-496; from France, 1905-901-148; from Japan, 0031-11-503, from Germany, 0130-811-672). Over 150 listings, in all parts of Manhattan. Prices include fee; when you make your reservation, you must pay 25% of the total bill as a deposit. Refundable up to 5 days before your visit, with $5 cancellation fee. Credit card payments accepted. Hosted accommodations: singles $55-70 (most around $65), doubles $60-95 (most around $80). Unhosted apartment $70-135.

Bed and Breakfast Network of NY Inc. (645-8134). Around 300 listings throughout the city. 25% deposit required when you make your reservations, refundable up to 10 days before your visit. Deposits payable by personal check, but only cash or traveler's checks accepted for the bill. Hosted accommodations: singles $50-60, doubles $70-90. Unhosted apartments from $80. Weekly and monthly rates available.

Urban Ventures (594-5650). The oldest and most established agency in the city. A whopping 700 listings covering most neighborhoods in Manhattan. Booking fee of $20 or, if booking with less than 5 days notice, one night's rent. 2 night min. Hosted accommodations: singles from $48, doubles from $60. Unhosted singles from $85.

Food

This city takes its food seriously. In New York, delis war. Brunch rules. Trendy dining has caught on. Supermarkets haven't—with so many bakeries, bistros, butcher shops, and greengrocers, who needs to stop and shop in a food mall? Don't be confused by the conflation of food and art. Certain eateries think they are galleries, while select delis look like museums. Assorted gourmet cooks pose as pushcart vendors. Sidewalk gourmands can stick with the old roving standbys on wheels (hot dogs, pretzels, roasted chestnuts), or try something more adventurous (shish kebabs, felafel, hot knishes).

New York's restaurants do more than the United Nations to promote international goodwill and cross-cultural exchanges. City dining spans the globe, with eateries ranging from relatively tame sushi bars to wild combinations like Afghani/Italian, or Mexican/Lebanese. In a city where the melting pot is sometimes less than tranquil, one can still peacefully sample Chinese pizza and Cajun knish. Be open-minded: you won't get very far in New York if you eat only what you can pronounce.

Chinese restaurants spice up every neighborhood and even fill up a town of their own. For a taste of bell'Italia, cruise to Mulberry Street in Little Italy. For the most realistic of post-post-revolutionary Russian cuisine, make a trip to Brighton Beach, where Soviet emigrès have built their community. Many Eastern European dishes have become New York staples: the plump traditional dumplings, or *knishes* make a great lunch; eat potato knishes with mustard or meat knishes with *yoich* (gravy). Fill up on *pirogi,* Polish dough creations stuffed with potato or cheese and garnished with fried onions and sour cream; sample some spicy Polish *kielbasa* (sausage), or pig out on *blintzes,* thin pancakes rolled around sweet cheese, blueberries, and other divine fillings. The *bialy* is a flat, soft, onion-flavored bagel cognate.

And of course there are always two old favorites: pizza and bagels. New Yorkers like their pizza thin and hot, with no shortage of grease. Warfare between pizzerias has been going on for years; the major issue is not the taste but the name. There are now a full 22 institutions fighting over the right to call themselves the Original Ray's. Who is Ray? Who cares? Innominate pizzerias can offer as fine fare as titled competitors. The humble bagel is mighty Brooklyn's major contribution to Western civilization. Bagels come in a rainbow of flavors—the most common being plain, egg, poppyseed, and onion—but only one shape, well suited for cream cheese spread thick. Exiles from the city often find bagel deprivation to be one of the biggest indignities of life outside of New York. Outsiders might wonder what the fuss is all about.

Those low on cash can take advantage of the inexpensive lunch specials offered by otherwise unapproachable restaurants—a large Hungarian lunch can be yours for $5. Almost any local coffeeshop will serve you a full American breakfast with eggs, bacon, toast, coffee, and the works for $2-3. Atriums and public parks throughout the city provide idyllic urban settings for picnics. Many of the larger museums provide picturesque, artwork-filled cafés to facilitate your digestion.

New Yorkers dine later than most Americans. In New York you can find a restaurant open and serving dinner almost anytime between afternoon and midnight. Make reservations or arrive before 7pm to beat the crowds to the best tables in the house. Don't be afraid to send back food that does not live up to your expectations; no one lets manners stand in the way of a good meal.

Follow your nose. Look before you eat. Read the writing on the menu on the wall. Don't judge a restaurant by its façade; good things often come in a dingy, spoilt package. Ask: where are the crowds? An empty restaurant is a good place tò avoid. A full restaurant is either very trendy or very good, and occasionally both. With so many eateries to choose from, those not up to par rarely last.

East Midtown

New York has six "four-star" restaurants, four of them (La Grenòuille, Hatsuhana, Lutèce, and The Quilted Giraffe) in this area. Tycoons dine here amòngst skyscraping office buildings, art deco monuments, and high rents. But it's just possible to eat here without the company card. East Midtown hosts many sidewalk food vendors and fast-food peddlers. You can drop by the **Food Emporium,** 969 Second Ave. (593-2224), between 51st and 52nd, or **D'Agostino,** Third Ave. (684-3133), between 35th and 36th. These upscale supermarket chains, with branches scattered throughout Manhattan, feature reliable, well-stocked delis, fresh fruit and salad bars, ice cold drinks, gourmet ice cream, tons of munchies, and lots more—all at reasonable prices. After you've stocked up, picnicking is free in the area's green cloisters: try **Greenacre Park,** 51st St. between Second and Third; **Paley Park,** 3rd St., between Fifth and Madison; or **United Nations Plaza,** 8th St. at First Ave.

Crystal Gourmet, 422 Madison Ave. (752-2910), between 48th and 49th St. Stunning buffet, topped with a watermelon dramatically chiselled into an eagle. Mounds of melons, cherries, and fresh salad material alongside pastas, chicken, and beef dishes—all at $4 per pound. Primarily takeout, but for $5 you can sit at the plain little tables in the back and engorge yourself on their "all-you-can-eat" dinner special (5-7pm). Open Mon.-Fri. 7am-7pm, Sat.-Sun. 8am-5pm.

Royal Canadian Pancake House, 1004 Second Ave. (219-3038) at 53rd St. "Pancakes make people happy," screams the slogan above the front door, and at this benevolent institution, one pancake can make up to three people happy. Pancakes the size of Saskatchewan are saturated with syrup, plunked with berries, titillated by exotic toppings, and spiked with Grand Marnier. Most are $9, but quite a deal. Bigfoot! Share charge on weekends 9am-5pm: $5. Open daily 7am-11pm. Another location in the Village.

Hsin Yu, 862 Second Ave. (752-9039), at the corner of 46th Street. In the heart of the commercial area. Businessmen crowd in at lunch, not for the fake flowers or charming tablecloths, but for good, inexpensive food. Intriguing special combination platters—like shrimp with lobster sauce, egg roll, and fried rice—cost $5-6; most other entrees $7-10. Begin with the ham and winter melon soup (for two) served in an excavated melon $3.50 and finish with, surprise, a fortune cookie. Open Mon.-Fri. 11:30am-10:45pm, Sat.-Sun. noon-10:45pm.

Zaro's Bread Basket, 466 Lexington Ave. (972-1560) at 46th St. The ambience created by the tiled floors and tiled walls of this busy bread and pastry emporium is as romantic as a 7-11, but you can take out a huge selection of food at reasonable prices. Meat sandwiches $3-5, cheese sandwiches $1-3, muffins $1.10, deli croissants $3.25, large coffee or iced tea $1.10. Open Mon.-Fri. 6am-10pm, Sat. 6:30am-6pm.

Madras Woodlands, 308 49th St. (759-2441) between First and Second. Amidst the subdued strains of the sitar, serpentine waiters glide you to your seat. The attentive maître d' guides you through the spicy and delicious mysteries of the 14-course vegetarian buffet ($7.95, weekdays noon-3pm). The favored haunt of Indian businessmen. Dinner prices somewhat steep. Kosher. Open daily noon-3pm, 5-10pm.

Le Croissant Shop, 459 Lexington Ave. (697-5580) at 45th St. A standard French-style bakery, but the price is right for this neighborhood. You can sit on stools and watch the passersby while munching on a hot, flaky, filled croissant ($1.10-1.95) or a croissant sandwich ($3-4). Baguettes ($1.30) and quiche ($2.50) abound. Open Mon.-Fri. 6:30am-7pm, Sat. 8am-6pm, Sun. 8:30am-4:30pm.

Dosanko, 135 E. 45th St. (697-2967), between Lexington and Third Ave. Wide-ranging chain with modest ambition. Japanese fast-food at relatively cheap prices. The main dish here is *lo mein*, a tubful of noodles and occasional vegetables, seasoned with butter or curry ($4.90). Six pork dumplings with rice and salad $5.70; chicken, fried and marinated, served with green salad and sauteed vegetables, only $6. Open daily 11am-9:30pm.

Coldwaters, 988 Second Ave. (888-2122) between 52nd and 53rd St. Seafood entrees ($6-11) under nautical paraphernalia and stained-glass lamps. The real attraction is brunch (served daily 11:30am-4pm): two drinks (alcoholic or non), choice of entree, salad and fries for $6.95. Open 11:30am-3am.

West Midtown

West Midtown smokes with summer heat, booms with construction, and buzzes with nocturnal promise, but has never promised anyone decent food at reasonable prices. Your best bets are Seventh and Eighth Avenues. Around Times Square and the Port Authority Bus Terminal areas, the number of fast-food chains nearly approaches the combined tally of pushers, pimps, tourists, and prostitutes—quite an achievement. In the Theater District, the stretch of Broadway from Times Square to 52nd St., you'll run into plenty of first-rate and ethnically diverse restaurants, from French to Japanese to Thai and back to Italian. While the food in these places can be mouthwatering, your check will probably be much harder to swallow.

Celebrities occasionally drift over to **Sardi's,** 234 W. 44th St., and take a seat on the plush red leather, surrounded by caricatures of themselves and their best friends. Traditionally, on the opening night of a major Broadway play, the main star makes an exalted entrance following the show—to hearty cheers for a superb performance, or polite applause for a bomb. If this exercise grows tedious, they may head west of Eighth Ave., to 46th St.'s "Restaurant Row," an appealing but expensive strip. Follow luminaries into **Joe Allen,** 326 W. 46th St., and marvel at posters of shows that closed in under a week. Farther uptown, near Carnegie Hall, lies the **Russian Tea Room,** 150

W. 57th St., a New York institution where dancers, musicians, and businesspeople meet to down caviar and vodka.

Lotfi's Couscous, 145 W. 45th St. on the 2nd floor (768-8738), between Broadway and Sixth Ave. A cozy Moroccan hideaway, unfairly overlooked by the busy throng outside. Tea-parlor ambience enhanced by dim lighting, traditional tapestries on the walls, and soothing piped-in Middle Eastern music. Fancy. Try the *tajine* (Moroccan stew) slowly cooked with herbs in its own juice ($11-12) or the couscous specialty topped with vegetables ($10), and complete the experience with a "snake"—a cigar-like pastry filled with ground nuts and spices ($2.25). Soups $2.50, salads $3.25, entrées $9-14, desserts $2-3.50. Open Mon.-Fri. noon-11:30pm, Sat. 3-11:30pm. Oct.-March also open Sun. noon-11:30pm.

La Bonne Soupe, 48 W. 55th St. (586-7650), between Fifth and Sixth Ave. Excellent lighter fare in a split-level "bistro" that doubles as a gallery for Haitian paintings. Hearty meals of aromatic soups served with bread, salad, dessert, and wine for $10. Minimum charge $7. Open Mon.-Sat. 11:30am-midnight, Sun. 11:30am-11pm.

Bengal Express, 789 Ninth Ave. (489-8036), between 52nd and 53rd St. Small Indian take out/ eat in that prides itself on healthful cooking: no MSG, sulfites, or artificial anything. *Mulligatawny,* otherwise known as lentil soup ($1.50) and other delicious unpronounceables served hospitably on pink tablecloths. Extensive vegetarian selection $5-5.50. Open daily 11:30am-11pm.

Ellen's Star Dust Diner, 1377 6th Ave. (307-7575), at 56th St. Archie, Marilyn, and Jimmy Dean icons populate this soda fountain 50s time warp. Old jukeboxes would sing "Teen Angel" if they still worked, but the stereo system does it for them. Freckled, friendly waiters serve nostalgically-named 3-scoop shakes ($3.50) with pinwheeled straws. Burgers, BBQ, and 15 types of salad (the only concession to modern times) are $5-9. Skip bifferty! Open Mon.-Thurs. 7:30am-11:30pm, Sun. 8am-11pm.

Ariana Afghan Kebab, 787 Ninth Ave. (262-2323), between 52nd and 53rd St. Bedecked with embroidered textiles, Arabic calligraphy, and, oddly, slick reproductions of Alpine snow scenes. Try the *Bandinjah Burani* ($2.50), an unusual spicy eggplant dish served with sour cream and bread. Entrees ($5-8) mock the indecisive. The default choice is *lamb tikka kebab* ($6.75), with chunks of marinated meat cooked in a wood charcoal oven, served on a bed of brown rice with bread and salad. BYOB. Open Mon.-Sat. 11:30am-3pm and 5-11pm.

Little Italy Pizza Parlour, 72 W. 45th St. (730-7575), corner of 45th St. and Sixth Ave. All of the pizzerias on 45th St. claim to be world famous, but this one takes the pie. Walls shine with the usual studio glossies, including the autographed color photo of a daring blonde: "Love ya pizza—Madonna." Hot crispy slice with plenty of mozzarella ($1.65). Large Neapolitan pie $12, pie with the works $21. Calzones clock in around $3.75. Open Mon.-Sat. 6:30am-8:30pm.

Chinatown Express, 427 Seventh Ave. (563-3559), between 33rd and 34th St. A Chinese-food, penny-pinching, picnic-lover's wet dream. A 25-foot bar of every imaginable dish—General Tsao's chicken, fried rice, shrimp, spare ribs—all hot and delicious, for $3.69 per pound. Take out is best, as the upstairs seating area is cramped with uninspiring decor. Open daily noon-9pm.

Carnegie Delicatessen, 854 Seventh Ave. (757-2245), at 55th St. *The* deli. Ceiling fans twirl gently above as photos of illustrious dead people stare out from the walls. Eat elbow-to-elbow at long tables. The incredible pastrami and corned beef sandwich ($9) could easily stuff two people, but sharing incurs a $3 penalty. First-timers shouldn't leave without trying the sinfully rich cheesecake, topped with strawberries, blueberries, or cherries ($5.45). Open daily 6:30am-4am.

La Parisienne, 910 Seventh Ave. (765-4590), between 57th and 58th St. The best deal in this part of town. Nondescript atmosphere, standard fare, but generous portions at reasonable prices. Good for a quick burger ($3.55) or a cup of coffee ($1). Try their breakfast specials 'til 11am. It's a short walk from here to Central Park—a nice place to sprawl out and digest. Open Mon.-Sat. 6am-10pm, Sun. 7am-10pm.

Uncle Vanya Café, 315 W. 54th St. (2626-0542), between Eighth and Ninth Ave. Marionettes hang from the ceiling and the samovar reigns in this cheerful yellow café. These delicacies of Czarist Russia range from Borscht ($1.75) to *Teftley,* Russian meatballs in sour cream sauce ($2.50) to caviar (market price—a concession to capitalism). Undiscovered, homey, and very good. Open Mon.-Sat. 10am-8pm.

Sapporo, 152 W. 49th St. (869-8972), near Seventh Ave. A Japanese translation of the American diner, with the grill in full view. A favorite snack spot for Broadway cast members and corporate types alike. Menu items listed on the wall in Japanese. Portions are huge and flavors astounding. The *Sapporo ramen* special ($5.60) is a big bowl of noodles with assorted meats and vegetables, all floating around in a miso soup base. Open Mon.-Sun. 11:30am-11pm.

The Brewburger, 814 7th Ave. at 53rd St. Giant antlers and deer heads join literally thousands of beer mugs as quaint ceiling decoration in this spacious, dark restaurant. A satisfied crowd salivates all over the Brewburger special—a burger, all-you-can-eat-salad, and mug of beer for $9.50—while mavericks try the pizza burger for $6.95. Open daily 7am until "late."

La Fondue, 43 W. 55th St. (581-0820) between Fifth and Sixth Ave. The dark wooden tables and chalet decor transport you to Lake Geneva. Share in the peculiar Swiss tradition of dunking for apples in a tub of cheese fondue ($10)—loser has to pucker up or pay for drinks. Bizarre but fun. For the more sober-minded, the chocolate fondue with fruit ($5.75) erases all Woes. Open Mon.-Thurs. noon-midnight, Fri.-Sat. noon-12:30am, Sun. noon-11pm.

Viva Pancho, 156 W. 44th St. (944-9747), between Sixth and Seventh Ave. Neon and cactus rule inside this restaurant; fajitas and Mexican drinks top its menu. Friendly folks down margaritas and sangria by the pitcher. Regular entrees are $9-11, but you can get a heaping cheesy order of nachos for $5 and drink Dos Equis at the bar. All-you-can-eat Mondays (4:30-11:30pm) for $8. Open Mon.-Fri. 11:30am-11:30pm, Sat.-Sun. 2pm-midnight.

Hard Rock Café, 221 W. 57th St. (495-9320), between Broadway and Seventh Ave. The trunk of a 50s Buick dangles from the entrance. Brass doors lead into a vast space crammed with expensive autographed guitars, tourists, and loud music. Burgers cost a hefty $7, but what can you expect from an international t-shirt franchise masquerading as a restaurant? Open daily 11:30am-2am.

Hourglass Tavern, 373 W. 46th St. (265-2060), between Eighth and Ninth Ave. A tiny, crowded, and dark triangular joint with a limited menu that changes weekly. David Lynch atmospherics. Wear black and talk funny. Entrees $13; full bar and cheap wine. Open Mon.-Thurs. 11:30am-2:30pm and 5-11:15pm, Fri. 11am-2:30pm and 5-11:30pm, Sat. 5-11:30pm, Sun. 5-10:30pm.

Meson Sevilla, 344 W. 46th St. (262-5890), between Eighth and Ninth Ave. Prices may be too high for those on a shoestring budget, but this is one of the best values on posh Restaurant Row. The pre-theater crowd dines here on white linen, savoring the favored choice and house specialty, Spanish *paella* ($11), yellow rice with carefully arranged seafood. The loaded bar up front can help nudge you along to that perfect buzz only Spanish food can render. Open daily 11:30am-midnight.

Lower East Midtown

Straddling the extremes, the Lower Midtown dining scene is neither coldly fast-food commercial nor haute-cuisine trendy. Instead, this slightly gentrified but ethnically diverse neighborhood features many places where an honest meal is wed to reasonable prices. On Lexington's upper 20s, Pakistani and Indian restaurants battle for customers, some catering to a tablecloth crowd, others serving take-out. Liberally sprinkled throughout are Korean corner shops that are combination grocery and buffet bars. You can often fill up on prepared pastas, salads, and hot entrees, paying for them by the pound. At 18th St. and Irving Pl., among rows of 19th-century redbrick houses, you'll run into **Pete's Tavern.** Operating since 1864, it claims to be the oldest saloon in New York. Legend has it that O. Henry, who lived nearby, wrote his "The Gift of the Magi" in one of the booths.

National Café, 210 First Ave. (873-9354) between 12th and 13th. Savor homemade Cuban cooking in this small undiscovered diner. Try their lunch specials of chicken fricassee ($3.25) or rice, beans, and meat ($3.75), and suck sweetly on a papaya or mango milk shake ($2.25). Open Mon.-Sat. 10:30am-10pm.

Ray's Famous Original Pizza, 77 Lexington Ave. (795-1186), at 26th St. One of the 22 "Original" Ray's Pizzas in NYC. Lovely grease-dripping, cheese-laden, crusty-doughed pizza. Slice $1.55, large pie $11.05. Open Mon.-Thurs. 10am-midnight, Fri.-Sat. 10am-1am, Sun. 11am-midnight.

Empire Szechuan Restaurant, 381 Third Ave. (685-6215), between 27th and 28th St. Mirrored walls and leafy plants rim this purple-trimmed, multi-tiered Chinese food emporium. The grub, though not dirt cheap, is cooked with no MSG, very little oil, and always *al dente.* Entrees $6-10, but the real draw is the all-you-can-eat *dim sum* brunch ($7.95) on weekends 11am-5pm. Open daily 11:30am-midnight.

Daphne's Hibiscus, 243 E. 14th St. (505-1180) at Second Ave. Large Day-Glo fish hover in the window; inside, Caribbean art adorns the walls of this spacious Jamaican restaurant. Try the chicken cooked in coconut milk or the special meat-filled pastries called "patties." Hibiscus colada for the adventurous. Entrees $7.50-12.95. Sometimes music at night. Open Tues.-Thurs. 11am-11pm, Fri. 11am-midnight, Sat. 4pm-midnight, Sun noon-10pm.

Shaheen, 99 Lexington Ave. (683-2139) between 27th and 28th St. Cheap cheap Pakistani, Indian, and Bangladeshi cuisine in an area loaded with Indian restaurants. Pink and blue turbaned patrons chew thoughtfully the many incarnations of vegetable curry ($2.75) and the *basmati chawall,* rice cooked with herbs and vegetables (large portion $2.50). Open 24 hours.

Albuquerque Eats/Rodeo Bar, 375 Third Ave. (683-6500), off 27th St. Cow skulls, a silo, and a fully stuffed bison decorate the place—take a wild guess at the theme. Tex-Mex cuisine, with large entrees $10-15. Late-night country-western entertainment. Dinner $5-14. Open daily 11:30am-3am, kitchen closes at midnight.

Chelsea

Finding food in Chelsea isn't always easy. Good food tends not to be cheap, and cheap food is rarely good. The best offerings are the products of the large Mexican and Central American community in the southern section of the neighborhood. From 14th Street to 22nd Street, restaurants offer combinations of Central American and Chinese cuisine as well as varieties of Cajun and Creole specialties. Eighth Avenue provides the best restaurant browsing. Pool sharks who are willing to pay a little more for their meal for the chance to play a game of eight ball should check out the echoing, cavernous **Billiard Club,** 220 W. 19th St. (206-7665), where you can get lunch for two and an hour on a table for $17.

Sam Chinita Restaurant, 176 Eighth Ave. at 19th St. A red 50s diner with turquoise curtains serves up Spanish-and-Chinese cuisine. Extensive menu has dozens of deals under $5. Try the yellow rice with chicken Latin style ($6). Open daily 11:45am-11pm.

Mary Ann's, 116 Eighth Ave. (633-0877). More expensive but well worth the prices. Benevolent waiters serve up huge portions in this white-walled, wood-finished restaurant hung with *piñatas* and slung with lights. Inventive and unusual Mexican cuisine. Try the swordfish, salmon, and scallops in red pepper sauce ($9.25) or the veggie tamale ($7.25). Open Mon.-Sat. 11:30am-11pm, Sun. noon-10pm.

Utopia-W-Restaurant, 338 Eighth Ave. (807-8052) at 27th St., in the boxy shadow of the Fashion Institute of Technology. The school's chic diner. Heavy-duty meaty burgers on toasted buns (cheeseburger with fries $4.40). Dinner comes with a complimentary glass of wine. Open daily 6am-9:30pm.

Empire Diner, 210 Tenth Ave. (243-2736) at 22nd St. A self-consciously hip diner harking back to the 1920s. Waitstaff are all out-of-work actors and actresses with attitudes. Lounge on patio furniture and drink in the thick atmosphere and a decent bottomless cup of coffee ($1). Sophisticated beers for a star-studded clientele. Open 24 hrs.

Cola's, 148 Eighth Ave. (633-8020). Classic Italian cuisine in a simple setting. Restaurant critic Jeff LeBeau calls it one of the best Italian places in the city. Try *fettuccini giardino,* wholewheat pasta with artichokes, zucchini, mushrooms, etc. ($9). Bring your own liquor. Open for dinner only Sun.-Thurs. 4-11pm, Fri.-Sat. 4-11:30pm.

Kitchen, 218 Eighth Ave. A real kitchen specializing in Mexican food, with hot red peppers dangling from the ceiling. All food to go: there is no dining room. Burrito stuffed with pinto beans, rice, and green salsa ($5.70). Other ambulatory delights include a Cajun meatloaf sandwich on Italian flat bread ($4). Eye-opening daily specials. Open Sun.-Thurs. 11:30am-9:30pm, Fri.-Sat. 11:30am-10pm.

Famous Original Ray's Pizza, 204 Ninth Ave. (243-1129) at 23rd St. Another of the many pizzerias seeking to be called authentic Ray's. Average slices with oversweet tomato sauce ($1.65). Also serves subs ($4-6) and pasta ($5-7). Open daily noon-midnight.

La Favorita, 114 Eighth Ave. Another example of that inexplicable culinary hybrid: Latin American and Chinese. Cheaper than Sam Chinita down the block. Wild chicken rice Dominican style ($4.40) glows fluorescent yellow. $3.50 lunch special is one of the best deals in Manhattan. Open daily 11am-midnight.

Galaxy Diner, 174 Eighth Ave. (463-7460). Neither the decor nor the food are out-of-this-world, but the waiters are funny and it's a real neighborhood hangout. French toast and other breakfasts $2-3, sandwiches $2-4. Open daily 6am-1:30am.

Eighteenth and Eighth, 8th Ave. at 18th St. (242-5000). Between the regular customers and the photography display, this slightly-cramped room has the feel of a downtown art gallery. The masterpiece, of course, is the constantly changing menu, which does wonderful things to chicken, fish, vegetables, and tropical fruit. Curry-mango chicken, always available, $9; other entrees $7-15. Desserts $3-5. Open daily 8am-midnight.

Upper East Side

Unless you feel like eating a large bronze sculpture or an Armani suit, you won't find many dining opportunities on Museum Mile along Fifth and Madison Ave., aside from some charming cappuccino haunts, brunch breweries, and near-invisible ritzy restaurants. You will find mediocre food at extraordinary prices in posh and scenic museum cafés where you can languish among ferns and sip espresso between exhibits.

For less glamorous and more affordable dining, head east of Park Ave. Costs descend as you venture toward the lower-numbered avenues, though many do not escape the Madison pricing orbit. Hot dog hounds shouldn't miss the 100% beef "better than filet mignon" $1.50 franks at **Papaya King,** 179 E. 86th St. (369-0648), off Third Ave. (Open Sun.-Thurs. 8am-1am, Fri.-Sat. 9am-3am.) For a real New York bagel, try **H&H East,** 1551 Second Ave. (734-7441), between 80th and 81st, which bakes them 24 hrs., still using their original formula. Impervious to fads, H&H continues to deliver on their promise to put you in heaven. Don't feel confined to restaurant dining. Grocery stores, delis, and bakeries speckle every block. You can buy your provisions here and picnic in honor of frugality in Central Park.

Afghanistan Kebab House, 1345 Second Ave. (517-2776), between 70th and 71st St. Behind a simple, inconspicuous sign lurks one of the most rewarding restaurants in New York. Tender meats are broiled to perfection in a charcoal oven. Rich smells waft, subdued hues of Afghani rugs soothe, and soft Middle Eastern music drifts in from an invisible source. Bring your own booze. Ask the owner about the establishment's fleeting first incarnation as New York's sole Afghani pizzeria. Youngish crowd, casual atmosphere, irresistible kebab. All kebab dishes $6.50-7.50, vegetarian entrees $6. Dinner about $2 more. Take out and free delivery ($10 minimum). Open Mon.-Sat. 11:30am-10pm.

Szechuan Hunan Cottage, 1433 Second Ave. (535-1471), between 74th and 75th St. The food might not astound you but the free free-flowing wine (before and during the meal) probably will. Plentiful lunch special (entree, soup, egg roll, and rice) $4.25, dinners $6-9. Open Sun.-Thurs. noon-11pm, Fri.-Sat. noon-11:30pm.

Ruby's River Road Café, 1754 Second Ave. (348-2328) at 93rd St. Electric Jello (made with vodka) and Mississippi River favorites. Alligators perch on the ceiling. Rowdy crowd downs Cajun popcorn ($5.50) and jambalaya ($7.50) by the gallon. Open Mon.-Sat. 5:30pm-1am, Sun. 5pm-midnight.

Zucchini, 1336 First Ave. (249-0559), between 71st and 72nd St. A nutrition-conscious triathlete runs this healthy establishment. No red meat, but fresh seafood, salads, pasta, and chicken dishes should satiate even militant carnivores. A steaming loaf of whole-wheat bread precedes dinner. Rough brick walls covered with naturalistic renderings of fresh fruits and veggies. Lunch for $7, most pasta and vegetable entrees (soup included) under $11. Before 7pm try the Early Bird Special for only $10. Open daily 10:30am-10:30pm, brunch Sat.-Sun. 11am-4:30pm ($10).

El Pollo, 1746 First Ave. (996-7810), between 90th and 91st. This secret Peruvian dive has mastered the practice of cooking chicken and potatoes, which they serve with complimentary wine in their tiny bowling alley of a restaurant. Plump chickens are marinated and spit roasted, topped with a variety of sauces. The french fries ($2.50) alone make it worth the trip. Half chicken $5. Open daily 11:30am-11pm.

Camelback and Central, 1403 Second Ave. (249-8380) at 73rd St. Beautiful people drink beer and chilled banana soup ($2.95) outside, or toy with chips and nouvelle-continental cuisine in the apricot-colored adobe-like interior. This is the spot for star-gazing: Arthur Ashe comes here often; Diane Keaton and Robert Redford have also been sighted. Lunch entrees $6.50-9, soups and salads $3.25-6. At dinner, light fare (burgers with fries, special salads) $7-10, pasta entrees $12. Brunch $13. Open Sun.-Thurs. 11:30am-3pm and 5-11pm, Fri.-Sat. 5pm-midnight. Brunch Sat.-Sun. 11:30am-4pm.

Istanbul Cuisine, 303 E. 88th St. (74406903) between First and Second Ave. The cook con-jures up Turkish delights at the counter in the back of this tiny lace-curtained restaurant. Sip your complimentary glass of wine with *cacik*, yogurt with cucumbers and fresh herbs ($2.50), and follow it up with *tas kebap*, peppers with lamb and rice. Entrees $8-9. Open daily 6-11pm.

Sarabeth's Kitchen, 1295 Madison Ave. (410-7335), at 92nd St.; also at 423 Amsterdam (496-6280), at 81st St. Well-dressed parents and children masticate in grand style in this erstwhile local bakery, now a bustling glossy duplex. Gourmet dinner prices are steep, but brunch addicts should join the masses, put their name down an hour early, stroll around the neighborhood, and return to sink their teeth into Dr. Seussian "green and white" eggs ($6.75), scrambled with cream cheese and scallions. Open Mon.-Thurs. 8am-3:30pm, Fri.-Sun. 9am-4pm and 6-11pm.

Jackson Hole Wyoming, 1611 Second Ave. (737-8788/9), between 82nd and 83rd St. This cu-linary institution, like its geographical namesake, attracts tan and lively urbanites on the roman-tic prowl. Half-pound burgers served in 37 variations amidst gleaming chrome for $4-8, $6-10 for a platter. Also at 64th St. between Second and Third Ave., and most importantly on Madison Ave. at 91st St. Open Mon.-Sat. 10am-1am, Sun. 10am-midnight.

Brother Jimmy's BBQ, 1461 First Ave. (547-7427), at 76th St. The sign proclaims "BBQ and booze, the stuff that makes America strong," and this greasy-chops kitchen serves up plenty of both under the watchful eyes of boars' heads nailed to the walls. Bible Belt Brunch Sat.-Sun. 11am-2pm features over 20 types of pancakes and waffles. Kitchen open Mon.-Sat. 5-11pm, Sun. 4-10pm. Bar open "late."

Mimi's Pizza and Ristorante, 1248 Lexington Ave. (861-3363) at 84th St. Also at 1049 Lex-ington Ave. (535-8400), between 74th and 75th St. Pizza the way it should be. Craved by New Yorkers, copied without success by impersonators (Mimmo's and Mimma's), and the favorite of at least one Brit in New York—Paul McCartney. Large pie $11, spaghetti with meatballs $6, veal *parmigiana* $7.50. If the pizzeria seems impersonal, dine in the cozy *ristorante* portion. Take out and free delivery. Open daily 11am-11pm.

ecco'la, 1660 third ave. (860-5609), corner of 93rd st. if you don't mind waiting with the rest of the neighborhood, you're in for a lowercase fantasy. sit at hand-painted tables, eating fresh pasta pockets filled with lobster, mushrooms, scallions, and parsley in an avocado cream sauce ($9). pricey, but interesting. open daily noon-11:30pm.

Mumtaz, 1493 Third Ave. (879-4797), near 84th St. Behind the mysterious façade, a dark, draped interior provides an unusual setting for traditional North Indian cuisine. Candles in red glass bowls suffuse food with romance. The *gulab jaman*, a fried pastry in honey sauce, is par-ticularly good. Hearty portions, prices a bit steep. Most entrees under $10. Lunch special $7. Open daily noon-11:30pm.

Sesumi, 222 E. 86th St. (879-1024), between Second and Third Ave. Small, romantic, and Jap-anese. One of New York's best-kept secrets. Inconspicuous outside, but a blizzard of ornate silk tapestries, paper lanterns, and winding greens inside, topped off by a full suit of samurai armor. Fresh food presented with a keen aesthetic sense. Entrees $9-12, sushi from $7.50. Dine early and take advantage of the generous Early Bird Special (5:30pm-7pm; $8). Open Mon.-Fri. noon-2:30pm and 5:30-11pm, Sat.-Sun. 4:30-11pm.

La Prima Strada, 1293 First Ave. (722-9333), between 69th and 70th St. Hole-in-the-wall piz-zeria serving generous, topping-laden slices of whole wheat pizza. They specialize in vegetar-ian. Slices $1.50. Large plain pie $10, with 1 topping $12. Another location at 263 Amsterdam Ave. (496-7300). Both open 11am-midnight.

Urban Grille, 1613 Second Ave. (744-2122) at 83rd St. Totally characterless, but this small, clean joint is a good deal. Beer $1; burger and soup or salad $5. Brunch Sat.-Sun. 11:30am-3:30pm ($6.50). Open daily 11am-11pm.

Budapest Pastry, 207 E. 84th St., between Second and Third Ave. A curious combination of Hungarian and Middle Eastern foods. Sit down at a small table and give the Hummus Plate ($4.50) a try, or buy the light, flaky *baklava* and an assortment of Hungarian strudels (90¢-

$2.25) to eat on the curbside. Open Mon. 8am-6pm, Tues. 7:30am-6:30pm, Wed.-Fri. 7:30am-7:30pm, Sat. 9am-7:30pm, Sun. 10am-5pm.

Chicken Kitchen, 301 E. 80th St. (517-8350) at Second Ave., 1177 Second Ave. (308-9400) at 62nd St., and 982 Second Ave. (980-5252) at 52nd St. No frills, fast-food style restaurants for those hornswoggled by exotic foods. Chicken a-roasting in the windows. Speedy and cheap. Half chicken with rice $4.55. Potato salad $1.70. Open daily 11am-11pm.

Dumpling Queen, 206 E. 85th St. (249-0362), off Third Ave. Not a place to impress your parents, but clean and filling enough to satisfy a late-night wonton craving. No surprises on the menu, just good food at low prices. Soups $1-3.25, *dim sum* $1-4, seafoods $7-9, vegetarian entrees $6.50. Take out and free delivery. Open Mon.-Thurs. 11am-11pm, Fri.-Sat. 11am-11:30pm, Sun. noon-11pm.

Burger Joy, 1332 Lexington Ave., between 88th and 89th St. Amidst smiling photos of Ronald Reagan and James Dean in their best Western wear these folks find 33 joyful ways to cook 8oz. of beef. Toppings include bacon, cheeses, ham, cream cheese, avocado, grilled pineapple, and anchovies ($3.70-7.55). Side orders like *chili con carne*, onion rings, or fries $1.60-2.25. Hands-on guide to saving choking victims on prominent display. Open Mon.-Fri. 6:30am-9pm, Sat.-Sun. 6:30am-6pm.

Ottomanelli's Café, 1559 York Ave., between 82nd and 83rd St., and a dozen other locations on the Upper East Side. Outposts of the vast and powerful Ottomanelli Empire that has supplied New York with meat and baked goods since 1900. No-frills setting, but extraordinary fresh-baked goods. An impressive coterie of bagels, breads, danish, and muffins 50¢-$1.25. Large iced coffee, a summertime must, $1. After 5pm, all danishes and muffins depreciate to 50¢. Open Mon.-Sat. 6:30am-7pm, Sun. 7:30am-3pm.

Paris Croissant, 609 Madison Ave. (319-0828) at 58th St. Join the Madison Avenue crowd for lunch or a snack of pizza strudel in this gold-trimmed, mirrored café. Bring your manners. Fresh soups, innovative salads, quiche, pizza, and every member of the croissant species. Pastries 80¢-$2.50, salads $4.15 per pound. Takeout downstairs, restaurant upstairs. Open Mon.-Sat. 7am-8pm, Sun. 8am-6pm.

Upper West Side

The Upper West Side stays up later than its austere counterpart to the east. Monthly rents are heading up, "in" bars are going out, and high-fashion boutiques multiply—but here, gentrification does not make for boredom. Old New York charms endure: fancy Central Park West buildings with refined names, outdoor Columbus cafés with fried zucchini and gleaming chrome, dollar-a-book Broadway peddlers, Riverside views of sunset on the Hudson. If browsing in Laura Ashley or Charivari makes you tired, go haggle at the Columbus Avenue Street Fair, happen onto a hidden gallery, or wander down the tempting aisles of **Zabar's**, 2245 Broadway (787-2002), the deli that never ends. The vast array of restaurants in the area offer meals for the solitary as well as the social.

Pizza Joint Too, 70 W. 71st St. (799-4444) at Columbus Ave. The ultimate. Will top pizza with "anything you can think of." Unless you have the belly of a whale, order Sicilian slices one at a time. This pizza joint makes 'em big. $1.55 per slice. Open 10am-5am, delivery until 4:30am.

Café Lalo, 210 83rd St. (496-6031) at Amsterdam Ave. Fabulously popular and new-looking dessert café attracts struggling artists, young people, and loaded professionals; it's worth the short wait to join them all at their high tables and antique chairs amid the strains of the Baroque era's top 40. Sixty-plus pastry or cake desserts, mostly excellent, $3-6; try any fruit tart. Not the best value for your café dollar, but probably the best food. Cappuccino $1.75. Peach, pear, or apricot nectar $1.25. Wine and beer from $2.75. Open Sun.-Thurs. noon-2am, Fri.-Sat. 11am-4am.

Café La Fortuna, 69 W. 71st St. (724-5846), between Central Park West and Columbus Ave. A wide range of excellent Italian pastries, including a fine *tiramisu*. The proprietor, a devout opera lover, has decorated the walls with autographed daguerreotypes of opera greats, and thick Victrola 78s of Caruso and Shalyapin. Justifiably mobbed about half-an-hour after the theaters downtown let out; come earlier. Pastries $2.50-4.50. Open Tues.-Thurs. 1pm-1am, Fri. 1pm-2am, Sat. noon-2am, Sun. noon-1am.

La Caridad, 2199 Broadway (874-2780) at 78th St. One of New York's most successful Chinese-Spanish hybrids. Feed yourself and a pack of burros with one entree. *Arroz con pollo* (1/

4 chicken with yellow rice) $4.90. Other entrees of the Americas, including *Chop suey de cerdo ahumada*, $5-6. Fast-food ambience, but so what? Open Mon.-Sat. 11:30am-1am, Sun. 11:30am-10:30pm.

The Opera Espresso, 1928 Columbus Ave. (799-3050), between 64th and 65th St. Across from Lincoln Center, this is the closest some symphony subscribers will ever get to an American diner (not very). Opera programs over the vinyl seats. Chicken salad $6, burgers $8, and omelettes $8. A few outdoor tables. Open Mon.-Sat. 7:30am-midnight.

Genoa, 271 Amsterdam Ave. (787-1094) at 73rd St. This tiny, family-owned restaurant serves some of the best food on the West Side. Wood beams, stucco walls, red candlelight, and Italian romance. Arrive before 6pm or wait in line with the rest of the neighborhood. *Pasta Festiva* or *Puttanesca* $8.50. *Veal Scallopine Francese* $11.50. Open Tues.-Sat. 5:45-10:30pm, Sun. 5:30-9:30pm.

Rikyu, 210 Columbus Ave. (799-7922), between 69th and 70th St. This modestly furnished Japanese restaurant lives up to the name: consume "eternal happiness" at one of three appetizing locations—in the main room, in the sushi bar watching the chef have his way with the fish, or in a kneel-as-you-eat *tatami* room. Noodle dishes $7-8, but come here for the seafood. Sashimi or Bluefish Teriyaki $8.95. $6 lunch special proffers sushi, tempura, and other dishes until 4pm. $10 takeout sushi packages. Open Mon.-Sat. noon-11:30pm, Sun. 12:30pm-11:30pm.

Diane's Uptown, 251 Columbus Ave. (799-6750), off 71st St. Large portions and reasonable prices make this popular, brass-railed, inexplicably dark café a student hangout. Spice up a 7-oz. burger ($4) with chili, chutney, or your choice of seven cheeses (85¢ per topping). Sandwiches $3-5, omelettes $3.90, onion rings and lots of fries $3. Open daily 11am-2am.

The Symposium, 544 W. 113th St. (865-1011). Plato competes with hippie maxims on the psychedelic menu. Longinus would have loved the *souvlaki, moussaka* and such ($7-10), especially after a pitcher of sangria. Lamb *arzerpilaf* $8.50. *Spanokopita* $6.50. Ask to sit in the back room, where a sturdy tree penetrates floor and ceiling. Open daily noon-11pm.

Dallas BBQ, 27 W. 72nd St. (873-2004), off Columbus Ave. Also at 21 University Pl. (674-4450) at 8th St. Georgia O'Keefe's horse skulls and Navajo rugs have migrated to the walls of this slightly cheesy-looking New York eatery. Authentic Texas-style chicken and ribs on the same bill with tasty tempura and homey chicken soup. Mountains of food and oceans of noise in this often crowded restaurant. Big breakfast featuring 50¢ coffee. Early bird special (Mon.-Fri. noon-6:30pm, Sat.-Sun. noon-5pm) features soup, half a chicken, cornbread, and potato for $8 per dining duo. 1/2-lb. burger $4.75, Texas-style chili $3 per bowl. Take out an entire barbecued chicken for $5. Open Sun.-Thurs. noon-midnight, Fri.-Sat. noon-1am.

La Rosita, 2823 Broadway (663-7804) at 108th St. You can't miss this big Dominican luncheonette; the food practically leaps out the window at you. Breakfast $2.50-4. Hamburgers $1.75, fried kingfish $6.25. Many dishes come with gigantic helpings of black beans and yellow rice. For dessert, have the famed Spanish flan ($1.40). Open daily 7am-1am.

The Blue Nile, 103 W. 77th St. (580-3232), between Columbus and Amsterdam Ave. No etiquette worries here; the waiter brings one tray and no silverware to your table. Sop up fine Ethiopian entrees with *injera,* a spongy pancake. Lunch buffet $7. Entrees from $6.50. Open Mon.-Thurs. 5-11pm, Fri. 5pm-midnight, Sat. noon-midnight, Sun. noon-11pm.

EJ's Luncheonette, 433 Amsterdam Ave. (873-3444) at 81st St. Popular retro diner with chrome, old Coca-Cola ads, and plenty of "regulars." Happily, 80s nouvelle ingredients replace the Spam, Skippy, and Campbell's of Warhol fame. Gargantuan chili burger $6. Grilled cajun chicken sandwich $6.50. Breakfast food all day, $5-6. Open Mon.-Thurs. 8am-11pm, Fri. 8am-midnight, Sat. 9am-midnight, Sun. 9am-11pm.

Original Ray's Pizza and Restaurant, 462 Columbus Ave. (873-1134 or -1135), between 82nd and 83rd St. Every branch of Ray's pretends to be the original one; this one's claims are no more authentic than any other's. But the pizza is outstanding, made with tender loving care using Neapolitan tomatoes, Wisconsin cheese, and fresh meat supplied by Neapolitan butchers. Large plain pie $12, with one topping $14.50. Just $2 for a slice the size of Manhattan. Alluring calzone $3-3.50. Takeout and free delivery. Open Mon.-Thurs. 10am-3am, Fri.-Sun. 10am-4am.

Panrella, 513 Columbus Ave. (799-5784), between 84th and 85th St. Two stories of ornate dining rooms with deep greens and reds predominating; you'll almost expect painted Baroque cherubs on the ceiling. The look may be heavy, but the Italian cuisine is varied, light, and skillfully prepared; dig the shrimp with black pasta ($11). Eat outside if you prefer pollution to ornament. Salads around $6.50, *antipasti* $4.50-7.50, and pasta dishes $7.50-11. Open Fri.-Sat. noon-4pm and 5:30pm-midnight.

The Armadillo Club, 2420 Broadway (496-1066) at 89th St. This urban chic/Tex-Mex bistro's masterstroke is a 7-ft. orange neon cactus mounted on a column in the center of the room. The menu croons with a heavy Texan drawl, sporting such regional staples as hot chili and barbecued chicken and beef. *Nachos con pollo* (with chicken) $6, fajitas $10, other entrees $8-15. Open Mon.-Fri. 4pm-2 or 4am, Sat.-Sun. noon-2 or 4am (depending on bar traffic).

Caramba!!!, Broadway and 96th St. (749-5055). The 3 exclamation points signify that this is the 3rd of many Carambas in this city. All guts, no-frills Mexican eatery the size of a small roller rink and about as loud. Good food, bountiful portions, and a festive atmosphere. Chili *Relleños* with rice, beans, and salad $7.95, bowl of chili $3.50. "Lunch at the bar" entree and frozen margarita or wine $5. Open Sun.-Thurs. noon-midnight, Fri.-Sat. noon-1am.

Empire Szechuan Gourmet, 2574 Broadway (663-6004, -6005, -6006 or 663-6340) at 97th St. A favorite of Upper West Siders (thus the 4 telephone numbers). Exhaustive menu features "revolution diet" section, hors d'oeuvres (mostly $1), and *dim sum* ($1-5 Sat.-Sun. 11am-3pm). Cold sesame noodles $3.95. Pint of soup $1.30. Beef with hot chili sauce $7.95. Lunch specials $5, 11:30am-3pm Mon.-Fri. Look for dinner coupons on takeout menus handed out in front of the restaurant. Open Mon.-Tues. 10:30am-midnight, Wed.-Sun. 10:30am-2am. Free delivery.

Empire-Szechuan Kyoto Sushi, 2642 Broadway at 100th St. (662-9404). Very spacious, bicultural restaurant with superior sushi ($1.75-3 per piece, $3.50 per roll) and no minimum order. Don't expect to fill up on it without busting your budget; do make a point of snacking here. Chinese entrees also look good ($7-9). Open Mon.-Sat. 11:30am-2am, Sun. 11:30-1am.

Au Petit Beurre, 2737 Broadway at 105th St. Spacious French café staffed by *garçons* with patent accents and frequented by a cosmopolitan student crowd and ordinary neighborhood folks. Deli menu with many incarnations of chopped liver, the New York equivalent of pâté. Hot or cold asparagus $4.50. Zucchini sauteed in olive oil with "snow beans" and carrots $7. Espresso $1.50, cappuccino $1.75. Open daily 7:30am-midnight.

Popover Café, 551 Amsterdam Ave. (595-8555), between 86th and 87th St. The city's quaintest café. Possibly a meeting place for pincushions. Bursting with violet, calico, paisley, teddy bears, and—most important—delightful popovers with strawberry butter, $1.50 each or $3.75 for 3. Excellent for breakfast despite the menu's general priciness. Melted brie sandwich with mushrooms, watercress, and tomatoes $5.50. Open Mon.-Fri. 8:30am-11pm, Sat. 9:30am-11pm, Sun. 9:30am-10pm.

Chez David, 494 Amsterdam Ave. (874-4974) at 84th St. Flanked by a Christian fundamentalist association and titled *en français,* David's serves up kosher food at plastic tables and counters styled after the blue and white of Israel's flag. Pizza and Middle Eastern specialties, in their kosher incarnations. The fresh felafel is a must-eat ($3). Hearty bowl of bean or split-pea soup $2.50. Pasta in the $6 range. Open Sun.-Thurs. 10am-11pm, Fri. 10am-4:30pm, Sat. 10pm-3am.

Cleopatra's Needle, 2485 Broadway (769-6969), between 92nd and 93rd St. Crackling jazzy vocals plagiarized from Woody Allen soundtracks suit the snappy decor. Floor-to-ceiling windows open on to Broadway. Go for lunch, when all food is served at deli prices. Egyptian burrito, hummus or felafel sandwich $2.50. 1/2 lb. spicy seafood to go, $4. Deli/takeout open daily 8am-11pm; restaurant open daily noon-midnight (later Fri.-Sat. as a bar). Jazz piano Fri.-Sat. nights.

Obento Delight, 210 W. 94th St. (222-2010), between Amsterdam and Broadway. Eating in? Consider sending out for fresh Japanese food at prices so low you'd think the dollar had overcome the yen. *Miso* soup $1; *yakitori* (2 skewers of chicken and onion) $5.50; sashimi $7.50. Sushi a la carte from under $2. Hot diggety! Electrify your senses with flamed eel in tantalizing sauce grounded in a heaping bowl of rice ($9). Lunch special daily 11:30am-3:30pm, $4.25-8. Free delivery with a $7 minimum. Open daily 11:30am-11pm.

Indian Café, 2791 Broadway (749-9200) at 108th St. and West End Ave. Cozy Indian joint. Vegetarian entrees $6-8, seafood like shrimp *muglai* (sauteed with fresh ginger and garlic in a creamy curry sauce with almonds) $9-10. Treat yourself to a mango shake for $2.25. Open daily 11:30am-midnight.

Mi Tierra, 668 Amsterdam Ave. (874-9514), between 92nd and 93rd St. The first Mexican restaurant on the Upper West Side and still one of the best. Authentic Yucatecan and Venezuelan food served in a simple setting dotted with fleamarket-style toreador paintings. Three enchiladas (beef, chicken, cheese, shrimp, or pork) $9-10. On the Venezuelan side, investigate *carne* *ranchera,* steak chunks with tomato sauce, peppers, onions, and olives ($8). *Pernil* (roast leg of pork with sauteed onions) $8.50. $5 weekend brunch (Mexican food only). Open daily 11am-midnight.

Ollie's, 2315 Broadway (362-3111 or -3712) at 84th St. The requisite whole-chickens hang inside the window, but the real marks of quality here are the wonderful smells of the noodle soups, most in the $5 range and the size of a meal. Come early to avoid the movie-going crowd. Brunch Sat.-Sun. 11:30am-4pm. Open Sun.-Thurs. 11:30am-midnight, Fri.-Sat. 11:30am-1am.

 H&H Bagels, 2239 Broadway (595-8000) at 80th St. 65¢ bagels with a string of awards behind 'em; stop in if only to *smell* this bagelry. Call 1-800-NY-BAGEL to ship them anywhere in the world [I did—Ass. Ed.]. Always open.

Café Mozart, 154 70th St. (595-9797). Twee, dainty, mock-sophisticate café featuring floral motifs, chairs a bit too small, and ever-poignant classical music. Good selection of Italian desserts (cannoli, zabaglione, etc.) $3.25-4.75. Lunch special—sandwich, quiche, or omelette, soda or coffee, and dessert, $6 (offered Mon.-Fri. 11am-2pm). The perfect spot to drink tea and read *Alice in Wonderland* after a hard day at Lincoln Center. Live classical music Mon.-Sat. 9pm-midnight, Sun. 3-6pm and 7-10pm. Open Sun.-Thurs. 11am-1am, Fri.-Sat. 10am-3am.

Orloff's, 2 Lincoln Square, across from Lincoln Center at Columbus and 65th (799-4000). Crowded and generic, but the best food deal in the predatory Lincoln Center eating environment. Hamburgers $5-7, pasta salad and special entrees $6, OK desserts $3. Open daily 6:30am-midnight.

Sakura of Japan, 2298 Broadway (769-1003) at 83rd St. Big Japanese restaurant distinguished by its $5 sushi, tempura, and combinatory dinners, available daily 5-7pm and Fri.-Sat. again from 11:30pm-12:30am. Open Mon.-Thurs. noon-11:45pm. Fri.-Sat. noon-12:45am., Sun. noon-11:30pm.

Positively 104th St., 2724 Broadway at 104th St. (316-0372). Slick neighborhood dinner cage with a neighbor's cubist paintings on the walls. Good *nouvelle* and Italian cooking. Leg of lamb with mozzarella, red peppers, and onions $6.75, at lunch. Any pasta dish $10 with salad and wine (1 glass) after 10pm (9pm on Sun.). Open Mon.-Sat. 8am-11pm, Sun. 8am-10pm.

The Hungarian Pastry Shop, 1030 Amsterdam Ave. (866-4230) at 111th St. The West Side's worst-kept secret: plain, friendly, Boho pastry shop (duh) with *hamentashen* $1.30. Eclairs, cake slices, and other goodies all around $2. Fine coffee, too. A good place to write or read. Open Mon.-Fri. 8am-11:30pm, Sat. 9am-10:30pm, Sun. 9am-11:30pm.

Columbia Bagels, 2836 Broadway (222-3200). Fresh if chewy 45¢ bagels in many varieties (one dozen $5.40). Open 24hrs.

Mingala West, 325 Amsterdam Ave. at 75th St. (873-0787). As ethnic strife spreads across Europe and Asia, New Yorkers can expect more and more exotic cuisines to become available in Manhattan. Burmese cooking involves rice noodles, peanut sauces, coconuts, and curries, yet tastes nothing like Thai or Indonesian food; this place, with its lavender walls, ebony elephants, and photo of Nobel laureate Aung San Soo Kyi, makes for a friendly introduction. $4.50 lunch specials noon-4pm weekdays; $6 "light meal" samplers 5-7pm. Or try glass noodles and beef dishes from the main menu $7-13. Open Mon.-Thurs. noon-11pm, Fri.-Sat. noon-midnight.

Bennie's Cafe, 321 Amsterdam Ave. at 75th St. (874-3032). Excellent selection of gourmet and homemade salad entrees, $4.95 each. Open daily 11am-11pm.

Greenwich Village

Whatever your take on the West Village's Bohemian authenticity, it's undeniable that all the free-floating artistic angst does result in many creative (and inexpensive) food venues. The aggressive and entertaining street life makes stumbling around, drunk and stupid, deciding where to go, almost as much fun as eating.

Try the major avenues for cheap, decent food. Wander by the posh row houses around Jane St. and Bank St. for classier bistro and café fare. The European-style bistros of **Bleecker Street** and **MacDougal Street,** south of Washington Square Park, have perfected the homey "antique" look. Amidst a clutter of collectibles, **Caffé Reggio,** 119 MacDougal St. (475-9557), south of W. 3rd St., offers a hip young college scene and demi-celebs galore (Open Sun.-Thurs. 10am-2am, Fri.-Sat 10am-4am).

Late night in the Village is a unique New York treat: as the sky grows dark, the streets quicken. Don't let a mob at the door make you hesitant about sitting over your coffee for hours and watching the spectacle—especially if the coffee is good. Explore twisting side streets and alleyways where you can join Off-Broadway theater-goers as they settle down over a burger and a beer to write their own reviews, or drop into a jazz club. Or ditch the high life and slump down 8th St. to Sixth Ave. to join the freak scene and find some of the most respectable pizzerias in the city. The crucial question: John's or Ray's?

John's Pizzeria, 278 Bleecker St. (243-1680). Loud NYU hangout caters to fratboys, freaks, and even U.S. presidents, if you believe the handwriting on the wall. Cooked in a brick oven, with a crisp crust and just enough cheese, pizza for 2 or 3 costs $8.40. If the place is full, they'll find room for you at **John's Too** next door. No slices; table service only. Open daily 11:30am-11:30pm.

Ray's Pizza, 465 Sixth Ave. (243-2253) at 11th St. Half of the uptown pizza joints claim to be the "Original Ray's," but any New Yorker will tell you that this is the real McCoy. People fly here from Europe just to bring back a few pies—it's the best pizza in town. Well worth braving the lines and paying upwards of $1.75 for a slice. Open Sun.-Thurs. 11am-2am, Fri.-Sat. 11am-3am.

Olive Tree Café, 117 MacDougal St. (254-3630), north of Bleecker St. Standard Middle Eastern food offset by seemingly endless stimulation. If you get bored by the old movies on the wide screen, rent chess, backgammon, and Scrabble sets ($1), or doodle with colored chalk on the slate tables. Falafel $2.25, chicken kebab platter with salad, rice pilaf, and vegetable $7. Delicious egg creams only $1.75. Open daily 11am-3am.

Ed Debevic's, 663 Broadway (982-6000), south of 3rd St. Endure the noise and gregarious waiters and you'll be rewarded: a huge meal at a good price. Front room is 40s-style bar; back room is full of 60s revolution graffiti. Great burgers $5-7 and fries (with gravy or cheese) $2.50. Open Sun.-Tues. noon-11pm, Wed.-Thurs. noon-midnight, Fri.-Sat. noon-2am.

Cucina Stagionale, 275 Bleecker St. (924-2707). Unpretentious Italian dining in a clean, pretty environment. Packed with loyalists on weekends—sample the soft *calamari* in spicy red sauce or pasta *puttanesca* ($5) to realize why. Open noon-midnight.

Trattoria Due Torri, 99 MacDougal St. (477-6063), north of Bleecker St. This tiny Italian treasure continues to offer excellent food at reasonable prices. Fresh pastas $7-8, entrees $8-9. Try the *capellini primavera.* Open Sun.-Thurs. 12:30pm-midnight, Fri.-Sat. 12:30pm-2am. A second, identical location opened recently at 136 Houston St.

Shopsin's, 63 Bedford St. (924-5760), between Commerce and Morton St. Quaint Ma and Pa joint serving wonderful home-cooked dishes for an eager band of Village regulars. A neighborhood favorite. Open Mon.-Fri. 11am-10pm.

Eva's, 11 W. 8th St. (677-3496), between MacDougal St. and Fifth Ave. Refreshing, fast-service health food with a seating parlor. Massive meatless combo plate with felafel, grape leaves, and eggplant $4.50. Open Sun.-Thurs. 11am-midnight, Fri.-Sat. 11:30am-1am.

Villa Florence, 9 Jones St. (989-1220), north of Bleecker St. A quiet, friendly spot with brick walls, checked tablecloths, and excellent food. The owner also runs the butcher shop next door; meat dishes are especially good. Pasta $6-12, Newport steak $9, rainbow salad (arugula, endive, and radicchio) big enough for 2, $3.50. *Maria tiramisu,* a trifle-like Sicilian dessert, $3. Open Tues.-Fri. 5-11pm, Sat. 4pm-midnight, Sun. 3-11pm.

Elephant and Castle, 68 Greenwich Ave. (243-1400). The avenue cuts diagonally northwest from Sixth Ave. at 8th St. Pleasant atmosphere makes this place consistently popular. Select from a page of omelette options ($5-7). The apple, cheddar, and walnut creation is weird but good. Delectable sesame chicken with spinach and cucumbers $9. Open Mon.-Thurs. 8:30am-midnight, Fri. 8:30am-1am, Sat. 10am-1am, Sun. 10am-midnight.

West 4th St. Saloon, 174 W. 4th St. (255-0518), between Sixth and Seventh Ave. Do late supper with a rowdy crowd in this pub's brick-walled, brass-railed decor. Salads and sandwiches $6-8. Catch-of-the-day priced according to season. Happy hour Mon.-Fri. 4-7pm: $1 off all drinks. Open daily 11am-4am.

Manhattan Chili Company, 302 Bleecker St. (206-7163) at Seventh Ave. The attraction here is pretty clear: chili. Spice barometer reads from mild to hot to "Texas Chainsaw" ($7-8). The red-meat-shy should try the turkey chili ($7.95). Beer $2.25. Open Sun.-Thurs. 11:30am-midnight, Fri.-Sat. 11:30am-2am.

Caffé Dante, 79 MacDougal St. (982-5275), south of Bleecker St. A Village staple. If you can't find a seat at Caffé Reggio, you'll be just as happy here. Try the *Frutta di bosco* ($3.50) and beware the espresso: it bites back. Nice gelati and Italian ices ($3.50). Open daily 10am-1am.

Mustafa, 48 Greenwich Ave. A no-frills Middle Eastern joint with a few tables inside and out. Not a place where you'll want to linger—just stop in and grab a felafel sandwich ($2.50). Open daily 11am-11pm.

Tutta Pasta, 26 Carmine St. (463-9653), at Sixth Ave. A modern establishment with glass doors that slide open in summer. The treat here is the fresh homemade pastas, including *tortellini, manicotti,* and *linguini* ($8). Open Mon.-Thurs. 11:30am-10:30pm, Fri.-Sat. 11:30am-11:30pm.

Caliente Cab Co., 61 Seventh Ave. (243-8517) at Bleecker St. A huge margarita glass and the rear ends of cabs adorn this clique-infested bar/restaurant. Kitschy and made for big crowds of ten- to twentysomething, who plan on eating burritos and drinking margaritas until they lose all motor coordination. Big brunch buffet, all you can eat, Mon.-Fri. 11:30am-4:30pm, $4.95. Bigger brunch buffet, drink til you drop, Sat.-Sun. noon-3pm, featuring bottomless Margaritas, Bloody Marys, screwdrivers, and mimosas, $6.95. Happy hour Mon.-Fri. 4:30-7pm features free food. Open Sun.-Thurs. 11am-3am, Fri.-Sat. 11am-4am.

The Whitehorse Tavern, 567 Hudson St. (243-5260) at W. 11th St. Boisterous students and screaming waiters pay a strange and twisted homage to the poet at Dylan Thomas's death site. D.T. drank himself to death here, pouring 19 straight whiskies through an already tattered liver. A bar/restaurant with a historical claim to fame (which they don't let you forget), heavenly food in the back, and the best burgers in the Village ($4). Open Sun.-Thurs. 11am-2am, Fri.-Sat. 11am-4am.

Caffé Borgia, 185 Bleecker St. (677-1100). Moody, dark café has the look and feel of mother Italy. Cult figures who frequent the place include Pacino, De Niro, and Fred Gwynne (of Munsters fame). Stick with the nigh-endless coffee list and the delicious desserts. Sun.-Thurs. 10am-2am, Fri. 10am-4am, Sat. 10am-5am.

The Pink Teacup, 42 Grove St. between Bleecker and Bedford. Soulfood in a small, pink, and friendly environment. $6 lunch special includes fried chicken, stew, or barbecued anything, soup or salad, two vegetables, and dessert. Coffee, eggs, and fritters can feed two well for under $10. BYOB. Open Sun.-Thurs. 8am-midnight, Fri.-Sat. 8am-1am.

The Ear Inn, 326 Spring St. (226-9060), near the Hudson. Once a big bohemian/activist hangout, this bar now tends to the SoHo stubble baseball-cap crowd. Dark wood, mellow blues, and tables with crayons. Back room functions as a restaurant during lunch and dinner hours. Try the rich and delicious mud pie ($3). Okay American food served from 11am-4:30pm, 6pm-1am every day. Appetizers and salads $2-6, specials and entrees $5-9. Bar open to 4am.

Murray Cheese Shop, 257 Bleecker St. (243-3289) at Cornelia St. You can't eat inside, but the 400-plus kinds of cheese justify a picnic. Delicious fresh bread and salads. Try the camembert in rosemary and sage ($3) on a loaf of wheat ($1.30). Open Mon.-Sat. 8am-7pm, Sun. 9am-5pm.

SoHo and TriBeCa

In SoHo, food, like life, is art. Down with the diner: food here comes in a variety of exquisite and pricey forms, with long and oft-unpronounceable names. Most of the restaurants in SoHo demonstrate an occasionally distracting preoccupation with art (some are practically indistinguishable from their neighboring galleries). Even the grocery stores get in on the act: **Dean and Deluca,** 60 Broadway, at Prince St., features gallery-quality art and gourmet-caliber food. With art, of course, comes money, so don't be surprised if you find it hard to get a cheap meal. Often the best deal in SoHo is brunch, when the neighborhood shows its most cozy and good-natured front. You can down your cantaloupe and coffee in any number of café/bar establishments.

Dining in TriBeCa means dinner. Many of New York's highest-priced restaurants hide behind closed curtains; inexpensive places are few and far between.

Elephant and Castle, 183 Prince St. (260-3600), off Sullivan. Also at 68 Greenwich Ave. Popular with locals for its excellent coffee and creative light food. Perfect for brunch. Prepare to wait for a table. Dinner around $10, brunch around $8. Open Sun.-Thurs. 8:30am-midnight, Fri.-Sat. 9am-1am.

Thai House Café, 151 Hudson St. (334-1085) at Hubert St. Not called the Bangkok House. This inconspicuous little place offers excellent Thai cuisine at a reasonable price (entrees $6-10). The waiter's suggestions are often astute. Open Mon.-Sat. 11:30am-11pm.

Lupe's East L.A. Kitchen, 110 Sixth Ave. (966-1326) at Watts St. Not elegant, but one of the cheapest, tastiest spots around. Burritos, enchiladas, and beer are standard. Better atmosphere than East L.A. Open Sun.-Thurs. 11:30am-11pm, Fri. 11:30am-midnight, Sat. 5:30pm-midnight.

Fanelli's Café, 94 Prince St. A very mellow neighborhood hang-out, where it always feels like late at night. Standard bar fare and sorta cheap brew ($2.50). Come to escape the gallery crowd. Open Mon.-Sat. 10am-2am, Sun. 11am-2am.

The Cupping Room, 359 West Broadway (925-2898) at Broome St. Drinks, dinner, and coffee in a low-key atmosphere. A great choice for a weekend brunch on either Sat. or Sun., but arrive early or be prepared to wait. On the bright side, brunch ($10) is served from 7am to 6pm, and therefore difficult to miss. During the week, the Cupping serves a full breakfast and dinner menu. Entrees around $14. Light menu with salads and burgers ($7-8) also available. Open Sun.-Thurs. 7:30am-midnight, Fri.-Sat. 8am-2am: but the kitchen still closes at midnight.

Berry's, 180 Spring St. (226-4354), near Thompson St. A small, dark, homey place with up-scale American food, full bar, outdoor seating, and reasonable prices. Sunday brunch 11am-4pm ($7-12). Entrees hover around $12. Hours: Mon.-Thurs. Open daily 11:30am-3:30pm and 5:30-11:30pm. Kitchen closes at 10pm.

Brother's BBQ, 228 Houston St. (727-2775), between Sixth Ave. and Varick St. Friendly service, 'liciious ribs, and mashed potatoes—what a combo. Bring a bib. Most entrees roll in at $8. Howitzer! Open Mon.-Thurs. 11:30am-11pm, Fri.-Sat. 11:30am-midnight, Sun. 5:30-11pm.

Prince St. Bar and Restaurant, 125 Prince St. (228-8130) at Wooster St. Overcrowded menu and overflowing, portly portions. Everything is big. Burgers ($6.50), breakfast ($4-7), vegetarian and Indonesian specialties. Cheap beer, too. Open Mon.-Sat. 11:30am-1am (kitchen closes at 12:30am), Sun. noon-midnight.

Royal Canadian Pancake, 145 Hudson St. (219-3038) at Hubert St. Yukon-sized pancakes compensate for the long lines. Big, big, big. Choose from over 50 kinds of hotcakes. Expect a wait for Sat. or Sun. brunch. Open daily 7am-midnight.

SoHo Kitchen and Bar, 103 Greene St. (925-1866), near Prince St. A quintessential SoHo hangout: sky-high ceiling, gigantic artwork, scores of wines by the glass, casual (but still calculated and hep) dress: the veritable definition of bourgeois tastefulness. Rich art crowd poses and struts while hapless tourists ogle. Chic pizza (topped with wild mushroom, roasted pepper, and grilled eggplant) $10, sandwiches $8. Open Mon.-Thurs. 11:30am-1am, kitchen closes at 12:45am; Fri.-Sat. 11:30am-3am, kitchen closes at 1:45am.

New Deal, 152 Spring St. (431-3663), between West Broadway and Wooster. A fine option for those with a hankering for nouvelle cuisine (a.k.a. pretentious American food). You can avoid the steep *prix fixe* by ordering from a bistro menu that allows you to sample the chef's specialties at $6.50 per item. Or nurse one of the bar specials from 4-7pm. Open Mon.-Thurs. 11:30am-10:30pm, Fri.-Sat. 11:30am-11:30pm, Sun. 11:30am-9:30pm.

La Petit Cafe, 156 Spring St. (219-9723). Atypical SoHo dining—small, unpretentious, inexpensive, zero modern art quotient; Fro Yo available. Large and tasty fresh mozzarella sandwich $4.50; Italian specialties change daily, average $6.50. Wonderful strawberry lemonade is pink plus strawberry juice, minus sugar. Outdoor tables in summer. No credit cards. Open Sun.-Thurs. 9am-midnight, Sat.-Sun. 9am-2am.

Cowgirl Hall of Fame, 519 Hudson St. (633-1133). Antelope chandeliers and leather saddles. Celebrated inductees include: barbecued chicken sandwich ($5.50), boisterous buttermilk pancakes ($5.25), demure fried chicken with mashed potatoes and gravy ($7.95). Sunday brunch 11:30am-4pm (with children's brunch menu). Open Mon.-Fri. noon-11pm, Sat.-Sun. 5pm-midnight.

Arturo's Coal Oven Pizza, 106 W. Houston St. (475-9828). Delicious but pricey pizza in a dark bunker atmosphere. Degas, Gaughin, Van Gogh ripoffs as well as frescoes of Italian streets and photos of Al Pacino cover the walls (and are for sale). You'll find art types and regulars here, and a full bar. Pianist plays dinner jazz nightly, 8pm-1am. Pizzas $11-$14, pasta $7-10, Italian entrees $10-12, wine $12 by the carafe. $20 min. on all credit cards. Open Mon.-Thurs. 4pm-1am, Fri.-Sat. 4pm-2am, Sun. 3pm-midnight.

East Village and Lower East Side

Culinary cultures clash on the lower end of the East Side, where pasty-faced punks and starving artists sup alongside an older generation conversing in Polish, Hungarian, and Yiddish. Observant Jews and slavophiles reach nirvana in the delis and restaurants here. The Eastern European restaurants distributed along First and Second Ave. serve up some of the best deals in Manhattan. The **9th St. Bakery,** 350 E. 9th St. (open daily 8:30-7pm), and **Kossar's Hot Bialys,** 367 Grand St., (473-4810) at Essex St. (Open 24 hrs.) daily sell cheap and unsurpassable New York bagels and bialys.

If you consider such delicacies bland, hurry on to one of the many cheap Indian restaurants in the East Village, particularly concentrated on 6th St. between First and Second Ave. Or you can try the newer, West Village-type restaurants that cater to a young and with-it crowd—often indistinguishable from their neighbors to the west.

Dojo Restaurant, 24 St. Marks Place (674-9821), between 2nd and 3rd Ave. Probably the most popular restaurant/hangout in the East Village, and rightly so. Offers an incredible variety of healthful, delicious, and inexplicably inexpensive food in a comfortable brick and darkwood interior. Tasty soyburgers with brown rice and salad $2.95. Spinach and pita sandwich with assorted veggies $1.95. Outdoor tables allow for interaction with slick passers-by. Open Sun.-Thurs. 11-1am, Fri.-Sat. 11-2am.

Life Café, Ave. B. and E. 10th St. (477-8791), in Alphabet City next to Tompkins Sq. Park. A hip restaurant/bar, popular with the local beats, which serves up huge portions of "Cal-Tex-Mex-veg" food. Beef, chicken, or ragout (veggie) tacos, burritos, and enchiladas $5-7. Try the hot almond soy drink ($2). Open Sun.-Thurs. 11am-midnight, Fri.-Sat. 11-1am.

Odessa, 117 Ave. A (473-8916) at 7th St. Beware of ordinary-looking coffee shops with slavic names. Lurking beneath the title may be an excellent, inexpensive restaurant serving Eastern European specialties. Choose your favorites from a huge assortment of *pirogi,* stuffed cabbage, *kielbasa,* sauerkraut, potato pancakes, and other delicacies for the combination dinner ($6). Spinach pie and small Greek salad $4.50. Open daily 7am-midnight.

Veselka, 144 Second Ave. (228-9682) at 9th St. Down-to-earth soup-and-bread Polish-Ukrainian joint. Blintzes $5.50. Cup of soup, salad, stuffed cabbage, and 4 melt-in-your-mouth *pirogi* $7. 25. Open 24 hrs.

Cucina di Pesce, 87 E. 4th St. (260-6800), between Second and Third Ave. Fish warrants the longish wait and highish prices. Friendly Italian seafood restaurant. Pasta dishes $6-9, and *bouilabaisse* fit for a king in the summer $15. Open daily 5pm-midnight.

Two Boots, 37 Ave. A (505-2276) at E. 2nd St. The two boots are Italy and Louisiana, both shaped remarkably like footwear. It may be Cajun Italian or Italian Cajun, but it sure is tasty. Menu changes twice a year, but pasta is $6-9 and the shrimp pizza ($7.50) is a mainstay. Open daily noon-midnight.

Second Ave. Delicatessen, 156 Second Ave. (677-0606) at 10th St. The definitive New York deli, established in 1954; people come into the city just to be snubbed by the waiters here. Have a pastrami or tongue on rye for $7, a fabulous burger deluxe for $6.75, or Jewish penicillin (a.k.a chicken soup) for $2.85. Note the Hollywood-style star plaques embedded in the sidewalk outside: this was once the heart of the Yiddish theatre district. But while their art form is all but forgotten, such personages as Moishe Oysher and Bella Meisel have gained a fragile foothold on immortality, embossed metallic tributes sunk in pocked pavement. Open Sun.-Thurs. 8am-midnight, Fri.-Sat. 8-2am.

Benny's Burritos, 93 Ave. A (254-2054) at 6th St. This Cal-Mex hot spot is dirt cheap and always hoppin'. Plump, tasty burritos with black or pinto beans, around $5. Open Sun.-Weds. 11am-midnight, Thurs.-Sat. 11am-2am.

Kiev, 117 Second Ave. (674-4040) at E. 7th St. Unparalleled *pirogi* and tons of heavy foods laced with sour cream and butter, generally around $8. Upscale deli decor. A popular late-night and early-morning pit stop for East Village club hoppers with the munchies. Open 24 hrs.

Passage to India, 308 E. 6th St. (529-5770), off Second Ave. Newer and classier than others on the block. Some of the city's best Indian food. Dine under chandeliers and brass-framed mirrors in British colonial style. Full *tandoori* dinner (soup, appetizer, main course, dessert, coffee) $13. Lamb curry $5.75. Open Sun.-Thurs. 12:30pm-12:30am. Fri.-Sat. noon-1am.

Kyber Pass Restaurant, 34 St. Mark's Pl. (473-0989), between Second and Third Ave. A dainty place on the central artery of the East Village, serving Afghani food. Basically Middle Eastern curries, soups, and dumplings, but with a subterranean Chinese influence. Sit on pillows and enjoy *Bouranee Baunjaun,* eggplant with mint yogurt and fresh coriander ($6.50) or *phirnee,* a delicate rice pudding with pistachios and rose water ($2). Open daily noon-midnight.

Ukrainian East Village Restaurant, 140 Second Ave. (529-5024), between 8th and 9th St. Pleasantly decorated, complete with chandeliers and large plants; excellent food at amazingly low prices. Cheese *pirogi* $4.50, stuffed cabbage with potato and mushroom gravy $5.55, *kielbasa* with sauerkraut and potato $5.25, hot *borscht* with vegetables $1.95. Open Sun.-Thurs. noon-11pm, Fri.-Sat. noon-midnight.

The Cloister Café, 238 E. 9th St. (777-9128). Dive into your bowl of cappuccino in a restaurant with more stained glass per square foot than any place this side of Rome. Or maybe lounge in a gorgeous outdoor garden complete with fish and a fountain, and order from an inexpensive, quality menu with light dishes (lunch platters $6-10, dinner $11-12). Open daily 11am-midnight.

Sugar Reef, 93 Second Ave. (477-8427), between 5th and 6th St. Enough fake fruit to stock a plastic plantation; loud music to match the color scheme. Wide selection of appropriately garish drinks; entrees $8-14. Open Mon.-Thurs. 5-11:45pm, Fri. 5pm-1am, Sat. 3pm-1am, Sun. 3-11:45pm.

The Sheik, 133 Ave. A between St. Marks and E. 9th St. Very cheap Middle Eastern food once provided good seats for riots in Tompkins Square Park; still a great deal. Burger on pita $1.50. Felafel $1.50. Open 11am-10pm.

Seekers of kosher food won't find much *traif* east of First Ave., especially south of East Houston St., where there has been a Jewish community since turn-of-the-century immigrant days.

Ratner's Dairy Restaurant, 138 Delancey St. (677-5588) just west of the Manhattan Bridge. The most famous of the kosher restaurants, partly due to its frozen food line. Despite the rundown surroundings, this place is large, shiny, and popular. Jewish dietary laws strictly followed; you will have to go elsewhere for a pastrami sandwich with mayo. But there's no better place to feast on fruit blintzes and sour cream ($8.50) or simmering vegetarian soups ($3.75). Potato pancake to go $6. Open Sun.-Thurs. 6am-midnight, Fri. 6am-sundown, Sat. sundown to 2am.

Katz's Delicatessen, 205 E. Houston St. (254-2246), near Orchard. Classic informal deli, established in 1888. The fake orgasm scene in *When Harry Met Sally* took place here. You'd better know what you want, because the staff here doesn't fool around. Have an overstuffed corned beef sandwich with a pickle for $6.45. Mail-order department enables you to send a salami to a loved one (or, perhaps, an ex-loved one). With testimonial letters from both Carter and Reagan, how could it be bad? (Don't think about that one too much.) Open daily 7am-11pm.

Yonah Schimmel Knishery, 137 E. Houston St. Rabbi Schimmel's establishment, around since the heyday of the Jewish Lower East Side (around 1910), has honed the knish to an art. Kasha and fruit-filled knishes (from $1.25) available too. Or try yogurt from a 71-year old strain (no, really). Open daily 8am-7pm.

Chinatown

You don't have to dig a hole to China to find authentic Asian food and groceries; you can hop on the subway and go to one of the oldest Chinatowns in the U.S. New Yorkers have long thrived on the delectable food in this area, whether dining in, taking out, or picking and choosing in grocery stores and spillover markets. You can find rare items like Chinese housewares, hermetically sealed whole fish, roots, and spices of all stripes in the numerous small stores that lurk on these streets. The neighborhood's 200-plus restaurants conjure up some of the best Chinese, Thai, and Vietnamese cooking around. And they don't make dumplings for Trumplings either—compared to prices in a French or Italian eatery, these restaurants are remarkably inexpensive. This is perhaps due to the fierce culinary competition. The great Vietnamese place you ate in last year may now be serving Malaysian cuisine under a different name. Such competition has been a boon for palates; once predominately-Cantonese cooking has now burgeoned into different cuisines from the various regions of China: hot and spicy Hunan or Szechuan food; the sweet and mildly spiced seafood of Soochow; or the hearty and filling fare of Peking. This competition has not diminished the popularity of Cantonese *dim sum,* however. In this Sunday afternoon tradition, waiters roll carts filled with assorted dishes of bite-sized goodies up and down the aisles. To partake, you simply point at what you want. (Beware of "Chinese bubblegum," a euphemism for tripe.) At the end of the meal, the number of empty dishes on your table are tallied up. To reach Chinatown, take the #4, 5, 6, J, M, Z, N, or R to Canal St., walk east on Canal to Mott St., go right on Mott, and follow the curved street toward the Bowery, Confucius Plaza, and E. Broadway.

Hunan Joy's, 48 Mott St. on the 2nd floor (267-4421), near Bayard St. Good and inexpensive Szechuan and Hunan food. Spicy hot and sour soup ($1.50), tasty beef with oyster sauce ($6.75) and interesting soft shell crab entree ($11.25) will fill you and please you. Open daily 11:30-2am.

Mweng Thai Restaurant, 23 Pell St. (406-4259), near Mott St. The curry comes in four different colors—good luck to those who choose hot green ($7). Try the Matsuman curry ($9) or the coconut chicken soup ($3). Lunch special weekdays 11:30am-3pm—your choice of curry with rice for $5. Open Sun., Tues.-Thurs. 11:30am-10pm, Fri.-Sat 11:30am-11pm. Closed Mon.

House of Vegetarian, 68 Mott St. (226-6572), off Bayard St. Faux chicken, faux beef, faux lamb and faux fish repopulate the menu: all the animals are ersatz, here, made from soy and wheat by-products. Try *Lo mein* with 3 kinds of mushrooms ($3.75) or seaweed fish ($8). An ice-cold lotus seed or lychee drink ($1.30) really hits the spot on hot summer days. Open daily 11am-11pm.

Nom Wah Tea Parlor, 13 Doyers St. (962-6047), a curved side alley off Pell St., near the Bowery. Open for 72 years. Airy, large, and quiet, especially during off hours. *Dim sum* served all day; small dishes $1, larger ones $2. Ask for *Ha Gow* ($2), a mixture of chopped shrimp and Chinese vegetables encased in rice flour dough and cooked in bamboo steamers. Rinse it all down with a pot of imported Chinese tea. Open daily 8:30am-8pm.

Pho Bang Restaurant, 6 Chatham Sq. (587-0870), on the corner of Mott and Bowery. Authentic Vietnamese food and a meat lover's paradise. Check out the full color menu, listen to the crazy disco music, and prepare to snarf. Try the chicken lemongrass ($5.95) or the delicious summer rolls ($3.25). The Sesame Beef is fun—roll your own dumplings with mint, lettuce, and lemongrass. Note the broad selection of tasty drinks at the end of the menu—go for the three-color sweet bean drink with jelly, mung beans, and coconut milk ($1.75). Open daily 10am-11pm.

Lung Fong Bakery, 41 Mott St. (233-7447), off Bayard St. A clean, spacious, airy place, unlike many other bakeries here. Almond cookies 50¢, pineapple sponge cake 50¢, chicken rolls 60¢, hot baked pork or sausage buns 50¢. Open daily 7am-9pm.

Chinatown Ice Cream Factory, 65 Bayard St. (608-4171), off Mott St. Some say Chinatown natives give equal business to the Häagen-Dazs down the street, but Häagen-Dazs doesn't have authentic homemade ice cream in flavors like lychee, mango, ginger, red bean, and green tea. One scoop $1.70, two $3, three $3.90. Open Mon.-Thurs. noon-11pm, Fri.-Sun. noon-12:30am.

Kam Kuo Food Corp., 7 Mott St. (349-3097), off Chatham Sq. Multitudinous wonders occupy this local supermarket. In the frozen meats section, London Broil is supplanted by pork toes, chicken feet, and duck wings. The produce section features Chinese versions of broccoli and eggplant. Look out for the sweetened, dried cuttlefish ($1-2). Upstairs, an entire floor of chinaware and cooking utensils rivals that of Zabar's. Open Mon.-Thurs. 9am-9pm, Fri.-Sat. 9am-10pm.

Hong Fat, 63 Mott St. (962-9588), off Bayard St. Suspiciously delicious. No-frills Cantonese meals in formica heaven, with a small, hot Szechuan menu. Try the *Kung Po Gai Ding* ($6.50), a tender, diced chicken dish with peppers and peanuts, or go straight for the fat noodle, a.k.a. *Chow Foon* ($5.50). With massive A/C support, Hong Fat stays chilly all night long. Open daily 10am-5am.

May May Gourmet Bakery, 35 Pell St. (267-0733), between Mott and Bowery. New, clean, and touristy. Countless interesting pastries (under 75¢) and fresh wontons ($3.75 for 10 pieces). Bring back some lotus seed or black bean paste pastries ($2.25 for 10 pieces) for future nibblings. Open daily 9am-7pm.

Peking Duck House, 22 Mott St. (227-1810), off Park St. You may not know it from the drab, lifeless decor, but this is the place which won seven stars from the *Daily News* and which former mayor Ed Koch called "the best Chinese restaurant in the world." If someone else is paying, order the *Peking Duck Extravaganza* ($28). Other poultry and pork entrees $8, beef dishes $8.50. 'Spensive. Open Sun.-Thurs. 11:30am-10:30pm, Fri.-Sat. 11:30am-11:30pm.

Yuen Yuen Restaurant, 61a Bayard St. (227-0862). The menu at this excellent new eatery is mostly in Chinese, but the specialty drinks, at least, are listed in English. Try a lychee ice, a milkshake with syrup and fresh lychees at the bottom ($1.50). Inexpensive Chinese food, sit-down and takeout, mostly $3-6.

Little Italy

A chunk of Naples seems to have migrated to this lively quarter roughly bounded by Canal, Lafayette, Houston St., and the Bowery. Raging Bull Robert De Niro stalked the *Mean Streets* here in 1973 and then returned a year later to cut a few slice-of-life scenes for the 1918 segments of *The Godfather Part II* (and you can still see the remnants of the set).

Immortalized by Billy Joel, who used to have dinner in the local *ristoranti,* Mulberry Street is the main drag and the appetite avenue of Little Italy. From Spring St. down to Canal St., Chinese ideograms gradually take over. During the day, Little Italy keeps quieter than most districts of New York; at night, evening crowds, tourists and neighborhood families alike, clog the sidewalk *caffè*. Stroll here after 7pm to catch street life but arrive earlier to get one of the better tables. For the sake of variety and thrift, sup at a restaurant but get your just desserts at a *caffè*. For Little Italy, take the #4, 5, 6, or J, N, R to Canal St. or the B, D, F, Q to Broadway-Lafayette.

On the second Thursday in September, Mulberry St. goes wild as Little Italy toasts the Saint of Naples during a raucous 10 days of merriment during the **Feast of San Gennaro.**

Luna, 112 Mulberry St. (226-8657), between Hester and Canal St. Enter through the small kitchen—where a halo of steam surrounds a generous platter of clams—to emerge into a narrow, somewhat haphazard dining room, furnished with stray photos. Come here to chat with the family who gossips in the kitchen. Don't be afraid to ask for translations and advice. Waiters give honest appraisals of vast menu. Spaghetti with white clam sauce $7, tumbler of wine $3, fish from $9. Open noon-midnight.

Paolucci's, 149 Mulberry St. (226-9653 or 925-2288). Family-owned restaurant with a penchant for heaping portions. The boss watches you from the front wall. Chicken *cacciatore* with salad and spaghetti $9, pasta from $6, daily lunch specials until 5pm $4.25-8.50. Open Sun. 11:30am-9:30pm, Mon.-Thurs. 11:30am-10:30pm, Fri.-Sat. 11:30am-11:30pm.

Ballato, 55 E. Houston St. (274-8881), off Mott St. Gracefully stemmed wine glasses and glistening chocolate-covered cherries greet you. Formerly a haunt of the beautiful people, now the breeding ground of impeccable Southern Italian cooking. Pasta $11.50, trout in olive oil $12.50. *Antipasti* $5.50-8. *Prix fixe* lunch (Mon.-Fri. noon-4pm; $12.50) and dinner (Mon.-Sat. 4-6:30pm; $17.50) include varied choice of appetizer, entree, and dessert. Open Mon.-Thurs. 11:45am-10pm, Fri. 11:45am-11pm, Sat. 4pm-midnight.

Ristorante Taormina, 147 Mulberry St. (219-1007, -1008, or -1009), between Grand and Hester St. No linoleum here; just large windows, graceful green plants, exposed brick walls, and blondewood fittings. Dressy but comfortable clientele enjoys gourmet food at reasonable prices. *Penne arrabiate* $10, *saltimbocca alla romana* (veal with *prosciutto,* white wine, and sage) $12.50. Open Mon.-Thurs. noon-11:30pm, Fri. noon-12:30pm, Sat. noon-1am, Sun. noon-10:30pm.

Il Fornaio, 132A Mulberry St. (226-8306). The clean white-tiled interior, with its perfectly symmetrical jars and tins of olive oil and its absence of garishness, suggests that Il Fornaio is the new kid on the block. Upbeat, reasonable menu. For lunch, mini-pizza costs $3. Hot sandwiches start at $4.50, pasta dinners at $5. Rumored to have the best *antipasti* in town. Open Sun.-Thurs. noon-11pm, Fri.-Sat. noon-11:30pm.

Trattoria Pietro and Vanessa, 23 Cleveland Pl. (226-8764 or 941-0286), off Spring and Lafayette St. Removed from the fray of Mulberry St. Large, quiet patio out back. Baked clam *antipasto* $5.25, pasta including spaghetti *filetto* (with *prosciutto* and onion) $7-9, veal, chicken, and fish $10. Open Mon.-Fri. noon-11pm, Sat. 4-11pm, Sun. 4-10pm.

Puglia Restaurant, 189 Hester St. (966-6006). Long tables mean fun and rowdiness. Venture into 3 separate dining rooms, ranging from diner-like to warehouse-like. A favorite with New Yorkers and bold tourists. Monstrous plate of mussels $8, entrees from $7. Live music nightly. Open Tues.-Sun. noon-1am.

Vincent's Clam Bar, 119 Mott St. (226-8133), off Hester St. A New York institution. Archaic photos line the walls of the restaurant which "Arnoldo the Great" established in 1904. Ravioli with Vincent's famous sauce $8, pasta from $6.50. Open Mon.-Thurs. 11:30am-2am, Fri.-Sat. 11:30am-4am, Sun. noon-1:30am.

Road to Mandalay, 380 Broome St. (226-4218), off Mulberry St. A rare Burmese pearl washed up on the Italian shores of Mulberry St. Refined Burmese cuisine, served in a cozy setting enhanced by baskets overflowing with fruit and vegetables. Start with the coconut noodle soup ($3.25), accompanied by the thousand-layered pancake, a delicate Burmese bread ($2.50). Entrees range from $7-9.50 with beef or chicken curry dishes laced with coriander checking in at $8. Lighter fare features street market noodle fried with duck and garlic $5.50-7. Open Mon.-Fri. 5-11pm, Sat.-Sun. noon-11pm.

Paesano, 136 Mulberry St. (966-3337). Foresaking subtlety for pomp, Paesano embodies the Southern Italian soul. Everything about this restaurant invites comparisons to big family reunions. Everyone seems familiar, portions are big enough to sink ships, and the piped tango seems a blood relative of the tune from *The Godfather.* White stucco and exposed brick straddle dark oak crossbeams wrapped in garlands and hung with hundreds of little Chianti bottles, diapered like babies in straw overalls. All pasta dishes $7, chicken *cacciatore* $7, *calamari* $7, veal $10. Open Sun.-Thurs. 11:30am-midnight, Fri.-Sat. 11:30am-1:30am.

Caffè Sorrento, 132 Mulberry St. (219-8634). Part of a new breed of M-Street eateries, Sorrento takes exotica off the walls and puts it on the menu. Fortunately the menu is equipped with a lengthy description of each entree. Pasta from $7.50, *capelli d'angeli primavera* (angel hair pasta with vegetables in cream) $9.50, *costat e salsicce di maiole alla calabrese* (pork chop and sausage with vinegar peppers) $10.75. Open daily noon-midnight.

La Mela, 167 Mulberry St. (431-9493 or 226-9623). If Little Italy believed in cult restaurants, La Mela would be the kingpin. Kitsch paintings and postcards dot the walls haphazardly; tables and chairs crop up here and there like mushrooms after a rain. Technically there's no menu; the boss talks you through your order. People travel from as far as Rapid City to sink their teeth into the famed chicken *scarpariello.* A wide assortment of pasta and *gnocchi.* Equally rambunctious outdoor seating in their backyard, complete with a guitar-touting bard, the final mark of "authenticity." The menu, a handwritten fly-swatter of a paper bag, beckons: "Come in side please, for sure we will not disappointed you." Pricey and unpredictable: the lack of fixed menu leaves them with lots of leeway. Open daily noon-11pm.

Benito I, 174 Mulberry St. (226-9171). A small no-nonsense trattoria churning out genuine cuisine. For a memorable appetizer, order *mozzarella in carozza* ($6), and follow it up with *pollo scarpariello* ($11), a chicken beak and feather above the rest. Open Sun.-Thurs. noon-11pm, Fri.-Sat. noon-11:30pm.

Rocky's Italian Restaurant, 45 Spring St. (226-8121) at Mulberry St. This Italian stallion punches out primo dishes a few blocks away from the heart of the action. Billy Crystal and his uncle are regulars in this place that's been cooking up consistently good Italian fare for over 20 years. Signed portraits of stars hung throughout. For lunch try a pizza hero $4, or sandwiches $4-7, served until 5pm. Pasta $8-13. For dessert, try their homemade Italian cheesecake, made with fresh ricotta tinted with anise ($3). Open Mon.-Sat. 11am-11pm.

Caffè

Caffè Roma, 385 Broome St. (226-8413) at Mulberry St. A good *caffè* gets better with time. A full-fledged saloon in the 1890s, Roma has kept its original furnishings intact: dark green walls with polished brass ornaments, chandeliers, and darkwood cabinets where liquor bottles used to roost. Since its saloon days, Roma has removed the imbibery and installed several elegant, Tuscan landscapes. The pastries and coffee, Roma's *raison d'etre,* prove as refined as the setting. Try the neapolitan *cannoli* or the *baba au rhum* ($1.20 to take out, $1.75 to eat in). Potent espresso $1.40; obligatory cappuccino, with a tiara of foamed milk, $2.25. Open Sun.-Thurs. 8am-midnight, Fri.-Sat. 8am-1am.

Caffè Biondo, 141 Mulberry St. (226-9285). Don't mistake the glass front and polished black-and-white checkered floor for a gallery. Sip espresso ($1.50) while surrounded by cornucopias and diabolical grimaces. Or try *caffè corretto* (espresso with Sambuca) $2.50, *cappuccino alla panna* (with whipped cream) $2.50. *Cannoli* $2.50. Open daily noon-1am.

La Bella Ferrara, 110 Mulberry St. (966-1488). Named after the city that brought you turbo power, La Bella Ferrara maintains the dual imperatives of power and grace in its dynamic production of *dolci*. The largest selection of pastries around. Sleek glass and checkered tile. Pastries $1-3, cappuccino $2.50. Continental breakfast $2.75. Lunch special (soup and sandwich) until 5pm, $5. Open Sun.-Thurs. 9am-1am, Fri. 9am-2am, Sat. 9am-3am.

Ferrara, 195-201 Grand St. A slick emporium where hundreds of tempting pastries vie for your attention. The espresso bar has become one of the city's most popular places for cappuccino and its creamy siblings. In good weather the bar extends onto the sidewalk, where a counter dispenses authentic Italian *gelati*. *Cannoli* $2.50, Lobster Tail (bavarian cream and flaky dough) $4.25, pizza *rustica* $4.25. Open Sun.-Thurs. 7:30am-midnight, Fri.-Sat. 7:30am-1am.

Lo Spuntino, 117 Mulberry St. (226-9280), between Hester and Canal St. Not the flashy type. Gorgeous desserts compensate for lackluster decor. Endless list of mousses includes pumpkin mousse (in season). Pears in white wine sauce $4, *torta di frutta* $3.75, espresso $1.50. Open Mon.-Sat 11:30am-1am, Sun.4pm-12:30am.

Financial District

Bargain-basement cafeteria joints here can fill you up with everything from gazpacho to Italian sausages. Fast-food joints pepper Broadway between Dey and John St., just a few feet from the overpriced offerings of the Main Concourse of the World Trade Center. In summer, food pushcarts form a solid wall on Broadway between Cedar and Liberty St., wheeling and dealing in a realm beyond hot dogs. Assorted vendors sell felafel and eggplant plates ($2.75), cheese nachos ($3), and chilled gazpacho with an onion roll ($3). You can sup or dine in Liberty Park, across the street.

At the pedestrian plaza at Coenties Slip, between Pearl and South William St., you can choose among small budget restaurants. Grab an *empanada* (turnover) for $2.50 at **Rubin's** or select from a bounteous buffet at **The Golden Chopsticks** for $4 per pound.

North of City Hall, food kiosks fill St. Andrew's Plaza, a no-frills alternative for the local crowd of office workers doing lunch. At the South St. Seaport you can choose from a collage of food-booths; dine formally on exquisitely prepared salmon, or chomp casually on fried clams. Up Fulton St., between Cliff and William St., the cost of dining dwindles.

Frank's Papaya, 192 Broadway (693-2763), at John St. Excellent value, quick service. Very close to World Trade Center. 1/3-lb. hamburger $1.50, hot dog with sauerkraut 60¢. Breakfast (egg, ham, cheese, coffee) $1.50. Stand and eat at one of the counters inside the room. Open daily 5:30am-10pm.

Happy Deli, 181 Broadway (587-1105), between John and Cortlandt St. A salad bar the size of Guam—choose your favorite greens, pasta, fruit ($4 per pound). Seating in rear. Open 24 hrs. Free delivery.

Big Kitchen, 5 World Trade Center (938-1153), Main Concourse near entrance to subway and PATH trains. Select from a ring of deli, pizza, and Thai food booths. Central seating for access to à la carte whims. Taco $2, 1/2-pint pork fried rice $1.95, frozen yogurt 43¢/oz. Open Mon.-Fri. 7am-7pm, Sat. 9am-5pm.

McDonald's, 160 Broadway (385-2063) at Liberty St. For the Wall St. McPower lunch. A double decker McPalace seating 250 at marble tabletops. A doorman in a tux and the strains of a baby grand piano greet you. Pick at grapes and strawberries with your breakfast, or down a pastry ($2.50) and espresso ($1.75). Fruit nectar ($1.50) and herbal tea ($1) to quench that Big Mac thirst. Prices run about 25% higher than at standard McDonald's. Drop in on the new gift boutique on your way out. Open Mon.-Fri. 6am-11pm, Sat.-Sun. 8am-9pm.

Wolf's Delicatessen, 42 Broadway (422-4141). A deli untainted by any trend in cuisine or decor that hit after the early 60s. Formica, pickles, no pretensions. Baked beans $1.10, BLT $3.75, turkey burgers $2.85-4.45. Open Mon.-Fri. 6am-7:45pm, Sat. 6am-3:45pm.

Hamburger Harry's, 157 Chambers St. (267-4446). Gourmet burgers for the connoisseur: 7-oz. patty, broiled over applewood with exotic toppings like avocado, alfalfa sprouts, chili, salsa, or bearnaise sauce, from $6. (You can have chicken breast done similarly for the same price.)

Regular burger $4, nacho cheese fries $3. Open Mon.-Thurs. 11:30am-10pm, Fri. 11:30am-11pm, Sat. noon-11pm, Sun. noon-9pm.

Top Floor, Pier 17 at South St. Seaport. Livelier than Fulton Market, with a better selection: South Philly Steaks and Fries (gourmet onion rings $2); The Salad Bowl (pita sandwich with tuna, chicken, or hummus $4.50, vegetable soup $2); Dumpling House (pan-fried Chinese dumplings $3). Open daily 11am-9pm.

Fulton Seaport Deli, 52 Fulton St. (393-1137). Select from the massive, high-quality salad bar at $4 per pound, or try a triple-decker sandwich for $4.25, then munch back at the seaport. Open 24 hrs.

Topside Shops and Cafés, Fulton Market, Fulton St. A partial survey of the highlights of this top-floor extravaganza: New York Pastrami Factory (Hebrew National hot dog $1.95); Fulton Market Fish and Clam Bar (6 oysters $7, fried shrimp on a bun $4.25); Burger Boys of Brooklyn (sirloin burger $3); Pizza Del Ponte (cheese calzone $3). Open daily 11:30am-9pm.

Brooklyn

Ethnic flavor changes every two blocks in Brooklyn. Brooklyn Heights offers nouvelle cuisine, but specializes in pita bread and *baba ganoush.* Williamsburg seems submerged in kosher and cheap Italian restaurants, while Greenpoint is a borscht-lover's paradise. And for those who didn't get enough in Manhattan, Brooklyn now has its own Chinatown in Sunset. Venture out to find a restaurant with food from another nation and prices from another century.

Downtown and North Brooklyn

Junior's, 986 Flatbush Ave. Extension (718-852-5257), across the Manhattan Bridge at De Kalb St. Subway: #2, 3, 4, 5, B, D, M, N, Q, or R to Atlantic Ave. Lit up like a jukebox and playing classic roast beef and brisket for hordes of locals. Brisket sandwich $6.25, entrees around $10. Suburban types drive for hours to satisfy their cheesecake cravings here (plain slice $3). Open Sun.-Thurs. 6:30am-12:30am, Fri.-Sat. 6:30am-2am.

Moroccan Star, 205 Atlantic Ave. (718-643-0800) in Brooklyn Heights. Subway: #2, 3, 4, 5, M, or R to Borough Hall, then down three blocks on Court St. Ensconced in the local Arab community, this restaurant serves delicious and reasonably cheap food. Try the *pastello* ($8.75, lunch $6), a delicate semi-sweet pigeon pie with almonds. Open Sun. noon-10pm, Tues.-Thurs. 10am-11pm, Fri.-Sat. 11am-11pm.

Fountain Café, 183 Atlantic Ave. (718-624-6764) in Brooklyn Hts. Subway: #2, 3, 4, 5, M, or R to Borough Hall, then down three blocks on Court St. This place, named for a rumbly little fountain in the center of the restaurant, serves up inexpensive and more-than-edible Middle Eastern food. Shwarma $4, kafta kebab $4, felafel sandwich $2.85, spinach meat pie $1.50. Open daily 10:30am- 10:30pm.

Near East Bakery, 183 Atlantic Ave. (718-875-0016) in Brooklyn Heights. Subway: 2, 3, 4, 5, M, or R to Borough Hall. Stairs lead down to a stone basement, a Saharan atmosphere, and meat and spinach pies ($1.25) straight from the *suk.* A dozen loaves of good pita cost $1.25. Open Tues.-Sat. 9:30am-4:30pm, Sun. 9:30am-1pm.

Teresa's, 80 Montague St. (718-797-3996) in Brooklyn Heights. Subway: 2, 3, 4, 5, M, or R to Borough Hall. Good, cheap Polish food in a pleasant wood and orange interior. Two pieces of stuffed pepper ($6) or some *pirogi* ($3.25) stuffed with cheese, potatoes, meat, or sauerkraut and mushrooms make a filling meal. Open daily 7am-11pm.

Promenade Restaurant, 101 Montague St. (718-522-7433), near promenade in Brooklyn Heights. Subway: 2, 3, 4, 5, M, or R to Borough Hall. Elderly clientele suits out-dated aqua and gold-leaf diner decor. Corned beef and cabbage with a boiled potato $7. Chicken croquette with mashed potatoes and peas $5. Open Sun.-Thurs. 6am-2pm., Fri.-Sat. 6-3:30am.

Milo's Restaurant, 559 Lorimer St. (718-384-8457) in Williamsburg. Subway: J or M to Lorimer St. In a neighborhood packed with Italian food this place stands out with its Sinatra-special jukebox selection (19 of his greatest!). Antipasto $3, several choices of pasta under $5. Why not try the Neapolitan specialty, *capozzelle,* an entire lamb's head served with lemon wedges? ($5.50)—*Mangiate bene!* [*trans.* good but mangy—Ed.] Open Wed.-Sun. 11am-9pm.

Stylowa Restaurant, 694 Manhattan Ave. (718-383-8993) in Greenpoint. Subway: G to Nassau Ave. Polish cuisine at its best and cheapest. Sample *kielbasa* (Polish sausage) with fried onions, sauerkraut, and bread ($4) or roast beef in homemade gravy with potatoes for $4. All other entrees ($4-6) served with a free glass of compote (pink, apple-flavored fruit drink). Delicious potato pancakes $2.50. Open Mon.-Thurs. noon-9pm, Fri. noon-10pm, Sat. 11am-10pm, Sun. 11am-9pm.

Central Brooklyn

Hungry, tired, low on funds, far from Manhattan, wearing sunglasses? Simmer down, O budget traveler. Satisfying and affordable meals abound. Eighth Ave. in Sunset is the heart of Brooklyn's Chinatown. The Park Slope area had a variety of ethnic restaurants and Avenue J in Flatbush is the place to go for Jamaican and other West Indian cuisine.

El Gran Castillo de Jagua, 345 Flatbush Ave. (718-622-8700), at Carlton St. near Grand Army Plaza. Subway: D or Q to 7th Ave. A terrific place for cheap, authentic Spanish food. Meat dinners with rice and beans or plantains and salad $5-7; exotic fruit drinks $1. Try the *mofungo* (crushed green plantains with roast pork and gravy; $3.50) Open daily 7am-midnight.

El Castillo de Jagua, 148 Fifth Ave. (718-783-9743), at Douglas St. in Park Slope. Subway: D or Q to Seventh Ave. The deafening jukebox pumps out the newest Latino rhythms. Excellent, cheap food with great breakfast specials. Try the *pasteles*, meat-filled green bananas, for $1.50. Fried plantains (Latin American french fries) are served with every meal. Open daily 7am-midnight.

Tom's Lucheonette, 782 Washington Ave. (718-783-8576), at Sterling Pl. Subway: #2 or 3 to Brooklyn Museum. The best breakfast place in Brooklyn—an old-time luncheonette complete with a soda fountain and 50s-style hyper-friendly service. Two eggs with fries or grits, toast, and coffee or tea $1.85. Famous golden challah french toast $2.75. Breakfast served all day. Open daily 4am-4pm.

Aunt Sonia's, 1123 Eighth Ave. (718-965-9526) at 12th St., near Park Slope. Subway: F to Seventh Ave./Park Slope. A tiny, very classy haven for the budget gourmand, with ceiling fans and black interior. Line up with the crowds awaiting the chef's newest creations. Besides providing daily specials, he creates a new menu every 2 months. Entrees $8-10. Open Mon.-Thurs. 5:30-10pm, Fri. 5:30-11:30pm, Sun. 10am-10pm, Sat. 10am-4pm, 5:30-10pm.

Oriental Palace, 5909 Eighth Ave. (718-633-6688), near 56th St. in Sunset. Subway: N or R to 59th St. New, authentic, and inexpensive. *Dim sum* $1.50 a piece, including chicken feet and bird's nest, from 7:30 to 4pm daily. Lunch for around $3, roast pork bun 50¢. Open Sun.-Thurs. 7:30am-11pm, Fri.-Sat. 7:30am-midnight.

Kar Chang, 5605 Eighth Ave. (718-854-3996), in Sunset. Subway: N or R to 59th St. Wide variety of seafood includes frogs and snails. Clay pot casseroles ($7.50-10) and the best hot and sour soup in town ($3.50). If you're still hungry, grab a roast pork bun (50-60¢) at a nearby bakery. Open daily 10:30am-11pm.

Taxco, 412 Fifth Ave. (718-832-1341), at 7th St. subway: R or F to 9th St/4th Ave. Tasty Mexican food: two tacos $6; taco, enchilada, and tostada $7. Try the house specialty, chicken enchiladas with molé sauce, and groove with the Latin music pumping from the jukebox. Sun.-Thurs. 10:30pm, Fri.-Sat. noon-2am.

Cafeteria of the Main Branch Library, Grand Army Plaza (718-780-7700). Subway: #2 or 3 to Grand Army Plaza. Unexciting food, but superior to McDonald's. Grilled chicken breast sandwich $1.75. Two pieces of chicken, french fries, and cole slaw $2. Open Tues.-Thurs. 9am-5:30pm, Fri. 10am-5:30pm

.Short Ribs, 9101 Third Ave. (718-745-0614), in Bay Ridge. Subway: R to 86th St. The best barbecue around, especially tasty if someone else foots the somewhat hefty bill. Try the French onion soup served in a round loaf of semolina bread ($4). A solid meal with onion rings costs $10-15. Incredibly popular; crowded even with two stories. Open Sun. noon-10pm, Mon.-Thurs. noon-11pm, Fri.-Sat. noon-1am.

South Brooklyn

The shores of Brooklyn present a true dining quandary: the choices are endless. Try knishes (Eastern European dough creations with filling) on Brighton Beach Ave., Italian *calamari* (fried squid) in spicy marinara sauce along Emmons Ave. in Sheepshead Bay, or tri-colored candy on Coney Island. Eat until you feel ill—it still won't make a dent in your wallet.

Mrs. Stahl's Knishes, 1001 Brighton Beach Ave. (718-648-0210), at Coney Island Ave. Subway: D or Q to Brighton Beach. World-famous knishes—if knishes can be world-famous—in 20 flavors, including pineapple cheese ($1.35; cheese flavors $1.50; seniors $1.10). Grab a *hamentashen* (a 3-cornered, fruit-filled pastry) for dessert (90¢). Open Sun.-Thurs. 10am-7pm, Fri.-Sat 10am-8pm.

Sea Lane Bakery, 615 Brighton Beach Ave. (718-934-8877), underneath the El. Subway: D or Q to Brighton Beach. The best Jewish bakery in Brighton. Try a little of everything (9 assorted pastries 85¢) or buy a loaf of honey cake, loaded with almonds and cherries ($4). Open daily 7am-9pm.

Lulu's Deli Restaurant, 107 Brighton Beach Ave. (718-372-6033), 1 block from Ocean Pkwy. Subway: D or Q to Brighton Beach. Eighty years of preparing Hebrew National meats have made them a trusted favorite among locals. Obligatory pastrami on rye with mustard $5.60. The lunch special ($4.25) includes soup, entree, french fries, cole slaw, pickle, and a drink. Greasy but memorable potato pancakes ($1) make a good snack. Open Tues.-Sun. 10am-9:45pm.

Primorski Restaurant, 282 Brighton Beach Ave. (718-891-3111). Subway: D or Q to Brighton Beach. Popular with natives, this bright red and blue restaurant serves the best Ukrainian borscht ($1.70) in this hemisphere. Menu is pot-luck, as many of the waiters struggle with English. That's okay—every dish is tasty. Eminently affordable lunch special ($4) available weekdays 11am-5pm, weekends 11am-4pm. At night, prices rise as the disco ball begins to spin and you pay for entertainment too. Open daily 11am-midnight.

Nathan's, Surf and Sitwell Ave. in Coney Island. Subway: B, D, F, or N to Coney Island. Seventy-four years ago, Nathan Handwerker became famous for undercutting his competitors on the boardwalk. His hot dogs cost a nickel; theirs were a dime. Today, a classic frank at Nathan's sells for $1.75. Unique, absurdly plump crinkle-cut french fries $1.55. Open Sun.-Thurs. 8am-4am, Fri.-Sat. 8am-5am.

Philip's Candy Store, 1237 Surf Ave., at the entrance to the B, D, F, or N train in Coney Island. Satisfy the child inside of you. Famous salt-water taffy (95¢ a quarter-pound). Candy or caramel apple 75¢. Cotton candy $1. Open Sun.-Thurs. 11am-3am, Fri.-Sat. 11am-4am.

Jimmy's Famous Heros, 1786 Sheepshead Bay Rd. (718-648-8001), across the street from El Greco diner. Subway: D or Q to Sheepshead Bay. Heros, New Yorkese for subs or grinders, cost about $5 and can be shared by two. Never mind what it entails; always ask for "the works" on whatever you order. Open Mon.-Fri. 7am-6pm, Sat. 7am-7pm, Sun. 7am-5pm.

Joe's Clam Bar, 2009 Emmons Ave. (718-646-9375), across the street from the bay. Subway: D or Q to Sheepshead Bay. Pricy, but the fish hail from the Atlantic and not from the toxic bay. Try the fried *calamari* ($12) and dip the chunks of chewy squid in hot or mild sauce. Raw clams served on the half-shell ($5.25 for 6) are especially good smothered in lemon juice and crackers. Open Sun.-Thurs. 11am-midnight. Fri.-Sat. 11am-2am.

Roll-n-Roaster, Nostrand Ave. and Emmons Ave. (718-769-6000), a half-mile walk east from Sheepshead Bay Rd. Subway: D or Q to Sheepshead Bay. Twenty years of quite remarkable roast beef ($3.30; $3.55 with cheese) have earned this semi-fast food joint a loyal following despite the plastic gas lamps and hollow stone walls. Cheese fries a perennial favorite ($1.70). Open Sun.-Thurs. 11am-1am, Fri.-Sat. 11am-3am.

Queens

Reasonably priced, authentic ethnic food is one of the best things about Queens. **Astoria** specializes in discount shopping and ethnic eating. Take the G or R to Steinway St. and Broadway and browse all the way down to 25th Ave., or turn up Broadway and walk toward the Manhattan skyline. The number of Greek and Italian restaurants increases right around the elevated station at Broadway and 31st St., where you can catch the N north to Ditmars Blvd. for even more Astorian cuisine. In **Flushing,** you can find excellent Chinese, Japanese, and Korean restaurants, but always check the prices. An identical dish may cost half as much only a few doors away. **Bell Boulevard** in Bayside, out east near the Nassau border, is the center of Queens night life, and on most weekends you can find crowds of young natives bar-hopping here.

In **Jamaica** and the other African-American and West Indian neighborhoods to its southeast, you can try fast food like Jamaican beef pattie or West Indian *rito* (flour tortilla filled with potatoes, meat, and spices). Jamaica Avenue in downtown Jamaica and Linden Blvd. in neighboring St. Albans are lined with restaurants specializing in this type of cuisine. Jamaica also holds a **farmer's market** at 90-24 160th St. (718-291-0282) Mon.-Sat. 7am-6pm, where the farmfolks offer their bounty indoors, next to a food court with local and nationally-known restaurants. To get to Jamaica, take the E or J train to Jamaica Center; from there the Q4 bus goes to Linden Blvd. in St. Albans.

Roumeli Taverna, 33-04 Broadway, Astoria (718-278-7533). Subway: G or R to Steinway St. (and walk four blocks west) or N to Broadway (and walk two blocks east). When in Astoria, do as the Astorians do. A taste of the Old Country, with Greek accents as authentic as the food. *Spanokopita* (spinach pie) appetizer $3, lamb stew $9.50. Open Sun.-Fri. 11am-midnight, Sat. 11am-1am.

Waterfront Crabhouse, 2-03 Borden Ave. Long Island City (718-729-4862). Subway: #7 to Vernon Blvd./Jackson Ave., then south on Vernon; walk all the way to the river on Borden Ave. Former home of the turn-of-the-century "Miller's Hotel," through which the rich and famous passed as they escaped to Long Island by ferry. Theodore Roosevelt, Grover Cleveland, and Lillian Russell all dined in this building, which lost its 3rd floor in a fire in 1975. Today the crabhouse attracts its own big names, such as Paul Newman and Ed Asner. Sliced shell steak $7. Sixteen oz. boneless shell steak $12.50. Double-cut prime rib on the bone $14. If someone is treating, try the famous Waterfront bouillabaisse, a whole steamed lobster on a bed of linguini, surrounded by a coterie of seafood in marinara sauce ($19). Daily entertainment. Reservations recommended. Open Mon.-Wed. noon-10pm, Thurs. noon-11pm, Fri.-Sat. noon-midnight, Sun. 1-10pm.

Woo Chon Restaurant, 41-19 Kissena Blvd., Flushing (718-463-0803). Subway: #7 to Main St., then walk south two blocks. Some of the finest Korean food in Flushing. Look for the waterfall in the window. Try the *chun jou gob dol bibim bab* ($9.95), an obscure and ancient rice dish served in a superheated stone vessel; mix immediately, or the rice will be scorched by the bowl. For lunch, try a filling bowl of *seol-lung-tang* ($6.50), fine rice noodles in a beef broth with assorted Oriental veggies. An unlimited supply of *kim-chi* (spicy marinated vegetables) accompanies every meal. Open perpetually.

Pastrami King, 124-24 Queens Blvd. (718-263-1717), near 82nd Ave., in Kew Gardens. Subway: E, F, or R to Union Tpke./Kew Gardens, then south on Queens Blvd. Everything here, from the meats to the coleslaw to the pickles, is made on the premises. The home-cured pastrami and corned beef is among the best in New York. Take out a sprawling, 3-inch-thick pastrami on rye for $6. Open Sun.-Fri. 8am-9pm, Sat. 8am-10pm.

Galaxy Pastry Shop, 37-11 30th Ave. (718-545-3181), in Astoria. Subway: N to 30th Ave. Make a right on 30th and continue until 37th St. Hypoglycemics can ascend to Mt. Olympus here. Honey-drenched *baklava* $1; bite-sized pieces 35¢. Gorge yourself on Greek pastries at a squeaky-clean table inside the slickly mirrored shop, or lounge in the ample outdoor seating. Open daily 7am-2am.

Rizzo's Pizza, 30-15 Steinway St., Astoria (718-721-9862). Subway: G or R to Steinway St. and Broadway. Walk up Steinway to 30th Ave. The restaurant is tiny, the seating makeshift, and the whole affair could easily go unnoticed in the endless row of discount stores and specialty shops lining Steinway. But the pizza deserves your attention: Sicilian rectangles based on a thin, crisp crust, and spread with an unforgettable tomato sauce. Ask for extra cheese. $1.20 per slice, $6.90 per 6-slice pie. 35¢ per extra topping per slice. Open Mon.-Thurs. 11am-8pm, Fri.-Sat. 11am-9pm, Sun. noon-6pm.

Uncle George's, 33-19 Broadway, Astoria (718-626-0593). Subway: G or R to Steinway St., then four blocks west, or N to Broadway, then two blocks east. This popular Greek restaurant, known as "Barba Yiogis O Ksenihtis" to the locals, serves inexpensive and hearty delicacies around the clock. Almost all entrees are under $10; try the rabbit stew or goat soup ($6), or lamb and potatoes ($7). The hanging plants and flowers on the table lend this place a cheery greenhouse effect. Open 24hr.

Empire Kosher Chicken Restaurant, 100-19 Queens Blvd. (718-997-7315), in Forest Hills. Subway: G or R to 67th Ave. Cheap chicken prepared according to ancient Jewish laws of ritual purity by one of the major kosher meat manufacturers. Fried, roasted, blanched, or barbecued. Meals $3-8; delicious chicken salad sandwich $3.70. Open Sun.-Thurs. 11am-9:30pm, Fri. 11am-2:30pm.

Kuala Lumpur, 135-31 40th Rd., Flushing (718-353-8333), just off Main St. Subway: #7 to Main St. Watch out for your chopsticks. Malaysian cuisine at extremely reasonable prices: the lunchtime special features 3 small dishes of your choice and a soup for $3.75 (Mon.-Fri. 11am-3pm). Open daily 7am-midnight.

Bronx

When Italian immigrants settled the Bronx, they brought their recipes and tradition of hearty communal dining with them. While much of the Bronx is a culinary disaster zone, the New York *cognoscenti* soon discovered the few oases along Arthur Ave. and in Westchester where the fare is as robust and the patrons as rambunctious as their counterparts in Naples. The enclave on Arthur Ave. and along 187th St. brims with pastry shops, streetside *caffè*, pizzerias, restaurants, and mom-and-pop emporiums vending Madonna 45s and battalions of imported espresso machines—all this without the schmaltzy tourist veneer of Little Italy. Established in 1910, **Ruggieri Pastry Shop,** under the dynamic leadership of Sam and Lurdes, produces mountains upon mountains of classic Italian pastries, though they're especially proud of their *sfogliatella* a flaky Neapolitan pastry stuffed with ricotta. Those nostalgic for the groovy golden 50s will be glad to know that Ruggieri operates one of the last authentic ice cream fountains in New York. Drag your sweetheart here for a real malted or an egg cream. Ruggieri blends and bakes at 2373 Prospect Ave., at E. 187th St. (Open daily 8am-10pm.) Revel in elaborate French and Italian pastries to the tune of a warm cappuccino in **Egioio Pastry Shop,** 622 E. 187th St. An octogenarian with modern flair, a trim, sexy interior, and inviting outdoor tables, Egioio makes the best *gelato* in the Bronx. To get to Arthur Ave., take the #2 or 5 train to Pelham Parkway, then Bronx bus #BX12 two stops west; or B, C train to Fordham Rd.

You can watch the rich and infamous stroll out of their limos and make a grand entrance into **Joe Nina's,** 3019 Westchester Ave., right under the subway platform of the Buhre Ave. #6 stop.

Ann & Tony's, 2407 Arthur Ave. (933-1469). Typical of Arthur Avenue, this bistro not only has an understated and comfortable decor, but excellent food. Unlike most restaurants in the area, however, Ann & Tony's has specials for dinner that run as low as $6, salad included. For lunch, sandwiches begin at $4.95. Open Tues.-Thurs. 11:30am-10pm. Fri. 11:30am-11pm. Sat. noon-midnight. Sun. 2-9pm. Closed Mon.

Dominick's, 2335 Arthur Ave. (733-2807). Small authentic Italian eatery. Vinyl tablecloths and bare walls, but great atmosphere nonetheless. Waiters won't offer you a menu or a check—they'll recite the specials of the day and bark out what you owe at the end of the meal. Try the linguini with marinara sauce ($7) and the special veal *francese* ($12). Open Mon. and Wed.-Sat. 10am-midnight, Sun. 1-9pm. Arrive before 6pm or after 9pm, or expect at least a 20-min. wait.

Mario's, 2342 Arthur Ave. (584-1188). Five generations of the Migliucci *famiglia* have worked the kitchen of this celebrated Southern Italian trattoria. The original clan left Naples in the early 1900s and opened the first Italian restaurant in Egypt, then came to the U.S. and cooked themselves into local lore: Mario's appears on the pages of Puzo's pre-cinema *Godfather*. Celebrities pass through, among them the starting lineups for the Yankees and the Giants. A room-length couch embraces patrons with familial arms. Try *spiedini alla romana,* a deep-fried sandwich made with anchovy sauce and mozzarella ($8). Notorious for pizza too. Traditional pasta $9-11, *antipasto* $5.50. Open Sun. and Tues.-Thurs. noon-10:30pm, Fri.-Sat. noon-midnight.

Pasquale's Rigoletto, 2311 Arthur Ave. (365-6644). A relative newcomer to the Arthur Ave. pasta scene, Pasquale's cooks with the best of them. As the name suggests, they do soothe you with potent arias; if you have a favorite in mind, they'll gladly play it for you. *Antipasto* $4, pasta $9, poultry $12.50. Open Tues.-Fri. noon-10pm, Sat.-Sun. noon-1am.

Taormina Ristorante, 1805 Edison Ave. (823-1646). Subway: #6 to Buhre Ave. Hearty Italian fare in the shadow of the subway tracks. Combine any pasta with any sauce to suit your fancies. Pasta $9.50-10, sandwiches $5-7.50. Chicken dishes from $10, veal from $12. Relax with a cup of espresso ($2) or cappuccino ($3). Open Mon.-Thurs. noon-10:30pm, Fri.-Sat. noon-11:30pm, Sun. noon-10pm.

Tony's Pizza, 34 E. Bedford Park Blvd. (367-2854). Subway: #4 to Bedford Park Blvd. Pizza so good that students from nearby Bronx High School of Science will skip class to grab a slice. Crisp crust slathered with generous amounts of cheese. $1.30 per slice, 65¢ per extra topping. Open Mon.-Sat. 10:30am-8:30pm.

Caffè

Delilo Pastry Shop, 606 E. 187 St. (367-8198), off of Arthur Ave. Although this small shop is often crowded, it's worth your while to sit here and sample the excellent baked goods, along with a cappuccino or espresso. Open Tues.-Sun. 8am-11pm.

Caffè Margherita, 689 E. 187 St. (no phone), off of Arthur Ave. In the late 70s the New York Times called Margherita's cappuccino the "best in the world." On hot summer nights, retreat from the city into the fantasies offered by this *caffè*, complete with an outdoor jukebox with tunes ranging from Sinatra and Madonna to Italian folk music. "Cold" espresso at $2. Alcohol served, but no desserts. Open daily 8am-midnight.

Caffè Egidio, 622 E. 187 St. (295-6077), off of Arthur Ave. In addition to *gelati,* cappuccino, espresso, and a fascinating interior complete with oversized portraits of the Borgias, this *caffè* has one of the largest selections of jellybeans in the city with flavors from Blueberry and Lemon Meringue to Banana and Cranberry. Also has inexpensive lunch and dinner specials. Open daily 7am to 10pm.

Sights

> *Far below and around lay the city like a ragged pur-*
> *ple dream, the wonderful, cruel, enchanting, bewil-*
> *dering, fatal, great city.*
>
> —*O. Henry*

The classic sightseeing quandary experienced by New York tourists is finding the Empire State Building. They've seen it in dozens of pictures and drawings, captured in sharp silhouettes or against a steamy pink sky as a monument of dreams. They've seen it towering over the grey landscape as their plane descends on to the runway, or in perspective down long avenues or from a river tour. But they can't see it when they're standing right next to it.

This optical illusion may explain why many New Yorkers have never visited some of the major sights in their hometown. When you're smack in the middle of them, the tallest skyscrapers seem like a casual part of the scenery. But no one—natives and tourists alike—knows what they're missing. Not all sights are as glaringly green and obvious as the Statue of Liberty. Sometimes you'll enter a modest doorway to find treasures inside, and sometimes you'll need to take a long elevator ride to see what everybody's raving about. If it's your first time in the big city, you'll notice even more subtle attractions—the neighborhoods and personalities jumbled together on shared turf, the frenzy of throngs at rush hour, the metropolitan murmur at dusk. And if it's your hundredth time in the city, there will still be areas you don't know too well, architectural quirks you've never noticed, and plain old doorways you have yet to discover and enter. Seeing New York takes a lifetime.

Sightseeing Tours

> *A bulger of a place [New York] is. The number of*
> *the ships beat me all hollow, and looked for all the*
> *world like a big clearing in the West, with the dead*
> *trees all standing.*
> — *Davy Crockett, Tour to the North and Down East*
>   *...in 1834*

The best way to discover New York City is on foot. A quick official tour can help set your bearings before you return to explore your favorite spots.

In spring and early fall, the **Museum of the City of New York,** Fifth Ave. and 103rd St. (534-1672), sponsors popular walking tours ($15) every other Sunday, starting at

1pm and lasting for a leisurely two or three hours. Areas surveyed include Chelsea, the Lower East Side, and Greenwich Village, with foci on the history and architecture of the particular district. Sign up a few days beforehand.

The **Municipal Art Society,** at the Urban Center, 457 Madison Ave. (935-3960) near 50th St., leads $10-15 guided walking tours and bus tours ($20-25); destinations change with the seasons. Their free tour of Grand Central Station meets every Wednesday at 12:30pm, in front of the Chemical Commuter Bank. Call in advance with an idea of where you'd like to go, or ask for a schedule of their tentatively-planned future tours.

Some knowledgeable New Yorkers are willing to share their love for the city with you. **Lou Singer Tours** (718-875-9084), now in their 23rd year, are still led by the colorful Mr. Singer, who regales his audience with zesty little nuggets while driving from place to place. The six-hour Manhattan Noshing Tour ($25, plus $17 food charge) is a multi-ethnic food sampling extravaganza, with 12 food stops peppered with Lou's intriguing commentaries on the history and architecture of the Lower East Side. Also offered is a tour of Brooklyn Brownstones ($25, plus $2 admission charges), including a jaunt through a historic house and a visit to a church with Tiffany windows. Advance reservations are required. The bus departs from 325 E. 41st St., between First and Second.

The friendly and knowledgdable John Wilson, a Yalie and a New Yorker for over 35 years, runs **City Walks** (989-2456). His walking tours of Manhattan cost $12, and usually last two hours, although he'll arrange for private trips. Specializing in Lower Manhattan and Harlem, Mr. Wilson's excursions focus on history and architecture. Unlike most guides, he gives tours during the week as well as on weekends. **Adventure on a Shoestring**, 300 W. 53rd St. (265-2663), runs walking tours of the Chinatown area, Greenwich Village, and the SoHo art swamp, among others. Their 90-minute tours try to incorporate chats with members of the various communities ($5). Some of their excursions—like touring backstage at the Met, or chatting with those who claim to have had out-of-body experiences—are open only to members ($3 per event; membership $40 per year).

For something even more offbeat, **Sidewalks of New York** (517-0201) offers anecdotal and amusing walking tours with titles like "Death Scenes of the Rich and Famous," and "All in the Family," a survey of popular Mafia hangouts. All tours cost $10 and last two hours. No reservations required: phone 517-0201 for a recorded message which will inform you of the next few forays.

The fact-oriented can enjoy a mass of more specialized tours. Imperial **Lincoln Center** sponsors guided tours of its theaters: The Metropolitan Opera House, New York State Theater, and Avery Fisher Hall. There are four to eight tours every day, from 10am to 5pm, and they last about an hour ($7.50, students $6.50, children $4.25). For information, and to make a reservation, call 875-5350. In addition, a free tour every Wednesday at 2pm instructs the curious in the art of locating items in the library's mammoth gathering of musical soundtracks and movie scores. The tour passes through the center's three art galleries. (For information, call 870-1670.)

Historic **Carnegie Hall,** at 57th St. and Seventh Ave., opens its doors to tourists Tuesdays and Thursdays at 11:30am, 2pm, and 3pm. Tours cost $6, seniors and students $5, children $3. (For information, call 247-7800.) A true shrine to an era long past, **Radio City Music Hall,** 50th St. and Sixth Ave. (632-4041), gives behind-the-scenes tours every day on nearly every hour for a mere $7.

Check out the still-wacky antics of Dave et. al. on the **NBC Studio Tour** (Mon.-Sun. 9:30am-4:30pm; admission $7.35). Tickets are sold on the Concourse Level of the RCA Building, 30 Rockefeller Plaza, and go on a first-come first-serve basis.

The **Petrel** (825-1976), a 70-foot pecan mahogany yacht, will take 40 passengers around New York Harbor, visiting Governor's Island, Ellis Island, the Brooklyn Bridge, or the Verrazano Narrows Bridge—depending upon Mother Nature's whims. There are four trips per day at noon, 1pm, 5:30pm, and 7:30pm. Sails range from 45 minutes to two hours, and cost $8-20 per person. The **Seaport Line** (233-4800) conducts 90-minute narrated sightseeing cruises of New York's essentials for $12, children $6. Even the vessel has a sense of history—it's a copy of Twain's Mississippi steamboat. In the summertime, boats leave from 11am to 5pm, on the hour. Twilight cocktail and jazz cruises run every Thursday at 7pm and 9:30pm. Purchase tickets directly at the Pier 16 Ticket Booth on the South Street Seaport.

A visit to the world's financial capital wouldn't be complete without a trip to the **New York Stock Exchange** (656-5167), on 20 Broad St. The tour of the building, including the zoo-like main trading floor, is free, but tickets are required. (Open Mon.-Fri. 9:15am-4pm.) Housing 1/4 of the world's gold reserves in facilities sinking five stories below street level, the immense **Federal Reserve Bank** (720-6130), 33 Liberty St., conducts hour-long free tours of the premises from Monday to Friday at 10:30am, 11:30am, 1:30pm, and 2:30pm. A minimum of one week's prior notification is required.

Circle Line Tours (563-3200) circumnavigates Manhattan island in a 3-hr. tour. A 3-hr. tour. Twelve cruises run daily 9:30am-4:15pm, but call for sailing times. Boats leave from Pier 83 at the Circle Line Plaza at W. 42nd St. and Twelfth Ave. (Tickets $16, seniors $15, under 12 $8.) From May 26 to September 2, the Circle Line conducts romantic "harbor lights" tours around Manhattan in the brassy light of sunset. You'll hear the sirens singing if you're not careful. Same rates as daily tour. Light snacks and cocktails served. Open March 8-Dec. 28.

Gray Line Sight-Seeing, 900 Eighth Ave. (397-2600) between 53rd and 54th St., or 166 W. 46th St. (354-5122) near Seventh Ave. Huge bus tour company offering 20 different trips, including jaunts through Manhattan and gambling junkets to Atlantic City. The tour of the lower half of Manhattan ($16.50) runs about 2 1/2 hr., and visits Times Square, Herald and Madison Squares, Greenwich Village, the World Trade Center, the U.N., Park Avenue, and Rockefeller Center. Other good bets include a 2-hr. trip through Harlem ($16.50), and the grand NYC-immersion tour ($26; 5hr). The launder-your-money voyage to Atlantic City costs $24.50. Reservations aren't required, but arrive at the terminal 1/2 hr. in advance.

Joyce Gold's Tours, 141 W. 17th St. (242-5762). The devoted Ms. Gold has read over 900 books on Manhattan, the subject she teaches at NYU and at the New School. Forty Sundays per year she and a company of intrepid adventurers set out on tours focusing on architecture, history, and the movements of ethnic groups within the city. Tours last 2-4 hr., depending on the subject, and cost $10.

Harlem Spirituals, Inc., 1697 Broadway (757-04254), at 53rd St. Offered are tours of upper Manhattan (in English, French, German, Spanish, and Italian) including the "Spirituals and Gospel" tour, highlighted by trips to historic homes and participation in a Baptist service ($28 for 4 hr., leaves Wed. at 9am). The "Soul Food and Jazz" tour ($65) runs from 7pm to midnight and features a filling meal at a Harlem restaurant. Call 24 hr. in advance for reservations.

Harlem Renaissance Tours (722-9534). The 4-hr. "Sunday Gospel Tour" features the history of Harlem, and involves one hour at a gospel church service and lunch or brunch at a local restaurant ($35). Call to make reservations.

The Empire State Building

> New York impressed me tremendously because,
> more than any other city in the world, it is the fullest
> expression of our modern age.
>
> —Leon Trotsky

The Empire State Building (slurred together by any self-respecting New Yorker into "Empire Statebuilding") has style. It retains its place in the hearts and minds of New Yorkers even though it is no longer the tallest building in the U.S. (an honor now held by Chicago's Sears Tower), or even the tallest building in New York (now the upstart twin towers of the World Trade Center). It doesn't have the best looks (the Chrysler building is more delicate, the Woolworth more ornate). But the Empire State remains New York's best-known and best-loved landmark and dominates the postcards, the movies, and the skyline.

The limestone and granite structure, with glistening mullions of stainless steel, stretches 1454 feet into the sky; its 73 elevators run on two miles of shafts. High winds can bend the entire structure up to a quarter-inch off center. The Empire State was among the first of the truly spectacular skyscrapers, benefiting from innovations like Eiffel's pioneering work with steel frames and Otis's perfection of the "safety elevator." In Midtown it towers in relative solitude, away from the forest of monoliths that has grown around Wall St. At festive times of year, the upper 30 floors light up in appropriate colors—from passion red for Valentine's Day to kelly green for St. Patrick's Day.

The Empire State was built on the site of two famous 19th-century mansions belonging to the prominent Astor clan. In the 1880s, William Waldorf Astor tore down one of the mansions to build the Waldorf Hotel, and in 1897, his cousin John Jacob demolished the other, building the Astoria Hotel. These hotels operated here until 1929, when they consolidated and moved uptown to make way for the Empire State Building.

The sleek grey building, with graceful setbacks and light art deco ornamentation, seems appropriate for the city—tall, not too garish, but so empirically impressive. The formula, though, came about more by chance timing than from one man's vision. In 1929, the Art Deco style was in vogue and zoning ordinances required setbacks on tall buildings; had it been built a few years later, with the International Style and a different set of zoning laws in full swing, the Empire State might have been just another dull box building.

The Empire State has always been in the limelight. It starred in the film classic *King Kong,* along with the jumbo-sized ape and his ravishing hostage. Its height brought involvement in several tragedies, beginning in 1933 with a rash of suicides. Twelve years later, a disoriented but earnest Army pilot crashed his B-25 into the 79th floor. A plaque on the observation deck commemorates his mishap.

The building is located on Fifth Ave. between 33rd and 34th St. (736-3100). It's within walking distance of Penn and Grand Central stations. The nearest subway stations are the B, D, F, N, Q, R at 34th St., the #6 at 33rd St., and the R at 28th St.

When you enter the building, check out the lobby, a shrine of art-deco interior decoration right down to the mail drops and the elevator doors. Don't miss the singularly tacky series of 1963 illustrations depicting the Seven Wonders of the Ancient World (plus you-know-which New York skyscraper), done in "textured light." Take the escalator down to the Concourse Level, where you can purchase tickets to the observatory. A sign here indicates the visibility level. On a day with perfect visibility you will be able to see 80 miles in any direction, but even on a day with a visibility of only five miles you'll still spot the Statue of Liberty. The nighttime view will leave you gasping. ($3.50, children and seniors $1.75.; observatory open daily 9:30am-midnight.)

If lines get long, you can also purchase observatory tickets at the **Guinness World's Records Exhibit Hall, Inc.,** (947-2335), located on the Concourse Level, but they must be bought in conjunction with exhibition tickets (see Museums).

Once on the main observatory, 1050 feet above Gotham, you can venture onto the windswept outdoor walkways, or opt to stay in the temperature-controlled interior. Whip out your map and get your bearings straight; you are pretty much in the center of the Manhattan street grid. Quiver at the gorgeous view to the north, which gives a feel for the monumental scale of Central Park.

East Midtown

The massive Beaux-Arts **Grand Central Terminal,** 42nd to 45th St. between Vanderbilt Pl. and Madison Ave., served as the gateway to New York for millions of travelers during the early 20th century. Fewer trains roll into and out of its depots today; nonetheless, it remains a starkly powerful symbol. It is an ideal place to begin a tour of East Midtown. Near the Vanderbilt entrance, you can see the famous 13-foot-wide clock mounted on the southern façade, surrounded by a statuary group designed by Jules Alexis Coutan. At the center stands winged Mercury, symbolic of the glory of

Midtown

Lincoln Center

W. 62nd St.

W. 61st St.

CENTRAL PARK

W. 60th St.

W. 59th St.

Central Park S.

W. 58th St.

COLUMBUS CIRCLE

W. 57th St.

W. 56th St.

Carnegie Hall

W. 55th St.

Eleventh Ave.

Tenth Ave.

W. 54th St.

Eighth Ave.

Seventh Ave.

W. 53rd St.

M
Mo

W. 52nd St.

C
Build

W. 51st St.

W. 50th St.

W. 49th St.

W. 48th St.

W. 47th St.

THEATER DISTRICT

W. 46th St.

W. 45th St.

W. 44th St.

DUFFY SQUARE

W. 43rd St.

W. 42nd St.

TIMES SQUARE

Port Authority Bus Terminal

W. 41st St.

W. 40th St.

Broadway

Lincoln Tunnel

Dyer Ave.

W. 39th St.

W. 38th St.

Eighth Ave.

Seventh Ave.

W. 37th St.

Javits Convention Center

W. 36th St.

W. 35th St.

Macy's

W. 34th St.

Eleventh Ave.

Tenth Ave.

W. 33rd St.

Ninth Ave.

General Post Office

Madison Square Garden

Penn Station

W. 32nd St.

W. 31st St.

W. 30th St.

GARMENT DISTRICT

E. 62nd St.

E. 61st St.

E. 60th St.

E. 59th St.

Bloomingdale's

Queensboro Br.

Grand Army Plaza

FAO Schwartz

Plaza Hotel

IBM Building

E. 58th St.

Trump Tower

E. 57th St.

Fifth Ave.

Madison Ave.

AT&T

E. 56th St.

E. 55th St.

Sutton Pl.

St. Thomas

Museum of Broadcasting

E. 54th St.

Citicorp Center

Second Ave.

First Ave.

m of Art

E. 53rd St.

Lever House

St. Peter's

E. 52nd St.

Seagram Building

E. 51st St.

Radio City Music Hall

St. Patrick's Cathedral

St. Bartholomew's

Third Ave.

E. 50th St.

Rockefeller Center

Saks

Waldorf Astoria

E. 49th St.

Lexington Ave.

E. 48th St.

E. 47th St.

DIAMOND ROW

(Sixth Ave.)

Vanderbilt Ave.

E. 46th St.

E. 45th St.

First Ave.

Pan Am Building

E. 44th St.

Chrysler Building

E. 43rd St.

(VEHICULAR TUNNEL BELOW STREET)

Grand Central Terminal

E. 42nd St.

Ford Foundation

United Nations

BRYANT PARK

New York Public Library

Chanin Building

E. 41st St.

Daily News Building

Madison Ave.

E. 40th St.

American Standard Building

E. 39th St.

Queens-Midtown Tunnel

Fifth Ave.

E. 38th St.

(VEHICULAR TUNNEL BELOW STREET)

Park Ave.

MURRAY HILL

E. 37th St.

Pierpoint Morgan Library

E. 36th St.

Empire State Building

E. 35th St.

Lexington Ave.

FDR Dr.

E. 34th St.

ERALD QUARE

E. 33rd St.

E. 32nd St.

0   1/4 mile

E. 31st St.

0   250 meters

E. 30th St.

N

commerce. To his right crouches Hercules (moral energy) and at his left, Minerva (mental energy). Down the steps, the Main Concourse—100 feet wide, 470 feet long, 150 feet high—covers more ground than the nave of Notre Dame de Paris. Constellations are depicted on the sweeping arced expanse of great green roof, while egg-shaped ribbed chandeliers light the secondary apses to the sides. This is an excellent spot for people-watching, as two-legged specimens of all descriptions hobble, stride, meander, and dash across the marble floor, but keep your eyes peeled for the bag-snatchers and pick-pockets who roam the halls.

Grand Central's construction was so monumental a project that two architectural firms ultimately collaborated on it. Railroad engineer William Wilgus first proposed in 1903 that a new terminal be built, envisioning it as a 16- to 30-story building. Out of the four firms who submitted designs (including powerful McKim, Mead, and White), Reed and Stem won. They were responsible for the ingenious separation of car, pedestrian, subway, and train traffic around the building, and the intricate series of elevated ramps connecting various levels within the complex. They didn't make the terminal as tall as originally planned; the reduced height adds to the feel of solidity and bulk. Later, the prominent Beaux-Arts firm of Warren and Wetmore was called in to give the place an extra touch of class; Whitney Warren designed much of the sumptuous exterior façade. The Municipal Art Society leads popular (and free) guided tours of the terminal every Wednesday at 12:30pm, starting next to the Chemical Commuter Bank in the Main Concourse.

Connected to Grand Central Terminal from within, the **Pan Am Building** stands on Park Ave., between 44th and 45th. Opinions vary on this 59-story monolith, which vaguely resembles an airplane wing section: some view it as a blight on the Park Ave. skyline (it blocks the view of everything behind it) and an abysmal low of high modernism unworthy of its co-designer Walter Gropius; others see it as an aging master's monument to turbulent modernity. The largest commercial office building ever built, it contains 2.4 million square feet of corporate cubicles. Deep inside the lobby, right above the escalators, hangs an immense Josef Albers mural. In the building's other lobby, at E. 44th and Vanderbilt, an intriguing wire and light sculpture encloses what appears to be an energized atom.

The bold columns and arches of the **Bowery Savings Bank,** at 110 E. 42nd St. between Park and Lexington, suggest that banking in New York City has become a liturgical ritual. Multiple pilasters engraved with intertwining patterns rise to form a majestic 3-story entrance arch, rosaries cover the air vents, and inlaid marble squares accent the vertical lines of the upper section. Inside, limestone and sandstone walls frame a high Romanesque banking chamber with a floor of fine French and Italian marble. This room has been intact for almost 70 years, and seems like a safe place to store your dollars in New York.

The gentle **Chanin Building** hovers right next door at 122 E. 42nd St. The 56-story skyscraper rises in a series of setbacks culminating in a tower, in accordance with the 1916 building code. The upper four stories of the tower are accented with buttresses. At the entrance, notice the flowery third-floor frieze depicting an orgy of curling botanical and fierce zoological life forms. Inside, the lobby glitters in art-deco gold, highlighted by stalactite chandeliers.

The New York skyline would be incomplete without the familiar art-deco headdress of the **Chrysler Building,** at 42nd and Lexington, built by William Van Allen as a series of rectangular boxes and topped by a spire modeled after a radiator grille. Other details evoke the romance of the automobile in the Golden Age of the Chrysler Automobile Company: a frieze of idealized cars in white and grey brick on the 26th floor; flared gargoyles at the fourth setback styled after 1929 hood ornaments and hubcaps; and stylized lightning bolt designs symbolizing the energy of the new machine. During construction, the Chrysler building engaged in a race with the Bank of Manhattan building for title of the world's highest structure. Work on the latter was stopped when it seemed as if the Bank had won. The devious machinists then brought out and strapped on the spire which had been secretly assembled inside. And so, when completed in 1929, this elegantly seductive building stood as the world's tallest. The Empire State topped it a year later.

Forty-Second St. also delivers the **Daily News Building,** the 1930 work of Raymond Hood with a little help from Howell. Above the entrance, an industrial-strength frieze tells the building's story. Inside, an immense globe rotates at the center, enveloped by a black-glass dome representing the night sky. A brass analog clock keeps time for 17 major cities world-wide, and frequent exhibitions breeze in and out of here. Home to the country's first successful tabloid, the building was innovative in its treatment of height: instead of the typical elevation in three stages corresponding to the base, shaft, and capital of a classical column, it rises in a series of monolithic slabs that lend it a sense of boundless verticality. In 1990, the paper became entangled in a bitter and drawn-out battle with its union workers that threatened to shut the presses down permanently. Now-dead multimedia mogul Robert Maxwell purchased the rag in March 1991 and took care of the labor dispute.

Farther east at 320 E. 43rd St., between First and Second Ave., lies the **Ford Foundation Building.** Glass and rust-colored steel enclose a 12-story garden atrium dense with vegetation. Most of the office windows face into the greenery—a welcome respite from the surrounding concrete.

For some outdoor vegetation, stroll in **Tudor Park,** between 42nd and 43rd St. on Tudor Pl. Small and charming, it sports benches, toylike gravel paths, and outsized oaks congregating in a refreshingly uncluttered silence. (Open daily 7am-midnight.)

Symbolic capital of the political world and flanked by the flags of its member nations, the **United Nations** (963-7713) overlooks the East River between 42nd and 48th St. Designed in the early 50s by an international committee including Le Corbusier, Oscar Niemeyer, and Wallace Harrison (whose ideas won out in the end), the complex itself makes a diplomatic statement—part bravura, part compromise. You can take a one-hour guided tour of the **General Assembly** and the **Security Council,** which starts in the main lobby of the GA every half-hour from 9:15am to 4:45pm. (Open daily 9am-6pm. Admission $5.50, students and children $3.50. Visitor's Entrance at First Ave. and 46th.) Visitors must take a tour to get past the lobby. From September through December, free tickets to GA meetings can be obtained in the main lobby about half an hour before sessions, which usually begin at 10:30am and 3pm Monday through Friday.

The U.N.'s other attractions include stained glass windows by Chagall in the lobby and a teeny park set in a sculpture garden by the East River. You can enjoy the delightful promenade above the riverbank. Or just relish the musclebound Socialist Realist statue showing a man beating a sword into a plowshare. The buff guy was a gift of the old USSR, which sent it to the U.N. in 1959.

The **Japan Society** is housed in **Japan House**, the first building of contemporary Japanese design in New York City, located at 333 E. 47th St. (832-1155), off First Ave. Designed by Junzo Yoshimura and completed in 1971, it serves as the headquarters of Japan Society, Inc., an association dedicated to bringing the people of Japan and America closer together. In the spirit of a traditional Japanese home, there is an interior pool garden on the first floor, complete with stones and bamboo trees. The second floor houses a sand garden and a gallery featuring three exhibitions per year of traditional and contemporary Japanese art. (Open Mon.-Fri. 9:30am-5:30pm, and on some weekends. Call for current information.)

The **General Electric Building,** at 570 Lexington Ave., was originally the headquarters of RCA. Designed by Cross and Cross, it was completed in 1931; General Electric moved in a year later when RCA shifted to the Rockefeller Center. Some RCA executives moved back in when, in 1986, GE swallowed the Radio Corporation of America. The famous orange-and-buff eight-sided brick tower is alive with bolts and flashes that crackle off the surface—an allegorical reference to the power of radio. G.E. keeps tight security (perhaps to prevent David Letterman and his camera crew from bothering their "pinhead" bosses at G.E.), but the elegantly designed art-deco lobby and elevators are worth a quick peek.

Right next door, on Park Ave. between 50th and 51st St., stands the Byzantine **St. Bartholomew's Church** (751-1616), whose design reflects the influences of medieval European ecclesiastical architecture. Designed by Bertram Goodhue and completed in 1919, the church incorporates a mottled Romanesque porch salvaged from a previous McKim, Mead, and White church. Inside, a large mosaic of the resurrection glitters with golden halos while less subtle paper flames dangle from the quilt-like dome. Pick up a copy of the comprehensive leaflet *St. Bartholomew's Church and Chapel Tour*. The church often hosts classical music concerts at 8pm. (Tickets around $10.)

The **Waldorf-Astoria Hotel,** at 301 Park Ave. between 49th and 50th, has an incomparable register: the Duchess of Windsor, King Faisal of Saudi Arabia, and the late Emperor Hirohito of Japan all stayed here. Every U.S. President since Hoover has spent a night or two at the hotel when away from the White House. Yet, any courteous mortal can tread the red carpet into the sumptuous main lobby. The Waldorf-Astoria clock, displayed at the 1893 World's Fair, is over nine feet tall and weighs a good two tons. The likenesses of Benjamin Franklin, six U.S. Presidents, and Queen Victoria stare back at you from different angles.

At the request of publisher Henry Villard, the tireless trio of McKim, Mead and White designed the six **Villard Houses,** clustered at 451-455 Madison Ave., between 50th and 51st. These powerful, graceful brownstones, completed in 1884, were roughly modeled in the neo-Italian Renaissance tradition after the Palazzo della Cancellaria in Rome. Their subsequent owner, the archdiocese of New York, sold them to Harry Helmsley, who proceeded to incorporate them into his **Helmsley Palace Hotel.** Leona and Harry restored the interiors to their turn-of-the-century rococo opulence, with chandeliers raining crystal, but the hotel's maudlin glass box now towers gracelessly over the mansions. Approach from Madison Ave. to gain the full effect of the tiny white lights strung all over the courtyard.

St. Patrick's Cathedral (753-2261), New York's most famous church and the largest Catholic cathedral in America, stands at 51st St. and Fifth Ave. Construction began on the Gothic Revival structure in 1858, and took 21 years to complete. Designed by James Renwick, the structure captures the essence of great European cathedrals like Reims and Cologne, yet retains its own spirit. The twin spires on the Fifth Ave. façade, captured in countless photos and postcards, streak 330 feet into the air. Artisans in Chartres and Nantes created most of St. Patrick's stained-glass windows, under which the controversial Cardinal O'Connor communes with God. The effect of both windows and O'Connor is unfortunately disrupted by the mid-day crush of summertime tourists. The shrine of the first male U.S. saint, St. John Neumann, rests in the north aisle. Today high society intermarries at the cathedral.

Back on 375 Park Ave., between 52nd and 53rd, is Mies Van der Rohe's innovative masterpiece: the dark and gracious **Seagram Building.** Completed in 1958, it remains the paragon of the International Style. Van der Rohe envisioned it as an oasis from the tight canyon of skyscrapers down Park Ave.: he set the tower back 90 feet from the plaza and put two great fountains in the foreground. The public approved; in 1961 the city altered its building code to encourage the further construction of tall box buildings with plazas; unfortunately this incentive resulted in a slew of trashy imitations. Off the main lobby, the lavish **Four Seasons** restaurant, designed by Philip Johnson, co-architect of the building, is in stark contrast to the austere Seagram exterior.

Across the street is a mediocre McKim, Mead and White construction, the **New York Racquet and Tennis Club.** Completed in 1918, 12 years after Stanford White's death, it lacks his soft touch and comes off looking like a warehouse. Yet this chunk serves as an important foil to the Seagram Building across the street, constituting the psychological western wall of the vast plaza and anchoring it down securely.

Lever House, at 390 Park Ave. between 53rd and 54th, may look like just another jolly glass giant, but the people at the Landmarks Office will tell you otherwise. Along with the Seagram Building down the street, this sleek building redefined the look and shape of the city. During the building's planning stages in the 50s, Park Avenue was lined by apartment blocks. Lever House changed it all by setting down two slabs of stainless steel and blue-green glass, one horizontally, the other poised vertically above it. Raised off the ground on columns, the building supports a rooftop garden.

As one of the big detergent makers in the United States, Lever Brothers Inc. wanted their headquarters to project an image of cleanliness. As a result, the building included unprecedented design features, including sealed windows and glass spandrels that made the exterior appear to be one continuous sheet of glass. Beside the aesthetic appeal of a sleek and uncluttered façade, it allows window-washing crews to sponge the outside of the building continuously and quickly, without obstructions from masonry. Just two men keep the glass of this 24-story building spic 'n span. In the ground floor lobby, you'll find year-round bright-white displays of company products and community art.

The interior of **Saint Peter's Church,** 619 Lexington Ave. (935-2200) at 53rd St., reflects the modern collapse of the boundaries between art and faith: along with its religious functions, the church serves as a movie theatre, art gallery, concert hall, dramatic stage, and public information forum. St. Peter's performs the social functions that great medieval churches once did, but it strives for a contemporary urban spirit and spirituality. Architecturally, it blends with its surroundings. The aerodynamic interior design does away with gratuitous ornamentation. Blondedwood furniture and enormous white walls complete the streamlined Bauhaus effect. In the central hall, artist Arnaldo Pomodore has rendered a crucifix in rich, rust-colored bronze. He incorporates a central, wedge-shaped "nail" into the otherwise homogeneous polished surface, making the rarified violence of the crucifixion palpable.

A Gothic church had stood on this site since 1905; by the late 60s, attendance had dwindled and the church faced extinction. Then corporate America stepped in. St. Peter's sold the land and air rights to Citibank, who in turn agreed to build a new church on the site, distinct from their headquarters rising above. The shiny, slanted **Citicorp Center** stands on four 10-story stilts in order to accommodate St. Peter's. The entire structure is sheathed in reflective greyish aluminum; at sunrise and sunset, the entire building radiates warmly. The 45-degree angled roof was originally intended for use as a solar collector. But this plan has not come to light. Instead the roof supports an intriguing gadget, the so-called TMD, or Tuned Mass Damper, which senses and records the tremors of the earth and warns of earthquakes.

Leave modernity behind and head north for the Central Synagogue, built in 1872 by Henry Fernbachn and located at 652 Lexington Ave. off 55th St. The Moor-revivalist architecture incorporates onion domes and intricate trim in the brownstone exterior, concealing an exquisite interior replete with stained-glass windows. It is the oldest continuously operating synagogue in the city.

The stylish **Madison Lexington Venture Building,** 135 E. 57th St., a little over five years old, has already garnered quite enough awards. The 32-story office complex, designed by the New York firm of Kohn, Pedersen and Fox, bears the bronzed initials of Holland's NMB Bank. The front of the main building posed at the corner of 57th and Lexington curves inward, creating an arc around four pairs of green Italian marble columns, arranged in a Stonehenge circle. Just add water from a sparkling fountain, gold trimmings on the green marble siding, and a first-floor arcade of art galleries and antique shops, and you get the building that makes New York architecture critics squirm with foam-flecked joy. Downstairs on the gallery row christened the **Place des Antiquaires,** 125 E. 57th St., you can browse through 45 separate antique shops designed to simulate a French château.

Back on Park Ave. and 56th St., the cramped-looking **Mercedes-Benz Showroom,** designed by Frank Lloyd Wright, showcases pricey prestige-cows. Philip Johnson's postmodern **AT&T Building** stands farther west, on Madison Ave. between 55th and 56th St. Although works by Johnson have been highly acclaimed in the past, most connoisseurs of Manhattan architecture agree that this black-striped building, its pinkish marble resembling a feta cheese spread, doesn't quite succeed. The cross-vaulted arcade underneath (open Mon.-Fri. 8am-6pm) features open cafés, the **AT&T Infoquest Center** (605-5555; see Museums), and the ritzy-ditzy four-star **Quilted Giraffe**, where tabs can sky-rocket up to $150 per person, even if you're not eating an endangered species. One block uptown, fellow blue-chipper IBM sits in the green granite **IBM Building** at 590 Madison Ave. between 56th and 57th St. It features a fine atrium with comfortable chairs and a dense bamboo jungle for the panda in you. The **IBM Gallery of Science and Art** is also here (see Museums).

Walking back to Fifth Ave. at 56th St., the garish yellow lettering on the bold face of **Trump Tower** spells fiscal abandon. A ludicrous five-story waterfall-on-a-wall washes down the atrium. There are enough fashion boutiques here to satisfy even the most depraved world leader. Trump Tower does, however, feature some of the city's finest public restroom facilities, located on the Concourse Level.

The **Fuller Building,** next to IBM on Madison Ave. between 57th and 58th St., displays the dark, brooding side of deco. Designed by Walker and Gilette and completed in 1929, it was one of the first office buildings to be situated so far north in Manhattan. It served as the headquarters of America's leading construction firm during the Great Depression. The slender tower reinterprets classical forms, with bold geometric patterns at the setbacks supplanting the traditional cornices.

Even a fanatical architect will feel like a kid again in **F.A.O. Schwarz,** 767 Fifth Ave. (644-9400) at 58th St., the Godzilla of toy stores. Six-foot-high dolls ($2000) of your favorite nursery heroes greet you at the entrance, and uniformed salespeople demonstrate the latest in videogames and multicolored ooze inside. Check out the gold Monopoly game (one million real dollars). Pretend you're Tom Hanks and dance on the Big keyboard. (Open Mon.-Wed. and Fri.-Sat. 10am-6pm, Thurs. 10am-8pm, Sun. noon-6pm.)

West Midtown

Pennsylvania Station crouches sadly at the bottom of West Midtown. The original Penn Station, a classical marble building modeled on the Roman Baths of Caracalla, was gratuitously demolished in the 60s. The railway tracks were depressed, and covered by the dreadfully depressing **Madison Square Garden** complex. The venue hosts a fine array of top entertainment, yet it is an architectural carbuncle, surrounded by bands of roving hustlers. Facing the Garden at 421 Eighth Ave., the immense main Post Office, or **James A. Farley Building,** luxuriates in its primary 10001 zip code. Completed in 1913, it mirrored the neoclassical magnificence of Penn Station across the street until the station's destruction. A lengthy swath of Corinthian columns shoulders broadly across the front, and a 280-foot frieze on top of the broad portico bears the bold motto of the U.S. Post Office: "Neither snow nor rain nor heat nor gloom of night stays these couriers from the swift completion of their appointed rounds."

Up Eighth Ave. the neighborhood gets more colorful (many would say seedier). On 41st St. shifting bands of homeless and more hustlers loiter outside the multistoried **Port Authority Bus Terminal,** departure point for a volley of buses. Despite the high profile police presence, this area can be dangerous, especially at night; stay on the major thoroughfares and try not to look like a tourist.

Head east to reach Seventh Ave. and the **Garment District.** Dodge the moving clothes racks and bins packed with striped and dotted polyester. Take a peek at the Garment Center Synagogue, 205 W. 40th St. Further along at 40 W. 40th St. stands the **American Standard Building,** a 21-story structure built in 1923. Raymond Hood's black brick building decorated with gold-colored stone combines Gothic detailing with art deco lines to form a stylized representation of the Tribune design. (Hood had, coincidentally, just won the commission to build the Chicago Tribune building). American Radiator, a heating equipment manufacturer, first owned this building, which retains an uncanny resemblance to a glowing coal lump when lit up at night. It now lies locked away, abandoned. Across the street, **Bryant Park** was the site of the World's Fair in 1853. The park has just undergone renovations, and on sundry afternoons people of all descriptions crowd into the large grassy tree-rimmed expanse to listen to free lunchtime jazz concerts. (Open daily 7am-8pm.)

The park shares the block with the **New York Public Library,** which reposes on the West side of Fifth Ave., between 40th and 42nd St. On sunny afternoons, throngs of people perch on the marble steps, which are dutifully guarded by the mighty lions Patience and Fortitude. The Grecian urns, sculptural groups, and fountains (the one on the right represents Truth, the other Beauty) anticipate the even more resplendent ornamentation inside. Belying the classical elements of the exterior façade, the ceilings in the main hall are flat, not domed. Because only two elevators serve the entire building, wide marble stairways run through all levels of the library. Specific areas or rooms have been named after the library's benefactors: Astor Hall wears garlands and rosettes; Gottesman Hall behind it flaunts a marvelous carved oak ceiling from the 16th century, complete with Renaissance iconography. The murals designed by Edward Lanning on the third floor were executed as a part of a WPA project. The library's art collection, kept in the Edna B. Salomon room, showcases the work of Gilbert Stuart, Sir Joshua Reynolds, and Rembrandt Peale. This is also the world's seventh largest research library; the third floor reading room is immense.

Carrère and Hastings erected the building in 1911 with the resources of two privately funded libraries—John Jacob Astor's general reference library (the first in the New World) and James Lenox's collection of literature, history, and theology. Samuel J. Tilden added a generous two million dollar bequest, Andrew Carnegie an even more generous $5.2 million donation for the establishment of the Public Library's 80 citywide branches. Free tours of the library take place Tuesday through Saturday, at 11am and 2pm, starting from the Friends Desk in Astor Hall. For information call 661-7220 (Open Tues.-Wed. 11am-7:30pm, Thurs.-Sat. 10am-6pm). Note that this library, devoted entirely to research, doesn't lend a thing. If you wish to borrow a book or just read away from the intimidating shadow of leonine virtue, you're better off across the street at the mid-Manhattan branch. (See Libraries under Practical Information.)

In the 20s, the **Algonquin Hotel,** on 44th St. between Fifth and Sixth Ave., hosted Alexander Woollcott's "Round Table," a regular gathering of the brightest luminaries of the theatrical and literary world. The Hotel's major attraction was proximity to the offices of the *New Yorker.* The Oak Room still serves tea every afternoon, but now exclusively to Algonquin guests (and their guests), regardless of the arts circles they inhabit. Inside the hotel, at the Blue Bar, James Thurber drawings adorn the walls deliciously.

Swing back down westward, and you'll soon find yourself in the flickering streets of soon-to-be renovated **Times Square,** at the intersection of 42nd St. and Broadway. If any place deserves to be called the dark and seedy core of the Big Apple, this is it. Big name Broadway stages and first-run movie houses compete with flashing neon, street performers, peep shows, and porn palaces. Marquees list lewd but nonsensical bills: "Penetrating/Buttwomen/Visualizer/Men Can Hump." Teens in search of fake IDs wait on street corners, while hustlers scrounge the streets for suckers. The area has a reputation for crime and physical decay, although much of the crime is "victimless." Women often find the area especially unnerving (approximately 85% of pedestrian traffic along 42nd St. is male), although the police presence is considerable. The carnival excitement here—the sense of bustle and chaos—is fairly unique, but also endangered. The entire area is presently undergoing a multi-year, $2.5 billion dollar demolition and reconstruction program, one of Ed Koch's parting gifts, the most ambitious of several attempts to "clean up" Times Square and settle an old puritanical business vendetta. The project hopes to build four new office buildings, open a hotel, restore a few historic theaters (including the Victory and the Apollo), and reconstruct and enlarge the Times Square subway station. The first member of the new generation, the ultra-modern **Marriott Marquis,** has replaced two historic but dilapidated Broadway stages. The new station, scheduled for completion in 1995, is slated to be equipped with a most unlikely rotunda and a computerized information center. A plethora of subway lines stop in Times Square (#1, 2, 3, 7, 9, or A, C, E, N, R, and S).

Just west of the Square, at 229 W. 43rd St., are the offices of the **New York Times,** founded in 1857, for which the square was named in 1904. Further west, on 42nd St. between Ninth and Tenth Ave., lies **Theater Row,** a block of renovated Broadway theaters. The adjacent **Theater District** stretches from 41st to 57th St. Some of the theaters have been converted into movie houses or simply left to rot as the cost of live productions has skyrocketed. Approximately 40 theaters remain active, most of them grouped around 45th St. (See Theater.) Between 44th and 45th, 1/2 block west of Broadway just in front of the Shubert Theater, lies **Shubert Alley,** a private street for pedestrians originally built as a fire exit between the Booth and Shubert Theaters. After shows, fans often hover at stage doors—generally labeled, several yards to the side of the main entrance—to get their playbills signed. Behind the scenes of every show are the playwrights, composers, and lyricists; protecting their interests is **The Dramatists Guild,** 234 W. 44th St., located in the former penthouse suite of J.J. Schubert. Members of the Guild include luminaries like Steven Sondheim, Peter Stone, and Mary Rodgers. "Producers, directors, agents, students, academicians and patrons of the arts" can all become subscribing members for $50 per year. Hardcore autograph hunters prey outside.

A few blocks uptown, at the helm of Restaurant Row (a strip of posh eateries catering to the free-spending pre-theater crowd) lies the graffiti-covered **Guardian Angels Headquarters,** off the corner of Eighth Ave. and W. 46th St. Wearing red berets rather than halos, these angels are self-declared vigilantes and martial artists who have taken city crime into their own hands. They carry no weapons, yet never hesitate to make a citizen's arrest. Angels are reknowned for their stamina; founder Curtis Sliwa managed to strike fear into his attackers even after being shot twice and thrown out of a taxi. If you fancy becoming an angel, write to Curtis or Lisa Sliwa, Guardian Angels, 982 E. 89th St., Brooklyn, NY 11236.

Between 48th and 51st St. and Fifth and Sixth Ave. stretches **Rockefeller Center,** a monument to the conjunction of business and art. Raymond Hood and his cohorts did an admirable job of glorifying business through architecture. On Fifth Ave., between 49th and 50th, the famous gold-leaf statue of Prometheus sprawls out on a ledge of the sunken **Tower Plaza** while jet streams of water pulse around it. The Plaza serves as an overpriced open-air café during the spring and summer and as an ice-skating rink in winter. Over 100 flags from the member nations of the U.N. flap in simultaneous obedience to the winds. Inside, hulking Social-realist proles heave, straining, on a heroic mural, mute and bulky testament to the glory of manual labor. The 70-story **RCA Building,** seated at Sixth Ave., remains the most accomplished artistic creation in this complex. Every chair in the building sits less than 28 feet from natural light. Nothing quite matches watching a sunset from the 65th floor as a coral burnish fills the room. The **NBC Television Network** makes its headquarters here, allowing you to take a behind-the-scenes look at their operations. The hour-long tour traces the history of NBC, from their first radio broadcast in 1926, through the heyday of tv programming in the 50s and 60s. The tour visits the studios of *Donahue, The Today Show, Late Night With David Letterman,* and even 8H, the hallowed halls of *Saturday Night Live.* Open daily 9:30am-4:30pm; admission $7.75, children under 6 not admitted; tours leave every 15 minutes, maximum 17 per group; tickets are first come, first served, so buy in advance.)

Despite possessing an illustrious history and a wealth of Art Deco treasures, **Radio City Music Hall** was almost demolished in 1979 to make way for new office high-rises. However, the public rallied and the music hall was declared a national landmark; it received a complete interior restoration (which, incredibly, took only a month to complete). Today, it thrives again as a multi-format entertainment venue. First opened in 1932, at the corner of Sixth Ave. and 51st St., the 5874-seat theater remains the largest in the world. The brainchild of Roxy Rothafel (originator of the Rockettes), it was originally intended as a variety showcase. A number of "gadgets" and architectural features especially adapted for its original function endure. Entering the Grand Foyer, note the 24-carat gold leaf ceiling and the huge mosaic carpet. In the theater auditorium, an immense proscenium arch formed by a series of increasingly larger arches gives, when lighted, a stylized representation of sunrise. The 144-foot wide stage is equipped with a revolving turntable comprised of three separate sections, each of which can be elevated or dropped 40 feet. The hydraulic stage elevator system was so sophisticated that during World War II, the U.S. Navy borrowed its design while developing aircraft carriers. Yet the hall functioned primarily as a movie theatre; over

650 feature films debuted here from 1933 to 1979. *King Kong, Breakfast at Tiffany's, To Kill a Mockingbird,* and *Doctor Zhivago* all came here first. The Rockettes, Radio City's chorus line, still dance on. The current dancers range in stature from 65 1/2 to 68 1/2 inches, but look of equal height on stage thanks to the marvels of perspective. People are blown away to this day by their complicated routines and eye-high kicks, a cut above the buck and wing shucksterism and little waist-high kicks of their competitors. Tours of the great hall are given Monday to Saturday, 10am-4:45pm and Sunday 11am-5pm ($7, children 6 and under $3.50). Call 632-4041 for more information.

At 51 W. 52nd St., the **CBS Building,** a skyscraper/black hole hybrid, maintains a cold but fervid watch over arch-enemy NBC. For greatest dramatic effect, view Eero Saarinen's smoke-colored granite tower from Sixth Ave. Down the block at 25 W. 52nd St. the newly relocated **Museum of Television and Radio** (621-6600), formerly the Museum of Broadcasting, just spent $50 million on its move and expansion. The new building, quadruple the size of its predecessor, broadcasts changing exhibits of artifacts and documents related to television and radio (see Museums).

St. Thomas's Church (757-7013), with its famously heavy lopsided left tower, anchors down the corner of Fifth Ave. and 53rd St. This Episcopal institution has occupied the site since 1911, and maintains among its treasures the statues of 50 saints, apostles, and missionaries on huge stone reredos reaching up to the overhead vaults. Try to spot St. Stephen, the first Christian martyr, St. Sebastian, the hopeless voluptuary, or Daniel Sylvester Tuttle, the presiding bishop in 1923. Guided tours are offered each Sunday following the 11am service. This church sits next to 666 Fifth Ave., a building with its numbers in big bright red neon facing the church. **Samuel Paley Plaza,** a pleasantly landscaped public space complete with waterfall, grants a reprieve from the noise of the city. The park nestles comfortably amongst tall buildings at 53rd and Fifth. Continue down W. 53rd St. towards Sixth Ave. and take in a handful of masterpieces in the windows of the **American Craft Museum** and the **Museum of Modern Art** (see Museums). Rest your tired dogs with a visit to the sculpture garden, featuring the works of Rodin, Renoir, Miro, Lipschitz, and Picasso.

The imposing **University Club,** on the northwest corner of Fifth Ave. and 54th St., is another turn-of-the-century McKim, Mead and White creation. This granite palace, with its lavish interior, was one of the first men's clubs that required its members to hold college degrees. Try to pick out the crests of over 20 prestigious universities carved above its windows. In June of 1987, the previously all-male club voted to admit women in accordance with a city ordinance (open to the great unwashed by appointment only; call 247-1000).

New York's most influential congregation, including the Walcotts, the Livingstons, and Theodore Roosevelt, once prayed in the pews of **Fifth Avenue Presbyterian Church,** built in 1875 by Carl Pfeiffer. The Gothic brownstone church was re-ordained at its present location on the corner of Fifth Ave. and 55th St. after making a pilgrimage from 19th St. At 130 W. 55th St., a former Muslim mosque was converted into the **City Center Theater** in 1943. Sickles and crescents still adorn each doorway; four tiny windows face Mecca from the limestone upper stories; and a Moorish dome caps the roof. Venture inside the lobby to see the elaborate tile mosaics surrounding the elevators.

For a view of an elaborate top, check out the **Crown Building,** located at the ultimate location—730 Fifth Ave. at 57th St. Designed by Warren and Wetmore in 1924, the upper façade has recently been overlaid with over 85 pounds of 23-carat gold leaf. At sunset, the reflected light results in a crown of fire.

On Fifth Ave. and 59th St., at the southeast corner of Central Park, sits the legendary **Plaza Hotel,** built in 1907 by Henry J. Hardenberg. Built at the then unprecedented cost of $12.5 million, its 18-story, 800-room French Renaissance interior flaunts five marble staircases, countless ludicrously named suites, and a two-story Grand Ballroom. Past guests and residents have included Frank Lloyd Wright, the Beatles, F. Scott Fitzgerald, and, of course, the eminent Eloise. When Donald Trump bought this national landmark in 1988, locals shuddered; so far, there has been little to fear. *Let's Go* recommends the $15,000-per-night suite. Double-billing as a forecourt to the Plaza Hotel and as an entrance to Central Park, the **Grand Army Plaza** absorbs the **Pulitzer Memorial Fountain** with Karl Bitter's statue of abundance, and an Augustus Saint-Gaudens gaudy gold equestrian statue of General Sherman.

How do you get to **Carnegie Hall**? Practice...lots of practice. This institution at 57th St. and Seventh Ave. was established in 1891, and remains New York's foremost sound stage, synonymous with musical success. During its illustrious existence, the likes of Tchaikovsky, Caruso, Toscanini, and Bernstein have played Carnegie; the Beatles and the Rolling Stones performed here within five months of each other in 1964. Other notable events from Carnegie's playlist include: the world premiere of Dvorak's Symphony No. 9 (*From the New World*) on 16 December 1893; Winston Churchill's landmark lecture *The Boer War as I Saw It* in 1901; ten-year-old Yehudi Menuhin's New York debut in 1927; and an energetic lecture by Albert Einstein in 1934. Apparently suffering from the same "Great Music Hall Syndrome" as Radio City, Carnegie Hall was in danger of being demolished in the 1950s and replaced by a large office building. Luckily, outraged citizens managed to stop the impending destruction through special state legislation in 1960. In 1985, in commemoration of the 25th anniversary of the rescue, a $50 million restoration and renovation program gave the worn façade a face-lift, enlarged the street-level lobby, and modernized the backstage.

Carnegie's exterior is done in a modified Italian Renaissance style, with reddish-brown Roman brick, belt courses, arches, pilasters, and terracotta decorations. The acoustics were pronounced "perfect" in 1890: the velvet-covered interior absorbed echoes, and boxes were laid out in sweeping curves instead of sharp lines to prevent sound from bouncing off at acute angles. During renovations, the stage ceiling, which had been damaged during the filming of "Carnegie Hall" in 1946, was finally repaired (it had always been left alone, covered with only some canvas and a curtain.) Legend says that it was this hole that gave Carnegie Hall its better-than-perfect acoustics; some critics contend that the Hall will never sound the same again. Tours are given Tuesdays and Thursdays at 11:30am, 2pm, and 3pm ($6, students $5).

Columbus Circle marks the end of West Midtown, the southwest corner of Central Park and the beginning of the Upper West Side. A smirking Christopher Columbus postures atop his pedestal, unmindful of the hubbub his anniversary celebration generated. The **Maine Monument** pays tribute to the seamen who died on the *USS Maine* in 1898 (the sinking of the ship sparked the Spanish-American War). The **New York Convention and Visitors Bureau,** at 2 Columbus Circle (397-8222; open Mon.-Fri. 9am-6pm, Sat.-Sun. 10am-6pm) assists tourists. Nearby is the **New York Coliseum,** built in 1954 by the Triborough Bridge and Tunnel Authority to serve as the city's convention center. Nowadays, the Jacob Javits Center has stolen the spotlight, leaving the Coliseum empty and its future uncertain. Its front has become an unofficial shelter for the homeless, protecting them from the winds whipping across the circle. The city periodically evicts these homeless people in order to clean up the area in preparation for special events, like the Democratic National Convention of 1992.

Hell's Kitchen is the name of the Midtown neighborhood that edges the Hudson, formerly a violent area inhabited by impoverished immigrants. Until the turn of the century, gangs, coppers, and pigs roamed its swarming streets. Now, the district's overcrowded tenements have been cleaned up and an artsier crowd has moved in. Ninth and Tenth Ave. are loaded with restaurants, delis, and pubs. The low-slung Gothic brownstone **Church of St. Paul the Apostle** sits placidly amidst the action at 415 W. 59th St., between Ninth and Tenth Ave. A high relief above a sky-blue mosaic offsets the cold blackness of the exterior, and dioramas of Christ's passion flank the interior. Services are given in both English and Spanish. (Entrance on Ninth Ave.)

Student protests over tuition hikes culminated in a two-week takeover of CUNY's **John Jay College of Criminal Justice** (899 Tenth Ave. at 58th St.) in May 1990, which ended with a violent reinstatement of power by administration officials. Renovations have given the 1903 neo-Victorian building, formerly the DeWitt Clinton High School (attended by Calvin Klein), a post-modern atrium and extension. Statues in niches, somber gargoyles, fretful nuthatches, and grape leaves adorn the building's white façade, while the American eagle stares blankly overhead.

Lower Midtown: Murray Hill, Madison Square, Union Square

Neither coldly commercial nor hotly trendy, lower Midtown, like the third little bear's bowl of porridge, seems just right. Neoclassical architecture and generous avenues create an aura of refinement suitable to classy monuments like the Empire State Building. At the Madison Square intersection, four of the earliest skyscrapers form a sub-skyline, one of the city's hidden visual treasures.

Late 19th-century "robber barons" took the lead in transforming the U.S. from a rural backwater into the world's leading industrial nation, amassing fortunes to rival the European monarchs' and creating lower Midtown in the process.

In the **Pierpont Morgan Library,** 29 E. 36th St. (685-0610), you can see stunning collections of rare books, sculpture, and artworks gathered by the banker and his son, J.P. Morgan, Jr. The omnipresent architectural firm of McKim, Mead & White naturally supervised the building of this low Renaissance-style *palazzo.* It was constructed with white marble bricks laid, in true Greek fashion, without mortar. The tree-shaded classical oasis may look familiar: it figured prominently in the movie *Ragtime.* Completed in 1907, the library remained private until 1924, when J.P. Morgan graciously opened it to the public. Its permanent collection, not always on display, includes drawings and prints from Blake and Dürer, illuminated Renaissance manuscripts, Napoleon's love letters to Josephine, a manuscript copy of Dickens' *A Christmas Carol,* and music handwritten by Beethoven and Mozart.

After taking in the exhibit, walk through the hall lined with medieval paraphernalia to a circular room, the former main entrance. The West Room on the right, Morgan Sr.'s opulent former office, has a carved ceiling made during the Italian Renaissance. It was common (well, not *common*) in the early days of the century to import large elements from European buildings for incorporation into domestic architecture.

Enter the library, a small but exquisitely planned space, its walls stacked with mahogany-colored bound volumes and encircled by a delicate balcony. Among the more notable items in the room: one of the three existing likenesses of John "Lady of Christ" Milton, a fabulous 12th-century jewel-encrusted triptych believed to contain fragments from the Cross, and one of 11 surviving copies of the Gutenberg Bible, the first printed book. (Subway: #6 to 33rd St. Open Tues.-Sat. 10:30am-5pm, Sun. 1-5pm. Suggested contribution $5, seniors and students $3. Free tours on various topics Tues.-Fri. 2:30pm.)

The **Church of the Incarnation,** 205 Madison Ave. at 35th St., lurks just around the corner from the Morgan Library. A comprehensive collection of late 19th-century art fills its sanctuary. Built in 1864, the church contains stained glass by Tiffany and sculptures and memorials by Augustus Saint Gaudens and Daniel Chester French in the nave. A handy pink pamphlet near the entrance can guide you to the church's art.

West on 34th St., Murray Hill refinement becomes Midtown chaos. On 34th St. at Herald Square looms **Macy's,** the largest department store in the world. With nine floors (plus a lower level) and some two million square feet of merchandise, it occupies an entire city block. Macy's has come a long way from its beginnings in 1857, when it grossed $11.06 on its first day of business. The store sponsors the Macy's Thanksgiving Day Parade, a New York tradition buoyed by helium-filled cultural icon-blobs, marching bands, floats, and general hoopla. Santa Claus always marches last in the parade, signalling the arrival of the Christmas shopping season and joy to kids (and merchants) everywhere.

Grab a store directory at the entrance to help you navigate Macy's mazes. Macy's has a separate Visitors Center, located on the first floor balcony, where the concierge service (560-3827) will assist anyone looking for anything. They will also make dining or entertainment reservations, provide information on upcoming entertainment events, and arrange for interpreters to accompany non-English speakers through the store. Those too busy making money to spend any of it themselves can hire others to spend it for them, using the "Macy's by Appointment" service on the third floor. A staff of fashion consultants, home accessories experts, and corporate specialists act as consumer therapists, walking clients through the store if necessary to help them discover what they really want (for an appointment, call 560-4181). All these services are free. (Open Mon. and Thurs.-Fri. 10am-8:30pm, Tues.-Wed. and Sat. 10am-7pm, Sun. 11am-6pm. Subway: #1, 2, 3, or 9 to Penn Station, or B, D, F, N, Q, or R to 34th St.)

To avoid the roar of the midtown crowds, walk back east on 34th St. to Madison Ave., and then downtown. On 29th St., at Madison Ave., the **Church of the Transfiguration,** better known as "The Little Church Around the Corner," has been the home parish of New York's theater world ever since a liberal pastor agreed to bury Shakespearean actor George Holland here in 1870 when no other church would. The diminutive Victorian brick structure features peculiar green roofs, cherub-like gargoyles, and a tangled garden out front. Check the stained glass windows: they may look like a scene from the Bible, but look again—the vignette is from *Hamlet.*

Madison Avenue ends, appropriately enough, at **Madison Square Park.** The park, opened in 1847, originally served as a public cemetery, and in recent years has grown decidedly seedy. Since developers have only just started to sink their cranes into this area, a number of the landmark buildings from years past remain, forming a miniature skyline. The area around the park, particularly to the south and east, sparkles with funky architectural gems.

The first of the old-but-tall buildings you will encounter, the **New York Life Insurance Building,** is located northeast of the park, occupying the block at 26th St. and Madison Ave. Built by Cass Gilbert (of Woolworth Building fame) in 1928, it wears its distinctive golden pyramid hat with an aplomb that should give modern box buildings pause. The site of P.T. Barnum's "Hippodrome," it was first rebuilt by Stanford White (the one who's not McKim or Mead) and renamed "Madison Square Garden" in 1879. It soon became the premier spot for New York's trademark entertainment spectacles. In 1906, the husband of Stanford White's reputed mistress shot the prolific architect to death on the roof. The building's present-day descendant, of the same name, now squats on top of Penn Station.

The clock faces of the 700-foot **Metropolitan Life Insurance Tower** survey the park from Madison Ave. and 23rd St. The tower, a 1909 addition to an 1893 building, also belongs to New York's I-used-to-be-the-tallest-building-in-the-world club.

Yet another distinguished club member is the eminently photogenic **Flatiron Building,** often considered the world's first skyscraper. It was originally named the Fuller Building, but its dramatic wedge shape, imposed by the intersections of Broadway, Fifth Ave., and 23rd St., quickly earned it its current *nom de plume.* The limestone façade is a rich tapestry of French Renaissance detailing, with slight window bays that break up the sense of a towering wall. *St. Martin's Press* currently occupies some of its floors. Whoopie.

Teddy Roosevelt lived in the 1840s brownstone at 28 E. 20th St. until he was 15. The **Theodore Roosevelt Birthplace** (260-1616) consists of five elegant period rooms from Teddy's childhood. While not the original rooms, they have been reconstructed along almost exactly the same lines. (Open Wed.-Sun. 9am-5pm. Guided tours 9am-3:30pm. Admission $1.)

Further east, on 20th St., is proof that not all New York real estate developers are as craven as The Donald. **Gramercy Park,** located at the foot of Lexington Ave. between 20th and 21st, was developed in 1831 by Samuel B. Ruggles, a developer fond of greenery. He drained an old marsh and then laid out 66 building lots around the periphery of the central space. Buyers of his lots received keys to enter the private park. Ruggles' idea was a glorious one; over 150 years later, little has changed, as the park, with its wide gravel paths, remains the only private park in New York, immaculately kept by its owners. The surrounding real estate is some of the choicest in the city.

The **Brotherhood Synagogue** flanks the park at no. 28. It was formerly a Friends Meeting House, commissioned in 1859 by the Quakers. They asked the firm of King & Kellum to design "an entirely plain, neat, and chaste structure of good taste, but

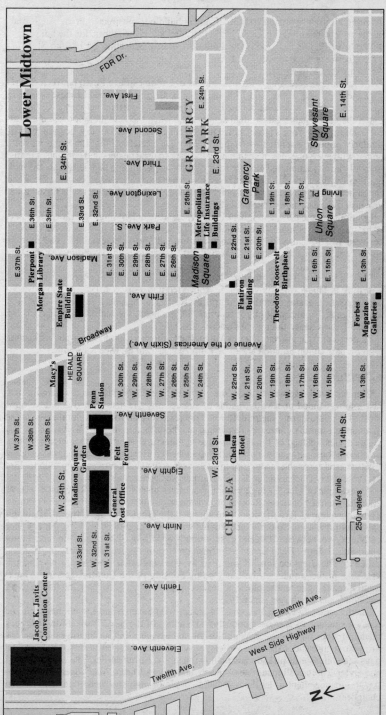

Lower Midtown

Jacob K. Javits Convention Center

Madison Square Garden

Penn Station

Felt Forum

General Post Office

Macy's

HERALD SQUARE

Empire State Building

Pierpont Morgan Library

Flatiron Building

Theodore Roosevelt Birthplace

Metropolitan Life Insurance Buildings

Madison Square

GRAMERCY PARK

Gramercy Park

Stuyvesant Square

Union Square

Irving Pl.

Forbes Magazine Galleries

Chelsea Hotel

CHELSEA

FDR Dr.

West Side Highway

0   1/4 mile
0   250 meters

avoiding all useless ornamentation." This tan building, constructed in the Anglo-Italianate style with simple cornices, pediments, and arched windows, fits the bill.

Way over on the east side is the **Police Academy Museum,** 35 E. 20th St. (477-9753), between Second and Third Ave., located on the 2nd floor of the NYC Police Academy (see Museums).

It's just a few increasingly off-beat blocks to **Union Square Park,** between Broadway and Park Ave. South, and 17th and 14th St. Originally named because two main roads merged here, the area boomed with high society intrigue before the Civil War. Later, the park's name gained dual significance when the neighborhood became a focal point for New York's large radical movement early in this century, hosting the particularly popular Socialist Movement's May Day celebrations. Later the workers united with everyone else in abandoning the park to drug dealers and derelicts. Finally, in 1989, the city attempted to reclaim it. After some rebuilding and de-toxing, the park has improved somewhat, although it retains an unsavory aftertaste. Now homeless and sunbather nap side by side on a blanket of pigeons. A farmers market sells fresh home-growns on the east side of the park.

Overlooking the park, a number of modern apartment buildings wear levitating party hats that glow at night. The **Zeckendorf Towers,** built in 1987, are at 1 Irving Pl., between W. 14th and 15th. The triangular caps and four-sided clock faces seem to be an obscene and mocking echo of Cass Gilbert's pyramid-topped buildings, such as the nearby New York Life.

Make a left onto 14th St. to reach **Palladium,** at 126 E. 14th St., between Third and Fourth Ave. This former movie palace, converted into a disco in 1985 by Japanese designer Arata Isozaki, contains a mural by Keith Haring and a staircase with 2400 round lights. Though well out of its brief "in" moment, the nightclub still boasts the world's largest dance floor. (See Dance Clubs.)

To get to the magnificent **Forbes Magazine Galleries** (206-5548), walk back along 14th St. past Union Square Park to 62 Fifth Ave. at 12th St. (See Museums.)

Chelsea

Clement Clark Moore of "Twas the Night Before Christmas" fame was more than just a long-winded poet with visions of sugarplums. He also owned and developed most of Chelsea during the mid-1800s. This relatively uniform development resulted in an architecturally consistent residential neighborhood in the Greek revival and Italianate styles, instead of the hodgepodge architectural stew that characterizes other neighborhoods. Strangely named after the Chelsea Hospital in London, the original Chelsea estate stretched from Eighth Ave. west to the Hudson river, from 14th to 23rd St. Present day Chelsea extends a few further blocks north and east.

An example of Moore's architectural work lives on at **Cushman Row,** #406-418 W. 20th St., a terrace of Greek Revival brownstones, complete with wrought-iron railings. These posh homes face the brick cathedral and the grounds of the **General Theological Seminary**, a grassy oasis that blooms with roses in summer (243-5150; entrance on Ninth Ave. between 20th and 21st; grounds open Mon.-Fri. noon-3pm, Sat. 11am-3pm, Sun. 2-4pm). Dean Eugene Hoffman erected this peaceful gateway in 1883 and called it "The Great Design." If you're lucky, you may catch some monks playing tennis. Take in the wonder of the fancy co-op housing of the **London Terrace Apartments,** spanning an entire block; it has occupied the area between 22nd and 23rd St. and Ninth and Tenth Ave. since 1929.

The historic **Chelsea Hotel**, on 23rd St. between Seventh and Eighth, has sheltered many a suicidal artist, most famously Sid Vicious of the Sex Pistols. Edie Sedgwick made pit stops here between Warhol films and asylums, before lighting the place on fire with a cigarette. Countless writers, as the plaques outside attest, spent their final days searching for inspiration and mail in the lobby. Arthur Miller, Vladimir Nabokov, and Dylan Thomas all made use of the abundant flat surfaces. Many over-zealous fans beg the management to let them spend a couple of nights in their superstar's former chamber.

Chelsea's **flower district,** on 28th St. between Sixth and Seventh, blooms most colorfully during the wee hours of the morning. Later in the day, if you wander around 27th St. and Broadway, you can witness the wholesale trading of cheap imports ranging from porn videos to imitation Barbie dolls to wigs made from 100% human hair.

Upper East Side

Until the close of the Civil War, 19th-century jetsetters chose this part of town for their summer retreats, building elaborate mansions in garden settings. By the late 1860s, simply summering uptown would not suffice. Landowners converted their warm-weather residences into year-round settlements; the building of elevated railroads soon brought an influx of the urban proletariat, and the East was won. In 1896, Caroline Schermerhorn Astor built a mansion on Fifth Avenue at 65th St., and the rest of high society soon followed. The Golden Age of the East Side Society flourished until the outbreak of World War I. The old-money crowd conspired with improvements in technology to produce sumptuous mansions outfitted with elevators, intercoms, and theatrical plumbing devices. Scores of the wealthy moved into the area and refused to budge, even during the Great Depression when armies of the unemployed pitched their tents across the way in Central Park.

So it was that select hotels, mansions, and churches first colonized the primordial wilderness of the Upper East Side. The lawns of Central Park covered the land where squatters had dwelt; **Fifth Avenue** rolled over a stretch once grazed by pigs. These days parades, millionaires, and unbearably slow buses share Fifth Avenue. Its **Museum Mile** includes the Metropolitan, the Guggenheim, the International Center of Photography, the Cooper-Hewitt, the Museum of the City of New York, and the Jewish Museum, among others. **Madison Avenue** means advertising: this is where artists, market psychologists, and salespeople conspire to manipulate America's buying habits. But these jingle factories are well concealed above an unbroken façade of expensive boutiques and superb galleries. The high-art and high-fashion windows of Madison afford endless hours of aesthetic bliss and materialistic glee.

The stately, dreary boulevard of **Park Avenue** was constructed around strict building codes. The architecturally unimaginative apartment blocks were termed "superslums" in the 1930s: they were equipped with every conceivable luxury, excepting air and light. Landscaped green islands now smother Park Avenue where railroad tracks once lacerated the thoroughfare. Admire the view down the Avenue to the hazy indigo outline of starscraping silhouettes in Midtown. Grittier **Lexington Avenue** injects a little reality into the East Side. Here and on Third, Second, and First Ave., you'll find the area's most vibrant crowds, a happening singles scene, and reliable public transportation. Farther north, highrise projects and grimmer urban settings replace the heartier party atmosphere of the streets of the 80s and 70s.

At 60th St. and Madison Ave. stands the infamous **Copacabana Club,** where Sammy Davis Jr. and Jerry Vale crooned in the 40s and Copa "Girls" like Lola danced with music and passion. Northwest of the Copa, at 1 E. 60th St., stands the **Metropolitan Club,** built by the dynamic trio of McKim, Mead & White on a commission from J.P. Morgan for his friends who had not been accepted at the **Union Club** (101 E. 69th St.). The **Knickerbocker Club,** at 2 E. 62nd St., was also founded by disgruntled Union men: Knickerbockers wanted to keep the club of pure Colonial stock.

Past residents of **810 Fifth Avenue** have included publisher Randolph Hearst and a pre-presidential Richard Nixon. Dick could go upstairs to borrow butter, eggs, and wire-taps from Nelson Rockefeller, a former shoeshine boy and anxious owner of New York's only fully equipped bomb shelter. Southeast at 47 E. 60th St. stands the **Grolier Club,** built in 1917 in honor of 16th-century bibliophile Jean Grolier. This Georgian structure houses a collection of fine bookbindings and a specialized research library. Though built and decorated in the 1930s, **Christ Church,** at 520 Park Ave. at 60th St., manages to appear quite ancient. Ralph Adams Cram ornamented this Byzantine-Romanesque hybrid with Venetian mosaics and onion-rippled marble columns. Note the iconic panels (taken from an old Russian church) above the altar. (Open daily

9am-5pm for meditation, prayer and respectful viewing. Occasional classical church music concerts given; call 838-3036 for information.) Just around the corner at 22 E. 60th St., the **French Institute** (355-6100), the cultural mission of the French Embassy, offers a variety of Gallic lectures and films. (Open Mon.-Thurs. 10am-8pm, Fri. 10am-6pm.)

Between Lexington and Park Ave. at 128 E. 63rd St., you'll find the **Society of American Illustrators** (838-2560) and their **Museum of American Illustration.** Back on Fifth Ave. at the corner of 65th St. stands **Temple Emanu-El,** ("God is with us"), the largest in the U.S. Outside, Eastern details speckle the limestone and otherwise Romanesque structure. Inside, the nave bears Byzantine ornaments and seats 2500—more than St. Patrick's Cathedral.

The Sarah Delano Roosevelt Memorial House, actually a pair of identical buildings executed by Charles Platt in 1908, sweeps #45-47 E. 65th St. between Park and Madison. The Roosevelt matriarch commissioned the constructions on the occasion of her son Franklin's wedding. In the bedroom on the fourth floor, Roosevelt recovered from polio in the early 1920s. He launched his political career in these buildings, now a community center for Hunter College students (see below).

Richard Hunt designed the **Lotos Club** on E. 66th St. between Madison and Fifth, an organization of actors, musicians, and journalists. Red brick rises from a base of rusticated limestone, capped by a two-story mansard roof in a style perhaps best described as Second Empire meets wedding cake. East 67th and 68th Streets between Madison and Fifth furnish more examples of turn-of-the-century mansion architecture with a distinct French accent.

Occupying virtually an entire block, the **Seventh Regiment Armory** makes its stand between 66th and 67th on Park Ave. The Seventh Regiment fought in every major U.S. campaign from 1812 on, including a valiant outing for the Union in the Civil War. Much of the armory's original 19th-century decoration and furnishing remain in place today. Notable rooms were designed by the Associated Artists under the baton of Louis Comfort Tiffany. The Veterans' room and the adjoining library-turned-display-room for the Regiment's silver are quite remarkable. The front hallway boasts a gargantuan staircase sheathed in venerable red plush, and a whole host of decomposing flags. The eerily impenetrable gloom makes it impossible to see the portraits, but they can see you. Since the Armory still serves as an active military facility, you should call ahead if you'd like a tour (744-8180).

The contrived ambience of fake-English luxury as interpreted by a New Yorker named Ralph has been conveniently summarized in the **Polo—Ralph Lauren** boutique quartered in a French Renaissance building at 867 Madison Ave. between 71st and 72 St. The store's atmosphere—complete with a live string quartet—has been so meticulously orchestrated that you may feel that you're on location for the shoot of the *Great Gatsby.* They'll be glad to dress you up.

Hunter College, part of the City University of New York, presents its unsightly modernist façade to Lexington and its more attractive posterior to Park Ave., between 67th and 69th St. The **Asia Society,** 725 Park Ave. at 70th St., increases cultural awareness of Asia with lectures, films, and an impressive art collection assembled by John D. Rockefeller, III.

Capitalist running-dog Henry Clay Frick's marvelous mansion, home of the **Frick Collection,** stands poised at 1 E. 70th St. on Fifth Ave. (see Museums). On Madison Ave. at 75th St., box-shaped and brutalist, stands the **Whitney Museum of American Art,** a shape as aloof as some of the art you will find inside. You don't even have to enter the lobby to enjoy Alexander Calder's whimsical wirefest of acrobatics; peek through the window and let Calder convince you that all the world's a circus (see Museums). Slightly removed from the mayhem of Madison where it once stood, **Sotheby Park Bernet Inc.** (606-7000) conducts its affairs and auctions at 1334 York Ave. near 72nd St. Viewings are open to the public, although admission to some auctions requires tickets. The front door of **900 Park Ave.** at 79th St. may look familiar: the once-wholesome cast of *Diff'rent Strokes* drove up in a limousine to Mr. Drummond's Park Ave. residence at the beginning of every episode.

Upper East Side

E. 106th St.
El Museo del Barrio
E. 105th St.
E. 104th St.
Museum of the
City of New York
E. 103rd St.
Conservatory
Garden
E. 102nd St.
E. 101st St.
E. 100th St.
Mt. Sinai
Hospital
E. 99th St.
E. 98th St.
E. 97th St.
E. 96th St.
E. 95th St.
International Center
of Photography
E. 94th St.
E. 93rd St.
Jewish Museum
E. 92nd St.
E. 91st St.
Cooper-Hewitt
Museum
National Academy
of Design
E. 90th St.
E. 89th St.
E. 88th St.
Guggenheim
Museum
E. 87th St.
Gracie
Mansion
E. 86th St.
Carl
Schurz
Park
E. 85th St.
E. 84th St.
E. 83rd St.
E. 82nd St.
E. 81st St.
E. 80th St.
Metropolitan
Museum
of Art
E. 79th St.
E. 78th St.
E. 77th St.
E. 76th St.
E. 75th St.
E. 74th St.
Whitney Museum
of American Art
E. 73rd St.
East
River
E. 72nd St.
E. 71st St.
Frick
Collection
Asia Society
E. 70th St.
Hunter
College
E. 69th St.
New York
Hospital
(Cornell
Univ.)
E. 68th St.
7th
Regiment
Armory
E. 67th St.
E. 66th St.
Temple
Emanu-El
China
House
E. 65th St.
Rockefeller
University
E. 64th St.
Museum of
American
Illustration
E. 63rd St.
Roosevelt
Island
E. 62nd St.
E. 61st St.
E. 60th St.
TRAMWAY
Bloomingdale's
E. 59th St.
Queensboro Bridge

Fifth Ave.
Madison Ave.
Park Ave.
Lexington Ave.
Third Ave.
Second Ave.
First Ave.
York Ave.
East End Ave.
FDR Dr.
Central Park

N

0   1/4 mile
0   250 meters

Even in death, celebrity New Yorkers manage to uphold their status, maintaining their coteries as they pass on to the Grand Ballroom in the sky. The grave roll call of the **Frank E. Campbell Chapel,** a prestigious funeral chapel (at 1076 Madison Avenue at 81st St.), reads like Who Was Who on the American Mount Olympus: Elizabeth Arden, James Cagney, Jack Dempsey, Tommy Dorsey, Judy Garland, Howard Johnson, Robert F. Kennedy, Mae West, John Lennon, and Arturo Toscanini, just to name a pew.

The **Metropolitan Museum of Art** manifests its majestic presence at 1000 Fifth Ave., flanked by long fountains and footsore museum-goers. The largest in the Western Hemisphere, the Met's art collection encompasses some 33 million works (see Museums). Across the street at 1014 Fifth Ave., **Goethe House, New York** (744-8310) offers a Germanic cultural respite from the *Sturm und Drang* of New York through film and lectures (library open Tues., Thurs. noon-7pm, Wed., Fri.-Sat. noon-5pm).

Located in the far east, between 84th and 90th St. along East End Ave. lies **Carl Schurz Park,** named in honor of a many-hatted German immigrant who served as Civil War General, Missouri senator, President Rutherford B. Hayes's Secretary of the Interior, and finally editor of the *New York Evening Post* and *Harper's Weekly.* The park, overlooking the East River, is a many-nooked haven of greenery for asphalt-weary metropolites. Dogs abound and bark. **Gracie Mansion,** at the north end of the park, has been the residence of every New York mayor since Fiorello LaGuardia moved in during World War II. David Dinkins occupies this hottest of hot seats. To make a reservation for a tour of the colonial mansion call 570-4751. (Tours given Wed. only; suggested admission $3, seniors $1.)

Originally settled by Germans, Yorkville (extending from the East River to Lexington Ave. from 77th to 96th St.) continued to welcome immigrants from the Rhine Valley over the first half of this century. The heavy German accent that once animated the local restaurant menus, beer gardens, pastry shops, and deli counters has thinned in the wake of newer chain stores and pizza parlors, but has not vanished. A few old of the old faithfuls remain, keeping the *Bratwurst* basting and the tradition going. **Henderson Place** lines East End Ave. at 86th St.; this series of Queen Anne-style houses decorated with multiple turrets, parapets, and dormers could have been wrought from Lego. Ghostbusters beware—rumor has it that some of these houses are haunted. All done up in reds, golds, and browns, the fanciful **Church of the Holy Trinity** all but hides from view at 316 E. 88th St. between First and Second Ave. Behind this late 19th-century church lies a small heavenly garden.

You can stop in at **Elaine's,** 1703 Second Ave., where Woody Allen makes the occasional appearance both on and off screen. Don't hold your breath. Still, media celebrities, gossips, and self-styled literati gather here. Elaine rules the place with an iron pan. The cuisine is allegedly Italian but the food fails to bear this out. Look self-important and they might let you in.

Back over on Fifth Ave. at 88th St., the newly-renovated prairie-white **Guggenheim Museum** is one of the few New York buildings designed by Frank Lloyd Wright. The **National Academy of Design** building, 1083 Fifth Ave. at 89th St., serves as both a school and a museum for the academy established in 1825. Work by 11 of the 30 founding members lodges at the Metropolitan Museum. (See Museums.)

When Andrew Carnegie requested that Babb, Cook, and Willard construct "the most modest, plainest, and most roomy house in New York" on 91st and Fifth, he received a large but formulaic Renaissance-Georgian combo of red brick and limestone, situated in a luxurious garden. Within, dark oak paneling, textured wallpaper, and demure atriums create the perfect setting for a society ball. When Carnegie moved out, the Smithsonian moved in, relocating their National Museum of Design here at the **Cooper-Hewitt Museum** (see Museums).

The **Jewish Museum,** at 92nd and Fifth, a French Renaissance structure with a modern wing added in 1962, contains the country's largest collection of Judaica (see Museums). At 60 E. 93rd St. between Park and Madison stands the haughty French mansion that served as a retreat for Mrs. William K. Vanderbilt after her dramatic divorce. The **International Center of Photography,** 130 Fifth Ave. at 94th, the first museum in the world to take photography seriously maintains a rich permanent collection and operates workshops, photolabs, and a screening room (see—yes, that's right—Museums).

The **Synod of Bishops of the Russian Orthodox Church Outside Russia** now inhabits the 1917 Georgian mansion at Park and 93rd. The bishops scattered a few icons about but left the interior decoration virtually unchanged, save a former ballroom they converted into a cathedral.

Before Manhattan builders got wise and turned to fireproof stone, they made all houses out of wood. A few of these mid-19th-century houses can be seen at 120 and 122 E. 92nd St. between Lexington and Park. Louise Nevelson's 1972 steel sculpture *Night Presence IV* stands on the island of Park Ave. at 92nd St.

The **Islamic Cultural Center,** at Third Ave. and 96th St., New York's most prominent mosque, was precisely oriented by computer to face the holy city of Mecca. Meanwhile the tenacious Russians continued their conquest of the Upper East Side with the construction of the **Russian Orthodox Cathedral of St. Nicholas** at 15 E. 97th St. The cathedral has a polychromatic Victorian body with a strong dose of authentic Russia, manifested in its five onion domes.

Central Park

> *There is no greenery; it is enough to make a stone sad.*
> —*Nikita Khrushchev, remark during visit to New York, October 1960*

Beloved Central Park has earned some moments in the sun. Recall Dustin Hoffman in *Marathon Man,* sprinting through the park to escape the hostile city, Laurence Olivier, and Olivier's dental instruments. The park has staged grand dramas throughout its history, from its heroic construction to the popular Shakespeare in the Park festival.

The campaign for a public park in New York began in the mid-1840s with William Cullen Bryant, a vociferous editor of the *New York Evening Post,* and received support from the acclaimed architect Andrew Jackson Downing in his magazine *The Horticulturist.* The creation of the park became a unifying issue in the mayoral campaign of 1851—both candidates were strongly in favor of the project. In 1853, the state authorized the purchase of land from 59th to 106th St. (The 106th to 110th St. addendum was purchased in 1863.) Alas, Downing met his death by drowning and was unable to design his dream project. The city held a competition to determine the new designer of the park.

The winning design, selected in 1858 from 33 competing entries, came out of a collaboration between Frederic Law Olmsted and Calvert Vaux. Because Olmsted had a day job heading the construction crews that cleared the debris and edifices from the proto-park, most of the plans for Central Park were drawn at night. Olmsted and Vaux transformed 840 acres of bogs, cliffs, glacial leftovers, bone-boiling works, and pig farms into a living masterwork they called *Greensward.* The whole landscape took 15 years to build and 40 years to grow.

The Park may be roughly divided north and south at the main reservoir; the southern section affords more intimate settings, serene lakes, and graceful promenades, while the northern end has a few ragged edges. Nearly 1400 species of trees, shrubs, and flowers grow here, the work of distinguished horticulturist Ignaz Anton Pilat. When you wander amidst the shrubbery, you need not get lost. Look to the nearest lamppost for guidance, and check the four-digit small metal plaque bolted to it. The first two digits tell you what street you're nearest (89, for example), and the second two whether you're on the east or west side of the park (an even number means east, an odd west). In an emergency, call the 24hr. emergency telephone line (800-834-3832).

You can observe some architectural and sculptural landmarks in the park, but the **Arsenal** at Fifth Ave. and 64th St., the nerve center of the New York Parks system since 1848, isn't one of them. The dumpy, ivy-covered brick building dispenses the *Central Park Calendar* and a glossy broadsheet generically called the *Leaflet*. The former prints a seasonal calendar of events sponsored by the park, a handy park map, and information on recreational activities. The latter has similar listings but includes a calendar of the joint efforts of the park in conjunction with the Met, the Symphony Orchestra, and the New York Shakespeare Festival. The Arsenal also houses an Arts Gallery (360-8111), displaying the work of contemporary artists. (Open Mon.-Fri. 9:30am-4:30pm. Free.)

Constructed in 1934, the **Central Park Zoo** (439-6500) still attracts flocks of visitors. Roving herds of wired children make even the drowsy reptiles of the Tropical Rainforest pavilion tremble in fear, and solitary tourists find a safe haven from sweat in the deliciously chilly Penguin room. (Admission $2.50, seniors $1.50, kids 3-12 50¢. Open daily 10am-5pm, last entry 4:30pm.) Above the archway, north of the main zoo, hangs the **Delacorte Musical Clock,** made in 1965 by Andrea Spaldini. Every half hour, bears, monkeys, and other bronze creatures perform a ritual hop and skip routine. North of the 65th St. transverse are the dried-up ponds and partially-gutted buildings of the recently-closed children's zoo, a victim of budget cuts.

Urban mothers in the late 19th-century had real troubles finding healthy milk for poor families. A particularly severe incidence of poisoning inspired Vaux in 1870 to design **the Dairy**, a cottage distributing purity-tested milk. Long-shuttered, the building reopened in 1979 as the **Central Park Reception Center**. Call 794-6564 or -6565, or come here for information on Sunday tours and events, lotsa brochures, and the dumbest video "touch-screen" display anywhere. We promise. (Open Tues.-Thurs. and Sat.-Sun. 11am-5pm, Fri. 1-5pm; Nov.-Feb. 11am-4pm and 1-4pm.) The **Chess and Checkers House,** a striped red brick concoction created by Robert Moses, realizes what Olmsted and Vaux called the *kinderberg*—the first ever children's playground. Today grandmasters and spunky amateurs square off at the 24 outdoor boards and 10 indoor boards (indoor tables available on the weekends; open Sat.-Sun. 11:30am-4:30pm).

The Wollman Skating Rink (517-4800) doubles as a miniature golf course in late spring. Trade your putter for a pair of skates, and **rollerdance** to your heart's content without having to leave the building. The complex also offers "bankshot," a half-court game of pseudo-basketball. (Ice- or rollerskating $5, kids and seniors $2.50, plus $2.50 skate rental or $5 rollerblade rental; 9-hole minigolf $4, kids $2; bankshot $5, kids $2.50; discounts for combining these activities. Ice-skating only in winter, since the rink is outdoors. Whole megillah open Mon. 10am-5pm, Tues.-Thurs. 10am-9:30pm, Fri.-Sat. 10am-11pm, Sun. 10am-9:30pm.) The best thing about the roller rink is undoubtedly the railed ledge overlooking it, from which an unparalleled (and actually quite pretty) view of midtown can be had free of charge. If you enjoy feeling you've been going in circles, visit the **Friedsam Memorial Carousel** (879-0244), located at 65th St. west of Center Dr. The 58 horsepower carousel was brought from Coney Island and fully restored in 1983. (Open Mon.-Fri. 10:30am-4:30pm, Sat.-Sun. 10:30am-5:30pm. Winter hours Sat.-Sun. 10:30am-4:30pm. Admission 90¢.)

Erroneously called Sheep's Meadow even by those in the know, **Sheep Meadow,** the largest chunk of Greensward, exemplifies the pastoral ideals of the park's designers and today's teenage crowds. Sheep did graze here until 1934, but after that the Park could afford lawn mowers and so terminated the flock. North of Sheep Meadow lie the bowling and croquet greens. Inside Sheep Meadow reclines the fun-loving frisbee generation, getting suntanned or stoned in the noonday sun.

West of Sheep Meadow, between 66th and 67th St., is **Tavern on the Green** (873-3200), said to be NYC's most profitable restaurant, specializing in over-priced food with a green view. (Lunch $11-25.50. Dinner $13-29. Open Mon.-Tues. and Thurs.-Fri. noon-3pm and 5:30pm-1am, Wed. 11:30am-3:30pm and 5:30pm-1am, Sat.-Sun. 10:30am-3:30pm and 5pm-1am.)

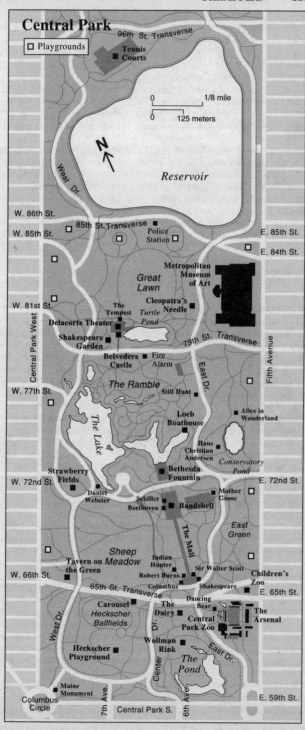

Along West Drive, at 67th St., stands the **Seventh Regiment Civil War Monument,** sculpted by John Quincy Adams Ward in 1870. Although bureaucrats deemed the Park "too chipper" for "sepulchral monuments," someone somewhere pushed the statue design through. In subsequent years it became a prototype for Civil War monuments throughout the country.

Across from the Dakota Apartments on 72nd St., the site of John Lennon's assassination, is **Strawberry Fields,** forever Yoko Ono's memorial to her husband. Ono battled valiantly against City Council members who had planned a Bing Crosby memorial on the same turf. She gathered 161 varieties of plants around the star-shaped mosaic that asks you to "Imagine."

To the east of Sheep Meadow lies **the Mall,** a path populated with statues of literary lions. Off the southwest end of the Mall, you can see the first American statue placed in the park: **The Indian Hunter** (1869), by J.Q.A. Ward, in extraordinary naturalistic bronze. At the **Hunt Memorial** at 70th St. on Fifth Ave., an elegant Beaux-Arts mishmash, Bruce Price's architectural musings mingle with sculptural groupings by **Daniel Chester French,** the Lincoln Memorial guy.

The broad **Terrace** leads down to **Bethesda Fountain,** the formal centerpiece of the Park, linking Mall with Lake. Designed by Vaux and Jacob Wrey Mould, sights boast elaborate ornamental carvings of plants, birds, and park animals. Descending the grand central staircase, you can look through a noble arch and spy the 1865 statue of **The Angel of the Waters,** sculpted in Rome by Emma Stebins. The bas-reliefs along the staircase depict the four seasons. The season of summer will likely also be well-represented by a cart in the vicinity selling soda and Italian ice. South of the Terrace, but north of the Mall, the old, cordoned-off Bandshell has been awaiting reconstruction or demolition for almost half a decade.

Located at 77th St. near the Lake, the graceful Balcony Bridge spans its stuff and features one of the most dramatic views from the Park: the Lake, the Ramble (a birdwatcher's paradise), and the heart of Midtown. The 1954 **Loeb Boathouse** (517-2233), a late but indispensable addition to the park, supplies all necessary romantic nautical equipment. Its mighty rental fleet includes rowboats, swanboats, and even gondolas. (Open daily late March-Nov. Mon.-Fri. noon-5pm, Sat.-Sun. 10am-5:30pm, weather permitting. Rowboats $8 first hr., $1.50 each additional 1/4hr., refundable $20 deposit; Gondola rides $35 per 1/2hr. per group. Call boathouse for reservations.) Aquaphobes can rent a bike from the boathouse and make their own journeys on *terra firma.* (Bike rental open late March-Nov. Mon.-Fri. 10am-7pm, Sat.-Sun. 9am-7pm, in clement weather. First hr. $6-8, $20 deposit on 10-speed; I.D. or additional $100 deposit required. Call 861-4137.)

Model boats set sail daily on the pacific swells of Conservatory Pond. The formal basin, site of the yacht race in E.B. White's little-known *Stuart Little,* vibrates in summertime with the careless joy of children and the plodding progress of their intrepid vessels. Clouds and sails sweep by on golden afternoons here in the most enchanting part of the park. A statue of **Hans Christian Andersen,** a gift from Copenhagen in 1956, stands next to dreamchild **Alice in Wonderland,** with several of her friends—another gift of the Danes, given in 1959. The Andersen statue has become a prime storytelling spot in the summer. Storytelling takes center stage at the **Swedish Cottage Marionette Theatre** (988-9093).

The high point of the Park, literally, is **Belvedere Castle,** a whimsical fancy designed by the restless Vaux in 1869. The castle of crossed destinies rises from the **Vista Rock,** commanding a view of the **Great Lawn,** the **Ramble,** the **Winter Drive.** For many years a weather station, Belvedere Castle has been reincarnated as an education center and serves as the stronghold of the green knights—the **Urban Park Rangers** provide visitor and emergency services for the park.

Encircled by joggers and larger than many towns, the shiny, placid Reservoir may be the most tranquil sight in Manhattan.

Visit the **Delacorte Theater** on midsummer nights to see **Shakespeare in the Park.** Come early: the theater seats only 1936 lucky souls (see Theater). The Dairy or the Arsenal can give you calendars for the '93 Central Park Summerstage program (assuming its funding comes through). In years past Summerstage has sponsored free concerts by big names in genres from opera to punk rock. Sonic Youth and jazz-bandleader-from-Saturn Sun Ra played to a spaced-out audience on July 4, 1992. (For recorded Summerstage info, call 360-2777.)

The madras-clad crowd plays **croquet** in Central Park from May through November north of Sheep Meadow at 67th St. [What *is* my damage?—Ed.] **Horseback Riding** operates out of Claremont Stables, at 175 W. 89th St. (724-5100). (Open Mon.-Fri. 6:30am-one hour before dusk, Sat.-Sun. 8am-5pm. $30 per hour.) The NYC Audubon Society outfits **bird-watching** expeditions in the spring, convening at 7:30am Monday and Wednesday at 72nd St. and Fifth Ave. Call 691-7483 to check times and find out about other events. The most popular place to run in the Park is on the track surrounding the Reservoir, where one lap measures 1.58 miles. Above the Reservoir, at 105th St. and Fifth Ave., is the attractive **Conservatory Garden** (860-1382; gates open spring-fall daily 8am-dusk).

Upper West Side

Along Central Park West the well-to-do residents can look down at doormen or across the park to their soulmates on the Upper East Side. The fancy apartment buildings here date mostly from before the Depression, some from the aptly-named gilded age of the 1880s. But the rest of the West Side is much less forbidding: the white-collar takeover that began in the 50s (with the construction of Lincoln Center) hasn't wiped out all the ethnic enclaves, though plenty of the antique stores, clothing emporia, and fern-colored singles bars attest to the comfortable West-Siders' tastes.

The original plan slated Broadway for residences and West End Ave. for business, but no one paid attention. Before long Broadway had become the principal and most colorful street on the West Side. Today the thoroughfare is crammed with delis, theaters, and boutiques; on the sidewalk desperate hawkers peddle everything from bun dumplings to worn copies of *Jugs* magazine to the kitchenware of yesteryear.

Columbus Circle, on Broadway at 59th St., is the symbolic entrance to the Upper West Side and marks the end of Midtown (see West Midtown Sights). At 1865 Broadway, off 61st, the **Bible House,** run by the American Bible Society, distributes the good book in nearly every tongue. Its exhibition gallery showcases rare and unorthodox bibles, plus a smattering of Gütenberg pages and an online *Good News Bible.* (Gallery open Mon.-Fri. 9:30am-4:30pm, free. Library open Mon.-Fri. 9am-4:30pm. Bookstore open 9:30am-5pm.) Between 61st and 62nd, the 27-story edifice at 45 Broadway once served as the Columbus Circle Automatic Garage and has since become a College Board facility whose lapis-lazuli-tinted first story celebrates the splendor of Art Deco.

Broadway intersects Columbus Ave. at **Lincoln Center,** the cultural hub of the city, between 62nd and 66th St. The seven facilities that constitute Lincoln Center—Avery Fisher Hall, the New York State Theater, the Metropolitan Opera House, the Library and Museum of Performing Arts, the Vivian Beaumont Theater, The Walter Reade Theater, and the Juilliard School of Music—accommodate over 13,000 spectators at a time. Power broker Robert Moses masterminded this project in 1955 when Carnegie Hall seemed fated for destruction. See all of Lincoln Center in its blanched expansiveness from the steps of 62nd St. (Look for the mini-Statue of Liberty atop a neighboring apartment building.)

The **plaza** is especially lively on weekend afternoons. The main entrance on Ninth Ave. features the fountain where Cher and Nicholas Cage were *Moonstruck,* and where the cast of *Fame* danced at the beginning of the show (before the first commercial). This open area is also a favorite spot for fashion photographers; watch as models sweat under fur coats in August. On your left, with your back to Columbus Ave., is the automated information booth. Marvel at the uniform white monumentality of the eight-block complex: planners may have been saying something about government sponsorship of the arts?

Avery Fisher Hall, on your right, designed in 1966 by Max Abramovitz, houses the New York Philharmonic under the direction of Kurt Masur, who recently inherited the baton from conductor Zubin Mehta. Previous Philharmonic directors have included Leonard Bernstein, Arturo Toscanini, and Leopold Stokowski (see Music below). Don't forget that the '92-93 season is the Philharmonic's 150th anniversary; watch out for special events.

Straight ahead, **The Metropolitan Opera House,** the 1966 work of Wallace K. Harrison, echoes behind a Mondrian-inspired glass façade. Chagall murals span the lobby. A grand, many-tiered staircase curves down to the humble opera buff. The Metropolitan Opera shop sells gift books, posters, libretti, and boxes of cough drops used and autographed by Caruso. Mmm. The shop also broadcasts performances live on house monitors; sneaky budgeteers can get a quick opera fix just browsing at the shop during performance time. (Open Mon.-Sat. 9am-8pm or until 2nd intermission of performance, Sun. noon-6pm.) The monolithic **New York State Theater** plays house to the New York City Ballet and the New York City Opera. December is *Nutcracker* month.

Henri Moore's 1965 *Lincoln Center Reclining Figure* sits gloomily in the reflecting pool on the south side of the Opera House. Across the pool squats the **Vivian Beaumont Theater,** a tidy glass box under a heavy cement helmet, built by Eero Saarinen in 1965. The **New York Public Library for the Performing Arts** (870-1630) bridges the Opera House and the theater and holds over eight million items, from videotapes to manuscripts. (Library open Mon. and Thurs. noon-8pm, Wed. and Fri. noon-6pm, Sat. 10am-6pm. See Libraries.)

The combined terrace and bridge leads across 66th St. to the halls of the prestigious **Juilliard School of Music,** Pietro Belluschi's brutalist-inspired building. Here Itzhak Perlman and Pinchas Zukerman fine-tuned their skills, and a drama major by the name of Robin Williams tried out his first comedy routines. For information on student concerts call 769-7406. Within the Juilliard building complex is the intimate **Alice Tully Hall,** where the Chamber Music Society of Lincoln Center resides. To your left as you face Juilliard and about 200 ft. away, a beige office building conceals Lincoln Center's newest offering, the **Walter E. Reade Theater.** Scan the film schedule in the front window.

Directly across from Lincoln Center, on a triangular plot between Broadway and Columbus Ave., is **Dante Park,** designed in 1921 to commemorate the 600th anniversary of the poet's death. Presiding over the minuscule park is an imposing bronze of the man himself, executed by the Denigris brothers. Juilliard students played jazz or chamber music here every Tuesday at 6:30pm during the summer of '92; maybe they'-ll come back.

The undistinguished modern façade of the **Museum of American Folk Art,** across from Lincoln Center, on Columbus between 65th and 66th, gives way to a cool interior, where you can rest on a bench when you've had your fill of 18th-century quilts. (See Museums.)

The mammoth, Moorish-inspired **West Side Y** hulks at 5 W. 63rd St. A block north at 2 W. 64th, the **New York Ethical Culture Society** (874-5210) gives sporadic lectures, readings, classical recitals, and schedules for the foregoing. This venerable organization helped found many others, including the American Civil Liberties Union. Another of New York City's armories holds the fort down at 56 W. 66th St., between Central Park West and Broadway. The one-time turrets and battlements of the **First Battery of the New York National Guard** now defend the ABC television studios hidden behind the Fisher-Price castle.

At 1 W. 67th St., poised between Central Park West and Columbus, stands the stately **Hotel des Artistes,** now a mass of luxury co-ops, originally designed to house bohemians who had moved beyond their romantic garret stage. Built by George Mort Pollard in 1913, the building has quartered Isadora Duncan, Alexander Woollcott, Norman Rockwell, and Noel Coward. The opulence is mostly on the inside; dig the ivy-shaped stonework, though. Here you will also find the chic **Café des Artistes.**

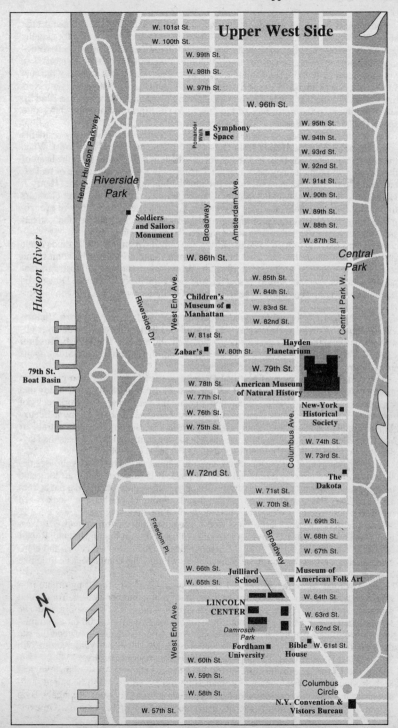

Upper West Side

W. 101st St.
W. 100th St.
W. 99th St.
W. 98th St.
W. 97th St.
W. 96th St.
W. 95th St.
W. 94th St.
W. 93rd St.
W. 92nd St.
W. 91st St.
W. 90th St.
W. 89th St.
W. 88th St.
W. 87th St.
W. 86th St.
W. 85th St.
W. 84th St.
W. 83rd St.
W. 82nd St.
W. 81st St.
W. 80th St.
W. 79th St.
W. 78th St.
W. 77th St.
W. 76th St.
W. 75th St.
W. 72nd St.
W. 71st St.
W. 70th St.
W. 69th St.
W. 68th St.
W. 67th St.
W. 66th St.
W. 65th St.
W. 64th St.
W. 63rd St.
W. 62nd St.
W. 61st St.
W. 60th St.
W. 59th St.
W. 58th St.
W. 57th St.

Henry Hudson Parkway
Riverside Park
Hudson River
79th St. Boat Basin
Riverside Dr.
West End Ave.
Broadway
Amsterdam Ave.
Columbus Ave.
Central Park W.
Central Park
Freedom Pl.
West End Ave.

Pomander Walk
Symphony Space
Soldiers and Sailors Monument
Children's Museum of Manhattan
Zabar's
Hayden Planetarium
American Museum of Natural History
New-York Historical Society
The Dakota
Juilliard School
Museum of American Folk Art
LINCOLN CENTER
Damrosch Park
Fordham University
Bible House
Columbus Circle
N.Y. Convention & Vistors Bureau

N

The stone-hewn glory of Imperial Egypt meets the principles of streamlined design at 135 W. 70th St., which flaunts sapphire-blue columns with bearded men for capitals and hawks whose lengthy wingspans any Grateful Dead fan will immediately recognize. The apartment house was the original home of the Knights of Pythias club.

Constructed in 1970 by the Talmudic tag team of Hausman and Rosenberg, the curvaceous, sunken **Lincoln Square Synagogue** at 69th St. and Amsterdam is a travertine cousin of Lincoln Center. The bow-tie shaped **Sherman Square** knots at 72nd St. and Broadway. In the north half of the cravat, **Verdi Square,** Giuseppe stares into space, hailed by four characters from his operas.

As Manhattan's urbanization peaked in the late 19th century, wealthy residents sought tranquility in the elegant **Dakota,** at 1 W. 72nd St. on Central Park West. When the apartment house was built in 1884, someone thought it so remote from the heart of the city that "it might as well be in Dakota Territory." In a rare convergence of real estate and humor, the idea caught on and became the building's official name. Henry J. Hardenburg designed the luxury complex, which featured the first passenger elevators in the city. The first floor has been veiled in scaffolds since 1991; if they're ever removed, you can gape at the sprouting turrets, gables, and oriels. John Lennon's streetside murder here in 1981 brought new notoriety to the mammoth building.

Between 73rd and 74th, at 2109 Broadway, the famed **Ansonia Hotel,** grande dame of Belle Apartments, bristles with heavy ornaments, curved Verona balconies, and towers. Its soundproof walls and thick floors proved most enticing to illustrious tenants like Enrico Caruso, Arturo Toscanini, and Igor Stravinsky. Theodore Dreiser did his own composing here while Babe Ruth, just a few doors away, meditated on his pinstripes.

Secure in their block-long neoclassical building, the staff of the **New York Historical Society,** at 77th St. and Central Park West (873-3400), will help you uncover obscure facts about the past or provide pop trivia about the present. The **Jewish Museum** (399-3344) is also quartered here until its new building (on the East Side) opens grandly sometime in early '93. (See Museums.)

The American Museum of Natural History waxes as unwieldly as a prehistoric mastodon at Central Park West from 78th to 81st St. Built in 1899 by J.C. Cady and Co. and since added to by like-minded architects, the rectilinear stonework reeks of romanesque. The museum's patron saint, Teddy Roosevelt, is honored by a Beaux-Artes triumphal arch and a racist bronze sculpture at the main entrance on Central Part West. Besides cool dinosaurs and innumerable dioramas, the museum boasts the Hayden Planetarium. Holden Caufield used to hang out here. (See Museums.)

Between 76th and 77th on West End Ave. are a block of Victorian townhouses designed by master masons Lamb and Rich in 1891. It is rumored that graft king and former Mayor Jimmy "Gentleman Jim" Walker's mistress once occupied a flat at 76th and Broadway above the townhouses, and that the doting mayor had the block zoned off to stop construction on highrises that might obscure the lovely view.

Dutch settlers constructed the **West End Collegiate Church and School,** 370 West End Ave. at 77th St., in 1637 as a reproduction of a market building in Holland. Robert Gibson overhauled it in 1893, using characteristically Dutch stepped gables and elongated bricks; with its one enormous stained-glass window, the church looks a little like a dyspeptic cyclops.

The **Apthorp Apartments** at 2207 Broadway and 79th St., featuring ornate iron gates and a spacious interior courtyard, have starred in a number of New York-based films: *Heartburn, Network, Eyewitness, The Cotton Club, The Changeling,* and *The Money Pit.* The apartments were built by Clinton and Russell in 1908 on a commission from William Waldorf Astor, who named them after the man who owned the site in 1763. Try to persuade the guard to let you take a peek at the courtyard. Across 79th St., the **First Baptist Church's** lopsided spires cavort asymmetrically.

The **West Park Presbyterian Church** has been a fixture at Amsterdam Ave. and 86th St. since 1890. It exhibits fine Romanesque styling, with a rough-hewn red sandstone surface that makes it look like it just popped out of a clay oven. Strangely, Byzantine doorways and capitals top off the Romanesque half-baked look. On ever-ecclesiastical 86th St. at West End Ave., you'll also find the **Church of St. Paul and St. Andrew,** dating from 1897. Check out the octagonal tower and the angels in the spandrels.

Central Park's Frederic Law Olmsted's other green contribution to Manhattan, **Riverside Park,** blooms down the stretch from 72nd to 145th St. along the Hudson River. As in the case of Central Park, Olmsted had a little help from Calvert Vaux. Directly across from the intersection of Riverside Drive and 89th St., the **Soldiers and Sailors Monument,** more tomb than memorial, mourns the Union lives lost in the Civil War. The **Carrére Memorial,** a small terrace and plaque at 99th St., honors one of the city's great architects, John Merven Carrére, who died in an automobile accident. His partner, Thomas Hastings, designed the monument. A brightly colored and moving mural "In Memory of Hector" (by "Chico") is worth looking for on 87th St. between Columbus Ave. and Central Park West.

Next to a vacant lot, at 175 W. 89th St. and Amsterdam Ave., stands the only surviving stable in Manhattan: the multi-story **Claremont Stables,** equine condos for high pedigree horses which also offer riding lessons (see Central Park). The appropriately-named **Eldorado** apartments, on Central Park West between 90th and 91st, showcase flashy Art Deco detailing in a full array of golds.

Originally a skating rink, the **Symphony Space** at 2537 Broadway at 95th St. (864-5400), has distinguished itself with brilliant if wacky programming. Their **Wall to Wall Bach** took a walk on the wild side, as did their gala birthday salute to the late avant-garde composer, John Cage. The space hosts a giant foreign-film-fest each summer to complement its classical music, world-beat, and literary programs during the year; stop in for a monthly program. (See Music and Film, both below.)

From the masters Carrére and Hastings comes the English Renaissance-style **First Church of Christ, Scientist,** on location at the corner of 96th and Central Park West. In the **Cliff Dwellers' Apartments** at Riverside and 96th St., Art Deco rampages through the Arizona desert. Two great tastes that taste great together? You decide. Cliff dwellers totemic symbols parade along the frieze.

Throughout the West Side, if not all over the City, apartment-dwellers have conspired to break the city's chromatic monotony by planting and maintaining cozy, informal public gardens. Especially verdant, varied, and flowerful is the **Lotus Garden** (580-4897), up a flight of stairs on 97th St. between Broadway and West End Ave. You can sit on the benches and admire the fat tulips, but only when gardeners are present.

If the antique barbershop window display of the Polo boutique has left you craving the real McCoy, check out the **Broadway Barber Shop** at 2713 Broadway, between 103rd and 104th. The gilt lettering on the windows has faded but the 1907 trappings remain.

Harlem

Half a million people are packed into the three square miles of Harlem's two neighborhoods. On the East Side above 96th St. lies Spanish Harlem, known as *El Barrio* ("the neighborhood"), and on the West Side lies Harlem proper. It begins in the gentrified region known as **Morningside Heights** above 110th St. and stretches up to 155th. Both poverty-ridden neighborhoods heat up with street activity, not always of the wholesome variety; visit Harlem during the day or go there with someone who knows the area. If you lack the street wisdom or can't find your own guide opt for a commercial tour (see Guided Tours).

But it is a colossal misconception that Harlem is merely a crime-ridden slum, devoid of worth. Although poorer, it is as culturally rich as any neighborhood in the city and, contrary to popular opinion, much of it is perfectly safe. Known as the city within the city, Harlem is considered by many to be the Black capital of the Western world. Media propaganda has made the place out to be a dump—you won't believe that hype after you've visited the place.

In recent years an influx of Dominicans has changed the culture of much of the western part of Harlem; the different ethnic communities stick largely to themselves.

Hamilton Heights, concentrated around St. Nicholas and Convent Ave. in the 140s is home to professionals of all kinds. The Harlem you read about is largely represented in Manhattan Valley, particularly along Lenox Ave. and Adam Clayton Powell Blvd.; you will want to avoid these avenues after dark. For more info on Harlem call the Uptown Chamber of Commerce.

During most of the 19th century, West Harlem held the large country estates of affluent Manhattanites. When subway construction began in the 1890s, speculators built expensive housing in Harlem, anticipating an influx of middle class residents. They never came. The owners rented the empty buildings to African-Americans, who for the first time could obtain respectable New York housing. Over the next 30 years Blacks flocked to Harlem by the thousands, more than doubling its population of 80,000 between 1920 and 1930 alone. With the increase in population came an unparalleled cultural flourishing. The 1920s were Harlem's Renaissance; a thriving scene of artists, writers, and scholars lived fast and loose, producing cultural masterworks in the process. The Cotton Club and the Apollo Theater, along with numerous other jazz clubs, were on the musical vanguard.

Music fans of the 50s could easily find themselves paralyzed by the offerings. In one bar Charles Mingus would be strumming on his dancing bass; next door Charlie Parker would be blowing solos over the newest bebop tune from a hocked horn, while across the street Billie Holiday would be mellifluously reducing her audience to pools of tears. Many small jazz clubs still exist. Ask around and you won't be sorry.

In the 60s, the radical Black Power movement flourished here. The Revolutionary Theater of LeRoi Jones performed consciousness-raising one-act plays in the streets. Malcolm X, Stokely Carmichael and H. Rap Brown spoke eloquently against racism and injustice. An attempt at redevelopment began in the 1970s and continues today as communities have bonded together to beautify their neighborhood and actively resist crime.

New York City's member of the Ivy League, **Columbia University,** chartered in 1754, is tucked between Morningside Dr. and Broadway, and 114th and 121st St. Now co-ed, Columbia has cross-registration with all-female **Barnard College** across West End Ave. Suggestively, this urban campus occupies the former site of the Bloomingdale Insane Asylum. The centerpiece of the campus is the magisterial **Low Library,** named after Columbia president Seth Low. Daniel Chester French's statue of the Alma Mater, stationed on the front steps of the building, became a rallying point during the riots of 1968. Tours of the campus are given by appointment. Call 854-2842 for info.

Columbia dominates the area west of Morningside Park and has developed it relentlessly, displacing some historically significant architecture and a few people in the process. Most recently, the university started a controversy when it decided to buy the abandoned **Audubon Ballroom,** on 165th St. between St. Nicholas Ave. and Broadway. The ballroom was the site of Malcolm X's assassination and protesters have covered the doorway with plaques calling for a memorial to the black power advocate. The silver dome of the **Masjid Malcolm Shabazz,** where Malcolm X was once minister, glitters on 116th St. and Lenox Ave. (Visit Fri. at 1pm and Sun. at 10am for services and info, or call 662-2200.)

Heading east of Columbia will take you to **Morningside Park,** a green patch that reaches up toward Amsterdam Ave. The **Cathedral of St. John the Divine,** between 110th and 113th, promises to be the world's largest cathedral when finished. Construction, begun in 1812, is still ongoing and not expected to be completed until the next century. At a stoneyard nearby, artisans carve blocks much as they would have in the age of the great medieval cathedrals. The original design called for a Byzantine church with some Romanesque ornamentation. Twenty years and several bishops later, Ralph Adams Cram drew up new designs that betrayed his admiration for French Gothic. The façade resembles Notre Dame, with its centerpiece rose window, symmetrical twin towers, and heavy arched portals. The nave measures 601 feet long, the towers will be 300 feet high, and the width will span 320 feet. The bronze door of the central portal was cast in Paris by M. Barbedienne, the same man who cast the Statue of Liberty. Amble down the overwhelming central nave to see the altar dedicated to AIDS victims, a 100 million-year-old nautilus fossil, a modern sculpture for 12 firefighters who died in 1966, and a 2000lb. natural quartz crystal. The church currently maintains an extensive secular schedule, hosting concerts, art exhibitions, lectures, theater, and dance events. For information call 662-2133. (Church open daily 7am-5pm.)

The complex has a homeless shelter, a school, and countless other community services. The **Children's Sculpture Garden,** at 12th St. and Amsterdam, crowned by a huge, grotesque fountain of a winged warrior on a smiling disc, explodes with spiralling jets of water. The Ring of Freedom surrounds the fountain, topped with small bronze sculptures created annually by schoolchildren. Enter the ground to the right of the main entrance to see the impressive stoneyard where raw marble is chiseled.

Near Columbia at 120th St. and Riverside Dr. is the **Riverside Church.** Its well-known pastor, William Sloane Coffin, uses his pulpit to champion the struggle for civil rights and the fight against AIDS (he was once a leading crusader against the war in Vietnam). The observation deck in the tower commands an amazing view of the bells within and the expanse of the Hudson and Riverside Park below. You can hear concerts on the world's largest carillon (74 bells), the gift of John D. Rockefeller Jr. (Open Mon.-Sat. 9am-4:30pm, Sun. service 10:45am, tours Sun. at 12:30pm. Observation deck may be closed for reconstruction; call first.)

Diagonally across Riverside Drive lies **Grant's Tomb** (666-1640). Once a popular monument, it now attracts only a few brave souls. The massive granite mausoleum rests in peace on top of a hill overlooking the river. Inside, the black marble sarcophagus of Ulysses S. Grant and his wife Julia are surrounded by the General's cronies cast in bronze. (Open Wed.-Sun. 9am-4:30pm. Free.) Take a rest on the Gaudí-inspired tile benches around the monument, added in the mid-70s.

Two blocks east at 120th St. and Broadway is the **Union Theological Seminary,** an interfaith school of theology. Up Broadway, on the northeast corner of 122nd St., you'll find the **Jewish Theological Seminary.** The library at this center for Jewish education has nearly 300,000 volumes of Judaica.

125th Street, also known as Martin Luther King Jr. Boulevard, spans the heart of traditional Harlem. Fast-food joints, jazz bars, and the **Apollo Theater** (864-0372; box office 307-7171) keep the street humming day and night. The recently built **Harlem Third World Trade Center** on 163 W. 125th St. has drawn even more life to 125th. The **Studio Museum in Harlem** displays at 144 W. 125th St. (see Museums). The former **Teresa Hotel,** on the northwest corner of 125th St. and Seventh Ave., has housed Fidel Castro and Malcolm X. Castro once preached solidarity and brotherhood to the people of Harlem from these balconies. An unconventional tourist, Castro felt safer in Harlem than other parts of New York; still, eternally paranoid, he transported live chickens from Cuba for his meals.

Off 125th St., at 328 Lenox Ave., **Sylvia's** (966-0660) has magnetized New York for 22 years with enticing soul-food dishes. Sylvia highlights her "World Famous talked about BBQ ribs special'" with "sweet spicy sauce" ($10), served with collard greens and macaroni and cheese. (Open daily 9:30am-10:30pm.) Try the smothered chicken for $9.45. Gospel Brunch on Sunday 1-7pm (live music and soul food) costs $12.95. Live music (no cover) Wed.-Fri. 7-9pm features jazz and R&B.

Sugar Hill (127th St. to 134th St. between Morningside Ave. and St. Nicholas Terrace) was at one time home to some of the city's wealthiest and most important gangsters. But today the striking buildings look as rundown as the rest of Harlem, and the neighborhood is better known for the Sugarhill Gang, the rap group that was born in its streets in 1979 and released the first real rap hit, "Rapper's Delight."

The Gothic **City College,** at 138th and Convent (650-5310), is the northernmost outpost of the City University of New York. Founded in 1849 as a free college, it accepted everyone and was populated primarily by Jewish students until after World War II. Today, the school, which has no dorms, educates mostly commuter students from the city. Over 50 languages are spoken on campus. The less appealing south campus lies between 130th and 135th St. The sharp angles of the **North Academia Center** form an optical illusion if viewed from the south on Amsterdam Ave. This mutant of the early 1970s was designed with no windows in order to extend students' attention spans—but unfortunately the air conditioning often fails. To the east on 135th St. and Lenox Ave., the **Schomburg Center,** a branch of the public library, houses the city's African archives and presents exhibits of local artists' work (see Libraries under Practical Information).

One notable upper-class Harlem neighborhood occupies 138th St. between Seventh and Eighth Ave.: **Striver's Row,** dominated by brownstones, was built by David King in 1891. Three different architects designed these buildings, now part of the St. Nicholas Historic District. Spike Lee filmed *Jungle Fever* here, and Bob Dylan owns a house on this street. At 132 W. 138th St. New York's oldest Black church, the Abyssinian Baptist Church, was at one time presided over by congressman Adam Clayton Powell Jr. The church has 14,000 members, and the pastor, Calvin Butts, is a well known NYC political leader.

Hidden by Harlem's noisy urban life lie vestiges of the nation's more serene colonial past. Alexander Hamilton built his two-story colonial-style country home, **Hamilton Grange** (283-5154) at what is now 287 Convent Ave. at 141st St. (Open Wed.-Sun. 9am-4pm. Free.) Hamilton's furniture, however, has been moved to the Museum of the City of New York. **Aunt Len's Doll and Toy Museum** nestles within Hamilton terrace at no. 6 (see Museums).

The Georgian **Morris-Jumel Mansion,** in Roger Morris Park at W. 160th St. and Edgecombe Ave. (923-8008), served as Washington's headquarters for the battle of Harlem Heights in the autumn of 1776 and later became the home of Gouverneur Morris, an influential member of the Second Continental Congress and a signer of the Declaration of Independence. Built in 1765, it is one of Harlem's oldest buildings. Don't be afraid to knock if it seems closed (open Tues.-Sun. 10am-4pm; admission $3; seniors and students $2).

Four buildings in **Audubon Terrace,** the Beaux-Arts complex at Broadway and 155th St., house the Numismatic Society Museum, the Hispanic Society of America, the Museum of the American Indian (see Museums), and **Boricua College,** a private Hispanic liberal arts college. The neo-Italian Renaissance courtyard has huge reliefs and sculptures. Diagonally across Broadway, you can wander around the graveyard that faces the Church of Intercession. A number of notables are buried in the **Trinity Cemetery,** at 153rd-155th St. between Amsterdam and Riverside Dr. The grave of John James Audubon is near the Church of the Intercession. John Jacob Astor and former mayor Fernando Wood are also rumored to be buried here. Exercise caution visiting the cemetery, especially if alone. Also check out the Liberation bookstore at 421 Lenox Ave. at 131st St. It has a great selection of African and African-American history, art, poetry, and fiction. (Open Mon.-Fri. 11am-7pm, Sat. 11am-6:30pm.) Nearby at 132nd and Lenox Ave. is the Lenox Terrace Apartment complex where many Black politicians live, including Percy Sutton.

East Harlem is better known as **Spanish Harlem,** or *El Barrio* (The Neighborhood). It hugs the northeast corner of Central Park and extends to the 140s, where it is framed by the Harlem River. At the main artery on 116th St., the streets bustle with people selling fruit, shirts, and diverse sorts of chow. The famous ice man flavors ground-up ice with mango, papaya, coconut, or banana syrup to save you from the summer heat. Anti-crack murals and memorials to its victims span the walls.

The area from 110th St. north is not safe unless you know which streets to stay on; below 110th you should be fine during the day. The northern tip of Fifth Avenue's Museum Mile stretches up to **The Museum of the City of New York** at 103rd St. and **El Museo del Barrio** at 105th St. (see Museums).

Washington Heights

Once upon a time the area north of 155th St. was an all-Irish enclave, but the sounds of rhumba and calypso soon drowned out those of the drum and bagpipes, as Puerto Ricans and Latin Americans began to claim the neighborhood for their own. Blacks, Greeks, and Armenians, as well as a large Jewish community, subsequently moved in.

Unfortunately, the newest accompaniment is the police siren; crack, ice, and other drugs litter the urban blightscape here, near the frontline of the war on drugs.

Come here during the day for a taste of urban life with a thick ethnic flavor. On the same block, you can eat a Greek dinner, buy Armenian pastries, purchase vegetables from a South African, and talk Talmud with a Jewish scholar at nearby Yeshiva University.

Bargain-shop along trinket-filled St. Nicholas Ave. or Broadway. Street vendors sell swimwear, Italian shoes, and household items for half the going rate. You'll find discount electronics stores here too. Prices go down as the street numbers go up.

The **United Church,** 4140 Broadway at 175th, may be the best example of architectural symbiosis between the Egyptian and Miami Beach schools. Originally Loew's 175th Street Theater, this old movie house now serves as a stage for the love-thyself sermons of Reverend Ike.

The **George Washington Bridge Bus Station,** on 178th St. between Broadway and Fort Washington Ave., resembles a huge Christmas tree cookie-cutter. The **George Washington Bridge,** a 1931 construction by Othmar Amman, is a 14-lane suspension bridge once pronounced "the most beautiful bridge in the world" by Le Corbusier. Just beneath it lies **Fort Washington Park,** home to the **Little Red Lighthouse** and the remnants of the original fort. Originally constructed to steer barges away from Jeffrey's Hook, the lighthouse became the thinly disguised subject of Hildegarde Hoyt Swift's obscure children's book, *The Little Red Lighthouse and the Great Grey Bridge.*

At 186th St. and Amsterdam Ave., surrounded by kosher bakeries and butcher shops, you'll find **Yeshiva University,** dating from 1886, the oldest Jewish studies center in the U.S. Its fanciful building has Romanesque windows and colorful minarets.

The journey north along Fort Washington Ave. (west of Broadway) takes you past a succession of mid-rise apartment buildings (c. 1920) to **Fort Tryon Park,** lovingly landscaped by Central Park's Frederic Law Olmsted. John D. Rockefeller donated this land to the city in exchange for permission to construct Rockefeller University. You can still see the crusty remains of Fort Tryon, a Revolutionary War bulwark. The park also contains a magnificent expanse of gardens and **The Cloisters,** the Met's sanctuary for medieval art (see Museums).

One block before the park, the **St. Francis Cabrini Chapel** shelters the remains of Mother Cabrini, the patron saint of immigrants. Her fleshy body lies in a crystal casket under the altar, but her smiling face is made of wax—Rome's got her head. Legend has it that shortly after her death, a lock of her hair restored the eyesight of an infant who has since grown up to be a Texas priest.

You can visit a modest but charming 18th-century Dutch dwelling at 204th and Broadway. Donated to the city as a museum in 1915, **Dyckman House** (304-9422) has been restored and filled with period Dutch and English family furnishings. (Open Tues.-Sun. 11am-noon, 1-4pm. Free.)

Greenwich Village

In "The Village," bordered by 14th St. to the north and Houston to the south, bohemian cool meets New York neurosis, resulting in the "downtown" approach to life. The buildings here do not scrape the skies, the street grid dissolves into geometric whimsy, and the residents revel in countercultural logics. Village people wear their slogans on their crotches and hang underwear in their galleries. Pop culture and P.C. politics thrive here, but both are secret slaves to the real arbiter of cool: fashion.

The Village's prominence began with Tom Paine, who in 1808 had the derring-do to live on Bleecker St. Herman Melville and James Fenimore Cooper wrote American masterworks here, and Mark Twain and Willa Cather explored the U.S. heartland from their homes near Washington Square. Henry James was born on the square (not a half-block away, as New York University has incorrectly indicated) during the Village's high-society days, and Edith Wharton lived nearby. John Reed, John Dos Passos, and e.e. cummings all made the Manhattan transfer straight from Harvard, followed by

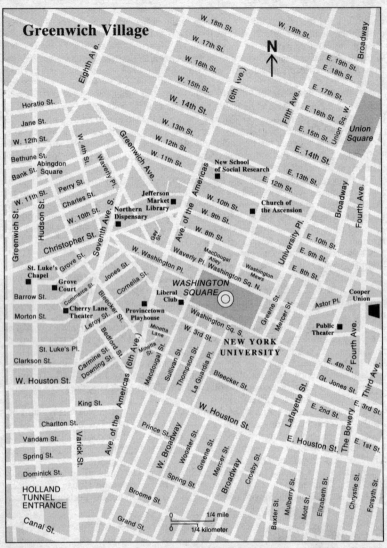

Greenwich Village

James Agee. Village rents were low then, and many writers came to this American Bohemia to begin their careers in poverty and obscurity. Eugene O'Neill created the Provincetown Playhouse in the West Village, and it created him in turn. Theodore Dreiser wrote here, as did Edna St. Vincent Millay and Thomas Wolfe. Tennessee Williams, James Baldwin, and William Styron found their way to small apartments in the area, and Richard Wright lived in the same building as Willa Cather, 35 years later.

"The Village" generally means the West Village and the Washington Square Park area, including everything west of Broadway. Bohemian residents pushed east by rising rents have taken to calling the area east of Broadway "The Village" rather than "The East Village" to imply that the real center of Bohemian life has shifted out of the "Old" West Village. The name "Greenwich Village" used to refer to the entire strip between Houston and 14th Streets (East and West) but now refers primarily to the West Village. Got it? Today there are fewer and fewer aspiring artists in Greenwich Village as young professionals take over one of the liveliest neighborhoods in Manhattan.

But the Village has not entirely sold out its old bohemian sense of fun—every year the wild **Village Halloween Parade** winds its way through the streets. If you ever wanted to see people dressed as toilets or carrots or giant condoms, this is your chance; if you're lucky, you may even receive a personal benediction from Rollerina, the city's cross-dressing fairy godmother on wheels.

The Villages of The City stay lively all day and most of the night. Those seeking propriety should head uptown immediately. Everyone else should revel in the rich and funky atmosphere, stores, and people-watching.

Washington Square Park Area

> *I know not whether it is owing to the tenderness of early associations, but this portion of New York appears to many persons the most delectable. It has a kind of established repose which is not of frequent occurrence in other quarters of the long, shrill city; it has a riper, richer, more honorable look than any of the upper ramifications of the great longitudinal thoroughfare—the look of having had something of a social history.*
>
> —Henry James, Washington Square

Washington Square Park has been the universally acknowledged heart of the Village since the district's days as a suburb. The marshland here served first as a colonial cemetery (around 15,000 bodies lie buried there) and then as a revolutionary hanging-grounds (people swung from trees which still stand today), but in the 1820s the area was converted into a park and parade ground. Soon high-toned residences made the area the center of New York's social scene.

Society has long since gone north, and **New York University** has moved in. The country's largest private university and one of the city's biggest landowners (along with the city government, the Catholic Church, and Columbia University), NYU has dispersed its administrative buildings, affiliated housing, and eccentric students throughout the Village. The university's signature purple banners concentrate around the park.

In the late 1970s and early 80s Washington Square Park was taken over by the drug trade and the homeless. The mid-80s saw a noisy clean-up campaign which has made the park fairly safe and allowed a more diverse cast of characters to return. A lot of people still buy drugs here, but *Let's Go* does not recommend it; you'll likely end up with oregano or supermarket-variety mushrooms. You will also certainly encounter several dozen of New York's unfortunate homeless; try to keep your distance, particularly at night. In the southwest corner of the park, a dozen perpetual games of chess wend their ways toward ultimate checkmate. The fountain in the center of the park provides an amphitheater for comics and musicians of widely varying degrees of talent. Judge for yourself how well Beethoven's Moonlight Sonata translates to the steel drum. (Subway: A, B, C, D, E, F, or Q to W. 4th St./Washington Sq.)

Across the street from the chess players, on the south side of the park, stands NYU's brick-arched **Vanderbilt Law School,** noted more for its scholarly than its architectural merits. Farther along Washington Sq. South you'll encounter the **Judson Memorial Baptist Church,** built in 1892 by the unflagging trio of McKim, Mead & White. Stained glass by John LaFarge panels the sanctuary. NYU's homely **Catholic Student Center** crowns the corner of Thompson St. and Washington Sq. South, neighboring the **Loeb Student Center,** an awkward shrunken likeness of the U.N. Building. On LaGuardia Pl. and Washington Sq. South looms a rust-colored monstrosity, the **Elmer Holmes Bobst Library,** another hideous progeny of the university, which for a time wanted all of its buildings to look like this so that the campus would have a common theme. Note two other buildings with the same red façade: the Tisch Building on W.

4th St. east of the park and the Meyer Physics building at Washington Pl. and Broadway. Luckily, NYU ended up opting for cheaper and more discreet purple flags instead. On the eastern side of the park, the main building of NYU contains the **Grey Art Gallery,** at 33 Washington Pl. The gallery shows both the standard student fare and unusual work from the art community. (Open Tues. and Thurs.-Fri. 11am-6:30pm, Wed. 11am-8pm, Sat. 11-5pm.)

On the south side of Washington Square Park at 133 MacDougal St. is the **Provincetown Playhouse,** a theatrical landmark. Originally based on Cape Cod, the Provincetown Players were joined by the young Eugene O'Neill in 1916 and brought here that same year to perform his successful play *Bound East for Cardiff.* The Playhouse went on to premier many of O'Neill's works, as well as the work of other Village writers such as Edna St. Vincent Millay. Farther south on MacDougal are the Village's finest (and most tourist-trampled) coffee houses, which had their glory days in the 1950s when Beatnik heroes and coffee-bean connoisseurs Jack Kerouac and Allen Ginsberg attended jazz-accompanied poetry readings at **Le Figaro** and **Café Borgia** (see Food). These sidewalk cafés still provide some of the best coffee and people watching in the city.

The north side of the park, called **The Row,** showcases some of the most renowned architecture in the city. Built largely in the 1830s, this stretch of elegant Federal-style brick residences soon became an urban center roamed by 19th-century professionals, dandies, and novelists. No. 18, now demolished, was the home of Henry James' grandmother, and the basic setting for his novel *Washington Square.*

Fifth Avenue splits The Row down the middle and arrives at its source, the grand Washington Memorial Arch, at the north side of the park. Some nostalgics built it in 1889 to mark the centennial of Washington's inauguration as President. The statues on top depict the multi-talented George in poses of war and peace. For many years, you could rarely pass the arch without encountering a gaggle of black-leathered and pink-mohawked youths. Today they, and the punk rock lifestyle, have moved on to the East Village.

A few steps north up Fifth Ave. on the East Side you'll find **Washington Mews,** a quirky, cobblestoned alleyway directly behind The Row. The boxy little brick houses, originally constructed as stables for the houses facing the park, are also worth seeing, as much for their charm as for their architectural curiosity.

Farther up Fifth Ave., on the corner of 10th St., rises the **Church of the Ascension,** a fine 1841 Gothic church with a notable altar and stained glass windows. (Open daily noon-2pm and 5pm-7pm.) Many consider the block down 10th St. between Fifth and Sixth. Ave. to be the most beautiful residential stretch in the city. This short strip plays out innumerable variations in brick and stucco, layered with wood and iron detailing. Ivy clothes the façades of many of the buildings, while windowboxes brighten others.

Balducci's, the legendary Italian grocery at 424 Sixth Ave., has grown over the years from a Sixth Ave. sidewalk stand to a gourmand's paradise. Enter its orgy of cheese barrels and bread loaves, live bug-eyed lobsters and chilled vegetables.

At 425 Sixth Ave. stands the landmark **Jefferson Market,** a Gothic structure complete with detailed brickwork, stained glass windows, and a turreted clocktower. Built as a courthouse in 1874, it occupies the triangle formed by the intersection of West 10th St., Sixth Ave., and Greenwich Ave. In the 1880s, architects voted it one of the 10 most beautiful buildings in the country. Changing tastes then threatened the site: in the early 1960s the remarkable structure faced a demolition plot. Carefully restored in 1967, the building reopened as a public library. Inside, the original pre-Raphaelite stained glass graces the spiral staircase. The brick-columned basement now serves as the Reference Room. An excellent pamphlet details the history of the site and the restoration. (Open Mon. and Thurs. noon-6pm, Tues. 10am-6pm, Wed. noon-8pm, Sat. 10am-5pm.)

Make a left out of the library on to 10th, cross the street, and you'll see an iron gate and a street sign which says "Patchin Place." Behind the gate lies a tiny courtyard, little more than a paved alley. The buildings here, constructed around 1850, later housed writers e.e. cummings, Theodore Dreiser, and Djuna Barnes.

Back on the other side of Sixth Ave. at 18 W. 11th St., a striking new building replaces the house destroyed in 1970 by a bomb-making mishap of the Weathermen, the radical group residing in the basement. Farther east at 47 Fifth Ave. is **The Salmagundi Club,** New York's oldest artists' club. Founded in 1870, the Club's building is the only remaining mansion from the area's heyday at the pinnacle of New York society. (Open during exhibitions, call 255-7740 for details.)

West Village

The bulk of Greenwich Village lies west of Sixth Ave., thriving on the new and different. In spite of rising property prices, the West Village still boasts an eclectic summer street life and excellent nightlife. The avant-garde has moved elsewhere, but the West Village puts on a pretty good show in its absence.

The West Village has a large and very visible gay community based around Sheridan Square—this is the native territory of the Guppie (Gay Urban Professional), although all kinds of gay males and lesbians shop, eat, and live here. The twisting streets host a remarkable variety of alternative clothing stores, clubs, bookshops, video stores, and even card shops. Same-sex couples can walk together openly. (See also Gay and Lesbian Nightlife.)

Christopher Street, the main byway to the south, swims in novelty restaurants and specialty shops. (Subway: #1 or 9 line to Christopher St./Sheridan Sq.) Christopher St. and Seventh Ave. intersect at tiny **Sheridan Square,** a carefully tended green traffic island/park. The square recently acquired sculptures of a gay and lesbian couple. Rioters against the Civil War draft thronged here in 1863, during some of the darkest days of New York City's history; some protesters brutally attacked freed slaves. A few street signs refer to Christopher St. as "Stonewall Place," alluding to **The Stonewall Inn,** the club where police raids in 1969 prompted the riots that sparked the U.S. gay rights movement. A plaque marks the former site of the club at 53 Christopher St.

Christopher St. runs into **Bedford Street,** a remarkably narrow old-fashioned strip. **Chumley's** bar and restaurant, at no. 86, between Grove and Barrow St., became a speakeasy in Prohibition days, illegally serving alcohol to literary Johns (Dos Passos and Steinbeck). As if in honor of its surreptitious past, no sign of any kind indicates that the neglected structure might be a commercial establishment.

One of the oldest buildings in the city, no. 77 Bedford St., on the corner of Commerce St., dates from 1799. Its handsome brick has tastefully faded. Next door, rundown, boarded-up no. 75 1/2, constructed in a former alley, is the narrowest building in the Village: it measures 9 1/2 feet across. Edna St. Vincent Millay lived there in 1850. In 1924 Millay founded the **Cherry Lane Theater** at 38 Commerce St. (989-2020), which has continued to showcase important off-Broadway theater ever since.

Across the way stand a pair of identical houses separated by a garden, known as the "Twin Sisters." Completely unsubstantiated legend has it that they were built by a sea-captain for his spinster daughters, who were not on speaking terms. At the other end of Bedford, look for the plaque near Seventh Ave. South marking the former home of Washington Irving, Jr.

SoHo and TriBeCa

SoHo (for "South of Houston"), the high-priced home of New York's artistic community, can come as quite a shock to the unwary, guileless budget traveler, who clings to the belief that art was for looking at—here, art is nothing if not for sale. Surely there remains no one who still supposes that among its many possible functions, art might somehow call into question setled social values, maybe even draw out of us moral and aesthetic preconceptions we had failed previously to see in ourselves. But if there were someone like that, wouldn't it be funny to take him or her to SoHo for a little stroll? Kinda like taking a little kid to a screening of *Snow White and the Seven Sailors.* Still, just because the art world sucks doesn't mean that you should avoid the historic (landmarked in 1973) and exciting district. Soho is the area bounded by Houston (pronounced HOUSE-ton), Canal, Lafayette, and Sullivan St. The architecture here is

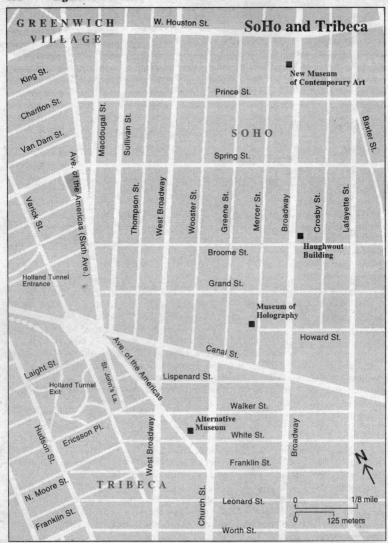

SoHo and Tribeca

GREENWICH
VILLAGE

W. Houston St.

New Museum
of Contemporary Art

King St.

Prince St.

Charlton St.

S O H O

Macdougal St.

Sullivan St.

Van Dam St.

Spring St.

Ave. of the Americas (Sixth Ave.)

Baxter St.

Varick St.

Thompson St.

West Broadway

Wooster St.

Greene St.

Mercer St.

Broadway

Crosby St.

Lafayette St.

Broome St.

Haughwout
Building

Holland Tunnel
Entrance

Grand St.

Museum of
Holography

Howard St.

Ave. of the Americas

Canal St.

Laight St.

St. John's La.

Lispenard St.

Holland Tunnel
Exit

Walker St.

West Broadway

Alternative
Museum

White St.

Broadway

Hudson St.

Ericsson Pl.

Franklin St.

N. Moore St.

T R I B E C A

Church St.

Leonard St.

0   1/8 mile

Franklin St.

0   125 meters

Worth St.

American Industrial (1860-1890), notable for its cast-iron façades. Architects used iron to imitate stone, often painting it to look like limestone, and they laced the columns and pediments with ornate detail. The iron frames made heavy walls unnecessary and allowed for the installation of vast windows. The sweatshops and factories that filled the structures were eventually outlawed, and in 1962 the City Club called the area "the wasteland of New York." Redevelopment plans were hatched soon afterwards, and residents fought against the construction of an intruding expressway.

Greene Street offers the best of SoHo's lofty architecture. Note the classic roof of No. 28-30, a bright blue building known as the Queen of Greene St. Its neighbor, No. 72-76, the King of Greene St., is actually two buildings designed to look like one, its Corinthian portico spread lavishly across five stories of painted metal. Once architects here made sweatshops look like iron palaces; now artists have converted factory lofts into studios. Every block has a gallery, an experimental theatre, or a designer clothing store. High-fashion sorts pay dearly (up to $500 for a pair of pants) for the right look, which is often quite vulgar. Excellent galleries line West Broadway; remember that most close on Sundays and Mondays (see Galleries). This is a great place for stargazing, too, so bring your autograph book and a bright flash for your cameras. Celebrities like that.

A mind-twisting mural by Richard Haas covers the southeast corner of Prince and Greene St. Try to pick out which windows are real and which are painted. To the south, on a lot at Wooster and Spring St., a daily fair makes its presence felt. Browse through the extensive selection of international goods. The bargain hunt continues on Broadway with a wide selection of used clothing stores. Flea market devotees should check out Sunday's market on the corner of Broadway and Grand St.

Art is not restricted to galleries here. At 583 Broadway, just north of Prince St., you'll find **The New Museum of Contemporary Art,** showing the newest and latest on the art scene. Electromagnetic radiation starts further south at 72 Wooster St. in the **Museum of Colored Glass and Light** and at the **Museum of Holography** at 11 Mercer St. (See Museums.)

If you're looking for genuine starving artists, you probably won't find them in SoHo—unless they're looking with envied longing though dark, plate-glass gallery windows. But you may find a few in young SoHo, called **TriBeCa** ("Triangle Below Canal"), an area bounded by Chambers St., Broadway, Canal St., and the West Side Highway. Still flanked by butter and egg warehouses, upstairs lofts here have undergone similar art gentrification to those in SoHo. Today Robert DeNiro owns a grill and a film company in the neighborhood, and the prices are heading up.

Admire the cast-iron edifices lining White St., Thomas St., and Broadway; the 19th-century federal-style buildings on Harrison St.; and the shops, galleries, and bars on Church and Reade St. For commercial goods, residents roam the streets of Hudson and W. Broadway. Duane St. has good food, if not great prices. Between Chambers and Northmore St. stands Manhattan Community College, part of the City University system.

The avant garde art world has migrated south from SoHo; new galleries offer exhibitions by less established artists. Art lovers should look to **Artists Space** at 223 West Broadway and to the **Franklin Furnace** at 112 Franklin St. (see Galleries), which battle fire regulations in their continuing quest to display the most alternative of alternative art.

East Village, Lower East Side, and Alphabet City

The old Lower East Side, once home to Eastern European immigrants, extended from Hester to 14th St. Now this area has developed a three-way split personality, encompassing the part south of Houston and east of the Bowery (commonly considered the Lower East Side), the section east of Broadway and north of Houston (known as the "East Village"), and the part of the East Village east of 1st Ave. (known as "Alphabet City"). Pick up a map to the area at a local bookstore, such as the Strand (see below).

Down below Houston in the somewhat deserted Lower East Side you can still find some excellent kosher delis and a few oldtimers who remember the time when the Second Ave. El ran from the power station at Allen and Pike St. Two million Jews arrived on the Lower East Side in the 20 years before World War I, and here are the remnants of the Jewish ghetto that inspired Jacob Riis' compelling work *How the Other Half Lives* (and more recently, the 80s epic musical *Rags* by Joseph Stein, Stephen Schwartz, and Charles Strouse). On **The Bowery,** you can haggle for lamps; on **Allen Street,** shirts and ties. Try the Orchard St. market on a Sunday morning for some real bargains. Off Delancey St., the Essex St. covered market is direct from Northern Africa. On The Bowery (which comes from the Dutch *bouwerie,* or farm) check out Stanford White's **Bowery Savings Bank,** at Grand St., a repository of wealth now surrounded by lots of homeless people. Built in 1894, it has kept the original carved check-writing stands inside. You'd probably feel safe leaving your money here, but don't go wandering around down here at night with a full wallet.

East Village

The East Village, a comparatively new creation, was carved out of the Bowery and the Lower East Side, as rents in the West soared and its residents sought accommodations elsewhere. Allen Ginsberg, Jack Kerouac, and William Burroughs all eschewed the Village establishment to develop their junked-up "beat" sensibility east of Washington Sq. Park. Billie Holiday sang here; more recently, the East Village provided Buster Poindexter and Red Transistor with their early audiences. The transfer of population has recaptured much of the gritty feel of the old Village, and the population here is less homogeneous than in the West, with older Eastern European immigrants living alongside new Hispanic and Asian arrivals. But it has been a difficult compromise, and many poorer denizens of the East Village feel they have been pushed out by the newcomers. These tensions have not been helped by glimmers of gentrification and rising rents in the East.

A fun stretch of Broadway runs through the Village, marking the western boundary of the East Village. Everyone and their grandmother knows about this browser's paradise. On summer weekends it overflows with shoppers known unaffectionately as the "B&T crowd," referring to the bridges and tunnels by which non-Manhattanites must reach the island.

Grace Church, constructed in 1845, asserts its powerful Gothic presence at 800 Broadway, between 10th and 11th. The church used to be *the* place for weddings. The dark, gorgeous interior has a distinctly medieval feel. (Open Mon.-Fri. 10am-5:45pm, Sat. noon-4pm.) Antique stores flock around the church, especially on 10th and 11th St. Most specialize in large, high-priced pieces of furniture or architectural elements (Greek-style columns and eagle-shaped statues).

One of the world's most famous bookstores is **The Strand,** at the corner of 12th St. and Broadway, which bills itself as the "largest used bookstore in the world" with over two million books on eight miles of shelves. At **Forbidden Planet,** directly across Broadway, you can browse through European space toys, vintage Superman comics, hundreds of science-fiction paperbacks, and a complete line of "Dungeons & Dragons" fantasy paraphernalia. (See Bookstores.)

Farther south on Broadway, the stores get funkier, with lots of "antique" (read: used yet expensive) clothing stores and accessory shops, where the trendy and their money are soon parted. Teeny-boppers trek miles for the fashion sense of **The Antique Boutique,** 217 Broadway. At Broadway and 4th St., you'll find another of the Village's spiritual landmarks: **Tower Records,** a store with an enormous (if limited) musical inventory. Open late (and often a privileged site for drug-induced meanderings), Tower has become not only a popular hangout, but also a sudden bonding ground for people of similar musical taste: "Wow, you're into Velvet Crush? I *love* Velvet Crush! Were you at their last concert?" (See Record Stores.)

Walk one block east of Broadway on East 4th to reach Lafayette St. To your right will be **Colonnade Row,** with the Public Theater across the street. Colonnade Row consists of four magnificently columned houses, built in 1833, once the homes of New York's most famous 19th-century millionaires: John Jacob Astor and Cornelius "Commodore" Vanderbilt, as well as the Delano family (as in Franklin Delano Roosevelt). There used to be nine of these houses; the ones that remain, at 428-434 Lafayette St., are a tad on the grubby side. The **Joseph Papp Public Theatre,** 425 Lafayette St. (598-7150), a grand brownstone structure, was constructed by John Jacob Astor in 1853 to serve as the city's first free library. After its collection moved uptown, the building became the headquarters of the Hebrew Immigrant Aid Society, an organization dedicated to assisting thousands of poor Jewish immigrants who came to New York in the early years of this century. In 1967, Joseph Papp's "New York Shakespeare Festival" converted the building to its current use as a theatrical center.

Up Lafayette St., Astor Place, both a small street and a large intersection, simmers with street life. The street signs were recently covered with the words "Peltier Place," in honor of a Native American man currently in prison for allegedly killing two FBI agents in 1985, and in protest of John Jacob Astor, whose fur trading is seen by some as exploitation of the Native American population.

At Astor/Peltier Place and Broadway you can complement your new Village wardrobe with a distinctive trim at the largest haircutting establishment in the world: **Astor Place Hair Stylists,** famous for its low-priced production-line approach to style. Scissors are passé here; expect to be mechanically clipped. A total of 110 people (including a DJ) are employed in this three-story complex at 2 Astor Pl. (475-9854; open Mon.-Sat. 8am-8pm, Sun. 9am-6pm; men's cut $10, women's cut $12; Sundays and holidays $2 extra).

Astor Place, the intersection, is distinguished by a sculpture of a large black cube balanced on its corner. If you and your friends push hard enough the cube will rotate, but somebody sleeping underneath may complicate the process. Note the subway kiosk, a cast-iron Beaux-Arts beauty which was built—believe it or not—in 1985 as part of a reconstruction of the station (the #6 train stops here).

Astor Place prominently features the rear of the **Cooper Union Foundation Building,** 41 Cooper Sq. (254-6300), built in 1859 to house the Cooper Union for the Advancement of Science and Art, a tuition-free technical and design school founded by the self-educated industrialist Peter Cooper. The school's free lecture series has hosted practically every notable American since the mid-19th century. Cooper Union was the first college intended for the underprivileged, the first coeducational college, the first racially open college, and the first college to offer free adult education classes. The American Red Cross and the NAACP were founded here. It's also the oldest standing building in the U.S. incorporating steel beams. Appropriately enough, its founder Cooper first laid down the steel rails that sped up railroad construction. On the second floor, the **Houghton Gallery** hosts changing exhibits on design and American history, but usually not during the summer. (Open daily, noon-7pm.)

Stuyvesant St. angles off from Astor Pl. cutting north over 9th St., and terminates at Second Ave. and 10th St., right in front of the pretty **St. Mark's-in-the-Bowery Church,** 131 E. 10th St. (674-6377). The church was built in 1799 on the site of a chapel in what used to be the estate of Peter Stuyvesant, the much-reviled last Dutch governor of the colony of New Amsterdam. He lies buried in the small cobblestoned graveyard here. Restored in the mid-70s, the church building burned to a near-crisp in a 1978 fire, and re-restoration was not completed until a few years ago.

Across from the church at 156 Second Ave. stands a famous Jewish landmark, the **Second Avenue Deli** (677-0606). This is all that remains of the "Yiddish Rialto," the stretch of Second Ave. between Houston and 14th St. that comprised the Yiddish theater district during the early part of this century. The Stars of David embedded in the sidewalk in front of the restaurant contain the names of some of the great actors and actresses who spent their lives entertaining the poor Jewish immigrants of the city. Order sublime chicken soup or splash out on a pastrami sandwich while you watch a schedule of Broadway shows flash by on what used to be an electronic stock-ticker. (See Food.)

St. Mark's Place, running from Third Ave. at 8th St., down to Tompkins Sq. Park, is the geographical and spiritual center of the East Village. In the 1960s, the street was the Haight-Ashbury of the East, full of pot-smoking flower children waiting for the next concert at the Electric Circus. In the late 1970s it became the King's Road of New York, as mohawked youths hassled the passersby from the brownstone steps off Astor Pl. Today things are changing again: a Gap store sells its conventional color-me-matching combos across the street from a shop stocking "YOU MAKE ME SICK" T-shirts. St. Mark's is the East Village's answer to a small town's Main Street. People know one another here—sometimes they even stop to talk to each other. Dark little restaurants and cafés elbow for space with leather boutiques and trinket vendors. People try to sell virtually anything here: new records, used underwear, aged red high-heeled shoes, hot stereo equipment, and four-year-old *Jugs* magazines.

The **St. Mark's Bookstore,** 12 St. Mark's Pl. (260-7853), is a nice spot for browsing and has a particularly wide selection of art periodicals, as well as large sections of books on socialism and philosophy. *Anarchists' Cookbooks* are also available. (Open daily 11am-11:30pm.)

Alphabet City

East of First Ave., south of 14th St., and north of Houston, the avenues run out of numbers and take on letters. This part of the East Village has so far escaped the escalating yuppification campaign that has claimed much of St. Mark's Place; in the area's heyday in the 60s, Jimi Hendrix and the Fugs would play open-air shows to bright-eyed love children. Rent here is still reasonable; here you'll find the stately residences of the East Village's deadbeatniks and hardcore anarchists, as well as girl-noise musical terrorists like God Is My Co-Pilot. (Regular old students reside here, too.) There has been a great deal of drug-related crime in the recent past, although the community has done an admirable job of making the area livable again. Alphabet City is generally safe during the day, and the addictive nightlife on Avenue A ensures some protection there, but try to avoid straying east of Avenue B at night.

Alphabet City's extremist Boho activism (and the inevitably brutish behavior of the NYPD) has made the neighborhood chronically ungovernable in the last several years, a little kernel of Amsterdam or old West Berlin set deep in the bowels of Manhattan. A few years ago, police officers set off a riot when they attempted to forcibly evict a band of the homeless and their supporters in **Tompkins Square Park,** at E. 7th St. and Ave. A. An aspiring video artist recorded scenes of wanton police depravity, setting off a public outcry and a further round of police-inspired violence. Today, the park is no longer a glum testament to the progress of gentrification—it has just reopened, and officials have high hopes for the area. The park still serves as a psycho-geographical epicenter for many a churlish misfit. One of the many riots that erupted in New York City following the Rodney King verdict in 1992 was led by the "East Side Anarchists," who humped down to Tompkins Square after tearing through St. Mark's Place.

Countless memorial murals attest to the scars left by drugs on this area. A mural on an old burnt-out crack house on Ave. C between 8th and 9th, pleads for action against drugs at home, not on the streets, and a mural on the northwest corner of 8th St. and Ave. C hangs "in memory of Cesar." Less solemn projects include the community gardens that bloom next to some of these murals and blasted buildings, including one on 9th St. between Ave. B and Ave. C. Krzyzstof Wodicko's mysterious Poliscar, a smug metal "war machine for people without apartments," has been repeatedly exhibited here. A good guide to current issues and events in Alphabet City and the entire East Village is the free *Downtown* newspaper, found at St. Mark's Bookshop and other stores in the area. Check out the often extravagant street art and read the neighborhood posters for an update on some of the current issues.

Little Italy and Chinatown

Little Italy, a touristy pocket of Naples and Sicily nestled in the lower spine of Manhattan, is roughly bounded by Houston St. to the north, Canal St. to the south, The Bowery to the east, and Lafayette St. to the west. The borders shift and recede; the neighborhood continues to shrink as Chinatown grows. Many young Italians are moving out; meanwhile, more authentic Italian neighborhoods flourish in Bensonhurst, Brooklyn and in Belmont, the Bronx. Nonetheless, until he landed in prison, alleged Mafia kingpin John Gotti still made his way around to the few social clubs that remain here for a deal or a meal. Around the intersection of Grand and Mulberry St., the flavor of the older Little Italy lives on.

The Little Italy experience revolves exclusively around food. Restaurants are horrendously overpriced—a full meal could run $40-50. Save money by dining on appetizers or grabbing a snack at one of the many shops and groceries. (See Food.)

A walk up Mulberry St. will have you ducking under the umbrellas of sidewalk cafés. At **Umberto's Clam House,** 129 Mulberry St. at Hester St., in the heart of Little Italy, "Crazy Joey" Gallo was slain in 1972 while celebrating his birthday; allegedly he offended a rival Family. Further north, at 264 Mulberry St. at Prince St., you'll find **St. Patrick's Old Cathedral,** finished in 1815. One of America's earliest Gothic revival churches, the façade was damaged in an 1866 fire and still hasn't been fully restored to its original grandeur.

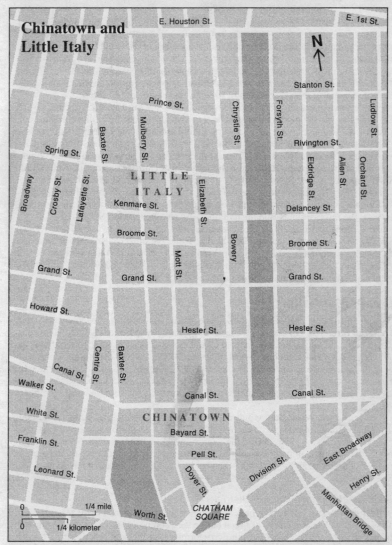

Chinatown and Little Italy

E. Houston St.

E. 1st St.

N

Stanton St.

Prince St.

Chrystie St.

Forsyth St.

Ludlow St.

Baxter St.

Mulberry St.

Rivington St.

Spring St.

Eldridge St.

Allen St.

Orchard St.

LITTLE ITALY

Broadway

Crosby St.

Lafayette St.

Kenmare St.

Elizabeth St.

Delancey St.

Broome St.

Bowery

Broome St.

Grand St.

Grand St.

Mott St.

Grand St.

Howard St.

Hester St.

Hester St.

Centre St.

Baxter St.

Canal St.

Walker St.

Canal St.

Canal St.

White St.

CHINATOWN

Franklin St.

Bayard St.

Pell St.

East Broadway

Leonard St.

Doyer St.

Division St.

Henry St.

Manhattan Bridge

0   1/4 mile

0   1/4 kilometer

Worth St.

CHATHAM SQUARE

At the corner of Lafayette St. and E. Houston St. stands the **Puck Building,** former home of the New York monthly magazine *Spy.* This beautiful, red brick building was constructed in 1889 to house the humor magazine *Puck*; a cute golden Puck stands over the Lafayette St. door.

Dotted with stores selling low-cost electronics and plastics, commercial **Canal Street** divides Little Italy and Chinatown. Stepping south across Canal St., the caffès and *gelaterie* of Little Italy give way to pagoda-topped phone booths, steaming tea shops, and firecracker vendors. New York's **Chinatown** has seven Chinese newspapers, over 300 garment factories, innumerable food shops, and houses the largest Asian community in the U.S. outside of San Francisco. Vaguely bounded by Worth St. and Canal St. to the south and north, and Broadway and Bowery to the west and east, Chinatown spills out further into the surrounding streets every year. The Chinese population in the area is now estimated at nearly 300,000.

Street life and businesses flourish. Don't be snookered by the low prices on merchandise; creative labelling abounds. Just because those Walkmen say Sony doesn't mean they're made in Japan. Gift shops line the streets, hustling to ply their overpriced miniature Buddhas and dragon-shaped clogs. During the Chinese New Year (in late Jan. or early Feb.), the area's frenetic pace accelerates. Be careful down here around the Fourth of July. You can buy fireworks of all stripes, but most are illegal, and dealing with the crafty sales techniques of fire-hawkers can be intimidating.

For a trippy freak of a hybrid religion, check out the **Ling Liang Church,** 173-175 E. Broadway, resting place of a postmodern Christ surrounded by biblical blessings on a bed of red Chinese characters. Scholars should ascend to the **Oriental Enterprises Company,** 13 Elizabeth St. (second floor), a bookstore serving those literate in Chinese. They also serve free tea. Sit in reading chairs as you sip and read or just admire the calligraphy equipment. Check out the selection of Chinese pop music. At the **Buddhist Temple,** 16 Pell St. off Mott St., the devout kneel in front of a porcelain statue, offering fresh fruit and shaking cans of incense. Visitors are welcome. Buddhists pray to *Kuinyin,* a multi-armed buddha who holds the symbol for Nirvana in his upper arms, at the Eastern states Buddhist Temple of America, 64 Mott St.

The **Chinatown Fair,** 8 Mott St., features video games and two woeful chickens. For 75¢ one is forced to "play" Tic Tac Toe while the other "dances" over what appears to be a spinning hot plate. (A sign above them claims that the chickens do not suffer.) Secular Confucius stands firm and wise on the plaza dedicated to him on the corner of Division St. and the Bowery, at the end of Mott St.

Lower Manhattan

Many of the city's superlatives congregate in the southern tip of Manhattan Island. The Wall Street area is the densest in all New York. Wall Street itself measures less than a half mile long. This narrow state of affairs has driven the neighborhood into the air, creating one of the highest concentrations of skyscrapers in the world. Along with density comes history: lower Manhattan was the first part of the island to be settled by Europeans, and many of the city's historically significant sights lie buried in the concrete canyons here. Omnipresent Heritage Trail markers indicate the most significant spots.

Touring Lower Manhattan won't cost you. Parks, churches, and temperature-controlled cathedrals of commerce such as the New York Stock Exchange and City Hall charge no admission. Visit during the working week, when suspendered and/or high-heeled natives rush around, brandishing *Wall Street Journals.* After hours, these titans of trade loosen ties and suck in the ocean breeze (and a few drinks) at the South Street Seaport.

Wall Street and the Financial District

Battery Park, named for a battery of guns the British stored there from 1683 to 1687, is now a chaotic chunk of green on the very southernmost toenail of Manhattan Island. The #1 and 9 trains to South Ferry terminate at the southern tip; the #4 and 5 stop at Bowling Green, just off the northern tip. You can take your morning constitutional here, admiring plaques and monuments on the way, or just inhaling some sea air. Usually mobs descend upon the park on their way to the Statue of Liberty ferry, to be preyed upon by parasitic peddlers. Try not to talk to strangers here.

Walk past the Netherlands Memorial Flagpole towards **Castle Clinton** and the water. On the way is Hope Garden, a living AIDS memorial dedicated in 1992, where 100,000 roses bloom each year. Castle Clinton, the main structure in the park, contains an information center and the circular pavilion where you can purchase tickets for the Liberty or Ellis Island ferries (see Statue of Liberty and Ellis Island). More than a glorified ticket booth, this structure was completed just before the war of 1812, as tensions between Britain and the newly independent United States were coming to a boil. It then stood in 35 feet of water, connected by a drawbridge to the shore 200 feet away. Not a single shot was ever fired from the fort, and by 1824 the city felt safe enough from British invasion to lease the area for public entertainment. First it was a theater for outdoor events: balloon ascents, scientific demonstrations, and fireworks. Later, in the 1840s, the castle was roofed over and turned into a concert hall. By 1855, enough landfill from nearby construction had accumulated to connect Castle Clinton to the mainland, and it became New York's immigrant landing depot. Between 1855 and 1889, more than seven million immigrants passed through these walls. In later years, when Ellis Island had assumed this function, Castle Clinton turned into the site of the beloved New York Aquarium; then the aquarium moved to Coney Island and the building was left vacant. When the city declared the fort a national historic site in 1950, wreckers had already removed the second story, the roof, and other expansions, leaving the building at its present dimensions, the same as those of 1811.

As you look out at the water from Castle Clinton, you'll have a clear view of lush New Jersey (on your right), Ellis Island (dominated by a large brick building), Liberty Island (she's waving at you), Staten Island (directly behind the Statue of Liberty), and Governor's Island, a command center for the U.S. Coast Guard (to the left). A short walk to your left as you face the water, south from Castle Clinton, brings you to the **East Coast Memorial,** a monument to those who died in coastal waters in World War II. A large sculpture of a vicious eagle stands in front of granite monoliths engraved with the names of the dead. Behind the eagle, the sheer, elegant—and largely empty—wedge of 17 State Street dominates the skyline. Built in 1989, this leviathan building stands on the site of the house where Herman Melville was born in 1819. Melville soon left to pen his masterpiece novel *Moby Dick* as well as "Bartleby the Scrivener," a maddeningly angst-ridden story of the life of a clerk in the 19th-century financial district. Beside 17 State St. and behind the church next door, you can explore a new (if kinda weird) exhibit called "New York Unearthed" (363-9327), a museum of Manhattan archaeology sponsored by the South Street Seaport Museum. Excavators have discovered most of the items here during preparations for new construction in the downtown area. The minuscule collection runs from clay pipes dated 1250 AD to wild boar, wildebeest, and other exotic mammal fragments found at the site of the 1830 marketplace. A set of dentures from 1880 is the star exhibit. (Open Mon.-Sat. noon-6pm; free.) The huge green buildings on the water near 17 State Street are hard to miss even if you try; the Coast Guard Building and the Staten Island Ferry Terminal redefine dreadful. Next door, a skulky black skyscraper—New York Plaza, home of the Chase Manhattan Bank—redefines monolith.

Before this area was landfilled, State Street was the shorefront, and by the 1790s it had become the most fashionable residential street in Manhattan. State Street's domestic glamor has vanished today, though you can feel its former elegance in the **Church of Our Lady of the Rosary** and the adjoining **Shrine of St. Elizabeth Ann Seton.** They stand out like brick and wooden ghosts against an expanse of streamlined glass and steel. The right-hand section, originally the James Watson House, was built in stages from 1792 to 1805 in the Federal style and retains its original façade, with columns supposedly cut from ship masts. St. Elizabeth Ann Seton, canonized in 1975 as the first U.S.-born saint, lived here with her family from 1801 to 1803. The adjoining church dates from 1883, when it served as a shelter for Irish immigrant women.

If you walk up State St. along the edge of Battery Park, you will come to the **U.S. Custom House,** off the northwestern corner of the park. This gorgeous building, designed by Cass Gilbert, was completed in 1907, when the majority of U.S. revenues came from customs duties, and the majority of customs duties came from New York. Come inspect this palace of trade. Fort Amsterdam stood here in 1626, facing out into the harbor and defending the then-Dutch colony. In 1790, a Georgian mansion was built here as the presidential residence, but Washington never moved in because the United States capital moved to Philadelphia the very same year. (Washington, DC didn't become the nation's capital until 1803.)

The Beaux-Arts masterpiece that stands here now combines Baroque and Renaissance inspiration with aggressive decoration. All of the sculpture and artwork on the building relates directly to its function. The 12 statues on top of the façade represent the 12 great trading centers of the world ("Germany," the third statue from the right, became "Belgium" in the years before World War I). On the ground level, four large

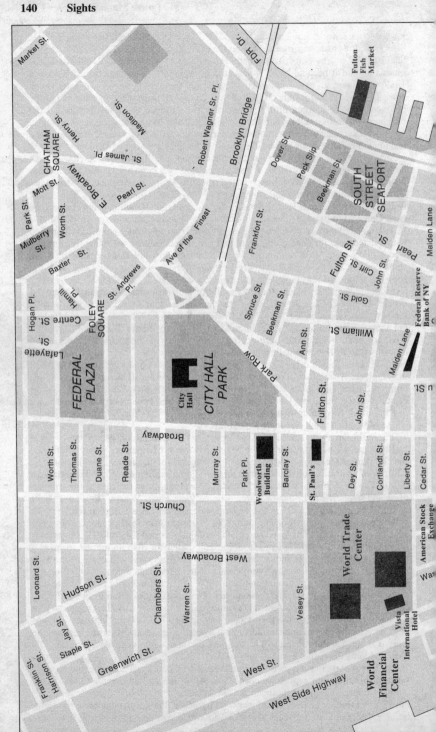

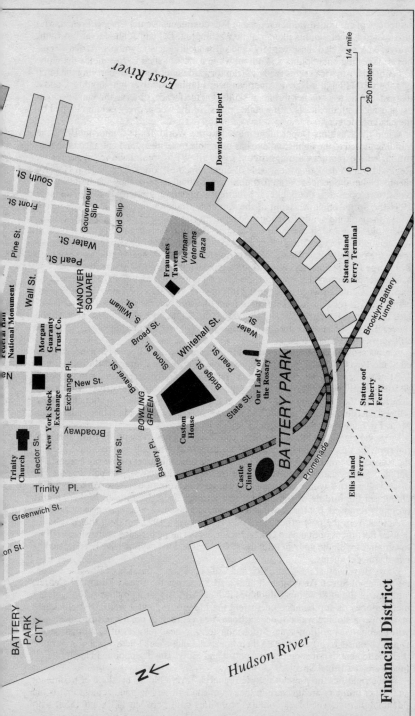

East River

South St.

Front St.

Pine St.

Wall St.

Gouverneur Slip

Water St.

Old Slip

Pearl St.

HANOVER SQUARE

Fraunces Tavern

Vietnam Veterans Plaza

Federal Hall National Monument

S. William St.

Morgan Guaranty Trust Co.

Broad St.

Whitehall St.

Exchange Pl.

New St.

Stone St.

Water St.

New York Stock Exchange

Beaver St.

BOWLING GREEN

Pearl St.

Bridge St.

Our Lady of the Rosary

Broadway

Custom House

State St.

Trinity Church

Rector St.

Morris St.

Battery Pl.

BATTERY PARK

Trinity   Pl.

Greenwich St.

on St.

Castle Clinton

Promenade

BATTERY PARK CITY

Downtown Heliport

Staten Island Ferry Terminal

Brooklyn-Battery Tunnel

Statue oof Liberty Ferry

Ellis Island Ferry

Hudson River

N

Financial District

1/4 mile

250 meters

0

0

sculptures of enthroned women represent four continents. Daniel Chester French, who also seated Lincoln on his memorial in Washington, DC and John Harvard in Cambridge, MA, chiseled these worldly (and offhandedly racist) symbols. Africa sleeps, her arms resting on a Sphinx and a lion, while a self-satisfied Europe holds the globe in her hands. America seems ready to leap forward out of her chair, carrying the torch of Liberty (although a Native American peeps ominously over her shoulder), and a distracted Asia rests on her throne of skulls. On the façade, observe the window arches, adorned with the heads of the eight "races" of the world, every column topped by the head of Mercury.

When the Customs Department moved to the World Trade Center in 1973, the building closed to the public; no one has been able to see the grand entrance or the rotunda, which features a magnificent cycle of WPA-commissioned frescoes by Reginald Marsh depicting the travels of eight famed explorers. The Federal Government's General Services Administration has decided to re-occupy the building and plans to re-open it to the public; it is currently undergoing intensive restorations. In 1994 the Smithsonian Museum of the American Indian will move in. In the meanwhile, the building's only functional department is, ironically, the Bankruptcy Court.

The old Customs House faces egg-shaped **Bowling Green,** the city's first park. It was rented out as a bowling green in 1733 for the price of one peppercorn a year—hence the oddball name. Here, colonists rioted in the 1760s against the taxes imposed by George III's Stamp Act. When George repealed the act in 1770, the forgiving New Yorkers commissioned a statue of the king on horseback and in 1771 protected the park with a gold-crowned fence made in England. But after the Declaration of Independence was read on July 9, 1776, in front of City Hall, the joyous (if fickle) populace raced to Bowling Green and tore down the statue, as well as the crowns on the fence. Bits of the statue were later used as bullets in the revolution. The 1771 fence still surrounds the park today.

A modest stone building across Broadway from Bowling Green says merely "United States Post Office—Bowling Green Station." This is the **Cunard Building,** built in 1921 as the central headquarters for the great transatlantic ocean liners, which departed from nearby piers. Make the effort to go inside. The humble post office facilities are dwarfed by the vasty classical rotunda in the grand booking hall. Antiquated maps, winged cherubs, acres of tubage, and frescoes of Viking ships adorn the walls. (Open Mon.-Fri. 6am-8pm, Sat. 6am-2pm.)

From the entrance to the post office, you'll have a good view of the Bull, poised to run from the tip of Bowling Green right up Broadway. The bull and bear have become the respective symbols of good and bad markets on Wall Street (some say because the bull attacks by raising its horns, the bear by lowering its claws). The bull was the gift of an Italian artist who mischievously planted it in front of the New York Stock Exchange in the middle of the night a few winters back. Unamused brokers had it promptly removed, but for now it stands here, at a distance, a compromise.

Across from the post office stands 26 Broadway, a 1922 building that originally housed the offices of Standard Oil. Its façade curves along the edge of the street, but its tower aligns with the uptown grid; the street level and the skyline have been treated as two distinct elements.

Cross Broadway at the post office and walk back down the side of Bowling Green, on Whitehall Street. At Whitehall and Pearl St. stands the **Broad Financial Center,** with one of the most whimsical lobbies in New York. Tapering pylons with revolving metal globes on top balance on surreal marble globes, and a wall-sized clockface stares over a sloping water-slide. Exit onto Pearl Street; at no. 85 and Broad St. you will encounter a million-square-foot monster, the headquarters of Goldman Sachs. Dutch colonists trying to recreate their homeland dug a canal here which ran through their settlement, but it soon became putrid and filthy. The disappointed Dutch filled it in and created Broad Street.

To the right lies the pseudo-historic Fraunces Tavern block, an island of traditional and rather ordinary architecture in the sea of modern self-aggrandizement that is the financial district. The block contains structures built between 1719 and 1883, with many 20th-century additions and reconstructions. **The Fraunces Tavern Museum** (425-1778) at 54 Pearl St. stands on the supposed site of one of George Washington's favorite New York hangouts. On this spot, or somewhere nearby, he said his final farewell to the officers of his victorious revolution. (See Museums.)

Continue up Pearl St. to Hanover Square, a paved-over intersection where you can sit down for a while. Note the statue of the Dutch goldsmith Abraham De Peyster, moved to this spot in the 1970s from Bowling Green. India House, a handsomely columned brownstone, faces the square; constructed in 1854 as the Hanover Bank, it has since become a private club.

Once the northern border of the New Amsterdam settlement, **Wall Street** takes its name from the wall built in 1653 to shield the Dutch colony from a British invasion from the north. By the early 19th century, it had already become the financial capital of the United States, and many a populist reformer used its name to refer to the entire financial district and its baleful menace to the nation. Its mystique endures today— Wall Street means big business, big money, loose lips, and lost illusions.

Citibank has deposited branch offices in the historic no. **55 Wall St.** (open Mon.-Fri. 9am-3pm). This building once housed the Second Merchants' Exchange (1836-1854), the predecessor of the modern stock exchange. Its 16 Ionic columns, each weighing 41 tons and cut from a single slab of stone, were dragged here by teams of oxen. In 1863, it became the United States Customs House. Originally only three stories tall, the structure grew in 1909 when the indefatigable firm of McKim, Mead & White added on the top four stories, and the **First National City Bank** moved in. A new row of smaller Corinthian columns gracefully complements the original façade.

Across the street at no. 60 hovers the unmistakable headquarters of the **Morgan Bank,** 52 stories of bizarre but eye-catching 1980s neo-neoclassicism. Some quick-witted critics point out that the building itself resembles a column. Wander through its vast public atrium of white and gray marble and gaze at the mirrored white latticework ceiling. The overall effect is that of a country-time front porch on steroids.

Down a bit on the same side of the street stands 48 Wall St., headquarters of the **Bank of New York,** originally founded in 1784 by Alexander Hamilton. This building, though constructed in the late 1920s, has somehow acquired tasteful colonial echoes. If you go quietly through the main entrance, you will probably be allowed to peek over the top of the sweeping marble staircases into the airy formal hall.

Just a bit farther down Wall St., at its intersection with Broad St. (which turns into Nassau St. to the north) cluster a mass of sights. Meet **Federal Hall** (264-8711) with its somewhat grotesque, larger-than-life statue of a tightly pantalooned George Washington on its steps. (Several historians have commented on the heft of Washington's rump.) After 1703, this classical building housed the original City Hall, where the trial of John Peter Zenger helped establish freedom of the press in 1735, and where the Stamp Act Congress met in 1765. It also served as the first seat of the constitutional government adopted in 1789; it was here that Washington was first sworn in (roughly on the spot where he stands today), that James Madison submitted the Bill of Rights to Congress, and that the House of Representatives and the Senate first met. Unfortunately, the original building was demolished in 1812. Its 1842 replacement functioned as a customs house (which building hasn't?) until 1862, when a branch of the U.S. Treasury Department moved there. In 1955 it became a national memorial, and its exhibits now include the illustrated Bible Washington used at his inauguration, a 10-minute animated program called "Journey to Federal Hall," and models of the building's predecessor. Tours and the animated film by request. (Open Mon.-Fri. 9am- 5pm; disabled entrance at 15 Pine St.)

Walk across from Federal Hall to the **Morgan Guaranty Trust Company,** built in 1913. On the Wall St. side of the building, underneath the fourth window over, pockmarks in the stone wall bear witness to a lunch-hour explosion on September 16, 1920, when a bomb left in a pushcart went off. Conspiracy theorists, cynics, and experts disagree on who to blame, but the consensus fingers an anarchist trying to destroy Morgan and his bank. The explosion killed 33 and injured 400, but the bank stood unscathed, as did Morgan, who happened to be abroad at the time.

On the southwestern corner of Wall and Broad St. stands the current home of the **New York Stock Exchange** (656-5168; open to the public Mon.-Fri. 9:15am-4pm). The main building, constructed in 1903, has a relief sculpture in its pediment titled "Integrity Protecting the Works of Man," made by J.Q.A. Ward, the man responsible for the statue of Washington outside of Federal Hall. The Stock Exchange was first created as a marketplace for handling the $80 million in U.S. bonds issued in 1789 and 1790 to pay Revolutionary War debts. In the course of the 19th century, the Exchange became increasingly formalized, and the 1867 invention of the stock ticker revolutionized the market; the ticker recorded every stock sale and made transaction information instantly available to the public (and, of course, provided the necessary material for "ticker tape" parades). The stock market cooked throughout the 1920s, only to collapse suddenly like a cheese soufflé on Black Monday, October 7, 1929. Many brokers bolted or went over the edge. The early 1980s saw another impressively "bullish" market, but its nosedive on October 19, 1987 gave traders an unwanted history lesson.

To get to the visitors' entrance to the stock exchange, walk to the left, down Broad St. to no. 20, where someone should be distributing free admission tickets and letting groups in on the hour. Arrive early in the morning, preferably before 9am, to ensure a convenient admission time. Tickets usually run out by around 1pm. Once admitted, you will be made to wait in a long line for the elevator—claustrophobes, take a deep breath. Upstairs, you can see exhibits detailing the workings of the stock market and the history of the exchange, along with a wide-screen "experience theater." Experience. But the real draw is the observation gallery, overlooking the zoolike main trading floor of the exchange. Under the 50-foot ceilings of the 37,000-square-foot room, you can observe frenetic activity from the glass-enclosed gallery while hearing recorded introductions to the floor activity in any of a number of languages. The visitors' gallery has been enclosed ever since the 60s, when leftist hooligans invented creative ways to disrupt trading activity, like throwing dollar bills at the traders.

Observe the chaos of murmuring and milling in this paper-strewn pen, as people huddle around honeycomb banks of green video screens. The TV monitors, grouped in clusters called "trading posts," nearly outnumber the people. 1700 companies deal at the New York Stock Exchange, the world's largest with 79 billion shares of stock valued at $3 trillion. Note the telling color-coded jackets sported by the folks on the trading floor; brokers are clad in yellow, reporters in navy, and pages in light blue. To your left, at the rostrum, the bell rings for opening at 9am and closing at 4pm.

Around the corner, at the end of Wall Street, rises the seemingly ancient **Trinity Church** (602-0773). Its Gothic spire was the tallest structure in the city when first erected in 1846. Two other churches have stood on this site; the Episcopal congregation here dates from 1696. The vaulted interior feels positively medieval, especially in contrast to the neighborhood temples of Mammon. Behind the altar is a small museum (open Mon.-Fri. 9-11:45am, 1-3:45pm, Sat. 10am-3:45pm, Sun. 1-3:45pm). Daily tours are given at 2pm. The church's 2 1/2 acre yard, dating from 1681, beds the graves of both Alexander Hamilton and Albert Gallatin, successive Secretaries of the Treasury. Hamilton, who served under Washington, committed himself to the development of the United States as a financial power, while Gallatin dedicated himself to the Jeffersonian vision of an agrarian republic. They now lie together, in a churchyard appropriately consumed by the vast financial establishment they spawned. North of Trinity, on the same side of the street, stand 111 and 115 Broadway, the Trinity and U.S. Realty Building. Gothic detail marks the lobbies of these twins. With all the stained glass and intricate gold leaf, you might as well be in a cathedral.

World Trade Center and Battery Park City

Walk up Broadway to Liberty Park, and in the distance you'll see the twin towers of the **World Trade Center.** The main plaza, on Church and Dey, offers two sculptures, a large fountain, ample seating space, daily lunchtime entertainment, and front-row views of the 1350-foot tall towers. The sleekly striped 1973 shafts dwarf practically every other building in the city, bosom companions at 110 stories each. They provided

10 million square feet of office space for their creator, the Port Authority of New York and New Jersey.

At Four World Trade Center, the **Commodities Exchange Center** (938-2018) does its thing on the ninth floor. The glass-enclosed visitors' gallery here overlooks the trading floor where gold, silver, sugar, coffee, and cotton change hands (no, not physically) from 9am to 3pm during the week. Seniors traveling together can take a guided tour; two weeks advance notice is required. The "floor show" can actually get more entertaining than the one at the Stock Exchange, since people here trade commodities in a bizarre dialect of sign language which must be seen to be believed. Screen the Murphy-Ackroyd classic *Trading Places* for an introduction to the frenzy.

Two World Trade Center has the **observation deck** (435-7397), and a banner to this effect hangs outside. When you enter the lobby, don't wait on the first line you see unless you want to get half-price tickets to a show (see Theater). Around the corner sits the observation ticket booth. (Open daily 9:30am-9:30pm, Oct.-May; 9:30am-11:30pm June-Sept. Admission $4, seniors $2.25, children $2.) Ride the elevator up to the 107th floor, where everyone ignores exhibits on trade history and economics to enjoy the best view in New York. Unfortunately, looking out the window can be difficult, since the stainless steel "stripes" on the building walls preclude any panoramic "picture window" views. The architects opted to place much of the skeleton of the building on the outside, in order to leave large, unbroken spaces inside the building. You may want to use the coin-operated telescopes or diagrams of landmarks distributed throughout the observatory. From the north, the Citicorp Building looks particularly impressive, a little like the neck of one of Jamie Reid's guitar swastikas, while the Citibank branch in Queens looks astray and diminutive. The green-capped Woolworth Building stands a bit to the north of the World Trade Center, and still appears attractive, even though its architects could scarcely have imagined that it would ever be appreciated from this angle. Note the gold-crowned federal court house and the hulking Municipal building astride the traffic of Chambers Street, topped off in a delicate wedding-cake fashion. And of course you'll see (as always) the pencilly Chrysler Building and the chunky Empire State Building, flaunting their fancy outlines at the more mundane edifices of Midtown.

To the west glimmers the golden-hued World Financial Center, obviously designed to be seen from above. Its crisp glinting angles and smooth curves look more like an architect's model than a real building. A flat New Jersey stretches into the distance across the river, on a majestic plane of radon. To the south, you can see (from right to left) Ellis Island, Liberty Island (with the Lady looking demure and sexy), and Governor's Island, with Staten Island in the distance behind them. You can also see the entrance to the Brooklyn-Battery Tunnel: look at the red paved area just north of Battery Park, where cars seem to disappear and re-appear from inside a boxy structure. To the east, the far-away Manhattan and Brooklyn Bridges steal the show. It's hard to believe that the arches of the Brooklyn Bridge once overshadowed the rest of the New York skyline.

In good weather, the rooftop observatory opens. Unless you're terrified of heights, take the escalator up to this extraordinary experience. The top of the neighboring twin seems only a few feet away (though really it's farther away at the top than at the bottom, a fact attributable to the curvature of the earth). You may have a distinct feeling of violating the divine order of things as you stand there, exposed to the elements, more than half a mile up in the sky. It doesn't get much higher than this. (Open daily 9:30am-8pm, weather permitting.)

The Trade Center elevator will let you off one level below ground, cleverly ensuring that all tourists encounter the underground mall here, the largest, and arguably most boring, underground mall in New York. If subterranean shopping fazes you, skip out of Hades and head back up the escalator to the plaza. Walk toward the Customs Building to the enclosed walkway which will take you to **Battery Park City** and the **World Financial Center.** Whatever the city tore up to construct the towering World Trade Center, it dumped west of West St. The 100 new acres were recently developed to form Battery Park City. Reached via the pedestrian overpass or a suicidal dash across

West. St., the area lies less than a mile from Wall St. With the stock market around the corner and the Statue of Liberty in full view, this neighborhood maintains the spirit of capitalism.

Cesar Pelli's **World Financial Center** towers with geometric shapes. Each of its 40-story towers has more footage than the 102-story Empire State Building because the buildings were built for computers requiring huge windowless rooms, not people who need a view to survive. Beneath the priceless electronics lies the glass-enclosed **Winter Garden,** an expanse of sixteen 40-foot tall palm trees and numerous expensive cafés. The garden points out onto the esplanade, which takes you right out to the water.

Head on the Battery Park City promenade past a series of postmodern residences. Sculptures by Fischer, Artschwager, Ned Smyth, Scott Burton, and Mary Miss line the esplanade. The loyal sentiments of two New York poets have been inscribed on the terrace here; their words give new meaning to the rhetorical technique of "railing." Frank O'Hara explains, "One need never leave the confines of New York to get all the greenery one wishes—I can't even enjoy a blade of grass unless I know there's a subway handy, or a record store or some other sign that people do not totally regret life." A less restrained Walt Whitman wrote, "City of the World (for all races are here, all the lands of the earth make contributions here;) city of the sea! City of wharves and stores—city of tall façades of marble and iron! Proud and passionate city—mettlesome, mad, extravagant city!"

The best way to get back on the street is to return the way you came, back through the Winter Garden to the walkway to the plaza.

City Hall and South Street Seaport

The aura of 19th-century New York, bulldozed out of existence elsewhere, still dominates this district. A number of magnificent municipal buildings stand near the rejuvenated South Street neighborhood.

The **Clocktower Gallery** (233-1096) stands at 108 Leonard St., between Broadway and Lafayette, as Chinatown fades into Lower Manhattan. The J, N, R and #4, 5, and 6 lines all stop on Canal St.; Leonard is four blocks down Broadway or Lafayette. The avant-garde gallery resides in the former home of the New York Life Insurance Company, on the 13th floor. Not only can you see some of the city's more ambitious reinterpretations of "art" here, you can climb inside the clocktower to observe its eyeboggling mechanism, as well as a fine view of lower Manhattan. For much of 1993 its sister gallery, PS 1 in Long Island City, takes over the studio space. (Open Thurs.-Sun. noon-6pm. Voluntary contributions.)

As you proceed down Lafayette to its intersection with Centre St., you can observe a group of sizable office buildings housing anonymous parts of the city bureaucracy. The pillared **United States Courthouse** at 40 Centre St., while unremarkable at street level, bears a gold roof that crowns the skyline. A little farther down, to the left on St. Andrew's Place and past a group of inexpensive food kiosks, the 1938 **Church of St. Andrew** (962-3972) stands in the shadow of the Municipal Building. Enter the serene space of the church to look at the altar's dark wood pillars with gold capitals and carved cross set against a deep crimson curtain. (Open daily 7am-5pm.)

Its towering neighbor, **One Centre Street,** also known as the **Municipal Building,** was completed in 1914. A bizarre free-standing colonnade distinguishes its enormous façade, while Chamber St. runs directly through its base. While fun-loving architects McKim, Mead & White outdid themselves on this one, creativity ultimately fails to soften the sheer bulk of the building. Across the intersection, you'll find the former **Hall of Records,** which now houses the Surrogate's Court. Two terribly municipal sculpture groups—"New York in Its Infancy" and "New York in Revolutionary Times"—grace the turn-of-the-century Beaux-Arts exterior. Twenty-four statues of notable New Yorkers also enliven the building. Come into the subdued marble entrance hall and step up to the balcony to get closer to the unique curvy ceiling. The lobby's ceiling is covered with Egyptian drawings and all the signs of the Zodiac.

This building faces the infamous **Tweed Courthouse,** diagonally across Chamber St., on the northern edge of City Hall Park. Builders laid the foundations of the courthouse on a $150,000 budget in 1862 and finished it a decade and $13 million later. Most of this cash found its way into the corrupt Tweed political machine, leading to a public outcry that marked the beginning of the end of the party's rule. Politics aside, today you can admire the building's Victorian reinterpretation of the classical rotunda, if that kind of thing suits you. The view from the ground floor affords an overview of the embellished space. (The building now houses the office of the mayor.)

Exit from the other side of the Tweed Courthouse and you'll find yourself in City Hall Park, facing the rear of **City Hall** itself. Go around to the other side to observe the front of the building, which still serves as the focus of the city's administration. The colonial chateau-style structure, completed in 1811, may be the finest piece of architecture in the city. It illustrates the idea that good things come in little baby packages; you can stand only a few feet away and comprehend the entire two-story building. During its restoration in 1956, a durable limestone replaced the original marble and the northern side was refinished and improved (originally left rough in the belief that the city would never really expand north of this point anyway). The vaulting rotunda here, while minuscule compared to the grand public spaces of lower Manhattan, wields a more restrained power. The winding stairs lead to the **Governor's Room,** originally intended for the use of said personage during his trips to New York, but now used to display a number of important early portraits, including ones of Jefferson, Monroe, Jackson, Hamilton, Jay, and Washington (who hated sitting for portraits because his rickety false teeth caused him so much pain). On one side of the Governor's Room sits the City Council Chamber, which resembles a lavish schoolroom with its rows of darkwood desks. A curving gold-banistered balcony overlooks the room, and a massive allegorical painting adorns the ceiling. On the other side of the Governor's Room, down the short hallway to the right, lies the **Board of Estimate.** Crystal chandeliers complement white wooden pews and blue carpeting, reproducing the seal of the city. There is no admission fee, and the building officially opens to tourists on weekdays from 10am to 4pm, but public meetings here often run later (sometimes through the night) and can be interesting.

City Hall Park itself has been a public space since 1686. It has been home to an almshouse, a jail, a public execution ground, and even a barracks for British soldiers. On July 9, 1776, George Washington and his troops encamped on the park to hear the Declaration of Independence. Today it has been prettily landscaped with colorful gardens and a fountain.

Towering at 233 Broadway, off the southern tip of the park, is the Gothic **Woolworth Building,** one of the most sublime and ornate commercial buildings in the world. Erected in 1913 by F.W. Woolworth to house the offices of his empire of corner stores, it stood as the world's tallest until the Chrysler Building opened in 1930. The lobby of this five-and-dime Versailles is littered with Gothic arches and flourishes, its glittering mosaic ceilings complemented by carved caricatures: note the one of Woolworth counting change and the one of architect Cass Gilbert holding a model of the building. Take one of the finely detailed elevators to the second-floor balcony, where you can get a closer look at the kitschy fresco of Queen Commerce receiving tribute from the subjects of the world.

A block and a half farther south on Broadway, **St. Paul's Chapel** was inspired by London's St. Martin-in-the-Fields. Constructed in 1766, with a spire and clocktower added in 1794, St. Paul's is Manhattan's oldest public building in continuous use. Gaze at the green churchyard and the surprising shades of the interior—baby blue, soft pink, and cream, with gold highlights. The human scale has a comforting effect, especially in contrast to the arrogance of the two brash "World" centers nearby. You can see George Washington's pew and a memorial to Major General Richard Montgomery, killed in the famous 1775 attack on Québec. For information call the office of the Trinity Museum (602-0773). (Open Mon.-Sat. 8am-4pm, Sun. 8am-3pm.)

Head across Broadway again, then east on Ann St., to the **Nassau Street pedestrian mall,** a little-known and slightly seedy shopping district characterized by fabulous

19th-century architecture and tacky ground-level clothing stores. Packed with shoppers during the day, the area has acquired a nice gritty feel (in spite of the restored building painted pink and green)—like many places in New York, it's worth avoiding at night. Make a right turn onto Nassau St. and walk down past John St. to Maiden Lane, where you will notice the lamely turreted skyscraper at 2 Federal Reserve Plaza. The basement here, the downtown branch of the **Whitney Museum of American Art**, usually hosts small exhibitions of an extraordinarily high caliber, drawn from the Whitney's permanent collection. (See Museums.)

Across Maiden Lane, the **Federal Reserve Bank** occupies an entire block. Built in 1924, this neo-Renaissance building was modeled after the Palazzo Strozzi of a 15th-century Florentine banking family. More than 200 tons of iron went into the decorative treatment. This building stores more gold than Fort Knox, since many nations store their gold reserves here, in facilities sinking to five levels below the street. International transactions are frequently conducted simply by taking gold out of one room, and bringing it to another. Free tours are available only by advance appointment (720-5000), but they're worth the trouble.

A trip one block back up Nassau St. and right onto John St. will bring you to **St. John's Episcopal Methodist Church** (269-0014). Established in 1766, St. John's is the oldest Methodist society in the country. (Sanctuary and museum of colonial and 19th-century memorabilia both open Mon.-Fri. 11:30am-3pm.) Fulton St. is one block further along William St. Turn right on to Fulton, heading past a large strip of moderately priced restaurants, and ultimately to the **South Street Seaport.** New York's shipping industry thrived here for most of the 19th century, when New York was the nation's prime port and shipping one of its leading commercial activities. Like many other waterfront areas of lower Manhattan, its size has increased considerably through the use of landfill. At the beginning of the 18th century, Water St. marked the end of Manhattan. Soon landfills had stretched the island to Front St., and by the early 19th century, to its present dimensions, South St. bordering on the water.

Zoning and development decisions made in the 70s rescued the neighborhood from the typical urban cycle of decay and development, steering it in the alternative direction of homogenized commercialization. If you get a feeling of *déjà vu* as you walk the cobbled streets or wander among the overpriced novelty shops, that may be because the Rouse Corporation, which designed the rejuvenated area, sponsored similar gentrification at Boston's Quincy Market and Baltimore's Harborplace.

The process succeeded, and the historic district, in all its fishy- and foul-smelling glory, became a ritzy Reagan-era playground. The fresh fish market became a yuppie meat market. Now the South Street Seaport complex has an 18th-century market, graceful galleries, and seafaring schooners. After 5pm, masses of crisply attired professionals flee their offices, ties trailing over their shoulders and sneakers lurking under their skirts, and converge here for long-awaited cocktails. The whole complex recalls a semi-formal frat party. Come observe the festive weekend atmosphere brought to you by the daiquiri-toasting Gucci-clad. And make sure to use the free and clean public toilets, if you have the wherewithal.

The seaport begins at the intersection of Fulton, Pearl, and Water Streets, as car traffic gives way to street performers. To your left stands the paradoxically miniature **Titanic Memorial Lighthouse**. To the left on Water St., a number of 19th-century buildings have been restored and now house precious little shops. Maritime buffs like the **Book and Chart Store**, 207 Water St. (669-9454; open Mon.-Sat. 10am-7pm, Sun. 11am-7pm), while a love of the printed word can be requited at **Bowne & Co.**, 211 Water St. (669-9400), a restored 19th-century printing shop where employees demonstrate a working letterpress. On the Fulton St. side of this block, you can enter Cannon's Walk, a sparklingly clean alley around the back of these shops.

Back on Fulton St., to the right as you face the water, huddles a row of novelty shops housed in the famous Schermerhorn Row, the oldest block of buildings in Manhattan, constructed mostly between 1811 and 1812. When Peter Schermerhorn purchased this land in the 1790s as an investment, it was a "water lot," and the city sold him the right to create the land by filling it in. Schermerhorn's just-add-landfill purchase proved to be profitable, as this spot rapidly became the focus of much of New York's sea-related commerce. At the **Museum Visitors Center** here (669-9424), you can buy tickets to many of the attractions at the Seaport (open daily 10am-5pm). You can also purchase these tickets at Pier 16.

Across Fulton St. from Schermerhorn Row stands one of the foci of the seaport, the **Fulton Market Building.** On the ground floor, you can smell the wonders of "Market Hall," a collection of bakeshops and exotic, expensive grocery-type establishments. At the end of Fulton St., you can see the river suddenly in view, as the spirits of dead fish pass through your nostrils. The stench comes from the **Fulton Fish Market,** the largest fresh fish mart in the country, hidden right on South St. on the other side of the overpass. The city has tried to dislodge the market, but it has been there for over 160 years, still opens at 4am, and resists all efforts at removal. New York's store and restaurant owners have bought their fresh fish here by the East River since the Dutch colonial period. Between midnight and 8am you can see buyers making their pick from the gasping catch, just trucked here in refrigerated vehicles. Those who can stomach wriggling scaly things may be interested in the behind-the-scenes tour of the market, given on the first and third Thursdays of the month at 7:45am, except during the winter. (Advance reservations required; call 669-9416.)

Behind Fulton Fish Market, you'll find the **Pier 17 pavilion** to your left, the **Pier 16 Ticketbooth** straight ahead, and a number of sailing ships docked to your right. At Pier 17 you can play on a three-story, glass-enclosed "recreation pier" filled with small unremarkable specialty shops, restaurants, and food stands. The top floor eating complex here has an even greater selection than Fulton Market, and a seating area with striking views of the Brooklyn Bridge. For marketplace info call 732-7678.

The Pier 16 kiosk, the main ticket booth for the seaport, stays open from 10am to 7pm (open 1hr. later on summer weekends). You can buy tickets here for some overpriced cruises, with predictably overstarched company aboard. The **Seaport Line's** authentic 19th-century paddlewheel steamboats (385-0791) offer 90-minute day cruises (call for a schedule that changes with the wind; fare $12, seniors $11, students $10, children 2-12 $6) and evening cruises to the live sounds of jazz, rock, and dixie ($18). Cruises leave from Pier 16. The air-conditioned boat circles around lower Manhattan to the Statue of Liberty, Ellis Island, and the World Trade Center. (The no-frills **Staten Island commuter ferry** gives you a similar view for 50¢—a sad spasm of inflation, as it used to cost a quarter.)

A museum admission ticket, sold at both the Pier 16 booth and the Museum Visitors Center, serves as a full-day pass to many small galleries, ships, and tours. The ticket includes entrance to **The Seaport Museum Gallery** on Water St., devoted to the city's evolution; **The Children's Center** on John St., craft workshops for kids; **Norway Galleries** on John St., exhibitions on the history of New York's seamen; and the ships *Ambrose, Wavertree,* and *Peking.* (See below.) Take a "Walk Through the Back Streets" to feel old New York in the district's unrestored areas (daily at 3pm) or board a "Ships Restoration Tour" (daily at 1pm). For recorded information about the museums, call 669-9417. (Admission $6, seniors $5, students $4, ages 4-12 $3.) Finally, if you want to take a cruise as well as visit the museums (and line the seemingly bottomless pockets of the Rouse Corporation while you're at it) you can pay a combination fare ($14, seniors $13, students $12, children $7).

Parked in Pier 16, next to the ticket kiosk, you'll find the **Peking,** the second largest sailing ship ever built. You can get in with your museum ticket or by paying $1 between 1 and 2pm. The *Peking,* built in 1911 by a Hamburg-based German company, spent most of its career on the "nitrate run" to Chile, a passage which involves going around Cape Horn, one of the most dangerous stretches of water in the world. Powered purely by shifting winds and brute force, ships like the *Peking* are the culmination of 2000 years of sailing history. Technological advances made in the years following its construction have made such ships obsolete.

On board, don't miss the 10-minute 1929 film of the ship during an actual passage around Cape Horn. This titanic movie plays daily at 12:30, 2:30, 3:30, 4:30, and 5:30pm. Also on board, you can see reconstructed living quarters, a photo exhibit about sailing life, and a documentary about the Fulton Fish Market, shown daily at noon. You can help the current crew raise one of the ship's 32 sails, Mon. through Fri. 12:30pm, weekends 2pm. On Sundays at 2:30pm, the staff demonstrates basic maritime duties.

Other ships seem docked for good in the seaport. Smaller ones include the *Wavertree,* an iron-hulled, three-masted ship built in 1885, and the *Ambrose,* a floating lighthouse built in 1907 to mark an entrance to the New York harbor. The *Pioneer* sailing ship gives two- and three-hour cruises on which you can assist with the sailing duties. Call the museum at 669-9417 for information ($15, children $7).

The Statue of Liberty

From its conception the Statue of Liberty has been a site for the projection of fantasies of America, a mythic archetype-in-progress. The list of famous names attached to those fantasies includes sculptor and conservative republican Frédéric-Auguste Bartholdi, publisher and yellow journalist Joseph Pulitzer, and parastatal auto tycoon Lee Iacocca on the one side, U2, Lou Reed, and Andy Warhol on another, and the films *Escape from New York, Working Girl, Splash, Planet of the Apes,* and *Brother from Another Planet* on yet another. But it's the chance to add one's own fantasy to the list, to partake of the myth, that makes the statue such a tourist draw.

The statue began as self-aggrandizer Bartholdi's idea for a lighthouse at the Suez Canal (see *Let's Go: Israel & Egypt* for more on the ditch), but he dropped the Africa plan when the prospect of building a monument to Franco-American friendship was mentioned. The new statue was to commemorate the victory of the Union (the North, the Yankees) in the Civil War and the constitutional extension of liberty to enslaved African-Americans; more pragmatically, the gift would improve the chances that America would oppose the government of Napoleon III in France. The reference to liberation was reduced over time as the project was delayed, and now remains only as a set of broken manacles at the statue's feet, invisible from the ground. Bartholdi finally came to America to line up support for his plan in 1871, when the Paris commune made things inhospitable for him in France. While his compatriots were plotting against the establishment of the worker's paradise in Paris, Bartholdi, along with President Grant and others, was plotting "Liberty Enlightening the World," the biggest statue the world had ever seen.

Bigness was the thing. Bartholdi was convinced that in America, size mattered. He wrote to his mother that everything was bigger here, "even the peas." Liberty is the embodiment of Kant's idea of the colossal—"the presentation of a concept almost too large for any presentation, bordering on the relatively monstrous." At 151 feet (300 with pedestal), with Bartholdi's moderate and academic talents to serve it and with a face modeled on Bartholdi's mother, relatively monstrous is an understandable description of Liberty. What Bartholdi had going for him was the publicist's eye for location, and Bedloe's (now Liberty) Island is, arguably, the best piece of real estate in the New World.

Even before its inauguration in October 1886, the monument to Franco-American friendship (something few Americans, then or now, get all that choked up about) had begun to acquire new significations: immigrants, not just French ones, had made a claim to the statue. Publishing magnate Joseph Pulitzer, a Hungarian immigrant made rich by the new journalism, raised the money for the pedestal by guilt-tripping ordinary New Yorkers into giving whatever they could. The fervent efforts included: "A lonely and very aged woman with limited means wishes to add her mite;" "Enclosed please find five cents as a poor office boy's mite to the pedestal fund;" and "We send you $1.00, the money we saved to go to the circus with." Emma Lazarus gave this new Liberty voice when she wrote *The New Colossus* as part an artists-for-Liberty campaign in 1883. The socialist-Zionist poet forever captured that monumental (and oedipal) solidity that Bartholdi envisioned with a mass migration and movement for liberation—"Mother of Exiles." This New Colossus wanted

Your tired, your poor,
Your huddled masses yearning to breath free,
The wretched refuse of your teeming shore.
Send these, the homeless, tempest-tossed to me.
I lift my lamp beside the golden door!

America's destiny as the home of the homeless, a nation of settlers, was sealed.

The rhythm of a colossus is carnivalesque spasm followed by grinding monotony. The last spasm occurred in 1986—the statue's centennial—with the relatively monstrous Liberty Weekend. (Critic Paul Fussell noted Liberty Weekend as an example of everything BAD about American Culture.) Chrysler Chairman and migrant-son-made-good Lee Iacocca was put in charge of efforts to restore the statue and Ellis Island, as well as the planning of the blow-out party. It was the pinnacle of Reaganaut bread-and-circus extravaganzas—overbudget, corrupt, dirty, televised, and riddled with Elvis impersonators—but at least it had an official snack food. And at least women could attend this celebration. Women were officially barred from the opening ceremonies in 1886, but a group of determined suffragettes chartered a boat and sailed themselves over to the statue, interrupting speakers by shouting about the irony of a female embodiment of Liberty in a country where women could not vote. Iacocca's fund drive was riven with political and administrative arguments; Lee was eventually fired from one of his jobs for conflict of interest. The restoration did fix the torch and some structural problems, but it made the statue newly attractive, and that means lines.

You will live with the legacy of Liberty Weekend in the summer—as lines take up to three hours. Winter is a good time to visit; springtime is dominated by howling packs of school children, who yearly reinvent the fine art of spitting on the heads of those climbing the statue below them. If you do try to go in the summer, get there on the first or second ferry, or forget it. The hotter and sunnier the day, the longer the line (and greater the number of heat exhaustion cases.) Eat before you go; the climb is harder than you think, and food on the island is priced according to international monopoly rules: whatever foreign tourists can bear.

An ideal summer trip will have you on the boat for Liberty at 9am, off the island by 10:30am and over to the air-conditioned comfort of Ellis Island by 11am. Ferries run in two loops, Manhattan-Liberty-Ellis, and Manhattan-Ellis-Liberty; listen for your stop. The ticket costs the same no matter how long you stay and regardless of whether you want to see only the statue or the immigration station, so you might as well do both.

The ferry ride is one long photo-opportunity—the awe-inspiring lower Manhattan skyline, the Brooklyn Bridge, and, of course, Liberty. The boat ride is geared to give you the best shots of the statue, and as it passes in front it will lean dramatically toward the island as the camera-ready rush to the rail. The copper sheeting (2.5mm thick) has acquired its green patina over the last 100 years as a form of self-protection. The symbols of the statue were chosen to promote the ideals of rational republicanism as Bartholdi saw it. Liberty was to enlighten the world; the seven points of the crown stand for the seven seas and seven continents. The toga recalls the ancient republics of Rome. The tablet in her left hand is the keystone of liberty and bears the inscription "July 4, 1776." More obscurely, each window in the visor represents one of the "natural minerals" of the earth. Finally, the torch was a symbol of the Masonic ideal, Enlightenment.

Once you're on the island, head straight for the entrance at the back of the statue. Enter through Fort Wood, once part of the system of New York harbor defenses during the War of 1812. The line on your left is the line up to the crown, the only way to get to the crown. It is all stairs: twenty-two stories, 300+ steps, many narrow and spiraling; over 110°F in the summer. There are only two reasons to go to the crown: 1. Like Mt. Everest, because it's there, and 2. You dig engineering. Gustave Eiffel of French tower fame designed the internal support system, and it is a thing of beauty and elegance. It was also one of the first curtain-wall constructions and inaugurated the skyscraper era. The only way to see the intricate and web-like structure is to clamber to the crown. Don't make the climb for the view: the windows at the top are small and look out not on Manhattan but the Brooklyn dockyards. One of the restorers wrote that the architectural team felt that a "grueling climb was an integral part of the visitor's experience" and should be preserved. Senior citizens, young children with a propensity to whine or spit, and anyone with a heart, respiratory, or leg ailment should avoid the climb. There are plenty of chances to stop climbing and go back if you feel you need to.

The line at the right as you enter is for the elevator. It goes to the top of Richard Morris Hunt's pedestal and the observation decks there. These are the beautiful views of New York, Ellis, and the statue above you. You cannot take the elevator halfway up and climb to the top. People with mobility problems can go to the lower observation decks and the museums. An exhibit on the history of the torch is located over the entrance doors on the second level. The torch has been closed to the public since 1916 when anti-American terrorists blew up a munitions barge in New Jersey and threatened to hinder the U.S. policies in those early days of World War I. Once a summer, without fail, something equally exciting happens at the statue. A protest, a parachuter, a bomb threat, a takeover—life in the big city.

Rangers are a friendly and knowledgeable lot and are surprisingly willing to answer any questions you have, even if you know they've been asked it before. With 3 million visitors a summer, they have been asked everything too many times. If they occasionally appear testy, rattled, or preoccupied with medical cases, it's only because they are so outnumbered: 15 of them to 10,000 tourists on a busy day. (Overheard: "How big are her boobies?")

The Statue of Liberty exhibit is well worth your time (it only takes about 20 minutes), but the immigration exhibit on the third floor is useless. If you want immigration, go to Ellis.

If you have some time before the next ferry departs and you're tremendously bored, stop in at the gift shop and cafeteria. In the former you can buy useful things like $70 Liberty hologram watches and 50¢ Statue of Liberty erasers. In the latter, see food names jumbled in a variety of languages by an indifferent staff (fried fish and french fries $4).

You can buy tickets for the ferry at Castle Clinton in the southwest corner of Battery park, the "toe" of Manhattan Island (see Financial District Sights). Ferries leave for Liberty Island from the piers on Battery Park every half hour from 9am-4pm, and the last ferry back runs at 5:15 pm (in July and Aug. at 7pm). Tickets cost $6, seniors $5, ages 3-17 $3, under 2 free.

Ellis Island

Ellis Island re-opened to huddled masses—just tourists this time—in 1990 after an infusion of hundreds of millions of dollars. During its heroic period (between 1890 and 1920) approximately 15 million people came through.

The exhibits on the island are divided between Ellis's history proper and the history of the peopling of America in general. Most of the first floor "Baggage Room" has been turned over to exhibits of America's roots, a study of its remarkable diversity— rivalled only by the diversity of tourists you will see milling about. Kodak sponsors "America's Family Album," which attracts mostly the self-obsessed, seeking people who have their name or look like them, but it's the exhibit of photos by immigration worker Augustus Sherman that is worth seeing. Sherman took all the famous moving images of newly arrived people, and his documentary style clashes with the real pathos of the newcomers, a disjunction that makes for a feeling of transparent attachment to the struggle for opportunity in the new world.

Ellis was known as the "Island of Tears," and almost everything about its history speaks of the arrival of the modern bureaucratic state's border control. There were physical and mental tests, quick exams for fitness, financial and criminal checks, and, of course, files. The volume of people at Ellis was so large and required such efficient processing that immigrants in effect became their own files, with their status (possible disease or acceptance) marked right on their bodies in chalk. The exhibit "Through America's Gate" on the second floor chronicles all this. Also on the second floor is the overwhelming Great Hall, where the majority of processing took place. The great windows flood the room with light, making it an ideal place to rest up on a hard day of touring.

The third floor houses the dormitory room, restored to its 1908 state. Triple-hung canvas cots, narrow enough for a thin adolescent, with about three feet of air space between the pancake stacks, supported detainees while they were under examination. While some saw Liberty upon arrival, those given free room and board here most likely conjured up images of prison. Offices and the extensive immigration library, open to researchers who have received advance permission, fill out the third floor.

One of the real achievements of the restoration of Ellis was an oral history program, which attempted to get immigrants to describe their experiences in their own words. Those moving words now serve as narration for the exhibits throughout the main hall. They are also the main text for the film "Island of Hope, Island of Tears," presented twice an hour in one of the two theaters (check for frequency) on the island. The film is free, but tickets must be picked up at the information desk near the entrance in advance of the showing. Do this as soon as you arrive if you want to see the film.

One of the lesser achievements of the restoration was a guided-tour-on-tape narrated by Tom Brokaw. It rushes you through everything fast and costs money. Read the signs for yourself. The restaurant is better than the one over on Liberty Island, but it, too, is overpriced and bland.

Most of the 27 1/2 acre island remains closed to the public. It was originally the site of a hospital complex—contagious disease wards and staff housing—and has not been restored. Iacocca wanted to tear it down and build an "ethnic Williamsburg;" someone then pointed out that Epcot Center was an ethnic Disneyland, so he scrapped the plan. The Park Service, to its discredit, wanted to build an international business conference center with swimming pool, racquetball, and first class hotel accommodations. Neither proposal has been adopted, and the hollowed-out old buildings are a silent reminder of the two million people turned away at America's golden door.

Two ferries bring you to and from Liberty and Ellis Island. One runs Battery Park-Manhattan-Liberty-Ellis, and the other Liberty State Park-Jersey City, NJ-Ellis-Liberty, approximately every 1/2 hour from 9:15am-4:30pm, seven days a week; on weekends and holidays the last boat may leave as late as 5pm. Tickets are $6, $3 for children under 17, and $5 for seniors. For recorded info call the Park Service at (212) 363-3200; otherwise call (212) 363-7620 or -3267.

The Brooklyn Bridge

You can stroll for a mile across the **Brooklyn Bridge** in the company of ambitious commuters in Reeboks. To get to the entrance on Park Row, walk a couple of blocks west from the East River to the City Hall area. Here a stairway leads to the promenade. Once on the bridge, you can do what you've always wanted to do while driving, but couldn't for fear of careening out of control—look straight up to the cables and Gothic arches.

Ahead stretch the piers and warehouses of Brooklyn's waterfront; behind, the cityscape that puts others to shame. The Gothic arched towers of New York's suspended cathedral, the greatest engineering achievement of their age, loomed far above the rest of the city back in 1883, the products of engineering wizardry and 15 years of steady work. Plaques on the bridge towers commemorate chief architect John Augustus Roebling, who, along with more than 20 of his workers, died of construction-related injuries. But Roebling's son, Washington, took over the management of the job, achieving in the end a combination of delicacy and power that made other New York bridges look cumbersome or scanty.

Like all great bridges, this one has had its share of poetry and death. A Mr. Brody leaped off the bridge in 1920, marking the first suicide. Locals say if only he had tucked and rolled, dived and not belly flopped, he might have lived. Stroll across the walkway and observe the sun weaving through the constantly shifting cobweb of cables. Suspended above traffic, close your ears and imagine the bridge when only horse-powered vehicles took its path over the East River. Make sure to walk on the left—the right is reserved for bicycles.

Roosevelt Island

This minute strip of land floating in the East River between Queens and Manhattan has had more names than a Spanish nobleman. When Dutch settlers bought the property from the Canarsie Indians in 1637, it was called "Long Island." The Dutch raised hogs here, giving the next title, "Hogs Island." In 1828, when the city purchased it from the Blackwell family, the island was referred to as Blackwell Island. The city has built hospitals, prisons, and the New York City Lunatic Asylum here; Boss Tweed served time on the island, and so did Mae West (for her role in a play called "Sex"). In 1921, the city christened the land mass Welfare Island, and in 1986 it was dubbed Roosevelt Island in honor of Franklin Delano.

The island has been the site of up to 26 hospitals, but only two remain today, as the island serves primarily as a state-planned residential quarter. By 1975 the residential building complexes of Eastwood, Westview, Island House, and Rivercross, completed under state supervision, provided housing for about 7000 people of mixed incomes. Now one of the nation's most successful planned and integrated communities, the island is virtually traffic- and crime-free, with tranquil views of the Manhattan skyline. Procuring an apartment requires a wait of several years. In 1989, the subway link to Midtown Manhattan at 63rd St. opened, 14 years behind schedule. Further construction projects at "Southtown" and Octagon Tower in the north part will soon complete the development of the island. Besides the subway and the tram, a bus runs from the Island over the Roosevelt Island Bridge to Queensboro Plaza.

The amusement-wracked tram ride over from Manhattan, rather than the island itself, draws visitors. This was the tram featured in the movie *Nighthawks*. Originally constructed in 1976 as a temporary alternative to subway service, the tram has faced an uncertain future since the subway finally opened. One of the only publicly operated commuter cable cars in the world, it operates at an annual deficit of $1 million.

You can pick up the tram at 59th St. and Second Ave. Look for the big red cable rotors next to the Queensboro Bridge. Round-trip fare costs $2.80 and the ride takes about four minutes each way. (Cars run every 15min., Sun.-Thurs. 6am-2am, Fri.-Sat. 6am-3:30am.) As you hover almost 250 feet above the ground, look to your right, downtown, and you can see the United Nations complex and the distinctive hats of the Chrysler Building and the Empire State Building.

Once on the island, take the mini-bus (10¢) up Main St. and roam around until you get bored. The northern half of the island is lined with playgrounds and jogging paths, and Lighthouse Park at the northern tip is a pleasant place to lie in the grass make out animal shapes in the clouds above Manhattan.

Brooklyn

When romantics ponder Brooklyn, they conjure up images of the rough stick-ball players who grew to become the Brooklyn Dodgers, or think of Woody Allen's boyhood home, presided over by his raucous mother and stubby aunt under the roller coaster in *Annie Hall*. To many Manhattanites, Brooklyn remains elusive. What goes on in Brooklyn tends to happen on the streets and out of doors, whether it's neighborhood banter, baseball games in the park, ethnic festivals, or gang violence.

Brooklyn's pride in its distinct culture has deep historical roots. The Dutch originally settled the borough in the 17th century. Although Brits shared the land, Dutch culture flourished well into the early 19th century. When asked to join New York in 1833, Brooklyn refused, saying that the two cities shared no interests except common waterways. Not until 1898 did Brooklyn decide, in a close vote, to become a borough of New York City.

In this hodgepodge of ethnic neighborhoods distinctly framed by avenues, each community has its own separate residential area and commercial zone. The Brooklyn-Queens Expressway pours into the Belt Parkway and circumscribes the borough. Ocean Parkway, Ocean Avenue, Coney Island Avenue, and diagonal Flatbush Avenue run from the beaches of Southern Brooklyn to Prospect Park in the heart of Brooklyn. Flatbush Ave. continues on and eventually leads to the Manhattan Bridge. The streets of Western Brooklyn (including those in Sunset, Bensonhurst, Borough Park, and Park Slope) are aligned with the western shore, not the south shore, and thus collide at a 45-degree angle with MacDonald Ave., which parallels Ocean Parkway and Central Brooklyn's other main arteries. In North Brooklyn, several avenues—Atlantic Avenue, Eastern Parkway, and Flushing Avenue—travel from downtown far east into Queens.

Brooklyn is spliced with subway lines. Most lines serving the borough pass through Atlantic Ave. Station downtown. The D and Q lines continue southeast through Prospect Park and Flatbush to Brighton Beach. The #2 and 5 trains head east to Brooklyn College in Flatbush. The B and N trains travel south through Bensonhurst, terminating at Coney Island. The J, M, and Z trains service Williamsburg and Bushwick and continue east and north into Queens. The Brooklyn-Queens crosstown G train shuttles from South Brooklyn through Greenpoint into Queens.

Downtown

Start a tour of downtown Brooklyn at the Atlantic Ave. subway station (#2, 3, 4, 5, D, and Q) or the Pacific Street station (B, M, N, and R). The **Williamsburgh Savings Bank,** at the corner of Flatbush Ave. and Hanson Place, is Brooklyn's tallest building at 512 feet. The building was completed in 1929 and has a gorgeous Romanesque interior with arches, pillars, patterned marble floors, and a gold and green tiled ceiling. There is also a huge painting of Brooklyn with the sun shining down on it, while a blackened Manhattan lurks in the shadows. Walk up Flatbush Ave. a few blocks to **Fulton St.** and take a left. The stretch of Fulton St. to Borough Hall of town is now called **Fulton Mall.** These eight blocks were renamed as part of a renewal project in the 70s designed to spark investment in the disintegrating street that was Brooklyn's main shopping thoroughfare in the 30s and 40s. Instead of the department stores of yesteryear, Fulton Street is now known for smaller, cheaper stores, with bargains galore on clothes, shoes, and electronics.

The **Dime Savings Bank,** 9 DeKalb Ave. at the junction of Fulton and DeKalb, presents a grand classical front, with monumental Ionic columns beneath a triangular pediment, two reclining figures, and a majestic domed roof. Pass through the relief-set bronze doors—one of which displays a Cubist vision of the New York skyline—and enter a marble interior filled with its original turn-of-the-century furniture. (Open Mon. and Thurs.-Fri. 9am-6pm, Tues.-Wed. 9am-3pm, Sat. 10am-3pm.)

While a meal at **Gage and Tollner,** 372 Fulton St., would be out of the budgetarian's range, the restaurant's 1892 landmark interior—decorated with cherry wood paneling, mirrors and imitation leather called Lincrusta (invented by the guy who brought you linoleum)—is worth a peek. The original gas lamps still light up every evening.

At the end of Fulton Mall, Fulton St. turns into Joralemon St. **Borough Hall** sits to your right at 209 Joralemon St. This eclectic Victorian/Greek Revival hulk was built in 1851, once housed the city hall of independent Brooklyn, and is now the oldest building in Brooklyn. (Tours Tues. at 1pm). If you walk to the opposite side of the building, into **Columbus Park**, you can see that Justice, standing firmly with scales and sword, on top of the hall, isn't wearing a blindfold. That's New York for you.

Just north of Borough Hall, past the statue of Columbus and a bust of Robert Kennedy, is the **New York State Supreme Court.** The building lies at the southern boundary of **Cadman Plaza Park,** a long stretch of greenery extending from Columbus Park to the Brooklyn Bridge. The Romanesque Revival lives on at the granite **Brooklyn General Post Office,** 271 Cadman Plaza East at Tillary St. At the northern end of the park is the **Brooklyn War Memorial,** which contains the **Rotunda Art Gallery** (718-875-4031; open Wed.-Fri. noon-5pm, Sat. 11am-4pm).

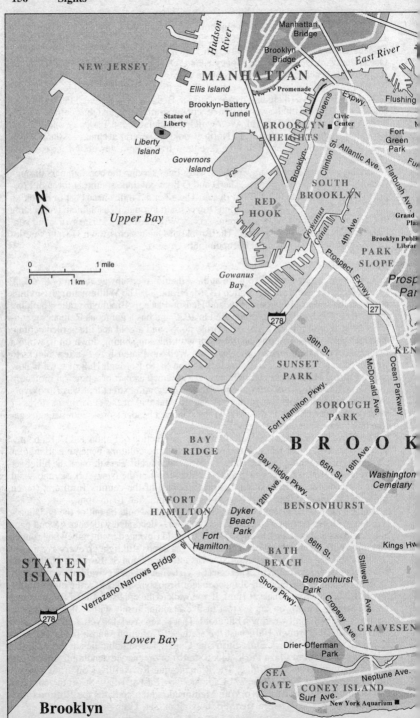

Brooklyn

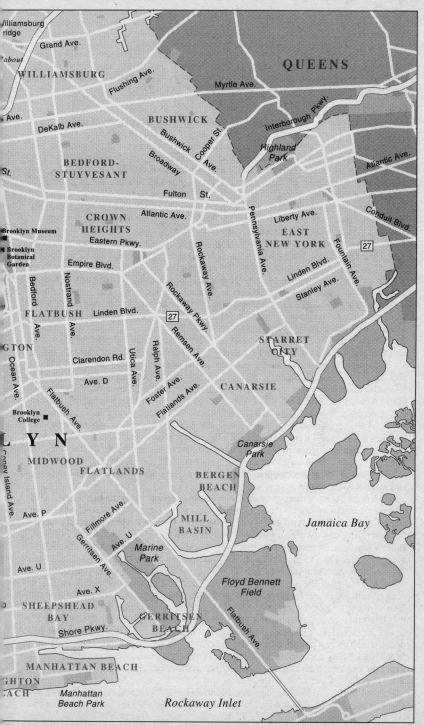

Williamsburg
Bridge

Grand Ave.

'abou

WILLIAMSBURG

Flushing Ave.

'Ave.

DeKalb Ave.

St.

**BEDFORD-
STUYVESANT**

QUEENS

Myrtle Ave.

BUSHWICK

Bushwick Ave.

Cooper St.

Broadway

Interborough Pkwy.

Highland
Park

Atlantic Ave.

Fulton   St.

**CROWN
HEIGHTS**

Atlantic Ave.

Pennsylvania Ave.

Liberty Ave.

Conduit Blvd.

**EAST
NEW YORK**

Brooklyn Museum

Brooklyn
Botanical
Garden

Eastern Pkwy.

Empire Blvd.

Bedford
Ave.

Nostrand
Ave.

Rockaway Ave.

Linden Blvd.

Fountain Ave.

27

Stanley Ave.

FLATBUSH

Linden Blvd.

Rockaway Pkwy.

27

GTON

Ocean
Ave.

Clarendon Rd.

Ave. D

Ralph Ave.

Ulica Ave.

Remsen Ave.

**STARRET
CITY**

Brooklyn
College

Flatbush Ave.

Foster Ave.

Flatlands Ave.

CANARSIE

LYN

MIDWOOD

FLATLANDS

Canarsie
Park

Coney Island Ave.

Ave. P

Fillmore Ave.

Ave. U

**BERGEN
BEACH**

Jamaica Bay

**MILL
BASIN**

Gerritsen Ave.

Marine
Park

Ave. U

Ave. X

Floyd Bennett
Field

**SHEEPSHEAD
BAY**

**GERRITSEN
BEACH**

Flatbush Ave.

Shore Pkwy.

MANHATTAN BEACH

GHTON
ACH

*Manhattan
Beach Park*

Rockaway Inlet

As Cadman Plaza Park ends at the entrance to the Brooklyn Bridge, Cadman Plaza West becomes Old Fulton St., and runs down to the waterfront, where you can catch a nice view of Manhattan. The **Eagle Warehouse and Storage Co.,** 28 Old Fulton St. at Front St., once housed Walt Whitman's *Brooklyn Eagle* and has been converted into apartments now. The entrance was once a passageway for delivery wagons. **Franklin House,** 1-5 Old Fulton St. at Water St., another dramatic 19th-century building, was originally a hotel and now houses the Harbor View Restaurant.

Brooklyn Heights

In 1814, when the invention of the steamboat made development in Brooklyn Heights possible, rows of now-posh Greek Revival and Italianate houses sprang up. The shady lanes of New York's first suburb were later the city's initial preservation target; Brooklyn Heights became New York's first Historic District in 1965. Brooklyn Heights is just west of Cadman Plaza Park and south of Old Fulton St. Today the brownstones of the 19th century house the young, upwardly mobile set and a diverse collection of families.

After supping on Middle Eastern food on Atlantic Ave., take a right onto Hicks St. for a stroll through the heart of historic Brooklyn. A few blocks down, **Grace Church,** 254 Hicks St. at Grace Ct., is bedecked with Tiffany windows depicting the life of Christ. Across from the church **Grace Court Alley,** a cul-de-sac intended for the motorless transport of the well-to-do, is flanked with the elegant apartments that recall a time when the pleasures of the bourgeois were simpler.

Take a right on to Remsen St. from Hicks St., and head to the **Our Lady of Lebanon Maronite Cathedral,** at the corner of Remsen and Henry St. The bronzed doors are decorated with boats and churches that seem eerily prophetic; they originally stood at the entrance to the main dining room of the *Normandie,* a grand French oceanliner which sank to the bottom of the Hudson River in 1942.

A left on Henry St., followed by a right on Montague St., will take you to **St. Ann's and the Holy Trinity Episcopal Church** (718-834-8794), on the corner of Clinton St. The church is presently undergoing a massive restoration, but tours are still available Tues. and Thurs. from noon to 2pm. This was the first church in America to have painted and stained glass windows, and it presently contains over 4000 sq. feet of glass. **Arts at St. Ann's** (854-2424) is also based here and brings great music from performers like Lou Reed and Marianne Faithfull to the acoustically superb church.

Take a left on Clinton St. to get to Pierrepont St., which parallels Montague St. and Remsen St. At 128 Pierrepont St. is the **Brooklyn Historical Society**, housed in a striking building lined with spooky gargoyle-busts of Shakespeare, Beethoven, and others. There is a museum and research library here for those interested in the esoterica of the borough. (Museum open Wed.-Sat. noon-5pm; admission $2.50, $1 children and seniors, Wed. free).

Pierrepoint St. leads directly to the **Promenade** (also known as the Esplanade). This waterfront walkway, which spans from Remsen St. to Orange St., also serves as the roof of the toxic Brooklyn-Queens expressway. The view of lower Manhattan exceeds the descriptive and evocative powers of all puny adjectives. To the left, the Statue of Liberty can be seen peeping out from past Staten Island. In fair weather, Ellis Island appears in full view, to the right of Liberty Island (see Statue of Liberty for more details and transportation information). The large green protrusion at the southern-most tip of Manhattan is the Staten Island Ferry Terminal. The bright orange ferry can be seen crossing back and forth regularly (see Staten Island Sights for more details on the ferry crossing). Only the tops of the World Trade Center are visible, but their proximity allows an intimate examination. Walk along the Promenade for a refreshing breath of sea air mixed with less-invigorating carbon monoxide from the cars shooting beneath you. You can continue on to the Brooklyn Bridge for the mile-long walk into Manhattan. Many commuters, including the lovely and talented Linda Rattner, prefer to get the exercise, the view, and the saving on subway fare that come from walking to work over the bridge.

Parallel to the Promenade, between Montague and Pierrepoint St., is **Pierrepont Place.** The addresses begin with No. 2 and end with No. 3. This exclusive street did have a #1, but three houses were deemed too plebeian. The two remaining Renaissance Revival brownstones overlook the water. You can see their large rear garden from the wrought-iron fence on the Promenade.

To see the potpourri of 19th-century styles that developed in Brooklyn and have come to represent U.S. architecture of that period, check out Willow Street between Clark and Pierrepont St. Numbers 155-159, in the Federal style, were the earliest houses here (c. 1825). Observe the dormer windows that punctuate the sloping roofs. The hand-hammered leadwork and small glass panes date the original doorways. Greek Revival fans should rally to the stone entrances of No. 101 and 103 (c. 1840) and the iron railings on No. 118-22. Numbers 108- 12, built by William Halsey Wood in 1884, are Queen Anne-style houses. Note how deftly Wood exploits the characteristics of each material, pushing stone, stained glass, and slate to their individual capacities and unique limits. Whew.

Continue along Willow and take a right on Orange St. to the **Plymouth Church of Pilgrims** (718-624-4743). The simple red brick church is set with stained-glass windows by Lamb Studios, the oldest glass studio in America. The church was the center of abolitionist sentiments before the Civil War under the leadership of its first minister, Henry Ward Beecher. His statue sits in the courtyard alongside a bas relief of Abraham Lincoln, who visited the church. The Tiffany windows from an earlier church now reside in the church's Hillis Hall.

To get to Brooklyn Heights, head down Atlantic Ave. from Borough Hall Station (#2, 3, 4, 5, M, R), or take the A, C train to High St.-Brooklyn Bridge, then walk across Cadman Plaza Park. Those in cars can head west on Atlantic Ave. to the docks. On your right hovers one of the Watchtower buildings: Jehovah's Witnesses own much of the property in this area and print their publications here. Head south (left) on Columbia St. over trolley tracks and cobblestones. Follow the truck route signs to Van Brunt St. At the end of this street, deep in **Red Hook,** take in a dazzling view of the harbor and the Statue of Liberty. To the right stands a turn-of-the-century warehouse. If you turn around and take a right on Beard St., you will pass a number of lovely decaying industrial complexes. A left on Columbia St. followed by a right on Bay St. will bring you to a football field that draws young crowds for pick-up soccer games and white-clad Haitian immigrants for cricket.

North Brooklyn

Hassidic Jewish culture thrives in **Williamsburg** (Subway: J, M, or Z to Marcy Ave.), north of downtown Brooklyn, just as it does on Manhattan's Lower East Side. Men wear long black coats and hats. The quarter is enclosed by Broadway, Bedford, and Union Avenues. Friday night and Saturday are celebrated as a day of rest, *Shabbat.* The austere Satmar sect observes the Sabbath religiously; if you intrude, you may feel unwelcome and conspicuous.

In recent years young artists have moved into old industrial complexes and converted them into lofts, and a hip SoHo-like bar scene has followed in their wake. To see the best of the struggling artists' work, stop by **Minor Injury,** 273 Grand St. (718-782-5259), a non-profit gallery specializing in challenging political art (open Fri.-Sun. 1-6pm).

Farther north, **Greenpoint** is the seat of an active Polish community (Subway: E or F to Queens Plaza, then G to Greenpoint Ave.). Manhattan Avenue intersects Greenpoint Ave. at the subway station and is at the heart of the neighborhood's bustling business district. Just west of Manhattan Ave. bounded by Java St. to the north, Meserole St. to the south, and Franklin St. to the west, is the **Greenpoint Historic District.** The Italianate and grecian houses were built in the 1850s, when Greenpoint was the home of a booming shipbuilding industry. The Union's iron-clad *Monitor*, which defeated the Confederacy's *Merrimac*, was built here.

If you take Manhattan Ave. south to Driggs Ave. and make a right, you will go through McCarren Park and meet up with the copper-covered domes and triple-slashed crosses of the **Russian Orthodox Cathedral of the Transfiguration of Our Lord,** at N. 12th St. Four blocks up N. 12th St. is Kent Ave., which runs through a seedy industrial zone and under the Williamsburg Bridge to the monstrous Brooklyn Naval Yard.

If you venture east into the neighborhoods of **Bedford-Stuyvesant, Brownsville, and Bushwick,** be cautious. Low public funding, high unemployment, and inadequate public works have created a high-crime ghetto. Major sights here are burnt-out buildings, patches of undeveloped land, and stagnant commercial zones. Still, social consciousness and political activism emerge from every pothole in these neglected streets. Wall murals portraying Malcolm X, slogans urging patronage of Black businesses, Puerto Rican flags, and leather Africa medallions all testify to a growing sense of racial and cultural empowerment. These are the explosive streets of Spike Lee's *Do the Right Thing.*

On July Fourth weekend each year, an African cultural celebration is held in Brownsville on the grounds of the Boys and Girls School, 1700 Fulton St. From noon to midnight for several days, you can hear rocking reggae bands and the slamming beats of local rap musicians. The Boys and Girls School is a community-controlled public school which grew out of the 1969 attempt to hand over control of the Ocean Hill-Brownsville School District to the community, a plan that was derailed by a teacher strike.

Institute Park

Brooklyn's cultural focus, **Institute Park,** lies between Flatbush Ave., Eastern Parkway, and Washington Ave. (Subway: 2 or 3 to Eastern Parkway-Brooklyn Museum.) The **Brooklyn Public Library** (718-780- 7700) has its main branch here, in a 1941 Art Deco building on the **Grand Army Plaza,** at the corner of Eastern Parkway and Flatbush Ave. The library has spawned 53 branches and contains 1,600,000 volumes. There are changing exhibitions on the second floor. (Open Tues.-Thurs. 9am-8pm, Fri.-Sat. 10am-6pm, Sun. 1-5pm). The **Brooklyn Museum** (718-638-5000) at the corner of Eastern Parkway and Washington Ave., has a large permanent collection and special exhibitions which regularly draw Manhattanites out of their borough. The building itself is a neoclassical wonder, with huge stone pillars and sculptures of 30 famous prophets and scholars (see Museums).

The **Brooklyn Botanic Garden** (718-622-4433) flowers next to the museum, at 1000 Washington Ave. This 50-acre fairy-land was founded in 1910 by the Brooklyn Institute of Art and Sciences for the pleasure of the public. Throughout the garden are little knolls of wonder. The **Fragrance Garden for the Blind** is an olfactory carnival—in mint, lemon, violet, and more exotic flavors. All are welcome. More formal, the **Cranford Rose Garden** crams in over 100 blooming varieties. Every spring, visitors can take part in the **Sakura Matsuri** (Japanese cherry blossom festival) at the Cherry Walk and Cherry Esplanade. The woodsy Japanese Garden (admission 25¢) contains weeping willows and a viewing pavilion, grouped around the turtle-stocked pond. Although artificial, the scenery here is realistic enough to fool the many water birds that flock to the site. The Shakespeare Garden displays 80 plants mentioned in his works. Towards the rear of the gardens are two cement pools of flowering lily-pads. The lilies create an intriguing combined effect: some come straight out of a Monet painting, while others are eerily reminiscent of the seed pods in *Invasion of the Body Snatchers.* (Garden open April-Sept. Tues.-Fri. 8am-6pm, Sat.-Sun. and holidays 10am-6pm; Oct.-March Tues.-Fri. 8am-4:30pm, Sat.-Sun. and holidays 10am-4:30pm. Free, except for a $2 entrance fee to the conservatory of tropical plants. Donations are appreciated, however.)

Park Slope and Prospect Park

The neighborhood called **Park Slope**, bounded by Flatbush Ave. to the north, 15th St. to the south, 5th Ave. to the west, and prospect Park to the east, combines a thriving business district with magnificent brownstone residences. Restaurants and stores line the north-south avenues, especially 7th Ave., and the east-west streets like Carroll St. are lined with beautiful homes. The entire neighborhood is starting to bulge with yuppies and young artists. One the corner of Sixth Ave. and Sterling Pl., owls and angels adorn the graceful, brownstone **St. Augustine Roman Catholic Church,** built in 1888. The attached academy has one entrance for "boys," on Sterling Pl., and one entrance for "girls," on Park Pl.

Just east of Park Slope, adjoining the southern border of institute Park, is **Prospect Park** (718-965-8961 or 965-8951). Take the #2 or 3 train to Grand Army Plaza, then head towards **Memorial Arch,** built in the 1890s to commemorate the North's victory over the South. The charioteer atop the arch is an emblem of Columbia, the Union—not of Victory, as is commonly believed. You can climb up to the top of the arch for free on weekends from noon to 4pm.

You can enter Prospect Park's north corner through Grand Army Plaza. Frederick Law Olmsted designed the park in the mid-1800s and supposedly liked it even more than his Manhattan project, Central Park. Exercise a measure of caution in touring the grounds. The park's largest area is the sweeping, 90-acre **Long Meadow,** the longest open urban parkland in North America. The **Friend's Cemetery,** a Quaker burial ground dating from 1846, remains intact in the west of the park. Natural glacial pools and man-made Prospect Lake lie south of Long Meadow. **Lookout Hill** overlooks Prospect Lake and marks the site of a mass grave where the British army deposited American casualties during the Revolutionary War.

In the eastern part of the park, at Flatbush Ave. and Ocean Ave., you can see old Brooklyn preserved in **Leffert's Homestead Historic House** (718-965-6505), a Dutch farmhouse burned by George Washington's troops and rebuilt in 1777. Nearby, saddle a horse taken from Coney Island on the **1912 Carousel,** which plays an odd version of the Beatles' "Ob-La-Di, Ob-La-Da." Open Sun.-Fri. noon- 5pm, Sat. noon-8pm. Admission 50¢). Park officials hope that the **Zoo** next door to the carousel, currently undergoing renovations, will become the East Coast's premier children's zoo when it reopens in 1993. In late summer, concerts are held at the bandshell in the northwest corner of the park. (Events hotline 718-788-0055; park tours 718-287-3400). Just southeast of Prospect Park is bustling Flatbush Ave.

On Flatbush Ave. and Clarkson St., down from Avi's Discount Center, you can spot the distinctive "tags" of graffiti artists Rock, Alan, Jew, and Picolo. At Flatbush and Church Ave. (subway: D to Church Ave.), you can see the oldest church in Brooklyn, **Flatbush Dutch Reformed Church** (c. 1654). A few of the sanctuary windows are Tiffany stained glass, including one of Samson. The church has tolled the death of every U.S. president. Next door stands the second oldest high school in North America, **Erasmus Hall Academy.** Not a single brick can be moved from the school's center building or the Dutch Reformed Church will repossess it. (Founding-father-figures Aaron Burr, John Jay, and Alexander Hamilton all contributed to the building of the school.) Although a strange concept today, the turn-of-the-century Manhattan aristocracy maintained summer homes in Victorian Flatbush (bounded by Coney Island, Ocean, Church, and Newkirk Ave.). You can wander around Argyle St. and Ditmas Ave. to see some of the old mansions, but be careful to avoid the crack houses on Church Ave. **Brooklyn College** (subway: #2 or 5 to Flatbush Ave./Brooklyn College), founded in 1930, includes the prestigious **Brooklyn Center for the Performing Arts** (718-434-2222).

South Brooklyn and Coney Island

On the southwest flank of Brooklyn lies **Sunset** (subway: N or R to 59th St.), a predominantly Latino neighborhood. Recently, Chinese immigrants have begun to establish a community on Eighth Ave. between 54th and 61st St., alongside a well-established Arab population. The unique egg-shaped towers of **St. Michael's Roman Catholic Church** rise above the sidewalk on 42nd St. and Fourth Ave. Nearby, on the southwest corner of 44th St. and Fourth Ave., you can check out a famous graffiti piece by the infamous artist Dare. Between 41st and 44th St., up the hill from 4th Ave. to 6th Ave., is **Sunset Park.** Here you'll find a sloping lawn with an extraordinary view of the Upper New York Bay, the Statue of Liberty, and Lower Manhattan. Avid consumers flock to Fifth Avenue, which is lined with discount stores and odd hybrid restaurants. On the northwest corner of Fifth Ave. and 54th St. is a colorful mural (presumably painted by children) of happy people in front of the Manhattan and Brooklyn skyline. On 59th St. and Fifth Ave. stands an immense grey-stoned church, **Our Lady of Perpetual Help.** If you're in a car, you can head down to First Ave. and explore the trolley-scarred streets, the setting for Vli Wedel's *Last Exit to Brooklyn.* Nearby, 19 huge white warehouses make up the six million square feet of **Bush Terminal,** the largest industrial park in Brooklyn. Exploring this desolate area by foot can be fun, but be extremely cautious...

Bay Ridge, south of Sunset, centers around Third Avenue, also called "Restaurant Row." If you're driving, venture down Shore Road and check out the mansions overlooking the Verrazano-Narrows Bridge and New York Harbor. **Bensonhurst** became a household word and rallying cry in the fight against racism, following the brutal murder of Yusef Hawkins. The predominantly Italian neighborhood centers around 86th Street, which hosted the dancing feet of John Travolta in the opening scene of *Saturday Night Fever.* This birthplace of disco is chock full of Italian bakeries, pizza joints, and discount stores.

The B, D, F, and N trains all plug into Stillwell Ave. Station at Coney Island, attesting to South Brooklyn's historic importance as a resort spot for the rest of the city. In the 1900s, only the rich could afford the trip here. Mornings, they bet on horses at the racetracks in Sheepshead Bay and Gravesend; nights, they headed to the seaside for fifty-dollar dinners. The introduction of nickel-fare subway rides to Coney Island made the resort accessible to the entire populace. Millions jammed into the amusement parks, beaches, and restaurants on summer weekends. In the late 40s, the area became less vigorous. Widespread car ownership allowed people to get even farther away from the city, and a few devastating fires in Coney Island soon paved the way for postwar city housing projects throughout the area.

Some vestiges of the golden era linger. The **Cyclone,** at 834 Surf Ave. (718-266-3434) and W. 10th St., built in 1927, remains the most terrifying roller coaster ride in the world. Enter its 100-second-long screaming battle over nine hills of rickety wooden tracks—the ride's well worth three dollars. The 1920 Wonder Wheel ($2.50), in Astroland on Surf Ave., has a special twist that surprises everyone, but make sure you get on a colored car. The El Dorado bumper car ($2.50), 1216 Surf Ave., the only ride that still plays thumping 70s disco tunes, also has a loudspeaker outside that invites you to "bump, BUMP, *BUMP* YO *ASS* OFF!!" The **New York Aquarium** (718-265-3400) on Surf and West 8th St. offers a ride-free environment. The first beluga whale born in captivity was raised in these tanks. Watch a solitary scuba diver be immersed in a tank full of feeding sharks. (Open daily 10am-4:45pm, holidays and summer weekends 10am-7pm. Admission $5.75, children and seniors $2.) A wooden wall lines the boardwalk side of the aquarium, painted with water-related questions for passers-by, including "Would you like to ride in George Bush's speedboat?" and "Does running water make you have to pee?"

· You can head west on Surf Ave. or take the boardwalk to the corner of W. 16th St., where the **Thunderbolt** coaster stands in ruins, overgrown with weeds and mongrel dogs. The tall, rusted skeleton of the **Parachute Jump,** relocated to the edge of the boardwalk in 1941, once carried carts to the top and then dropped them for a few seconds of freefall before their parachutes opened. Once a year, on Puerto Rican National Day, a flag somehow gets tied to the top. The pier that juts out into the water from here makes a good place for fishing or taking a stroll.

East of Coney Island, Ocean Parkway runs on a north-south line through half of Brooklyn. An extension of Olmsted's Prospect Park, this avenue was constructed to channel traffic to the seaside. Beyond the parkway lies **Brighton Beach** (subway: D or Q to Brighton Beach), nicknamed "Little Odessa by the Sea" because of the steady stream of Russian immigrants who moved there in the early 80s. Take a stroll down Brighton Beach Ave. or the parallel boardwalk along the sea. In late June and early July, old Eastern Europeans complaining about their bodily ailments, Spandex-clad girls listening to Top 40 music on their Walkmen, and middle-aged couples drowning sunburns in Noxema are all wowzered by the Blue Angels air shows. On the weekend of the Fourth of July, parachutists land near cheering seaside crowds.

To the east lies **Sheepshead Bay** (subway: D or Q to Sheepshead Bay), named after the fish that has since abandoned its native waters for the cleaner Atlantic. Emmons Avenue runs along the bay and faces **Manhattan Beach**, a wealthy residential section of doctors and mafioso just east of Brighton Beach. You can go after some blues (the fish, not the music) on any of the boats docked along Emmons Ave. (Boats depart daily 6am; trip $30.) Traditionally, a couple of dollars are collected from each passenger and the wad goes to the person who lands the biggest fish.

If you have a car, you can drive east along the Belt Parkway, which hugs Brooklyn's shores. Stop off at **Plumb Beach** for a more intimate sun and sand experience. At night, the parking lot here fills with big green Cadillacs and loving couples. Exit the Belt at Flatbush Ave., which leads south to Queens and the Rockaway beaches. Turn left just before the bridge and you can drive around the immense abandoned air strips of Floyd Bennett Field. Here, you will find information about **Gateway National Park** (718-338-3687).

Continuing on the Belt will take you to **Starett City**, based around Pennsylvania Ave. This development has its own schools, its own government, and its own source of electricity and heat. Originally, rent here was based on how much each resident's salary allowed. State legislators soon revoked this un-American policy.

Queens

Archie and Edith Bunker (and the employees of the Steinway Piano Factory) now share the brick houses and clipped hedges of their "bedroom borough" with immigrants from Korea, China, India, and the West Indies. In this urban suburbia, the American melting pot bubbles away with a foreign-born population of over 30%. Immigrant groups rapidly sort themselves out into neighborhoods where they try to maintain the memory of their homelands while living out "the American Dream."

The rural colony was baptized in 1683 in honor of Queen Catherine of Braganza, wife of England's Charles II. At the beginning of the 19th century, the small farms here began to give way to industry, and by the 1840s the area along the East River in western Queens had become a busy production center. In 1898, Queens officially became a borough of the City of New York, and with political linkage came physical growth. Between 1910 and 1930, the population of the borough quadrupled to one million; in 1938, Queens accounted for almost three-quarters of all new building in the city. The building boom of the 50s effectively completed the urbanization of Queens, establishing it as the new (old) Lower East Side, home to a wave of late 20th century immigrants. Today, in this medley of distinct neighborhoods, you can trace the history of ethnic settlement from block to block. An area predominantly Korean one year may become mostly Indian the next. Even houses of worship change hands as neighborhoods evolve: synagogues become churches become New Age lounges.

The ongoing immigration and relocation of ethnic groups in Queens—while contributing to an impressive cultural, culinary, and spiritual diversity—has not been accomplished without racial and ethnic tensions. Archie Bunker's xenophobic provincialism is a reality; like much of New York City, Queens resists interracial relationships.

Much of Queens feels like another city. It even styles itself one, sometimes: in response to ongoing concerns about taxes and city benefits (Queens maintains that it pays too much of the former and receives almost none of the latter), some uptight natives have lately called for secession. The city, meanwhile, has made noises about prioritizing outerborough tourism. The Dinkins-inspired "New York: Yours to Discover" campaign is supposed to divert flows of funds and people to Queens and other "neglected treasures." Until this program gets underway and Queens establishes its own tourism council, places like the **Queens Historical Society** (143-35 37th Ave., Flushing, NY 11354 (718-939-0647)) pick up the slack. The society can suggest self-guided tours of historically important neighborhoods (such as the "Freedom Aisle") and frequently leads its own guided tours. Call Mon.-Sat., 9am-5pm; membership $15 per year.

Orientation

Queens is easily New York's largest borough, covering over a third of the city's total area. To understand Queens' kaleidoscopic logjam of communities is to understand the borough. Just across the East River from Manhattan lies the Astoria/Long Island City area, the northwest region of Queens. **Long Island City,** spliced with subway lines and covered in grime, has long been Queens' industrial powerhouse. In the 1930s, 80% of all industry in the borough was based here; Newtown Creek saw as much freight traffic as the Mississippi River. The area has recently acquired a reputation as a low-rent artist community, though it remains to be seen whether the avant-garde will cross the river. **Astoria,** known as New York's Athens, is by some estimates the second largest Greek city in the world. Many Italians live here too.

Southeast of this section, in the communities of Woodside and Sunnyside, new Irish immigrants join more established ones. **Sunnyside,** a remarkable "garden community" built in the 20s, now commands international recognition as a model of middle-income housing. However, during the Great Depression, over half the original owners were evicted due to non-payment of mortgages. South of Sunnyside lies **Ridgewood,** a neighborhood founded by Eastern European and German immigrants a century ago. More than 2000 of the distinctively European attached brick homes there receive protection as landmarks, securing Ridgewood a listing in the National Register of Historic Places.

East of Ridgewood, **Forest Hills** and **Kew Gardens** contain some of the most expensive residential property in the city. The Austin Street shopping district imports the luxury of Manhattan. New York State Governor Mario Cuomo has a home in Forest Hills, as does former Vice Presidential candidate Geraldine Ferraro. Originally called Whitepot, the land of Forest Hills was bought from the Indians for some white pots—a deal almost as unreal as Peter Minuit's Manhattan purchase. Just north of this area, **Flushing Meadow-Corona Park,** site of the World's Fair in both 1939 and 1964, still attracts crowds, both for its museums and for its outdoor facilities. To the east and downtown, **Flushing** has become a "Little Asia" with a large Korean, Chinese, and Indian population, as well as a sizable number of Central and South American immigrants. Many go to **Bayside,** east of Flushing, for bar-hopping in a relaxed, north shore atmosphere.

In the central part of the borough, industry booms and African-American pride swells in **Jamaica.** Many of the middle- and upper-class neighborhoods to its southeast, such as St. Albans and Laurelton, are primarily West Indian and African-American. In the south shore of Queens, the site of mammoth Kennedy Airport, you can find the **Jamaica Bay Wildlife Refuge**. Relatively-rural eastern Queens has same easy feel Long Island's Nassau County.

Queens suffers from neither the monotonous grid of upper Manhattan nor the slipshod angles of the streets in the Village. Most neighborhoods here developed independently, without regard for an overriding plan. Nevertheless, streets generally run north-south and are numbered from east to west, from 1st St. in Astoria to 271st St. in Glen Oaks. Avenues run perpendicular to streets and are numbered from north to south, from 2nd Ave. in the north to 165th Ave. in the south. But named streets sometimes intrude into the numerical system, and sometimes two different numbering systems collapse into one another (as in these consecutive thoroughfares in Long Island City: 31st Road, 31st Drive, Broadway, 33rd Avenue). The address of an establishment or residence usually tells you the closest cross-street; for example, 45-07 32nd Ave. is near the intersection with 45th St. For added fun, roads and drives are frequently inserted between consecutive avenues, while Places are sometimes inserted between consecutive Streets. Occasionally a street is named rather than numbered, probably to throw your calculations.

Flushing

If you only have time to visit one place in Queens, you might choose Flushing. You'll find some important colonial landmarks, a bustling downtown, and the largest rose garden in the Northeast. Transportation couldn't be easier: the #7 Flushing line

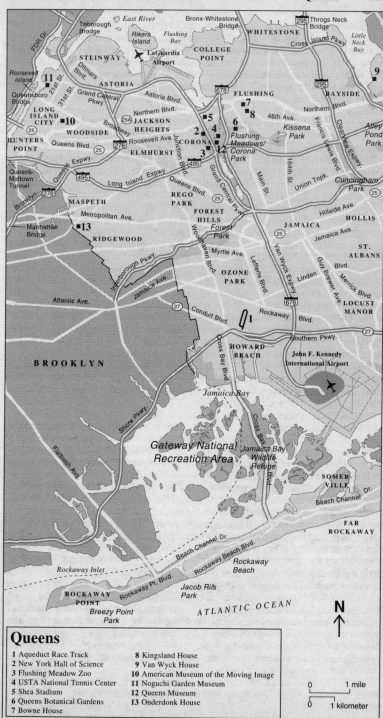

Queens

1 Aqueduct Race Track
2 New York Hall of Science
3 Flushing Meadow Zoo
4 USTA National Tennis Center
5 Shea Stadium
6 Queens Botanical Gardens
7 Bowne House
8 Kingsland House
9 Van Wyck House
10 American Museum of the Moving Image
11 Noguchi Garden Museum
12 Queens Museum
13 Onderdonk House

0   1 mile
0   1 kilometer

runs straight from Times Square. Just get on and sit back for about half an hour, until you reach the last stop (Main St., Flushing) in the northeastern part of the borough. Manhattan it isn't, but the streets are usually congested. Walk past the restaurants, discount stores, and businesses, and feel the crush of people and cultures on Main St.

A walk through downtown Flushing will provide a sense of the city's historical roots. Up Main St. toward Northern Boulevard stands **St. George's Episcopal Church.** The present structure was built in 1853 to replace the original, where Francis Lewis, a signer of the Declaration of Independence, was once a vestryman. Past the church about four blocks up and to the right, on Northern Boulevard, sits an inconspicuous shingled building at #137-16. This **Friends Meeting House,** a national historic landmark went up in 1694 and still serves as a place of worship for local Quakers (718-358-9636). Meetings are held here every Sunday morning, and the main room, a severe and simple hall, is open on the first Sunday of every month. Across the street, at 137-35 Northern Blvd., the **Town Hall,** built in 1862, has recently been restored in the Romanesque Revival tradition.

For other points of historical interest, continue down Northern Blvd., past the Gothic monstrosity known as Flushing High School, to Bowne St., and make a right. About two blocks down, at #37-01, is the **Bowne House** (718-359- 0528). This low, unassuming structure, built in 1661, is the oldest remaining residence in New York City. Here, John Bowne defied Dutch governor Peter Stuyvesant's 1657 ban on Quaker meetings—and was exiled for his efforts. Back in Holland, Bowne persuaded the Dutch East India Company to demand of the colony tolerance for all religious groups. This, along with the famous Flushing Remonstrance of 1657, helped to establish the tradition of religious freedom that Buddhist and Hindu newcomers to Flushing enjoy today. The house preserves furnishings used by Bowne and his descendents, who resided in the house until 1945. You can see a beehive oven, clay peace pipes, bone-handled utensils, and a walking stick old man Bowne used to kill wandering bears. (Open Tues. and Sat.-Sun. 2:30-4:30pm. Admission $3, seniors and ages under 14 $1.)

Next to the Bowne House lies a small park; head through it and past a playground on your left to the **Kingsland Homestead,** 143-35 37th Ave. (718-939-0647). This large, decrepit house, built in 1775, holds a permanent collection of antique china and memorabilia that belonged to the early trader Captain Joseph King. There is also a permanent collection of antique dolls and a fully furnished "Victorian Room." Don't be embarrassed to take a peek into "Aunt Marie's Secret Closet." As home of the Queens Historical Society, the house offers three or four temporary exhibits each year concerning aspects of the borough's history. It also serves as an archival research center for Queens. (Open Tues. and Sat.-Sun. 2:30-4:30pm. Admission $2, seniors and children $1.) In back of the house stands New York's only living landmark, a weeping beech tree planted in 1849 by nurseryman Samuel Parsons upon returning from Belgium. The first of its species in North America, it has a height of 65 feet and a circumference of 14 feet. The venerably twisted patriarch is comforted by a group of fine fledgling trees. A neglected garden complements the charm of the leafy cascades.

Five blocks down Main St. from the #7 station is the regal **Queens Botanical Garden** (718-886-3800). (The Q44 bus toward Jamaica stops right in front of the Garden.) Begun as a part of the 1939-40 World's Fair in nearby Flushing Meadow—Corona Park, the garden had to move when the park was being redesigned for the 1964-65 World's Fair. With the help of state-planning mastermind Robert Moses, the garden was relocated to its present site, where it now boasts a six-acre rose garden (the largest in the northeast), a 23-acre arboretum, and more than nine acres of "theme gardens." One of the more remarkable areas, the **Wedding Garden,** encompasses a three-acre oasis with a rose-lined walk, flowering fruit trees, and a pool filled by a running stream. Park officials estimate that more than 10,000 romantic New Yorkers have trysted here on their wedding days. Other attractions include a bee garden, a crabapple garden, and a gorgeous cherry garden. Make an effort to visit during the spring (and during the day), when 80,000 color-coordinated tulips make their grand entrance. (Open Tues.-Sun. 10am-7pm. Suggested donation $1, children 50¢.)

Kissena Park, on Rose Ave. and Parsons Blvd. in Flushing, preserves nature on a more modest scale. The **Historic Grove** was planted here in the 19th century as part of Parson's Nursery and contains many exotic foreign tree species. As you enter from Rose Ave., pass tennis courts and a nature center; down the hill is beautiful Kissena Lake, circled by picnickers, bicyclists, and even a few fisherfolk (fisherfolk?). Urban park rangers give walking tours (718-699-4204); you can call the Kissena Park Nature Center for more information (718-353-2460. Open Wed.-Sun. 10am-4am). From the #7 stop at Main St. pick up the Q17 bus in front of Model's. Take the Q17 down Kissena Blvd. to Rose Ave., and get out in front of Kissena Park.

To the east of Flushing, the 600-acre **Alley Pond Park/Environmental Center** (718-229-4000) offers guided tours of natural trails in the park, a greenbelt of wetlands, woodlands, and marshes. To get there, take the #7 to Main St., Flushing. Then take the Q12 bus from Stern's department store on Roosevelt Ave. along Northern Blvd. to the center.

Flushing Meadow—Corona Park

Queens has hosted a pair of World's Fairs, both in Flushing Meadow—Corona Park, a 1275-acre former swamp sliced out of the middle of the borough. The park, developed during the 1939 Fair, was cultivated on the tip of a huge rubbish dump. Most of the present-day facilities are left over from the 1964-65 Fair; the crumbling concrete bears witness to better days. Like downtown Flushing, the park is on the #7 line from Times Square; you can get off at the dilapidated 111th St. elevated station. (One stop further on, the mundanely named Willets Point/Shea Stadium station was called the World's Fair Station in 1939.) Before leaving the platform, take a look at the large, space-age mushroom-shaped structures in the distance. Walk straight toward these, and you will come to a parking lot about five blocks down.

The building that houses **New York Hall of Science,** at 111th St. and 48th Ave. (718-699-0675 or 718-699-0005), futuristic in 1964, stands on a neglected site, surrounded by rusty rockets. Its vision of the future has not aged well. But this "museum" deserves a visit, especially if you bring children. Over 150 hands-on, updated displays demonstrate a range of scientific concepts. Go to the second floor to climb in the distorto-room, look at the veins in your own bloodshot eye, reflect rainbows with prisms, or alter water waves by controlling the volume and frequency of a speaker. If you time your visit just right, you may witness one of the regularly scheduled cow's-eye dissections performed by one of the young and spirited "Explainers" on the staff. The museum also screens films and offers tours of local scientific centers such as power plants. (Open Wed.-Sun. 10am-5pm. Suggested admission $3.50, seniors and children $2.50. Free Wed.-Thurs. 2-5pm.)

East of the building, across the parking lot and overpass, lies the heart of the park and the **New York City Building.** The south wing houses winter ice skating (718-271-1996), and the north wing is home to the **Queens Museum** (718-592-5555). In the museum, you can see the "Panorama of the City of New York," the world's largest scale model of an urban area, clocking in at 1800 square feet. One hundred feet of New York correspond to one inch on the model, which re-creates over 865,000 buildings in miniature. As you exit the museum you may possibly notice a 380-ton steel globe in the pavilion to your right. It's the "Unisphere," the centerpiece of the 1964 World's Fair. The fountain is drained and the foundation decayed, but the globe remains a sight to behold. You can imagine what this place must have looked like 30 years ago, when women in wigged-out hairstyles and miniskirts and men in polyester turtlenecks and beads did little pagan dances around it.

The rest of the park's grounds are fun, too. Just south of the Hall of Science is a restored **Coney Island carousel** (718-592-6539) that pipes out mischievously off-key music at ear-splitting volume, 75¢ a ride. The **Queens Zoo** next door has recently reopened and features North American animals like elk, bison, and bear. You can try your hand at pitch-and-putt golf (a short course—par 3; 718-271-8182) for $5.50 a game, or cavort in a playground accessible to disabled children. In the southern part of the park, **Meadow Lake** offers paddle boating, rowboating, and duck-dunking, while

Willow Lake Nature Area offers guided tours; call the Urban Rangers at 718-699-4204 for more information.

Shea Stadium, to the north of the park, was built for the 1964 Fair, though the Mets now slug it out here. The **USTA National Tennis Center,** nearby, courts the U.S. Open tennis championship each year. (See Entertainment: Sports.)

Astoria, Long Island City, and Hunter's Point

In Astoria, Greek, Italian, and Spanish-speaking communities mingle amidst lively shopping districts and top-flight cultural attractions. Astoria lies in the upper west corner of the borough, and Long Island City is just south of it, across the river from the Upper East Side. The N line services the area. A trip on the N from Broadway and 34th St. in Manhattan to Broadway and 31st St. in Queens should take about 25 minutes. As you climb down from the El stop you will find yourself in the middle of the Broadway shopping district, a densely packed area where an average block includes three specialty delis, a Greek bakery, and an Italian grocery. Discount shoppers, you've been lusting for this.

Sculpture City and the Isamu Noguchi Garden Museum provide a remarkable diversion from consumerism. Walk down Broadway for about 15 minutes toward the Manhattan skyline, leaving the commercial district for a more industrial area. At the end of Broadway, cross the intersection with Vernon Boulevard. **Socrates Sculpture Garden** is located right next to the steel warehouse. The sight is stunning, if somewhat discomfiting: modern day-glo and rusted metal abstractions *en masse* in the middle of nowhere. Wander among the 20-odd sculptures on this six-acre waterfront plot; behold a junked car suspended in air and a collection of wooden posts listing today's environmental problems such as wetland destruction, soil erosion, and the Army Corps of Engineers. (The attached shovels presumably call for their burial.) Don't miss the "Sound Observatory" right on the edge of the East River. You could spend hours pitty-pat pattering on the tin drums and honking into the "vocal amplifier," which faces out onto the water. Miss Teen Schnauzer comes here often.

To your left as you face the river, two blocks down Vernon Blvd. at 32- 37, stands the **Isamu Noguchi Garden Museum** (718-204-7088 or 718-721-1932), established in 1985 next door to the world-renowned sculptor's studio. Noguchi (1904-88) designed and built this space, one of the only world-class museums that presents a comprehensive survey of the work of a single sculptor. Inside 12 galleries display Noguchi's breadth of vision. Take a look at the model of his proposed "Sculpture to Be Seen From Mars," a two-mile-long face to be carved in the dirt next to Newark International Airport as a monument to man in the post-atomic age. His most inspired works, the smaller stone sculptures, are worth seeing, too. Noguchi once said that he wanted "to look at nature through nature's eyes, and so ignore man as a special object of veneration;" he worked with stones to help them reveal their true souls, not to reshape them. The outdoor sculpture garden bears witness to his success. In "The Well," Noguchi left large parts of the boulder uncut, but bored a large circular "belly button" into the top; water perpetually wells over the top and shimmers down the sides of the stone. Touch its moving surface. The curators at the Metropolitan Museum liked this work so much, they commissioned one of their own. (Open April-Nov. Wed. and Sat. 11am-6pm. Suggested contribution $4, students and seniors $2. A shuttle service (718-721-1932) from Manhattan ($5) leaves from the Asia Society on Park Ave. and 70th St. on Sat. every hr. on the hr. from 11:30am to 3:30pm. It returns every hr. on the hr. until 5pm. An informative but long guided tour kicks off at 2pm.)

Astoria is also the home of the Kaufman-Astoria Studio; part of a 13-acre plant with eight sound stages, it is the largest studio in the U.S. outside of Hollywood. Paramount Pictures used these facilities to make such major motion pictures as *Ragtime*, *Arthur*, and *Secret of My Success*. The studios are closed to the public, but the complex contains the **American Museum of the Moving Image** (718-784-0077), at 35th Ave. and 36th St. The museum is said to be "dedicated to the art, history, and technology of motion picture and television." To get to the museum from the El stop on Broadway, walk five blocks away from Manhattan to 36th St.; make a right and walk two blocks through the residential neighborhood. A gallery with changing exhibitions occupies the ground floor of the museum, and an eclectic group of permanent exhibits is found upstairs. Look in a Magic Mirror to see yourself as Marilyn Monroe, or gaze at a wall of Bill Cosby's sweaters (he never wears the same one twice). The video avalanche of cultural icons and entertainment buzz clips is a reminder of how much cultural baggage we lug around with us, as is the memorabilia collection, which includes Mork and Mindy lunch boxes, Fonzie paper dolls, and the Leave it to Beaver "Ambush" game. Also upstairs is "King Tut's Fever Movie Palace," which shows flicks like "Batman and Robin," while the screening room downstairs regularly plays vintage films and rare collections of film shorts. (Open Tues.- Fri. noon-4pm, Sat.-Sun. noon-6pm.) Tours by appointment (718-784- 4520). For travel directions, call 718-784-4777. Admission $5, seniors $4, students $2.50.

More than anything else in the borough, the **Steinway Piano Factory**, at 19th Ave. and 30th St. in Northern Astoria (718-721-2600), puts Queens on the map. The Steinways moved their famous operation out to Astoria in the 1870s, and had the place to themselves for quite some time. The area was named after pioneering William Steinway, who built affordable housing for his workers around the factory in the 19th century. The thoughtful and considerate Mr. Steinway threw in a library, a kindergarten, and athletic grounds. You can still see some "piano houses" that he had constructed on 20th Ave. between Steinway and 41st St.

The world-famous Steinway pianos continue to be manufactured in the same spot, in the same way. The 12,000 parts of the piano range from a 340lb. plate of cast iron to tiny bits of the skin of a small Brazilian deer (Frootscootchie!). Over 95% of public performances in the U.S. are played on Steinway grands. (Tours Fri. 9am-noon. Try to make reservations at least 2 months before you want to go. Tours are sometimes booked a year in advance, but try anyway; people sometimes cancel.) If you're in the area, you can also take a look at the **Steinway House,** at 18-33 41st St., the spacious mid-19th-century mansion that belonged to William Steinway. Today it stands next to an auto shop and an assortment of Junkyard dogs.

You can gain some perspective on Manhattan from **Hunter's Point** on the East River, in Long Island City. Take the E or F to 23rd St. and Ely Ave., the first stop in Queens. (An another option is the #7 to Courthouse Square). You'll come up from the subway right in front of the brand-new **Citicorp Building,** the tallest building in New York outside of Manhattan, completed in 1989. Its sleek glass exterior hulks, looming over diminutive brick row houses, as if a butter-fingered planning official slipped somewhere, plopping a midtown monolith down on the wrong side of the river. The skyscrapering of the boroughs is probably the shape of the future; as Manhattan development reaches its saturation point, companies are starting to look elsewhere.

To get to the cutting-edge museum/gallery **ICA/PS1** from the Citicorp Building, turn toward the Manhattan skyline and walk two blocks down 45th Ave. (See Museums). Between 23rd and 21st Streets are the well-kept brownstones of the **Hunter's Point Historic District**. Check out the facing of Westchester stone on the 10 Italianate row houses, rare examples of late 19th Century architecture. Make a left on 21st St., go three blocks, and you will come to a red stone Victorian building, at 46-01 21st St. This is the **Institute for Contemporary Art/PS1** (718-784-2084). The building housed the first public school in Queens; you can still see the word "Girls" cut into the stone lintel above the entrance. To enter the unconventional museum you must be buzzed (in). The partially restored, partially decayed hallways form a maze of empty rooms and makeshift exhibition spaces—sometimes it's hard to tell them apart. Besides providing inexpensive studio spaces to lure artists out of Manhattan, PS1 hosts excellent changing exhibitions, like the strangely timeless "Painting in New York Now." Recently a special exhibit in memory of the Chinese students killed in Beijing in 1989 featured hundreds of door-sized panels, each designed by a different artist in materials ranging from goldfish bowls to candle-wax. There are three permanent exhibits over in the studio wing of the building. Ask a curator to take you up to the roof, where Richard Serra created an untitled piece for the 1976 opening. He took an unusual room of exposed beams and bricks and left it completely intact, constructing only a channel in the floor that runs from one corner of the room to the other. Today pigeon droppings complement the piece. Alan Saret's contribution, also designed for the opening, is more accessible (though somewhat difficult to distinguish from the general decay of the building). Called *Fifth Solar Chthonic Wall Temple,* after an old Blue Öyster Cult song, its walled excavation records the movement of the sun as shadows move around the inside of the third floor hallway. In James Turrell's well-known *Meeting,* you can sit on high-backed benches in a room where the ceiling rolls back, then watch the skies shift colors at sunset. The design celebrates the interplay between natural and artificial light. The piece reflects Turrell's Quaker background, and, like a Quaker meetinghouse, provides a simple environment for contemplation. *Meeting* opens only at prime sunsetting time for two hours between 5 and 9pm. Call in advance for reservations. (Museum open Wed.-Sun. noon-6pm. Suggested donation $2.)

Long Island City commands an outstanding view of Manhattan and the East River. To get to the shorefront, walk toward the skyline. Go right on Vernon Blvd., and then make a left onto 44th Dr. To your right as you face the river lies the Queensboro Bridge, better known to Simon and Garfunkel fans as the 59th St. Bridge. Directly in front of you, on the southern tip of Roosevelt Island, you can see the romantically turreted ruins of 19th-century hospital facilities. Besides the conventional highlights of the Manhattan skyline (the angular Empire State Building, the Art Deco Chrysler Building, and the Twin Towers of the World Trade Center in the distance to your left), there is a fine view of the United Nations Complex, the wide gray tower facing out into the river, connected to a smaller domed annex with a satellite dish. The Citicorp Building stands out boldly directly behind you.

Central Queens: Jamaica and Ridgewood

The historic Ridgewood neighborhood, in west-central Queens, was founded 100 years ago, when German and Eastern European immigrants fled ramshackle tenements in Manhattan. German architect Louis Berger designed most of the two- and three-story attached brick homes.

The best thing about the **Onderdonk Farmhouse,** 18-20 Flushing Ave. (718-456-1776), in northwest Ridgewood, is its doinker of a name. Built in 1709, Onderdonk is the oldest stone house in New York City, with charming colonial features like a brick fireplace *and* a hot Dutch oven. (Open Tues.-Sat. 9:30am- 4:30pm. Suggested donation $2, children $1.) Also the home of the Ridgewood Historical Society, the house has an annex that serves as a library on Ridgewood and Long Island history. To get to Ridgewood, take the M train to Seneca or Forest Ave.; to get to Onderdonk, take the L train to Jefferson St., walk one block to Flushing Ave., then up Flushing five blocks more. To the east of Ridgewood, **Forest Park** is a densely wooded area with miles of park trails, a bandshell (718-520-5918), a golf course (718-296-0999), a carousel (718-326-7999), baseball diamonds, tennis courts, and horseback riding (718-261-7679 or 718-263-3500). The Queens Greenhouse is also located here, off Woodhaven Blvd. For information on upcoming park events, call 718-520-5941. Take the L or M train to Myrtle/Wyckoff Ave., then the Q55 bus.

You can get a little taste of Old New York at the **Queens County Farm Museum** (718-347-3276), 73-50 Little Neck Parkway, in Floral Park on the Nassau Border. Built by Jacob Adriance in 1772 on 50 acres of land, this is the only working farm of its era that has been restored. Cows, duckers, chickens, and sheep graze here. Take the E or F train to Kew Gdns./Union Turnpike, then the Q46 bus to Little Neck Pkwy. Walk three blocks north. (Farmhouse/museum open Sat.-Sun. noon-5pm. Grounds open 9am-5pm daily. Donations requested.)

Jamaica, named for the Jameco Indians, lies in the center of Queens and is the heart of Queens' African-American and West Indian community. To get here, take the E or J train to Jamaica Center. The main strip on Jamaica Ave. is constantly bustling with activity, and the pedestrian mall on 165th St., from Jamaica Ave. to 89th Ave. is lined with restaurants selling succulent Jamaican beef patties, stores selling Malcolm X baseball caps and African clothing, and 50-ft.-tall metal men with arms outstretched.

The **Jamaica Arts Center,** 161-04 Jamaica Ave. (718-658-7400) at 161st St., offers workshops in dance, photography, and pottery, and often displays visual art exhibitions dealing with aspects of African-American or urban life. In 1990, the Center was awarded the New York State Governor's Arts Awards by Governor Mario Cuomo, who grew up in Jamaica. (Open Mon.-Sat. 9am-5pm. Free.)

If white colonial history is more your style, the **King Mansion** (718-291-02820, on Jamaica Ave. and 152rd St.) may be of interest. Recently renovated, this was the colonial residence of King Rufus, signer of the Constitution, one of New York's first senators and the first U.S. ambassador to Great Britain. His son was Governor of New York. The house, set in eleven-acre King Park, dates back to 1733 and combines examples of Georgian and Federal architecture. South of the mansion and the Long Island Railroad, just behind the Jamaica Center Subway station, at 159th St. and Archer Ave., is **Prospect Cemetery.** It was established in 1668, making it Queens' oldest burying ground; the first attorney general of New York was buried here. Today, despite its designation as an historic landmark, it is caged in, overgrown, filled with scrap tires, noisome fumes, and junked car doors. (In recent years decay has become a stock feature of historic sights in New York City, as maintenance funds are slashed and upkeep shrifted.) Two buildings on Jamaica Ave. are of architectural and historical note, though they, too, have been neglected. Though boarded up these days, the former **Jamaica Savings Bank** at 161-02 Jamaica Ave., right next to the Arts Center, is regarded by some as "the finest Beaux Artes building in Queens." Across the street at Jamaica Ave. and 165th St. is the former **Valencia Theater,** now the "Tabernacle of Prayer." It was built in 1929 as one of several atmospheric "Wonder Theaters;" if you can't get inside, a peek through the door into the front lobby will give you the idea. While the area directly south of downtown Jamaica is fairly barren except for food-processing factories and crime activity, the upper-class African-American communities to its southeast are well-kept residential areas with a fair amount of interesting history. After WWII **St. Albans,** the area centered on Linden Blvd. just east of Merrick, became the home of newly-mobile African-Americans, many of whom were empowered by the GI Bill and the work of the NAACP. St. Albans in the 1950s recalled Harlem in the 1920s; jazz greats Count Basie and Fats Waller, as well as James P. Johnson and baseball stars like Jackie Robinson and Roy Campanella, all lived here—mostly in the Addisleigh Park area of western St. Albans. Today, wealthier African-Americans have moved southeast to communities like Laurelton, but most of St. Albans' homes remain beautiful, and the Linden Blvd. shopping district is alive with West Indian bakeries and restaurants. To get to St. Albans, take the E or J trains to Jamaica Center, then take the Q4 bus to Linden Blvd.

Southern Queens

The **Jamaica Bay Wildlife Refuge** (718-474-0613), near the town of Broad Channel in Jamaica Bay, is about the size of Manhattan and ten times the size of Flushing Meadows-Corona Park. The refuge's western half dips into Brooklyn, and the entire place constitutes one of the most important urban wildlife refuges in the U.S., harboring more than 325 species of shore birds, water fowl, and small animals. Miles of paths around the marshes and ponds are lined with benches and birdhouses. You can see Manhattan from here, but you hear nothing save the roaring of planes leaving from nearby JFK to join the birds in flight. Beached wooden rowboats, a trout-mask replica, and the frequent egret or swan make this place a real oasis. Environmental slide shows and tours are available on weekends. (Nature Center open daily 8:30am- 4:30pm. Free.) To get here by subway, take the A, C, or H line to Broad Channel. Walk west on Noel Rd. to Crossbay Blvd., and then north (right) about 3/4 of a mile to the center. Or take the E,F,G, or R line to Roosevelt Ave., in Jackson Heights and then the Q53 express bus to Broad Channel, which involves the same walk.

Just south of the refuge lies Rockaway Peninsula, named after a Native American word for "living waters." Here you'll find **Rockaway Beach,** immortalized by the Ramones in one of their formulaic pop-punk tributes. A public beach (718-318-4000) extends from Beach 1st. St. in Far Rockaway to Beach 149th St. in the west, with a boardwalk extending to Beach 126th St. Between Beach 126th St. and Beach 149th St., it is unclear whether the beach is public or not; no street parking is allowed there during the summer so that the residents of million-dollar homes in Belle Harbor and Neponsit can avoid the riff-raff like us who come to the beach for a little fun and sun.

Just west of Rockaway Beach (and separated from it by a huge chain-link fence) is **Jacob Riis Park** (718-338-3338), part of the 26,000-acre **Gateway National Recreation Area** (718-474-4600), which extends into Brooklyn, Staten Island, and New Jersey. The park was named for Jacob Riis, a photographer and journalist who brought attention to the need for school playgrounds and neighborhood parks in the early 1900s; he persuaded New York City to turn this overgrown beach into a public park. Today the park is lined with its own gorgeous beach and boardwalk and contains basketball and handball courts, a golf course, and concession stands.

Adjoining the park to the west is **Fort Tilden,** also a part of Gateway, where you can walk through the sand dunes past old Nike missile sites from the Cold War days, as well as the sites of 16-in. shore guns from WWI and WWII, when this was a naval base. The **visitors center** (718-474-4600) for Riis Park and Fort Tilden is on Murray Rd. off Beach 169th St. and is open daily, 9am-5pm. To get to Rockaway Park, take the C or H train to Beach 105th or 116th St. To get to Riis Park, take the #2 or #5 train to Flatbush Ave., then pick up the Q35 bus on Nostrand Ave., in front of Lord's Bakery. The Q22 bus connects Riis Park to the Beach 116th subway station in Rockaway Park.

The Bronx

The Bronx?—No thonx.

—Ogden Nash

The Bronx has long exercised an unhealthy attraction on the American imagination, joined to Detroit, Watts, and Anacostia as a dark specters of urban decay, apocalyptic cities of doom. The reality here sometimes seems to warrant the grim comparisons: exiting the subway, rising from the gnarly bowels, one looks out on the far from pacific sight of bombed-out skeletal remains plastered over with imitation windows, the half-baked efforts of urban planners anxious to conceal obvious, systemic decay. The South Bronx *is* a misbegotten tribute to the delusional ambition of the postwar urban empire-builders, who succeeded in providing thousands of units of low-income housing, but only by creating nightmarish prisons of concrete and steel, dense, airless blocks projected upwards into space. But the Bronx is more than the sum of its representations, more than mere blight and phantasmagoric decadence. While the media presents the Bronx as a crime-ravaged husk, the borough offers its few tourists over 2000 acres of parkland, a great zoo, turn-of-the-century riverfront mansions, grand boulevards more evocative of Europe than late 20th-century America, and thriving ethnic neighborhoods, including a Little Italy to shame its counterpart to the south.

The only borough on the U.S. mainland, the Bronx took its name from the Bronx River, which in turn took its name from early Dutch settler Jonas Bronck who claimed the area for his farm in 1636. Until the turn of the century, the area consisted largely of cottages, farmlands, and wild marshes. Then the tide of immigration swelled, bringing scores of Italian and Irish settlers. The flow of immigrants (now Hispanics and Russians) has never stopped.

The southern part of the Bronx has become home to a large Black and Latino population. If you're not heading for Yankee Stadium, stay out of the South Bronx unless you're in a car and with someone who knows the area. The northern and eastern parts of the borough are largely middle class, with single-family houses and duplexes on peaceful, tree-lined streets. Pelham Bay Park in the northeastern Bronx, the city's largest park, used to be a private estate owned by the Pell family. In the center of the Bronx, on the banks of the Bronx river, Bronx Park contains the Bronx Zoo and the

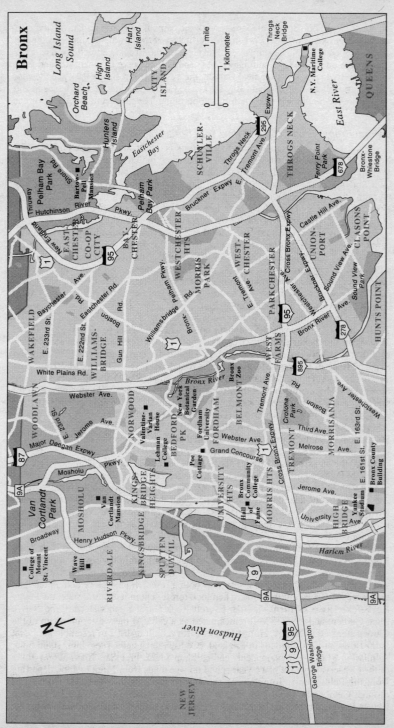

Bronx

Long Island Sound

Hart Island

High Island

Orchard Beach

Hunters Island

Eastchester Bay

CITY ISLAND

1 mile

1 kilometer

SCHUYLER-VILLE

Throgs Neck Bridge

N.Y. Maritime College

THROGS NECK

East River

QUEENS

Pelham Bay Park

Bartow Pell Mansion

Shore Rd.

Hutchinson River

Pelham Bay Park

Pkwy.

Bruckner Expwy.

E. Tremont Ave.

Castle Hill Ave.

Ferry Point Park

Bronx-Whitestone Bridge

678

UNION-PORT

CLASONS POINT

Thruway

New England Thruway

EAST CHEST. CO-OP CITY

BAY-CHESTER

WESTCHESTER HTS.

WEST-CHESTER

Cross Bronx Expwy.

Sound View Ave.

Sound View Park

HUNTS POINT

95

1

MORRIS PARK

PARKCHESTER

WAKEFIELD

Baychester Rd.

E. 233rd St.

E. 222nd St.

Eastchester Rd.

Boston Rd.

Williamsbridge

Pelham Pkwy.

Bronx Rd.

E. Tremont Ave.

Westchester Ave.

Bruckner Expwy.

95

278

WILLIAMS-BRIDGE

Gun Hill Rd.

1

Bronx River

WEST FARMS

895

White Plains Rd.

WOODLAWN

Webster Ave.

Bronx River

Bronx Zoo

New York Botanical Garden

BELMONT

Tremont Ave.

Crotona Park

Boston Rd.

MORRISANIA

Third Ave.

Westchester Ave.

E. 233rd St.

Jerome Ave.

NORWOOD

Valentine-Varian House

BEDFORD PK

Fordham University

FORDHAM

Webster Ave.

Grand Concourse

Cross Bronx Expwy.

1

TREMONT

Melrose Ave.

E. 163rd St.

87

Major Deegan Expwy.

Mosholu Pkwy.

Lehman College

Poe Cottage

UNIVERSITY HTS.

MORRIS HTS.

Jerome Ave.

E. 161st St.

Bronx County Building

9A

Van Cortlandt Park

MOSHOLU

Van Cortlandt Mansion

KINGS-BRIDGE HEIGHTS

Bronx Community College Hall of Fame

University Ave.

HIGH BRIDGE

Yankee Stadium

Mosholu

Broadway

Henry Hudson Pkwy.

KINGSBRIDGE

SPUYTEN DUYVIL

Harlem River

9

College of Mount St. Vincent

Wave Hill

RIVERDALE

9

9A

Hudson River

9A

95

9

1

George Washington Bridge

NEW JERSEY

N

excellent New York Botanical Garden, with the campus of Fordham University at its western edge. Van Cortlandt Park, in the northwest of the borough, completes the trio of major open spaces. The subway will take you to the Bronx's attractions: The #1, 9 and 4 reach up to Van Cortlandt Park; the C and D lines serve Fordham Rd. and Bedford Park Blvd., near the Botanical Garden; the #2 and 5 skirt Bronx Park and the zoo; and the #6 stretches into Pelham Bay Park. The C, D, and #4 trains whisk fans in and out of Yankee Stadium in the south of the borough. The **area code** for the Bronx is 718.

Central Bronx: Bronx Zoo and New York Botanical Garden

The most obvious reason to come to the Bronx is the **Bronx Zoo,** also known as the New York Zoological Society. The largest urban zoo in the United States, it husbands over 4000 animals. While it has some architecturally sound buildings, the animals and their fans prefer the 265-acre expanse of natural habitats created for their dwelling pleasure. While the Timber Rattlesnake has been sentenced to life in the Reptile House, more benign beasts have been loosed; Indian elephants inhabit the Wild Asia exhibit and White-Cheeked Gibbons treehop in the JungleWorld.

Noteworthy natural habitats include: the Himalayan Highlands, home to endangered snow leopards and fiery red pandas; Wild Asia, stalked by rhinoceroses, muntjacs, sambars and nilgais and rare Sika Deer; South America, roamed by guanacos, babirusas, and pygmy hippos; and the World of Darkness, swarming with scores of bats and bushbabies. Kids imitate animals at the hands-on Children's Zoo, where they can climb a spider's web or try on a turtle shell. If you tire of the children, the crocodiles are fed Monday and Thursday at 2pm.

You can explore the zoo on foot or ride like the king of the jungle aboard the Safari Train which runs between the elephant house and Wild Asia (one-way $1, children 75¢). Soar into the air for a funky cool view of the zoo from the **Skyfari** aerial tramway that runs between Wild Asia and the Children's Zoo (one-way $1.25, children $1). The **Bengali Express Monorail** glides round Wild Asia (20min.; $1.50, children $1). If you find the pace too harried, saddle up a camel ($2). **Walking tours** are given on weekends by the Friends of the Zoo; call 220-5142 three weeks in advance to reserve a place. Parts of the zoo close down during winter (Nov.-April); call 367-1010 or 220-5100 for more information. (Open Mon.-Fri. 10am-5pm, Sat.-Sun. 10am-5:30pm; Nov.-Jan. daily 10am-4:30pm. Admission Tues.-Thurs. free; Fri.-Mon. $5.75, seniors and children $2. For disabled access information call 220-5188.) If you're driving, take the Bronx River Pkwy. or (from I-95) the Pelham Pkwy. By subway take the #2 express to Bronx Park East (or, as the Chamber of Commerce recommends, to Pelham Parkway, though it takes longer), or the Lexington Ave. #5 Express to E. 180th St. and transfer there to the #2. Walk west to Bronxdale entrance to the zoo. Alternatively, take the D express to Fordham Rd., then the Bx12 bus to Southern Blvd. Walk east on Fordham Rd. to the Rainey Gate entrance. The express BxM11 bus leaves from Madison Ave. in midtown for the Bronxdale entrance to the zoo; call 652-8400 for details.

North across East Fordham Rd. from the zoo sprawls the labyrinthine **New York Botanical Garden** (220-8700). Snatches of forest and virgin waterways allow you to imagine the area's original landscape. The 250-acre garden, one of the world's outstanding horticultural preserves, serves as both a research laboratory and a plant and tree museum. Scope out the 40-acre hemlock forest kept in its natural state, the Peggy Rockefeller Rose Garden, the T.H. Everett Rock Garden and waterfall, the Native Plant Garden, and a Snuff Mill reincarnated as a café. At the westernmost tip of the Garden stands the **Enid A. Haupt Conservatory,** built in 1902 to resemble the Great Palm House at Kew Gardens in England. (Conservatory open Tues.-Sun. 10am-5pm. Admission $3.50; seniors, students and children $1.25. Free Sat. 10am-noon.) Tours of the Conservatory take place year-round on weekends from 11am to 4pm, departing from the Palm Court. Tours sweep the garden grounds on weekends from April through October, at 1 and 3pm, departing from the steps of the Visitor Information Center. If you go exploring by yourself, get a garden map; it's a jungle out there for the mapless. The three mile perimeter walk skirts most of the major sights. (Garden Grounds open April-Oct. Tues.-Sun., 10am-7pm, Nov.-March 10am-6pm. Donation ($3) suggested; parking costs $4. Call 220-8779 for information.) If you're driving, the Garden is easily reached via the Henry Hudson, Bronx River, or Pelham Parkways. By subway, take the D or #4 to Bedford Park Blvd. Walk eight blocks east or take the Bx26 bus to the Garden. The Metro-North Harlem line goes from Grand Central Station to Botanical Garden Station, right outside the main gate (call 532-4900 for details).

Fordham University (579-2000), begun in 1841 by John Hughes as St. John's College, has matured into the nation's foremost Jesuit school. Robert S. Riley built the campus in classic collegiate Gothic style in 1936. It spans 80 acres on Webster Ave. between E. Fordham Rd. and Dr. Theodore Kazimiroff Blvd. (Subway: C or D to Fordham Rd.)

Traditional immigrant cultures thrive in the Bronx, away from Manhattan's fervid glare. One of the more celebrated lies along the "Appian Road" that leads to Arthur Avenue, the uptown "Little Italy." In this neighborhood of two-story row houses and byzantine alleyways you'll find some of the best Italian food west of Naples. Outside the **Church of Our Lady of Mt. Carmel,** at 187th and Belmont, stand a pair of ecclesiastical shops where you can buy a statuette of your favorite saint. The portable martyrs come in all sizes and every color of the rainbow. Arthur Avenue itself is home to some of the best homestyle southern Italian cooking in the world. At **Dominick's,** between 186th and 187th, boisterous crowds at long communal tables put away pasta without recourse to ordering, prices, or menus. For the same dish on three different days you may pay three different prices, but you'll never leave kvetching. (Subway: C or D to Fordham Rd.; see Bronx Food.)

The enthusiastic Bronx Historical Society maintains the **Edgar Allan Poe Cottage** (881-8900), built in 1812 and furnished in the 1840s. The morbid writer and his tubercular wife lived spartanly here at 2640 Grand Concourse off Kingsbridge Rd. from 1846-48. Here Poe wrote *Annabel Lee, Eureka,* and *The Bells,* a tale about the neighboring bells of Fordham. The museum displays a slew of Poe's manuscripts and other macabrabilia. (Open Wed.-Fri. 9am-5pm, Sat. 10am-4pm, Sun. 1-5pm. Call in advance. Admission $2. Subway: D or #4 to Kingsbridge Rd.)

The **Herbert H. Lehman College** (960-8000), founded in 1931 as Hunter College, is a fiefdom in the CUNY empire. The U.N. Security Council met in the gymnasium building in 1946. In 1980, the Lehmans endowed the first cultural center in the Bronx, **The Lehman Center for the Performing Arts,** on Bedford Park Blvd. West (between Jerome and Goulden Ave.), a 2300-seat concert hall, experimental theater, recital hall, library, dance studio, and art gallery in one. (Subway: #4 to Bedford Park Blvd. Lehman College.) The **Bronx High School of Science,** nearby, is an unlikely center of academic excellence. The school has produced several Nobel prize-winning scientists.

At the **Bronx Community College Hall of Fame** at University Ave. and W. 181st St. (220-6003), gape at the granite busts of 102 great Americans set on beds of granite and weeds. Predictably, McKim, Mead and White designed this turn-of-the-century hall, a property of the City University of New York. (Open Mon.-Fri. 9am-5pm. Free. Subway: #4 to Burnside Ave.)

Northern Bronx: Van Cortlandt Park

Van Cortlandt Park (430-1890), the city's third-largest jolly green giant, spreads across 1,146 acres of ridges and valleys in the northwest Bronx. The park contains golf courses, tennis courts, baseball diamonds, soccer, football and cricket fields, kiddie recreation areas, and a large swimming pool. Van Cortlandt Lake teems with bustly fish; big rocks and stone formations speak volumes about the park's fiery prehistoric origins. Hikers have plenty of clambering options. The Cass Gallagher Nature Trail in the park's northwestern section leads to rock outcroppings from the last ice age and to damp corners, home to an assortment of the park's little creatures. The Old Putnam Railroad Track, once the city's first rail link to Boston, now leads past the quarry that supplied the marble for Grand Central Station. The Indian Field recreation area was laid on top of the burial grounds of pro-rebel Stockbridge Indians ambushed and massacred by British troops during the Revolutionary War.

In the southwest of the park stands the **Van Cortlandt Mansion** (543-3344), a city and national landmark built in 1748 by the prominent political clan that divided their time between politics and farming. It's the oldest building in the Bronx. George Washington made frequent visits here, including his 1781 meeting with Rochambeau to determine the final strategy of the war. George began the triumphant march into New York City from here in 1783. Vague British nobility, aristocratic French, solitary Hessians, and continental Americans all showed up with their forces for a brief, historic sojourn. Musty masonry and peeling paint add a few flakes of authenticity to this repeatedly restored mansion. The strange *gorbels* above the windows reveal the Dutch heritage of the builder; grimacing countenances like these showed their faces frequently in Holland, but rarely in the New World. The house also has the oldest dollhouse in the U.S. (Museum open Tues.-Fri. 10am-3pm, Sat.-Sun. 11am-5pm. Scheduled public tours occur Fri. 1-3pm and Sun. at 2pm. Admission $2, students and seniors $1.50. The park and the mansion can both be reached by subway—#1 or 9 to 242nd St.)

En route to Van Cortlandt Park stop off at **Manhattan College** (920-0100), a 100-year-old private liberal arts institution that began as a high school. Starting from the corner of Broadway and 242nd St. (Subway: #1 or 9 to242nd St.), take 242nd up, up, *up*hill. As you scale the tortuous mound past Irish pubs and Chinese laundries, watch for the college's pseudo-federalist red brick buildings and chapel. The campus sprawls over stairs, squares, and plateaus, like a life-sized game of Snakes and Ladders. The second staircase on campus brings you to a sheer granite bluff crowned with a kitsch plaster Madonna, a likely kidnapping victim for a suburban garden. Hardy souls who attain the campus peaks can take in a cinemascopic view of the Bronx. Continue up the hill to the sheltered **Fieldston School,** featured in Francis Ford Coppola's short in *New York Stories.*

Wave Hill, 675 W. 252nd St., a pastoral estate in Riverdale, commands an astonishing view of the Hudson and the Palisades. Samuel Clemens, Arturo Toscanini, and Teddy Roosevelt all resided in the Wave Hill House. Donated to the city over 20 years ago, the estate currently offers concerts and dance amidst its greenhouses and spectacular formal gardens. Picnic on the splendid lawns. (Open Wed.-Sun. 10am-4:30pm. Admission $4, seniors and students $2. Call 549-2055 for information.)

The 1758 **Valentine-Varian House** (881-8900), the second oldest building in the Bronx (Van Cortlandt got there first), saw light action during the revolution. It has since become the site of the **Museum of Bronx History** run by the Bronx County Historical Society. The museum, at Bainbridge Ave. and E. 208th St., functions as the borough archive, profiling its heritage. The house has retained a few period furnishings but negligible revolutionary ambience. (Open Sat. 10am-4pm, Sun. 1-5pm, otherwise by appointment. Admission $2. Subway: D to 205th St., or #4 to Mosholu Pkwy.)

Northeastern Bronx: Pelham Bay Park

Pelham Bay Park has over 2100 acres of green saturated with fun activities for the entire family. The omniscient Park Rangers lead a variety of history- and nature-oriented walks for creatures great and small (call 430-1890 for a schedule). Inside the park, the Federal **Bartow-Pell Mansion Museum** (885-1461) sits among prize-winning formal gardens landscaped in 1915. The interior decorator doted on the Empire/Greek Revival style. (Open Wed. and Sat.- Sun. noon-4pm. Closed three weeks in August. Admission $2, seniors and students $1. Subway: #6 to Pelham Bay Park.)

For a whiff of New England in New York, visit **City Island,** a community of century-old houses and sailboats, complete with a shipyard. The **City Island Historical Nautical Museum** and the **North Wind Undersea Institute** (885-0701) can chart a tour better than Julie McCoy any day. The ancient mariner's heart will be warmed at the sight of a 100-year-old tugboat, antiquated diving gear, exotic sea shells, and bundles of whale bones. Take #6 to Pelham Bay Park and then board the #21 bus outside the station. Get off at the first stop on City Island.

South Bronx

Sports fans and stair-master freaks will enjoy a visit to historic **Yankee Stadium,** on E. 161st St. at River Ave., built in 1923. Frequent remodeling has kept the aging stadium on par with more recent constructions. The Yankees played the first night game here in 1946; the first message scoreboard tallied points here in 1954. Inside the 11.6-acre park (the field measures only 3.5 acres), monuments honor Yankee greats Lou Gehrig, Joe DiMaggio, and Babe Ruth. (Subway: C, D, or #4 to 161st St.)

The **Bronx Museum of the Arts** (681-6000), at 161th St. and Grand Concourse near Yankee Stadium, is another good reason to go South. Set in the rotunda of the Bronx Courthouse, it exhibits works of old masters and local talent. Open Wed.-Fri. 10am-5pm, Sat., Sun. 1-6pm. Suggested admission: Adult $3, student $2, seniors $1; Sundays free.

Staten Island

In 1524, 32 years after Columbus patented the New World, a Florentine named Giovanni Da Verrazano sailed into New York Harbor and entered the history books as the godfather of what would later be known as Staten Island. The name (originally *Staaten Eylandt*) comes courtesy of Henry Hudson, who plied his sail in the neighboring waters while on a voyage for the Dutch East India Company in 1609. In 1687, the sportive Duke of York sponsored a sailing contest, generously offering Staten Island as the prize. Manhattan won and has since called the island its own.

For the first 440 years of the its existence, the only way to get from the island to New York proper was by boat. In 1713, a public ferry started running from Staten Island to the rest of the city. In spite of the new link, Staten Islanders still tended to look west to New Jersey, just a stone's throw away across the Arthur Kill, rather than north and east to the city. In 1964, builder Othmar "George Washington Bridge" Amman spanned the gap between Staten Island and Brooklyn with a 4260-foot suspension baby, the **Verrazano-Narrows Bridge.** Visible from virtually everywhere on the island, the bridge has the distinction of being the world's second longest suspension bridge, outspanned only by the Humber bridge in England. Amman's construction measures 60 feet longer than San Francisco's Golden Gate Bridge: between the epic bridge and the island's impossible hills, San Franciscans will feel right at home.

Even though traffic now flows more easily between Manhattan and Staten Island (via Brooklyn), the two boroughs exchange nothing save the barest cordiality. Life drains away on Staten Island. Manhattanites tend to think of Staten Island as part of New Jersey; most only go to the island in order to ride the ferry and come right back or to take driving tests (the waiting list for appointments is shorter than in Manhattan). In recent years Staten Islanders have unsuccessfully lobbied borough, state, and city governments to have Staten Island declared an independent municipality. Many resent the higher taxes they pay to subsidize the poorer neighborhoods in Manhattan.

To get to the ferry terminal, take the Westside 1 or 9 to South Ferry Station or take the N or R to Whitehall Station, then walk west about three blocks. Don't stop to wonder why the ferry ride to Staten Island is free, but it costs 50¢ to leave. Instead take in the splendid breeze and the famous views that the ferry ride affords. Look at the lower Manhattan skyline, Ellis Island, the Statue of Liberty, and Governor's Island; the views here might be the best in the city–it's like looking at 3D postcards. The rest of the waterscape is spectacular as well; New York scale is imprinted even on the boats, which are *huge*, and on the giant industrial structures shaped like headless giraffes which line the horizon. If you can arrange it, don't miss taking the 30-minute ride at night; the ferry runs 24 hrs.

The **Tourist Information Center** burned down not long ago, and has yet to be replaced; have good directions ready if you plan to go out onto the island, or ask a friendly bus driver for assistance. Because of the hills and the distances (and some very dangerous neighborhoods in between), it's a bad idea to *walk* from one site to the next. Make sure to plan your excursion with the bus schedule in mind.

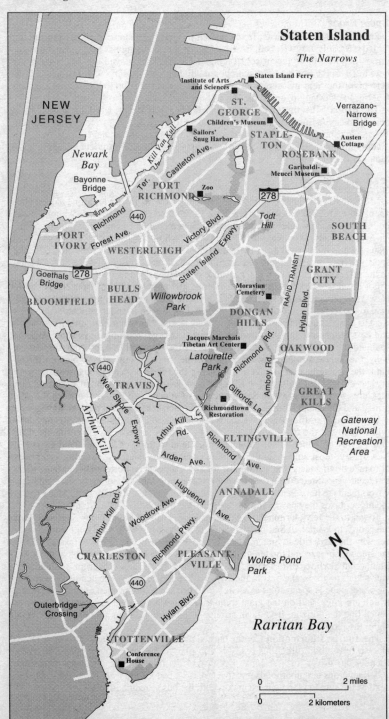

Staten Island

The Narrows

Staten Island Ferry

Institute of Arts
and Sciences

NEW
JERSEY

ST.
GEORGE

Children's Museum

Verrazano-
Narrows
Bridge

Sailors'
Snug Harbor

STAPLE-
TON

ROSEBANK

Austen
Cottage

*Newark
Bay*

Castleton Ave.

Garibaldi-
Meucci Museum

Bayonne
Bridge

PORT
RICHMOND

Zoo

278

Kill Van Kull

Ter.

Richmond

440

*Todt
Hill*

SOUTH
BEACH

PORT
IVORY

Forest Ave.

WESTERLEIGH

Victory Blvd.

Staten Island Expwy.

RAPID TRANSIT

GRANT
CITY

Goethals
Bridge

278

BULLS
HEAD

*Willowbrook
Park*

Moravian
Cemetery

Hylan Blvd.

BLOOMFIELD

DONGAN
HILLS

Jacques Marchais
Tibetan Art Center

*Latourette
Park*

Richmond Rd.

OAKWOOD

440

Amboy Rd.

West Shore Expwy.

TRAVIS

Giffords La.

GREAT
KILLS

Richmondtown
Restoration

Arthur Kill

Arthur Kill
Rd.

Richmond

ELTINGVILLE

*Gateway
National
Recreation
Area*

Arden   Ave.

Ave.

ANNADALE

Huguenot

Arthur Kill Rd.

Woodrow Ave.

Ave.

Richmond Pkwy.

N

CHARLESTON

PLEASANT-
VILLE

*Wolfes Pond
Park*

440

Hylan Blvd.

Outerbridge
Crossing

Raritan Bay

TOTTENVILLE

Conference
House

0   2 miles

0   2 kilometers

Just up the hill from the terminal, the second street on the right is Stuyvesant Place, site of the imposing Federalist **Town Hall** and its clocktower. You will also find here the **College of Staten Island,** the local colony of the City University of New York system. Its main building, a white institutional construction in the style of a Florentine *palazzo,* makes an attractive landmark inside and out. In the back courtyard, rises a sculpture of some guy named Frank D. Paolo. There's also a terrace with a nice view of the harbor.

Not far off at Stuyvesant Pl., the **Staten Island Museum** (718-727-1135), run by the S.I. Institute of Arts and Sciences, features displays of natural history and fine arts as well as nifty dioramas on Native American life. (Open Tues.-Sat. 10am-5pm, Sun. 2-5pm. Suggested donation $2; seniors, students, and ages under 12 $1.)

At 1000 Richmond Terrace, the **Snug Harbor Cultural Center** has been designated a National Historic Landmark District. Once a mariner's lair, it includes 26 architecturally significant buildings and the **Newhouse Center for Contemporary Art** (718-448-2500), which showcases the work of contemporary U.S. artists. (Open Wed.-Sun. noon-5pm. Free.) Also on the premises is the free **Staten Island Children's Museum** (718-273-2060; grounds open Wed.-Fri. 1- 5pm, Sat.-Sun. noon-5pm. $3 for all except children under 3). The **Staten Island Botanical Garden** occupies 28 acres of the Cultural Center's 80-acre spread. Hungry? Grab a bite at **Melville's Cafe,** located in the Visitors Center (open Wed.-Fri. 11am-2pm, weekends 12:30-3:00pm) which serves cafeteria style lunch for under $5. Or walk out of the Harbor, down Richmond Terrace less than 1/4 of a mile and try eating outdoors at **R.H. Tugs Restaurant** at 1115 Richmond Terrace (718-447-6369) and enjoy a waterfront lunch with flowers on the tables. Stick to the sandwiches and salads, tasty at $7 and under. Entrees run to $12. Budgeteers should bolt for the **Getty Mart Gas Station and Convenience Store**, right next door to Tugs, which contains a Deli/Pizzeria dear to the locals. Sandwiches under $5, outdoor tables (on the parking lot). Open Mon.-Sat. 6am to midnight, Sun. 6:30am-midnight.

The **Staten Island Zoo** (718-442-3101), in Barrett Park at Broadway and Clove Rd., has moved all of its big animals permanently to Mexico. (Hmmm...) You can still toy with some of the world's finest reptiles for $3 ($2 for children under 11). (Open daily 10am-4:45pm. Take the S48 bus from St. George Terminal.)

Built to resemble a Tibetan temple, an illusion abetted by its hilltop placement, the **Jacques Marchais Center of Tibetan Art** displays the finest collection of Tibetan art in the Western Hemisphere (see Museums). Take the #74 bus from the ferry to Lighthouse Ave.

The Vanderbilt saga comes to an end at the **Moravian Cemetery,** on Richmond Rd. at Todt Hill Rd. in Donegan Hills. Commodore Cornelius Vanderbilt and his clan lie in this ornate crypt, built in 1886 by Richard Morris Hunt. Central Park's Frederic Law Olmsted obliged with the landscaping. Alas, the crypt can be viewed only from the outside. Adjacent to the cemetery is the 72-acre **High Rock Park Conservation Center** (718-667-2165), with miles of well-marked trails, perfect for an afternoon stroll. You'll have to drive to get here; the buses steer clear of the grave-strewn paths of the Donegan Hills. (Park open daily 9am-5pm. Tours Sunday at 1pm, Call first.)

In the mid-1800s Giuseppe Garibaldi, an Italian patriot and mastermind of Italy's reunification, took refuge on the island following his defeat at the hands of Napoleon III. He settled in an old farmhouse in Rosebank and proceeded to amass enough memorabilia to make the place into a museum: the **Garibaldi-Menucci Museum** (718-442-1608) is located at 420 Tompkins Ave. (Open Tues.-Fri. 9am-5pm, Sat.-Sun. 1-5pm. Free.) At one time the house belonged to Antonio Menucci, the celebrated inventor of the telephone (he had developed his first working model by 1851 and finally received a U.S. patent caveat in 1871, but died before being recognized as the inventor—lucky for A.G. Bell). The S79 bus should, with any luck, drop you right at the door.

Historic Richmond Town, a huge museum complex, documents three centuries of Staten Island and its culture and history. Reconstructed 17th- to 19th-century dwellings are populated by "inhabitants," costumed master-craftspeople and their apprentices. Thanks to budget cuts, only 10 of these buildings, spread over 100 acres, are permanently open to the public. Head for **The Voorlezer's House** (1996), the oldest surviving elementary school in the U.S. (also a church and home), the **General Store** (1840), and an 18th-century farmhouse. The buildings that open to the public rotate, so call in advance to find out what is open, as well as to find out about the "living history" events. Tours of Richmond Town are available Wed.-Sun., 1-5pm, on the hour. Call 718-351-1611 in advance for tours or info about special events. To get here take a 40-minute ride on the $74 bus from the ferry.

The only peace conference ever held between British forces and American rebels transpired on Staten Island in the **Conference House.** At the summit on September 11, 1776, British commander Admiral Lord Howe met with three Continental Congress representatives—Benjamin Franklin, John Adams, and Edward Rutledge. Located at the foot of Hyland Blvd. in Tottenville, the house has become—what else?— a National Historic Landmark. Inside, you can see period furnishings and refresh your knowledge of Revolutionary War minutiae. (Admission $1, seniors and children 50¢. Guided tours by appointment Wed.-Sun. 1-4pm. Take the S103 bus to the last stop on Craig Ave.)

Museums

New York has accumulated more stuff in more museums than any other city in the New World. Come witness a culture collecting itself. Swoon under a life-sized replica of a great blue whale at the American Museum of Natural History. Control a 900-ft. aircraft carrier at the Intrepid Sea-Air-Space Museum. Slip into the world of the 2000-year-old Egyptian Temple of Dendur or of Van Gogh's 100-year-old *Café at Arles* at the Metropolitan Museum of Art. Relax alongside Monet's *Water Lilies* at the Museum of Modern Art.

Many museums request a donation instead of setting a fixed admission charge. No one will throw you out or even glare at you for giving less than the suggested donation; more likely, you'll feel slightly cheap, or maybe guilty. Enjoy that sneaky feeling. Recently the Met has extended its hours so you can stay longer or take a break and come back for more. (Always keep your pin.) Some museums have regular, weekly "voluntary contribution" (read: free) times.

During the annual **Museum Mile Festival** in June, Fifth Avenue museums keep their doors open till late at night, stage popular, engaging exhibits, involve city kids in mural painting, and fill the streets with the gritty lyricism of jazz.

The Metropolitan Museum

In 1866, a group of eminent Americans in Paris enthusiastically received John Jay's proposal to create a "National Institution and Gallery of Art." They probably never imagined that one day their project would span 1.4 million sq. feet and house 3.3 million works of art, mounted on a hill of steps crawling with popsicle, knish, and hot dog vendors. But whatever their vision, the New York Union League Club pressed hard under Jay's leadership, rallying civic leaders, art collectors, and philanthropists to the cause. In April 1870, the Metropolitan Museum showed its first collection, containing 174 paintings (mostly Dutch and Flemish), and assorted antiquities.

After a nomadic barf, the museum finally came to settle at its present location in Central Park at 82nd St. and Fifth Ave. on March 30, 1880. Although Frederic Olmsted, the designer of Central Park, was peeved at the intrusion of the building onto his landscape, different stages of construction continued for over a century. In the Lehman Wing, you can still see the west façade of the first building, a Gothic structure designed by Calvert Vaux and Jacob Wrey Mould. In 1902, Richard Morris Hunt, Richard Howland Hunt, and George B. Post erected the neoclassical façade. The Hunts also designed the magnificent central pavilion. McKim, Mead & White contributed the north and south wings, while Kevin Roche, John Dinkeloo & Associates created the Lehman Wing (1975), the Sackler Wing (1978), the American Wing (1980), the Rockefeller Wing (1982), and the Lila Acheson Wallace Wing (1987)—a high-tech glass curtain. A new addition is the Iris and B. Gerald Cantor roof garden, site of a (changing) sculpture garden and an incredible view of the park and the NYC skyline. The museum (879-5500) is located at Fifth Ave. and 82nd St.; subway: #4, 5, or 6 to 86th St.

Practical Information

After you catch your breath, stop by the **Visitors Center,** located at the Information Desk in the Great Hall. Stock up on brochures—make sure to grab a copy of the floor plan and the latest museum calendar, which should have descriptions of current exhibits, a handy Practical Information section, and a schedule of concerts, lectures, and other special events. In the Great Hall, the **Foreign Visitors Desk** distributes maps, brochures, and assistance in French, German, Italian, Spanish, Chinese, and Japanese. For information on disabled access, call Disabled Visitors Services (535-7710); for services for hearing-impaired visitors, call 879-0421. **Wheelchairs** are available upon request at coat check areas. **The Museum Cafeteria** is open Sun. and Tues.-Thurs. 11:30am-4:30pm, Fri.-Sat. 9:30am-8:30pm. The way-overpriced **Museum Restaurant** (570-3964) is open Sun. and Tues.-Thurs. 11:30am-3pm, Fri.-Sat. 11:30am-10pm.

If you feel like you need special direction, you can rent **recorded tours** of the museum's exhibitions, or follow the multilingual tour guides, footstepping lightly. For tour information go to the Recorded Tour Desk in the Great Hall. **Gallery tours** in English roam daily. Inquire at the Visitors' Center for schedules, topics, and meeting places. For recorded information on upcoming **concerts** and **lectures,** call 535-7710. Single tickets go on sale one hour before the event.

Admission is free to members, as well as to children under 12 accompanied by an adult. Suggested donation is $6 for adults, $3 for seniors and students; if you can stomach the shame, disregard their suggestion and plunk down as little as a quarter. The museum is open Sun. and Tues.-Thurs. 9:30am-5:15pm; Fri.-Sat. 9:30am-8:45pm. You can write to your favorite painting at 1000 Fifth Ave., New York, NY 10028-0198.

The museum's holdings sprawl over three floors. The **ground floor** houses the Costume Institute, European Sculpture and Decorative Arts, the Robert Lehman collection, and the Uris Center for Education, where public lectures, films, and gallery talks take place.

The **first floor** contains the extensive American Wing, the Arms and Armor exhibit, Egyptian Art, more European sculpture and decorative arts, Greek and Roman Art, Medieval Art, Art of the Pacific Islands, Africa, and the Americas, the Lila Acheson Wallace Wing with its footloose collection of 20th-century art, plus all the information facilities, shops, and restaurants.

The **second floor** brings you more of the American Wing, Ancient Near Eastern Art, Asian Art, a collection of drawings, prints, and photographs, yet another dose of European painting, sculpture, and decorative arts, a Greek and Roman Art encore, more Islamic art, musical instruments, the second installment of 20th-Century Art, and the R.W. Johnson Recent Acquisitions Gallery. Due to budget cuts some of the galleries will be only be open half-days on Tuesdays, Wednesdays, and Thursdays; call ahead.

Don't rush the Metropolitan experience; you could camp out in here for a month. No one ever "finishes" it. If you only have a few hours, the Greeks and Egyptians should keep you occupied (the dawn of civilization is reliably interesting, if only because we put their dead people on display). Or dip into one of the funkier smaller collections. If you plan to be in the city for awhile, you may want to plan on several short trips to the Met. After a couple hours of nonstop aesthetic bombardment, all the paintings start to look alike, anyway.

Collections

The **American Wing** houses one of the nation's largest and finest collections of American paintings, sculptures, and native decorative crafts. The paintings cover almost all phases of the history of American art from the late 18th to the early 20th century. You can get some celebrated glimpses of early America in Matthew Pratt's *The American School,* Gilbert Stuart's regal portrait of George Washington, Bingham's pensive *Fur Traders Descending the Mississippi,* and the heroic if precariously perched *George Washington Crossing the Delaware* by Emanuel Gottlieb Leutze. Of the 19th-century paintings, the pearl of the collection is Sargent's *Madame X,* a stunning portrait of a notorious French beauty, Mme. Gautreau, who allegedly consumed small doses of arsenic in the fashion of the time to give her skin that delicious, classical marble-like pallor.

The samples of decorative art date from the early colonial period to the beginning of the 20th century and include furniture, silver, pewter, glass, ceramics, and textiles. Twenty-five period rooms document the history of American interior design. Note the especially fun, sinuously curved Victorian tête-à-tête—an "S"-shaped love seat that looks like a pair of Siamese armchairs. Art Nouveau fans will gush at the ample selection of Louis Comfort Tiffany's glasswork, while admirers of American modernism can pay their respects at the Frank Lloyd Wright Room. The room was ingeniously designed to be an integral and organic part of the natural world outside the windows, an example of Wright's concept of total design.

To the left of the entrance (and out of sequence) are pieces from an Imperial villa which was covered in volcanic ash when Mt. Vesuvius erupted in A.D. 79. Beautiful ochre wall paintings are preserved next to sarcophagi and other Roman art. Nearby is the art of the Cyclades islands (neolithic and bronze age) where you can view some beautiful stone miniatures.

The collection of **Ancient Near Eastern Art,** located on the second floor, features artwork from ancient Mesopotamia, Iran, Syria, Anatolia, and a smattering of other lands, all produced during the period from 6000 BC to the Arab conquest in 626 AD. Notice that the *Human-Headed Winged Lion,* an Assyrian limestone palace gateway piece, has five legs. Viewed from the front, the beast stands firmly in place; viewed from the side, it appears to stride forward. The eerie *Standing Male Figure* stands in the first gallery.

Notable in the **Asian Art** collection is the *Yashoda and Krishna* sculpture, a moving work. It depicts a cowherdess, Yashoda, breastfeeding the infant Krishna. According to legend, newborn Krishna was exchanged for an unlucky cowherding couple's baby in order to prevent his death at the hands the wicked King Kamja. To witness the subtle workings of yin and yang in Chinese architecture, direct your sandals to Astor Court, modeled on a Ming scholar's garden. Here light meets dark and hard balances soft; the architecture recreates the harmonies of nature.

The **Department of Egyptian Art** occupies the entire northeast wing of the main hall, spanning thousands of years—from 3100 BC to the Byzantine Period (700 AD)—and containing a galaxy of artifacts, from earrings to *whole temples.* You can see the Tomb of Perneb, the Lord Chamberlain of the Fifth Dynasty. Sun gods now smile upon the Temple of Dendur through a shrine of glass. It looks much as it did back when Isis was worshiped inside, before the days of Shazam. Preserved in its entirety, the temple was a gift from Egypt to the United States in 1965 in recognition of U.S. contributions to the preservation of Nubian monuments. Tons of mummies—spooky fun for kids young and old.

Bring along your art anthologies to compare the illustrations with the originals, nearly 3000 of which congregate here in the museum's astounding hoard of **European Paintings.** The Italian, Flemish, Dutch, and French schools dominate the collection, but British and Spanish works make cameo appearances.

The Italian collection is particularly strong in paintings from the early Renaissance. A later gem is Bronzino's *Portrait of a Young Man,* one of the greatest works by this master of mannerism. The Spaniards are less numerous, but El Greco and Goya are well-represented. Goya's portrait of Don Manuel, a dough-eyed boy in red vestments, is shot through with allegory. The boy holds a magpie (a favorite pet since the Middle Ages), an oddball Christian symbol wherein the bird represents the soul. Cats, embodying evil, stare menacingly at the bird, while caged birds (incarcerated innocence) are separated from the cats by thin gilded bars.

In the Flemish quarters, you'll find Jan Van Eyck's *Crucifixion* and the macabre *Last Judgement,* where an undernourished Christ presides over the heavens as reptiles munch on writhing sinners in Hades below. The enigmatic Hieronymus Bosch makes a rare American appearance with his *Adoration of the Magi.*

The Dutch make a strong showing, led by Rembrandt, whose most emblematic *chiaroscuro* canvasses converge at the Metropolitan. Here are *Flora,* the *Toilet of Bathsheba, Aristotle with a Bust of Homer,* and a *Self Portrait.* The Metropolitan is one of the foremost repositories for the works of yet another esteemed Dutch master of light, Johannes Vermeer. Of less than 40 widely acknowledged Vermeer canvasses, the Museum can claim five, including the celebrated *Young Woman with a Water Jug,* the *Allegory of Earth,* and the vaguely fetal *Portrait of a Young Woman.*

The French contingent of the European collection may be the most comprehensive section of the museum, spanning the 16th-19th centuries. The Post-Impressionist trio makes a bang with Cézanne's landscapes and *Card Players,* Van Gogh's *Cypresses* and multi-million dollar *Irises,* and Gauguin's familiar Tahitian canvasses, one with an unusual twist. In *La Orana Maria,* Gauguin paints a tropical version of the Annunciation. A winged angel lurks amidst the semi-clad women and fruit trees. The central duo, the blessed mother and a small child, have halos above their heads. The name of the painting means "I hail thee, Mary"—the first words of the angel Gabriel at the Annunciation.

The **European Sculpture and Decorative Arts** department contains about 60,000 works, ranging from the early labors of the Renaissance to the early 20th century. The collection covers nine areas: sculpture, woodwork, furniture, ceramics, glass, metalwork, horological and mathematical instruments, tapestries, and textiles.

The Italian sculptures feature della Robbia's blue and white glazed terracotta relief *Madonna and Child,* hanging by the admission desk in the Great Hall. French sculptor Carpeaux stands out with *Voolino and his Sons* (1865-67), which illustrates the story from Canto XXXIII of Dante's *Inferno.* Pisan traitor Voolino, his sons, and his grandsons were imprisoned and then killed by starvation. Voolino's pose, face, and anatomical intensity bespeak Carpeaux's reverence for Michelangelo.

The museum's holdings of **Greek and Roman Art** span several millennia and the sweep of both empires. In addition, the collections illustrate the pre-Greek art of Greece and the pre-Roman art of Italy. Cypriot sculpture, Greek vases, Roman busts, and Roman wall paintings fill the rooms. Don't miss the tiny *Seated Harp-Player,* a simple, moving Cycladic statuette that influenced 20th-century styles. Remarkable amidst virile and perfectly proportioned Greek youths is the 2nd-century BC statue of an old, tired woman strolling to market—a notable reminder that life in Ancient Greece was not a constant Olympiad.

The museum offers a comprehensive overview of **Islamic Art.** You can see an intact mid-14th-century Iranian *mihrab* (a niche in a house of worship that points in the direction of Mecca), covered entirely in blue glazed ceramic tiles.

The **Robert Lehman Wing,** which opened to the public in 1975, houses the extraordinary collection assembled by the acquisitive Lehman clan. Italian paintings from the 14th and 15th centuries flank canvasses by Rembrandt, El Greco, and Goya. French painters from the 19th and 20th centuries are led by Ingrès, Renoir, standard Impressionists, and frivolous Fauves.

The **Jack and Belle Linsky Galleries** emphasize precious and luxurious objects. The highlights of the collection include canvasses by Lucas Cranach the Elder, Rubens, and Boucher; more than 200 Rococo porcelain figures from such renowned factories as Meissen and Chantilly; and exquisite 18th-century French furniture.

The arts of **Africa, the Pacific Islands,** and the **Americas** populate the **Michael C. Rockefeller Wing.** The African collection has bronze sculpture from Nigeria and wooden sculpture by the Dogan, Bamana, and Senufo of Mali. From the Pacific comes sculpture from Asmat, the Sepik provinces of New Guinea, and the island groups of Melanesia and Polynesia. A group of Inuit and Native American artifacts tells the other story of the arts of America.

Since its inception, the museum has been reluctant to invest in controversial modern art; the Museum of Modern Art had to be built to house works that the Metropolitan would not accept. But in 1967, the museum relented, establishing the **Department of 20th-Century Art,** which has since welcomed Picasso, Bonnard, and Kandinsky. The Americans flex the most muscle in here, with paintings by The Eight, the modernist Stieglitz Circle, abstract expressionists, and color field artists. Make sure to visit the **Lila Acheson Wallace Wing** of 20th-century art. Among the works of the regulars (Picasso, Kandinsky, Rothko) are some fascinating pieces by lesser-knowns. Marisol's vastly complex *Self-portrait Looking at the Last Supper* is here, as is Elizabeth Murray's whimsical *Terrifying Terrain*. Picasso's famed *Gertrude Stein* hangs across from Valdi's *Portrait of a Woman*.

The Museum of Modern Art (MoMA)

MoMA commands one of the world's most impressive collections of post-Impressionist and 20th-century art. Founded in 1929 by scholar Alfred Barr in response to the Met's wariness of what was then cutting-edge work, the Museum's was originally a minority stand; as the groundbreaking works of 1900, 1910, and 1950 have become accepted masterpieces, MoMA has shifted from revolution to institution, telling the more or less completed story of the Modernist revolt against Renaissance ways of seeing. Rotating galleries and temporary exhibits keep the museum-goer posted on current developments, but little can overshadow the permanent displays.

Cesar Pelli's 1984 glass additions to the 1939 museum building flood the halls with natural light. The admissions desk, besides collecting your dough, dispenses various interesting brochures as well as two printed guides to the collection, which aren't worth their $2 price. Past the admission desk lies the Abby Aldrich Rockefeller Sculpture Garden, an expansive patio with a fountain, a drooping willow, and a world-class assemblage of modern sculpture, featuring works by Matisse, Picasso and Henry Moore. Rodin's tormented, ultramasculine Balzac overshadows its neighbors; the roughly-finished, oversized bronze was rejected by Parisians, who expected a more conventionally heroic statue. Juilliard School affiliates populate the garden during summer evenings of free avant-garde music (see Classical Music).

Indoors, to the right, a small space presents changing exhibitions by contemporary artists. Last year's lineup included the skewed greeting cards of Erika Rothenberg ("SURPRISE! Our nation has just declared war on your nation!") To the left of the admission desk, the glass-walled Education Center shows a few films and posts a schedule of gallery talks. Nearby are bathrooms, phones, and the overpriced but crowded Garden Café. Beyond it, a set of five or so rooms presents more changing exhibitions. Take the escalator downstairs to still more temporary shows or to art films in the Roy and Niuta Titus theaters. (Pick up afternoon tix at 11am, evening tix at 1pm in the theater lobby.) The permanent display of paintings and sculptures, MoMA's core and raison d'etre, begins on the second floor: to do it "right" (complete and in chronological order), go in through the large opening to the left of the escalator.

You'll find yourself in Gallery 1, where the "modern" aesthetic begins: the post-Impressionists tried to find new and more individual ways of seeing the world, while still producing representations of what they saw "out there." Cezanne's scrawny *Bather* looks introverted and even depressed by a seashore almost devoid of water. In Gallery 2 swirls Van Gogh's well-loved *Starry Night*. They say the layers of paint are so thick that patches near the bottom of the frame are still wet. The lion lies down with the mandolin in the perspectiveless "naive painting" of Henri Rousseau's *Sleeping Gypsy*. Several landscapes by Georges Seurat round out the room; his perfectionism, ascetic lifestyle, and early death inspired a Stephen Sondheim musical, while his style, "pointillism," may have inspired television. In Gallery 3, another serene Rousseau balances works by James Ensor, a Belgian obsessed with death and deep red. Post-Impressionism outdoes itself in Gallery 4 with Vienna's Gustav Klimt; in *The Park*,

Klimt depicts a carpeting of treetops on a canvas filled with endlessly tesselating leaves. Only the tiny brown trunks at the bottom allow the painting to "depict" at all. There's also work by Andre Derain, whose "Fauve" school (the name means "Wild Beast") turned faces orange, apples blue, and gallery owners purple.

By the 1900s "content"—trees, people, whatever—had become more and more an excuse to investigate colors, forms, and emotions; for the painting of objects to stay interesting, some new way of seeing them had to be invented. Pablo Picasso and his pal Georges Braque came up with one: Analytical Cubism, which tried to show people and things on canvas from more than one angle at once, making paintings at once disturbingly fractured and mysteriously 3-D. The dawn of Cubism is now the star of Gallery 6: Picasso's giant *Demoiselles d'Avignon*, a painting he kept hidden for years until he felt Paris was ready to understand it. Smaller, purer and almost monochromatic, Cubist studies of violins, newspapers, and whatnot line the walls. It's almost impossible to tell Picasso from Braque in many paintings from this period.

At the far end of Gallery 6, turn left to enter the Water Lilies Room: Claude Monet's enormous screens depict the pond flora in dreamy, rough, and unmasked brushstrokes. Each of Monet's studies in light was choreographed by the sun's slant and the air quality. Monet would put aside a painting until the light and haze he wanted came back. His late style, like Matisse's, was partly the result of failing health. Picture windows overlook the sculpture garden and douse you, and the screens, in natural light; show up in early afternoon, and the screens seem perversely washed-out. At other times, the effect can be magical.

Cross back behind the Demoiselles to Gallery 7,where Picasso and Braque's Cubism becomes "synthetic"—more playful, less fine-grained, and a lot more colorful. Scope out the *Harlequin*, the sculpted *Guitar,* and the (apparently imploding) *Card Player.* Fernand Léger, whose cylindrical people, buildings and animals all bear an unfortunate resemblance to color-coded plumbing, dominates Gallery 8.

While Picasso and Co. were playing with representation in Paris, several Russian painters were itching to dispense with it altogether: their story starts in Gallery 9. Malevich tried to produce purified abstraction, like black or white squares on a white background. Though he wanted to transcend the physical and personal, his work seems almost crude and handmade today next to computer graphics or even good silkscreens; the real story of these Suprematist paintings is how their imperfections and barely visible brushstrokes strive toward, but don't reach, the Absolute.

Gallery 10 shows off big works by Marc Chagall, whose El Greco-damaged *Calvary* is more interesting than the more famous *I and the Village.* Gallery 11 boasts *Dresden Street,* Ernst Ludwig Kirchner's nightmare-vision of high society; his Dresden style included the fluorescent face-tracings Andy Warhol would later make familiar. The next room is devoted to the Italian Futurists, whose obsessions with speed and shrapnel set the pace for the avant-garde. Return to abstraction in the spacious Gallery 13, whose dozen-odd paintings follow Piet Mondrian's career; if the vague, tan grids of his earliest work resemble vertical slums, the crisp lines, primary colors and right angles to which he confined himself later suggest that design, precision, and harmony ought to drive out conflict and emotion. His more populated last works, like 1944's *Broadway Boogie-Woogie,* are sometimes read as celebrations of his adopted country and city (guess where). Hidden away beside the staircase in G13 are two worthwhile paintings by Czech colorist Franz Kupka.

Past the stairwell, in airy Gallery 14, you can follow Henri Matisse's 1909 bacchanal *Dance (First Version),* or fear the hidden teacher in his disturbing *Piano Lesson.* The next room can barely hold 14 canvases by Swiss painter and etcher Paul Klee, with his giggly squiggles and improvisational geometry. Klee once said his fantasy works were efforts at "taking a line for a walk." Gallery 16 incubates several items by the Romanian Constantin Brancusi: streamlined, simplified, and polished, these sculptures, once the height of abstract daring, now seem weirdly corporate and tame. Later Picassos dominate the walls, some almost cheerful (*Interior with a Girl Drawing*), some anguished, startled-looking, and skeletal—*Seated Bather* could be the corpse of a Blue Period subject. It's as if Picasso in the 20s and 30s, tired of formal innovation, had decided to expand his emotional range instead.

The next few rooms plumb the Surrealist depths. Gallery 17 presents the elaborate, 1890s-inspired Max Ernst and the early works of high-concept prankster Marcel Duchamp, whose mathematical obsessions eventually led him out of painting and sculpture and into incessant games of chess. Duchamp painted and signed some works as his female alter ego, Rrose Selavy; sometimes he also dressed the part. Take a right turn for Giorgio de Chirico, an Italian interested in dreams, mannequins, dark green skies, and Classical architecture; he later turned reactionary and painted apples, mom, and suchlike. Joseph Cornell's multifarious boxes merit at least the display case here. Straight ahead from Gallery 17 lies Gallery 20 (hey, this is the Surrealist section, after all) devoted to the sexually charged curves, bulging balloons and mustache whips of Catalan weirdo Joan Miró.

Gallery 21, the last of the sequence, collects mostly European pre-'45 misfits who didn't fit well into any movement. Balthus (it's like "Prince" or "Madonna") produced unsettling, sketchy pictures of children, cats, and everyday life; his portrait of *André Derain* makes the Fauvist look like a surprised criminal. Pavel Tchetlitchew's horrific *Hide and Seek* shows that some Surrealist works can still shock; the giant-veined fetuses and fleeing teenage girl evoke a traumatic abortion. The Belgian René Magritte painted dozens of fascinating if cerebral canvases, though nothing here even approaches his best. By hanging Wyeth's famous *Christina's World* here, among troubled Europeans, the curators have brought out the dreamy, puzzlelike qualities in what might otherwise seem sentimentally "American."

To the left as you exit from Gallery 21 are MoMA's exhibits of photograpy. With hundreds of photos in under ten rooms, the arrangement is rather daunting: temporary exhibits are in the front, parts of the permanent photo collection in back. The photography in the permanent collection, much of it originally affiliated with journalism, has a social and political dimension most of the rest of MoMA lacks.

Escalate to the third floor to keep seeing painting and sculpture; this time, enter the gallery directly in front of the escalator. The permanent exhibits here track American and European painting from the end of World War II to the late 60s. Gallery 23 showcases the late Francis Bacon's demonic judges and silent slabs of meat. Alberto Giacometti's spindled sculptures, said to represent the loneliness of postwar Europeans, and Jean Dubuffet's rude primitivism (his paintings sometimes included gravel and sand) also menace or sadden viewers here. Scoot to Gallery 25 for Rothko and Pollock in their early Surrealist mode, then watch Pollock's ascent into primal chaos in the next two rooms, from *She-Wolf* to *One (#31)* and *Number One,* gigantic "all-over" canvases created by pouring and flinging industrial-quality paint. (If they just look like random drips, look again: Pollock had a sense of composition that makes his forgers easy to catch.)

Calm down next door with Matisse's *Swimming Pool,* a cut-paper mural that originally covered the walls of his dining room. MoMA constructed a special room specifically to display this work, with its blue bodies cavorting joyously in a band of white water. Then, in Galleries 28-29, home to the Abstract Expressionists, return to the hectic, anguished, deadbeat heroism of New York in the 1950s. Check out Robert Motherwell's *Elegy to the Spanish Republic*, Franz Kline's angry calligraphy, and Willem de Kooning's scrawly *Woman.* In Gallery 30 you'll find Ad Reinhardt's *Number 87,* seemingly black-on-black, but actually (squint) deep violet on dark blue on black. There are also Barnett Newman's vertically-striped paintings, like large-scale, mystically resonant Universal Price Code tags, and the haunted hues of Mark Rothko. The history lesson ends, or peters out, with Pop Art: find Jasper Johns' *Flag* and *Target,* Lichtenstein's enlarged comic strips, and Warhol's gold Marilyn Monroe. Last of all is Frank Stella's "antihumanist" pinstripe painting, the chilling, absurd touchstone for this century's theorists of impersonality.

MoMA owns tons more 20th-century art than it will ever have space to display; an ever-changing assortment of works cavorts past the third-floor stairwell. Continue on to find a chamber full of work from the past 15 years; the selection here also changes rapidly, but there will surely be plenty to interest. To the right of the exit from the contemporary art is a small room which shows video compositions; to the right (and to the right of the escalator) is the museum's display of modern drawings, some sketches for masterworks, some masterworks themselves. Seek out Kupka's *Girl with Ball*. Directly above the photography exhibits and to the left of the escalator on the third floor is MoMA's prints dept.; again, there are lots of works, and they rotate frequently. A "reading room" lets you investigate old catalogs and defunct exhibitions.

Rise up to the design exhibits on the fourth floor; scale models and blueprints for Bauhaus buildings accompany up-to-this-decade displays of elegant furniture, Finnish tableware, and enough *chaise longues* to satisfy every psychoanalyst in New York.

The bookstore on the first floor (708-9702) sells art books, 50-cent postcards, and cool posters. The MoMA Design Store, across the street at 44 W. 53d St., sells high-priced objects like the ones on the fourth floor. (Both open 11am-5:45pm Fri.-Wed., 11am-8:45pm Thurs.)

The Museum of Modern Art will always be at 11 West 53d St., between Fifth and Sixth Ave. (708-9400; information and film schedules 708-9480). Subway: E or F to Fifth Ave. Open Fri.-Tues. 11am-6pm, Thurs. 11am-9pm. Admission $7.50, seniors'n'students $4.50, kids under 16 free. Films require free tickets obtained in advance from the information desk.

From late fall 1992 until early January 1993, MoMA hosts the largest Matisse exhibition ever, with over 450 paintings, cutouts, drawings and other works; the permanent exhibits will almost all be taken down to make room. Entrance fees for MoMA during the Matisse extravaganza will rise to $12.50, students $10, kids $2; hours will expand to Fri.-Tues. 10:30am-6pm, Wed. noon-6pm, Thurs. 10:30am-9pm. 500 tickets will be available daily at 10am to those who've lined up outside the museum; the rest will be sold weeks or months in advance. Expect a zoo. For Matisse-specific info, call 708-9850.

The Cooper-Hewitt Museum

Since 1976, Andrew "Shrimper" Carnegie's regal Georgian mansion has been the setting for the Smithsonian Institute's National Museum of Design. Pieces from the museum's vast permanent collection are culled in topical, fascinating shows on aspects of contemporary or historical design.

This design museum has an impressive design itself. Cast-iron archways alternate with intricately carved ceilings and an operatic staircase; everything basks in the pale, gilded glow of muted candelabras. You can pick out the Scottish bagpipes, an homage to Carnegie's heritage, in the moldings of the music room. An unusually low doorway leads to what was once 5'2" Carnegie's west library.

The collection dates back to 1859, when Peter Cooper opened the Cooper Union for the Advancement of Science and Art. Cooper's granddaughters opened a museum in 1897, which was donated wholesale to the Smithsonian Institution in 1963. In 1972, the collection found a new home in the Carnegie mansion. The largest group of holdings are the drawings and prints, primarily of architecture and design. Glass, furniture, porcelain, metalwork, stoneware, and textiles complete the catalogue.

Exhibitions at the Cooper-Hewitt are often sly and provocative. The museum has staged such playful offerings as a show of doghouses and a history of the pop-up book. Recent guest-curated shows have featured intricate cups and saucers from Denmark, and a review of designer fabrics. The museum's library is one of the largest and most accessible scholarly resources for design in America, with over two million volumes. At the museum shop on the first floor you can buy postcards, gifts, and books on art and design.

The museum is located at 2 E. 91st St. (860-6868) at Fifth Ave. Subway: #4, 5, or 6 to 86th St. Open Tues. 10am-9pm, Wed.-Sat. 10am-5pm, Sun. noon-5pm. Admission $3, seniors and students with ID $1.50, under 12 free. Free Tues. 5-9pm.

The Frick Collection

Pittsburgh steel magnate and robber baron Henry Clay Frick left his house and art collection to the city, and the museum retains the elegance of his French "Classic Eclectic" white marble chateau. It showcases Old Masters and decorative arts in an intimate setting, making a refreshing break from the warehouse ambience of New York's larger museums. The written guide to the Frick can lead you informatively from room to room ($1); paintings have not been comprehensively labeled in this most private of collections.

The collection has some natural highlights. Two of the 35 Vermeer paintings extant hang in the South Hall: *Officer and Laughing Girl* and *Girl Interrupted at Her Music,* both suffused with a uniquely warm light. The Octagon Room has Fra Filippo Lippi's 15th-century *Annunciation,* a work of spiritual power and luminous coloring. A number of early works also hang in the anteroom, including El Greco's *Purification of the Temple* and an anonymous 15th-century *Pietà* with a coldly surreal tone à la Salvador Dalí. Bruegel's painting *The Three Soldiers* was once owned by Charles I and Charles II of England.

In the Dining Room, feast your eyes on Thomas Gainsborough's 1783 masterpiece *The Mall in St. James's Park.* In this work the painter melds his love of nature with his mastery of the elaborate vanities of 18th-century portraiture. Leaves and gowns swish about the canvas complementing one another, as if corsets were the most natural thing in the world. In the Living Hall hang El Greco's *St. Jerome* clasping his Latin translation of the Bible, Titian's pensive *Portrait of a Man in a Red Cap,* and Giovanni Bellini's extraordinary *St. Francis in the Desert,* a 15th-century masterpiece of symbolic naturalism. The Library walls display Gainsborough and Reynolds portraits, a Constable landscape, a Turner seascape, a Gilbert Stuart likeness of George Washington, and a portrait of a benign if club-footed Henry Clay Frick surveying his domain. In the largest room in the Frick, the West Gallery, three works represent Rembrandt: the *Polish Rider,* owned by the last king of Poland; *Nicholaes Ruts,* one of Rembrandt's earliest portrait commissions; and his sensitive 1658 *Self-Portrait,* one of many (over 60) such meditations painted during his lifetime. Also note the works by Van Dyck (an elegant 1620 portrait of a close friend), Vermeer (an unfinished rendering of the opening of a letter), and Velazquez (a famous portrait of King Philip IV of Spain, painted in the town of Fraga following his military victories there against the French). Goya's *The Forge,* a depiction of blacksmiths at work, seems strangely out of place—perhaps the workers managed to sneak their way into this predominantly aristocratic collection on account of their esteemed previous owner, King Louis-Philippe of France. The Enamel Room contains a collection of Limoges enamels from the 16th and 17th centuries, as well as a penetrating evocation of Satan in Duccio di Buoninsegna's 1308 *The Temptation of Christ on the Mountain.*

The Oval Room has fine Gainsborough portraiture as well as an entrancing life-size terracotta sculpture of *Diana the Huntress,* executed in 1776 by Jean-Antoine Houdon. The East Gallery holds some more notable 19th-century work, including portraits by Whistler with unusually descriptive names: *Symphony in Flesh Color and Pink, Harmony in Pink and Grey,* and *Arrangement in Black and Brown* should be easy to tell apart. A fine Goya portrait of a young *Officer* pouts here. Downstairs, basement galleries added in 1977 feature special exhibits.

After walking through the least exhausting museum in New York, you can relax in the cool Garden Court and watch fountains of water burble up from the mouths of the little stone frogs.

The museum is located at 1 E. 70th St. at Fifth Ave. (288-0700). Subway: #6 to 68th St. Open Tues.-Sat. 10am-6pm, Sun. 1-6pm. Admission $3, students and seniors $1.50. No children under 10 admitted, and children under 16 must be accompanied by an adult. Group visits are by appointment only. Coats, cameras, and large handbags must be checked in the coat room.

The Guggenheim Museum

The Guggenheim's most famous exhibit is surely the building itself: the original, seven-story corkscrew of a museum dates to 1959 and is one of the only New York edifices Frank Lloyd Wright deigned to design. Sleek yet blunt, futuristic yet outdated, it's a 3-D memento of a design style that survives mostly in science-fiction illustration (right down to the *sans-serif* letters of the museum's name out front). However cool-looking it is though, as the museum's programmers tried for more and better exhibits, Wright's design offered insufficient space; from 1990-92, the museum shut down for restoration and expansion. Offices moved out of the corkscrew, skylights, and windows were replaced, and a new ten-story "tower gallery" sprouted behind the original structure, nearly doubling potential exhibit space. When the Guggenheim reopened last June, wags compared the new building to a Modernist toilet, and the Village Voice savaged the museum's fundraising methods. The gallery-goers, however, voted with their feet, mobbing the museum, the patio, the elevators, the restaurant, and the street outside. The huddled masses were treated to a dazzling if uneven sampler of the permanent collection in the tower galleries, and to the "minimalist" sculptor Dan Flavin, who decorated the display spaces (called "bays") along the spiral ramp with nothing but a repeating pattern of colored fluorescent tubes. Despite the chain of pastel lights from floor to ceiling (surely one of New York's tallest sculptures), visitors seem to prefer to study the 20th-century paintings in the new building.

By the time this book hits the stores, neither Flavin nor most of the permanent collection will be on display; most of the space will hold temporary and touring exhibits. The winter of 1992-93 brings tons of art from the Russian avant-garde of 1915-32, much of it borrowed from the collections of the Commonwealth of Independents States; shows of forged-iron sculpture by Picasso, Calder, Giacometti, and Smith and of multi-media work by Wim Wenders and Laurie Anderson begin in Feb., 1993. Pop artist Roy Lichtenstein and German sculptor/filmmaker/oddball Rebecca Horn prevail in the summer, while "Abstraction in the Twentieth Century" takes over in Sept. '93, reminding everybody that the Guggenheim was once dubbed "The Musuem of Non-Objective Painting."

Every Manhattan-bred child dreams of skateboarding down the Guggenheim's spiralling hallway. Since the exhibitions are sometimes arranged in ascending chronological order, you might at least consider trudging *up* the ramp instead. Bays along the ramp hold one sequence or exhibit: Tower Galleries 4, 5, and 7, each accessible by ramp or elevator, may present a different sequence or show. (Because the side rooms have higher ceilings than the ramp levels, there is no Tower Gallery 3 or 6). Tower Gallery 2, near the bottom, holds the Thannhauser Collection of pre-1920s work; Delaunay's famous exploding Eiffel Towers, Marc Chagall's "Fiddler on the roof" painting (actually entitled *Green Violinist*) and a gaggle of minor Picassos and Impressionists hang out here indefinitely. The rest of the permanent collection is especially strong on cerebral, geometric art, showcasing Mondrian and his Dutch *De Stijl* school, the Bauhaus experiments of Hungarian Moholy-Nagy, and the Russian modernists. The collection also holds an amazing Barnett Newman, Miró's well-known *Tilled Field,* and some mindbending collage/paintings from Jim Dine and Robert Rauschenberg; you might ask if any of these happen to be on display. Tower Gallery 5 adjoins a puny (900-sq.-ft.) outdoor terrace from which you can look over Central Park or study a sculpture. Or two. The postcard-happy gift shop adjoins Tower Gallery 7.

The museum described above spirals away at 1071 5th Ave. and 89th St. (recording 423-3500, human being 423-3600, TDD 423-3607). There is also a new **Guggenheim Museum SoHo** (see below). The Guggenheim (5th Ave.) open Fri.-Wed. 10am-8pm. Admission $7, students and senior $4, kids under 12 free; Tues. 5-8pm "pay what you wish." Two-day pass to both Guggenheim museums (5th Ave. and SoHo) $10, students and seniors $6; if you buy one in SoHo on Wednesday, it remains valid uptown for Fri. Coats, cameras, handbags must be checked in the coatroom. And don't forget to stare at the building for a while.

The Whitney Museum

When the Metropolitan Museum of Art declined the donation of over 600 works from Gertrude Vanderbilt Whitney in 1929, Ms. Whitney, a wealthy patron and sculptor, decided to form her own museum. Opened on 8th St. in 1931, the Whitney museum has since moved twice, most recently in 1966 to an unusual and forbidding futuristic fortress designed by Bauhauser Marcel Breuer. The museum's collection is devoted solely to American art, including some 8500 sculptures, paintings, drawings, and prints.

Turn right as you enter and stop short before the playful shapes of Calder's *Circus,* one sculptor's fantasy world. A videotape allows you to see these many-hatted dolls put on a three-ring sword-swallowing extravaganza, with a little help from their creator. The first and second floors are devoted to a wide range of changing exhibitions including theme shows, retrospectives, and contemporary work by artists like Julian Schnabel and Nam Jun Paik. The theater periodically shows film and video from independent American artists. Call or ask at the information desk about these and other special events, lectures, and guided tours.

The museum has assembled the largest collection of 20th-century American art in the world; if the varied (and often excellent) temporary exhibits don't toot your horn, something in the permanent collection is bound to. Be warned: although the musuem has dozens of American masterworks (including Ad Reinhardt's *Abstract Painting, Number 33,* Jasper John's *Three Flags,* Frank Stella's famous *Brooklyn Bridge,* Robert Raushenberg's *Satellite,* Willem De Kooning's *Woman on Bicycle,* and Georgia O'Keefe's *Flower Collection*), don't expect to see them all. The Whitney's permanent collection is shown in bits and pieces; some selection of it is always on display, but specific works are called in and out of retirement on a rotating basis. Works by Cindy Sherman, Alexis Smith, David Salle, Kiki Smith, and many others will probably satisfy your aesthetic cravings, even if you can't see your favorite. Blasted by the Guerilla Girls ("the conscience of the art world") for failing to present women artists, the museum claims to be making an effort to include more women in its shows, even as it takes heat on the right from Hilton Kramer and the neo-con art crowd for abandoning time-honored high-Modernist standards.

The Whitney is located at 945 Madison Ave. at 75th Street (information 570-3676; special tours 570-3652; films 570-0537). Subway: #6 to 77th St. Call 570-3652 for information about tours, 570-0573 for film info. Open Wed. 11am-6pm, Thurs. 1pm-8pm, Fri-Sun 11am-6pm. Adults $6, students 'n seniors $4, children under 12 free; Thurs. 6pm-8pm free.

Another branch of the Whitney is in the Philip Morris building, 120 Park Ave. at 42nd St., where a sculpture court features a changing array of installation pieces. Free. Gallery Talks Mon.-Fri. at 1pm are also free. Call 878-2453 for updates.

Food is available at **Sarabeth's at the Whitney** (560-3670), delicious but expensive ($10 minimum per person for lunch). Open Tues. 1pm-7:30pm, Wed.-Fri. 11am-4:30pm, Sat. 10am-4:30pm, Sun. 10am-5:30pm. It's cheaper to knosh on a knish, always available down on the corner.

The Store Next Door, right next door at 943 Madison Ave., sells postcards (60¢) and all sorts of arty stuff, including a clock with a chalkboard face that you can draw on ($25), and a hot pink aluminum CD case. Open Tues.-Sun. 10am-6pm; Thurs. 10am-8pm.

American Museum of Natural History

The largest science museum in the world broods in a suitably imposing Romanesque structure. The building, four blocks long, holds 36 million items of varied appeal. Why not see them all in a day? Charm your toddler friends with a stop at the dinosaur fossils and poignant preserved-mammal dioramas; impress your partner by nonchalantly stomaching the explicit display on the biology of invertebrates.

The original building, built in 1877, has been almost entirely walled in by 21 additions. A statue of Theodore Roosevelt—on horseback and in uniform, flanked by a naked African man and a feather-clad Native American, both on foot—holds the reins over the newer Central Park West entrance. Efforts to ditch or alter this boldly racist monument have been frustrated by its status as a national landmark. In the cavernous Rotunda, just inside, a 40-foot Barosaurus skeleton fights for her life against a fierce but fossilized predator Allosaurus. Grab a map from the information desk to the left of the entrance. The quotations and murals along the walls depict, or issue from, Teddy Roosevelt. His interests, background, and hunting hats are displayed on the first floor, in Hall 12.

Teddy's distant ancestors can be seen in the Ocean Life and Biology of Fishes display in Hall 10, also on the first floor. A two-story high blue whale replica casts shadows on the black-lit fish in the surrounding tanks. Admire the largest unexploded Pop Rock on earth in Hall 6—the 34-ton *Ahnghito,* the largest meteorite ever retrieved.

Stuffed stuff representing thousands of species can be discovered on floors 1-3. (The fourth floor, future home of the dinosaurs, will reopen in '94.) A modest King Kong beats his breast in the Hall of African Mammals (Hall 13). A herd of Indian elephants runs riot through Hall 9, Asiatic Mammals. But as neat as a few dioramas may be, the real story here is biodiversity itself; in that light a roomful of short-horned ruminants can impress just as easily as a Komodo dragon. [He's so right—Ed.] Towards the back of the second floor dwell huge and colorful anthropology exhibits; don't miss the costumed mannequins of African "Dance and Belief," and try not to wince at the more dated placards.

Hall 2, on the third floor, demonstrates the evolutionary chain from tree shrew to you. Also on the third floor, through January '94, is "Global Warming," a temporary exhibit whose photos, puzzles and video screens show how bad for the planet our car exhaust can be.

This dino-centric museum will reopen the doors to its star attraction—the skeletons themselves—in 1994, and the world will see interactive videos and the dinosaur *mummy* along with the beloved fossil reconstructions. In the meantime, the first floor's Gallery 77 will give you a taste of the great lizards' bones along with a preview of their reorganized array.

The Alexander White Natural Science Center, the museum's only room to hold live animals, explains the ecology of New York City to kids, while the Discovery Room gives them artifacts they can touch. (Both open erratically, usually afternoons; call ahead to check.) The People Center hosts scholarly talks and demonstrations of traditional peoples' arts at scheduled times during the academic year.

The museum is located at Central Park West (769-5100), at 79th to 81st St. Subway: B or C to 81st St. Open Sun.-Thurs. 10am-5:45pm, Fri.-Sat. 10am-8:45pm. Suggested donation $5, children $2.50; Fri.-Sat. 5-9pm free. Excellent access for the disabled.

The museum also houses **Naturemax** (769-5650), a cinematic extravaganza on New York's largest movie screen, four stories high and 66 feet wide. Ahnghito! Admission $5, children $2.50; Fri.-Sat. double features $7, children $3.50. The **Hayden Planetarium** (769-5920) offers outstanding multi-media presentations. Seasonal celestial light shows twinkle in the dome of the **Theater of the Stars,** accompanied by astronomy lectures. Admission $5, seniors and students $3.75, children $2.50. Electrify your senses with **Laser Rock** (769-5921) on Fri.-Sat. nights. Admission $6.

Other Major Collections

Alternative Museum, 17 White St. at Sixth Ave. (966-4444). Subway: #1 or 9 to Franklin St. Founded and operated by artists for non-established artists. New visions, social critique, and funky productions are the name of the game. Poetry reading and folk/jazz/traditional concerts, with an emphasis on the international, the unusual, and the socially-conscious. Open Nov.-June Tues.-Sat. 11am-6pm. Suggested donation $3.

American Craft Museum, 40 W. 53rd St. (956-3535), across from MoMA. Subway: E or F to Fifth Ave./53rd St. Not the old-fashioned quilts and Shaker furniture you might expect. This museum revises received notions of craft, showing modern pieces in wood, glass, metal, clay, plastic, paper, and fabric. Regular, ingenious exhibitions are shaped around particular subjects or materials. Past shows have included "Made with Paper," "American Glass Now," and the outrageous "Plastic as Plastic." Open Tues. 10am-8pm, Wed.-Sun. 10am-5pm. Admission $4.50, seniors and students $2.

The Asia Society, 725 Park Ave. (288-6400), at 70th St. Subway: #6 to 68th St. The Asia Society brings you the best of the East. Exhibitions, musical performances, popular and independent Asian cinema, an acclaimed "Meet the Author" series, and informative cultural symposia on topics such as Buddhist art or the political survival of Cambodia. Open Tues.-Sat. 11am-6pm, Sun. noon-5pm. Admission $2, seniors and students $1. Free Fri. 6-8pm.

AT&T Infoquest Center, 550 Madison Ave. (605-5555) at 56th St. Subway: E, F, N, or R to Fifth Ave. Learn about "microchips and you" from a multi-lingual robot named Gordon: this hands-on exhibition educates while it entertains. Sponsored by the pseudo-monopoly with the soothing voice. Guests are given personal AT&T cards as they enter the space-age center, granting them access to over 40 interactive computer displays on photonics, microelectronics, and computer software. The displays are neither too technical nor too self-serving, and some, like the one where you rearrange a scrambled shot of your face, are downright fun. Open Tues. 10am-9pm, Wed.-Sun. 10am-6pm. Free.

Audubon Terrace Museum Group, at Broadway and 155th St. in Harlem. Subway: #1 to 157th St. Once part of John James Audubon's estate and game preserve, the terrace now contains a number of museums and societies. The **National Museum of the American Indian** (283-2420), part of the Smithsonian Institution, is the world's largest collection of Native American artifacts. In recent years, the museum has been faced with demands by Native American groups seeking the return of many exhibits; for the moment, you can still see Geronimo's warrior cap and cane, Sitting Bull's war club, and Crazy Horse's headdress. Treaty belts given to William Penn are here, as well as a full array of masks, dolls, clothes, and weapons. Shrunken heads on the third floor. Open Tues.-Sat. 10am-5pm, Sun. 1-5pm. Admission $3, seniors and students with ID $2. The **Hispanic Society of America** (926-2234) is a museum devoted to Spanish and Portuguese culture, including paintings, mosaics, and ceramics. The most notable works here by Spanish greats El Greco, Velázquez, and Goya. Spanish scholars will enjoy the 100,000 volume research library. Open Tues.-Sat. 10am-4:30pm, Sun. 1-4:30pm. Free. The **American Numismatic Society** (243-3130) presents an extraordinary, nay mindblowing, collection of coinage, from prehistoric times to the present. The earliest coins date from 1000 BC, originating in China and India. Open Tues.-Sat. 9am- 4:30pm, Sun. 1-4pm. Free. Finally, the **American Academy of Arts and Letters** (368-5900) honors American artists, writers, and composers, and offers occasional exhibits of manuscripts, paintings, sculpture, and first editions. Call for current exhibition details and times.

Aunt Len's Doll and Toy Museum, 6 Hamilton Terrace (281-4143) at 141st St. Subway: A, B, C, or D to 145th St. Who was Aunt Len? What does Len stand for? Mystery surrounds the large collection of dolls and toys from all eras and locales. Call Aunt Len for appointment.

Black Fashion Museum, 155-157 W. 126th St. (666-1320). Subway: #2 or 3 to 125th St. Founded in 1979, the BFM maintains a permanent collection and mounts two yearly exhibits devoted to garments designed, sewn, or worn by Black men and women from the 1860s to the present. Alongside the creations of popular contemporary Black designers you'll find two slave dresses, an inaugural gown designed for Mary Todd Lincoln by Elizabeth Keckley, a dress made by Rosa Parks, and costumes from Broadway musicals like *The Wiz.* See award-winning costumes from the Canadian Miss Behaving Contest. Open by appointment Mon.-Fri. noon-8pm. Suggested donations $1.50, students $1.

The Bronx Museum of the Arts, at 165th St. and Grand Concourse (681-6000). Subway: #4, C, or D to Yankee Stadium/161st St. Set in the rotunda of the Bronx Courthouse. The museum focuses on young talent, collecting works on paper by minority artists and sponsoring twice-yearly seminars for local artists which culminate in group showings.

Brooklyn Museum, 200 Eastern Pkwy. at Washington Ave. (718-638- 5000). Subway: #2 or 3 to Eastern Pkwy. The little sibling of the Metropolitan Museum—but not that little. Check out the outstanding ancient Greek, Roman, Middle Eastern, and Egyptian galleries on the 3rd floor; larger Egyptian collections are found only at the British Museum and in Cairo. Crafts, textiles, and period rooms on the 4th floor provides respite from "higher" pursuits; the Moorish Room, a lush bit of exotica from John D. Rockefeller's Manhattan townhouse, is especially amusing. Gems from Sargent and the Hudson River School shine in the American Collection on the 5th floor. Nearby, the small, unusual, contemporary gallery contains noteworthy works by Bacon. On the same floor is European art from the early Renaissance to Post-Impressionism, including works by Rodin, Renoir, and Monet. Multi-media Asian art fills the 2nd floor; note the McMullan rugs in the Islamic gallery. The enormous Oceanic and New World art collection takes up the central 2-story space on the first floor; the towering totem poles covered with human/animal hybrids could go nowhere else. The impressive African art collection here was the first of its kind in an American museum, when it opened in 1923. Galleries downstairs put on temporary exhibits. Due to budget restraints, the museum is only open Wed.-Sun. 10am-5pm. Gift shop with fine jewelry and large art and travel book collection open same hr. Gallery talks Fri. at 2pm. Café open 10am-4pm. Suggested donation $4, students $2, seniors $1.50.

The Center for African Art, 54 E. 68th St. (861-1200), off Fifth Ave. Subway: #6 to 68th St. Three exhibitions a year profile African history and culture. Displays include West African tribal artifacts and "Africa Explored" (20th-century African art). Also conducts scholarly research and organizes guided expeditions to Africa. Open Tues.-Fri. 10am-5pm, Sat. 11am-5pm, Sun. noon-5pm. Suggested donation $2.50, seniors and students $1.50.

China House Gallery, 125 E. 65th St. (744-8181), between Park and Lexington Ave. Subway: #6 to 68th St. This minute gallery within the China Institute showcases a broad spectrum of Chinese art, including calligraphy, ceramics, and bronzes, as well as occasional cultural-anthropological exhibits. Open Mon.-Sat. 10am-5pm. Suggested contribution $3.

City Gallery, 2 Columbus Circle (841-4239), in the Visitors Center at 58th and Broadway. Subway: #1, 9, A, B, C, or D. A gallery devoted to depicting the metropolis at its finest and at its direst. From the nuts that hold together New York bridges to the nuts who design the city's skyscrapers, they've got it covered. Open Mon.-Fri. 10:30am-6pm. Free.

The Cloisters, Fort Tryon Park, upper Manhattan (923-3700). Subway: A through Harlem to 190th St. From the train station take a right and head through the park, or take the #4 bus. Buses leave regularly from the Metropolitan Museum's main building on Fifth Ave. In 1938, Charles Collen brought the High Middle Ages to the edge of Manhattan: building a monastery from pieces of 12th- and 13th-century French and Spanish cloisters, he established an offshoot of the Metropolitan Museum. John D. Rockefeller, never short of a few bob, donated the entire site and many of the contents. Retreat to the air-conditioned Treasury to admire the Met's rich collection of medieval art. Fifteenth-century playing cards trump with symbols based on dog hunting instead of hearts and clubs. Examine countless books drawn by neurotic monks; when healthy people were off rampaging through the countryside looking for dragons, the monks were carving intricate 3-D biblical scenes in boxwood miniature. Follow the allegory told by the priceless Unicorn Tapestries, and wander through airy archways and manicured gardens bedecked with European treasures like the ghoulish marble fountain in the Cuxa Cloister. (Open March-Oct. Tues.-Sun. 8:30am-5:15pm, Nov.-Feb. Tues.-Sun. 9:30am-4:45pm. Museum tours daily at 3pm, in winter Wed. at 3pm. Suggested donation $6 adults, $3 students and seniors. Donation includes, and is included with, admission to the Metropolitan Museum's main building.)

Forbes Magazine Galleries, 62 Fifth Ave. (206-5549), at the corner of 12th St. Subway: #4, 5, 6, L, N, or R to 14th St.-Union Sq. The holdings here, like those in the Frick Museum and Morgan Library, were acquired by a multimillionaire financier for his own amusement and then turned over to the public. The late Malcolm Forbes's irrepressible penchant for the offbeat permeates this 20th-century collection. Eclectic exhibits occupy the ground floor of the late magnate's publishing outfit: 12,000 toy soldiers assuming various battle positions in the military miniatures collection; a rotating exhibit of Presidential paraphernalia (including the opera glasses and stovepipe hat Lincoln was wearing when he was shot); and the world's largest private collection of Fabergé Easter eggs. Open Tues.-Sat. 10am-4pm. Free, but entry is limited to 900 persons per day; children under 16 must be accompanied by an adult. Thurs. is reserved for advanced-notice group tours.

Fraunces Tavern Museum, 54 Pearl St. (425-1778) on second and third floors. Subway: #4 or 5 to Bowling Green, #1 or 9 to South Ferry, or R to Whitehall St. While some exhibits in the museum convey the spirit of old New York, the building itself is neither a restoration nor a genuine reconstruction of the original Fraunces Tavern—no one knows what it looked like. Instead, the structure, constructed between 1904 and 1907, is a piece of architectural guesswork, based upon generalizations about the typical tavern of the period. The second floor features two period rooms, along with the room where George Washington said good-bye to his troops after the Revolutionary War. The third floor features changing exhibits on the culture and history of early America. Open Mon.-Fri. 10am-4pm. Suggested contribution $2.50; seniors, students, and children $1.

Guinness World of Records, 350 Fifth Ave. (947-2335), located in the Concourse Level of the Empire State Building. Subway: #6 to 33rd St. Synthesizer pop music and enthusiastic recorded voices lure the unwary into the goofy world of Guinness. Primary colors exemplify the level of sophistication. See plastic replicas of the world's tallest man, heaviest man, and longest neck. Yowza. Open daily 9am-8pm, longer hours in summer. Admission $7, children $3.50.

Hall of Fame for Great Americans, 181st St. (220-6003) and University Ave. Subway: #4 to Burnside Ave. Located on the grounds of City University of New York in the Bronx. Spurning the flimsiness of wax, this poignant though decrepit hall features nearly 102 bronze busts of America's immortals, among them Alexander Graham Bell, George Washington Carver, Abraham Lincoln, Booker T. Washington, and both(!) Wright brothers. Open Mon.-Fri. 10am-5pm. Free.

IBM Gallery of Science and Art, 590 Madison Ave. (745-6100) at 56th St. Subway: E, F, N, or R to Fifth Ave. Another blue-chip gallery trying to expose the masses to the worlds of art and science. Some exhibits are unrelated to computers, like the recent retrospective "Theater in Revolution: Russian Avant-Garde Stage Design." Of course, they also have a permanent show titled "Mathematica: A World of Numbers and Beyond," featuring topological phenomena like the Möbius strip. Open Tues.-Sat. 11am-6pm. Free.

International Center of Photography, 1130 Fifth Ave. (860-1778) at 94th St. Subway: #6 to 96th St. Housed in a landmark townhouse built in 1914 for *New Republic* founder Willard Straight. The foremost exhibitor of photography in the city, and a gathering place for its exponents. Historical, thematic, contemporary, and experimental works, running from fine art to photojournalism. The bookstore sells bimonthly booklet *Photography in New York*, a comprehensive guide to what is shown where ($2.95). Midtown branch at 1133 Sixth Ave. (768-4680) at 43rd St. Both open Tues. 11am-8pm, Wed.-Sun. 11am-6pm. Admission $3.50, seniors and students $2.

Intrepid Sea-Air-Space Museum, Pier 86 (245-2533), at 46th St. and Twelfth Ave. Bus: M42 or M50 to W. 46th St. One ticket allows access to the veteran World War II and Vietnam War aircraft carrier *Intrepid,* the Vietnam War destroyer *Edson,* and the first guided missile submarine, *Growler.* On the main carrier, Pioneers Hall shows mock-ups, antiques, and film shorts of flying devices from the turn of the century to the 30s. Technologies Hall recounts the exploration of the depths of the ocean and the far reaches of space. Catch the wide-screen flick that puts the viewer on a flight deck as jets take off and land–a Navy glory-flying gimmick, but breathtaking nonetheless. You can also climb onto the Intrepid's 900-ft. flight deck. Open Memorial Day-Labor Day daily 10am-5pm; Labor Day-Memorial Day Mon.-Fri. 10am-5pm. Admission $7, under 12 $4, under 6 free.

The Jewish Museum, 1109 Fifth Ave. (860-1889, recorded information 860-1888), at 92nd St. Subway: #6 to 96th St. The permanent collection of over 14,000 works details the Jewish experience around the house and throughout history and ranges from antiques and ceremonial objects to contemporary masterpieces by Marc Chagall and Frank Stella. Numerous exhibitions, such as "Gardens and Ghettoes: the Art of Jewish Life in Italy," trace the threads of history and culture of Jewish communities dispersed around the world; other exhibitions examine Jewish themes in contemporary art. Until early 1993 this location is closed for renovations; the Jewish Museum temporarily occupies the first floor of the New-York Historical Society (see below).

Kostabi World, 544 W. 38th St. (268-0616), off Eleventh Ave. across from the Javits Center. Subway: A, C, or E to 34th St. The "world" is a 3-story former stable, a bustling factory of modern merchandisable art, in which a crew of multimedia artists realizes the inspirations of the master schemer. Kostabi signs all the works himself, which explains how he has managed more than 33 one-person shows in the last few years. Unfortunately, only the gallery is open to the public. Open daily 10am-6pm.

Jacques Marchais Center of Tibetan Art, 338 Lighthouse Ave., Staten Island (718-987-3478). Take bus #74 from Staten Island ferry to Lighthouse Ave., then turn right and walk up the hill. Almost 2hr. from Manhattan but worth the trip for the largest private collection of Tibetan art in the West. Bronzes, paintings, and sculpture from Tibet and other Buddhist cultures. Tours, lectures, and classes on everything from Tibetan family rituals to origami. Set amid dramatic cliffs, the museum, itself a replica of a Tibetan monastery, exudes serenity. It's got a goldfish pond! $3 adults, $2.50 seniors, $1 kids. Open April-Nov. Wed.-Sun. 1-5pm.

El Museo del Barrio, 1230 Fifth Ave. (831-7272) at 104th St. Subway: #6 to 103rd St. The only museum in the U.S. devoted exclusively to the art and culture of Puerto Rico and Latin America. Begun in an East Harlem classroom, the project has blossomed into a permanent museum that features video, painting, sculpture, photography, theater, and film. Permanent collection includes pre-Columbian art and *Santos de Palo,* hand-crafted wooden saint figures from Latin America. Open Wed.-Sun. 11am-5pm. Admission $2, seniors and students $1.

Museum of American Folk Art, 2 Lincoln Center (595-9533 or 977- 7298), on Columbus Ave. between 65th and 66th St. Subway: #1 or 9 to 66th St. Three bright, white rooms devoted to crafts, from European-influenced quilts, needlepoint, and folk portraits to Navajo rugs and Mexican polychrome wooden animals. The museum provides special programs for children and crafts demonstrations for everyone, often enlivened by folk dancers and storytellers (977-7170). The gift shop provides inspirational hand-made baskets, dolls, and antiquated signs for the collector, as well as cards and novelties. Gift shop open Mon.-Tues. and Sat. 11am-6pm, Wed.-Fri. 11am-7:30pm, Sun. noon-6pm. Museum open Tues.-Sun. 11:30am-7:30pm. Wheelchair access. Suggested donation $2.

Museum of American Illustration, 128 E. 63rd St. (838-2560) between Park Ave. and Lexington. Subway: #4, 5, or 6 to 59th St. N or R to Lexington Ave. Changing exhibitions of illustration for books, advertising, and institutions. Open Sept.- July Mon. and Wed.-Fri. 10am-5pm, Tues. 9am-8pm. Free.

Museum of Bronx History, at Bainbridge Ave. (881-8900) and 208th St. Subway: D to 205th St., or #4 to Mosholu Pkwy. Run by the Bronx Historical Society on the premises of the landmark Valentine-Varian House, the museum presents historical narratives of the borough of Bronx. Exhibitions change regularly; call for schedule. Open Sat. 10am-4pm, Sun. 1-5pm; otherwise by appointment. Admission $2.

Museum of the City of New York, 103rd St. and Fifth Ave. (534- 1672), in East Harlem next door to El Museo del Barrio. Subway: #6 to 103rd St. Originally located in Gracie Mansion, the museum moved to its own roomy neo-Georgian quarters in 1932. It tells the story of New York City from the 16th century to the present through historical paintings, Currier and Ives prints, period rooms and furnishings, Duncan Phyffe furniture, Tiffany silver pieces, ship models, and exquisitely made toys and dolls. Lectures, symposia and walking tours for adults. Suggested contribution $5, seniors and students $3. Open Wed.-Sat. 10am-5pm, Sun. 1-5pm.

Museum of Colored Glass and Light, 72 Wooster St. (226-7258), between Spring and Broome St. Subway: #6 to Spring St. Go west on Spring and turn left on Wooster St. Don't just sit in the dark; come see glass panels, made from thousands of delicately colored fragments, that channel, refract, and diffuse light to an imagination-startling extent. Created by Raphael Nemeth, these compositions reflect the breakthrough of a new artistic medium. Nemeth, dissatisfied with the reflective poverty of natural light, uses 10,000 volts of pure electricity to highlight the artwork. It's worth the charge. Open daily 1-5pm. Admission $2.

Museum of Television and Radio, 25 W. 52nd St. (621-6600), between Fifth and Sixth Ave. Subway: B, D, F, Q to Rockefeller Center, or E, F to 53rd St. Formerly the Museum of Broadcasting. A collection of muppets greets you in the lobby as you head into the Steven Spielberg galleries. Boob tube relics and memorabilia, as well as over 40,000 programs in the museum's permanent collection. [Yes, they have *The White Shadow*—Ed.] Individual TV and radio consoles allow visitors to watch or listen to anything from a 1935 broadcast of *La Traviata* to a 1976 *Saturday Night Live*. Special screenings can be arranged for large groups. Open Tues.-Wed. and Fri.-Sun. noon-6pm, Thurs. noon-8pm. Suggested admission $5, students $4, seniors and children $3.

National Academy of Design, 1083 Fifth Ave. (369-4880), between 89th and 90th St. Subway: #4, 5, or 6 to 86th St. Founded in 1825 to advance the "arts of design" in America: painting, sculpture, architecture, and engraving. Currently the academy hosts exhibitions, trains young artists, and serves as a fraternal organization for distinguished American artists. The collection includes paintings, sculptures, drawings, prints, and architectural designs. Winslow Homer, Frederic Edwin Church, John Singer Sargent, Thomas Eakins, and others represent the 19th century in the permanent collection. The impressive assortment of contemporary artists and architects includes Isabel Bishop, Richard Estes, Robert Rauschenberg, Robert Ventura, and Philip Johnson. Regular exhibitions explore the history of American design and its European influences. The Academy is quartered in a 19th-century dollhouse mansion, remodeled by Ogden Codman in 1913. Inside you will find all the ingredients of a classic townhouse: checkered floors, ornate ceilings, columns, and, of course, a winding Cinderella staircase. Open Wed.-Thurs., Fri., Sat.-Sun. noon-8pm. Closed Tues. Admission $3.50, seniors and students $2.

New Museum of Contemporary Art, 583 Broadway (219-1222), between Prince and Houston St. Subway: R to Prince, #6 to Bleecker, or B, D, F to Broadway/Lafayette. Dedicated to the destruction of the canon and of conventional ideas of "art," the New Museum supports the hottest, the newest, and the most controversial. Interactive exhibits, video tricks aplenty. Many works deal with the politics of identity—sexual, racial, and ethnic. And once a month an artist sits in the front window and converses with passersby. Open Wed.-Thurs. and Sun. noon-6pm, Fri.-Sat. noon-8pm. Suggested donation $3.50; artists, seniors, and students $2.50; ages under 12 free.

The New-York Historical Society, 170 Central Park West (873-3400), from 76th to 77th St. Subway: B or C to 81st St. Permanent collection and special exhibits celebrate urban history and culture in New York City and throughout America. The hyphen in the name, which dates back to 1804, recalls the original spelling of "New York." The historical society delights in preserving and documenting every historical object, no matter how trivial. As a result, the collection achieves an unusual kind of personal warmth. Permanent displays upstairs include 18th and 19th century portraits, Audubon's original "birds of America" watercolors, and dozens of shimmering bankable Tiffany lamps. Temporary exhibits shuffle in and out. Until 1993 the Historical Society's first floor will serve the **Jewish Museum** (399-3344) as temporary exhibit space. NYHS open Tues.-Wed., Fri. and Sun. 11pm-5pm, Thurs. 11am-8pm; Jewish Museum exhibits open Tues.-Wed., and Sun. 11pm-5pm, Thurs. 11am-8pm, Fri. 11am-3pm until early 1993. NYHS and Jewish Museum admission $4.50, seniors or students $3, kids $1.

Parsons Exhibition Center, at Parsons School of Design, 2 W. 13th St. (229-8987) at Fifth Ave. Subway: L, N, R or #4, 5, 6 to 14th St. A variety of exhibitions, many of student work, including photography, computer art, painting, and sculpture. Open Mon.-Fri. 8am-10pm. Sat. 8am-6pm.

Police Academy Museum, 235 E. 20th St. (477-9753), off Second Ave. Subway: #6 to 23rd St. On 2nd floor of the city's police academy. Intriguing displays of counterfeit money and firearms, including Al Capone's personal machine gun. Call ahead. ID required. Open Mon.-Fri. 9am-2pm, closed holidays. Free.

Nicholas Roerich Museum, 319 W. 107th St. (864-7752), between Broadway and Riverside Dr. Subway: #1 or 9 to 110th St. A friend and close collaborator of Stravinsky on Diaghilev's *Ballets Russes,* Nicholas Roerich painted, philosophized, archaeologized, studied things Slavic, and founded an educational institution to promote world peace through the arts. Located in a stately old townhouse, the museum brims with Roerich's landscapes, books, and pamphlets on art, culture and philosophy. Open Tues.-Sun. 2-5pm. Free.

Schomburg Center for Research in Black Culture, 515 Lenox Ave. (491-2200) at 135th St. Subway: #2 or 3 to 135th St. This branch of the New York Public Library has one of the largest collections of documentation on Black history and culture in the world, including taped oral history, photographs, and personal papers. Shows by African and African-American artists. Open Tue.-Wed. noon-8pm, Fri.-Sat. 10am-6pm. Free.

Abigail Adams Smith Museum, 421 E. 61st St. (838-6878) at First Ave. Subway: #4, 5, or 6 to 59th St.; N or R to Lexington Ave. Although the house bears her name, Abigail never actually lived (or even slept) here. In fact, this building was once her stable. Now refurbished with 9 rooms of 18th-century articles, including a letter from George Washington. Open Sept.- July Mon.-Fri. noon-4pm; Sun. 1-5pm. Admission $2.

Studio Museum in Harlem, 144 W. 125th St. (864-4500). Subway: #2 or 3 to 125th St. A remarkable museum, founded in 1967 at the height of the Civil Rights Movement and dedicated to the collection and exhibition of works by Black artists. Large and impressive displays of photographs and paintings in a dramatic building donated by the New York Bank for Savings. Everything from early American crafts to contemporary work by Black artists. Open Wed.-Fri. 10am-5pm, Sat.-Sun. 1-6pm. Admission $3, seniors and students $1.50; seniors free on Wed.

Ukrainian Museum, 203 Second Ave. (228-0110), between 12th and 13th St. Subway: L to Third Ave. This tiny upstairs museum exhibits late 19th- and early 20th-century Ukrainian folk art, including pottery, handcarved candelabra, and traditional embroidered ceremonial clothing. Interesting for Ukraine buffs and those in the neighborhood. Seasonal exhibits on Christmas and Easter crafts. Open Wed.-Sun. 1-5pm. Admission $1, seniors and students 50¢.

Whitney Branch, Equitable Center (544-1000), at Seventh Ave. and 52nd St. Subway: N or R to 49th St. A prodigious Roy Lichtenstein mural spans the lobby of this small museum devoted solely to modern American art. There are 5 exhibitions per year, featuring the works of sculptors like Carl André and Alexander Calder and painters like Ad Reinhardt and Jackson Pollock; the recent "Dirt and Domesticity" explored issues of women in art. Open Tues.-Wed. and Fri. 11am-5pm, Thurs. 11am-7:30pm, Sat. noon-5pm. Additional branches with similar exhibitions at **Philip Morris,** 120 Park Ave. (878-2453) at 42nd St. Subway: #4, 5, 6, 7, or S to 42nd St. (open Mon.-Wed. and Fri.-Sat. 11am-6pm, Thurs. 11am-7:30pm), and at **Federal Reserve Plaza,** 33 Maiden Lane (943-5657), Subway: #4, 5 to Wall St., J, M, Z to Broad St. or R to Rector St. (open Mon.-Fri. 11am-6pm).

Galleries

The city overflows with small galleries. Some focus on buying and selling, others on exhibiting small-scale shows. While gallery-hopping can be great fun, remember that many of the commercial galleries have an elite image to maintain, and may not be the most accommodating places for tourists not planning to shell out five grand for a 200-lb. granite porcupine. Always ask before invading the premises, especially if you travel in a pack of two or more.

SoHo is a wonderland of galleries, with a particularly dense concentration lining Broadway between Houston and Spring St. The 79 different establishments in this two-block stretch can keep you busy for a while. Madison Ave. between 84th and 70th has a generous sampling of ritzy showplaces, and another gaggle of galleries festoons 57th St. between Fifth and Sixth. Most of these places are open from Tuesday to Saturday, from 10 or 11am to 5 or 6pm. One of the nicest things about gallery-hopping is that during the week, especially in the summer, the galleries are relatively empty. Try to go during off hours to enjoy some of the widest open spaces in Manhattan—for free.

Pick up a free copy of the *Gallery Guide* at any major museum or gallery; it lists the addresses, phone numbers, and hours of virtually every showplace in the city, and comes equipped with several handy maps to orient you on your art odyssey. Extensive gallery information can also be found in the "Art" section of *New York* magazine as well as in the omniscient "Goings On About Town" in *The New Yorker*.

SoHo

Due to hard economic times, the galleries in SoHo are in a state of flux. Not only do they open and close with amazing rapidity, but many of them have had to cut their losses and sell what they call "bread and butter" art—a landscape that goes well with a yuppie sofa, for instance, or a soothing sunset to remind the investment banker of his upcoming Club Med holiday. The avant-garde is having trouble getting its foot into the door of the ground-level, more commercial galleries that line West Broadway.

Because there are many galleries packed into a tiny neighborhood, it's easy to get lost; look over your Gallery Guide carefully, so that you don't miss a show that leaves tomorrow. Some galleries can always be relied upon for good shows. You may want to start your journey at the **Alternative Museum** (966-4444) at 594 Broadway–which, unlike most SoHo galleries that bill themselves as alternative, actually *is* alternative, focusing on socially-conscious art. (Open Tues.-Sat. 11am-6pm, closed August. See Museums.) On the third floor of the same building is the **Richard Meyer Gallery of African Art** (941-5968), which holds a fascinating collection of Western and Central African art, including masks, tapestries, and sculpture. (Open Tues.-Sat. 11am-6pm, closed Aug. 1-Sept. 8.) On the 2nd floor of the building is **American Primitive** (966-1530). This patronizingly-named gallery holds works by folk artists and self-taught American artists of the 19th and 20th centuries. Rene La Tour, a retired tin worker, built a tin dog and a huge robot, quirky works of great skill and creativity. (Open Mon.-Fri. 10am-6pm, Sat. noon-6pm; Summer, Mon.-Fri. 10am-6pm.) Down the street at 578 Broadway is a branch of the famed **Leo Castelli Gallery** (431-6279). Here you can see the smaller work of big names in peace and quiet. Rauschenberg, Oldenburg, Stella, and Johns are just a few standouts. (Both branches open Tues.-Sat. 10am-6pm). Around the corner, at 63 Crosby near Spring St. is the **A.I.R. Gallery** (966-0799), a gallery for women artists. (Open Tues.-Sat. 11am-6pm, closed July and August.) Walk back to Spring, then 5 blocks west to West Broadway, and take a right. You might want to check out the **O.K. Harris Gallery**, 383 W. Broadway (431-3600), which has a range of artists and mediums from installation pieces to photographs, and four one-person shows a month. (Open Tues.-Sat. 10am-6pm, summer Tues.-Fri. noon-5pm, closed July 18-Sept. 8.) Now walk up past Spring to **Mary Boone**, 417 W. Broadway (431-1818), where the likes of Sean Scully and Yoko Ono are featured, as well as Barbara "You are where you are shown" Kruger and David Salle. (Open Tues.-Sat. 10am-6pm). Next door, at 415 W. Broadway, are seven galleries; the **James Danzinger** (226-0056) shows many well-known photographers, including Mapplethorpe, Leibowitz, and Weber, as well as artists working in other media. Across the street at 420 W. Broadway is the main branch of the **Leo Castelli Gallery**, which sur-

veys the works of individual artists, including James Brown and the fabulous Starn
Twins. This big, established gallery probably should not be missed. (Open Tues.-Sat.
10am-6pm.) In the same building is **Sonnabend** (966-6160), which features (duh)
contemporary paintings by American and European artists. Jeff Koons, John Baldessari, Robert Rauschenberg top the bill.

Take a right onto Prince Street, a left onto Wooster, and stop in at the hard-to-find
Gagosian Gallery (228-2828) where David Salle, James Rosenquist, and Peter Halley are featured. (Open Tues.-Sat. 10am-6pm; summer Mon.-Fri. 10am-6pm. The gallery is closed for part of the summer, call to find out when.) If you're not so sick of art
that you're going to yench if you see another oil, acrylic, sand, and rubber on stretched
canvas, think about the mess you'd make, then proceed to the excellent **Paula Cooper
Gallery**, 149/155 Wooster St. (674-0766), which represents Jackie Winsor, Elizabeth
Murray, Jennifer Bartlett, Julian Lethbridge, Dara Birnbaum, and Dara Mayers. (Open
Tues.-Sun. 10am-6pm, summer Mon.-Fri. 9:30am-5pm.) If you can bear it, hop over
to Greene St. off Houston and check out the famed **Pace Gallery**, 142 Greene St.
(431-9224), where hang the works of biggies like Julian Schnabel, Chuck Close, and
Claes Oldenburg. (Open Tues.-Sat. 10am-6pm; July-Aug. Mon.-Thurs. 10am-6pm,
Fri. 10am-4pm) Further down on Greene St., near Spring, is the **Blum Helman Warehouse,** 80 Greene St., (226-8770). Artists lesser known but important show here right
along side the brand names. Spend some time with the work of Chuch Agro, Karin
Davie, and Richard Serra. Get to know these paintings. (Open Tues.-Sat. 10-6pm;
summer, Mon.-Fri. 10am-5:30pm.)

A fixture of the New York art scene, **Artists Space**, 223 W. Broadway (226-3970),
is a non-profit gallery that brings new talent to light. See them while they're hatching—especially in September. Every year 10 or 15 artists are chosen from the organization's slide file of unknown artists for a group exhibition. (Open Sept.-June Tues.-
Sat. 11am-6pm.)

At 580 W. Broadway, directly below Houston St., numerous small galleries inhabit
the first two floors. The **Rebecca Tate Gallery,** #1109 (219-5219), shows contemporary works by a lesser-known crowd. (Open Sept.- June Tues.-Sat. 10am-6pm, July
Mon.-Fri 10am-6pm.) Down a couple of doors in the **Prince Building,** 578 Broadway,
eight prestigious galleries inhabit large loft spaces. A branch of the famed complex exhibits monthly contemporary shows on the 3rd floor. (Open Sept.-June. Tues.- Sat.
10am-6pm, July Tues.-Fri. 11am-5pm.) Upstairs on the 11th floor, the **Lorence Monk
Gallery** (431-3555) presents contemporary group shows within its clean, open interior. (Open Sept.-June. Tues.-Sat. 10am-6pm, July Tues.-Fri. 10am-6pm.)

A few blocks west, **Metro Pictures,** 150 Greene St. (925-8335), corner of Houston,
is a flashy haven for photographers and select sculptors and painters, well stocked
with the biggies: Cindy Sherman, Robert Longo, and Louise Lawler. (Open Sept.-June
Tues.-Sat. 10am-6pm, July Tues.-Fri. 10am-6pm.)

Wooster Street's warehouse air nurtures cheaper crafts galleries. A few noteworthy
art spaces can be found on the upper floors. The **Brooks-Alexander Gallery,** 59
Wooster St. (925-4338), between Spring and Broome St., shows the trendy favorites.
(Open Sept.-June Tues.-Sat. 10am-6pm, July-Aug. Mon.-Fri. 10am-5pm.) Across the
street is a fine print gallery by the same name.

Galleries concentrate along West Broadway. A random stroll can be disappointing,
since a lot of mediocre art clusters along this commercial strip. Be selective. **Martin
Lawrence Galleries,** 457 W. Broadway (995-8865), and **Martin Lawrence Modern,**
426-428 W. Broadway (941-5665), both near Houston St., are most fun. Both specialize in Pop Art: Warhol, Lichtenstein, Rosenquist, and others. (Open Mon.-Thurs.
10am-7pm, Fri.-Sat. 10am-8pm, Sun. noon-6pm.) Six galleries stack at 420 W. Broadway, down the block. **Leo Castelli** (431-5160) has a branch on the 2nd floor, mixing
new works by young and old artists. See the wonder twins Mike and Doug Starn with
re-run stars Ellsworth Kelly, Frank Stella, Rauschenberg, and Warhol. (Open Sept.-
June Tues.-Sat. 10am-6pm, July to mid-Aug. Tues.-Fri. 11am-5pm.) Upstairs, **49th
Parallel** (925-8349) introduces the best of contemporary Canadian art—something

you may not have thought much about. (Open Sept.-June Tues.-Sat. 10am-6pm, July Tues.-Fri. 10am-5pm.)

Across the street at 415 W. Broadway, eight galleries flaunt big names. See works by Jennifer Bartlett, David Hockney, Francisco Clemente, and Larry Rivers at **Stuart Levy Gallery** (941-0009; open Sept.-July Tues.-Sat. 10am-6pm). The **Helander Gallery** (966-9797) has similar fare (open Tues.-Fri. 10am-6pm, Sat. 11am-6pm). Down the street, **Nahan Galleries,** 381 W. Broadway (966-9313), mainly represents French contemporary artists, including Chagall, Tobias, and Pepart. (Open Mon.-Fri. 10am-6pm, Sat. 11am- 6pm, Sun. noon-6pm.)

Upper East Side

M. Knoedler & Co., Inc., 19 E. 70th St. (794-0550). One of the oldest and most respected galleries in the city, it shows abstract expressionists like Olitski and Motherwell as well as Stella, Rauschenberg, Smith, and Diebenkorn. Open Tues.-Fri. 9:30am-5:30pm, Sat. 10am-5:30pm.

Hirschl and Adler Galleries, 21 E. 70th St. (535-8810). A wide variety of 18th- to 20th-century European and American art. Good contemporary work. Open Tues.-Fri. 9:30am-5pm. Also **Hirschl and Adler Modern** at 851 Madison Ave., between 70th and 71st St.

57th Street

André Emmerich Gallery, 41 E. 57th St. (752-0124), between Madison and Park Ave. Important contemporary work by Hockney et al. Open Oct.-May Tues.-Sat. 10am-5:30pm, April-Sept. Mon.-Fri. 10am-5pm.

Marlborough Gallery, 40 W. 57th St. (541-4900), between Fifth and Sixth Ave. English and North American artists like Francis Bacon, Larry Rivers, Red Gosmos, and Rufino Tamayo. Open Mon.-Sat. 10am-5:30pm.

Holly Solomon Gallery, 724 Fifth Ave. (757-7777) between 56th and 57th St. An important gallery showing avant-garde conceptual and performance artists as well as painters and sculptors. Joe Zucker, Rodney Ripps, and Kim MacConnel show here. Open Oct.-May Mon.-Sat. 10am-6pm, April-Sept. Mon.-Fri. 10am-5pm.

Pace Gallery, 32 E. 57th St. (421-3237). An uptown heavy, not afraid to show Picasso and Rothko. **Pace Editions** and **Pace Primitive,** under the same roof, offer an even larger selection of prints and primitive art. Open Tues.-Fri. 9:30am-5:30pm, Sat. 10am-5pm.

Sidney Janis Gallery, 110 W. 57th St. (586-0110), between Sixth and Seventh Ave. Spanning artistic epochs from Cubism to Minimalism, this gallery has hosted one-man shows by de Kooning, Gorky, Gottlieb, Pollock, and Rothko. Open Mon.-Sat. 10am-5pm.

Entertainment

Theater

Broadway is currently undergoing a revival—ticket sales are booming, and these mainstream musicals are receiving more than their fair share of attention. Dorky, old-fashioned productions such as *Crazy For You* and *Guys and Dolls* are very popular and tickets can be hard to get. Broadway tickets cost about $50 each when purchased through regular channels, although some theaters have recently introduced $15 seats on the farthest reaches of balcony. TKTS (Times Square Theater Center, 354-5800) sells half-price tickets to Broadway shows on the same day of the performance. TKTS has a booth in the middle of Duffy Square (the northern part of Times Square, at 47th and Broadway). Tickets are usually about $25 each (plus the $2 service charge per ticket). Pay in cash or traveler's checks. (Tickets are sold Mon.-Sat. 3-8pm for evening performances; Wed. and Sat. 10am-2pm for matinees; and Sun. noon-8pm for matinees and evening performances.) The line can be long, snaking around the traffic island a few times, but it moves fairly quickly. To beat the lines, arrive before selling time. The board near the front of the line posts the names of the shows with available tickets. Consult *The New Yorker* for superior short descriptions of current shows, or try *The New York Times.*

The lines are often shorter downtown, where TKTS has an indoor branch in the mezzanine of 2 World Trade Center. (Booth operates Mon.-Fri. 11am-5:30pm, Sat. 11am-1pm.) You can also buy matinee tickets here one day before the show.

StarTix, on the Main Concourse at Grand Central (687-4545), offers discount tickets for Broadway, Off-Broadway and Off-Off-Broadway shows. Call 932-1000 to check availability. (Open Mon.-Fri. 8am-7pm, Sat. 11am-3pm.) Take into account any registration fees or service charges when working out how much money you are (or are not) saving.

You can get a similar discount with "twofers," (i.e. two fer the price of one) ticket coupons that float around the city at bookstores, libraries, and the New York Visitors and Convention Bureau. They are usually for the old Broadway warhorses—shows which have been running strong for a very long time.

For information on shows and ticket availability, call the **NYC/ON STAGE hotline** at 768-1818, **Ticket Central** between 1 and 8pm at 279-4200, the **Theater Development Fund** at 221-0013, or the **New York City Department of Cultural Affairs** hotline at 956-2787. *Listings,* a weekly guide to entertainment in Manhattan ($1), has listings of Broadway, Off-Broadway, and Off-Off-Broadway shows.

Off-Broadway theaters are a group of smaller theaters, mostly located downtown. Officially, these theaters have between 100 and 499 seats; only Broadway houses have over 500. Off-Broadway houses frequently offer more offbeat or quirky shows, with shorter runs. Occasionally these shows have long runs or jump to Broadway houses (tickets cost $10-20). The best of the Off-Broadway houses huddle around the Sheridan Square area of the West Village. They include the **Circle Rep,** at 99 Seventh Ave. S. (924-7100), the **Circle in the Square Downtown,** at 159 Bleecker St. (254-6330), the **Lucille Lortel,** at 121 Christopher St. (924-8782), the **Cherry Lane,** at 38 Commerce St. (989-2020), and the **Provincetown Playhouse,** at 133 MacDougal St. (477-5048). Eugene O'Neill got his break at the Provincetown; and Elisa Loti made her American debut at the Actors Playhouse. TKTS also sells tickets to the larger Off-Broadway houses. Off-Off-Broadway is not a comical designation (at least not deliberately) but an actual category of theaters, where shows play limited, cheaper engagements. For years, the **Joseph Papp Public Theater,** 425 Lafayette St. (598-7150), was inextricably linked with founder Joseph Papp, one of the city's leading producers and favorite sons (he died in 1991). The six theaters present a wide variety of shows; the theater is in the middle of presenting its Shakespeare Marathon, which includes every single one of the Bard's plays down to *Timon of Athens.* Ticket prices $15-35. The Public Theatre saves about one quarter of the seats for every production to be sold at its **Quixtix** for about $10 on the day of performance (starting at 6pm for evening performances, and 1pm for matinees).

Papp also founded the **Shakespeare in the Park** series, a New York summer tradition which practically everybody in the city has attended (or attempted to, anyway). From June through August, two Shakespeare plays are presented at the Delacorte Theater in Central Park, near the 81st St. entrance on the Upper West Side, just north of the main road (861-7277). The glorious outdoor amphitheater overlooks Belvedere Lake and its mini-Dunsinane. Top-notch productions—plus the opportunity to perform Shakespeare in the great outdoors—attract the most important actors around. Recent performances have included *The Taming of the Shrew* with Morgan Freeman and Tracey Ullman, *Richard III* with Denzel Washington, and *Othello* with Raoul Julia and Christopher Walken. For free tickets, wait in line at the Delacorte Theater (you should get there by noon; 2 tickets per person).

The city also boasts the widest variety of ethnic theater in the country. The **Repertorio Español,** currently housed in the Gramercy Arts Theater at 138 E. 27th St. (889-2850) presents many of its productions in Spanish. The **Negro Ensemble Company** (575-5860) is located on the fifth floor of 155 W. 46th St. The **Pan Asian Repertory Theater** (245-2660) is located at Playhouse 46, 423 W. 46th St.

New York has birthed exciting and controversial developments in alternative theater, including that elusive amalgam called "performance art," a combination of stand-up comedy, political commentary, theatrical monologue, and video art. Beside the Brooklyn Academy of Music's famous Next Wave festival, a number of Manhattan institutions specialize in this distinctive art form, including **The Kitchen**, at 512 W. 19th St. (255-5793), **Franklin Furnace**, at 112 Franklin St. (925-4671), **Performance Space 122 (P.S. 122)**, at 150 First Ave. (477-5288), and the **Theater for the New City**, at 155 First Ave. (254-1109). **La Mama** at 74A E. 4th St. (254-6468), the most venerable of the lot, helped Sam Shepard get started.

Broadway Houses

Broadway theaters are only open when a play is in production. **Telecharge (239-6200) handles tickets and information for all theaters except for the Brooks Atkinson (691-5914).**

Ambassador Theater, 215 W. 49th St., between Broadway and Eighth. Built on a slant. Spencer Tracy played here in *The Last Mile* in 1930. In *The Straw Hat Revue* (1939), Danny Kaye, Jerome Robbins, and Imogene Coca parodied the rest of the shows playing on Broadway, anticipating *Forbidden Broadways* to come.

Ethel Barrymore Theater, 243 W. 47th St., between Broadway and Eighth. In 1927 the celebrated Ethel was blithely appearing in a Maugham play at another theater when playwright Zoe Atkins approached her and promised that the Shuberts would build her a theater if she would agree to do a play called *The Kingdom of God*. Ethel Barrymore read and liked it, and soon found herself starring in this play and a series of others. Alfred Lunt, Lynn Fontanne, and Noel Coward appeared here in Coward's *Design for Living*. Described as "a kettle of venom" by Brooks Atkinson, Claire Booth Luce's scathing play *The Women*, with a cast of 40 females, nonetheless ran for 657 performances. *A Streetcar Named Desire* opened here in 1947, starring Jessica Tandy and Marlon Brando, as did Lorraine Hansbery's acclaimed *Raisin in the Sun*, starring Sidney Poitier.

Belasco Theater, 111 W. 44th St., between Sixth and Seventh Ave. Built in 1907 by David Belasco, a producer extraordinaire who acted, designed, directed—and fervently believed in spectacle. He equipped the place with an elevator stage that could lower for set changes and a backstage elevator that would ascend to his private apartments. In 1935, the legendary Group Theater brought Clifford Odet's *Awake and Sing* to the Belasco. The Group Theater proved the most politically explicit act on Broadway, and 4 decades later the very nude revue *Oh! Calcutta!* exploded here as the most sexually explicit.

Booth Theater, 222 W. 45th St., between Broadway and Eighth. Designer Herts dressed it up in early Italian Renaissance in 1913 and Melanie Kahane modernized it in 1979. Kaufman and Hart's *You Can't Take It With You* opened here, as did Noel Coward's *Blithe Spirit*. Ntozake Shange's poetic *For Colored Girls Who Have Considered Suicide When the Rainbow is Enuf* lasted 742 performances.

Broadhurst Theater, 235 W. 44th St., between Broadway and Eighth. Designed in 1917 by Herbert J. Krapp, the man who churned out these theaters at the top of the century. Helen Hayes crowned the place with her legendary performance in *Victoria Regina* back in 1935. *Grease* first rocked here, as did *Godspell*. And *Dancin'* hoofed here for 3 years. Ian McKellan played Salieri to Tim Curry's Mozart and Jane Seymour's Constanze in the American premier of *Amadeus*.

Broadway Theater, 1681 Broadway, between 52nd and 53rd St. Built as a moviehouse in 1924, with a whopping capacity of 1765. Its first theatrical venture, *The New Yorkers* by Cole Porter and Herbert Fields, closed in 20 weeks—it was hard to sell tickets for $5.50 during the Depression. Benefits, including Irving Berlin's *This Is the Army* with a cameo by Irv himself, raised money for the Emergency Relief fund during World War II. Soon Oscar Hammerstein did a jazzed-up all-black *Carmen*. A few operas and dance troupes later, the stage saw another musical: *Mr. Wonderful*—starring Sammy Davis Jr. and Sr. Soon *The Most Happy Fella* dropped in, *The Body Beautiful* dropped out, and Les Ballets de Paris, the Beryozka Russian Dance Company, and the Old Vic flew in to do Shakespeare. Then Ethel Merman brought musical comedy belting back with *Gypsy*. In 1972, *Fiddler on the Roof* ended its run here, breaking previous records with its tally of 3242 performances. Harold Prince revived Leonard Bernstein's *Candide* with labyrinthine staging and multi-level seating, and went on to stage *Evita* here. Here Anthony Quinn starred in the revival of *Zorba*.

Brooks Atkinson Theater, 256 W. 47th St. (691-5914), between Broadway and Eighth. Designed in 1926 as the Mansfield by very busy architect Herbert J. Krapp. In 1930, *The Green*

Pastures opened here, setting southern blacks amidst Old Testament events; it played 640 performances and won the Pulitzer Prize. Marc Blitzstein's revolutionary *The Cradle Will Rock* opened here during the memorable snowstorm on December 26, 1947. In the 50s, the struggling theater served as a TV playhouse. Then in 1960, it was named for the much-loved *New York Times* theater critic and Harvard grad who had retired from reviewing plays that spring. John Steinbeck's *Of Mice and Men* was revived here with James Earl Jones as Lenny. Ellen Burstyn and Charles Grodin conducted their annual fling here in *Same Time, Next Year* for 1453 performances.

Circle in the Square Theater, 1633 Broadway, between 50th and 51st St. Delightfully in the round, a charming hotbed of things Shavian and Shepardian. Modeled after the downtown theater by the same name but half the size, it opened with *Mourning Becomes Elektra* in 1972. The circular stage has brimmed with sand for Tina Howe's *Coastal Disturbances* and has been strung up with laundry for a recent production of *Sweeney Todd*. Much Moliére here.

Cort Theater, 138 W. 148 St., between Sixth and Seventh Ave. Built in the style of Louis XVI, with a lobby of Pavanozza marble and 999 seats. Katherine Hepburn made her debut here in 1928 in *These Days*; it closed in a week, but she returned in the 50s to star in a blockbuster run of *As You Like It*. Grace Kelly made her first Broadway appearance here too.

Gershwin Theater, 1633 Broadway, between 50th and 51st St. Neo art nouveau. It started up in 1972 as the Uris, hosting *Porgy and Bess*, *Sweeney Todd*, and the *Pirates of Penzance*, who spent the summer in Central Park. Both *The King and I* and *Mame* were revived here.

Golden Theater, 252 W. 45th St., between Broadway and Eighth. Built by Krapp, commissioned by the production whiz-kids Chanin brothers who wanted the 800-seat space to accommodate intimate artistic work. When *Angel Street*, a strange piece of Victoriana, opened here, skeptical producers ordered only 3 days' worth of playbills—but the show ran 1293 (3 x 431) performances. Some revues swept through—starring Mike Nichols and Elaine May, Yves Montand, and finally the likes of Peter Cook and Dudley Moore in *Beyond the Fringe*.

Helen Hayes Theater, 240 W. 44th St., between Broadway and Eighth. It opened in 1912 with only 299 seats and was soon appropriately christened the Little Theatre. Originally designed to stage intimate and noncommercial works, it didn't do too well commercially and closed. It served as New York Times Hall from 1942-1959 and as the ABC TV Studio from 1959-1963, but then went on to host the long-running comedy *Gemini* and Tony Award-winning *Torch Song Trilogy*.

Mark Hellinger Theater, 237 W. 51st St., between Broadway and Eighth. On April 22, 1930, it opened as the Hollywood Theater Moviehouse. It became the 51st Street Theater in 1936. In 1940, Laurence Olivier and Vivian Leigh were Romeo and Juliet here, but soon the movies started playing again. Then, in 1949, Anthony Farrell bought the place and named it for Broadway columnist Mark Hellinger. The 50s saw revues and Gilbert and Sullivan. Musical comedy reared its feathered head in 1955 with *Plain and Fancy*, a stylish musical about the Amish. In 1956, *My Fair Lady* won innumerable awards and ran for 2717 performances. *Jesus Christ Superstar* opened here.

Imperial Theater, 249 W. 45th St., between Broadway and Eighth. Built in 1923, it entered the big leagues with *Oh, Kay!* by the Gershwins, together with book by P.G. Wodehouse and Guy Bolton. Rodgers and Hart, and George Abbot, conflated American musicals and Russian ballet in their 1935 hit *On Your Toes*. Cole Porter's *Leave It To Me* introduced to the Broadway stage Mary Martin and a chorus blue-boy named Gene Kelly. Martin returned in *One Touch of Venus*, a show by unlikely collaborators Kurt Weill, S.J. Perelman, and Ogden Nash. Ethel Merman proved there's no business like show business in *Annie Get Your Gun*. *Fiddler on the Roof* opened here on September 22, 1964. *Cabaret* had a brief stint, followed by *Zorba* and *Minnie's Boys*, a musical about the Marx Brothers.

Lunt-Fontanne Theater, 205 W. 46th St., between Broadway and Eighth. Built in 1910 as the Globe. Carrière and Hastings planned the seating and equipped the place with an oval ceiling panel that could be removed in fair weather. Fanny Brice dazzled here in the *Ziegfeld Follies of 1921*. *No, No Nanette*, featuring the song "Tea for Two," was a hit here in the 20s. The Globe went dark during the Depression, and then became a moviehouse. In 1957, the City Investing Company fixed it up and named it after dashing drama couple Alfred Lunt and Lynn Fontanne. The restored house hosted new musicals *The Sound of Music* and *The Rothschilds*, and revivals *A Funny Thing Happened on the Way to the Forum* and *Hello, Dolly!* Sandy Duncan flew here as *Peter Pan*.

Lyceum Theater, 149 W. 45th St., between Sixth and Seventh Ave. The oldest of the lot, designed by Herts and Tallant back in 1903, topped by a 10-story tower with scene shops, carpentry studios, and extra dressing rooms galore. It faced demolition in 1939; playwrights George S. Kaufman and Moss Hart chipped in with some friends, bought it in 1940, and sold it to the Shubert Organization in 1945. *Born Yesterday,* with Judy Holliday, opened here in 1946. *Look Back in Anger* stormed over from England in 1957. In 1980 the 1939 flop *Morning's at Seven* was revived here—and won a Tony Award.

Majestic Theater, 247 W. 44th St., between Broadway and Eighth. The largest legit theater in the district and the last of the former Chanin chain. Rodger and Hammerstein's *Carousel* opened here, as did their short-lived *Allegro* and their hot ticket *South Pacific,* which ran 1925 performances. *Camelot,* with Julie Andrews and Richard Burton, charmed Broadway for 873 performances.

Martin Beck, 302 W. 45th St. (246-0102), between Eighth and Ninth Ave. When built in 1924, it was the only Byzantine-style American theater. The Abbey Irish Theater Players performed here in 1932 in classics like *Juno and the Paycock* and *Playboy of the Western World.* Katharine Cornell played Juliet here to Basil "Sherlock" Rathbone's Romeo and Orson Welles' Tybalt. Tennessee Williams found his way here with *The Rose Tattoo,* starring Maureen Stapleton and Eli Wallach, and *Sweet Bird of Youth,* starring Geraldine Page and Paul Newman. Liz Taylor made her Broadway debut in *The Little Foxes* here in 1981.

Minskoff Theater, 200 W. 45th St. at Broadway. Less streamlined than its neighbor, the Gershwin, but equally high-tech. Its 1621 seats are 35 ft. in the air. It opened on March 13, 1973, with Debbie Reynolds in a revival of *Irene.* Nureyev pirouetted through here with the Murray Lewis Dance Company in 1978, followed by a series of short-lived musicals: *The King of Hearts,* a *West Side Story* revival, and *Can-Can,* a fast-stomping extravaganza that closed after 5 days.

Music Box Theater, 239 W. 45th St., between Broadway and Eighth. Cute, charming, built in 1921 by Sam Harris and Irving Berlin to house Berlin's *Music Box Revues.* This stage braved the Depression with French comedy *Topaze* by Marcel Pagnol and Noel Coward's "Mad Dogs and Englishman" ditty sung by Beatrice Lillie in *The Third Little Show.* Music Box production *Of Thee I Sing* became the first musical comedy to win the Pulitzer Prize. When romantic comedies upstaged revues, the Music Box churned out tuneless *I Remember Mama,* introducing the young Marlon Brando to the stage; Tennessee Williams' *Summer and Smoke;* and William Inge's *Bus Stop.* *Sleuth* mysteriously endured for 1222 performances, *Deathtrap* for a prime 1609. Irving Berlin maintained a lively financial and emotional interest in the theater until he died.

Nederlander Theater, 208 W. 41st St., between Seventh and Eighth Ave. It opened as the National Theater in 1921. Noel Coward and Gertrude Lawrence trod the stage in a group of plays called *Tonight at 8:30.* Orson Welles and John Houseman transported their Shakespearean productions from the smaller Mercury Theater. Here Sir John Gielgud and Lillian Gish starred in a failed production of *Crime and Punishment,* and Edward Albee premiered his successful *Who's Afraid of Virginia Woolf*—starring Uta Hagen and directed by Alan Schneider—and his more obscure *Tiny Alice.* The Royal Shakespeare Company's *A Midsummer Night's Dream* directed by Peter Brook, came to visit, as did Tom Stoppard's *Jumpers* and Harold Pinter's *Betrayal.* In 1980 the National-turned-Billy Rose-turned-Trafalgar was dubbed *The Nederlander* in honor of late theater owner David Tobias Nederlander.

Neil Simon Theater, 250 W. 52nd St., between Broadway and Eighth. Built in 1927 as the Alvin Theater with a capacity of 1400 by tireless designer Herbert J. Krapp. The Lunts' *The Taming of the Shrew,* staged for the Finnish Relief Fund, was followed by Pulitzer Prize-winning *There Shall Be No Night* by Robert E. Sherwood, about Russia's invasion of Finland. The Alvin found lighter fare with long-running *A Funny Thing Happened on the Way to The Forum* and Stoppard farce *Rosencrantz and Guildenstern Are Dead.*

Eugene O'Neill Theater, 230 W. 49th St., between Broadway and Eighth. Using the Georgian style, Krapp designed this one too, when it was born as the Forrest Theater back in 1925. In 1959, it was renamed in honor of playwright Eugene O'Neill who had died in 1953. Arthur Miller's *All My Sons* opened here, as did his *A View From the Bridge.* A slew of musicals have come and gone here, followed by a host of Neil Simon plays and some sterner stuff.

Palace Theater, 1564 Broadway at 47th St. Sarah Bernhardt, Ethel Barrymore, you name it, they played at the Palace. Once a vaudeville haunt for Houdini, W.C. Fields, and the Marx Brothers, the Palace became a movie house with few spells of musical theater from the 30s to the 50s. Then in 1965, James Nederlander restored it. Lauren Bacall stopped by to be *The Woman of the Year,* later followed by the more outrageous men of the year in *La Cage aux Folles.*

Plymouth Theater, 236 W. 45th St., between Broadway and Eighth. Built in 1917. Krapp designed it to seat 1000. Thornton Wilder's *Skin of Our Teeth* played here in 1942. A British invasion began with *Equus, Piaf,* and *The Real Thing;* English visitors completely reconstructed the house for the Royal Shakespeare Company's Dickensian 8-hr. marathon *Nicholas Nickleby,* which won Tonys for inspiring actor Roger Rees and directors Trevor Nunn and John Caird.

Richard Rodgers Theater, 226 W. 46th St., between Broadway and Eighth. Prolific architect Herbert J. Krapp sloped the seats L-Z upward for short people in the back. Here *Finian's Rainbow* charmed Broadway with an Irish lilt--725 performances worth. *Guys and Dolls* opened here in 1950, won 8 Tony Awards, and lasted 1194 performances. Audrey Hepburn transmogrified into Jean Giraudoux's lyrical sprite in *Ondine* in 1954. In 1975, Sir John Gielgud directed Maggie Smith in a revival of *Private Lives,* and Bob Fosse staged the hit *Chicago.* The 80s brought the sizzling musical *Nine,* based on Fellini's *8 1/2.*

Theater Royale, 242 W. 45th St., between Broadway and Eighth. Designed by Krapp. This house seats over 1000 and caters mostly to musicals. Tennessee Williams's first Broadway play, *The Glass Menagerie,* moved here from the Off-Broadway Playhouse, starring Laurette Taylor. Julie Andrews made her debut in *The Boy Friend,* a 1954 take-off on 1920s musicals. Thornton Wilder's *The Matchmaker* previously flopped as *The Merchant of Yonkers* and later got musicalized as *Hello, Dolly!* here in 1955. Mary Tyler Moore took the man's role in *Whose Life Is It Anyway?* continuing the tradition of profuse gender confusion initiated by Bowie, glam, and Glitter in the 70s.

St. James Theater, 246 W. 44th St., between Broadway and Eighth. Built in 1927. Seats 1600 in Georgian splendor. Here "April in Paris" was first sung and Hamlet first soliloquized on an American stage. John Houseman and Orson Welles collaborated on Richard Wright's chilling *Native Son. Oklahoma!* whirled in 1943, dazzling New York, running for 2248 performances and launching Rodgers and Hammerstein. Yul Brenner first took the Broadway stage here in *The King and I* in 1951. Laurence Olivier and Anthony Quinn even traded roles at whim in their remarkable production of Anouilh's *Becket.* Joseph Papp brought his musical version of *Two Gentleman of Verona* here.

Shubert Theater, 225 W. 44th St., between Broadway and Eighth. Built in 1913 by Lee and J.J. Shubert in memory of their deceased brother Sam. The Shubert exemplifies Venetian Renaissance. Paul Robeson played Othello here in 1943, with Uta Hagen and José Ferrer. 1932 brought *Americana,* with its depression song, "Brother, Can You Spare a Dime?" Katherine Hepburn thrilled audiences with *The Philadelphia Story* for 417 sold-out performances. *A Chorus Line* opened and closed here after its record-breaking run.

Virginia Theater, 245 W. 52nd St., between Broadway and Eighth. On April 13, 1925, President Coolidge pushed a button in Washington, D.C. that set the floodlights flowing over Shaw's *Caesar and Cleopatra,* starring Helen Hayes and Lionel Atwill. Next, Lunt and Fontanne came here with Shaw's *Arms and the Man.* Edward G. Robinson graced the stage in 1927 in Pirandello's *Right You Are If You Think You Are.* A series of flops forced the Theater Guild to lease out the place as a radio playhouse from 1943-50. The American National Theater and Academy (ANTA) then took over, and started sponsoring experimental productions and straight plays such as *J.B., A Man For All Seasons,* and a revival of *Our Town* with Henry Fonda.

Walter Kerr Theater, 225 W. 48th St. Built in a record 66 days in 1921 as the Ritz, and only recently christened the Walter Kerr in honor of the gentle critic. When it was the WPA Theater, the Federal Theater Project staged *Pinocchio* and T.S. Eliot's *Murder in the Cathedral* here. Renovated in 20s style by Karen Rosen, the Kerr reopened in 1983 with the juggling, entertaining *Flying Karamazov Brothers.*

Winter Garden Theater, 1634 Broadway, between 50th and 51st St. It opened in 1911 as a hall "devoted to novel, international, spectacular and musical entertainment." Al Jolson first appeared in blackface here. The Winter Garden has always been graced by new musical successes, from *Wonderful Town* to *West Side Story* to *Funny Girl.* Here Zero Mostel revived *Fiddler on the Roof,* Angela Lansbury revived *Gypsy,* and the multimedia blitz *Beatlemania* revived Beatles nostalgia. Most recently, designer John Napier clawed the place apart to create his fantasy set for *Cats.*

Off-Broadway Houses

Actors Playhouse, 100 Seventh Ave. S. (691-6226).

American Place Theater, 111 W. 46th St. (840-3074).

Astor Place Theater, 434 Lafayette St. (254-4370).

Cherry Lane, 38 Commerce St. (989-2020).

Circle in the Square Downtown, 159 Bleecker St. (254-6330).

Circle Repertory Company, 99 Seventh Ave. S. (924-7100).

Criterion Theater, 1514 Broadway (354-0900)

Douglas Fairbanks Theater, 432 W. 42nd (239-4321)

Ensemble Studio, 549 W. 52nd St. (247-3405)

Harold Clurman Theater, 412 W. 42nd (594-2370).

Hudson Guild, 441 W. 26th (760-9810).

John Houseman Theater, 450 W. 42nd (967-9077).

Lamb's, 130 W. 44th (997-1780).

Lucille Lortel, 121 Christopher St. (924-8782).

Manhattan Theater Club, 453 W. 16th St. (645-5590).

Orpheum, 126 Second Avenue. (477-2477).

Playhouse 91, 316 E. 91st St. (831-2000).

Playwrights Horizon, 406 W. 42nd St. (279-4200).

Promenade Theater, 2162 Broadway (580-1313).

Provincetown Playhouse, 133 MacDougal St. (477-5048).

Public Theater, 425 Lafayette St. (598-7150).

Ridiculous Theatrical Company, 1 Sheridan Sq. (691-2271).

Roundabout Theater, 00 E. 17th St. (420-1360).

Samuel Beckett Theater, 412 W. 42nd. St. (594-2826).

Sullivan Street Playhouse, 181 Sullivan St. (674-3838).

Theater at Saint Peter's Church, 619 Lexington Ave. (935-2200).

Westside Theater, 407 W. 43rd St. (315-2244).

Village Gate Theater, 160 Bleecker St. (475-5120).

Movies

New York City does, quite frankly, give a damn about film. Most movies open in New York weeks before they're distributed across the country, and the response of Manhattan audiences and critics can shape a film's success or failure nationwide. Dozens of revival houses show motion picture classics year round. And independent filmmakers from around the reel world come to New York to flaunt their work.

First run movies show all over the city. Big screen fanatics should check out the cavernous **Ziegfeld**, 141 W. 54th St. (765-7600), one of the largest screens left in America, which shows first-run films of interest. Consult local newspapers for complete listings. Tickets run $6-7. For more extensive listings of revival houses and independent films check *The Village Voice* or *The New Yorker.*

The Kitchen, 512 W. 19th St. (255-5793) at Tenth Ave. Subway: C or E to 23rd St. World-renowned showcase for the off-beat happening. Features experimental and avant garde film and video, as well as concerts, dance performances, and poetry readings. Most shows are from New York-based struggling artists. Season runs from October til end of June: call for information or check advertisements in *The Village Voice*. Ticket prices vary by event.

Film Forum, 209 W. Houston St. (727-8110). Subway: C or E to Spring St. Three theaters showing the best in independent filmmaking, movie classics, and foreign films. Tickets $7 seniors $4. 50.

Angelika Film Center, 18 W. Houston St. (995-2000) at Mercer St. Subway: #6 to Bleecker St. or B, D, F, Q to Broadway/Lafayette. A new arrival on the film scene: six screens of entertainment showing a diverse selection of new, old, double features, and retrospectives. Try the excellent espresso while you wait. Tickets $7; students, seniors and children under 12 get in for $3.50 before 5pm.

Theater 80, 80 St. Mark Pl. (254-7400), between First and Second Ave. Subway: #6 to Astor Pl. A great revival house running a nightly double bill of all your favorite chisel-nosed actresses. Tickets $7.

Joseph Papp Public Theater, 425 Lafayette St. (598-7150). Subway: #6 to Astor Pl. Quirky selection of old movies, particularly "art" classics and film history milestones. There is also a theater auditorium featuring live "experimental" performance pieces. No Monday screenings. For info call 598-7107. Tickets $5-7.

Anthology Film Archives, 32 Second Ave. (505-5181) at E. 2nd St. Subway: F to Second Ave. A forum for independent filmmaking, focusing on the contemporary, off-beat, and avant-garde chosen from U.S. and foreign production. The resident cinema guru has created the Archives' most enduring series—"The American Narrative"—featuring 300 great American films. Tickets $6, students with ID $5.

Millenium Film Workshop, 66 E. 4th St. (673-0090). Subway: F to Second Ave. More than just a theater, this group presents an extensive program of experimental films and offers classes and workshops. Tickets $6.

The Collective for Living Cinema, 41 White St. (925-2111). The collective combines two cinematic specialties—Hollywood legends and new productions by the local avant garde. It also runs exhibits, workshops, and seminars related to modern cinema. Call ahead for updated info.

If movie house offerings seem limited, remember that most of New York's museums run their own film programs. Check out the **Metropolitan Museum of Art,** Fifth Ave. at 82nd St. (570-3949), which shows free films in the summertime (with museum admission) on Fridays and Saturday at 7pm, usually fairly standard silver screen and foreign classics (box office opens at 5pm on the day of the performance; limit 4 tickets per person). The **Museum of Modern Art: Roy and Nivta Titus Theaters**, 11 W. 53rd St. (708-9490), serves up an unbeatable diet of three great films per day (free with museum admission). The **American Museum of the Moving Image,** 35th Ave. at 36th St., Astoria, Queens (718-784-4520) has three full theatres showing everything from silent classics to retrospectives of great directors. (Admission $5, seniors and students $2.50.)

Lincoln Center, New York's performing arts octopus, flexes yet another cultural tentacle with its year-old **Walter Reade Theater** (875-5600) in the Rose Building to the left of the Juilliard School in the Lincoln Center complex. Foreign, famous, and critically-acclaimed American independent films dominate. The expanding canon of quality foreign films plays here every July and August at **Symphony Space's** Foreign Film Festival ($6; see Classical Music).

Try **Adam Clayton Powell, Jr., State Office Building,** at 163 W. 125th St. (873-5040) off Seventh Ave. for contemporary and classic cinema created by and about African-Americans as well as work done by Black filmmakers from South America, Africa, and the Caribbean. (Admission $5, seniors and students with ID $3. Lectures by contemporary filmmakers $5.)

For a real deal, check out the library. All New York Public Libraries show free films: documentaries, classics, and last year's blockbusters. Screening times may be a bit erratic, but you can't beat the price (see Libraries under Practical Information).

Followers of Eastern European cinema should contact the **Ethnic Folk Arts Center,** 66 W. 12th St. (691-9510) for details on their popular annual series of notable Czech, Hungarian, Soviet, and Polish films. The **Goethe Institute,** 1014 Fifth Ave. (439-8700) offers weekly German films, usually with English subtitles, at locations around the city; ticket prices vary. Francophiles can satisfy their craving for Godard by inquiring at the **French Institute/Alliance Française** about current film offerings. The institute is located at Florence Gould Hall, 55 E. 59th St., but its films are screened at Tinker Auditorium, 22 E. 60th St. (Tickets $5.50, $4 students.) Each year, **The Japan Society** mounts five prodigious retrospectives of the greatest Japanese achievements in film. The film schedule can be obtained by visiting the society at 333 E. 47th St. or by calling 752-0824. (Tickets $7.) For cinematic exposure to Chinese culture, go to the **Sun Sing Theater,** 75 E. Broadway (619-0493).

If you've grown tired of the reifying cinematic offerings of the crypto-fascist bourgeois capitalist culture industries, you may wish to learn of the subversive activities transpiring unsuspected at **Revolution Books,** 13 E. 16th St. (691-3345). On auspicious nights, films, videos, and lectures are presented in the crowded bookstore. The schedule varies unpredictably, but dedicated revolutionaries and budget fellow travellers have been known to make do; the price ($2) is nice.

Television—Live in the Studio

If you didn't get enough tv before you took this big vacation of yours, New York is the place to dose up. Here in the City you can pass right through television's fourth wall—the tv screen itself—and plop down directly in front of your favorite actors and most beloved talkshow hosts. For free. Plan ahead, though. It's best to order your tickets 2-3 months in advance, although standby tickets are often available. Here's a little sampler of what the Big Three are offering and how to get on the ticket.

Two of **CBS's** most popular talkers are Joan Rivers and Geraldo "Lips" Rivera. For up-to-date ticket info on Joan, call 975-5522; she usually tapes on Mon. and Wed. Geraldo's people can be reached at 265-1283; he tapes on Mon., Wed., and Fri. We recommend that you call ahead to find out about times and ticket availability. At the time this book went to press, Joan's and Geraldo's were the only two shows to which CBS admitted guests. **NBC** has a whole slug of shows to sit in on, including *Late Night with David Letterman, The Phil Donahue Show,* and *Saturday Night Live.* Call 664-3055 for general info. Order tickets well in advance by sending a postcard to 30 Rockefeller Plaza, 10012, but be warned: not only do you *not* have the option to choose specific dates, but also, because requests are lotteried, you might not find out you've been rejected until four months after you send off your request. You just might want to get in line on the Mezzanine level of Rockefeller Center (50th St. side) at 8am, the morning of the show. One ticket per person, please. For general info on **ABC's** offerings call 456-7777. When this book went to press, *Regis and Kathy Lee* was the only show to which ABC admitted guests. If you write to Reg and Kath, expect an eight-month wait for tickets. For standby tix, line up at the corner of 67th St. and Columbus Ave. at 8am. Or before. No one under 18 admitted to this one.

Classical Music

Musicians advertise themselves vigorously; you should have no trouble finding the notes. Begin with the ample listings in the *New York Times, The New Yorker,* or *New York* magazine. Remember that many events, such as outdoor music, are seasonal.

The **Lincoln Center Halls** have a wide, year-round selection of concerts. **Avery Fisher Hall** (875-5030) paints the town ecstatic with its annual Mostly Mozart Festival, featuring performers like Itzhak Perlman, Alicia de Larrocha, Jean-Pierre Rampal, and Emanuel Ax. Show up early; major artists and rising stars usually give half-hour pre-concert recitals, beginning one hour before the main concert and free to ticketholders. The festival runs from July to August, with tickets to individual events running $12-25. **The New York Philharmonic** (875-5700) begins its regular season in mid-September. The 1992-93 season celebrates the Philharmonic's 150th Anniversary with world premieres of works by Olivier Messiaen, David Diamond, and others; "Remembering Lenny," a tribute to Leonard Bernstein (June); a signal performance of Bach's monumental *St. Matthew Passion* (February); and weeks of gala festivities. In addition to Music Director Kurt Masur, former directors Zubin Mehta and Pierre

Boulez will conduct. Tickets range from $10-50. (Call CenterCharge at 721-6500 Mon.-Sat. 10am-8pm, Sun. noon-8pm) During the Philharmonic's regular season, students and seniors can sometimes get $5 tickets; call ahead to check availability, then show up 1/2hr. before the concert (Tues.-Thurs. only). $5 tickets are also sold for the odd morning rehearsal; again, call ahead (anyone is eligible for these). In mid-July, the Philharmonic heads for the hills and lawns of New York's parks. Kurt Masur and friends lead the posse at free concerts on the Great Lawn in Central Park, in Prospect Park in Brooklyn, in Van Cortland Park in the Bronx, and around the city. Select nights are enlivened by fireworks after the program. For information call 875-5709.

Alice Tully Hall (875-5050) serves up an eclectic mix of music, dance, theater, video, and performance art. Composer Philip Glass is a regular here. Founded five years ago, the Serious Fun! Series brings big-name avant-garde, mixed-media, and performance artists into the realm of corporate sponsorship. 1992's program included playwright/designer Robert Wilson, *Talk Radio* monologist Eric Bogosian, and yamless Karen Finley. Serious Fun! lasts three weeks in July; tickets start between $10-20 per event. (Box office open Mon.-Sat. 11am-6pm, Sun. noon-6pm; for tickets call CenterCharge at 721- 6500.)

The Lincoln Center complex also includes the **Juilliard School**, one of the world's leading factories of classical musicians. Juilliard's **Paul Recital Hall** hosts free student recitals almost daily during the school year (Sept.-May); Alice Tully Hall holds larger student recitals, also free, most Wednesdays at 1pm Sept.-May. Orchestral recitals, faculty performances, chamber music, and dance or theater events take place constantly at Juilliard and never cost over $10—you can see the next generation's Yo-Yo Ma for a third of the cost of seeing this one's. Call 769-7406 for a complete Juilliard schedule.

The Great Performers series, featuring musicians famous and foreign, packs the Avery Fisher and Alice Tully Halls and the Reade Theater, from Oct.-May (call 721-6500; tickets from $11). The Chamber Music Society offers students and seniors heavily discounted seats for its performances in Alice Tully Hall (students from $7.50, seniors from $12, others from $15; call 875-5788). Free outdoor events at the Lincoln Center boggle the mind every summer, with everything from modern dance premieres to country music festivals; call 875-5400 for the daily bogglement. All of Lincoln Center's halls are wheelchair accessible.

Carnegie Hall, Seventh Ave. (247-7800) at 57th St., the New York Philharmonic's original home, was saved from demolition in the 1960s by Isaac Stern, and is still the favorite coming-out locale of musical debutantes. Big soloists and chamber groups are still booked regularly. (Open daily 11am-8pm Sept.-June; tickets $10-40.)

Cultural life on the Upper East Side revolves around **The 92nd Street Y** (996-1100), located on Lexington Ave. The Y's Kaufmann Concert Hall seats only 916 people and offers an intimate setting unmatched by New York's larger halls, with flawless acoustics and the oaken ambience of a Viennese salon. The Y is the home of the **New York Chamber Symphony** under the fiery direction of Gerard Schwartz. The Chamber Symphony's repertoire covers everything from Telemann and Rameau to the works of contemporary masters like Pijton, Diamond, and Stravinsky. In addition, the Y hosts a panoply of world-class music. The Distinguished Artists Series, dating back to the late 30s, has featured all the big names from Segovia and Schnabel to Yo-Yo Ma, Alfred Brendel, and Schlomo Mintz. Other notable series include Chamber Music at the Y, Mastersingers, Fascinatin' Rhythm (featuring hot jazz), Brandenburg Festival, Young Concert Artists, and annual installments of the decade-long restrospective of the music of Franz Schubert (series currently in its sixth year.) Other events include the ongoing series of literary readings at the Poetry Center, and some of most engaging lectures in New York. (Lectures $14; concerts $25-40.)

The landmark **Town Hall** 123 W. 43rd St. (840-2824), between Sixth Ave. and Broadway, is an elegant pavilion with excellent acoustics. Tenacious trio McKim, Mead & White designed the place in 1921; it has since hosted a wide variety of cultural events, including lectures, jazz festivals, and concerts of all kinds. Joan Sutherland made her debut here. The building has a seating capacity of 1498. (Year-round programs; tickets $15-35.)

Quartered in Abraham Goodman House at 120 W. 67th St. between Broadway and Amsterdam, the **Merkin Concert Hall** (362-8719) offers eclectic, ethnic, and contemporary music alongside more conventional selections. A typical week at the Merkin might include love songs and laments spanning 400 years, classical and modern Chinese music, and the choral, folk-inspired works of Bartok and Shostakovich. Traditional Jewish and 20th-century classical musics seem to be Merkin specialties. One of New York's best spaces for chamber music, the intimate theater seats a juicy 457. (Tickets $10-30; season Sept.-June.)

The misleadingly-named **Symphony Space** (864-5400) at Broadway and 95th, is a former skating rink and cinema which now hosts all manner of cultural events: the performance season, from Sept.-June, corrals classical and traditional ethnic musical performances along with plays, dance companies, and the "Selected Shorts" program of fiction readings by famous actors. An annual Gilbert and Sullivan operetta packs the space; during the summer, it sponsors an ambitious program of old and new foreign films. Pick up a Symphony Space program guide at the Space itself; though they've promised to put NYC hostels on their mailing list, the invaluable listings are currently available nowhere else. (Box office open Tues.-Sun. noon-7pm; tickets free-$35, depending on event.) Free concerts at the **World Financial Center Plaza,** Battery Park City (945-0505), occasionally include classical artists.

Museums do their bit for metropolitan music. The **Metropolitan** posts a schedule of performances covering the sound spectrum from traditional Japanese music and Russian balalaika to all-star classical music recitals. Some concerts are free with museum admission; others charge $10 and up for tickets. (For ticket information or brochure, call Concerts and Lectures at 535-7710.) The **Museum of Modern Art**'s "Summergarden" program (708-9480) presents free concerts of "avant-garde" contemporaryclassical music in the museum's Sculpture Garden most summer weekends, Fri. and Sat., at 7:30pm. Enter the Sculpture Garden through the (normally locked) back gate at 14 W. 54th St. between 6-10pm. **The Frick Collection** (288-0700) hosts occasional Sunday afternoon chamber music concerts, with music piping into the idyllic garden court. You can sit back in the lush, marmoreal setting and imitate Cicero listening to the Muses in a Roman courtyard. Or you can just enjoy the music. Free concerts come to the garden of the **Cooper-Hewitt Museum** (860-6868) from June through August. (See Museums.)

One of the best ways for the budget traveler to absorb New York musical culture is by visiting a music school. Except for opera and ballet productions ($5- 12), concerts at the schools listed below are free and frequent. **Juilliard School of Music,** Lincoln Center (see above); **Mannes School of Music,** 150 W. 85th (580-0210), between Columbus and Amsterdam Ave.; **Manhattan School of Music,** 122 Broadway (749-2802); **Bloomingdale House of Music,** 323 W. 108th St. (663-6021), off Broadway.

The **Cathedral of St. John the Divine** (662-2133), Amsterdam Ave. and 112th St., presents an impressive array of concerts, art exhibitions, lectures, theatre, and dance events. Farther uptown, between 120th and 122nd St. on Riverside Drive, the **Theater at Riverside Church** (864-2929), capacity 275, hosts theater, music, dance, and video performances. On a smaller scale, **St. Paul's Chapel** (602-0747 or 602-8073), built in 1766 and located on Broadway between Church and Fulton St., is Manhattan's only surviving pre-Revolutionary War church. George Washington came here to pray after his inauguration. The exquisite interior, lit by Waterford crystal chandeliers, provides the perfect setting for concerts of classical and church music. (Concerts Mon. and Thurs. at noon. Suggested donation $2.)

Founded in 1859, the **Brooklyn Academy of Music (BAM),** 30 Lafayette St. (718-636-4100), between Felix and Ashland Pl., has compiled a colorful history of magnificent performances: here Pavlova danced, Caruso sang, and Sarah Bernhardt played Camille. The oldest performing arts center in the country, it focuses on new, non-traditional, multicultural programs (though is sometimes features classical music as well). Jazz, blues, performance art, opera, and dance can be enjoyed here. Every May brings Dance Africa, which features West African dancing as well as crafts. Call for the constantly-changing schedule. BAM's annual Next Wave Festival, held October through December, features contemporary music, dance, theater, and performance art; it broke artists like Mark Morris and Laurie Anderson. BAM is home to the Brooklyn Philharmonic Orchestra, which performs from September to March and hosts a brief opera season from March through June. (Orchestra and Opera tickets $10-40.) Manhattan Express Bus makes the round trip to BAM from 51st and Lexington for each performance ($4); Subway: #2, 3, 4, 5, D, Q to Atlantic Ave or B, M, N, R to Pacific St.

The **Brooklyn Center for Performing Arts At Brooklyn College (BCBC)** (718-434-1900 or 718-434-2222), is one block west of the junction of Flatbush and Nostrand Ave., on the campus of Brooklyn College. The BCBC prides itself on presenting many exclusive events each year. In 1992-93 it brings Itzahk Perlman and a Siberian dance company. (Season Oct.-May; tickets $20-30; Subway: #2 or 5 to Flatbush Ave.)

The **Colden Center for the Performing Arts** (718-793-8080) at Queens College in Flushing, Queens, has a beautiful theater and a program of excellent jazz and dance concerts. (Season Sept.-May; tickets $12-25; Subway: #7 to Main St., Flushing, then Q17 or Q25-34 bus to the corner of Kissena Blvd. and the Long Island Expressway.) Fans of old-fashioned Americana may prefer the **Yankee Tunesmiths Ancient Fife and Drum Corps** (718-845-3133). **The Ukrainian Bandura Ensemble of New York,** 84-82 164th St. (718-658-7449) in Jamaica, Queens, keeps the 56-stringed *bandura* alive, playing at parades and various other events around the city.

Opera and Dance

Lincoln Center (875-5000) is New York's one-stop shopping mall for high-culture consumers; there's usually opera or dance at one of its many venues. Write Lincoln Center Plaza, NYC 10023, or drop by its Performing Arts Library (870-1930) for a full schedule and a press kit as long as the *Ring* cycle. The **Metropolitan Opera Company** (362-6000), opera's premier outfit, plays on a Lincoln Center stage as big as a football field. Upper balcony seats (around $15; the cheapest have an obstructed view) are not for fraidy cats. You can stand in the orchestra ($12) along with the opera freakazoids who've brought along the score, or all the way back in the Family Circle ($9). (Regular season runs Sept.-May Mon.-Sat.; box office open Mon.-Sat. 10am-8pm, Sun. noon-6pm.) In the summer, watch for free concerts in city parks (362-6000). The Met also plays host to dance companies like the Kirov Ballet. The 1992-93 opera season will include a world premiere, Philip Glass' *The Voyage*, and works by Strauss, Wagner, Janacek, and tons of Italians.

At right angles to the Met, the **New York City Opera** (870-5570), under the direction of Christopher Keene, has a new sound. Under Beverly Sills, its previous head, the opera was reknowned for beating old masters into the ground. Keene's first season got rave reviews, although the opera's financial problems may soon force it out of Lincoln Center. The company now performs pop classics and contemporary U.S. operas, in addition to the old faithfuls. "City" now offers a summer season (July-Nov.) and keeps its ticket prices low year-round ($10-62; top balcony, back row, standing room $10). Call on the night before the performance you want to attend to check the availability of rush tickets, then wait in line the next morning.

Look for free performances by the **New York Grand Opera** at Central Park Summerstage (360-2777) from June to early August. Check the papers for performances of the old warhorses by the **Amato Opera Company,** 319 Bowery (228-8200; Sept.-May; tickets $16, seniors $13). Music schools often stage opera as well; see Classical Music for further details.

When the City Opera isn't using the New York State Theater (870-5570), the late great George Balanchine's **New York City Ballet,** the oldest dance company in the U.S., steps in. (Performances Nov.-Feb. and April-June. Tickets $11-55, standing room $8.) The **American Ballet Theater** (477-3030) dances at the Met during May

1993. Under Mikhail Baryshnikov's guidance, ABT's eclectic repertoire has ranged from grand Kirov-style Russian to experimental American. (Tickets $12-65.)

The **Alvin Ailey American Dance Theater** (767-0940) bases its repertoire of modern dance on jazz, spirituals, and contemporary music. It often takes its moves on the road, but always performs at the **City Center** in December. Tickets ($15-40) can be difficult to obtain. Write or call the City Center, 131 W. 55th St. (581-7907), weeks in advance, if possible. The **Martha Graham Dance Co.,** 316 E. 63rd St. (838-5886), performs original Graham pieces during their October New York season. The founder of modern dance, Graham revolutionized 20th-century movement with her psychological, rather than narrative, approach to choreography (tickets $15-40). **Anna Sokolov's Players' Project** dances the acclaimed Russian choreographer's modern pieces to the sounds of Satie, Kurt Weill, and Jelly Roll Morton. Without sacrificing the integrity of the dance medium, Sokolov has incorporated theater, narration, and references to the visual arts in works like "The Evolution of Ragtime" and "Matisse, Matisse." (Sporadic year-round season; see newspaper listings for concerts.)

Keep an eye out for performances of the **Merce Cunningham Dance Company,** of John Cage fame, and the **Paul Taylor Dance Company,** usually in the spring. Two companies in Queens specialize in traditional ethnic folk dance: the **Ballet Folklorica de Dominican Republic,** 25-28 89th St. (718-651-8427) in Jackson Heights, and **The Yori African Dance Ensemble,** 89-21 169th St. (718-657-4264) in Jamaica. Central Park Summerstage (320-2777) hosts dance companies from around the world. In 1991, it featured Eric Hawkins, as well as troops from Bali and Zaire. Ballet connoisseurs should call the Brooklyn Center for Performing Arts at Brooklyn College (see Classical Music), which introduces a major foreign ballet company to New York every year.

Half-price tickets for many music and dance events can be purchased on the day of performance at **Bryant Park,** on 42nd St. (382-2323) between Fifth and Sixth Ave. (Open Tues. and Thurs.-Fri. noon-2pm and 3-7pm, Wed. and Sat. 11am-2pm and 3-7pm, Sun. noon-6pm.) Monday concert tickets are available on the Sunday prior to the performance. Call for daily listings.

Rock

New York City has a long history of producing bands on the vanguard of rock music and performance, from the New York Dolls to DNA to Deee-Lite. If New York City's home-grown bands fail to satisfy the craving for live rock, keep in mind that virtually every band that touches down on American soil comes to New York City. The annual **New Music Nights Festival** (473-4343, ex. 296) is a six-night summer music orgy, usually in late June, that brings over 350 of the world's best new artists to over 20 of the city's clubs, discos, and theaters. Nirvana and Jane's Addiction played here way back when, and 1992's festival brought Superchunk, Pavement, and Small Factory to the Big Apple. Passes include admission to all shows and cost around $70. If arena rock is your favorite band's style, **Madison Square Garden**, Seventh Ave. and W. 33rd St. (465-6000), perhaps America's premier entertainment facility, hosts over 600 events and nearly six million spectators every year. Apart from rock concerts, regular offerings include exhibitions, trade shows, boxing matches, rodeos, monster trucks, dog, cat, and horse shows, circuses, tennis games, and the odd presidential convention (tickets $20-50). **Radio City Music Hall** (247-4777) and New Jersey's **Meadowlands** (201-935-3900) also occasionally stage equally high-priced performances. Some of the best medium-sized performances take place at the West Side's **Beacon Theater** (496-7070), with alternative rock offerings for the college-aged crowd.

Punk, Rock, and Folk

CBGBs 313 Bowery (982-4052) at Bleecker St. Subway: #6 to Bleecker St. The initials stand for "country, bluegrass, blues, and other music for uplifting gourmandizers," but everyone knows that since 1976 this club has been all about punk rock. Blondie and The Talking Heads got their starts here, and the club continues to be *the* place to see great alternative rock. CB's has adjusted to the post-punk 90s with more diverse offerings, but the punk spirit lives on in the decidedly non-glitzy interior, the multi-colored layers of graffiti on the bathroom walls, and the wistful eyes of some of the clientele. Shows nightly at around 8pm, Sun. (often hardcore) matinee at 3pm. Cover $5-10.

Maxwell's, 1039 Washington St. (201-798-4064) at 11th St., in Hoboken. High-quality underground rockers from America and abroad have plied their trade in the back room of a Hoboken restaurant for going on 15 years; New Order played their first U.S. show here, the Feelies were once regulars, and Ira Kaplan of Yo La Tengo manned the soundboard for a while. Now it's graced by the likes of Pavement, Wingtip Sloat, Some Velvet Sidewalk, and Tsunami. Cover $6-9; shows occasionally sell out, so get tix in advance from Maxwell's, Pier Platters (see Shopping: Records) or, yes, Ticketron. (Sandwiches $6, entrees $7-9. Restaurant open Tues.-Sun. 2pm-midnight. To get here, take the PATH train ($1) from 33rd, 23rd, 14th, 9th or Christopher St. and 6th Ave. to the Hoboken stop, then walk ten blocks down Washington to 11th St.) Subway: B, D, F, N, Q, or R to 34th St., then PATH train ($1) from the 34th St.

Knitting Factory, 47 E. Houston St. (219-3055), near Mulberry St. Subway: #6 to Spring St. or B, D, F, Q to Broadway-Lafayette St. Free-thinking musicians anticipate the Apocalypse with a wide range of piercing-edge performances, complemented by great acoustics. Several shows nightly. Big names from Sun Ra to Laibach share space with Joe Coleman and Brinssly Slopchop. The last Sunday of each month features "Cobra", a musical genre invented by avant-garde jazz composer John Zorn. The earlier you come, the cheaper the beer. Cover usually $9.

Cat Club, 76 E. 13th St. (505-0090). Subway: #4, 5, 6, L, N, or R to 14th St. Burly teens bang heads here. A well-worn stepping stone for bands on their way to success. Sunday night (8pm-1am) is Big Band Jazz Night for the New York Swing Dance Society. Doors open 9:30pm; shows after 11pm. Cover $5-15.

The Marquee, 547 W. 21st St. (929-3257) at Tenth Ave. Subway: #1, 9, C, or E to 23rd St. Bands who've escaped the small club scene but don't have enough corporate backing to go big-time come to this large, awkwardly glitzy club. The height of the stage discourages intimate banter with the performers. Door opens 7-8pm. Cover $5-20.

The Bitter End, 174 Bleecker St. (673-7030) at Thompson St. Subway: #1, 9 to Christopher St. or A, B, C, D, E, F, Q to West 4th St.. Small space hosts sweetsounding rock, folk, and country music. Call for show times. Cover $5-15.

Ballroom, 253 W. 28th St. (244-3005) at Eighth Ave. Subway: C or E to 23rd St. A slinky cabaret on the edge of Chelsea, near the Flower and Fleece Market. Borderline Art-Deco decor with a funky, vegetable-heavy Tapas Bar. Eclectic offerings range from Long Island Retro to Village Avant-Garde. Often dance, comedy, or performance art tactics enrich the music. Open in summer Tues.-Sat. 4:30pm-1am, Sun. from noon. Showtime Tues.-Sat. 8:30pm, Sun. 3pm. Cover $15-20, plus 2-drink min.

Bottom Line, 15 W. 4th St. (228-7880 or 228-6300) at Mercer St. in Greenwich Village. Subway: #1, 9 to Christopher St. or A, B, C, D, E, F, or Q to W. 4th St. A somber, loftlike space where rainbows weave on the walls, set against black. If you can't find a seat, you can sit at the comfy bar (even without ordering a drink), surrounded by old show photos. A mixed bag of music and entertainment—from jazz to kitsch to country to theater to good ol' time rock and roll by over-the-hill singer/songwriters. Double proof of age (21 and over) required, but some all-ages performances. Shows nightly at 8 and 11pm. Cover $15.

Continental Divide, 25 Third Ave. (529-6924) at St. Marks Pl. Subway: #6 to Astor Pl. Punks, posers, artists, literati and the occasional skinhead. Terribly East Village. Very loud music in a blackened interior. Shows nightly at around 10:30pm. No cover, Sun.-Thurs.; Fri.-Sat. $2.

Lone Star Roadhouse, 240 W. 52nd St. (245-2950). Subway: #1 or 9 to 50th St. Friendly Tex-Mex cantina where good old boys and square dancing gals mix it up with Macy's cowboys and silver-spurred posers. Solid entertainment with no-frills rock, R&B, country, funk, and zydeco. Red-checkered table cloths, roadside kitsch, and long-neck Buds. Music nightly at 9:30 and 11:30. Cover $10-15.

The Ritz, 254 W. 54th St. (541-8900), off Broadway. Once a rough warehouse-like club on the street. Now *the* New York club for minor music industry stars. Everything from De La Soul to Sonic Youth. Occupies the space of the late, great Studio 54. Showtimes vary. Cover $10-25.

Academy, 234 W. 43rd St. (840-9500) at Seventh Ave. Subway: #1, 2, 3, 7, or 9 to 42nd St. Broadway theater turned concert club. Wide variety of rock styles. Call for showtimes. Tickets $15-15.

Palladium, 126 E. 14th St. (473-7171) at Third Ave. Subway: #4, 5, 6, L, N, or R to 14th St. Started by megaclub moguls Steve Rubell and Ian Schrager. Once notorious; now the largest crowds are on the videoscreens. Club MTV used to be filmed here. Funky, funky, funky. Look for mainstream alt-rock shows in the alternative Michael Todd Room. Open 10pm-4am. Cover $10-30.

Roseland, 239 W. 52nd St. (245-3240) at Eighth Ave. and Broadway. Subway: C or E to 50th St. Decently-priced concert club featuring mostly They-Might-Be-Giants-style major-label college rock. Tickets $15-25.

World Beat

Sounds of Brazil (S.O.B.), 204 Varick St. (243-4940), at the corner of Seventh and Houston in the Village. Subway: #1, 9 to Houston (a local stop only). This luncheonette-turned-dance-club presents bopping musicians playing the sounds of Brazil, Africa, Latin America, and the Caribbean in a setting inflicted with tropicana. Open for dining Tues.-Thurs. 7pm-2:30am, Fri.-Sat. 7pm-4am. Music from 9pm Tues.-Thurs., Fri.-Sat. from 10pm. Cover Mon.-Thurs. $12-18, Fri. $17, Sat. $18.

Wetlands Preserve, 161 Hudson St. (966-4225). Subway: #1, 9, A, C, or E to Canal St. A giant Summer of Love mural in the back room sets the tone, a Volkswagen bus curio shop swims in tie dyes, and mood memorabilia harken to the Woodstock years in this 2-story whole earth spectacular. Chill downstairs in a flowerchild's love patch. Mondays and Fridays Wetlands brings you reggae; Tuesdays Grateful Dead tribute; Wednesdays mixes things up; Thursdays blues and rock; Saturday nights psychedelic mania kicks in and Sundays things are back to the mellow groove with folk. Shows start nightly after 9:30. This eco-night club does some canvassing on the side, sponsoring benefits in the cause of a healthier earth. Opens Sun.-Thurs. 5pm, Fri.-Sat. 9pm. Cover $5-15 (no drink min.).

Tramps, 45 W. 21st St. (727-7788). Subway: F, N, or R to 23rd St. Screaming violins and clattering washboards pack the sweaty dance floor. Louisiana Zydeco rocks nightly with help from blues, reggae, and rock bands. Surprisingly agile crowd. Doors open at 7pm. Sets at 8:30 and 11pm. Cover $5-15.

Bentley's, 25 E. 40th St. (684-2540), between Park and Madison Ave. Subway: #4, 5, 6, 7, or S to 42nd St. Predominantly Black crowd dancing to incredible rhythms at impossible speed. Even the yuppies have a good time. First floor has a house DJ. Upstairs cools down with reggae music. Free buffet Thurs.-Fri. at 5pm. Thursday (6pm-2am) is Reggae-Soca-Calypso Night. Open daily at 5pm. Fri. 5-11pm free, $10 after 11pm; free for women until 11pm Sat.; otherwise cover $10.

Jazz

Jazz in New York comes in two versions: smoky or smoke-free. You can check out one of the many hazy dens that bred lingo like "cat" and "hip." (A "hippie" was originally someone on the fringes of jazz culture who talked the talk but was never in the know.) The summertime spawns cleaner but humid sets in parks and plazas.

Central Park Concerts/Summerstage, at 72nd St. (360-2777) in Central Park divides its attentions between many performing arts, including jazz, opera, and folk. (Season: mid-June-early Aug. Free.) The **World Financial Center Plaza** (945-0505) hosts free concerts from July to September. The range of jazz styles is wide: 1992 brought Charlie Bird, Ruth Brown, and the incomparable Tito Puentes and his Latin Jazz All-Stars. The **South Street Seaport** (732-7678) sponsors a series of outdoor concerts from July to early September at Pier 17, Ambrose Stage, and the Atrium.

For the price of an orchestra seat at the New York Opera, you can·take yourself and your eight closest friends to the **Lincoln Center Plaza, Damrosch Park,** or the **Guggenheim Bandshell** to hear jazz, salsa, and big band delights. (Fountain Plaza concerts cost $6.) The Lincoln Center's new midsummer Night Swing Dancextravaganza, held late June to late July every Wednesday to Saturday night, invites couples and singles to tango, swing, shimmy, or foxtrot. The Center provides dance floor, café, and bands fronted by bandleaders like Illinois Jacquet. (Dancing Wed.-Sat. 8:15-11pm, Wed. at 6:30pm.) **Alice Tully Hall,** also at Lincoln Center, presents a summer jazz series (875-5299). Guest soloist Wynton Marsalis trumpeted the inaugural season.

In the heart of Rockefeller Center, entertainment palace **Radio City Music Hall** (247-4777) has a bill of great performers that reads like the invitation list to the Forbes Anniversary bash: Ella Fitzgerald, Frank Sinatra, Ringo Starr, Linda Ronstadt, and Sting, among others. The Rockettes still kick out the lights here. (Box office at 50th St. and Sixth Ave. Open Mon.-Sat. 10am-8pm, Sun. 11am-8pm.) Tickets range from $20 to $1000 for the "Night of 100 Stars." The **Beacon Theater,** 2124 Broadway (496-7070) at 75th St., hosts special films, dance groups, international performing arts groups, and mainstream soul and rock artists.

New York's churches wed the pristine to the upbeat in their capacity as music halls. Though the true godfathers of gospel keep the faith farther uptown, the Midtown sacred jazz scene belongs to **Saint Peter's,** 619 Lexington Ave. (935-2200) at 52nd St. On the first Sunday of every month, St. Peter's hosts a gala jazz mass. On other Sundays, jazz vespers are intoned at 5pm, followed at 7 or 8pm by a full-fledged jazz concert. ($5 donation for the concert.) In addition, the hippest ministry in town brings you art openings and exhibits, theater, lectures, and more. (See Theater and Midtown Sights.) John Garcia Geyel, Pastor to the Jazz Community, oversees all tuneful good deeds. Most of the music schools and halls listed under Classical Music have jazz offerings.

Although primarily a rock festival, the **Coca Cola Concert Series** (307-7171) also brings jazz and reggae concerts to **Jones Beach** (516-221-1000; June-early Sept.; tickets $20-27.50).

Jazz clubs

Expect high covers and drink minimums at the legendary jazz venues. Most of them crowd tables together and charge $5 a drink. Of the upscale clubs, Condon's lets you sit at the bar with a drink minimum, but no cover. Hearing the jazz gods costs an arm and a leg; however, there are a few bars, like Augie's, which supply a reliable selection of no-names free of charge.

J's, 2581 Broadway (666-3600), between 97th and 98th St., 2nd floor. Subway: #1 or 9 to 103rd St. A classic jazz bar. Top-notch music, dim lighting over red brick walls: intimacy without claustrophobia. Owner Judy Barnett, a respected jazz singer, ropes in well-known talent; as you'd expect, there's more focus on singing here than at most clubs. Some swing; blues on Sundays. After the set, the musicians schmooze at the bar. Open Mon.-Thurs. 5pm-12:30am, sets from 8:30pm; Fri. 5pm-1am, sets from 9pm; Sat. 7pm-1am, sets from 9pm; Sun 7pm-1am, sets from 10pm. No cover; $7 min. at bar; $12 at tables.

Augie's, 2751 Broadway (864-9834), between 105th and 106th St. Subway: #1 or 9 to 103rd St. Small and woody. Jazz all week until 3am. The saxophonist sits on your lap and the bass rests on your table. Quality musicians and a cool, unpretentious crowd. No cover; $3 drink min. Sets start around 10pm. Open daily 8pm-3am.

Blue Note, 131 W. 3rd St (475-8592) at MacDougal St. Subway: A, B, C, D, E, F, or Q to Washington Sq. The Carnegie Hall of jazz clubs. Now a commercialized concert space with crowded tables and a sedate audience. They often book top performers. Sets at 9pm and 11:30pm. Fri. and Sat. at 1:30am also.

Bradley's, 70 University Pl. (473-9700) at 11th St. Subway: #4, 5, 6, L, N, or R to Union Sq. Nightly piano and bass duos (and other small ensembles) cut through the smoke. Usually crowded. Sets at 10pm, midnight, 2am. Music daily 9:45pm-4am. Cover $8 weekdays, $12 weekends. $8 min. at tables. Two-drink min. at bar.

Dan Lynch, 221 Second Ave. (667-0911) at 14th St. Subway: #4, 5, 6, L, N, or R to Union Sq. Dark smoky room with Casablanca fan, long bar, and "all blues, all the time." Swinging, beautifully friendly, deadhead crowd envelops the dance floor. Pool table in back. Open daily 8pm-4am; blues and jazz start at 10pm. Jam session Sat.-Sun. 4-9pm. Cover Fri.-Sat. $5.

Village Vanguard, 178 Seventh Ave. (255-4037), south of 11th St. Subway: #1, 2, 3, or 9 to 14th St. A windowless cavern shaped like a wedge, as old and hip as jazz itself. The walls are thick with memories of Lenny Bruce, Leadbelly, Miles Davis, and Sonny Rollins. Sets at 9:30 and 11:30pm, Fri.-Sat. also at 1am. Every Monday the Vanguard Orchestra unleashes their torrential big band sound on the sentimental journeymen at 10pm and midnight. Cover: Mon.-Thurs. and Sun. $12 plus $7.50 min., Fri.-Sat. $15 plus $7.50 min.

Indigo Blues, 221 W. 46th St. (221-0033), between Broadway and Eighth. Subway: C or E to 50th St. Located in the basement of the Hotel Edison. Jazz and blues served up nightly in a high modernist glass and brick den. Heavyweight guests have included Milt Jackson, Freddie Hubbard, Frank Bruno, Betty Carter, and Stanley Jordan. Music starts after 9pm. Cover $10-20 depending on the attraction, plus a variable min. if you sit at a table (no ingestive min. at the bar).

Village Gate, 160 Bleecker St. (475-5120), near Thompson St. Subway: #6 to Bleecker. This landmark entertainment complex houses 3 bars, a jazz terrace, and two theaters staging concerts, off-Broadway shows, musical revues, and nightly jazz music. Dark, old village hangout. Every Monday salsa meets jazz downstairs in the big room 9pm-2am, same on the Terrace Tues.-Sun. from 10pm. Jazz regulars play Monday and Tuesday nights. Sat.-Sun. 2-6pm open mike for college jazz prodigies; Sat.-Sun. 6-10pm professionals take over. Open daily 6pm-2am. Salsa Meets Jazz $15-20; original plays $20-33. Comedy upstairs $8, jazz on the terrace free with a $6.50 drink min.

Sweetwater's, 170 Amsterdam Ave. (873-4100) at 68th St. Subway:#1 or 9 to 66th St. Cool jazz blended with uptown chic. Open Mon.-Fri. noon-4am, Sat.-Sun. 4pm-4am. Cover $10 plus 2-drink min. downstairs; $10 cover plus $10 dinner min. upstairs. Fri.-Sat cover $20 plus $10 min.

Michael's Pub, 211 E. 55th St. (758-2272), off Third Ave. Subway: #4, 5, or 6 to 59th St. New Orleans traditional jazz. Woody Allen played his clarinet here instead of picking up his 3 Academy Awards for *Annie Hall*. He still sneaks in some Mon. nights. Sets Mon. at 9 and 11pm, Tues.-Sat. at 9:15 and 11:15pm. Open Mon.-Sat. noon-1am. Cover $15-25. No cover Mon. Substantial food and drink min. at tables.

Birdland, 2745 Broadway (749-2228) at 105th St. Subway: #1 or 9 to 103rd St. A supper club serving reasonably good food and top jazz. The place feels Upper-West-nouveau but the music is smoked-out-splendid-52nd St. Blue Note Records makes recordings here. Sun. jazz brunch. Open 4pm-4am, Sun. noon-4pm and 5pm-4am. First set nightly at 9pm. Fri.-Sat $5 cover, plus $5 min. per set at bar; $10 cover and $15 min. per set at tables. Sun.-Thurs. $5 cover plus $5 min. per set at tables, no cover at bar. No cover for brunch. Appetizers $7, entrees $12-16, sandwiches $8-10.

Condon's, 117 E. 15th St. (254-0960), east of Union Sq. Subway: #4, 5, 6, L, N, or R to Union Sq. All flavors of jazz, including Brazilian and big band sounds, in an intimate setting. Menus (in Japanese, French, Spanish, Italian, and German) range from $7.50 burgers to $18 steak. Bar from 4pm. Dinner Sun.-Thurs. 5:30pm-midnight, Fri.-Sat. 5:30pm-1am. Sets at 9 and 11pm, Fri.-Sat. also at 1am. Cover at tables $12.50-20. No cover at bar. Two-drink min.

Apollo Theater, 253 W. 125th St. (864-0372). Subway: #1 or 9 to 125th St. Historic Harlem landmark has heard Duke Ellington, Count Basie, Ella Fitzgerald, Lionel Hampton, Billie Holliday, and Sarah Vaughan. A young Malcolm X shined shoes here. Now undergoing a revival. Show tickets $5-30. Arrive at least one hr. early for cheap tickets. Amateur night Wed. at 7:30pm. Call for more information.

Fat Tuesday's, 190 Third Ave. (533-7902), between E. 17th and 18th St. Subway: L to Third Ave. A small club with big names. Dependable mainstream jazz artists have included Betty Carter, Astrud Gilberto, and the Les Paul Trio. Sets Mon.-Fri. 8 and 10pm, Sat.-Sun. 8pm, 10pm, and midnight. Cover $12.50.

Sweet Basil, 88 Seventh Ave. (242-1785), between Bleecker and Grove St. #1 or 9 to Christopher St./Sheridan Sq. Serves mostly traditional jazz with dinner. Lots of tourists, some regulars. Check *Village Voice* for occasional star sets. Shows Mon.-Fri. 10pm and midnight. Sat.-Sun. 10pm, 12pm, and 1:30am. Cover $15, plus $6 min.

Red Blazer Too, 349 W. 46th St. (262-3112), between Eighth and Ninth Ave. Subway: A, C, or E to 50th St. Dance cheek to cheek in the stardust of fab golden oldies. Tuesdays are a musical romp through 20s and 30s. Thursday Big Bands take the stage, Fri.-Sat. is blistery Dixieland. Jazz Age crowd. Sunday jazz brunch noon-5pm; Wed. and Fri. twilight jazz 5:30-8:30pm (with free hors d'oeuvres). Music nightly: Sun. at 6pm, Mon.-Thurs. 8:30pm-12:30am, Fri.-Sat. 9pm-1am. Cover $5, except Mon.

Greene Street, 101 Greene St. (925-2415). Subway: R to Prince St. This restaurant/bar recalls the setting for *The Sting* or *The Untouchables:* splendid gilded decor just asking to be riddled by bullets. Twi-lit, leafy, and cavernous, with a piano stationed somewhere far below. Jazz is their forte, with an accent on piano music. No cover charge. Open 6pm-midnight, weekends 6pm-1am. Closed during the summer; opens Labor Day. Cover $3, weekends $5.

Dance Clubs

> *A wilderness of human flesh; Crazed with avarice,*
> *lust and rum, New York, thy name's Delirium.*
> —Byron R. Newton, Ode to New York, 1906

The New York dance club is an unrivaled institution. The crowd is uninhibited, the music unparalleled and the fun unlimited—as long as you uncover the right place. Homing into the hippest club in New York isn't easy as a tourist. Clubs rise, war, and fall, and even those "in the know" don't always know where to find the hot spot. The best parties are often "raves" or "outlaws," advertised only by word of mouth. They convene late at night on subway platforms, in abandoned warehouses, or at closed bars and unknown clubs. Many clubs move from space to space each week, although true clubbers still manage to find them. Make friends with someone on the inside.

The rules are simple. You have to have "the look" to be let in. Doormen are the clubs' fashion police, and nothing drab or conventional will squeeze by. Wear black clothes and drape your most attractive friends on your arms. Don't look worried or fearful; act like you belong. Come after 11pm unless you crave solitude; things don't really get going until 1 or 2am.

Most good clubs are good on only one or two nights a week. The right club on the wrong night can be a big mistake, particularly if you've already paid the $5-15 cover charge. The cover can rise to $20 on weekend nights when the too-cool B&T crowd (who reach Manhattan from New Jersey and Long Island by bridge and tunnel) attempt to get past the bouncers *en masse.*

Alternative and downtown nightlife often blend; the hippest clubs have one or two "gay nights" a week, and same-sex couples can go "clubbing" in most places without any hassle. The following suggestions could well have changed by the summer of '93. Call ahead to make sure that you know what (and whom) you'll find when you arrive. Most clubs open their doors around 9pm and stay open until 4am; a few non-alcoholic after-hours clubs keep getting busy until 5 or 6am, or later.

Building, 51 W. 26th St. (576-1890), between Broadway and Sixth Ave. Subway: R to 28th St. One of the foundations of the New York club scene. Converted power plant with 50-ft. ceilings and a great crowd. If it's empty there is no place worse to be, but a full house is quite a party. Friday is Industrial Alternative. Open Thurs.-Sun.

Nell's, 246 W. 14th St. (675-1567), between Seventh and Eighth Ave. Subway: #1, 2, 3, or 9 to 14th St. A legendary hot spot; some faithful admirers hang on even through its decline. Dingy neighborhood belies the opulence of the huge Victorian-style sitting room inside. Overstuffed chairs, chandeliers, and bejeweled Beautiful People upstairs. Angular dance floor downstairs. Not a gay club, but a popular gay spot. Open daily 10pm-4am. Cover Sun.-Wed. $6, Thurs. $10, Fri.-Sat. $12.

China Club, 2130 Broadway (877-1166) at 75th St. Subway: #1, 2, 3, or 9 to 72nd St. Rock and roll hot spot where Bowie and Jagger come on their off nights. Models and long-haired men make it a great people-watching spot. Monday nights are best. Go elsewhere for great dancing. Cover around $10.

Rex, 246 Fifth Ave. (725-6997). Subway: R to 28th St. A restaurant with good (if expensive) food downstairs and a hopping dance floor upstairs. Live music downstairs until late on Friday and Saturday nights. On weekends a very young crowd (sweet sixteen-ish) bops to generic but loud as hell dance music. Reliable back-up for a slow night.

Limelight, 47 W. 20th St. (807-7850) at Sixth Ave. Subway: F or R to 23rd St. Once a church and some nights are about as much fun as Sunday School. The real attraction is Wednesday night's Disco 2000 party, where funky things happen. Queer on Fri. and Sat. nights. Sunday night is heavy metal. Cover $12, Fri.-Sat. $15.

Au Bar, 41 E. 58th St. (308-9455), between Park and Madison Ave. Subway: #4, 5, 6 to 59th St., or N, R to Lexington Ave. Au dear. Très Euro. Gypsy Kings music on the dance floor. Lots of thirtysomething men in Armani suits, cigars in hand, put the moves on willing women. Open daily 9pm-4am. Cover Sun.-Wed. $10, Thurs.-Sat. $15.

Laura Belle, 120 W. 43rd St. (819-1000). Subway: #1, 2, 3, 7, or 9 to 42nd St. Au Bar's sister. Very chi chi. Women with Chanel bags, gold jewelry, and black dresses. Men with jeans and more of those Armani jackets. Everyone with daddy's credit card. Dinner until 10pm, at which point the tables are cleared away and it becomes a dance floor. Cover Wed.-Sat. $10.

Copacabana, 10 E. 60th St. (755-6010) at Madison Ave. Subway: #4, 5, 6 to 59th St., or N, R to Lexington Ave. Several levels, with a dark and dancy lower floor. Music and passion are still in fashion on the last Thursday of the month, when weirdness abounds. Cover Tues.-Thurs. $5-10, Fri.-Sat. $10-15.

Metropolis Cafe, 31 Union Square (675-2300). Subway #4, 5, 6, L, N, R to 14th St. Across from the Coffee Shop this expensive restaurant hides a downstairs party late Thursday night (live jazz upstairs most other times). Come between 1-2am.

Quick, 6 Hubert St. off Hudson, 5 blocks south of Canal. Subway: #1 or 9 to Franklin St. Designed by Broadcast Arts, the same animators responsible for Pee Wee Herman's playhouse. In its previous incarnation, this club was called "Area," and was Palladium's arch-rival and evil double. Current gimmicks include large ceramic pigs and small porcine go-go dancers. Thursday's gay night has a $10 cover—the entertainment features a drag queen lip-syncher and hip house music. Beware: with no A/C, this place gets too hot for comfort in summer. Open Wed.-Sun. 10pm-4am. Cover Thurs. "Gay Night" $5-10, Fri.-Sat. $15.

The Bank, 225 E. Houston St. (505-5033) at Essex. Subway: F to Delancey St. A stately bank converted to a slick club. Clear sight lines make it great for live music. Reliable, if standard, music. Underground vault a great spot for the wee hours. Call for information on the erratic schedule. Cover $6.

Amazon Club, Pier 25 at North Moore St. (227-2900). Outdoor summer extravaganza so big and tacky that it's actually fun. Palm trees, grass huts, and an outdoor waterfall. The dancing isn't the main attraction, but things do heat up if the right person is throwing a party. Admission Sun.-Wed. $5, Thurs.-Sat. $10.

SOBs, 204 Varrick St. (243-4904) at Houston. Subway: #1 or 9 to Houston. SOBs often hosts "Soul Kitchen" on Tues., one of the absolute best parties around. If you can find it (it moves), go. You might need a date to get by the doorman.

The Pyramid, 101 Ave. A (420-1590) at 6th St. Subway: #6 to Astor Pl. No sign over the door, just a pink triangle. Transvestite punk and 60s lighting. Those seeking the unusual will fit right in. Avant-garde performances nightly. This is mostly a gay club, though Friday nights are straight. Transvestite go-go dancers on the bar (yes, on the bar), Sun. night gay cabaret. Cover $5-10.

Mission, 531 E. 5th St. (473-9096), between Ave. A and B. Subway: #6 to Astor Pl. Depeche Mode and Cure fans, complete with hairspray and ticket stubs from New Jersey, fill this tiny club. Major-label alternative music tends towards Gothic and industrial. Those who can't muster up the energy to dance head for the couches in the back room to stare at the fluorescent-painted walls. Open Thurs.-Sun. at 10pm. Cover $5-10.

Gay and Lesbian

The New York gay scene extends visibly throughout the city. The West Village, especially around Christopher St., has long been the hub of the city's alternative life. A harder-core gay crowd occupies the lower East Village on First and Second Ave. south of E. 12th St. Wealthier types cruise the Upper West Side in the upper 70s; Columbus Ave. on Sundays is a great place to drive. Gay communities are not restricted to Manhattan; Park Slope in Brooklyn has long been home to a large and important lesbian community.

Each week the *Village Voice* and *New York Native* publish full listings of gay events. The Gay and Lesbian Student Organization of Columbia University sponsors a huge dance on the first Friday of each month in Earl Hall at 116th St. and Broadway (Subway: #1 to 116th St.; Cover around $5). The *Pink Pages* is a phone book for the queer community with all sorts of listings, including bars and clubs. You can pick one up in some of the gay/lesbian bars. Or call them at 427-8224 to get information on where to pick one up.

The Spike, 120 11th Ave. (243-9688) at W. 20th St. Subway: C or E to 23rd St. Caters to an adventurous crowd of leather-clad men (and some women) who know how to create a spectacle. Open daily 9pm-4am. Cover varies.

DTs Fat Cat, at W. 4th St. and W. 12th St. (243-9041). Subway: A, C, E, or L to 14th St. Yes, these two streets do intersect, in the non-Euclidean West Village, near Eighth Ave. Piano bar with a large straight clientele; relaxed scene for lesbians. Open daily until 4am. No cover.

Pandora's Box, 70 Grove St. on 7th Ave. south. Dark bar with older lesbian scene. Crowded on weekends, popular hangout and meeting place. Dyke dance club some nights. Beer starts at $3.50. Occasional cover ($7). Open 4pm-4am.

Building, 51 W. 26th St. (576-1890) between Broadway and Sixth Ave. Subway: #1 or 9 to 23rd St. This former generating plant has 50-ft. ceilings and a mix of straight and gay dancers grooving to house/Hi-NRG mixes. Thurs. and Sun. are the best nights for the gay crowd. Open 9pm- 4am. Cover $5-10.

Limelight, 47 W. 20th St. (807-7850) at Sixth Ave. Hosts a club within a club, **Lick It!,** on weekend nights, plus a gay back room always. Check out the Plexiglas "feel-me" booth. Cover $12, Fri.-Sat. $15.

The Clit Club. Hard to find. Traveling lesbian club moves every week or so; ask at one of the other bars about its present whereabouts. Exotic celebs: Annie Sprinkle is occasionally sighted here.

The Monster, 80 Grove St. (924-3557) at 7th Ave. Subway: #1 or 9 to Christopher St. Piano bar with downstairs disco; heats up on Fri. and Sat. nights. Open daily 4pm-4am. Cover Fri.-Sat. $5.

The Pyramid, 101 Ave. A (420-1590) at 6th St. Subway: #6 to Astor Pl. Also known by its street address, this dance club mixes gay, lesbian, and straight folks. Vibrant drag scene. Continues to push the limits of exotic with the freshest mixes. Fri. is straight night. Open 9pm-4am. Cover $5-10.

Henrietta Hudson, 438 Hudson St. (924-3347). New clean bar with good jukebox featuring women artists. Mellow in the afternoon, packed and perky at night and on the weekends. Young lesbian crowd. No cover ever. Open 3pm-4am.

Crazy Nanny's, 21 7th Ave. South (926-8356). Mixed lesbian crowd, lively bar. Open 4pm-4am daily.

Uncle Charlie's, 56 Greenwich Ave. (255-8787), at Seventh Ave. Subway: #1 or 9 to Christopher St. Biggest and best-known gay club in the city. Mainstream and preppy, with some exclusive types. It's still fun, if a bit crowded on the weekends. Women are welcome, but few come. Delectable bathrooms. Open daily 4pm-4am. No cover.

The Roxy, 515 W. 18th St. (645-5156). A mixed club with a heavily gay crowd on Sat. and Sun. (sometimes Tues.) in a good space. Music mix is sometimes tired, but the crowd makes up for it with serious moves on the dance floor. Security can be tight. Open 10am-4am. Cover $7-15.

The Works, 428 Columbus Ave. at 81st. (799-7365). Cheerfully dim, long, narrow, and popular spot for gay men, behind a one-way window (from the outside it always looks closed). Amusing mural. Faint tropical theme. Good age range. On Sundays guzzle all the beer you can for $5. Open daily 2pm-4am.

Bars

New York soaks in bars. Every major street has a couple of dark holes where the locals burrow on weeknights. Because of laws discouraging heavy drinking, bars no longer offer official happy hours, but most keep prices tied down and music pumped up. To capture the essence of a particular New York subset, venture into the wild Venn diagram of the city's bar life.

The Village (Greenwich)

Automatic Slims, 733 Washington St. (645-8660) at Bank St. Subway: A, C, or E to 14th St. Simple bar in the West Village with the best selection of blues and screamin' soul, complemented by the guitars and pensive faces of South-side stars. Twentysomething Villagers sit at tables with classic 45s under the glass top. Packed on weekends with a more diverse crowd. American cooking, served 6pm-midnight (entrees $7.50-14). Open Sun.-Mon. 5:30-2:30am, Tues.-Sat. 5:30-4:30am.

Peculiar Pub, 145 Bleecker St. (353-1327). Subway: #6 to Bleecker St. Over 300 kinds of beer from 43 countries. Interesting soccer-scarf-clad crowd. Fiona McKenna occasionally comes here for a swifty. A neighborhood crowd during the week, but packed with tourists and the "bridge and tunnel" crowd on weekends. Beer can get a little pricey here. Open Mon.-Wed. 5pm-2am, Thurs. 5pm-3am, Fri. 4pm-4am, Sat. 2pm-4am, Sun. 5pm-1am.

Pool Bar, 643 Broadway at Bleecker St. Subway: #6 to Bleecker St. A flight of stairs leads down to a dance floor and pool table. Beautiful bartenders serve expensive drinks while psychedelic funk attempts to get the place grooving. Open Mon.-Thurs. 6pm-4am, Fri.-Sat. 6pm-3am. Cover Thurs.-Sat. $2-3.

Eagle Tavern, 355 W. 14th St. (924-0275) at Ninth Ave. Subway: A, C, or E to 14th St. A true Irish pub in the heart of the meat-packing district. Barside blarney and poignant folk music swell in the air. Mon. and Fri. nights promise traditional Irish music. There's rock on Tues. and Sat., bluegrass on Thurs. Cover $2-10 with one drink min. Open daily 8pm-4am. Music at 8pm.

Barrow Street Ale House, 15 Barrow St. (206-7302) near 7th Ave. and 4th St. Ignore the paintings on the wall and enjoy this roomy neighborhood bar. Don't miss the tremendous deals: $1 drafts all day Sunday and Monday and 5:30-9:30pm on Tues. and Wed. You'll be laughing and stumbling all the way to the bank. Pool and pinball downstairs. Have a black and tan. Open Sun.-Thurs. 3pm-2am, Fri. and Sat. 3pm-4am, Sun.

East Village, Alphabet City, TriBeCa

The International Bar, 120 1/2 1st Ave. (777-9214) between 7th St. and St. Marks Place. This long and skinny bar has only two tables in the back, but the large, friendly counter seats many. Christmas lights and yellow-sponge-painted walls give this bar a firey glow. Grimy and authentic East Village. Clientele includes immigrants, lost youths, and college kids. Lots of regulars and history. Open Mon.-Fri. 10:30am-4am, Sat and Sun. noon-4am.

Downtown Beirut, 158 First Ave. (260-4248). Subway: L to First Ave. Hardcore but friendly East Village crowd gathers under a large inflatable man to listen to the jukebox belt out hits by Mudhoney, the Avengers, and the Clash. Draft beer for $1. Mon.-Fri. mixed drink specials $2. Open daily noon-4am.

The Edge, 95 3rd. St. (477-2940) between 1st and 2nd. Hell's Angels abound here (visit their homestead across the street). Crowd is a mix of regulars and downtownies. Gritty yet strangely upscale atmosphere, but don't go here alone—especially if you're a woman. Pitcher of Bud $9 (zoinks!). Open Mon.-Fri. 4pm-4am, Sat. and Sun. noon-4am.

Sophie's, 507 E. 5th St. (228-5680), between A and B Ave. Subway: F to Second Ave. or #6 to Astor Pl. Packed with leather jackets, t-shirts, jeans, and baseball-caps on weekends. Unpretentious downtown artists friendly to the lone tourist. Pool table and soulful jukebox. Open daily noon-4am.

Siné, 122 St. Mark's Pl. (982-0370), between First and A Ave. Subway: #6 to Astor Pl. Name means "That's it" in Gaelic. Down to earth, folksy crowd comes here after a long day at the farm. Live folk, blues, and Irish music 10pm-2am nightly. Open daily 11am-2am. No cover.

Dan Milano's, 51 E. Houston (226-8632), near Mulberry St. Subway: F to Second Ave. The celebrity crowd drifts in here on the weekends; Madonna stopped here with Sean in happier days. Sit at the long oak bar and check out the photo of Marciano about to knockout Louis. Guinness Stout on tap for $2.75 a half-pint. Open Mon.-Sat. 8am-4am, Sun. noon-4am.

King Tut's Wah Wah Hut, 112 Ave. A (254-7772), in the East Village. Subway: #6 to Astor Pl. In the middle of the scene a few years ago; now only a vestigial East Village crowd remains. Punkish crowd plays pool. Antique couches melt into surreal psychedelic walls. Platinum hair, and wrinkled tattoos. Infidel shrine with Jesus, Mary, angels, and skull lights. Draft $2, hot dog $1.50. Open daily 4pm-4am.

Ludlow St. Café, 165 Ludlow St. (353-0536), right below E. Houston St. Subway: F to Delancey St. or J, M, Z to Essex St. Fashionable downtown bag ladies and men with shorn hair and nerdy glasses come to this dark ghetto to hear loud live music. Music varies in quality and tends toward folk, rock, and strange; the schedule is painted fluorescent on the wall. Dinner 6pm-midnight ($2.50-7). Draft beer $1.50; free with dinner. Open until 3 or 4am. Cover Fri.-Sat. $3.

Max Fisch, 178 Ludlow St. (529-3959) at Houston St. Subway: F to Delancey St. or J, M, Z to Essex St. Wall covered with found art, and original cartoons. Plastic skulls line the wall/ceiling juncture. The crowd is hip if a bit pretentious, and the all-CD jukebox is easily the best in town: Pavement, Dustdevils, Scratch Acid, Superchunk, and the Minutemen. Beer is steep at $2.25 a glass. Open daily 5:30pm-4am.

International Bar, 120 First Ave. (977-9244), between 7th St. and St. Mark's Pl. Subway: #6 to Astor Pl. Charming small bar run by an old Finnish woman. A quieter spot where downtowners taking a break from the boisterous life mix with a friendly older crowd. Year-round Christmas lights, tin ceilings, and old Wurlitzer jukebox. Open daily 11am- 4am. Call in July.

SoHo

The Ear Inn, 326 Spring St. (226-9060), near the Hudson. Once a big bohemian/activist hangout, this bar now tends to the SoHo baseball-cap crowd. Dark wood, mellow blues, and tables with crayons. Back room functions as a restaurant during lunch and dinner hours. Try the rich and delicious mud pie ($3). Good American food served from 11am-4:30pm, 6pm-1am every day. Appetizers and salads $2-6, specials and entrees $5-9. Bar open to 4am.

Lucky Strike, 59 Grand St. (943-0479), off W. Broadway. Subway: #1, 9 or A, C, E to Canal St. SoHo prices attract droves of the ultra-magna-beautiful, scantily clad in black. Super-attractive waitstaff. $3.50 Budweisers with similarly scaled food prices in the back makes this more of a sight than a watering hole. Open daily noon-4am.

Upper West Side

The Shark Bar, 307 Amsterdam Ave. between 74th and 75th (496-6600). High-class and enjoyable bar and soul-food restaurant; possibly the only truly interracial establishment on the West Side below 110th St. Live jazz on Tuesdays with a $5 cover; "gospel brunch" Sat. 12:30 and 2pm (no cover). Reasonable drink prices (bottled beer from $3). Entrees from $11. Open Mon.-Fri. 11:30am-2am, Sat.-Sun. 11:30am-4:30pm and 6:30pm-4am.

Westend, 2911 Broadway (662-8830) at 113 St. Subway: #1 or 9 to 116th St. Columbia University and prep school hangout once frequented by Kerouac. Huge sitting areas, indoors and outdoors, give way to the small dance room with rock and funk bands in the back—6 bands every Fri.-Sat. night (cover $5 and up). Cheap pitchers with a great beer selection. Comedy club downstairs (no cover, but 2-drink min.) Open until 4am.

Marlin, 2844 Broadway (678-8743), between 109th and 110th St. Subway: #1 or 9 to 110th St. A watering hole with inexpensive drinks and a well-rounded crowd. Rolling Rock $1. Happy hour Mon.-Fri. 5-7pm (all drinks $2). Open daily 8am-4am.

The Bear Bar, 2156 Broadway at 76th St. (362-2145). A bit removed from the Amsterdam Ave. yupbar scene—thus cheaper and less boring. Stuffed black bears beside and over the door. Lots of cheap drink promotions, like $1 Moosehead on Sun., and a "drink early" scheme whereby beer starts at 50¢ at 5pm and goes up 25¢ every hour. Open Mon.-Fri. 5pm-4am, Sat.-Sun. noon-5am.

Lucy's Retired Surfers Bar and Restaurant, 503 Columbus Ave. (787-3009) at 85th St. Subway: B or C to 86th St. Loud and packed to frothing with young Upper West Siders and people who heard it was fun. Surfers and surfboards on the walls and on TV screens. Happy hour 3-7pm daily. Open 24 hr.

McAleer's Pub, 425 Amsterdam Ave. (874-8037). Lively wood-and-brick pub. Often a line outside; twentysomething white people on the inside. Bottled beer from $4. Open Mon.-Sat. 8am-4am, Sun. noon-4am.

Upper East Side

American Trash, 1471 First Ave. (988-9008) between 76th and 77th St. Cavernous barroom hung with "trash" oddities from Christmas stockings to prize ribbons. Swinging singles having a wild 'n crazy time. Open daily noon-4am.

Electric Café Bar, 1608 Third Ave. (360-6036) between 90th and 91st. Psychedelic posters pulsate on the walls, and planets swirl in color on the ceiling. Rowdy neon-sporting patrons. Come here if the word electric turns you on. Open 3pm til "late."

Subway Inn, 143 E. 60th St. (223-8929) at Lexington Ave. Dusty and dark, with a red glow emanating from the bar, this threadbare joint serves up some of the cheapest beer in NYC. Patrons gaze philosophically at dust-coated ET figurines and model ships, or talk neighborhood gossip over the Spanish music. A dollar a Bud. Open daily 11am-2pm.

Midtown, Lower Midtown, and Chelsea

Gough's Chop House, 212 W. 43rd St. (221-9460) between 7th and 8th St. Cheap, unpretentious bar right off the titillating action of Times Square. The old heroes—Babe Ruth, Joe Dimaggio, Jack Dempsey—stare down from the walls, as a full counter of guys drink to their memories. Pitcher $5. Open daily 11am-4am.

Buckets of Beer, on 23rd St. at Madison Ave. The self-conscious, alcohol-related storefront graffiti advertises the bonanzas of drink specials that change nightly: $1 drafts until 7pm, $10 all-you-can-drink Sat. 8-10pm. A bar for the dedicated drinker. Open Mon.-Tues. noon-3:30am, Wed.-Thurs. noon-3:45am, Fri. noon-4am, Sat. 4pm-4am, Sun. 6pm-1:30am.

Old Town Bar and Grill, 18th St. (473-8874), between Park and Broadway. Subway: #4, 5, 6, L, N, or R to Union Sq. A quieter hideaway with wood and brass. As seen on *Letterman*. Cheeseburger with fries $6. Open Mon.-Thurs. 11:30am-midnight, Fri. 2pm-midnight, Sat. noon-midnight, Sun. 2-11pm.

O'Lunney's, 12 W. 44th St. (840-6688), between Fifth and Sixth Ave. Subway: B, D, F, or Q to 42nd St. A steak and burgers place that serves up live country and western as a digestive. Folk music occasionally thrown into the stew. Open Sun.-Fri. 11am-2am, Sat. 6pm-2am. Music Sun.-Thurs. 7-11:30pm, Fri.-Sat. 7pm-2am. Music at 7pm.

Coffee Shop Bar, 29 Union Sq. West (243-7969), facing Union Sq. Park. Subway: #4, 5, 6 or L, N, R to Union Sq. A chic diner for fashion victims, owned by three models. Open 23 hours daily.

Peter McManus, 152 Seventh Ave. (929-9691) at 19th St. Made famous by a NY Times article on the timeless appeal of ordinary bars, of which this is the epitome. The carved mahogany bar and leaded glass windows add to its charm.

The Other Boroughs

It's true that we only list one bar below. Don't get all testy, though; *Let's Go: New York* lists a whole kaboodle of pubs, taverns, bars with menus, and well-liquored restaurants located in other boroughs (o.k., not Staten Island) in the Food and Clubs sections (above and below). But wherever you go to swill, remember not to drive intoxicated.

Teddy's, N. 9th St. and Berry St. (718-384-9787), in Greenpoint, Brooklyn. Subway: G to Nassau Ave. The new artiste crowd starts drinking here, and only you can find out where they end up. True adventures often born in this bar. Jazz on Thurs. during winter months. Open Mon.-Tues. 3:30pm-2am, Wed.-Sun. 10am-2am.

Comedy Clubs

The Next Big Thing only a few years ago, comedy clubs are now on the wane. While venues vary tremendously in size and atmosphere, they nearly all impose a hefty cover and a minimum that's more like a maximum on Fridays and Saturdays. Invariably, there'll be an annoying emcee who'll jab at the Kansans in the front row between acts; if you dare to sit up close, be prepared.

The Original Improvisation, 358 W. 44th St. (765-8268), between Eighth and Ninth Ave. Subway: A, C, or E to 42nd St. A quarter century of comedy—acts from Saturday Night Live, Johnny Carson, David Letterman. Richard Pryor and Robin Williams got started here. Shows Sun.-Thurs. at 9pm, Fri. and Sat. 9:15, midnight. Cover: Mon.-Tues. $8 and $8 min., Wed., Thurs., Sun. $11 and $9 min., Fri., Sat. $12 and $9 min.

Comedy Cellar, 117 MacDougal St. (254-3630), between W. 3rd St. and Bleecker St. Subway: A, B, C, D, E, F, or Q to W. 4th St. Subterranean annex of the artsy Olive Tree café. Dark, intimate, atmospheric, packing the people in late on early Saturday morning. Features rising comics like John Manfrellotti, established ones like George Wallace, and drop-ins by superstars like Robin Williams. Shows Sun.-Thurs. at 9pm-2am, Fri. at 9 and 11:30pm, Sat. at 9pm, 10:45pm, and 12:30am. Cover Sun.-Thurs. $5, plus 2-drink min.; Fri.-Sat. $10, plus $5 drink min. Make reservations on weekends.

Chicago City Limits, 351 E. 74th St. (772-8707), between First and Second Ave. Subway: #6 to 77th St. If you're looking for something a little different from the usual stand-up, check out New York's longest running comedy revue. Shows are careful syntheses of cabaret, scripted comedy sketches, and improvisation, often with a political bent. Extemporaneous skits are heavily dependent on audience suggestions for plot direction, allowing the crowd to get into the act. 4500 improvised performances already. No alcohol served. Shows Mon. and Wed.-Thurs. at 8:30pm, Fri.-Sat. at 8 and 10:30pm. Cover Mon. $10, Wed.-Thurs. $12.50, Fri.-Sat. $15. New Years Eve and Labor Day are big laff-a-thon nights.

Mostly Magic, 55 Carmine St. (924-1472), between Sixth and Seventh Ave. Subway: #1 or 9 to Houston St. Holograms decorate the walls of the restaurant out front. Sparse but appreciative crowd enjoys a superb fusion of comedy/magic vaudeville acts in the back. Open Tues.-Thurs. 6-11pm, Fri.-Sat. 6pm-1am. Shows Tues.-Thurs. at 9pm, Fri.-Sat. 9 and 11pm. Cover Tues.-Thurs. $10, plus $8 food or drink min.; Fri.-Sat. $15, plus $8 food or drink min. Children's magic matinees Sat. at 2pm for $10. Also open for lunch Sat.

Catch a Rising Star, 1487 First Ave. (794-1906), near 77th St. Subway: #6 to 77th St. No more a showcase of "rising stars" than any other comedy club. Yuppies laughing at themselves, mostly. Shows Sun.-Thurs. at 9pm, Fri. at 8:30 and 11pm, Sat. at 8pm, 10:15pm, and 12:30am. Cover Sun.-Thurs. $8, Fri.-Sat. $12. Two-drink min. for all shows. Make reservations before 5pm on previous day.

Stand Up NY, 236 W. 78th St. (595-0850) at Broadway. Subway: #1 or 9 to 79th St. Headliners from Carson, Letterman, Star Search, HBO, and Showtime dish out handsomely-appointed fun. Steven Wright tries out new material here on occasional visits. Shows Sun.-Thurs. at 9pm, Fri. at 9 and 11:30pm, Sat. at 8pm, 10:15pm, and 12:30am. In the summer there are also shows Sat. at 9 and 11:30pm. Cover Sun.-Thurs. $7, Fri.- Sat. $12. Two-drink min. for all shows.

The Comic Strip Inc., 1568 Second Ave. (861-9386), between 81st and 82nd St. Subway: #6 to 77th St. Sunday comics characters Dagwood and Dick Tracy line the walls of this well-established pub-style stand-up joint. Jim Morris honed his Reagan impressions here. Monday is audition night, when lucky wanna-bes who signed up the previous Friday are chosen by lottery for their brief moment in the spotlight. Shows Sun. 8:30pm, Mon.-Thurs. 9pm, Fri. 9 and 11pm, Sat. 8:30 and 10:30pm. No cover charge Mon. Sun. and Tues.-Thurs. $8 cover and 2 drink min., Fri. and Sat. $10 cover and 2 drink min. Make reservations.

Dangerfield's, 1118 First Ave. (593-1650), between 61st and 62nd St. Subway: #4, 5, or 6 to 59th St. or N, R to Lexington Ave. Rodney's respectable comic launching pad commands one of the heaviest covers and minimums in the city. Rising stars from throughout the country perform here, and HBO specials featuring the likes of Roseanne Barr, Sam Kinison, and Jerry Seinfeld have been taped at the club. Surprise guests appear now and then in addition to the scheduled lineup. Shows Sun.-Thurs. at 8:45pm, Fri. at 9 and 11:30pm, Sat. at 8pm, 10:30pm, and 12:30am. Cover Sun.-Thurs. $12.50, Fri.-Sat. $15.

The Boston Comedy Club, 82 W. 3rd St. (477-1000), between Thompson and Sullivan. Subway: A, B, C, D, E, F, or Q to W. 4th St. Coarse humor with a funny accent. Boston memorabilia everywhere. Shows Sun.-Thurs. at 9:30pm, Fri. at 9:30 and 11:30pm, Sat. at 10pm and midnight. Cover Sun.-Thurs. $5-7, Fri.-Sat. $10. Two-drink min.

Radio

Classic Rock: WBAB 102.3, WNEW 102.7, WRCN 103.9, WXRK 92.3
Top 40: WRKS 98.7, WHTZ 100.3, WBLS 107.5, WPLJ 95.5
Oldies: WCBS 101.1
Country: WYNY 103.5
Classical: WQXR 96.3, WNCN 104.3
Jazz: WJAZ 96.7, WBGO 88.3
News: WCBS 880AM, WINS 1010AM, WABC 770AM
Public Radio: WNYC 93.9, WBAI 99.5
Sports: WFAN 660AM

Rap shows tend to show up at night on stations like WRKS 98.7 or WBLS 107.5. Some of the most interesting programming is on the college stations between 89.1 and 90.5, where you'll find jazz, country, Latin, Caribbean, blues, classical, heavy metal, and underappreciated rock. WFMU 91.1 from Upsala College in New Jersey has amazing underground rock shows scattered generously through their programming, and WNYU 89.1 collects the best indie rock for its New Afternoon show (weekdays 4-7:30pm). WSOU 89.5 from Seton Hall specializes in heavy metal, and WXCR 89.9 from Columbia University fills the airwaves with an eclectic mix of non-rock.

Spectator Sports

While most cities would be content to field a major league team in each big-time sport, New York opts for the Noah approach: there are two baseball teams, two hockey teams, and two NFL football teams (although the Giants and Jets are now quartered across the river in New Jersey). In addition to local teams' regularly scheduled season games, New York hosts a number of celebrated world-class events like the New York Marathon and the United States Tennis Association Open. The city papers overflow with information on upcoming events.

Baseball

The national pastime thrives in New York from late March to early October, when two high-exposure teams make their exploits off the field almost as melodramatic as those on it. The **New York Mets** lost their slugging rightfielder Darryl Strawberry to the Los Angeles Dodgers, but remain the city's darlings, with stars like Dwight Gooden, Bobby Bonilla, and Howard "Hashbrown" Johnson. Watch them go to bat at Shea Stadium in Queens (718-507-8499). Tickets range from $6 for bleacher seats to $15 for lower box seats, although the better ones are often difficult to obtain. On promotion dates, sponsors give away baseball cards, action figures, wallets, helmets, banners, and other memorabilia. Avoid family days unless you really love screaming kids.

The legendary but mortal **New York Yankees** play ball at Yankee Stadium in the Bronx (293-6000). Now that idiosyncratic boss George Steinbrenner has been relieved of some of his duties, managers can breathe easier and fans can dream again of another dynasty, led this time by Don Mattingly, Mel "the Dashboard" Hall, and other sluggers. Plenty of tickets are usually available, from $5.50 for bleacher seats to $14.50 for lower box seats. On Family Day every Monday, the deserving brood can get half-priced seating.

Football

Though both New York teams once battled in the trenches at Shea Stadium, nowadays they play across the river at Giants Stadium in East Rutherford, New Jersey. The mighty **New York Giants** (201-935-3900) are looking for their third Super Bowl ring. Meanwhile, the **Jets** (526-538-7200), long seeking to return to the glory of the Namath years, rose from the basement to second in their division in 1991. Just where will they be in 1993? Tickets for the Jets start at $25, for the Giants, $26. The former are hard to come by; the latter nigh impossible, with a ten-year waiting list. During the spring, the New York/New Jersey Knights (644-1991) play in Giants Stadium against other teams from the NFL-backed World League of American Football. Tickets $12 and $16.

Basketball

After years of mediocrity, the **New York Knickerbockers** finally appeared to be a force in the NBA, winning the Eastern Conference title in 1989 with their best record since the dream 1971-72 season. Center Patrick Ewing decided not to skip town and instead led the Knicks to the conference semifinals in 1992. The Knicks do their dribbling at Madison Square Garden (465-6741 or 751-6130) from late fall to late spring; tickets, which start at $12, aren't too hard to get, except during the playoffs. On the college level, the second-tier N.I.T. and Big East collegiate tournaments take place at Madison Square Garden (465-6741) in March.

Hockey

In a town known for its speed and turbulence, it's not hard to understand why New Yorkers attend hockey games with such fervor. The **New York Rangers** play at Madison Square Garden (465-6741 or 308-6977) from late fall to late spring. Faithful fans have endured the 50 years since their Rangers last brought home the Stanley Cup. The team did make it to the division finals in 1992. Meanwhile, the **New York Islanders,** winners of four consecutive Stanley Cups in the early 80s, but now stranded near the bottom of the league, hang their skates at the Nassau Coliseum (516-794-9300) in Uniondale, Long Island. Tickets start at $12 for the Rangers and $14 for the Islanders.

Tennis

Tennis enthusiasts who get their tickets three months in advance can attend the prestigious **United States Open,** held in late August and early September at the United States Tennis Association's (USTA) Tennis Center in Flushing Meadows Park in Queens (718-271-5100). Tickets start at $12. The **Virginia Slims Championship**, featuring the world's top women players, comes to Madison Square Garden (465-6000) in mid-November. Tickets for the opening rounds start at $15.

Horseracing

Forsake the rat race for some equine excitement. Thoroughbred fans can watch the stallions go at **Belmont Park** (718-641-4700) every day except Tuesday, from May to July and September to mid-October, and may even catch a grand slam event. The Belmont Special leaves from Penn Station every twenty minutes from 9:45am to noon. ($7 round-trip, including $1 off admission.) Meanwhile, **Aqueduct Racetrack** (718-641-4700), next to JFK (take the A or C train to Aqueduct), has races from late October to early May, every day except Tuesday. Grandstand seating at both tracks costs $2. Racing in New York is suspended during the month of August when the action goes upstate to Saratoga.

Running

On the third Sunday in October, two million spectators line rooftops, sidewalks, and promenades to cheer 22,000 runners in the **New York City Marathon** (16,000 of whom actually finish). The race begins on Verrazano Bridge and ends at Central Park's Tavern on the Green.

Participatory Sports

Amateur and recreational athletes also do their thing here. Although space in much of the city is at a premium, the City of New York Parks and Recreation Department (360-8111) manages to maintain numerous playgrounds and parks in all boroughs, for everything from baseball and basketball to croquet and shuffleboard.

Swimming

Beaches

Coney Island Beach and Boardwalk (2 mi.), on the Atlantic Ocean, from W. 37th St. to Corbin Pl., in Brooklyn (718-946-1350). Subway: B, D, F, or N to Coney Island.

Manhattan Beach (quarter mi.), on the Atlantic Ocean, from Ocean Ave. to Mackenzie St. in Brooklyn (718-946-1373).

Orchard Beach and Promenade (1 1/4 mi.), on Long Island Sound in Pelham Bay Park, Bronx (885-2275). Subway: #6 to Pelham Bay Park.

Rockaway Beach and Boardwalk (7 mi.), on the Atlantic Ocean. From Beach 1st St., Far Rockaway, to Beach 149th St., Neponsit, Queens (718-318-4000). Subway: A, C, or H to any Beach St. stop.

Staten Island: South Beach, Midland Beach, and **Franklin D. Roosevelt Boardwalk** (2 mi.), on Lower New York Bay. From Fort Wadsworth to Miller Field, New Dorp. Take bus #51 from the ferry terminal.

Outdoor Pools

All pools, inside and out, open Memorial Day Through Labor Day from 11am to 7 or 8pm, depending on the weather.

Manhattan: Highbridge, Amsterdam Ave. and W. 173rd St. (397-3173); **Jackie Robinson,** Bradburst Ave. and W. 146th St. (397-3146); **Sheltering Arms,** Amsterdam Ave. and W. 129th St. (397-3126); **West 59th Street,** 533 W. 59th St. (397-3159); **Dry Dock,** E. 10th St. (397-3110), between Ave. C and D; **Carmine St.,** Clarkson St. and Seventh Ave. (397-3107).

Brooklyn: Betsy Head, Hopkinson and Dumont Ave. (718-965-6581); **Kosciuszko,** Marcy and DeKalb Ave. (718-965-6585); **Red Hook,** Bay and Henry St. (718-965-6579); **Sunset Park,** Seventh Ave. and 43rd St. (718-965-6578); **Commodore Barry,** Flushing Ave. and North Elliot Plaza (718-965-6584); **Douglass and De Graw,** Third Ave. and Nevins St. (718-625-3268).

Queens: Astoria, 19th St. and 23rd Dr. (718-626-8620); **Fisher,** 99th St. and 32nd Ave. (718-520-5375); **Liberty,** Liberty Ave. and 172nd St. (718-520-5354).

The Bronx: Claremont, E. 170th St. and Clay Ave. (822-4217); **Crotona,** E. 173rd St. and Fulton Ave. (822-4440); **Mullaly,** E. 165th St. and River Ave. (822-4343); **Van Cortlandt,** W. 242nd St. and Broadway (822-4222); **Haffen,** Ely and Hamsley Ave. (822-4176); **Mapes,** E. 180th St. and Mapes Ave. (822-4249).

Staten Island: Joseph L. Lyons, Pier 6 in Tomkinsville (718-816-9571); **Faber Park,** 2175 Richmond Terrace, Port Richmond (718-442-9613); **West Brighton,** Henderson Ave., between Broadway and Alaska St. (718-816-5507); **Tottenville,** 6960 Hylan Blvd. and Joline Ave. (718-356-8242).

Indoor Pools

Manhattan: Asser Levy, E. 23rd St. and Ave. A (447-2020); **Carmine Street,** Seventh Ave. South and Clarkson St. (397-3107); **East 54th Street,** 342 E. 54th St. (397-3154); **John Rozier Hansborough, Jr.,** 35 W. 134th St. (397-3134); **West 59th Street,** 533 W. 59th St. (397-3159).

Brooklyn: Brownsville (requires $10 membership), Linden Blvd. and Christopher St. (718-345-2706); **Metropolitan,** Bedford and Metropolitan Ave. (718-965-6541).

Queens: Roy Wilkins, 119th St. and Merrick Blvd. (718-276-4630).

Bicycling

From spring to fall, daily at dawn and dusk and throughout the weekend, packs of dedicated (and fashion-conscious) cyclists dressed in biking shorts navigate the trails and wide roads of Central Park. (The circular drive is car-free Mon.-Thurs. 10am-3pm and 7-10pm, and Fri. 7pm to Mon. 6am.) Over on the west side, along the Hudson bank, **Riverside Park** between 72nd and 110th draws more laid-back riders. Other excellent places to go on weekends include the deserted **Wall Street** area or the unadorned roads of Brooklyn's **Prospect Park.** For quick same-day excursions, plenty of bike shops around Central Park rent out two-wheelers by the hour (see Practical Information).

Bowling

There's only one place left for strikes and spares in Manhattan—the 44-lane **Bowlmor,** 110 University Pl. (255-8188), off 13th St. With such limited alley space, call ahead to check lane availability. ($3 per game each person; open Sun.-Thurs. 10am-1am, Fri.-Sat. 10am-4am.)

Golf

While New York golf courses don't quite measure up to those at Pebble Beach, New Yorkers nonetheless remain avid golfers, jamming all of the 13 well-manicured city courses during the weekends. Most are found in the Bronx or Queens, including **Pelham Bay Park** (885-1258), **Van Cortlandt Park** (543-4595), and **Forest Park** (718-296-0999).

Ice Skating

The first gust of cold winter air brings out droves of aspiring Brian Boitanos and Katarina Witts. While each of the rinks in the city has its own character, nearly all have lockers, skate rentals, and a snack bar. The most popular and expensive is the tiny sunken plaza in **Rockefeller Center,** Fifth Ave. and 50th St. (757-5730), which doubles as the chic American Festival Café during the spring and summer months. You can do your Bolero thing at the Donald Trumped **Wollman Memorial Rink** (517-4800), located in a particularly scenic section of Central Park near 64th St. The city's highest and largest year-round indoor skating spot is **Sky Rink,** 450 W. 33rd St. on the 16th floor (695-6555), between Ninth and Tenth Ave. Weekend crowds are unpredictable, so call in advance.

Jogging

In New York, joggers and cyclists go hand in hand—not exactly a harmonious combination. When running in **Central Park** during no-traffic hours (see Bicycling above), stay in the right-hand runner's lane to avoid being mowed down by some reckless pedalpusher. Despite the recent publicity about the assaulted jogger, crime in the park isn't as much of a problem as long as you stay in well-lit, populated areas. Avoid venturing beyond 96th St. unless you have a companion or are familiar with the route. Recommended courses include the 1.58 mile jaunt around the Reservoir and a picturesque 1.72 mile route starting at Tavern on the Green along the West Drive, heading south to East Drive, and then circling back west up 72nd St. to where you started. Another beautiful place to run is **Riverside Park,** which stretches along the Hudson bank from 72nd to 116th; don't stray too far north.

Cricket and Croquet

The two bastions of British civilization, cricket and croquet, are both played in this most un-English of cities. You won't see Ian Botham swinging his chunk of willow, but you can turn your arm over for a few overs of off-spin at **cricket fields** throughout the boroughs. Fields include: **Flushing Meadow-Corona Park** in Queens (call 718-520-5932 for permits); **Canarsie Beach Park** in Brooklyn (718-965-8919); and **Van Cortlandt Park** in the Bronx (430-1830).

For a quick dose of mallet and wicket, head to the croquet lawn in Central Park, north of Sheep Meadow (call 360-8133 for permits; open May-Nov.).

Shopping

At the Whitney Museum, you can buy a $60 canvas sack imprinted with a bold, constructivist message that reads "I Shop Therefore I Am." As Descartes would recognize, image is what sells in this City of Images, whether that image is an "I love Brooklyn" sweatshirt on the street or a Polo-emblazoned pair of socks from Ralph Lauren's believe-me-or-not *palazzo* on Madison.

Clothing

In SoHo, enormous **Canal Jean,** the original home of the surplus clinic, at 504 Broadway (226-1130), brims with neon ties, baggy pants, and silk smoking jackets. Fashion-conscious (public) high school students buy their black here. Poke around in the bargain bins out front. (Open Sun.-Thurs. 10am-8pm, Fri.-Sat. 10am-9pm.) On weekends, check out the flea market at the western end of Canal for honest-to-goodness antiques along with the usual funk junk. Back up Broadway, in Greenwich Village, the **Antique Boutique,** 712 Broadway (460-8830), near Astor Pl., sells both stunning vintage clothing and interesting new designs. (10% discount for students with ID. Open Mon.-Thurs. 10am-10pm, Fri.-Sat. 10am-midnight. Sun. noon8pm.) **Reminiscence,** 175 MacDougal St. (979-9440), may spark high school memories. But now it's even cheaper—most items under $10. (Branches at 109 Ave. B near 14th St. (353-0626) and 74 Fifth Ave. near 14th St. (243-2292); open Mon.-Sat. 11:30am-8pm, Sun. 1-6pm.)

At the very bottom of SoHo hover two relatively unknown stores with great bargains. **Three Wishes,** 355 W. Broadway (226-7570) above Canal St., sells lots of unusually-cut, quality women's clothes and chunky costume jewelry at bottom rates. (Open daily noon-7pm.) Close by **Debris,** 341 W. Broadway (941-1959), is a vintage store with a twist. Clothes are cleaned, sized, and categorized—making try-ons less frustrating. (Open daily 11am-9pm.) Check the market on the corner of Spring and

Wooster St. for clothes, handmade belts, jewelry, and hats; it's open in fair weather from late morning until sundown.

The garment district to the east packs outlets on Orchard St., from Houston to Grand St. The selection tends towards business dress, but hip items can be found. **Vectal,** 86 Rivington St. (674-7260) at Orchard, carries undamaged Betsey Johnson and Bob Mackie stuff at slashed prices (open daily 9:30am-6pm). Known for its large selection of cashmere, **Fishkin Knitwear Co.,** 314 and 318 Grand St. (226-6538), also carries Adrienne Vittadini and others at 30-50% markdowns.

Uptown, those with the stamina to burrow through mountains of clothes can find some amazing bargains at **Gabay's,** 225 First Ave. (254-3180) between 13th and 14th, which sells seconds from major New York department stores (open Mon.-Fri. 9am-5:30pm, Sat. 9am to 5pm, Sun. 10am-4pm). Go early: the best buys are gone by 11am. You can also find clothes and shoes of all descriptions, generally in very good condition, at the mammoth **Salvation Army** in Chelsea, on Eighth Ave. between 20th and 21st.

The shopping experience in the Upper West Side along Columbus Ave. is designed primarily for those with Roman numerals after their names. Hit the boutiques during the January and July sales. A few havens for the not-so-rich or famous do exist. Still a favorite of the young and hip is **Alice Underground,** 380 Columbus Ave. (724-6682) at 78th St. (also at 481 Broadway (431-9067)). Nothing more curious than a purring cat named Alice recalls the store's namesake. Alice Underground offers wonderful cummerbunds, bow ties, and silk dinnerjackets to give men that Bond, James Bond sheen. Women have choices galore, from chic to funk to Victorian. Enjoy pre-rock pop music of the 30s and 40s as you finger through the racks of dresses. (Open on Columbus, Sun.-Fri 11am-7pm, Sat. 11am-8pm; on Broadway daily 11am-7:30pm.) Daryl Hannah, Diane Keaton, and Annie Lenox stop at **Allan and Suzi,** 416 Amsterdam Ave. (724-7445) at 80th St. From new Gaultier Madonna-wear at 70% off to $40 original Pucci dresses, this store is cheap chic chaos. A large assortment of platform shoes surrounds the chaos. Swim among *mondains* in the world of the mundane. No men's clothes.

Across town, buy highfalutin' designer clothes second-hand at **Encore,** 1132 Madison at 82nd St. (879-2850; open Mon.-Wed. and Fri.-Sat. 10:30am-6pm, Thurs. 10:30am-7pm, Sun. 12:30-6pm), or at **Michael's,** on Madison (on the second floor) between 79th and 80th (737-7273; open in summer Mon.-Fri. 9:30am-6pm, otherwise Mon.-Sat.). For new designer clothes, head down to the two-story **Daffy's,** 335 Madison Ave. (557-4422) at 44th St., or 111 Fifth Ave. (529-4477) at 18th St. (Open Mon.-Fri. 9am-5pm, Sat. 10am-6pm, Sun. 11am-5pm.)

Department Stores and Malls

New York has more ritzy department stores than Beverly Hills. Start with the world's largest department store: "If you haven't seen **Macy's,** you haven't seen New York," proclaims the sign out front. You can eat breakfast, lunch, and dinner at Macy's, get a facial and a haircut, mail a letter, have your jewelry appraised, purchase theater tickets, and get lost. Of course, you can also shop. The colossus sits at 151 W. 34th St. (695-4400), between Broadway and Seventh (see Midtown Sights above). (Open Mon. and Thurs.-Fri. 10am-8:30pm, Tues.-Wed. and Sat. 10am-7pm, Sun. 11am-6pm.)

Courtly **Lord and Taylor,** 424 Fifth Ave. (391-3344), between 38th and 39th St., has made a specialty of stocking clothes by American designers, but its furniture department transcends the trendy with such *couture* classics as Henredon sofas, Chinese porcelain lamps, and reproductions of Louis XV tables. Scores of New Yorkers come to be shod at the legendary shoe department, and to be treated in Lord's manner: caring service, free coffee in the early morning, and unsurpassable Christmas displays. The first in history to use the picture window as a stage for anything other than merchandise, the store began this custom in 1905, during an unusually balmy December that had failed to summon the appropriate pre-Christmas meteorological garnish. Lord and Taylor filled its windows with mock storms and blizzards, reviving the Christmas spirit for the gloomy city-dwellers. (Open Mon. and Thurs. 10am-8:30pm, Tues.-Wed. and Fri.-Sat. 10am-6:30pm, Sun. noon-6pm.)

Also renowned for its window displays, **Barney's New York** (945-1600). The mother store, a 10,000-square-foot coliseum, overlooks the Hudson at 2 World Financial Center. Barney's features collections of sportswear, formal wear, shoes, and oh-so-fine shirts from Truzzi. (Open Mon.-Fri. 10am-7pm, Sat. 10am-6pm, Sun. noon-5pm.) Another outlet (929-9000) does business at Seventh Ave. and 17th St. (Open Mon.-Thurs. 10am-9pm, Fri. 10am-8pm, Sat. 10am-7pm; also Sept.-June Sun. noon-6pm.)

Saks Fifth Avenue, 611 Fifth Ave. (753-4000), between 49th and 50th St., is subdued and chic: this institution has aged well and continues to combine good taste with smooth courtesy. The perfume-sprayers are more restrained, although no less canny, than those in Bloomingdale's. Sales make the whole affair vaguely affordable. (Open Mon.-Wed. and Fri.-Sat. 10am-6:30pm, Thurs. 10am-8pm, Sun. noon-6pm.)

Bloomingdale's, 1000 Third Ave. (705-2000) at 59th St., affectionately known as Bloomie's, is a wild shopping adventure in the spirit of a safari. With show business pizazz, the store's buyers have scoured the markets of China, India, Israel, and the Philippines and returned with ideas for rugs, clothes, and furniture. The store also stocks Western classics by Yves Saint Laurent, Ralph Lauren, and Calvin Klein. The festive atmosphere borders on the chaotic, as walls of simulcasting televisions coo about products; perfume commandos squirt passersby, fumigator-style; and rakish music wafts amidst the scent of Giorgio. See the young and the spoiled congregate here on Sundays. Don't miss Petrossian, the czar of caviar, whose entire store pays homage to the fishy extravagance. (Open Mon.-Wed., Fri. 10am-6:50pm, Thurs. 10am-9pm, Sat. 10am-6:30pm, Sun. 11am-6pm.) Sit in luxury's lap at the legendary, extortionate **Bergdorf-Goodman** clothing mansion, where expensive people purchase pricey jewelry by the crystal light of chandeliers. 754 Fifth Ave. (753-7300), between 57th and 58th St. (Open Mon.-Wed. and Fri.-Sat. 1am-6pm, Thurs. 10am-8pm.)

If the name doesn't set you rolling, the smorgasbord of bizarre merchandise will; **Hammacher Schlemmer,** 157 E. 57th St. (421-9000), between Third and Lexington Ave., is a gadget fancier's fantasyland. Marvel at such essential items as a self-stirring French saucepan, a computerized fortune teller, and the Whiz Bang Popcorn Wagon. More redeemingly, Hammacher's zeal for automated convenience has also provided the world with the steam iron, electric razor, and pressure cooker. Masquerade as a serious consumer while test driving the floor models of the various massage machines. (Open Mon.-Sat. 10am-6pm.)

Abraham & Strauss (594-8500), the inventor of the vertical shopping mall, ascends to commodity heaven with eight levels of fashion, toys, electronics, and hard-to-find items. **A&S Plaza's** (Sixth Ave. and 33rd St.) colored lights and fantasy-land exterior appear to herald an amusement park—a first guess that's not far wrong. All is movement inside, with the silver escalators and the constant parade of humanity. Four glass elevators haloed in lightbulbs slide—apparently without support—up and down the walls, eliciting the same sinking will-I-make-it feeling as an advanced technology ferris wheel. The building has twisted itself into doughnut shape, so that the seven-story central atrium forms a space as vacuous as the shoppers who spend on its perimeters. The top level, called "Taste of the Town" is an international food court, an entire floor of noshing and funk. (Plaza open Mon. and Thurs.-Fri. 9:45am-8:30pm, Tues.-Wed. and Sat. 9:45am-6:45pm, Sun. 11am-6pm.)

As the Trump empire crumbles, to the celebratory crowing of righteous peoples everywhere, you may want to catch a glimpse of one of the tycoon's last major ostentations before it is bought by raiders and converted into condos. The **Trump Tower** (832-2000) gleams with marble and gold. Inside, a fountain of plenty climbs the walls of a six-story atrium of upmarket boutiques and restaurants. Capitalism is alive and well here, though slightly feverish. (Open Mon.-Sat. 10am-6pm, Atrium open daily 8am-6pm.)

At the **SoHo Emporium,** 375 Broadway (966-7895), between Broome and Spring St., some 25 independent boutiques vie tooth and claw with each other for your patronage. Everything goes on sale here, from furs and jewelry to crafts and crystal. A fortune teller on hand can help you define your most urgent shopping needs. (Open Mon.-Sun. noon-8pm.) Mall shopping on a global scale transpires daily at the 60 shops and restaurants in the concourse of the **World Trade Center** at West and Liberty St. (466-4170).

Specialty Stores

Want something special? Go to a specialty store.

Godiva Chocolatier, Inc., 560 Lexington Ave. (980-9810), between 50th and 51st St. Subway: #6 to 51st St., or E, F to Lexington/Third Ave. You'd think they were selling jewelry with all the mini-chandeliers and gold; instead, nuggets of chocolate repose in the glass cases. The rich substance has been molded to reproduce all forms of nature and all manner of corporate whims, like golfballs, tennis rackets, and cubist sculpture. Even if you don't buy it, come take a calorie-free look at the best-pressed chocolate in the world. Open Mon.-Sat. 10am-6pm.

The Erotic Baker, 582 Amsterdam Ave. (362-7557), between 88th and 89th St. Subway: #1 or 9 to 86th St. Decadent baked goods, shaped to approximate nature's designs. Some PG-13 baking too. Place custom orders 24 hr. in advance. Open Mon.-Thurs. 11am-7pm, Fri.-Sat. 11am-8pm.

The Last Wound-Up, 1595 Second Ave. (529-4197) between 83rd and 84th St. If you can wind it, you'll find it here. Egg-laying chickens, ambulatory elephants, bouncing genitals, and rolling eyeballs. Wind-up basketballs, baseballs, and footballs. Demure turn-of-the-century music boxes and disk music boxes grind their way through oldie tunes. The NY Press voted it the "Best One-Stop Toy Store" in the city. Open Mon.-Thurs. 10am-7pm, Fri.-Sat. 10am-10pm, Sun. 11am-6pm.

Rita Ford Music Boxes, 19 E. 65th St. (535-6717), between Madison and Fifth Ave. Subway: #6 to 68th St. Wind them up and hear them go. Dappled stallions surge up and down as tiny lanterns glow. Mostly figurines, fastidious and delicate, but Daffy Duck and Mickey Mouse for the less Victorian. Open Mon.-Sat. 9am-5pm.

Mythology Unlimited, 370 Columbus Ave. (874-0774), between 77th and 78th St. Subway: B or C to 81st St. A weird potpourri of rubber stamps, tin soldiers, old postcards, art books, and antique toys for occultists of all ages. A loyal following. Open Mon.-Sat. 11am-11pm, Sun. 11am-6pm.

Maxilla & Mandible, Ltd., 451-5 Columbus Ave. (724-6173) between 81st and 82nd St. Shelves and boxes of well-displayed shells, fossils, eggs, preserved insects, and most of all, bones from every imaginable vertebrate (including *Homo sapiens*). A giant walking stick insect under glass, an 11-foot alligator skeleton, and a $350 human spinal column stand out prominently among the merchandise; malachite-colored jewel beetles "for the kids" $9. Caters to international collectors. Macabre but neato—Nell's favorite store on the East Coast. Open Mon.-Sat. 11am-7pm, Sun. 1-5pm.

The Ballet Shop, 1887 Broadway at 62 St. (581-7990). LPs, CDs, photographs, books, posters, and memorabilia related to ballet. Open Mon.-Sat. 11am-7pm; during ballet season, also open Sun. noon-5pm.

The Soldier Shop, 1222 Madison Ave. (535-6788). Subway: #4, 5, or 6 to 86th St. If you dream in battle formations, you've met your match. If not, salute boredom. The humble tin soldier brings in a lot of business here. Painted little infantrymen of all times and empires march, fire, bang drums, and play the fife throughout the store. Wall-to-wall bookshelves stocked with military memoirs, battle and campaign accounts, and histories of conquest. Weapons and military regalia complete the martial ensemble. Mon.-Fri. 10am-6pm, Sat. 10am-5pm.

Dollhouse Antics, 1343 Madison Ave. (876-2288) at 94th St. Subway: #6 to 96th St. First-class doll real estate plus most mundanities miniaturized: coffee sets, Scrabble boards, toilets, napkins, and tables covered by artfully stitched baby tablecloths. Come to start a collection or just to feel like Gulliver. Mon.-Fri. 11am-5:30pm, Sat. 11am-5pm; July-Aug. closed Sat. and Mon.; in Dec., also open Sun.

Mouse 'N Around Too, 901 Sixth Ave., 7th floor, at the A&S Plaza (947-3954), between 32nd and 33rd St. Subway: B, D, F, N, Q, N, or R to 34th St. Favorite latter-day cartoon greats march off the screen and onto every imaginable merchandizable surface. Mickey imitates Dan Quayle on the clocks, Bugs Bunny docs on shirtfronts and telephones, and Betty Boop does her Marilyn impressions on beach towels. The biggest collection of cartoon watches outside the Disney research labs. Open Mon. and Thurs.-Fri. 9:45am-8:30pm, Tues.-Wed. and Sat. 9:45am-6:45pm, Sun. noon-6pm.

Economy Candy, 108 Rivington St. (254-1531). Imaginatively named store purveys sugar in all its most attractive forms. Imported chocolates, jams, oils, and spices, plus countless bins of confections, all at rock bottom prices. Open Sun.-Fri. 8:00am-6pm, Sat. 10am-5pm.

Little Rickie, 49 First Ave. (505-6467) at 3rd St. Subway: F to Second Ave. Collectible off-beat cultural icons, like topical Pee Wee Herman decals, Madonna tapestries, and Elvis lamps. With both ant farms and Mexican day-of-the-dead statues, this is the only place that really de-livers. Open Mon.-Sat. 11am-8pm, also in summer Sun. noon-7pm.

Tiffany & Co, 727 Fifth Ave. (755-8000), between 56th and 57th St. Subway: E or F to Fifth Ave. So revered for its high-quality jewelry that many of its wares sit in permanent exhibits of museums. Strings of pearls, diamonds, and emeralds draped gracefully in gleaming white cas-es. Gaze at creations by Elsa Peretti and precocious Paloma Picasso. Check out the windows, especially at Christmas time. Open Mon.-Sat. 10am-5:30pm.

Tender Buttons, 143 E. 62nd St. (758-7004), between Third and Lexington Ave. Subway: #4, 5, or 6 to 59th St. or N, R to Lexington Ave. A treasure-trove of billions of buttons, fashioned from materials ranging from lucite to taqua nut to abalone to silver. If you carelessly lost the button on your favorite Renaissance doublet, you will find a replacement here. Fork out $1000 for a button off of one of George Washington's coats. Open Mon.-Fri. 11am-6pm, Sat. 11am-5pm.

Connoisseur Pipe Shop, 1285 Sixth Ave. (247-6054) at 51st St., on the Concourse level of the PaineWebber building. Subway: B, D, F, or Q to 47-50th St. A selection of graceful and gen-tlemanly pipes, some subdued, some flamboyant, with all flavors of tobacco. Owner Edward Burak makes his pipes by hand, using unstained and unvarnished woods. His pieces have been displayed in MoMA, The American Craft Museum, and 12 European museums. Prices start at $27.50; a personal pipe "sculpture" fetches $4000. Open Mon.-Fri. 8am-6pm.

J.J. Hat Center Inc., 1276 Broadway (502-5012) at 33rd St. Subway: B, D, F, N, Q, or R to 34th St. Fedoras, stetsons, caps, and homburgs to cover your noggin. Swing out of there with your own Indiana Jones number. Open Mon.-Sat. 8:45am-5:45pm.

Bird Jungle, 401 Bleecker St. (242-1757) at 11th St. Subway: #1 or 9 to Christopher St. Col-orful, gregarious parrots fly around the shop window, schmoozing with passersby. (They're not dead.) Take home domestically-bred rainforest birds from ordinary canaries to the $10,000 Hy-acinth Macaw. Open Mon.-Fri. 12:30-6:30pm, Sat. 11am-6:30pm, Sun. 11am-5:30pm.

Just Cats, 244 E. 60th St. between Second and Third Ave. Instead of ringing like a bell, the door skreeks "meow" when you walk in. Cat pets, cat clocks, cat figurines, cat rocks, and the fancy mechanized tail-waving, meow-saying kind. Large rhinestone pin saying "Purrfect" only $25. (Open Mon.-Sat. 10am-6pm.)

Record Stores

If you're not the scrounge-and-search type, go straight to **Tower Records,** 692 Broadway (505-1500) at E. 4th St. This one-stop music emporium, nearly a block long with four full floors of merchandise, is one of the largest on the East Coast. Gadgets like the music video computer let you preview select songs before purchasing them, while a touch-screen store directory makes tracking down that elusive album by your favorite mainstream artist a cinch. (Open daily 9am-midnight; Subway: #6 to Bleecker St.)

For those music enthusiasts on the lookout for more obscure titles or labels, at least a dozen smaller stores can be found around Tower Records in the East Village and roundabout Bleecker St. in the West Village. Though they may lack the stock and or-ganization of larger stores, many of these places specialize in hard-to-find alternative rock imports, dance remixes, rare oldies, and the insurgent 7" single. Several of these smaller stores also sell used records, cassettes, and CDs at bargain prices. Perserver-ance pays off in this city; if you can't find what you want here, you're probably not looking hard enough.

Your first stop should be **Pier Platters,** 56 Newark St. (201-795-4785), in Hoboken. (Subway: B, D, F, N, Q, or R to 34th St., then the PATH train ($1) to the first stop in Hoboken. Walk up Hudson St. one block, then left on Newark St.) The store features the best alternative rock selection in the greater New York City area, if not the Western hemisphere; celebrated members of the musical underground shop here regularly, perusing the incredibly extensive, high-quality collection of rare singles and full-length records, with an emphasis on independent releases from the U.S. and New Zealand. **Pier Platters CDs** (201-795-9015), down the adjacent alley behind this store, features an equally comprehensive selection of CDs. Both stores open Mon.-Sat. 11am-9pm, Sun. noon-8pm.

Kim's Underground, 144 Bleecker St. (260-1010), 2 blocks west of Broadway. Subway: A, B, C, D, E, F, or Q to West 4th St. Mostly a tremendous video showcase specializing in foreign films (organized by director's surname), the rear of the store contains a small, startlingly strong selection of independent and import CDs for almost reasonable prices. Also carries a few contemporary 7" releases. Occasionally hosts small concerts in-store. Open daily 10am-midnight.

The Record Hunter, 507 Fifth Ave. (697-8970) at 42th St. Subway: #7 to Fifth Ave. or E, F to 53rd St. Frequent and substantial discounts on CDs and cassettes. Large inventory of major label titles, from rock to jazz to classical music. Best bargains on older titles, as low as $6 per CD. Open Mon.-Sat. 9am-6:30pm. Sun. 11am-6pm.

Sounds, 20 St. Mark's Pl. (677-3444), between Second and Third Ave. Subway: #6 to Astor Pl. CD & Cassette Annex at 16 St. Mark's Pl. (677- 2727). Good fair-priced selection of alternative and dance music. Used CD folders offer the best values. Racks of used LPs. New CDs $9-13, used ones $5-9. They'll pay cash for used CDs, up to 50% of their resale value. Open Mon.-Thurs. noon-10pm, Fri.-Sat. noon-11pm, Sun. noon-9pm.

Rebel Rebel, 319 Bleecker St. (989-0770), between Grove and Christopher St. Subway: #1 or 9 to Christopher St. A small store specializing in British Top-40 and dance imports; LPs, CDs, and 7" singles. Rare stuff. Open Sun.-Thurs. 12:30-8pm, Fri.-Sat. 12:30-9pm.

Disc-O-Rama, 186 W. 4th St. (206-8417), between Sixth and Seventh Ave. Subway: #1, 9 to Christopher St. or A, B, C, D, E, F, or Q to W. 4th St. Cheap popular albums. Upstairs, album CDs from Billboard's Top-30 are $10. Small sections for classic rock, alternative rock, and import labels. Downstairs, vinyl city stacks house and R&B singles for $4 and all kinds of used LPs for $3-5. Open daily 11am-10:30pm.

Midnight Records, 263 W. 23rd St. (675-2768), between Seventh and Eighth Ave. Subway: #1, 9 or C, E to 23rd St. The world's largest rock mail-order service; also a retail store. Posters plaster the walls; every last mildewy nook is crammed with records—over 10,000 in stock. Prices aren't cheap, but if you're looking for the Prats' album, *Disco Pope,* this may be the only place to find it. Lots of 60s and 70s LPs. Most LPs $9-20. Open Tues.-Sat. noon-8pm.

Vinyl Mania, 43 Carmine St. (463-7120) near Bleecker St. and Sixth Ave. Subway: A, B, C, D, E, F, or Q to W. 4th St. Carries import and domestic rock, a small jazz collection, and the latest in club, house, and rap. Open Mon.-Fri. noon-9pm, Sat.-Sun. 11am-7pm.

Revolver Records, 45 W. 8th St. on the 2nd floor (982-6760), between Fifth and Sixth Ave. Subway: A, B, C, D, E, F, or Q to W. 4th St. From Deep Purple to Guns-N-Roses, this place specializes in guitar rock through the decades, whether classic, metal, or thrash. New releases are mostly American metal. Bargains on non-metal items that slip through the cracks. Also a large collection of bootlegs and books on Elvis and The Beatles. Open Sun.-Thurs. 11am-10pm, Fri.-Sat. 11am- midnight.

Music Factory, 1476 Broadway (221-1488), between 42nd and 43rd St. in Times Square. Subway: #1, 2, 3, 7, 9, N, R, or S to Times Sq. Straight from the pages of C&C, this joint deals primarily in rap, house, R&B, and special extended remixes heard at many popular night spots. Open Mon.-Thurs. 10am-7:30pm, Fri.-Sat.10am-9:30pm.

Smash Compact Discs, 33 St. Mark's Pl. (473-2200), between Second and Third Ave. Subway: #6 to Astor Pl. Come here if you can't find a 60s or classic rock album at Sounds. Used CDs $8. Open Mon.-Wed. 11am- 10pm, Thurs. 11am-11pm, Fri.-Sat. 11am-midnight, Sun, noon-10pm.

Rocks in Your Head, 157 Prince St. (475-6729), between Thompson and West Broadway. Subway: C or E to Spring St. Yet another one of the many alternative rock/import record stores in the area. Average prices. They buy used vinyl and CDs: $4 for selected CDs, $1.50 per LP, $1 per 12 inch single. Used CDs $8 and LPs $5 worth a quick browse. Open Mon.-Thurs. 1-8pm, Fri. 1-10pm, Sat. noon-10pm., Sun. noon-8pm.

Gryphon Record Shop, 251 W. 72nd St., #2F (874-1588) near West End Ave. A second-floor apartment with walls, tables, and crates of classical LPs, many rare or out-of-print. Real collector atmosphere; proprietor seems to have the knowledge to match. Open Mon.-Sat. 11am-7pm, Sun. noon-6pm.

Bleecker St. Jazz, 237 Bleecker St. (255 7899). Basement full of jazz LPs; street-level full of rock, reggae, country, and "oldies." Not an especially discriminating selection, but there are so many LPs that there's probably something here you've been seeking. Some bootlegs. Open Mon.-Sat. 11:30am-6:15pm, Sun. 1-5:30pm.

Electronics

Amps, CD players, cameras, tape decks, VCRs—you name it, New York sells it for less. Every other block has a combo camera/electronics/luggage store. With few exceptions, avoid these tourist traps; the salesmen will likely sell you something you'll regret buying. When dealing with equipment costing several hundred dollars or more, make sure you're getting the best possible merchandise for your money, since no one likes to spend more than they have to. Try to stick to new goods with original manufacturer's American warranties.

To eliminate most hassles, shop at two of the bigger and more reputable electronics stores in NYC: **The Wiz** and **J & R Music World.** Recently, The Wiz has been publicizing their long-held but formerly obscure policy of matching advertised competitors' prices. They proudly proclaim that "Nobody Beats The Wiz" and then dare you to find a lower-priced ad on anything sold in their stores. If you find a valid ad, they'll beat it, and return 10% of the price difference. Take them up on that price challenge. Get hold of the Sunday *New York Times* or the latest copy of the *Village Voice.* In both, you'll find ads from 6th Ave. Electronics City and Uncle Steve, two stores that consistently beat The Wiz's prices. In Manhattan, The Wiz locations include 337 Fifth Ave. (684-7600), on 33rd St. opposite the Empire State Building; 871 Sixth Ave. (594-2300), off 31st St.; 12 W. 45th St. (302-2000), between Fifth and Sixth; and 17 Union Sq. West (741-9500), at the corner of 15th St.

J & R Music World, 23 Park Row, near City Hall; take #4,5,or 6 to City Hall (732-8600; open Mon.-Sat. 9am-6:30pm, Sun. 11am-6pm), will also meet most of your electronic needs. Though there is no price protection plan, prices tend to be competitive.

Bookstores

Whether your taste runs to European fine art or Third World revolution, whether you seek a Serbo-Croatian dictionary or a first-edition copy of Freud's *On the Interpretation of Dreams,* Manhattan is the island for you. Barnes and Noble (897-0099), B. Dalton (674-8780), Doubleday (397-0550), and Waldenbooks (269-1139) have a number of hard-to-avoid stores throughout the city. These chains sell current best-sellers for good prices. If the books you want are harder to find, you can try either one of the larger shops like the Strand (over two million volumes) or a specialized shop like Murder Ink. (See listings.)

General Interest

Strand, 828 Broadway (473-1452) at 12th St. Subway: #4, 5, 6, L, N, or R to 14th St. New York's biggest and most-loved used book store. A must-see. Eight miles of shelf space holding nearly 2 million books. Staffers will search out obscure titles at your bidding. Ask to see a catalog, or better yet, get lost in the shelves on your own. The best of the best. (Be prepared to sweat in the summertime as they don't have A/C.) Open Mon.-Sat. 9:30am- 9:30pm, Sun. 11am-9:30pm.

Gotham Book Mart, 41 W. 47th St. (719-4448). Subway: B, D, F, or Q to Rockefeller Center. Legendary, venerable bookstore selling new and used volumes. Largest selection of contemporary poetry in the city, huge stock of drama, art, and literary journals. Upstairs an art gallery hosts changing exhibitions. Open Mon.-Fri. 9:30am-6:30pm, Sat. 9:30am-6pm.

Books and Company, 939 Madison Ave. (737-1450), between 74th and 75th St. Subway: #6 to 77th St. Excellent selection of literature, criticism, and literary periodicals. Friendly and knowledgeable staff. Open Mon.-Sat. 10am-6pm, Sun. noon-5pm.

Endicott Book Sellers, 450 Columbus Ave. (787-6300), between 81st and 82nd St. Subway: B or C to 81st St. Carpeted and wood-paneled. Lounge on the couch in the back room as you browse and skim. Mostly modern literature. Open Sun.-Mon. noon-8pm, Tues.-Sat. 10am-9pm.

Shakespeare & Company, 2259 Broadway (580-7800) at 81st St. Subway: #1 or 9 to 79th St. A decent selection of new and travel books, but no chairs or space for browsing. Open Sun.-Thurs. 10am-11:15pm, Fri.-Sat. 10am-12:15am.

St. Mark's Bookshop, 12 St. Mark's Pl. (260-7853) at Third Ave. Subway: #6 to Astor Pl. Small shop with a great selection of leftist journals, poetry, and very hip new releases. The ultimate East Village bookstore. Open daily 11am-11:30pm.

Burlington Book Shop, 1082 Madison Ave. (288-7420) at 81st St. Subway: #6 to 77th St. Charming neighborhood shop with new and out-of-print books. Great staff knows what's worth reading, so don't be shy about asking for advice. Open Mon.-Fri. 9:30am-6pm, Sat. 10am-6pm, Sun. noon-5pm.

Barnes & Noble, 107 5th Ave. (897-0099), at W. 18th Street. Although part of a chain, this store began it all. With the distinction of being the "biggest bookstore in the world" you'll find tons of titles. This store compares well with both Shakespeare and Coliseum bookstores. Open Mon.-Fri. 9:30am-7:45pm, Sat. 9:30am-6:15pm, and Sun. 11am-5:45pm.

Barnes & Noble Bargain Annex, 128 5th Ave. (633-3500), across from the main store. Great for browsing, this store has an often odd and sometimes remarkable collection of seconded and used books. Be prepared to spend time looking through the stacks and piles of texts. There's an entire room of bargain scholarly books. Same hours as the main store.

Rizzoli, 31 W. 57th St. (759-2424), between Fifth and Sixth Ave. Subway: B or Q to 57th St. Beautiful, with many discounted old prints. Open Mon.-Sat. 9am-8pm, Sun. noon-8pm.

Ruby's Book Sale, 119 Chambers St. (732-8676) at W. Broadway. Subway: #1, 2, 3, 9, A, or C to Chambers St. You might have a lot of trouble finding something specific, but if you're looking for nothing in particular you'll find it very cheap. Great old magazines. Open Mon.-Fri. 10am-6pm, Sat. 10am-5:30pm.

Gryphon, 2246 Broadway (362-0706), between 80th and 81st St. Subway: #1 or 9 to 79th St. Small and homey, with used books and records. Excellent annex with wider selection and lower prices at 246 W. 80th St., just 1 block down off Broadway, on the 4th floor. The Annex has the philosophy, lit-crit, and social science holdings. The main store is almost exclusively fiction and art. Open daily 10am-midnight.

Spring St. Books, 169 Spring St. (219-3033) near W. Broadway. Subway: C or E to Spring St. Casual; lots of periodicals. Open Mon.-Fri. 10am-11pm, Sat. 10am-1am, Sun. 11am-9pm.

Coliseum Books, 1771 Broadway (757-8381) at 57th St. Subway: #1, 9, A, B, C, or D to 59th St. A big bookdom with a little of everything. Browser unfriendly: new releases are wrapped in plastic and untouchable. Open Mon. 8am-10pm, Tues.-Thurs. 8am-11pm, Fri. 8am-11:30pm, Sat. 10am-11:30pm, Sun. noon-8pm.

Specialty Books

Pageant Print and Book Shop, 109 E. 9th St. (674-5296). Subway: L to Third Ave. Promises hours of pleasurable browsing among its wide selection of fine books and prints. Open Mon.-Thurs. 10am-7pm, Fri. 10am-8pm, Sat. 11am-7:30pm.

Argosy Bookstore, 116 E. 59th St. (753-4455). Subway: #4, 5, 6 to 59th St. or N, R to Lexington Ave. Hoards rare and used books, along with modern first editions, autographed editions, and medical books. Open Mon.-Fri. 9am-5:30pm.

Applause Theater and Cinema Books, 211 W. 71st St. (496-7511) at Broadway. Subway: #1, 2, 3, or 9 to 72nd St. Great selection of scripts, screenplays, and books on everything from John Wayne to tap dancing. Over 4000 titles. Open Mon.-Sat. 10am-6pm, Sun. noon-6pm.

Drama Bookshop, 723 Seventh Ave. (944-0595) at 48th St. Subway: #1 or 9 to 50th St. New York's most extensive bookstore on the theater. Sheer joy for theater people. Open Mon.-Fri. 9:30am-7pm, Sat. 10:30am-5:30pm, Sun. noon-5pm.

Skyline Books & Records, 13 W. 18th Street (675-4773), off of 5th Ave. Although the size of a large walk-in closet, this bookstore has an excellent selection of poetry, philosophy, movie books, and country music records. Open Mon.-Sat. 9:30am-9pm. Sun. 11am-7pm.

Academy Books, 26 W. 18th Street (242-4848), across the street from Skyline. This is Skyline's sister store and has a large selection of art books, used CDs, video tapes, and classical records. Open Mon.-Sat. 9:30am-9pm, Sun. 11am-7pm.

The Complete Traveller Bookstore, 199 Madison Ave. (685-9007) at 35th St. Lots of books about places you probably haven't visited. Possibly the widest selection of guidebooks on the Eastern seaboard. The perfect place to get your second copy of *Let's Go,* when some well-informed thief steals the first. Open Mon.-Fri. 9am-7pm, Sat. 10am-6pm, Sun. noon-5pm.

Biography Bookstore, 400 Bleecker St. (807-8655) at W. 11th St. Subway: #1 or 9 to Christopher St. Rediscover your previous incarnations. Biography browsing at its best. Open Mon.-Fri. noon-8pm, Sat. noon-10pm, Sun. noon-6pm.

Murder Ink, 2486 Broadway (362-8905), between 92nd and 93rd St. Subway: #1, 2, 3, or 9 to 96th St. New and used, happily cluttered. Mystery everywhere. Open Mon.-Wed. 10am-7pm, Thurs., Fri. 10am-9pm.

Kitchen Arts and Letters, 1435 Lexington Ave. (876-5550) at 93rd St. Subway: #6 to 96th St. Playground for the budding chef. Hundreds of new and out-of-print cookbooks, plus books on wine, cheese, and mushrooms. Equally delicious photographs and prints. Open Mon. 1-6pm, Tues.-Fri. 10am-6:30pm, Sat. 11am-6pm.

The Dictionary Store, 115 Fifth Ave. (673-7400) at 19th St. Subway: R to 23rd St. Start at aardvark and work your way through. Relief for problem spellers in over three dozen languages. Open Mon.-Sat. 10am-6pm.

A Photographer's Place, 133 Mercer St. (431-9358), between Prince and Spring St. Subway: R to Prince St. Photographic books, photo this and photo that. Open Mon.-Sat 11am-6pm, Sun. noon-5pm.

Revolution Books, 13 E. 16th St. (691-3345), off Fifth Ave. Subway: #4, 5, 6, L, N, or R to 14th St. Ironically one of the most successful chains of independent booksellers, a real entrepreneur in books on Marx, Mao, and Martin Luther King, Jr. Open Mon.-Sat. 10am-7pm, Sun. noon-5pm.

A Different Light Bookstore, 548 Hudson St. (989-4850) at Charles St. Subway: #1 or 9 to Christopher St. Catering specifically to the West Village gay community with books, t-shirts, and an active bulletin board. Open Sun.-Thurs. 11am-9pm, Fri.-Sat. 11am-11pm.

Oscar Wilde Memorial Bookstore, 15 Christopher St. (255-8097) at Gay St. Subway: #1 or 9 to Christopher St. Stocks a wide selection of books by, for, and about gay men. Open Sun.-Fri. noon-7:30pm, Sat. 11am-8pm.

Judith's Room, 681 Washington Pl. (727-7330) at Charles St. Subway: #1 or 9 to Christopher St. A bookstore by, for, and about women (gay and straight). Large selection of non-sexist and non-hetero-sexist children's books. Open Mon.-Thurs. noon-8pm, Fri.-Sat. noon-10pm, Sun. noon-7pm.

Pathfinder Books, 191 Seventh Ave. (727-8421), between 21st & 22nd St. Small Trotskyite bookstore with an esoteric and sometimes provocative selection of political tracts, from book-length interviews with Fidel to the complete works of Marx and Engels and Trotsky. A must for all failed revolutionaries. Open Mon., Tues., Thurs. noon-3pm and 5:30-8:30pm, Wed., Fri., Sat. 5:30-8:30pm.

Hacker Art Books, 45 W. 57th St. (688-7600), between Fifth and Sixth Ave. Subway: B or Q to 57th St. A multi-lingual den of texts on fine and applied art. Buy coffee-table covers here. Open Mon.-Fri. 9am-6pm.

Forbidden Planet, 227 E. 59th St. (751-4386) or 821 Broadway (473- 1576) at W. 12th St. Science fiction and fantasy buffs will go into orbit over the selection of new and out-of-print titles. Cool toys and a huge selection of sci-fi comic books dating from the 1920s. Open Mon.-Wed., Sat. 10-7pm, Thurs.-Fri. 10am-7:30pm, Sun. noon-7pm.

Pomander Bookshop, 955 West End Ave. (866-1777) at Broadway and 108th St. Cozy used bookstore with a booksearch service and a cute, if hyperactive, collie. Open daily 11am-9pm.

Daytripping from NYC

*This city drives me crazy, or, if you prefer, crazier;
and I have no peace of mind or rest of body till I get
out of it.*

—Lafcadio Hearn, 1889

Atlantic City

The riches-to-rags-to-riches tale of Atlantic City began half a century ago when the beachside hotspot was tops among resort towns. Vanderbilts and Girards graced the boardwalk that inspired *Monopoly*, the Depression-era board game for coffee-table high rollers. Fans of the game will jizz to see the real Boardwalk and Park Place they've squabbled over for years. But the opulence has faded. With the rise of competition from Florida resorts, the community chest closed. Atlantic City suffered decades of decline, unemployment, and virtual abandonment.

In 1976, state voters gave Atlantic City a reprieve by legalizing gambling. Casinos soon rose out of the rubble of Boardwalk. Those who enter soon forget the dirt and dank outside, especially since the managers see to it that you need never leave. Each velvet-lined temple of tackiness has a dozen restaurants, big-name entertainment, even skyways connecting it to other casinos. The chance to win big draws everyone to Atlantic City, from international jet-setters to seniors clutching plastic coin cups. One-quarter of the U.S. population lives within 300 miles of Atlantic City, and fortune-seeking foreigners flock to its shore to toss the dice. Budgeteers can even take a casino-sponsored bus from Manhattan—pay $15 for the trip and get it all back in quarters upon arrival. How can you lose?

Practical Information

Emergency: 911.

Visitor Information: Public Relations Visitors Bureau, 2308 Pacific Ave. (348-7100), conveniently located near Mississippi Ave. Open Mon.-Fri. 9am-4:30pm. Just next door is the **Atlantic City Convention and Visitors Bureau,** 2310 Pacific Ave. (348-7100 or 800-262-7395), home of the Miss America pageant. Open Mon.-Fri. 9am-5pm. There is also a booth on Boardwalk at Mississippi Ave.; personal assistance daily 10am-6pm; leaflets available 24 hrs.

Pamona Airport: 800-428-4322. Serves Washington, Philadelphia, and New York.

Amtrak: (800-872-7245) at Kirkman Blvd. off Michigan Ave. Follow Kirkman to its end, bear right, and follow the signs. To: New York City (1 per day, 2 1/2 hr., $28); Philadelphia (2 per day, 1 1/2hr., $13); Washington, DC (2 per day, 3 1/2hr., $40). More connections to DC and NYC through Philly. Open Sun.-Fri. 9:30am-7:40pm, Sat. 9:30am-10pm.

Buses: Greyhound, 971-6363 or 344-4449. Buses every hr. to New York (2 1/2hr., $19) and Philadelphia (1 1/4hr., $9). **New Jersey Transit,** 609-348-7130. Runs 6am-10pm. Hourly service to New York City ($21.50) and Philadelphia ($10), with connections to Ocean City ($1.50), Cape May ($3.50), and Hammonton ($3.25). Also runs along Atlantic Ave. (base fare $1). Both lines operate from **Atlantic City Municipal Bus Terminal,** Arkansas and Arctic Ave. Open 24 hrs. Both offer casino-sponsored round-trip discounts, including cash back on arrival in Atlantic City. In Manhattan, go to a local pharmacy and ask where you can buy bus tickets to Atlantic City. Bally's has a particularly good deal—you get your full fare ($15) back in quarters upon arrival.

Pharmacy: Parkway, 2838 Atlantic Ave. (345-5105), 1 block from TropWorld. Delivers locally and to the casinos. Open Mon.-Fri. 9am-7pm, Sat. 9am-6pm, also July-Aug. Sun. 10am-4pm.

Hospital: Atlantic City Medical Center (344-4081), at the intersection of Michigan and Pacific Ave.

Bookstore: Atlantic City News and Book Store (344-9444), at the intersection of Pacific and Illinois Ave. Most comprehensive collection of gambling strategy literature east of Las Vegas. Buy with your head, not over it. Open 24 hrs.

Help Line: Rape and Abuse Hotline, 646-6767. 24-hr. counseling, referrals, and accompaniment.

Post Office: Martin Luther King and Pacific Ave. (345-4212). Open Mon.-Fri. 8:30am-5pm, Sat. 10am-noon. **ZIP code:** 08401.

Area Code: 609.

Atlantic City lies about half-way down New Jersey's coast, accessible via the **Garden State Parkway,** and easily reached by train from Philadelphia and New York. Hitching is not recommended—in fact, in these parts it's exceptionally stupid.

Gamblers' specials make bus travel a cheap, efficient way to get to Atlantic City. Many casinos will give the bearer of a bus ticket receipt $10 in cash and sometimes a free meal. Specials change frequently, depending on business and season, although Trump seems unusually generous these days. Deals are hard to miss at any bus station, tourist info center, or casino lobby. Look for deals in the Yellow Pages under "Bus Charters" in New Jersey, New York, Pennsylvania, Delaware, and Washington, DC. Also check the Arts and Entertainment section of the *New York Times.*

Getting around Atlantic City is easy on foot. The casinos pack tightly together on the Boardwalk along the beach. When your winnings become too heavy to carry, you can hail a **Rolling Chair,** quite common along the Boardwalk. Though a bit of an investment ($1 per block for 2 people, 5-block min.), Atlantic City locals or erudite foreign exchange students chat with you while they push. The less exotic and less expensive **yellow tram** runs continuously for $1.25. On the streets, catch a **jitney** ($1.25), running 24 hrs. up and down Pacific Ave., or a NJ Transit Bus ($1) covering Atlantic Ave.

Accommodations and Camping

Large, red-carpeted beachfront hotels have bumped smaller operators out of the game. Expect to pay a hundred bucks for a single. Smaller hotels along **Pacific Avenue,** a block from the Boardwalk, have rooms for less than $60, and rooms in Ocean City's guest houses are reasonably priced, though facilities there can be dismal. Reserve ahead, especially on weekends. Many hotels lower their rates mid-week. Winter is also slow in Atlantic City, as water temperature, gambling fervor, and hotel rates all drop significantly. Campsites closest to the action cost the most; the majority close September through April. Reserve a site if you plan to visit in July or August.

Irish Pub and Inn, 164 St. James Pl. (344-9063), off the Boardwalk, directly north of Sands Casino. Clean, cheap rooms fully decorated with antiques. Victorian sitting rooms open on to sprawling porch lined with large rocking chairs. Laundry in basement. Singles $25. Doubles $40, with private shower $60. Quads $60. Cot in room $10. Key deposit $5. Breakfast and dinner $10, children $8. Open Feb.-Nov.

Hotel Cassino, 28 S. Georgia Ave. (344-0747), just off Pacific Ave. Named after a *cassino* in the Italian hometown of kindly proprietors Felix and Mina. Multi-cultural atmosphere. A little run-down, but no sleaze. Strictly a family business. Rates negotiable depending on specific room, day, time of year, and number of people. Singles $30-45. Doubles $35-50. Key deposit $10. Open May-Oct.

Birch Grove Park Campground, Mill Rd., in Northfield (641-3778). About 6 mi. from Atlantic City. 50 sites. Attractive and secluded. Sites $15 for 2 people, with hookup $18.

Pleasantville Campground, 408 N. Mill Rd. (641-3176). About 7 mi. from the casinos. 70 sites. Sites $24 for 4 people with full hookup.

Food

After cashing in your chips, you can visit a cheap **casino buffet.** Most casinos offer all-you-can-eat lunch or dinner deals for $10-12; sometimes you can catch a special for around $5. Trump charges $11 for lunch and $13 for dinner. The town provides higher quality meals in a less noxious atmosphere. For a complete rundown of local dining, pick up a copy of *TV Atlantic Magazine, At the Shore,* or *Whoot,* all free, from a hotel lobby, restaurant, or local store.

Pacific Avenue is cramped with steak, sub, and pizza shops. Since 1946, the **White House Sub Shop,** Mississippi and Arctic Ave. (345-1564 or -8599), has served world-famous subs and sandwiches. Celebrity supporters include Bill Cosby, Johnny Mathis, and Frank Sinatra, rumored to have subs flown to him while he's on tour ($6-8, half-subs $3-4; open Mon.-Sat. 10am-midnight, Sun. 11am-midnight.) For renowned Italian food, including the best pizza in town, hit **Tony's Baltimore Grille,** 2800 Atlantic Ave. at Iowa Ave. Feel like Donald Trump as you sit in a booth and twiddle the knobs on your own personal jukebox. (Open daily 11am-3am; bar open 24 hrs.) Though the crowds may put you off, you can get great slices of pizza ($1.75) from one of the many **Three Brothers from Italy** joints on the Boardwalk. The **Inn of the Irish Pub,** at 164 St. James Pl., serves hearty, modestly-priced dishes like deep-fried crab cakes ($4.25), honey-dipped chicken ($4.25), and Dublin beef stew ($5). This oaky, inviting pub has a century's worth of Joycean élan and Irish memorabilia draped on the walls. (Open 24 hrs.) For a traditional and toothsome oceanside dessert, try custard ice cream or saltwater taffy.

Entertainment

Casinos

Inside, thousands of square feet of flashing lights and plush carpet stupefy the gaping crowds; everyone pretends not to notice the one-way ceiling mirrors concealing big-brother gambling monitors. Chumps in formalwear yearn to re-live Atlantic City's glamorous past. In vain, though. Winnebago pioneers in matching tees easily outnumber the dipsticks in butterfly bowties. The luring rattle of chips and clicking of slot machines never stops. Occasionally these are joined by the clacking of coins. Outside the gambling matrix, coffee shops and lounges teem with con-men, bargain-blazing seniors, and dealers. Glittery crooners crow all day.

The casinos on the Boardwalk all fall within a dice toss of one another. Even if you tried, you couldn't miss the newest beanstalk on the block, the **Taj Mahal** (449-1000), Donald Trump's meditation on sacred Indian art and architecture. Limestone elephants greet you at the entrance. The dayglow onion domes wreathed in flickering yuletide lights confirm that you have arrived at the heart of the American dream. Ironically, it was missed payments on this tasteless tallboy that cast the financier into his billion-dollar tailspin. Trump has two other casinos, each screaming out his name in humongous, lighted letters—the **Trump Castle** (441-2000) and **Trump Plaza** (441-6000). Other peacocks include **Bally's Park Place** (340-2000), and **Resorts International** (344-6000). **Caesar's Boardwalk Regency** (348-4411) and **Harrah's Marina Hotel** (441-5000) are hot clubs. Rounding out the list are the **Clairidge,** at Indiana Ave. and the Boardwalk (340-3400), and **Showboat,** at States Ave. and the Boardwalk (343-4000). The **Sands,** at Indiana Ave. and the Boardwalk (441-4000) and **Trop-World Casino,** at Iowa Ave. and the Boardwalk (340-4000), have extensive facilities that include golf and tennis. You may be amused by the two "moving sidewalks" that carry customers from the Boardwalk to the only two casinos without a Boardwalk entrance. These sidewalks move in only one direction.

Open nearly all the time (Mon.-Fri. 10am-4am, Sat.-Sun. 10am-6am), casinos lack windows and clocks, denying you the time cues that signal the hours slipping away. Free drinks and bathrooms at every turn keep you stupid and satisfied. To curb inevitable losses, stick to the cheaper games: blackjack, slot machines, and the low bets in roulette and craps. Stay away from the cash machine room. A book like John Scarne's *New Complete Guide to Gambling* will help you plan an intelligent strategy, but keep your eyes on your watch or you'll have spent five hours and five digits before you know what hit you.

The minimum gambling age of 21 is strictly enforced. Even if you sneak by the bouncers posted at the doors, you cannot collect winnings if you are underage. When an underage gambler hit a $200,000 jackpot, claiming his father had won, the casino reviewed videos to discover the kid had pulled the lever. It was the casino's lucky day, not his.

High-priced casino entertainment, featuring magicians, comedians, songstresses, and musicals, can sometimes be endured at a discount. Call casinos to find out or consult *Whoot,* the weekly free "entertainment and casino newspaper." Atlantic City and adjacent shore towns maintain an active nighttime schedule, and many clubs host solid rock and jazz outfits [My brother saw Stevie—Ass't Ed.]: consult *Whoot* or *Atlantic.*

Beaches and Boardwalk

You can bet the ocean is just a few spaces away. Atlantic City squats on the northern end of long, narrow **Absecon Island,** which has seven miles of beaches—some pure white, some lumpy gray. The **Atlantic City Beach** is free and often crowded. Adjacent **Ventnor City's** sands are nicer. The legendary **Boardwalk** of Atlantic City has given itself over to junk-food stands, souvenir shops, and carnival amusements. Take a walk, jog, or bike in Ventnor City, where Boardwalk development tapers off.

New Haven

Today New Haven is simultaneously university town and depressed city. Academic types and a working class population live somewhat uneasily side by side—bumper stickers proclaiming "Tax Yale, Not Us" embellish a number of street signs downtown. But there is more than mere political tension here. New Haven has a reputation as something of a battleground, and Yalies tend to stick to areas on or near campus, further widening the rift between town and gown. The difference between the controlled, wealthy academic environment and the rest of the town is apparent in every facet of the city—from architecture to safety.

Practical Information and Orientation

Visitor Information: New Haven Visitors and Convention Bureau, 195 Church St. (787-8822), on the Green. Free bus and street maps, and information about current events in town. Open Mon.-Fri. 9am-5pm. **Yale Information Center,** Phelps Gateway, 344 College St. (432-2300), facing the Green. Free campus maps. Pick up a 75¢ walking guide and *The Yale,* a guide to undergraduate life ($3). Bus maps and a New Haven bookstore guide available. Open daily 10am-4pm. Free 1-hr. tours Mon.-Fri. at 10:30am and 2pm, Sat.-Sun. at 1:30pm.

Trains: Amtrak, Union Station, Union Ave. (800-872-7245). Newly renovated station, but area is unsafe at night. To or from Yale, take city bus A ("Orange St."), J, or U ("Waterbury"), or walk six blocks northeast to the Green. Trains to Boston ($36), Washington, DC ($69), and New York ($22). **Metro-North Commuter Railroad,** Union Station (800-638-7646), runs trains to New York's Grand Central Station for half of Amtrak's fare ($9.25-12.75). Ticket counter open daily 6am-10:30pm.

Buses: Greyhound, 45 George St. (772-2470). In a rough area. Walk there with a companion, or take a cab. Frequent bus service to: New York ($11), Boston ($19), Providence ($17.50), Cape Cod/Hyannis ($28), and New London ($9.50). Ticket office open daily 7:30am-8:15pm. **Peter Pan Bus Lines,** Union Station (878-6054) offers buses to Boston ($28). **Connecticut Transit** serves New Haven and the surrounding area from 470 James St. (624-0151). Most buses depart from the Green. Open Mon.-Fri. 8am-4:30pm. Information booth at 200 Orange St. open Mon.-Fri. 9am-5pm.

Car Rental: Thrifty Rent-a-Car, 37 Union St. (562-3191 or 800-367-2277). Economy cars start at $42.95 per day ($29.95 on the weekend), with 125 free mi., 29¢ each added mi. for those 25 and over with major credit card; 21-25 add $5 surcharge. Open Mon.-Fri. 8am-6pm, Sat. 8am-2pm, Sun. 10am-2pm.

Taxis: Metro Cab (777-7777). Downtown to the airport for $8-9.

Area Code: 203

New Haven is a cinch to get to. The city lies at the intersection of I-95 (110 miles from Providence) and I-91 (40 miles from Hartford). At night, don't wander too freely out of the immediate downtown and the campus areas, as surrounding sections are notably less safe. The Yale area is well patrolled by campus police. The downtown area is also patrolled by police mostly on the lookout for illegally parked cars. Around 4pm on weekdays tow trucks are out in full force, so be sure to read parking signs carefully.

New Haven is laid out in nine squares. The central one is **The Green,** which, despite the fact that it lies between **Yale University** and City Hall, is a pleasant escape from the hassles of city life. A small but thriving business district borders the Green, consisting mostly of bookstores, boutiques, cheap sandwich places, and other services catering to students and professors. Downtown New Haven, and particularly the Yale campus, is littered with distinctive buildings. The omnipresence of American Collegiate Gothic in spires, towers, and ivy-covered buildings lends the campus a unity of design that its Cambridge role-model lacks.

Accommodations

Inexpensive accommodations are sparse in New Haven. The hunt is especially difficult around Yale Parents weekend (mid-Oct.) and graduation (early June).

Hotel Duncan, 1151 Chapel St. (787-1273). Decent singles for $40 and doubles for $55, both with bath. May need reservations on weekends.

Nutmeg Bed & Breakfast, 222 Girard Ave., Hartford 06105 (236-6698). Reserves doubles in New Haven B&B's at $35-45. Open Mon.-Fri. 9am-5pm.

Bed & Breakfast Ltd. (469-3260). Mon.-Fri. 4pm-9pm, Sat.-Sun. anytime.

The nearest parks for camping are **Cattletown** (264-5678, sites $10), 40 minutes away, and **Hammonasset Beach** (245-2755, sites $12), 20 minutes away.

Food

Food in New Haven is reasonably cheap, catering to the student population.

Atticus Café, 1082 Chapel St. (776-4040). A charming bookstore/café with friendly if harried service. Try their soups served with swell half-loaves of bread ($3-4); lunch specials $5. Eat amidst books. Open 8am-midnight.

Naples Pizza, 90 Wall St. (776-9021 or 776-6214). A Yale tradition, updated with a video jukebox. Try a pizza with broccoli, pineapple, or white clams ($7.25) and a pitcher of beer ($5.50). Open June-Aug. Mon.-Wed. 7-10pm, Thurs.-Fri. 7-11pm; Sept.-May Sun.-Thurs. 7pm-1am, Fri.-Sat. 7pm-2am.

Daily Caffè, 376 Elm St. (776-5063). Started by a Yale graduate; quickly becoming the haunt of the university's coffee and cigarette set. Selection of coffees. Mon.-Thurs. 8am-midnight, Fri.-Sat. 9am-1am, Sun. 9am-midnight.

Claire's, 1000 Chapel St. (562-3888). A homey restaurant that touts its gourmet vegetarian menu, with Mexican and Middle-Eastern selections. The real draw is Claire's rich cake ($2.25 per slice). Outdoor dining in the summer. Open daily 8am-10pm.

Yankee Doodle Coffee Shop, 258 Elm St. (865-1074). A tiny, diner-like place, squeezed into a 12-ft.-wide slice just across the street from the Yale Boola-Boola Shop. Eggs, toast, and coffee are yours for $1.54. So damn good. Open Mon.-Sat. 6:30am-2:30pm.

Louis Lunch, 263 Crown St. (562-5507). The wife-and-husband team serves the best flame-broiled burger on the East Coast for $2.50. They claim the menu has not changed in 40 years. Open Mon.-Fri. 9-11am and 11:30am-4pm.

Sights

James Gambel Rodgers, a firm believer in the sanctity of printed material, designed **Sterling Memorial Library,** 120 High St. (432-1775). The building looks so much like a monastery that even the telephone booths are shaped like confessionals. Rodgers spared no expense to make Yale's library look "authentic," even decapitating the figurines on the library's exterior to replicate those at Oxford, which, because of decay, often fall to the ground and shatter. (Open summer Mon.-Wed. and Fri. 8:30am-5pm, Thurs. 8:30am-10pm, Sat. 10am-5pm; academic year Mon.-Thurs. 8:30am-midnight, Fri. 8:30am-5pm, Sat. 10am-5am, Sun. 1pm-midnight.) The massive **Beinecke Rare Book and Manuscript Library,** 121 Wall St. (432-2977), has no windows. Instead this intriguing modern structure, the design of Louis Khan, is panelled with Vermont marble cut thin enough to be translucent; supposedly its volumes (including one Gutenberg Bible and an extensive collection of William Carlos Williams's writings) can survive a nuclear war. (Open Mon.-Fri. 8:30am-4:45pm, Sat. 10am-4:45pm.) Along New Haven's own Wall St., between High and Yale St., the Neo-Gothic gargoyles perched on the **Law School** building are in fact cops and robbers.

Most of New Haven's museums are on the Yale campus. The **Yale University Art Gallery,** 1111 Chapel St. (432-0600), opened in 1832, claims to be the oldest university art museum in the Western Hemisphere. Its collections of John Trumbull paintings and Italian Renaissance works are especially notable. (Open Tues.-Sat. 10am-5pm, Sun. 2-5pm. Closed Aug. $3 donation requested.) The **Yale Center for British Art,** 1080 Chapel St. (432-2800), sponsors some pretty thought-provoking exhibits—two years ago they displayed a collection of snuff boxes. For anglophiles. Yench. (Open Tues.-Sat. 10am-5pm, Sun. noon-5pm. Free.) The **Peabody Museum of Natural History,** 170 Whitney Ave. (432-5050; 432-5799 for recorded message), houses Rudolph F. Zallinger's Pulitzer Prize-winning mural, which portrays the North American continent as it appeared 70 to 350 million years ago. Other exhibits range from Central American cultural artifacts to a dinosaur hall displaying the skeleton of a Brontosaurus. (Open Mon.-Sat. 10am-5pm, Sun. noon-5pm. Admission $2.50, seniors $2, ages 3-15 $1. Free Mon.-Fri. 3-5pm.)

Entertainment

New Haven offers plenty of late-night entertainment. Check **Toad's Place,** 300 York St. (562-5589; recorded information 624-8623), to see if one of your favorite bands is in town. While you get tickets, grab a draft beer ($1) at the bar. (Box office open daily 11am-6pm; tickets available at bar after 8pm. Bar open Sun.-Thurs. 8pm-1am, Fri.-Sat. 8pm-2am.) The **Anchor Bar,** 272 College St. (865-1512), just off the Green, is the kind of bar that serves Corona and St. Pauli Girl Dark; a local paper rated its jukebox the best in the region, though we're skeptical. Harrumph. (Open Mon.-Thurs. 11am-1am, Fri.-Sat. 10am-2am.)

Once a famous testing ground for Broadway-bound plays, New Haven's thespian community carries on today at a lesser scale. The **Schubert Theater,** 247 College St. (624-1825, 800-228-6622), a large part of the town's on-stage tradition, still mounts shows. (Box office open Mon.-Fri. 10am-4:30pm, Sat. noon-3pm.) Across the street, **The Palace,** 246 College St. (784-2120, box office 624-6497), hosts concerts and revues. New Haven's **Long Wharf Theater,** 222 Sargent Dr. (787-4282), received a special Tony Award for achievement in Regional Theater in 1978. (Tickets $21-26, student rush $5. Season June-late Sept.)

Yale itself accounts for an impressive loogie of the theater activity in the city. The **Yale Repertory Theater** (432-1234) has turned out such illustrious alums as Meryl Streep, Glenn Close, and James Earl Jones, and continues to produce excellent shows. (Open Oct. to May.) The **University Theater,** at 22 York St., stages undergraduate plays throughout the academic year and graduation. Tickets are usually under $8. In summer, the Green is the site of free **New Haven Symphony** concerts (865-0831), the **New Haven Jazz Festival** (787-8228), and other free musical series. The Department of Cultural Affairs (787-8956), 770 Chapel St., can answer questions about concerts on the Green.

On the banks of the Housatonic River south of New Haven, the smaller town of **Stratford** is home to the **American Shakespeare Theater,** 1850 Elm St. (375-5000), exit 32 off I-95. (Tickets $19-29.) During the summer Shakespeare Festival, some of the country's ablest actors and directors stage the Bard's plays while strolling minstrels, musicians, and artists grace the grounds.

Princeton

Princeton slumbers peacefully 50 miles southwest of New York City off Rte. 1 in New Jersey. This disarmingly quiet and preppy town's only attraction, say some students, is Ivy League Princeton University, which has turned out presidents (James Madison and Woodrow Wilson), tycoons (J.P. Morgan), writers (F. Scott Fitzgerald), movie stars (Jimmy Stewart), and jeans models (Brooke Shields). The commercial section of the town itself, which, surprisingly, does not cater to the student population, is small but upscale. The town, too, has produced famous alums, including, most recently, the band Blues Traveller. But don't let their white-bread blues wheezings discourage a trip to this charming locale.

Practical Information

Visitor Information: Princeton University Communication/Publication Office, Stanhope Hall (258-3600). Campus maps and current information, including the *Princeton Weekly Bulletin,* with a calendar of events. Open Mon.-Fri. 8:30am-4:30pm. **Orange Key Guide Service,** 73 Nassau St. (258-3603), in the back entrance of MacLean House. Free campus tours, pamphlets, and maps. 1-hr. tours Mon.-Sat. at 10am, 11am, 1:30pm, and 3:30pm, Sun. at 1:30 and 3:30pm. Office open Mon.-Sat. 9am-5pm, Sun. 1-5pm. **Princeton University Telephone Information,** 258-3000. Open daily 8am-11pm.

Trains: New Jersey Transit. (In state 800-772-2222; out of state 201-762-5100, hearing impaired 800-772-2287). Leaves NYC about every hour, leaves Princeton less frequently. 1-hr. trip starts at 6am ($9.85 one way, $14 roundtrip). Prices include a five-minute ride on the "dinky," probably the shortest commuter train in the world, which runs directly to the Princeton campus, stopping across from the McCarter theater. **Amtrak,** 800-872-7245. Connects Princeton Junction, 3 mi. south of Princeton on Rte. 571, to New York City. Seven trains run daily run from New York to Princeton, nine from Princeton to New York. 1-hr. trip costs $22 oneway, $36 round-trip.

Buses: New Jersey Transit, 800-772-2222. Runs 6am-midnight. Buses stop at Princeton University and Palmer Sq. Take bus #606 to Trenton (every 1/2hr., $1.90 exact change). **Suburban Transit** (908-2491100) has two Princeton locations, in Palmer Square and Princeton Shopping Center, about five blocks from the center of town. Departures every half hour; call for times. One-way $7.15, round-trip $13.95.

Taxi: Associated Taxi Stand, 924-1222. Open Mon. 5:30am-midnight, Tues.-Fri. 6am-midnight, Sat.-Sun. 7am-midnight.

Post Office: in Palmer Sq. behind Tiger Park (921-9563). Open Mon.-Fri. 8am-4:30pm, Sat. 8:30am-12:30pm. **ZIP code:** 08542.

Area Code: 609.

Located in the green heart of the "Garden State," Princeton is within commuting distance of both New York City and Philadelphia. Driving from New York City, take the Holland Tunnel to the New Jersey Turnpike and exit at Hightstown. **Nassau Street** is Princeton's main strip, with shops clustered on one side and the university set back on the other. **Palmer Square,** the center of Princeton's business district, lies right off of Nassau between Witherspoon and Chambers St.

Accommodations

While there are no budget accommodations in the town of Princeton, cheap motels clutter Rte. 1 and the environs of giant Quaker Bridge Mall—four miles south of Princeton but served by local bus (see Practical Information above).

Sleep-E-Hollow Motel, 3000 U.S. 1, Lawrenceville (896-0900). Five mi. south of Princeton. Beds in small, well-worn rooms. $29.50 for two people, one bed; $34.50 for two people, two beds.

McIntosh Inn, U.S. 1 and Quaker Bridge Mall (896-3700). Ideal for more than one person. Rooms come clean, large, and user-friendly. Singles $39.95. Doubles $46.95.

Food

Most of Princeton's reasonably priced restaurants line Nassau and Witherspoon St.

P.J.'s Pancake House, 154 Nassau St. (924-1353). Old wooden tables etched with student graffiti. Typical college hangout—loud, crowded, inexpensive. Fresh, tasty food. Try the 3-pancake sampler with fresh fruit ($5.50). Lines for Sunday brunch during school year. Most meals $5-7. Open Mon.-Thurs. 7:30am-10pm, Fri. 7:30am-midnight, Sat. 8am-midnight, Sun. 8am-1am.

The Athenian, 25 Witherspoon St. (921-3425). Bizarro hybrid: coffee shop collides with Greek pastry shop and Italian pizzeria. Good pizza by the slice ($1.50) and by the pie (sm. $5.50, med. $7.25, lg. $8.95). Gaze at the Parthenon while you gnarl on a wedge of pepperoni. Top it all off with *baklava.* Sandwiches and entrees under $7. At $5.25 the Greek special *is* special. Open Mon.-Wed., Sun. 11am-10pm; Thurs. 11am-11pm; Fri. and Sat. 11am-midnight. No liquor license.

The Tempting Tiger, 14 Witherspoon St. (609-924-0634, -0644). Very crunchy. Fresh, healthy food for purists. Try the California Dream sandwich (cheese, avocado, red onion, alfalfa sprouts) with the creamy house dressing ($5.25). Good hummus ($4.95) and other healthy items, including veggie burgers and the "sproutie special." Small and clean. Open Mon.-Fri. 11am-8:30pm, Sat. 11am-5:30pm.

Teresa's Pizetta Caffé, 21 Palmer Sq. East, (608-921-1974). Personalized gourmet pizzas with poetic toppings in a clean, well-lit, modern café. Try the spinach, eggplant, fresh garlic pizza ($5.50). Entrees $6 and under. Open Mon.-Thurs. 10am-11pm, Fri. and Sat. 10am-midnight, Sun. 10am-10pm.

The Annex, 128 1/2 Nassau St. Popular student hangout and bar. Darker and often quieter than P.J.'s. Serves Italian entrees ($5-7), as well as omelettes and sandwiches ($2-4). Open Mon.-Sat. 11am-1am.

Marita's Cantina, 138 Nassau St. Average Mexican food. Collegiates come here mostly to drink. The $6 all-you-can-eat lunch buffet (Mon.-Fri. 11:30am-2pm) attracts starving students. Go *à la carte* for $2-5. Restaurant open Mon.-Thurs. 11am-10pm, Fri.-Sat. 11am-11pm, Sun 11am-10pm. Live bands on Thursdays. Open daily 11am-11pm. Bar closes around 1:30am.

Thomas Sweet's Ice Cream, Palmer Sq. (609-683-1655) across from the Nassau Inn. Have them blend a topping into their homemade ice cream ($2-3). Be sure to sample the Snickers and cookie dough flaves. A scoop will run you $1.60. Open Sun.-Thurs. 11am-11pm, Fri.-Sat. 11am-midnight.

Sights

The 2500-acre landscaped campus of Gothic Princeton University will wowzer you with its offerings. The **Orange Key** (see Practical Information above) provides free tours geared toward prospective students intent on hearing the myths and legends of the nation's fourth oldest school (founded in 1746). The school's graduating classes place commemorative plaques and patches of ivy on the outer wall of **Nassau Hall.** Upon completion in 1756 it stood as the colonies' largest stone edifice and Princeton's original university building; it also served as the capitol building of the original U.S. colonies for several months in the summer of 1783. The two magnificent bronze tigers represent the school's mascot. **Whig** and **Clio Hall** are home to the oldest college literary and debating club in the U.S. **Prospect Gardens,** a huge bed of flowers in the shape of Princeton's shield, grows particularly beautiful in the summertime.

Princeton's art collection is astounding. The **University Art Museum**(258-3778) holds everything from the Renaissance masters to Jean Michel Basquiat. There is also a fine contemporary collection in which women artists such as Louise Nevelson and Nancy Graves are well-represented. Also of interest is Cezanne's *La Montaigne Sainte Victoire*. The museum's fine exhibitions turn over rapidly, so call to find out what's on display.

The sculptures scattered about campus come from the $11 million **Putnam Collection.** The profile of one modern piece behind Nassau Hall bears a striking and comical

Place
Stamp
Here

LET'S GO Travel

Harvard Student Agencies, Inc.
Harvard University
Thayer B
Cambridge, MA 02138 U.S.A.

resemblance to former President Richard M. Nixon. Picasso's *Head of a Woman* stands in front of the University Art Museum (258-3778). Tours of the outdoor sculptures (which include doilies by Alexander Calder, Henry Moore, Pablo Picasso, and David Smith) or of the museum's permanent indoor collection can be arranged through the university. (Open Tues.-Sat. 10am-5pm, Sun. 1-5pm. Free.)

Entertainment

On May 17, 1955, Princeton students held one of the first pro-rock 'n' roll demonstrations in the U.S., blaring Bill Haley and the Comets' "Rock Around the Clock" until 1am, when the Dean woke up and told them to knock it off. For some of that distilled white, male, Ivy League tradition, down a drink in **The Tap Room,** in the basement of the Nassau Inn in Palmer Sq. (921-7500). A Princeton tradition since 1937, the pub sports aging but freshly polished wooden booths. (Open Mon.-Thurs. 11:30am-10pm, Fri.-Sat. 11:30am-12:30am.) Lovey Williams plays guitar Fri.-Sat. nights (7:30-midnight). Whoever he is. Check Princeton's *Weekly Bulletin* for the scoop on films, concerts, and special events. Students and professional actors perform at **McCarter Theater** (683-8000). The **Princeton Record Exchange** (609-921-0881), at 20 Tulane Street, sells new and used records, cassettes, and CDs. Prices start at 99¢. Good stuff, cheaply. (Open Mon.-Sat. 10am-8pm, Sun noon-6pm.)

Long Island

Long Island is easy to stereotype, but difficult to grasp. For some, the Island evokes images of sprawling suburbia, dotted with malls and office buildings; others see it as the privileged retreat of New York WASPs; for still others it is a summer refuge of white sand and open spaces. Fewer see the pockets of poverty on Long Island, or its commercial and cultural centers.

While in theory "Long Island" includes the entire 120-mile-long fish-shaped land mass, in practice the term excludes the westernmost sections, Brooklyn and Queens. The residents of these two boroughs, at the head of the "fish," will readily remind you that they are officially part of the City. This leaves Nassau and Suffolk counties to constitute the real Long Island. East of the Queens-Nassau line, people read *Newsday,* not the *Times* or the *Daily News;* they back the Islanders, not the Rangers, and they enjoy their role as neighbor to, rather than part of, the great metropolis.

Until the 20th century, Long Island was a sparsely populated, typically Northeastern jambalaya of farms and villages on land considered especially good for potato farming. Its docks and ports sustained a strong maritime industry. Parts of Suffolk County still preserve the rural tradition. Some towns "out on the island" might as well be in New England, with their white clapboard churches and village squares.

In the early part of the 20th century, the eastern end of Long Island became the playground of Manhattan's rich and famous. New York millionaires built their country houses on the rocky north shore, creating the exclusive "Gold Coast" captured in its 1920s heyday by F. Scott Fitzgerald's *Great Gatsby.* The 1950s were a turning point for the Island; New York City expanded, cars became more affordable, and young couples enjoying post-war prosperity sought dream houses for their baby-boom families. The new Long Island neighborhoods provided an escape from the city and a safe, wholesome environment in which to raise children. Soon tidy "development" neighborhoods emerged, plaided out with street after street of identical houses framed by manicured shrubbery. The 10,000 units of identical Levit box houses, finished in 1951, made "Levittown" the first housing development in the world built using mass production techniques; some workers did nothing but install doorknobs, while others only painted front stoops. The completed residences were put on the market at a total cost of $7990 per unit (a $90 down payment and monthly payments of $58).

The 50s also saw the creation of Long Island's transportation system, the essential link to New York City for hordes of commuters. For years, the Long Island Railroad (LIRR) provided the only major connection between the city and the island. While many islanders still commute to the city by train, Long Island is best seen by car. Also during the 50s the Island's main artery, the Long Island Expressway (LIE, officially called State Highway 495) grew to include 73 exits on the 85-mi. stretch from Manhattan to Riverhead. This expansion, along with the creation of the rest of the Island's "parkway" system, was supervised by Robert Moses, a legendary state planning official. Today the Island's population has outgrown all its forms of transportation, and traffic tends to jam during rush hour on the expressway.

Although the island gives the impression of uninterrupted suburbia, parts of the east end are quite rural, while other towns, like Hicksville, are quite urban (in spite of the name). Dozens of mega-malls dot Long Island; it is no mistake that they appear on road maps, highlighted as points of interest. The cluster of communities along the south fork, known collectively as the Hamptons, is home to summering Manhattanites and modern day Gatsbys. The area jams in July, as traffic backs up miles on Highway 27. Each Hampton has its own sands, style, and stereotype. Look in Southampton for old money, Westhampton for new money, and East Hampton for artistes. Don't look for Northampton. Bridgehampton, appropriately enough, lies between Southampton and East Hampton. All are full of freshly waxed imported cars. Even the towns without Hampton in their name have Hampton in their hearts; don't expect to find the Clit Club in Quogue, Amagansett, or Water Mill.

Practical Information

Area Code: 516.

Visitor Information: Long Island Tourism and Convention Commission (794-4222), Eisenhower Park, Hempstead Turnpike, East Meadow, or on the LIE South between Exits 51 and 52 in Commack.

Airports: John F. Kennedy Airport (see New York City listing). LaGuardia Airport (see New York City listing). Long Island MacArthur Airport, Ronkonkoma, Suffolk. LIE Exit 57S. For general information call 467-3210, for airline telephone numbers 467-6161 or -6162. A small local airport, offering regular flights to other east coast cities. Suffolk's other small airports are the Brookhaven Airport (281-5100) and the East Hampton Airport (537-1631).

Trains: Long Island Railroad (LIRR), train information 822-5477, tour information 718-990-7948, lost articles 718-990-8384. The Island's main public transportation facility has four central lines. Fares vary according to destination and time of day ("peak" or "off-peak"). Peak fares (5:30-9am on trains from Long Island to Manhattan and 4:30-8pm on trains from Manhattan to Long Island) range from $4.25-14. Off-peak fares, charged at all other times (duh), range from $3-9.50. The LIRR also offers educational and recreational tour programs, as well as escorted sightseeing tours from May to November. Call 718-990-7498.

Buses

Metropolitan Suburban Bus Authority (MSBA): daytime bus service in Queens, Nassau, and Western Suffolk (542-0100). Bus information 766-6722. Service runs along most major highways, but the routes are complex and irregular—make sure you confirm your destination with the driver. Some buses run every 15 min., others every hour. In Nassau, the fare is $1.50, but crossing over into Queens costs an additional 50¢, and transfers cost 25¢. Disabled travelers and senior citizens pay half-fare. Children under 44 inches tall ride free. The MSBA has daily service to and from Jones Beach during the summer months.

Suffolk Transit: (360-5700, open Mon.-Fri. 8am-4:30pm). Fare policy same as Nassau. The S-92 bus loop-de-loops back and forth between the tips of the north and south forks, with nine runs daily, most of them between East Hampton and Orient Point. Call to confirm stops and schedules. The route also connects with the LIRR at Riverhead, where the forks meet. No service Sunday. The fare is $1.50; 50¢ for senior citizens and the disabled. Transfers are 25¢ for everyone. Children under 5 ride free.

Greyhound: 66 W. Columbia St. (483-3230) in Hempstead; 90 Broadhollow Rd. (427-6897) in Melville; 307 E. Main St. (727-7488) in Riverhead; and 1684 Expressway Dr. (234-2445) in Islip.

Hampton Jitney Inc.: 800-447-7748, on Long Island 283-4600, in Manhattan 212-936-0440. 15-25 upscale buses daily from Manhattan to the South Fork and back. On Fri. and Sat. they

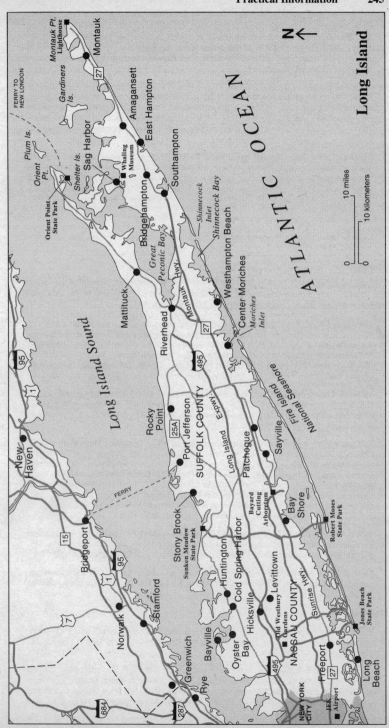

run every half-hour. One-way fares $15-20, same-day round-trip $36. Senior citizens pay $10 for a one-way ticket. Catch buses on 41st St. between Lexington and Third Ave. They go directly to Westhampton, but then stop at almost all villages and towns on the South Fork, up to Montauk. Call their suave operators for detailed schedule and fare information. Reservations are suggested but not required.

Hampton Express: (212-861-6800, on Long Island 874-2400). Buses almost every hour. on Friday, five times per day most other days. Buses depart Manhattan from 86th and Columbus; 81st and Third; and 42nd and Third; 72nd and Madison; 72nd and Lexington to destinations on the South Fork. Thurs.-Mon. $18; Tues.-Wed. $15. Reservations required (1-7 days in advance). $5 discount for senior travel club members. Children under 10 pay $10 and lapkids ride for free.

Sunrise Express: 800-527-7709, in Suffolk 477-1200. Their "NY Express" runs four times per day from Manhattan to the North Fork ($15, $28 round-trip). Catch buses on the corner of 44th St. and Third Ave. or in Queens (LIE exit 24, Casino Blvd. in front of Queens College Golden Center at the Q88 bus stop.) They go directly to Riverhead, then stop at almost all villages on the North Fork up to Greenport. The buses service the Shelter Island Ferry. Disabled travelers pay $22 round-trip and lapkids ride free. Reservations required. Bicycles ($10) and pets ($5) allowed. Call for schedule information.

Long Island Airports Limousine Service: 234-8400; Queens 718-656-7000. Buses and vans available 24 hrs.

Ferries

Many of the smaller islands off the shore of Long Island are popular with vacationers. Listed below are several of the ferry services from Long Island to various islands. Included are points of departure, departure times, and rates.

To Shelter Island: from North and South Fork about every 15 min. from 5:40am (5:15am on Mon.) to midnight (1am Fri. and Sat.). **North Fork: Greenport Ferry,** 749-0139. North Ferry Rd., on the dock. For passenger and driver $6, $6.50 round-trip, 75¢ each additional passenger, 75¢ for a walk-on (without a car). **South Fork: North Haven Ferry,** 749-1200. South Ferry Rd., on the dock. Same fares as Greenport Ferry, but $1 for each additional passenger and $1 for walk-ons.

To Block Island: Viking Lines, P.O. Box 730, Montauk (668-5709). Call for reservations. $29.50 same day roundtrip, $15 one way; ages 5-12 $15 round-trip, $10 one way; bicycles $5 round-trip. Mopeds and motorcycles $10 round-trip. Ferry leaves daily at 10am, returns from Block Island at 4:30pm.

To Connecticut (next 3 listings): Steamboat Co., 102 West Broadway, Port Jefferson (473-0286). To Bridgeport (1 1/4hr.): car and driver $24-$30, each additional passenger $8, unlimited passengers $30. Walk-ons and children ages 6-12 $6. Tuesday is Gentlemen's day, and walk-ons of the appropriate gender pay $8 round-trip; Thursday is Ladies's day and same rules apply for women. Ferries leave every hour or so from 6am-7pm. Call for exact times and reservations. **Fisher's Island Ferry:** 203-443-6851 or 203-442-0165. State Street, New London, CT. Fisher's Island to New London: car and driver $12, each additional passenger $3.50. Children 5-12 pay $1.75. Any trip leaving New London after 3:45pm costs $1 extra.

Viking Lines, P.O Box 730, Montauk (668-5709). Montauk to New London: Fri.-Sun., earliest ferry departs from Montauk at 7am; the latest return trip leaves New London at 9pm. $15, $19.50 roundtrip; children under 12 pay $10, $15 roundtrip. Call for reservations.

Sayville Ferry Service: 589-0810 or -0822. Sayville to Pines or Cherry Grove ($9 roundtrip, seniors $8, children $4.50), to Sailor's Haven or Sunken Forest ($7.50 roundtrip, children $4.50).

Getting Around

Taxis: Ollie's Airport Service, in Nassau. North Shore 829-8647, South Shore 937-0505. Open 24 hrs. Vans, limousines, and cars. **All-Island Taxi Service,** 177 Jackson St., Hempstead (481-1111). Open 24 hrs.

Car Rental: Avis Rent-a-Car, nationwide reservations 800-331-1212. In Nassau, 357 Old Country Rd., Westbury (222-3255). In Suffolk, 20 East Jericho Turnpike, Huntington Station (271-9300). **Hertz Rent-a-Car,** worldwide reservations 800-654-3131. In Nassau, 225 Northern Blvd., Great Neck (482-5880). In Suffolk, Long Island MacArthur Airport (737-9200). See also New York City listings.

Bike Rental: Country Time Cycles, 11150 Main Rd. (298-8700), in Mattituck. All bikes $15 first day, $10 second day. $5 each following day. Credit card required. **Piccozzi's Service Station,** Rte. 114 (749-0045), in Shelter Island Heights. A 10-min. walk from the north ferry. Three-speeds $12 for 4 r., $17 for 8hr.; 12-speeds $14 for 4hr., $19 for 8hr.; 21-speeds $17 for 4hr., $21 for 8hr. Cash deposit or credit card required.

Hotlines

Help Line: Rape Hotline, 222-2293.

Accommodations

Finding a place to stay on the island can be a daunting prospect for the budget traveler. Daytrippers in Nassau will probably be better off heading back to the city to crash for the night. Most of the decent hotels in Nassau exact indecent rates ($100-150 per night). Likewise, the majority of the smaller motels do not cater to tourists but to business travelers and romantic couples (some advertise special rates for "short stays"). Suffolk County provides a wider variety of accommodations, many of them more attuned to the demands of the tourist market. In general, however, places close during the off-season and fill up quickly during the summer. Still, with some planning, you can find a good Island deal.

Nassau

Hicksville Motor Lodge, Duffy Ave. (433-3900), in Hicksville. LIE Exit 41S. A decent motel–used to be a Howard Johnson's. Singles $65, doubles $75. During the off-season singles $60, doubles $65.

Days Inn, 828 South Oyster Bay Rd. (433-1900), in Hicksville. LIE Exit 43. Part of a chain. Many business types, courtesy of nearby Grumman defense plant. Singles $62, doubles $68.

Gateway Inn, 1780 Sunrise Hwy. (378-7100), in Merrick. LIE Exit 38 (Meadowbrook Pkwy.). Comfortable 60-room inn on the South Shore, convenient to Jones Beach. Singles $75, doubles $80 (motel) and $90 (hotel). Complimentary continental breakfast and free satellite TV.

Olsen's Motel, 400 Carman Mill Road (795-4800), in Massapequa, LIE Exit 44S. A pleasant little motel, not far from Jones Beach and the LIRR. HBO and complimentary coffee. Singles $55, doubles $75.

Freeport Motor Inn and Boatel, 445 South Main St. (623-9100) in Freeport. LIE Exit 38. Right on the water, only 5 minutes from Jones Beach. Clean and comfortable. Singles $60, doubles $62 on weekdays. Singles and doubles $65 on weekends. Continental breakfast, cable TV.

Suffolk

Montauket, Tuthill Rd. (668-5992). Follow the Montauk Hwy. to Montauk. At the traffic circle take Edgemere, which becomes Flamingo, and make a left onto Fleming and then another left. From March-May and Oct. 1-Nov. 15, only 4 rooms are open; the whole hotel opens for the summer season. Make reservations for summer weekends starting March 1st—it fills up quickly. The Island's best bargain. Almost always full on weekends. Doubles $35, with private bath $40.

Pines Motor Lodge, corner of Rte. 109 and 3rd St. (957-3330), in Lindenhurst. LIE to Southern State Pkwy. East, Exit 33. Doubles $40-70.

Vineyard Motor Inn, Rte. 25 (722-4024), in Jamesport on the North Fork. At end of LIE, take Rte. 58 and then Rte. 25. Singles $55 weeknights, $65 weekends. Doubles $60 weeknights, $70 weekends. During off-season singles $45, doubles $55.

Ranger Guest House/Anchor's Rest, 74 Old Riverhead Rd. (728-8955), in Hampton Bays. LIE Exit 70 to Sunrise Highway Exit 65N. Private residence with 3 rooms on the 2nd floor and a shared bathroom. Guests receive a house key. Continental breakfast included on weekends. Call for rates; weekend package $100.

132 North Main Guest House, East Hampton (324-2246 or 324-9771), 1 mi. from the beach. LIE Exit 70 to Sunrise Hwy., which becomes Montauk Hwy. Main house, cottages, and cabana on 2 acres of grounds. $60-90; summer weekend rate for doubles $100-150.

Easterner Resort, 639 Montauk Hwy. (283-9292), in Southampton. Sunrise Hwy. Exit 66. 1- and 2-bedroom cottages, tennis court, pool, cable TV, and A/C. Weeknights $60, summer week-end package $125. Open Memorial Day through Labor Day.

Oceanside Beach Resort, Montauk Hwy. (668-9825), in Montauk. Refrigerators and kitchen areas in each room. Swimming pool. Friendly service. Close to town and beach. Often crowded. Singles $79. Doubles $88.

Malibu Motel, Elmwood Ave. (668-5233) in Montauk. Near town and beach. Clean and friendly, family owned and operated. Unpretentious and relatively affordable. Doubles $85-95.

Shelter Island

Azalea House, 1 Thomas Ave. (749-4252). At the center of the island. Doubles $50 (Mon.-Thurs.), $65 (Fri.-Sun.), off-season $50. Two night min. during summer weekends, but they'll work with you if you make reservations early enough (2-3 weeks in advance).

The Belle Crest House, 163 North Ferry Rd. (749-2041), in Shelter Island Heights. Country inn with lovely garden. Rooms infested with American antiques. Open March-Dec. Singles $65-75. Doubles $80-165.

Referral Services

Twin Forks Reservation, P.O. Box 657, Hampton Bays, NY 11946 (728-5285). B&B on East End. Doubles: South Fork $80, North Fork $85.

A Reasonable Alternative, Inc., 117 Spring St., Port Jefferson, NY 11777 (928-4034). Rooms in private homes all along the shores of Nassau and Suffolk. Doubles $60-80.

Camping

Camping makes financial sense if you plan to spend any amount of time on the Is-land without spending too much money. On the down side, there are only a few months when the weather blows fair enough for comfort, and even then the humidity can be oppressive. You will also find the Island's campsites tangled in a mystifying web of local, state, and federal regulations. Most Island camping facilities are restrict-ed to local residents; you can camp on most of the Island only if you already live there. But at least a few places will welcome visitors to these shores.

Battle Row (293-7120), in Bethpage, Nassau. Eight tent sites and 50 trailer sites available on a first come, first serve basis. Electricity, restrooms, showers, grills, and a playground. Tent sites $5. Trailer sites $8 for Nassau residents, $12 for visitors. 21 and over–unless you're a family.

Heckscher Park (800-456-2267 or 581-4433), in East Islip, Suffolk. A state-run facility. Make reservations by calling the toll-free state number. 69 tent and trailer sites. Restrooms, showers, food, grills, fishing, a pool, and a beach. Open May-Sept. $11 per night. Reservations must be made at least 7 days in advance.

Hither Hills (668-2554 or 668-5000), in Montauk. Carl G. Fisher, creator of Miami Beach, bought 10,000 acres here in 1926, but the Depression forestalled his development plans and he sold the lands to the state. 165 tent and trailer sites. Restrooms, showers, food, grills, fishing, tennis, and a beach. Reservations required 90 days in advance. Open April-Oct. for a week stay ($83.25).

Fire Island National Seashore (597-6633), in Watch Hill. Adjacent to the only area in New York State formally designated by the Federal government as "wilderness." Restrooms, show-ers, food. Reservations necessary (call Wed.-Fri. 10am-1pm).

South Haven Park (854-1418), in Brookhaven. Campground, rowboats. Suffolk residents $12, others $16. Open Memorial Day to the close of the autumn duck-hunting season.

Wildwood Park (800-456-2267 or 929-4314), at Wading River. Location of Mackay Radio Station, source of Voice of America and one of the largest stations in the country (not open to the public). Former estate of Charles and John Arbuckle, multimillionaire coffee dealers who, brilliantly, packaged coffee instead of selling it in bulk. 322 tent and trailer sites, restrooms, showers, food, fishing, and a beach. Tent sites $10. Trailer sites $12. Reservations advisable (at least one week in advance).

McCann Trailer Park (477-1748 or 734-5459), in Greenport. Privately run. Within walking distance of the beach (a long walk though). 50 tent and trailer sites. Laundry rooms, restrooms, showers, food, beach, pool, hay-rides, and a game room. Tent sites $10, trailer sites $18. Reservations required. Open April-Oct.

Food

If you are already on Long Island, you might as well eat there. Tourist food, found mostly in the fashionable resorts out east, is wonderful if you have already made your first million, but otherwise not worth discussing. Restaurants catering to Islanders, on the other hand, do very well for themselves without droves of rich Manhattan patrons. Many of these Island favorites specialize in ethnic fare—Chinese, Italian, Greek. You might have to overcome your hang-ups about style, decor, and locale, though: if you refuse to eat in a shopping center, you are seriously limiting your options. By the way, for some of the best food on the Island, we recommend scoping out the bountiful farm stands of the East End and the infallible seafood restaurants of Suffolk.

Nassau

An amazing variety of reasonably priced restaurants, from Turkish to Viennese, help to diversify Nassau, pleasing those whose wallets have been depleted in New York. You are practically always assured of a good meal at one of the Chinese eateries found at virtually every shopping center in Nassau: some good *moo shi* vegetables or beef and broccoli should send you on your way with a full stomach for about $5. Naturally, every shopping-center Chinese restaurant has its Italian equivalent, often next door; Long Island lasagna is worth a second sniff.

No trip to Long Island is complete without a stop at one of its regionally unique diners. Originally, decommissioned dining cars parked on streetsides to provide short-order cooking; the diner on Long Island has since become (largely under Greek management) a fieldstone-modernist extravaganza, with potted palms, hosts, mints, and utterly preposterous menus. Whether you are rolling out of bed for an early start or returning from the late show, you should be able to find something savory on that 2-foot glossy menu tossed in front of you by the curt waitron. A Greek salad costs around $6 and can be depended upon to feed two. If you order a complete dinner (about $10) you'll probably end up with some leftovers for Schlongdorff, your dog.

Long Island Seafood Dumpling House, 2126 Merrick Ave., Merrick (867-6060). LIE Exit 38 to Meadowbrook State Pkwy. Specializes in satisfying big appetites. Perfect for large groups on their way back from Jones Beach. Nothing sensational, but plenty to fill you up. Open Mon.-Fri. noon-3pm and 5-10pm, Sat.-Sun. noon-10pm.

Christiano's, 19 Ira Rd., Syosset (921-9892). LIE to Exit 41N (South Oyster Bay Rd.), go north, cross the Jericho Tpke., continue on Jackson Ave. for 1 mi., and hang a right onto Ira Rd. Legend has it that this unassuming eatery inspired local youth Billy Joel to write his hit "Italian Restaurant." (It's not true, but on a lucky day you might have the good fortune to glimpse the Piano Man himself, nursing a tallboy at the bar.) Order a bottle of blush chablis to enjoy with the excellent food and prices (most entrees around $6). Open Mon.-Thurs. 11:30am-1am, Fri.-Sat. 11:30am-2am, Sun. noon-1am. The sequel, **Christiano's II** (933-7272), pastaletizes in Plainview at 361 South Oyster Bay Rd. Open Mon.-Thurs. 11am-midnight, Fri.-Sat. 11am-1am, Sun. noon-1am.

Raay-Nor's Cabin, 550 Sunrise Hwy., Baldwin (223-4886). Southern State Pkwy. Exit 20. Real home cooking at dirt cheap prices. Amazing southern fried chicken ($10). Top it off with key lime pie. Open Mon.-Fri. 5-9:30pm, Sat. 4-10pm, Sun. 1-9pm.

Pizza Delight, 1048 Old Country Rd., Plainview (931-3910). LIE to Exit 41S. Go through Hicksville on Rte. 107, make a left onto Old Country Rd. and go 1/4mi. past the Seaford-Oyster Bay Expwy. Pizza for the ultra-sophisticated. Try the "white pizza," which has olive oil, mozzarella, and ricotta—but no tomato sauce. One pie ($15) serves 3 or 4. Praiseworthy broccoli rolls, fit for a president. Open Mon.-Thurs. 10am-10pm, Fri. 10am-11pm, Sat. 11am-11pm, Sun. 11am-10pm.

Alfredo's Pizza, 163 Post Ave., Westbury (333-7877). Northern State Pkwy. Exit 32. Long Islanders will send Alfredo up against any Manhattan pizzeria with understandable confidence.

Tangy tomato sauce and heavy cheese. The restaurant is open daily from 10:30am-10:30pm, but the pizza craver can satisfy that urge until 1am Sun.-Thurs. and as late as 2am Fri.-Sat.

Empire Diner, 42 Jerusalem Ave., Hicksville (433-3350). LIE to Exit 41S (Route 107), go through Hicksville and take the left fork to Jerusalem Ave.; the diner is on the right. Excellent dinner fare. Humbler than its name suggests. A bit greasy, but awfully tasty. Open daily 6am-1am.

Fuddruckers, 725 Merrick Ave., Westbury (832-8323). LIE to Exit 40 (Jericho Tpke.). Go south and turn left onto Post Lane, which after 4 mi. will become Merrick Ave. Carefully engineered to produce the best all-around hamburger experience a human can have. Look through the glass walls to see freshly ground beef being prepared in the kitchen or examine the mini bun-bakery while you wait for your order. Listen to the cows not being slaughtered out back. Then garnish that burger at the gourmet fixings bar. 1/3-lb. burger $4.18, 1/2-lb. burger $4.78. Open Mon.-Thurs. 11am-10pm, Fri. 11am-11pm, Sat. 11am-midnight, Sun. 11am-9pm.

Stango's, 19 Grove St., Glen Cove (671-2389). LIE Exit 39N to Rte. 107. Since 1914, this neighborhood southern Italian restaurant has been serving up delicious bargain food. Red checked tablecloths and garlic bread. Open Tues.-Sun. 4-11pm.

To Fu, 8025 Jericho Tpke., Woodbury (921-7981 or 921-7983). Take LIE Exit 43 N. (South Oyster Bay Rd.), go north, make a right onto Jericho Tpke., travel about 1 1/2mi. It's on the left just past the Finast shopping center. Chinese and Japanese food to rave about. Friendly (if a bit overzealous) service. Praiseworthy To Fu, and some of the best sushi on Long Island. Entrees start around $9. Open Mon.-Thurs. 11:30am-10pm, Fri. 11:30am-11pm. Sat. 12:30-11pm, Sun. 1-10pm.

Suffolk

On the north and south forks, upscale seafood eateries abound. Don't trust decor as an indicator of price; there are a lot of expensive dives lurking about.

For a truly wholesome food experience, visit one of **Lewin Farms'** two separate pickin' patches. At the one on Sound Ave. in Wading River (929-4327), you can pick your own apples, nectarines, and peaches. (Open May-Dec. daily 9am-5pm. LIE to Exit 68, go north to Rte. 25A and east to Sound Ave.—it's the first farm on Sound Ave.) At the other (727-3346), 123 Sound Ave. in Calverton, you can pick strawberries, raspberries, plums, pears, peaches, nectarines, beans, onions, peas, squash, and tomatoes. Pumpkins too. (Open June-Nov. daily 8am-6pm. LIE to Exit 71N, drive on Edwards Ave. to Sound Ave.; the farm is 1/4mi. down on the left.)

Seasons Restaurant, 3845 Veteran's Memorial Hwy., Ronkonkoma (585-950, ext. 316). LIE Exit 57 south on to Veterans' Memorial Hwy. Bright restaurant with a traditional light menu. Fish and chips $7, great quiche of the day $5. Open Sun.-Thurs. 6:30am-10pm, Fri-Sat. 6:30am-11pm.

Grace's, Rte. 111, Manorville (874-2833). LIE Exit 70. Used to be a hot dog stand; good business swelled its size. Still the best hot dogs on the island ($1.25). Open Mon.-Thurs. 5am-9:30pm, Fri.-Sat. 5am--11pm., Sun. 7am-11pm.

Driver's Seat, 62 Jobs Lane, Southampton (283-6606). Rte. 27E to Southampton town center. A well-known Hamptons meeting place. Eat indoors, outdoors, or at the bar. Entrees like jumbo burgers, quiche, and local seafood run $5-16. Open daily 11:30am-11pm or last call.

Fish Net, 122 Montauk Hwy., Hampton Bays (728-0115). Some of the best fish on the South Fork. Served on paper plates, eaten with sleeves rolled up. Often a wait. Open Sun.-Thurs. 11:30am-10pm, Fri.-Sat. 11:30am-11pm.

Lotus East, 416 North County Rd., St. James (862-6030). LIE Exit 56, then north on Rte. 111 to Rte 25A. Delicious Chinese food. Noisy and crowded. Quite remarkable fried dumplings. Open Sun.-Thurs. 11:30am-10:30pm, Fri. 11:30am-11pm, Sat. 11am-11pm, Sun. 11am-10pm.

Lobster Roll Restaurant, Montauk Hwy., Amagansett (267-3740). LIE to Exit 70, Rte. 3S to Sunrise Hwy., which becomes Montauk Hwy.; the restaurant lies about 3 mi. out of town center, on the right. Lyrical seafood shack surrounded by dunes and seagulls. Dinner $10. Open Sun.-Thurs. 11:30am-10pm, Fri.-Sat. 11:30am-11pm.

Meeting House Inn, Meeting House Creek Rd., Aquebogue (722-4220). LIE to Exit 73, Rte. 25E to Aquebogue, cross Rte. 105 and make a right onto Edgar, cross the railroad tracks and bear left onto Meeting House Creek Rd. Seafood and steaks alongside Meeting House Creek.

Reservations suggested. Dinners around $12. Open Mon.-Thurs. 11:30am-10pm, Fri.-Sat. 11:30am-11pm, Sun. 11:30am-3pm.

56th Fighter Group, Republic Airport, Rte. 110, Farmingdale (694-8280). LIE to Exit 49 on to Rte. 110 south; follow signs to the airport. English farmhouse in the midst of a World War II encampment, complete with bunkers, sandbags, low-flying planes, and Glenn Miller's trombone-tugging dance tunes. Lunches from $5.50; dinners from $11. Open daily 11am-midnight.

Spinnaker's, Main St., Sag Harbor (725-9353). LIE Exit 70 to Rte. 27, left at the monument on Bridgehampton Tpke. Stay to the right, follow it all the way into Sag Harbor town—it's in the middle of the block on the right. This airy, inviting American/Italian eatery is quite a draw—there's usually a wait on weekends. Maybe it's the primavera (the most popular dish by far) or the unlimited supply of warm, delicious homemade bread at every table. Maybe it's the friendly service. Any one of these alone is reason to check this restaurant out. A filling meal will run you about $12. Open Sun.-Thurs. 11:30am-10pm, Fri.-Sat. 11:30am-11pm. On "theater nights" (when the nearby Sag Harbor Theater has a show) the place stays open until 10:30pm.

Peter's Pasta Specialties, 132 W. Main St., Babylon (422-9233). Take the Southern State Parkway East to 109 S. and follow it to the end. Fork left on Montauk Highway, make a left onto Main St. A cozy Italian restaurant where, if nothing on the menu makes your mouth water, you can dream up your own meal and then watch the chef prepare it. The specials are always special, and the service is amazing. Entrees cost about $9. On weekends, the lines sometimes stretch out the door. Open Mon.-Thurs. 5-9pm, Fri.-Sat. 5-10:30pm, Sun. 2-8pm.

Sights

Nassau

Nassau has lots of sights you don't know about. The Blue Ribbon of the Atlantic, an eight-foot-tall onyx, gold, and silver trophy, is awarded to the nation that holds the speed record for transatlantic ship travel. This title has been held by the U.S., and the trophy kept in the **United States Merchant Marine Museum** (773-5000) in King's Point, since 1952—although Richard Branson's British *Virgin Atlantic Challenger* beat the record only to be denied the trophy on a technicality. The museum stows away in a beautiful Gold Coast mansion overlooking the Long Island Sound, just over the Throgs Neck Bridge. Take LIE to Exit 33N, then Lakeville Rd., which becomes Middleneck Rd., and turn left on Steamboat Rd.

The **Sands Point Preserve,** on Middleneck Rd. in Port Washington, is notable for its astounding architecture. Originally, this densely forested 216-acre property was home to railroad heir Howard Gould. His Hempstead House, built here in 1910, was modeled after a Tudor period English castle. He also built some of Long Island's most lavish stables; called **Castlegould,** they are modeled after Ireland's turreted Kilkenny Castle. Daniel Guggenheim purchased the estate in 1917, and in 1923 his son Harry built **Falaise** on the cliffs overlooking the Long Island Sound. A Norman-style manor house, Falaise includes medieval and Renaissance architectural elements in its design. Together these buildings form one of the most remarkable surveys of European architecture this side of the Atlantic.

The grounds now attract families and young children on school trips. Castlegould is part visitors' reception center and part children's exhibition; the grounds host other special events (call 883-1610 for information). One-hour escorted tours of Hempstead House are offered Monday through Wednesday; advance reservations are encouraged. (Open May to mid-Nov. Sat.-Wed. 10am-5pm.) If you can escape the howling children, the grounds offer six peaceful nature walks. (Open early April to mid-December, 10am-5pm.) Take LIE to Exit 36N (Searingtown Rd., which becomes Port Washington Blvd., then Middleneck Rd.).

The **Polish American Museum,** at 116 Bellevue Ave. in Port Washington (883-6542), maintains hundreds of volumes, along with church artifacts and army items. (Open Mon.-Fri. 10am-4pm, Sat.-Sun. 1-4pm). The museum stands two blocks from the Port Washington LIRR stop. By car, take LIE to Exit 36N (Searington Rd.), go north about five miles, and make a left onto Main St., which connects with Bellevue Ave.

The **Nassau County Museum of Art** (484-9338) in Roslyn Harbor offers great exhibits from museums around the country. Summer 1993 promises an exhibit entitled "La Belle Epoque," featuring paintings, drawings, prints, sculpture, and furniture from 1870-1914. Even if you aren't interested in the art inside the museum, walk around the gardens. (Open Tues.-Sat. 11am-5pm; take the LIE to Exit 35, then go north to 25A west.)

Just north of Roslyn Harbor is the beautiful seaside town of **Sea Cliff**, only a mile square and full of charming streets lined with little gingerbread houses. Follow Glen Cove Rd. north off the LIE (Exit 39) and look for the signs.

Those tired of manicured gardens and delicately pruned trees can find nature in a more untamed condition at one of the preserves scattered throughout the county. The **Garvies Point Museum and Preserve** (671-0300), one of the best of its kind, includes a small museum (with exhibits on regional geology, archeology, and anthropology) and 60 acres of woods, thickets, fields, and ponds. Nice at sunset in autumn. (Museum open May-Oct. daily 9am-4:45pm. Preserve open year-round Mon.-Fri. 8am-dusk, Sat.-Sun. 9am-dusk.) Take LIE to Exit 39N, follow Glen Cove Rd. north for five miles, then take the left fork (Rte. 107) to its end, and turn right. Go left on Cottage Rd. and follow the signs. The museum hosts a popular annual **Indian Feast** the weekend before Thanksgiving.

Several other lavish Gold Coast properties, now open to the public, boast extravagant gardens. Among the largest is the **Planting Fields Arboretum,** site of insurance magnate William Robertson Coe's Oyster Bay home, Coe Hall (922-0479 or -9206). Constructed in 1921 in the Tudor Revival style, the residence has rows upon rows of mind-boggling windows. Only eight decorated rooms are open to the public; unless you are an interiors enthusiast, you may be better off using your imagination and admiring the building from the outside. (House open Mon.-Fri. 1-3:30pm.) Take LIE to 41N, go north on U.S. 106 to Rte. 25A and follow the signs. The massive Arboretum consists of 409 acres of some of the most valuable real estate in the New York area. Two huge greenhouses, covering 1 1/2 acres, contain the largest camellia collection in the northeast. The flowers burst into bloom during the unlikely months of January, February, and March, when most city-dwellers have begun to forget what flora look like. Other quirky highlights include a "synoptic garden" of plants obsessively arranged according to their Latin names, from A to Z—every letter is represented, except "J" and "W." The **Fall Flower Show,** held in mid-October, attracts huge crowds every year. (Grounds open daily 9am-5pm.) If you're around in the summer, check out the concert series hosted by the Arboretum. Past seasons have seen the likes of Joan Baez and the Indigo Girls. Spyro Gyra too.

At **Old Westbury Gardens,** on Old Westbury Rd. (333-0048), yet another extravagant estate, nature overwhelms architecture. You can feel the setting take over as you pass through the wrought iron gates and drive down the gravel road lined with towering evergreens. The elegant house, built by John Phipps in 1906 and modeled after 19th-century English country manors, sits in the shadow of its surroundings. These grounds are smaller than the Planting Fields, but they are better organized and full of flowers. The two lakes are ornamented by sculptures, gazebos, and water lilies. A vast rose garden adjoins a number of theme gardens (such as the "grey garden," which contains only plants in shades of silver and deep purple). Take LIE to Exit 39S (Glen Cove Rd.), make a right onto Old Westbury Rd., and continue another 1/4mi.

Budding botanists should also visit **Clark Gardens** and the **Bailey Arboretum.** Clark Gardens, at 193 I.U. Willets Rd. in Albertson (621-7568), set on much smaller grounds, has over 20 special displays and three ponds, as well as five honey-producing beehives. (Open Mon.-Fri. 8am-4:30pm, Sat.-Sun. 10am-4:30pm.) Take LIE to Exit 37S, go south 1mi. on Willis Ave. and then left onto I.U. Willets Rd. for about 1/4mi. The Bailey Arboretum (676-4497) blossoms on Bayville Rd. in luxurious Locust Valley. Here you can find some of the largest trees on the Island, a miniature castle carved by a German master craftsman, and one garden with wheelchair access. (Open May-Oct. Tues.-Sun. 9am-4pm. Admission $1.) Take LIE to Exit 41N (U.S. 107N), go right on U.S. 25A, then left onto Wolver Hollow Rd., and follow the signs.

Of course, if you happen to be driving around these gardens, you have an excuse to tour the ritzy North Shore. Take a few turns off the major roads to drive past some breathtaking (and some breathtakingly vulgar) homes of the rich and anonymous. Make sure your gas tank is full; it's easy to lose track of time as you argue with your car-mates over the comparative merits of Tudor Revival and Contemporary.

The **Tackapausha Museum and Preserve** (785-2802), on Washington Ave., just south of the Sunrise highway in Seaford, offers 80 acres of lush greenery and local wildlife. A museum pamphlet details the 200 species of insect and animal life in the region. The museum itself has a variety of animals in artificial habitats, including a number of nocturnal animals in a reversed night-day cycle. (Museum open daily 9:30am-4:45pm. Preserve open daily dawn-dusk.) LIE to Exit 44S, follow the Seaford-Oyster Bay Expwy. to its end, go east on U.S. 27A (Merrick Rd.), and turn left on Washington Ave.

Nassau does have some activities involving people rather than shrubs. Quite a few places in the county keep a sense of local history alive. Don't miss Nassau's top cultural attraction, **Old Bethpage Village Restoration** (420-5280), on Round Swamp Rd. in Old Bethpage. In this "history preserve," fragments of Long Island's 19th-century heritage have been gathered and reassembled in the form of a typical pre-Civil War village. As you enter the general store or the blacksmith's shop, employees clad in period costume will explain their occupations. The hatter is especially informative. Special events take place every weekend afternoon; stick around for sheep shearing. Ahnghito! Overall, the village seems to succeed quite well in recreating the 1850s, and because it is county-run, Bethpage manages to avoid being obnoxiously commercial. Of course, charm of Americana can wear out, especially in summer when this place packs solid with tourists. Winter visitors may have to dodge school groups. Columbus Day weekend brings the **Long Island Fair,** a popular old-fashioned festival. Take LIE to Exit 48, then hang a right onto Round Swamp Rd. and a left onto the winding driveway. I wouldn't kick the fondue here out of bed.

Relive history on a more modest scale at two attractions near one another in Oyster Bay, a small and sleepy town on the North Shore. Take LIE to Exit 41N and go north past U.S. 25A on U.S. 106, which becomes first Pine Hollow Rd. and then 6th St. You can get to **Sagamore Hill** (922-4447) perhaps the most important residence in Nassau County, by turning right off 6th St. in the town center and then following the signs to Cove Neck Rd. A National Historical Site, Sagamore Hill was the summer residence of Theodore Roosevelt during his presidential term. Roosevelt met here with envoys from Japan and Russia during the summer of 1905 to set in motion negotiations that would lead to the Treaty of Portsmouth, which ended the Russo-Japanese War. Despite a few recent robberies, the house remains jam-packed with "Teddy" memorabilia, and its Victorian clutter evokes a powerful sense of Roosevelt's era; the collection of antlers reflects his sporting interests. (Open Wed.-Sun. 9:30am-5pm.)

While in Oyster Bay, check out **Raynham Hall** (922-6808), 20 West Main St., a left turn off 6th St. in the town center. A lesson in architectural epoque-clashing incongruity, this house has a colonial salt-box façade in front, and a rear preserved in an overlaid Victorian style. Inside you will find Colonial and Victorian rooms side by side. Discover for yourself how home life evolved during the 18th and 19th centuries.

Since the days of Melville, U.S. culture has given a suitably prominent place to that longest of mammals, the whale. To indulge a cetacean obsession or merely to catch up on what you have been missing, nothing compares to the **Cold Spring Harbor Whaling Museum** (367-3418), on Main St. in Cold Spring Harbor. Built in honor of a small whaling fleet that sailed from Cold Spring Harbor in the mid-19th century, the museum features a 30-foot-long fully rigged vessel, one of only six remaining whaleboats of its kind in the world. The collection of scrimshaw, detailed whalebone carvings done to pass the long hours at sea, testifies to the joys of the seafaring tradition. (Open Labor Day-Memorial Day daily 11am-5pm. Wheelchair access.)

Harpoons and creaky old houses do not tell the whole of Nassau's history. The **African-American Museum,** at 110 North Franklin St. in Hempstead (485-0470), houses a permanent collection on the history of African-Americans on Long Island, as well as traveling exhibits, films, lectures, and educational programs on the contributions of African-Americans to the region and to the nation. (Open Tues.-Sat. 9am-4:45pm, Sun. 1-4:45pm.) Take LIE to Exit 39S and go south to the town center on Hempstead Ave., which becomes Fulton Ave.; turn left onto Franklin St. and continue four lights down.

While Long Island remains unrivaled in the field of Long Island history, its traditional fine arts museums must go head to head with those in Manhattan. Art museums on the Island tend to be small and modest, offering a welcome change from cavernous New York galleries. The cutting-edge "computer imaging facility" at the **Fine Arts Museum of Long Island,** 295 Fulton Ave. in Hempstead (481-5700), is actually interesting. Five computers feature the interactive graphic design of contemporary computer artists. The work is mesmerizing. Local artists get their own shows in the summer, and exhibits change every two months. (Open Wed.-Sat. 10am-4:30pm, Sun. noon-4:30pm.) Take LIE to Exit 39S onto Hempstead Ave., which turns into Fulton Ave. The nearby **Hofstra Museum** (463-5672), on the campus of Hofstra University, has galleries of ethnology and Modern American and European art as well as a 42-piece sculpture garden. The museum is famous for its innovative exhibitions, and recently hosted a popular Henry Moore retrospective. (Open Tues.-Fri. 10am-5pm; off-season Tues. 10am-9pm, Wed.-Fri. 10am-5pm, Sat.-Sun. 1-5pm.) Take LIE to Exit 38S and Meadowbrook Pkwy., go west on Hempstead Tpke. for four traffic lights, turn left onto the campus and follow the signs.

Jones Beach State Park (784-1600) is the best compromise of convenience and crowd for daytrippers from the city. There are nearly 2500 acres of beachfront here and the parking area accommodates 23,000 cars. Only 40 minutes from the City, Jones Beach packs in the crowds in the summer months. The beach becomes a sea of umbrellas and blankets with barely a patch of sand showing. Along the 1 1/2-mile boardwalk you can find deck games, roller-skating, miniature golf, basketball, and nightly dancing. The **Marine Theater** inside the park hosts rock concerts (see Nassau: Entertainment). There are eight different bathing areas on either the rough Atlantic Ocean or the calmer Zachs Bay, plus a number of beaches restricted to residents of certain towns in Nassau County. During the summer you can take the LIRR to Freeport or Wantaugh, where you can get a bus to the beach. Call 212-739-4200 or 212-526-0900 for information. **Recreation Lines, Inc.** (718-788-8000) provides bus service straight from mid-Manhattan. If you are driving, take LIE east to the Northern State Pkwy., go east to the Meadowbrook (or Wantaugh) Pkwy. and then south to Jones Beach.

Suffolk

For a comparatively rural and undeveloped place, Suffolk County is superchunk-full of first-rate and offbeat attractions. Many of Suffolk's colonial roots have been successfully preserved, so the county offers some fine colonial house-museums. Salty old towns, full of shady streets—refreshing retreats from the din of New York—line the lazy coast.

On the other hand, Suffolk transforms during the summer, when the water warms, the sun shines, the hotels double their rates, and it seems as if half of New York is tagging along as you stroll along the streets. On sunny weekends thousands of other people will have the same bright idea as you. Ordinarily most places in Suffolk are about two or three hours away from Manhattan by car, bus, or LIRR. But the easy ride gets hard on Friday afternoons and even harder on Sunday evenings, when flocks of urban dwellers clog the roads. The traffic nightmare can be avoided by traveling at off-peak hours. If you are going for the weekend, leave before 3pm or after 10pm on Friday. Or visit mid-week when lodging is cheaper and beaches are all but empty. The drawback to this last plan is that many of the county's most interesting sites are open only on the weekend.

Break up your trip by stopping at one of numerous roadside farm stands, where you can pick your own produce. Better yet, pull over and take a tour of one of Long Island's vineyards and wineries, many of which offer free tours and tastings (see Wine Country).

After shopping at the **Walt Whitman Mall,** the nearby **Walt Whitman's Birth-place** (427-5240) will seem a more appropriate memorial to the great American poet whose 1855 *Leaves of Grass* brought forth a democratic free-verse style that revolutionized poetry. The small, weathered farmhouse at 246 Old Walt Whitman Rd., Huntington Station, was built in 1816 by Walt Whitman, Sr., the Bard of Long Island's dad. You can find a several-hundred-volume library of Whitmanalia here amid simple rusted and worn furnishings. (Open Wed.-Fri. 1-4pm, Sat.-Sun. 10am-4pm.) Take LIE to Exit 49N, drive 1 3/4mi. on Rte. 110 and turn left onto Old Walt Whitman Rd.

On the edges of Heckscher State Park lies a stop well-worth the art-lover's time. The **Heckscher Art Museum** (351-3250), Rte. 25A and Prime Ave. in Huntington, houses European and U.S. paintings and sculptures dating from the 16th century to the present. (Open Tues.-Fri. 10am-5pm, Sat.-Sun. 1-5pm.) Take LIE to Exit 49N, go north on Rte. 110, and make a right onto 25A followed by a left onto Prime Ave.

The **Vanderbilt Museum** (262-7888), on Little Neck Rd. in Centerport, preserves some American extravagance to contrast with Whitman simplicity. Built by William Kissam Vanderbilt II (1918-1944), great-grandson of the famed "Commodore" Cornelius Vanderbilt, the 43-acre North Shore estate enjoys a great view of Northport Harbor and the Long Island Sound. (House open May-Oct. Tues.-Sat. 10am-4pm, Sun. noon-5pm.) The **Vanderbilt Planetarium** (262-7888), also on the grounds, is one of the largest and best-equipped in the country. The magnificent four-ton projector can simulate the night sky from any place on earth at any season of the year, all the way back to the dawn of humankind. On a clear evenings the 16-inch reflecting telescope sometimes opens to the public. Call ahead.

Sagtikos Manor (665-0093), on Rte. 27A in Bay Shore on the South Bay, built on 10 acres of land in 1692, remains the finest example of colonial architecture on the Island. The hub of Long Island's pre-revolutionary aristocracy, the 42-room mansion housed the commander of British forces during the revolution and perfidiously hosted George Washington during his presidency. Built by the Van Cortlandt family, it soon passed into the hands of the Thompsons, who lived there until the 20th century. Its current owner, Robert Gardiner, descends from another family of early Suffolk settlers. The only part of the building open to the public includes an exhibit of the 18th-century postal system used by revolutionary leaders as well as the old kitchen with its original paint made of lime, buttermilk, and blueberries. (Open July-Aug. Wed.-Thurs., Sun. 1-4pm; June and Sept. Sun. 1-4pm.) Take the Southern State Pkwy. to Exit 40 (the Robert Moses Causeway) and drive 1 1/2mi. south. The house is on the left, after Manor Lane.

Your scientific interests may be sparked by the **Brookhaven National Lab Exhibit Center,** located on the William Floyd Pkwy. in Brookhaven (282-2345). See old fashioned reactors, huge magnets, and an experiment show with lots of impressive explosions. (Open July-Aug. Sun. 10am-3pm, or by appointment weekdays.) Take LIE to Exit 68N onto William Floyd Pkwy.; the lab experiments about 1 1/2 miles down.

The **William Floyd Estate** (399-2030), at 245 Park Dr. in Mastic Beach, yet another magnificent and historic site, is the furnished home of a signer of the Declaration of Independence—William Floyd—and eight of his descendants. Floyds lived here from 1724 to 1975. The 25-room furnished mansion is set on 613 acres of South Shore property facing Fire Island. You're not actually reading this. Here, instead of being restored, hidden, or closed off, the modernized sections of the house have been preserved and adjoin the older sections, documenting the evolution of family life in an ancestral home. There are guided tours of the house, but don't miss the self-guided tours of the grounds and the family cemetery. (Open July-Aug. Fri.-Sun. 10am-4pm; June Sat.-Sun. 10am-4pm. Groups by reservation only.) Take LIE to Exit 68S, then the William Floyd Pkwy. for seven miles. Make a left onto Havenwood Dr. which becomes Neighborhood Dr., and a left onto Park Dr.

One of the more unusual sights on the east end is the American Armored Federation's **Tank Museum** in Mattituck. Take the LIE to Exit 73 and follow Rte. 25 into

Mattituck. Turn left onto Love Lane and you can see a whole range of armored vehicles from throughout the last century. (Open Sun. 11am-4pm.)

At the **Mattituck Historical Society Museum** on Rte. 25 in Mattituck, an 19th-century homestead has been maintained as a lived-in home—complete with clothes; children's toys, rope beds, musical instruments, and kitchen artifacts. (Open July-Aug. Sat.-Sun. 2-4pm. Write P.O. Box 766, Mattituck, NY 11952 for a calendar of events like Victorian teas, flea markets, antique shows, and doll shows.)

The **Corwith House** (537-1088) in Bridgehampton, on the corner of Montauk Hwy. and Corwith Ave., was built by the Corwith family in the late 1700s. This Greek Revival structure exhibits a multitude of period objects in rooms set up to show the way they might have looked during different eras. Next door stands the **George W. Strong Blacksmith and Wheelwright Shop,** with a working forge and many blacksmith's tools. The shop was moved here from its original site in Wainscott, a few towns to the east. (Both open June-Labor Day Mon. and Thurs.-Sat. 10am-4pm.) The **Guild Hall Museum,** at 158 Main St. in East Hampton, ensures that sophisticated New Yorkers escaping to the Hamptons do not have to suffer art withdrawal. The collection specializes in well-known artists of the eastern Island region from the late 19th century to the present. Guild Hall hosts changing exhibitions, films, lectures, concerts, plays, art classes, and special events.

For those who have had their fill of museums, art exhibits, and historical sites, the **Long Island Game Farm and Zoological Park** (878-6644) in Manorville, 2 miles south of LIE Exit 70, is the perfect place to go for a more interactive, hands-on good time. Stroke the goats in the petting zoo, which, along with countless other tame and exotic animals, make the game farm their home. The **Oceanarium Sea School Theater** presents sea lion shows several times a day. (Open mid-April-mid-Oct. 9am-5pm daily.)

Wine Country

No one ever said that Long Island wines were famous, or even really good, but visiting one of the North Fork's 40 vineyards can be a positive experience. Twelve wineries and 40 vineyards produce the best Chardonnay, Cabernet Sauvignon, Merlot, Pinot Noir, and Riesling in New York State. Local climate and soil conditions rival those of Napa Valley. Two Long Island wines were even chosen to be served at President Bush's inauguration. Quite a few of the Island wineries offer free tours and tastings; call ahead and make an appointment.

To get to the wine district, take LIE to its end (Exit 73), then Rte. 58, which becomes Rte. 25 (Main Rd.). North of and parallel to Rte. 25 is Rte. 48 (North Rd. or Middle Rd.), which has a number of wineries. Road signs announce tours and tastings.

> **Palmer Vineyards,** 108 Sound Ave., Riverhead (722-9463). Take a self-guided tour of the most advanced equipment on the island and see a tasting room with an interior assembled from two 18th-century English pubs. On Oct. weekends you can take a hayride to the vineyards.

> **Bridgehampton Winery,** Sag Harbor Tpke., Bridgehampton (537-3155). Guided tours June-Sept. daily 11am-6pm. The winery holds special summer events, including the effervescent Chardonnay Festival in mid-July.

> **Bedell Cellars,** Rte. 25, Cutchogue (734-7537). Offers tastings, tours and sales by appointment.

> **Mattituck Hills Winery,** Bergen and Sound Ave., Mattituck (298-9150). Hosts both a Strawberry Festival and a Pre-Harvest Festival, as well as daily tours and tastings.

Sag Harbor

Out on the South Fork's north shore droops Sag Harbor, one of the best-kept secrets of Long Island. Founded in 1707, this port used to be more important than New York Harbor; its deep shore made for easy navigation. In 1789, Washington signed the document creating Ports of Entry to the United States, and, of the two named, "Sagg Harbour" appeared before New York. At its peak, this darling village was the fourth largest of the world's whaling ports. It boasts the second-largest collection of colonial

buildings in the U.S., as well as cemeteries lined with the gravestones of Revolutionary soldiers and sailors. James Fenimore Cooper began his first novel, *Precaution,*
while staying in a Sag Harbor hotel in 1824. During the Prohibition years the harbor
served as a major supply spot for smugglers and rum runners from the Caribbean.

Today it is hard to imagine bustling activity on the quiet, tree-lined streets of salt-
box cottages and Greek Revival mansions. In town, catch the **Sag Harbor Whaling
Museum** (725-0770), in the former home of Benjamin Hunting, a 19th-century whale
ship owner. Enter the museum through the jawbones of a whale. Note the antique
washing machine, made locally in 1864, and the excellent scrimshaw collection.
(Open May-Sept. Mon.-Sat. 10am-5pm, Sun. 1-5pm. Tours by appointment.).

The **Whaler's Presbyterian Church**, built in 1844 in the Egyptian Revival style, is
a hodgepodge of Greek, Chinese, and Turkish architectural influences. Its old burying
ground was used as a fort when the British occupied the town during the Revolution.
Imagine this building with the 187-foot-tall steeple that crowned it until the hurricane
of 1938. Sag Harbor is also home to **Temple Adas Israel**, the oldest synagogue on
Long Island. Constructed in 1989 on a plot of land costing $350, it served the early
Jewish immigrants who arrived when Joseph Fahys started a watchcase factory here.

Montauk

At the easternmost tip of the South Fork, Montauk is one of the most popular destinations on Long Island. The place generates natural exhilaration, as you look out at
the Atlantic Ocean and realize that you can go no farther, that you have reached the
end, that there is nothing but water and a handful of sharks between you and Kerry.
The image of Montauk's famous lighthouse is what comes to mind for many people
when they think of Long Island. But Long Island sights don't get any farther away than
this: the trip from Manhattan can take up to four hours. On the bright side, though, life
gets substantially less congested once you get past the Hamptons. Take LIE to Exit 70
(Manorville), then go south to Sunrise Hwy. (Rte. 27), which becomes Montauk Hwy.,
and drive east. You will know you've arrived when water sloshes around your brake
pedal.

Montauk offers numerous accommodations and activities, but the **Montauk Point
Lighthouse and Museum** (668-2544) is the really the highpoint of a trip here. Like
the marker that greets a mountain climber who has reached a summit, the lighthouse
marks the end of the line for the weary driver. This lighthouse is exactly as it should
be: set on the rocky edge of the water, its sloping white sides adorned bluntly by a single wide band of brown. Its bulky, solid form rises with a utilitarian elegance from a
cluster of smaller, weaker buildings. The builders knew exactly what they were doing
back in 1796, when the 86-foot structure went up by special order of President George
Washington. Back then, the lighthouse was 297ft. away from the shoreline.

On a clear day, you should climb the 138 spiraling steps to the top, where you can
look out over the seascape, across the Long Island Sound to Rhode Island and Connecticut. The best seasons for viewing are the spring and fall, when the sea has scarce-
ly a stain on it; the thick summer air can haze over the view. You may want to climb
up, even on a foggy day, to see if you can spot the so-called "Will o' the Wisp," a clip-
per ship sometimes sighted on hazy days under full sail with a lantern hanging from its
mast. Experts claim that the ship is a mirage resulting from the presence of phospho-
rus in the atmosphere, but what do they know anyway? (Open May to mid-June and
early Oct.-Nov. Sat.-Sun. 10:30am-4pm; mid-June to mid-Sept. daily 10:30am-6pm;
mid-Sept. to early Oct. Fri.-Mon. 10:30am-5pm.)

Fishing and whale-watching are among Montauk's other pleasures. **Lazybones'**
half-day fishing "party boat," which is more party than boat, makes two trips daily,
from 7am to noon and from 1 to 5pm, leaving from Tuma's Dock next to Grossman's.
Call Captain Mike at 668-5671 for information. The **Okeanos Whale Watch Cruise**
is one of the best in the business, though a tad expensive. The cruises are run by the
non-profit Okeanos Research Foundation, which helps finance its studies of whales by
taking tourists out on its 90-foot ship, accompanied by a biologist and research team
of whale experts. You may see Fin, Minke, and Humpback whales.

The Island's Islands: Fire and Shelter

Fire Island, one of the more extraordinary natural sites off of Long Island's shores, is a 32-mile-long barrier island protecting the South Shore from the roaring waters of the Atlantic. The state has designated most of Fire Island as a state park or federal "wilderness area," legally protected from development, but 17 summer communities have designated the rest of it as their resort area and have forged their own niche here. Fire Island's unique landscape will make you forget there ever was such a city as New York. Cars are allowed only on the easternmost and westernmost tips of the island; there are no streets, only "walks." Fire Island was a hip counterculture spot during the 60s, and today maintains a laid-back atmosphere; predominantly gay communities thrive in two of Fire Island's many resorts, Cherry Grove and the Pines.

The **Fire Island National Seashore** is the main draw here, and in summer it offers fishing, clamming, and guided nature walks. The facilities at **Sailor's Haven** include a marina, a nature trail, and a famous beach. Similar facilities at **Watch Hill** include a 20-unit campground, where reservations are required. **Smith Point West** has a small visitor information center and a nature trail with disabled access (289-4810). Here you can spot horseshoe crabs, whitetail deer, and monarch butterflies, which flit across the country every year to winter in Baja California.

The **Sunken Forest,** so-called because of its location down behind the dunes, is another of the Island's natural wonders. Located directly west of Sailor's Haven, its soils support an unusual and attractive (visually, at least) combination of gnarled holly, sassafras, and poison ivy. From the summit of the dunes, the forest looks like a well-tended lawn: the trees are laced together in a hulky, uninterrupted mesh.

Ferries shuttle between the South Shore and the park from May through November. From Bay Shore, they sail to Fair Harbor, Ocean Beach, Dunewood, Saltaire, and Kismet. From Sayville (589-8980), ferries leave for Sailor's Haven, Cherry Grove, and Fire Island Pines. From Patchogue, ferries go to Davis Park and Watch Hill. LIRR stations lie within a short distance of the three ferry terminals, making access from New York City relatively simple. (See Practical Information.)

Shelter Island bobs in the protected body of water between the North and South Forks. Accessible by ferry (see Practical Information) or by private boat, this island of about 12 square miles offers wonderful beaches and a serene sense of removal from the intrusions of the City. That doesn't mean you'll have to rough it here, because the island has virtually everything that you might need, including a coalyard, four insurance agencies, and a real estate attorney.

Entertainment and Nightlife

The best nightlife for most Long Islanders is in Manhattan. The selection is severely limited out on the island, but there's still no reason to sit at home reading a book after the sun sets over the Long Island Sound. Huge multi-screen theaters pepper the island, and tickets are cheaper than in the city. *Newsday* has full listings.

Nassau

Nassau has never been known as a late-night paradise; post-movie options are limited. You can relax to some live jazz at **Sonny's Place,** 3603 Merrick Rd., Seaford (826-0973). Sonny extracts an $8 cover charge here on Friday and Saturday nights and enforces a two-drink minimum. During the week the music plays on, without the cover or minimum. For dancing, try **Gatsby's,** a fashionable spot on a stretch past the green light at 1067 Old Country Rd. in Westbury (997-3685). The DJ starts spinning at 9pm Tues.-Sat., and there are occasional live shows on Thurs. and Sat. nights.

Nassau's comedy clubs feature unknown but rising talents as well as established New York names. Chuckles, at 159 Jericho Tpke. in Mineola (746-2770), has a $5-12 cover and a two-drink minimum, with shows Wednesday through Sunday. Belly laughs ripple through Governor's Comedy Shop, 90A Division Ave., Levittown (731-3358) Tuesday through Saturday. (Cover $8-17, 2-drink min.)

Nassau also bows to the more refined. **The Great Neck Symphony** (466-5155) gives regular concerts throughout the county, and the **Long Island Philharmonic** (239-2222), a highly respected orchestra, performs at the Tilles Center for the Performing Arts. Located on the C.W. Post Campus of Long Island University, on Northern Blvd. in Greenvale, the **Tilles Center** (299-2600) has recently been renovated. Enjoy a concert under its slopy white ceiling. The **Arena Players Repertory Theater,** 296 Rte. 109 in East Farmingdale (293-0674) and the **Broadhollow Theater** at 229 Rte. 110, Farmingdale (752-1400), have full calendars of productions. Performances can be uneven, especially by New York standards, and shows are often overly commercial. Still, the theaters have matured, and are worth a look when a favorite goes up. Local universities also have active theaters–notably the **Olmstead** at Adelphi University in Garden City (741-2313) and the **John Cranford Adams Playhouse** at Hofstra University, on Fulton Ave. in Hempstead (560-6644).

National rock concert tours stop during the summer at the **Jones Beach Marine Theater,** Jones Beach State Park, Wantaugh (785-1600). Joining the bandmembers for some slam-dancing is impossible here unless you have a rowboat; the stage is separated from the bleachers by a wide stretch of water. In a production of "Showboat," the actors made their entrances and exits by motorboat. Now the theater hosts concerts exclusively. The **Westbury Music Fair,** on Brush Hollow Rd. in Westbury (334-0800), has a tremendous theater in the round, and usually hosts traditional big names on tour.

Suffolk

The most exciting nighttime entertainment in Suffolk (besides breathing the night air and listening to the crickets) can be found on the grounds of the parks and museums, which host harpsichord and piano recitals. This outdoor musical life, as with most things in Suffolk, becomes much more active in the summer. Performance dates and times vary; call the parks for schedules (see Suffolk: Sights). Some of these parks restrict admission to local residents, or charge exorbitant fees to keep out tourists like yourself—get the dope before setting out. *Dan's Papers,* published in Bridgehampton, provides information on concerts and other nighttime happenings.

If music by dead Europeans is unappealing, watusi over to one of the clubs on Long Island, like **Spize II**, at 1058 Broadhollow Rd., Farmingdale (753-2096). (Cover $5-10. Open Thurs.-Sat. 10pm-4am.) Techno-industrial-alternative music for the local college scene. Farther out on the Island, **CPI** (the Canoe Place Inn), located on the East Montauk Hwy. in Hampton Bays (728-4121), caters to a more mature crowd. Drop by the piano lounge, listen to live patio jazz, or shake your love thing on the sprawling dance floor. You must be 21 or over and wearing proper attire to enter.

One of the newer, hipper clubs for the post-college crowd is **Co-Co's Water Café,** at 117 New York Ave., Huntington (271-5700). (Open 11:30-4am daily. Beware: the minimum age for the nightclub goes *up* on the weekends (from 21 to 23 for women, 25 for men). The South Fork has a number of New Yorky clubs, but the covers are steep ($10-20) and the dancing, uneven. Try **Plastic Bananafish** (283-8298) on Rte. 27 at the Omnicenter in Southampton.

For stand-up comedy in Suffolk, look to: **Boomer's,** 1509 Main St., Port Jefferson (473-9226), with shows from Thursday to Saturday nights and an $8-15 cover; **Joker's Wild,** 503 Lake Ave., St. James (584-9565) with a cover of $5; and **Thomas McGuire's Comedy,** 1627 Smithtown Ave., Bohemia (467-5413), with a $9 cover and shows Friday and Saturday nights; and **East Side Comedy Club,** at 1815 Rte. 110, Farmingdale (249-6061), with shows Wed.-Sun. and a $6-22 charge.

The **New Community Cinema** in Huntington (423-7653), just over the Nassau border, is a local secret and one of the only places on Long Island where you can safely call your movie a "film." It provides a great alternative to the huge, more commercial theaters by screening offbeat documentaries and foreign art flicks. Shows are often preceded by introductions or concluded with question-and-answer sessions with the filmmakers themselves (Wim Wenders, among others, has stopped by for this purpose) or simply those in the know. Eat brownies and siphon herbal tea while you wait for the lights to go down (they won't start the film until everyone is seated). Bye.

Appendices

Free New York

New York may cost an arm and a leg to live in, but you can visit it without having the Midas touch. Free entertainment abounds; you just need to know where to look.

Some museums--the Cooper-Hewitt, the Fraunces Tavern Museum, the International Center of Photography, MoMA, and the Whitney--have weekly free times, often on Tuesday evenings. Others have voluntary donation policies; if you're on a budget, you can choose to pay less at the Alternative Museum, the Black Fashion Museum, the Brooklyn Museum, the Center for African Art, the Cloisters, the Fraunces Tavern Museum, the Metropolitan Museum, the Museum of Television and Radio, and the New Museum of Contemporary Art. Smaller galleries and some museums never charge admission; without spending a penny, you can visit the American Numismatic Society, the AT&T Infoquest Center, Bible House, the China House Gallery, the City Gallery, the Forbes Magazine Galleries, the Garibaldi-Meuci Museum on Staten Island, the Hall of Fame for Great Americans, the Hispanic Society of America, the IBM Gallery of Science and Art, the Museum of American Folk Art, the Museum of American Illustration, the Nicholas Roerich Museum, the Police Academy Museum, the Schomburg Center for Research in Black Culture, and the Staten Island Children's Museum. For those who prefer more animate entertainment, the Bronx Zoo is free Tuesday through Thursday, and the Staten Island Zoo is free on Wednesday.

For free, you can tour Grand Central Station, the Lincoln Center Library, the New York Stock Exchange, and the Commodities Exchange Center at the World Trade Center. Paying your respects at Grant's Tomb and the U.N. General Assembly (Sept.-Dec.) costs nothing. And colonial dwellings like the Dyckman House and Hamilton Grange welcome their modern-day visitors free of charge.

Shakespeare shows for free in Central Park, if you can wake up early enough to obtain a ticket. Music schools don't charge for their concerts: try Juilliard, the Greenwich Music School, and the Bloomingdale House of Music. You can listen to a prestigious free lecture series at the Cooper Union, or to free poetry at the 92nd Street Y.

Come summertime, troopers willing to brave the heat enjoy concerts, dances, comedy, theatre, and film at absolutely no charge. The *Summer in New York* brochure, available free at the Visitors Bureau and other info booths (see Practical Information), presents a full catalog of gratis summertime events. The **Market at CitiCorp Center** (559-2330), on the corner of 53rd St. and Lexington Ave., brings out the big drums at dinnertime (6-7pm) to entertain musically attuned yuppies. The summer 1992 menu included jazz, big bands, and country-western. The **Mark Goodson Theatre** (841-4100) sponsors free midday classical concerts from October to June at 2 Columbus Circle, near 58th St. and Eighth Ave.

Assorted corporate magnates mount their own musical agendas. From June to August, **Rockefeller Center** (698-8901) holds concerts on Tuesday and Thursday at 12:30pm at the Garden at 1251 Avenue of the Americas. On Wednesdays, the Rockefeller series moves to the McGraw Hill Minipark at 48th St. and Sixth Ave. (also at 12:30pm). **The World Financial Center** (945-0505) hosts its own summer bash from June to September, mostly free: a fittingly global parade of art, chamber music, contemporary dance, and jazz greats like Dave Brubeck. The Duke Ellington Orchestra, the Artie Shaw Orchestra, and Buster Poindexter have all played here in the past. Serious classical music wafts alongside strains of classic rock-and-roll: the Shostakovich String Quartet shared the bill with Flash Cadillac, the beat boys from *American Graffiti*.

The **World Trade Center** (466-4170) also maintains a full summer entertainment schedule at its Austin J. Tobin Plaza, July 4 through August 31. Each day has a different theme, such as oldies, comedy, or jazz. In August, **Lincoln Center** (875-5400) holds a series of music and dance concerts six days a week, day and evening, on the plazas. Offerings include folk, blues, and classical music.

The **South St. Seaport Museum** (669-9424) presents summer outdoor concerts June through August on Saturdays at 8pm on Pier 16. The Museum of Modern Art (708-9850) holds its free **Summer Garden Series** of classical music in its delightful sculpture garden at 14 W. 54th St. (July-Aug. Fri.-Sat. at 7:30pm). And the **Washington Square Music Festival** (431-1088) presents excellent orchestra concerts every Tuesday in July. All performances are at 8pm in Washington Square.

The Central Park **Arsenal** (360-8111) provides information on free New York Parks activities, like the Central Park Dairy's calcium-enriched Sunday afternoon recitals. **The Lower Manhattan Cultural Council** (432-0900) stages music and dance performances and public readings at various downtown sites. **American Landmark Festivals** (866-2086) include a series of free summertime concerts at various locales.

Other boroughs host private fiestas which they invite you to join. Every Sunday in August, the **Bronx Arts Ensemble** (601-7399) performs at Fordham University. The Bronx sponsors a music festival (590-3199) in July and/or August (depending on the budget), with free concerts on weeknights and weekend days in Bronx parks.

The **Brooklyn Summer Series** fills the bill with concerts in Brooklyn parks, playgrounds, and even shopping malls. **Celebrate Brooklyn** (718-788-0055), a multimedia extravaganza, swarms the Prospect Park Bandshell in Brooklyn with jazz, rock, worldbeat, blues, and big brass as well as dance, ballet, and theatre. The **Brooklyn Botanical Garden** (718-622-4433) hosts Pappless summer Shakespeare and outdoor chamber music.

The borough of **Queens** Arts Council (718-291-1100) organizes its own "Arts in the Park Festival" at Forest Park Seufert Bandshell, at Forest Park Dr. and Woodhaven Blvd. Concerts take place July through August; concerts for children are held on Thursdays. Check the Council's bimonthly calendar of events, the *Queens Leisure Guide,* or call its Culture Hotline (718-291-1100).

Opening Times of Sights

Alternative Museum	Nov.-June Tues.-Sat. 11am-6pm
American Craft Museum	Tues. 10am-8pm, Wed.-Sun. 10am-5pm
American Museum of the Moving Image	Tues.-Fri. noon-4pm, Sat.-Sun. noon-6pm
American Museum of Natural History	Sun.-Tues. and Thurs. 10am-5:45pm, Wed. and Fri.-Sat. 10am-9pm
American Numismatic Society	Tues.-Sat. 9am-4:30pm, Sun. 1-4pm
Arsenal Arts Gallery	Mon.-Fri. 9:30am-4:30pm
Asia Society	Tues.-Sat. 11am-6pm, Sun. noon-5pm
AT&T Infoquest Center	Tues. 10am-9pm, Wed.-Sun. 10am-6pm
Bartow-Pell Mansion Museum	Wed. and Sat.-Sun. noon-4pm, closed 3 weeks in Aug.
Bible House	Mon.-Fri. 9:30am-4:30pm
Black Fashion Museum	By appointment Mon.-Fri. noon-8pm
Bowne House	Tues. and Sat.-Sun. 2:30-4:30pm
Bronx Community College Hall of Fame	Mon.-Fri. 9am-5pm
Bronx Museum of the Arts	Wed.-Sat. 10am-5pm
Bronx Zoo	Mon.-Fri. 10am-5pm, Sat.-Sun. 10am-5:30pm; Nov.-Jan. daily 10am-4:30pm
Brooklyn Botanic Garden	April-Sept. Tues.-Fri. 8am-6pm, Sat.-Sun. and holidays 10am-6pm; Oct.-March Tues.-Fri. 8am-4:30pm, Sat. Sun. and holidays 10am-4:30pm
Cathedral of Saint John the Divine	Daily 7am-5pm
Center for African Art	Tues.-Fri. 10am-5pm, Sat. 11am-5pm, Sun. noon-5pm
Central Park Zoo	Mon. and Wed.-Fri. 10am-5pm, Tues. 10am-8pm, Sat.-Sun. 10am-5:30pm
China House Gallery	Mon. and Wed. 9am-5pm, Tues. and Thurs. 9am-8pm, Fri. 9am-11:30pm
Christ Church	Daily 9am-5pm
Church of the Ascension	Daily noon-2pm, 5pm-7pm
Citibank, no. 55 Wall St.	Mon.-Fri. 9am-3pm

City Gallery	Mon.-Fri. 10:30am-6pm
Clocktower Gallery	Thurs.-Sun. noon-6pm
Cloisters	March-Oct. Tues.-Sun. 8:30am-5:15pm; Nov.-Feb. Tues.-Sun. 9:30am-4:45pm
Commodities Exchange Center	Mon.-Fri. 9:30am-3pm
Cooper-Hewitt Museum	Tues. 10am-9pm, Wed.-Sat. 10am-5pm, Sun. noon-5pm
Cunard Building	Mon.-Fri. 8am-6pm, Sat. 8am-2pm
Dime Savings Bank	Mon. and Thurs.-Fri. 9am-6pm, Tues.-Wed. 9am-3pm, Sat. 10am-3pm
Dyckman House	Tues.-Sun. 11am-5pm
Edgar Allan Poe Cottage	Wed.-Fri. 9am-5pm, Sat. 10am-4pm, Sun. 1-5pm
Ellis Island Museum of Immigration	Sept.-July 4 daily 9am-5:30pm; July 4-Aug. 9am-6:30pm
El Museo del Barrio	Wed.-Sun. 11am-5pm
Empire State Building	Observatory daily 9:30am-midnight
Federal Hall	Mon.-Fri. 9am-5pm
Forbes Magazine Galleries	Tues.-Sat. 10am-4pm
Fraunces Tavern Museum	Mon.-Fri. 10am-4pm; Oct.-May also Sun. noon-5pm
French Institute	Mon.-Thurs. 10am-8pm, Fri. 10am-6pm, Sat. 10am-1:30pm
Frick Collection	Tues.-Sat. 10am-6pm, Sun. 1-6pm
Garibaldi-Menci Museum	Tues.-Fri. 9am-5pm, Sat.-Sun. 1-5pm
General Theological Seminary grounds	Mon.-Fri. noon-3pm, Sat. 11am-3pm. Sun. 2-4pm
Grey Art Gallery	Sept.-June Tues. and Thurs. 10am-6:30pm, Wed. 10am-8:30pm, Fri. 10am-5pm, Sat. 1-5pm; July-Aug. Mon.-Fri. 10am-6pm
Guggenheim Museum	Closed until early 1992
Guinness World of Records	Daily 9am-8pm, later during peak periods
Hall of Fame for Great Americans	Mon.-Fri. 10am-5pm
Hamilton Grange	Wed.-Sun. 9am-4:30pm
Hispanic Society of America	Tues.-Sat. 10am-4:30pm, Sun. 1-4:30pm
Hugh Rock Park Conservation Center	Daily 9am-5pm
IBM Gallery of Science and Art	Tues.-Sat. 11am-6pm
Institute for Art and Urban Resources	Wed.-Sun noon-6pm
International Center of Photography	Tues. noon-8pm, Wed.-Fri. noon-5pm, Sat.-Sun. 11am-6pm
Intrepid Sea-Air-Space Museum	Memorial Day-Labor Day daily 10am-5pm; Labor Day-Memorial Day Mon.-Fri. 10am-5pm
Jacques Marchais Center of Tibetan Art	April-Nov. Wed.-Sun. 1-5pm
Jamaica Bay Wildlife Refuge	Daily 8:30am-5pm
Japan House	Mon.-Fri. 9:30am-5:30pm
Jefferson Market	Mon. and Thurs. noon-6pm, Tues. 10am-6pm, Wed. noon-8pm, Sat. 10am-5pm
King Mansion	Thurs. 1-4pm
Kingsland Homestead	Tues. and Sat.-Sun. 2:30-4:30pm
Kostabi World	daily 10am-6pm
Metropolitan Museum	Sun. and Tues.-Thurs. 9:30am-5:15pm, Fri.-Sat. 9:30am-8:45pm.
Metropolitan Opera House	Mon.-Sat. 9am-8pm, Sun. noon-6pm
Minor Injury	Fri.-Sun 1-6pm
Morris-Jumel Mansion	Tues.-Sun 10am-4pm
Museum of American Folk Art	Daily 9am-9pm
Museum of American Illustration	Sept.-July Mon. and Wed.-Fri. 9am-5pm, Tues. 9am-8pm
Museum of Bronx History	Sat. 10am-4pm, Sun. 1-5pm
Museum of the City of New York	Wed.-Sat. 10am-5pm, Sun. 1-5pm
Museum of Holography	Tues.-Sun. 11am-6pm

Museum of Modern Art	Fri.-Tues. 11am-5:45pm, Thurs. 11am-8:45pm
Museum of Television and Radio	Tues.-Wed. and Fri.-Sun. noon-6pm, Thurs. noon-8pm
NBC	Daily 9:30am-5:30pm
National Academy of Design	Tues. noon-8pm, Wed.-Sun. noon-5pm
National Museum of the American Indian	Tues.-Sat. 10am-5pm, Sun. 1-5pm
New Museum of Contemporary Art	Wed.-Thurs. and Sun. noon-6pm, Fri.-Sat. noon-8pm
New York Aquarium	Daily 10am-4:45pm, holidays and summer weekends 10am-7pm
New York Botanical Garden	April-Oct. Tues.-Sun. 10am-7pm; Nov.-March 10am-6pm
New York Hall of Science	Wed.-Sun. 10am-5pm
New-York Historical Society	Tues.-Sun. 10am-5pm
New York Stock Exchange	Mon.-Fri. 9:15am-4pm
"New York Unearthed"	Mon.-Fri. noon-6pm
Nicholas Roerich Museum	Tues.-Sun. 2-5pm
Isamu Noguchi Garden Museum	April-Nov. Wed. and Sat. 11am-6pm
Onderdonk Farmhouse	April-Nov. Sun. 2:30-4:30pm
Pierpont Morgan Library	Tues.-Sat. 10:30am-5pm, Sun. 1-5pm
Police Academy Museum	Mon.-Fri. 9am-3pm, closed holidays
Queens Botanical Garden	Tues.-Sun. 10am-7pm
Queens County Farmhouse Museum	Sat.-Sun. noon-5pm
Richmondtown Restoration	Wed.-Fri. 10am-5pm, Sat.-Sun. and Mon. holidays 1-5pm
Riverside Church watchtower	Mon.-Sat. 11am-3pm, Sun. 12:30-4pm
St. Paul's Chapel	Mon.-Sat. 8am-4pm, Sun. 8am-3pm
Schomburg Center for Research in Black Culture	Tues.-Wed. noon-8pm, Fri.-Sat. 10am-6pm
Abigail Adams Smith Museum	Sept.-July Mon.-Fri. noon-4pm, Sun. 1-5pm
Snug Harbor Cultural Center	Thurs.-Fri. 1-5pm, Sat.-Sun. noon-6pm
Staten Island Children's Museum	Wed.-Fri. 1-5pm, Sat.-Sun. 11am-5pm
Staten Island Museum	Tues.-Sat. 10am-5pm, Sun. 2-5pm
Staten Island Zoo	Daily 10am-4:45pm
Statue of Liberty	Daily 9am-5:15pm
Studio Museum in Harlem	Wed.-Fri. 10am-5pm, Sat.-Sun. 1-6pm
Theodore Roosevelt Birthplace	Wed.-Sun. 9am-5pm
Tudor Park	Daily 7am-midnight
Ukrainian Museum	Wed.-Sun. 1-5pm
United Nations	Daily 9am-6pm
Van Cortlandt Mansion	Tues.-Fri. 11am-3pm, Sun. 1-5pm
Whitney Museum	Tues. 10am-8pm, Wed.-Sat. 10am-6pm, Sun. noon-6pm
Wollman Skating Rink	Mon. 10am-9pm, Tues.-Thurs. 10am-9:30pm, Fri.-Sat.10am-11pm; winter Sat.-Sun. 10:30am-4:30pm
2 World Trade Center	Observation deck daily 9:30am-9:30pm

Major Annual Events

January	Chinese New Year (sometimes early Feb.), Chinatown; Martin Luther King, Jr. Memorial Day Parade, Fifth Avenue; National Boat Show, New York Coliseum
February	Washington's Birthday Parade, Fifth Avenue; Black History Week, American Museum of National History; Queens Purim Parade
March	Ringling Bros. and Barnum & Bailey Circus, Madison Square Garden, kicked off by Parade of Circus Animals from Twelfth Ave. and 34th St. at 10am the day before the first performance; St. Patrick's Day Parade, Fifth Avenue; Greek National Day Parade, Fifth Avenue
April	Easter Day Parade, Fifth Avenue, informal Easter parade near St. Patrick's Cathedral; Japanese Cherry Blossom Festival, Brooklyn Botanic Garden; Great Easter Egg Event, Bronx Zoo

May	Armed Forces Day Parade, Fifth Avenue; Israel Parade, Fifth Avenue; Ukrainian Festival, East 7th St.; Ninth Avenue International Food Festival (37th-57th St.); SoHo Festival, Prince St.; Washington Square Outdoor Art Show, Greenwich Village; Norwegian Independence Day Parade, Bay Ridge, Brooklyn (67th-90th St.); Memorial Day Weekend: Czechoslovak Festival, Bohemian Hall, Astoria; Asian Pacific-American Festival, Queens Botanical Garden; Bronx Day, Van Cortlandt Park
June	Kool Jazz Festival; Newport Jazz Festival; Puerto Rican Day Parade, Fifth Avenue; Museum Mile Celebration, Fifth Ave. (82nd-105th St.); Metropolitan Opera performances in parks; Weekend Summergarden concerts at MoMA's sculpture garden; New York Women's Jazz Festival and Guggenheim Concerts, Damrosch Park, Lincoln Center; 52nd Street Festival; Summer Pier Concerts, Fri. and Sat., South Street Seaport; Indian Festival, Central Park; Jewish Festival (usually 2nd Sun.), E. Broadway (Rutgers-Grand St.); Gay Pride March from Columbus Circle; Lexington Avenue Street Fair (23rd-34th St.); Shakespeare Day, Brooklyn Botanical Garden; Queens Day, Flushing Meadow Park; Queens Ethnic Music Festival, Bohemian Hall
July	Macy's Firework Display (July 4) from Hudson River barges (79th-125th St.); Mostly Mozart Music Festival, Avery Fisher Hall, Lincoln Center; Harbor Festival, Battery Park; American Crafts Festival, Lincoln Center Plaza; Irish Festival, 116th St. in Rockaway; Summer Festival, Sailors Snug Harbor Cultural Center, Staten Island
August	Greenwich Village Jazz Festival; New York Folk Festival; New York Philharmonic concerts in parks; Lincoln Center Out-of-Doors Festival; Harlem Week; New York Ecuadorian Parade, 37th Ave., Jackson Heights
September	Labor Day Parade, Fifth Avenue; New York Film Festival, Lincoln Center; Festival of San Gennaro, Mulberry St. (Houston St.-Washington Sq. Park), Little Italy; U.S. Open Tennis Championships, USTA National Tennis Center, Flushing Meadow; Washington Square Outdoor Art Show; Columbus Avenue Festival (66th-79th St.); Annual Fifth Avenue Mile Race (82nd-62nd St.); Governor's Cup Race, New York Bay; Richmond County Fair, Richmondtown Restoration, Staten Island
October	Columbus Day Parade, Fifth Avenue; Halloween Parade, Greenwich Village; Hispanic American Parade, Fifth Avenue; New York City Marathon (from Verrazano Bridge to Tavern on the Green)
November	Veteran's Day Parade, Fifth Avenue; Macy's Thanksgiving Day Parade, Broadway (Huge balloon floats assembled the previous evening at 79th and Central Park West)
December	Christmas Tree lighting, Rockefeller Center; Christmas Tree and Baroque Creche, Metropolitan Museum; Chanuka candle lighting at City Hall; Christmas in Richmond Town, Richmond Town Restoration, Staten Island; Korean Harvest and Folklore Festival, Flushing Meadow-Corona Park; Yuletide Festival, Wave Hill, Bronx; New Year's Eve, Times Square—at midnight, a big apple drops from Times Tower, ushering in the new year.

Index

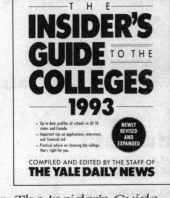

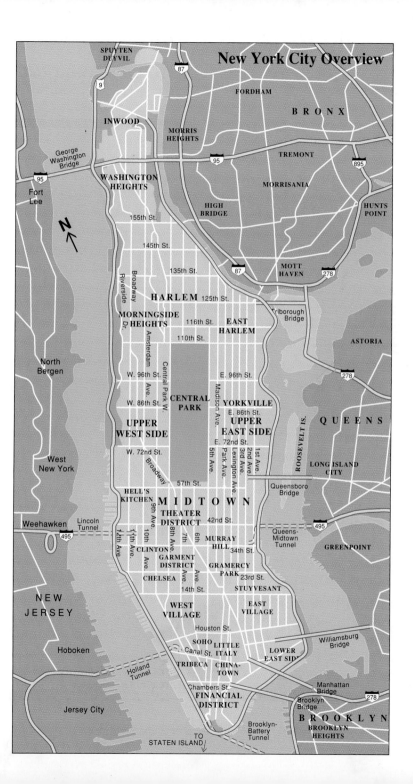

Subways

Stops are not served by all trains at all times.
Refer to Transit Authority map for descriptions
of express, local, and limited service.

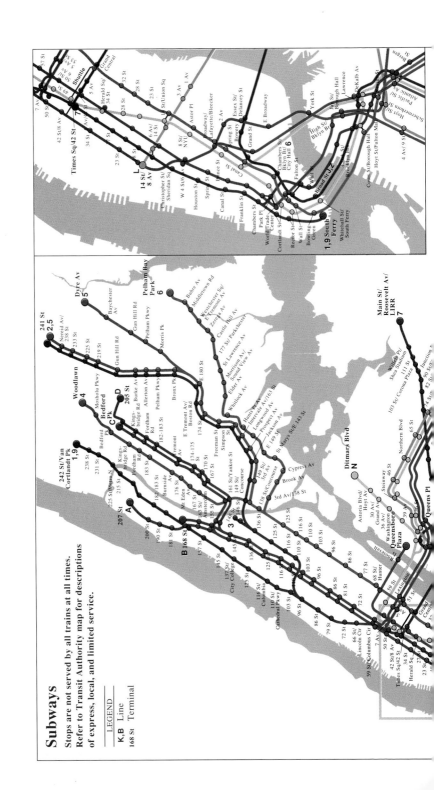

Downtown

Alternative Museum, 22
Anthology Film
Archives, 27
Buddhist Temple, 21
Castle Clinton, 1
CBGB's, 26
Cherry Lane Theatre, 29
Chinatown Fair, 20
Church of the
Ascension, 38
City Hall, 18
Clocktower Gallery, 19
Cooper Union, 32
Downtown Heliport, 4
East Coast Memorial, 2
Federal Hall, 10
Federal Reserve Bank, 11
Forbidden Planet, 37
Fraunces Tavern
Museum, 5
Fulton Fish Market, 12
Grace Church, 35
Jefferson Market
Library, 39
Joseph Papp Public
Theater, 31

Knitting Factory, 25
Morgan Guaranty Trust
Company, 8
Museum of Holography, 23
New Museum of
Contemporary Art, 24
New School of Social
Research, 40
New York Stock
Exchange, 9
Our Lady of the Rosary
(Church of), 3
Second Avenue Deli, 33
St. John's Episcopal
Methodist Church, 13
St. Luke's Chapel, 30
St. Mark's in the Bowery
Church, 34
St. Paul's Chapel, 14
The Strand, 36
Tower Records, 28
Trinity Church, 7
U.S. Custom House, 6
Woolworth Building, 17
World Financial Center, 16
World Trade Center, 15

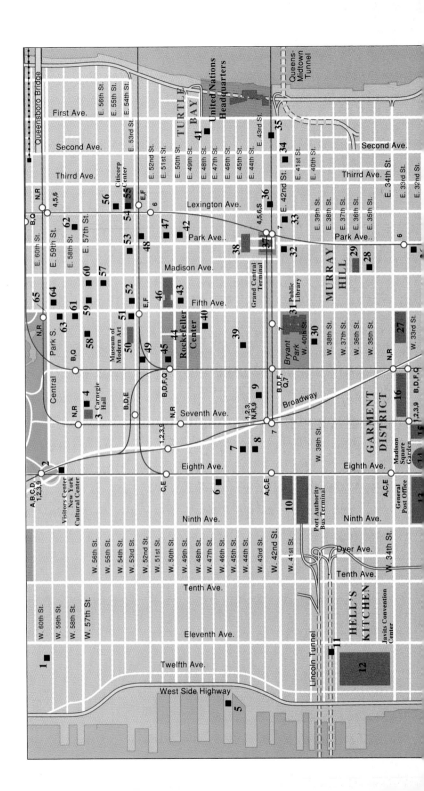

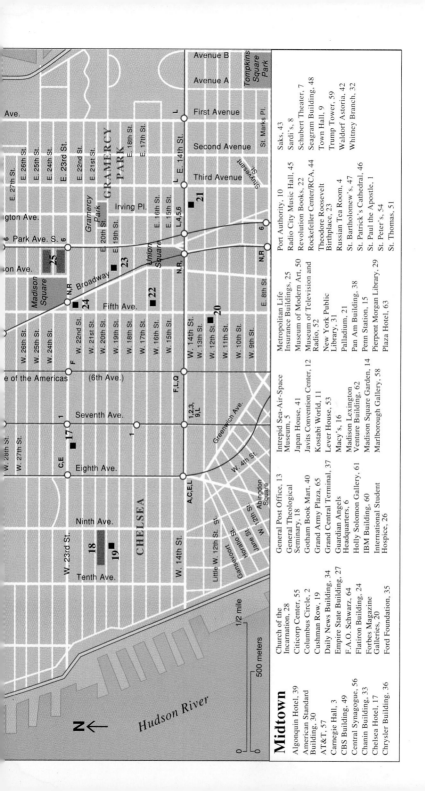

Uptown

American Museum of Natural History, 47
The Ansonia, 49
The Arsenal, 25
Asia Society, 14
Belvedere Castle, 32
Bethesda Fountain, 29
Bloomies, 22
Cathedral of St. John the Divine, 41
Central Park Zoo, 24
Children's Museum of Manhattan, 45
Children's Zoo, 26
China House, 19
Cleopatra's Needle, 34
Columbia University and Barnard College, 40

Conservatory Garden, 2
Cooper-Hewitt Museum, 7
The Dakota, 50
Delacorte Theater, 33
El Museo del Bario, 1
Fordham University, 54
Frick Museum, 13
Gracie Mansion, 10
Grant's Tomb, 39
Guggenheim Museum, 9
Hayden Planetarium (at the American Museum of Natural History), 47
Hector Memorial, 44
Hotel des Artistes, 51
Hunter College, 16
International Center of Photography, 5

Jewish Museum, 6
The Julliard School (at Lincoln Center), 53
Lincoln Center, 53
Loeb Boathouse, 30
Masjid Malcolm Shabazz , 37
Metropolitan Museum of Art, 11
Mt. Sinai Hospital, 4
Museum of American Folk Art, 52
Museum of American Illustration, 21
Museum of the City of New York, 3
National Academy of Design, 8
New York Convention & Visitor's Bureau, 55
New York Historical Society, 48

New York Hospital, 15
Police Station (Central Park), 35
Rockefeller University, 20
7th Regiment Armory, 17
Shakespeare Garden, 31
Soldiers and Sailors Monument, 43
Strawberry Fields, 28
Studio Museum in Harlem, 38
Symphony Space, 42
Tavern on the Green, 27
Temple Emanu-El, 18
Tennis Courts, (Central Park), 36
Whitney Museum of American Art, 12
Wollman Rink, 23
Zabar's, 46

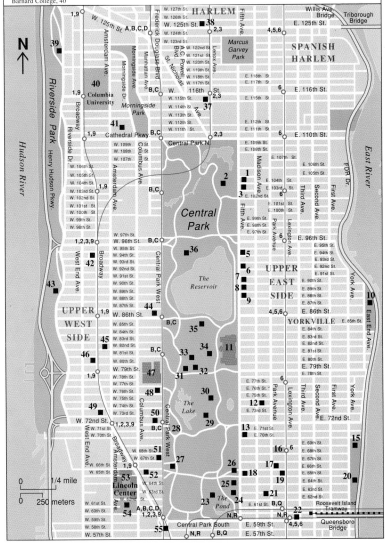